Cisco Exam Objectives
Exam 640-505: Remote Access

Cisco Remote Access Networks Introduction	Chapter
Specify and/or identify the Cisco products that best meet the WAN connection requirements for permanent or dialup access connections	1, 2

Selecting Cisco Products for Remote Connections	Chapter
Explain and/or identify the advantages and disadvantages of WAN connection types	1
Select the appropriate WAN connection types that address specific site connection considerations	1
Select Cisco equipment that will suit the specific needs of a WAN topology	2

Assembling and Cabling the WAN Components	Chapter
Identify the components and connections necessary to allow WAN connections such as frame relay and ISDN PRI from the central site to a branch office, and to allow WAN connections such as frame relay and ISDN BRI from a branch office telecommuter site to the central site	2

Configuring Asynchronous Connections to a Central Site with Modems	Chapter
Specify the commands and procedures necessary to configure an access server for modem connectivity so telecommuters can access the central site, and to configure the central site for dial out connections	3
Specify the commands used to reverse Telnet to the modem, configure the modem for basic asynchronous operations, and set up the modem autoconfiguration feature	3

Configuring PPP and Controlling Network Access with PAP and CHAP	Chapter
Specify the commands and syntax to configure a PPP connection between the central site and a branch office	4
Specify the commands and syntax to configure PAP or CHAP authentication to allow access to a secure site	4
Configure Multilink PPP to increase the data throughput and specify the commands to verify proper PPP configuration and troubleshoot an incorrect PPP configuration	4
Access the central site with Windows 95 and specify the commands and procedures to configure a PC to complete a dialup call to the central site router through the traditional telephone network	5

Using ISDN and DDR Technologies to Enhance Remote Connectivity	Chapter
Identify when to use ISDN BRI and PRI services and select the service that best suits a set of given requirements	6, 8
Identify the Q.921 and Q.931 signaling and call setup sequences	6
Specify the commands to configure ISDN BRI, PRI, and DDR	6, 8

Optimizing the use of DDR Interfaces	Chapter
Specify or select appropriate dialup capabilities to place a call, specify the commands and procedures to configure rotary groups and dialer profiles, and specify the commands to verify proper dialer profile or rotary group configuration and troubleshoot an incorrect configuration	7

Using X.25 for Remote Access	Chapter
Specify the commands and procedures to configure an X.25 WAN connection between the central office and branch office	9
Specify proper X.121 addresses and the commands to assign them to router interfaces	9
Specify the commands and procedures used to verify proper X.25 configuration and troubleshoot incorrect X.25 configuration	9

Establishing a Dedicated Frame Relay Connection and Control Traffic Flow	Chapter
Specify the commands and procedures to configure a frame relay WAN connection between the central office and branch office	10
Specify the commands to configure subinterfaces on virtual interfaces to solve split horizon problems	10
Specify the commands to configure frame relay traffic shaping and the commands and procedures to verify proper frame relay configuration and troubleshoot an incorrect configuration	10

Enabling a Backup to the Permanent Connection	Chapter
Specify the procedure and commands to configure a backup connection that activates upon primary line failure and when the primary line reaches a specified threshold, and to configure a dialer to function as backup to the primary interface	11

Managing Network Performance with Queuing and Compression	Chapter
Determine why queuing is enabled, identify alternative queuing protocols that Cisco products support, and determine the best queuing method to implement	12
Specify the commands to configure weighted-fair, priority, and custom queuing, and the commands and procedures used to verify proper queuing configuration, troubleshoot incorrect configuration, and effectively select and implement compression	12

Scaling IP Addresses with Network Address Translation	Chapter
Describe how NAT and PAT operate, specify the commands and procedures to configure NAT and PAT to allow reuse of registered IP addresses in a private network, and verify proper configuration of NAT and PAT with available Cisco verification commands	13

Using AAA to Scale Access Control in an Expanding Network	Chapter
Specify, recognize, or describe the security features of CiscoSecure and the operation of a CiscoSecure server, specify the commands and procedures to configure a router to access a CiscoSecure server and to use AAA, and specify the commands to configure AAA on a router to control access from remote access clients	14

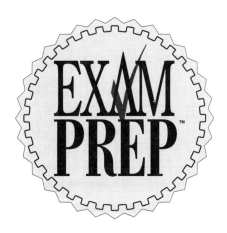

CCNP™
Remote Access

Barry Meinster
Richard A. Deal

CCNP™ Remote Access Exam Prep

Limits of Liability and Disclaimer of Warranty

The author and publisher of this book have used their best efforts in preparing the book and the programs contained in it. These efforts include the development, research, and testing of the theories and programs to determine their effectiveness. The author and publisher make no warranty of any kind, expressed or implied, with regard to these programs or the documentation contained in this book.

The author and publisher shall not be liable in the event of incidental or consequential damages in connection with, or arising out of, the furnishing, performance, or use of the programs, associated instructions, and/or claims of productivity gains.

Trademarks

Trademarked names appear throughout this book. Rather than list the names and entities that own the trademarks or insert a trademark symbol with each mention of the trademarked name, the publisher states that it is using the names for editorial purposes only and to the benefit of the trademark owner, with no intention of infringing upon that trademark.

The Coriolis Group, LLC
14455 N. Hayden Road, Suite 220
Scottsdale, Arizona 85260

(480)483-0192
FAX (480)483-0193
www.coriolis.com

Library of Congress Cataloging-in-Publication Data
Meinster, Barry
    CCNP remote access exam prep / by Barry Meinster and Richard Deal.
      p.   cm.
    Includes index.
    ISBN 1-57610-692-6
    1. Electronic data processing personnel--Certification.   2. Computer networks--Examinations--Study guides.   3. Computer terminals--Remote terminals. I. Title.
QA76.3.M345 2000
004.67--dc21   00-058926
                                               CIP

President and CEO
Keith Weiskamp

Publisher
Steve Sayre

Acquisitions Editor
Sharon Linsenbach

Development Editor
Deb Doorley

Product Marketing Manager
Brett Woolley

Project Editor
Karen Swartz

Technical Reviewer
Michael Jennings
Warren Heaton

Production Coordinator
Todd Halvorsen

Cover Designer
Jesse Dunn

Layout Designer
April Nielsen

CD-ROM Developer
Chris Nusbaum

Printed in the United States of America
10 9 8 7 6 5 4 3 2 1

The Coriolis Group, LLC • 14455 North Hayden Road, Suite 220 • Scottsdale, Arizona 85260

ExamCram.com Connects You to the Ultimate Study Center!

Our goal has always been to provide you with the best study tools on the planet to help you achieve your certification in record time. Time is so valuable these days that none of us can afford to waste a second of it, especially when it comes to exam preparation.

Over the past few years, we've created an extensive line of *Exam Cram* and *Exam Prep* study guides, practice exams, and interactive training. To help you study even better, we have now created an e-learning and certification destination called **ExamCram.com**. (You can access the site at **www.examcram.com**.) Now, with every study product you purchase from us, you'll be connected to a large community of people like yourself who are actively studying for their certifications, developing their careers, seeking advice, and sharing their insights and stories.

I believe that the future is all about collaborative learning. Our **ExamCram.com** destination is our approach to creating a highly interactive, easily accessible collaborative environment, where you can take practice exams and discuss your experiences with others, sign up for features like "Questions of the Day," plan your certifications using our interactive planners, create your own personal study pages, and keep up with all of the latest study tips and techniques.

I hope that whatever study products you purchase from us—*Exam Cram* or *Exam Prep* study guides, *Personal Trainers*, *Personal Test Centers*, or one of our interactive Web courses—will make your studying fun and productive. Our commitment is to build the kind of learning tools that will allow you to study the way you want to, whenever you want to.

Help us continue to provide the very best certification study materials possible. Write us or email us at **learn@examcram.com** and let us know how our study products have helped you study. Tell us about new features that you'd like us to add. Send us a story about how we've helped you. We're listening!

Visit *ExamCram.com* now to enhance your study program.

Good luck with your certification exam and your career. Thank you for allowing us to help you achieve your goals.

Keith Weiskamp

Keith Weiskamp
President and CEO

Look for these other products from The Coriolis Group:

CCNP Remote Access Exam Cram
by Craig Dennis, Eric Quinn

CCNP Routing Exam Cram
by Eric McMasters, Brian Morgan, Mike Shroyer

CCNP Switching Exam Cram
by Richard Deal

CCNP Support Exam Cram
by Matthew Luallen

CCNP Routing Exam Prep
by Corwin Low, Bob Larson, Paul Rodgriguez

CCNP Switching Exam Prep
by Sean Odom, Doug Hammond

CCNP Support Exam Prep
by Sean Odom, Gina Galbraith

Dedicated to my wife, Amy.
—Barry Meinster

❧

I would like to dedicate this book to my wife, Natalie,
whose continual support has inspired me to strive harder
to reach goals that I thought were impossible.
—Richard A. Deal

❧

About the Authors

Having spent over 32 years in education and IT training, **Dr. Barry Meinster** (Ph.D., MCT, MCSE, CCNA, CCNP) brings an enormous number of teaching techniques along with an immense breadth of technical knowledge to the field of Cisco training.

Richard A. Deal has over 13 years experience in the computing and networking industry, including networking, training, systems administration, and programming. In addition to a B.S. in Mathematics and Literature from Grove City College, Richard has the following certifications from Cisco: Cisco Certified Training Instructor (CCSI), Cisco Certified Network Associate (CCNA), Cisco Certified Design Associate (CCDA), and Cisco Certified Design Professional (CCDP). For the last four years, Richard has operated his own company, The Deal Group, Inc., recently relocated to Orlando, FL. Richard's company provides network consulting and training services nationwide. As a Cisco Instructor, Richard teaches not only the Building Cisco Remote Access Networks (BCRAN) class, but these other courses as well: Interconnecting Cisco Network Devices (ICND), Building Scalable Cisco Networks (BSCN), Building Cisco Multilayer Switched Networks (BCMSN), Cisco Campus ATM Solutions (CATM), Cisco Internetwork Design (CID), Multiband Switch and Service Configuration (MSSC), and BPX Switch and Services Configuration (BSSC). This is Richard's third book with The Coriolis Group. His first book was titled *CCNP Cisco LAN Switch Configuration Exam Cram* and his second one was *CCNP Switching Exam Cram*.

Acknowledgments

I would like to thank the personnel at Information Management Systems, especially Curtis Watts, for supporting me in my teaching endeavors. I want to thank my grandmother, Sarah Simms, who has just reached the young age of 90 this year. The example she has lead throughout her life always brings warmth to my heart. And I would also like to thank my family: my mother and father, and my two sisters, Kristen and Kimberly, and their families. And last, and most important, I would like to thank my wife, Natalie, for giving me the strength and resolve to complete this book, for giving me that cock-eyed smile that I always have on my face, and for bringing true love into my life…I am forever in your debt.
—*Richard A. Deal*

Contents at a Glance

Table of Contents

Chapter 11
Configuring Dial Backup for WAN Redundancy 353

Chapter 12
Bandwidth-Saving Strategies 381

Exam Insights

Welcome to *CCNP Remote Access Exam Prep*! This book aims to help you get ready to take—and pass—Cisco certification Exam 640-505, Remote Access. This Exam Insights section discusses exam preparation resources, the testing situation, Cisco's certification programs in general, and how this book can help you prepare for Cisco's certification exams.

Exam Prep books help you understand and appreciate the subjects and materials you need to pass Cisco certification exams. Our aim is to make sure all key topics are clearly explained and to bring together as much information as possible about Cisco certification exams.

Nevertheless, to completely prepare yourself for any Cisco test, we recommend that you begin by taking the Self-Assessment included in this book immediately following this Exam Insights section. This tool will help you evaluate your knowledge base against the requirements for a CCNP under both ideal and real circumstances.

Based on what you learn from that exercise, you might decide to begin your studies with some classroom training or some background reading. You might decide to read The Coriolis Group's *Exam Prep* book that you have in hand first, or you might decide to start with another study approach. You may also want to refer to one of a number of study guides available from Cisco or third-party vendors.

We also strongly recommend that you install, configure, and fool around with the network equipment that you'll be tested on, because nothing beats hands-on experience and familiarity when it comes to understanding the questions you're likely to encounter on a certification test. Book learning is essential, but hands-on experience is the best teacher of all!

How to Prepare for an Exam

Preparing for any Cisco career certification test (including CCNP) requires that you obtain and study materials designed to provide comprehensive information about Cisco router operation and the specific exam for which you are preparing. The following list of materials will help you study and prepare:

➤ *Instructor-led training*—There's no substitute for expert instruction and hands-on practice under professional supervision. Cisco Training Partners, such as Information Management Systems (IMS), offer instructor-led training courses for all of the Cisco career certification requirements. These companies aim to help prepare network administrators to run Cisco routed and switched internetworks and pass the Cisco tests. Although such training runs upwards of $400 per day in class, most of the individuals lucky enough to partake find them to be quite worthwhile.

➤ *Cisco Connection Online*—This is the name of Cisco's Web site (**www.cisco.com**), the most current and up-to-date source of Cisco information.

➤ *The CCPrep Web site*—This is the most well-known Cisco certification Web site in the world. You can find it at **www.ccprep.com** (formerly known as **www.CCIEprep.com**). Here, you can find exam preparation materials, practice tests, self-assessment exams, and numerous certification questions and scenarios. In addition, professional staff members are available to answer questions that you can post on the answer board.

➤ *Cisco training kits*—These are available only if you attend a Cisco class at a certified training facility or if a Cisco Training Partner in good standing gives you one.

➤ *Study guides*—Several publishers—including Certification Insider Press—offer study guides. The Certification Insider Press series includes:

  ➤ *The Exam Cram series*—These books give you information about the material you need to know to pass the tests.

  ➤ *The Exam Prep series*—These books provide a greater level of detail than the *Exam Cram* books and are designed to teach you everything you need to know from an exam perspective.

  Together, the two series make a perfect pair.

➤ *Multimedia*—These Coriolis Group materials are designed to support learners of all types—whether you learn best by reading or doing:

  ➤ *The Exam Cram Personal Trainer*—Offers a unique, personalized, self-paced training course based on the exam.

  ➤ *The Exam Cram Personal Test Center*—Features multiple test options that simulate the actual exam, including Fixed-Length, Random, Review, and Test All. Explanations of correct and incorrect answers reinforce concepts learned.

By far, this set of required and recommended materials represents an unparalleled collection of sources and resources for preparing for the CCNP exam. We anticipate that you'll find that this book belongs in this company. In the next section, we explain how this book works and give you some good reasons why this book counts as a member of the required and recommended materials list.

Taking a Certification Exam

Alas, testing is not free. Each computer-based exam costs between $100 and $200, and the CCIE laboratory exam costs $1,000. If you do not pass, you must pay the testing fee each time you retake the test. In the United States and Canada, computerized tests are administered by Sylvan Prometric. Sylvan Prometric can be reached at (800) 755-3926 or (800) 204-EXAM, any time from 7:00 A.M. to 6:00 P.M., Central Time, Monday through Friday. You can also try (612) 896-7000 or (612) 820-5707. CCIE laboratory exams are administered by Cisco Systems and can be scheduled by calling (800) 829-6387.

To schedule a computer-based exam, call at least one day in advance. To cancel or reschedule an exam, you must call at least 24 hours before the scheduled test time (or you may be charged regardless). When calling Sylvan Prometric, have the following information ready for the telesales staffer who handles your call:

➤ Your name, organization, and mailing address.

➤ Your Cisco Test ID. (For most U.S. citizens, this is your Social Security number. Citizens of other nations can use their taxpayer IDs or make other arrangements with the order taker.)

➤ The name and number of the exam you wish to take. For this book, the exam name is "CCNP Remote Access" and the exam number is 640-505.

➤ A method of payment. The most convenient approach is to supply a valid credit card number with sufficient available credit. Otherwise, Sylvan Prometric must receive check, money order, or purchase order payment before you can schedule a test. (If you're not paying by credit card, ask your order taker for more details.)

When you show up to take a test, try to arrive at least 15 minutes before the scheduled time slot.

The Exam Situation

When you arrive at the testing center where you scheduled your exam, you'll need to sign in with an exam coordinator. He or she will ask you to show two forms of identification, one of which must be a photo ID. After you've signed in and your time slot arrives, you'll be asked to deposit any books, bags, or other items you brought with you. Then, you'll be escorted into a closed room.

All exams are completely closed book. In fact, you will not be permitted to take anything with you into the testing area. However, you are furnished with a blank sheet of paper and a pen. We suggest that you immediately write down on that sheet of paper all the information you've memorized for the test. Although the amount of time you have to actually take the exam is limited, the time period does not start until you're ready, so you can spend as much time as necessary writing notes on the provided paper. If you think you will need more paper than what is provided, ask the test center administrator before entering the exam room. You must return all pages prior to exiting the testing center.

You will have some time to compose yourself, to record this information, and even to take a sample orientation exam before you begin the real thing. We suggest you take the orientation test before taking your first exam, but because they're all more or less identical in layout, behavior, and controls, you probably won't need to do this more than once.

Typically, the room will be furnished with anywhere from one to half a dozen computers, and each workstation will be separated from the others by dividers designed to keep you from seeing what's happening on someone else's computer. Most test rooms feature a wall with a large picture window. This permits the exam coordinator to monitor the room, to prevent exam-takers from talking to one another, and to observe anything out of the ordinary that might go on. The exam coordinator will have preloaded the appropriate Cisco certification exam—for this book, that's Exam 640-505—and you'll be permitted to start as soon as you're seated in front of the computer.

All Cisco certification exams allow a certain maximum amount of time in which to complete your work (this time is indicated on the exam by an on-screen counter/clock, so you can check the time remaining whenever you like). All Cisco certification exams are computer generated and most use a multiple-choice format. Although this may sound quite simple, the questions are constructed not only to check your mastery of basic facts and figures, but they also require you to evaluate one or more sets of circumstances or requirements. Often, you'll be asked to give more than one answer to a question. Likewise, you might be asked to select the best or most effective solution to a problem from a range of choices, all of which technically are correct. Taking the exam is quite an adventure, and it involves real thinking. This book shows you what to expect and how to deal with the potential problems, puzzles, and predicaments.

When you complete a Cisco certification exam, the software will tell you whether you've passed or failed. All tests are scored on a basis of 100 percent, and results are broken into several topic areas. Even if you fail, we suggest you ask for—and keep—the detailed report that the test administrator should print for you. You can use this report to help you prepare for another go-round, if needed. Once you see your score, you have the option of printing additional copies of the score report. It's a good idea to print it twice.

If you need to retake an exam, you'll have to call Sylvan Prometric, schedule a new test date, and pay another testing fee.

Note: *The first time you fail a test, you can retake the test the next day. However, if you fail a second time, you must wait 14 days before retaking that test. The 14-day waiting period remains in effect for all retakes after the second failure.*

In the next section, you'll learn more about how Cisco test questions look and how they must be answered.

Exam Layout and Design

Whichever type of test you take, questions generally belong to one of four basic types:

➤ Multiple-choice with a single answer

➤ Multiple-choice with one or more answers

➤ Multipart with a single answer

➤ Multipart with one or more answers

A few of the questions may be in a different format, such as fill in the blank. We've included a few such questions in the sample test in Chapter 15 to familiarize you with these question types as well.

Always take the time to read a question at least twice before selecting an answer, and always look for an Exhibit button as you examine each question. Exhibits include graphics information related to a question. An exhibit is usually a screen capture of program output or GUI information that you must examine to analyze the question's contents and formulate an answer. The Exhibit button brings up graphics and charts used to help explain a question, provide additional data, or illustrate page layout or program behavior.

Not every question has only one answer; many questions require multiple answers. Therefore, it's important to read each question carefully, to determine how many answers are necessary or possible, and to look for additional hints or instructions when selecting answers. Such instructions often occur in brackets immediately following the question itself (as they do for all multiple-choice questions in which one or more answers are possible).

The following multiple-choice question requires you to select a single correct answer. Following the question is a brief summary of each potential answer and why it is either right or wrong.

Question 1

Which router prompt indicates that you are in interface configuration mode?

○ a. Router>

○ b. Router#

○ c. Router(config)#

○ d. Router(config-if)#

The correct answer is d. The interface configuration command prompt is "Router(config-if)#". Answers a and b are prompts for the User and Privileged EXEC modes, respectively. Answer c is the Global Configuration mode command prompt.

This sample question format corresponds closely to the Cisco certification exam format—the only difference on the exam is that questions are not followed by answer keys. To select an answer, you would position the cursor over the radio button next to the answer. Then, click the mouse button to select the answer.

Let's examine a question where one or more answers are possible. This type of question provides checkboxes rather than radio buttons for marking all appropriate selections.

Question 2

What are the two ways that frame relay performs address resolution? [Choose the two best answers]

❏ a. Via static routes

❏ b. Via inverse-ARP

❏ c. Via **map-class** statements

❏ d. Via **frame-relay map** statements

Answers b and d are correct. Before your DTE can start sending information across the VC, your DTE needs to know who it is connected to at the other end. To perform manual resolution, you use **frame-relay map** statements. Inverse-ARP, however, will do this resolution for you dynamically. When your DTE receives the full status report, for all VCs that are active, it will generate an inverse-ARP across those VCs. Inside the inverse-ARP it includes its layer-3 addressing information. When the destination DTE receives the inverse-ARP, it examines the VC that it came from—more specifically, the DLCI number of the VC—and the layer 3 address and adds this information to its resolution table. Answer a is incorrect because static routes resolve layer-3 address routing path decisions. Answer c is incorrect because frame relay **map-class** statements are used for congestion control and traffic shaping.

For this particular question, two answers are required. As far as the authors can tell (and Cisco won't comment), such questions are scored as wrong unless all the required selections are chosen. In other words, a partially correct answer does not result in partial credit when the test is scored. For Question 2, you have to check the boxes next to items b and d to obtain credit for a correct answer. Notice that picking the right answers also means knowing why the other answers are wrong!

Question-Handling Strategies

Based on exams we have taken, some interesting trends have become apparent. For those questions that take only a single answer, usually two or three of the answers will be obviously incorrect, and two of the answers will be plausible—of course, only one can be correct. Unless the answer leaps out at you (if it does, reread the question to look for a trick; sometimes those are the ones you're most likely to get wrong), begin the process of answering by eliminating those answers that are most obviously wrong.

Almost always, at least one answer out of the possible choices for a question can be eliminated immediately because it matches one of these conditions:

➤ The answer does not apply to the situation.

➤ The answer describes a nonexistent issue, an invalid option, or an imaginary state.

After you eliminate all answers that are obviously wrong, you can apply your retained knowledge to eliminate further answers. Look for items that sound correct but refer to actions, commands, or features that are not present or not available in the situation that the question describes.

If you're still faced with a blind guess among two or more potentially correct answers, reread the question. Try to picture how each of the possible remaining answers would alter the situation. Be especially sensitive to terminology; sometimes the choice of words ("remove" instead of "disable") can make the difference between a right answer and a wrong one.

Only when you've exhausted your ability to eliminate answers, but remain unclear about which of the remaining possibilities is correct, should you guess at an answer. An unanswered question offers you no points, but guessing gives you at least some chance of getting a question right; just don't be too hasty when making a blind guess.

Numerous questions assume that the default behavior of a particular utility is in effect. If you know the defaults and understand what they mean, this knowledge will help you cut through many Gordian knots.

Note: Once you answer a question and proceed to the next one, you cannot return to a previous question. Therefore, make sure you answer every question, and make your best educated choice for an answer of every question.

Mastering the Inner Game

In the final analysis, knowledge breeds confidence, and confidence breeds success. If you study the materials in this book carefully and review all the practice questions at the end of each chapter, you should become aware of those areas where additional learning and study are required.

After you've worked your way through the book, take the practice exam in the back of the book and test yourself with some of the varying exam formats on the CD-ROM. This will provide a reality check and help you identify areas to study further. Make sure you follow up and review materials related to the questions you miss on the practice exams before scheduling a real exam. Only when you've covered that ground and feel comfortable with the whole scope of the practice exams should you set an exam appointment. Only if you score 80 percent or better should you proceed to the real thing (otherwise, obtain some additional practice tests so you can keep trying until you hit this magic number).

Armed with the information in this book and with the determination to augment your knowledge, you should be able to pass the certification exam. However, you need to work at it, or you'll spend the exam fee more than once before you finally pass. If you prepare seriously, you should do well. Good luck!

The next section covers the exam requirements for the various Cisco certifications.

The Cisco Career Certification Program

The Cisco Career Certification program is relatively new on the internetworking scene. The best place to keep tabs on it is the Cisco Training Web site, at **www.cisco.com/certifications/**. Before Cisco developed this program, Cisco Certified Internetwork Expert (CCIE) certification was the only available Cisco certification. Although CCIE certification is still the most coveted and prestigious certification that Cisco offers (possibly the most prestigious in the internetworking

Table 1   Cisco Routing and Switching CCNA, CCNP, and CCIE Requirements.

CCNA

Only 1 exam required	
Exam 640-507	Cisco Certified Network Associate 2.0

CCNP*

All 4 of these are required	
Exam 640-503	Routing 2.0
Exam 640-504	Switching 2.0
Exam 640-505	Remote Access 2.0
Exam 640-506	Support 2.0

★ You need to have your CCNA before you become a CCNP.

CCIE

1 written exam and 1 lab exam required	
Exam 350-001	CCIE Routing and Switching Qualification
Lab Exam	CCIE Routing and Switching Laboratory

industry), lower-level certifications are now available as stepping stones on the road to the CCIE. The Cisco Career Certification program includes several certifications in addition to the CCIE, each with its own acronym (see Table 1). If you're a fan of alphabet soup after your name, you'll like this program:

Note: *Within the certification program, there are specific specializations. For the purposes of this book, we will focus only on the Routing and Switching track. Visit* ***www.cisco.com/ warp/public/10/wwtraining/certprog/index.html*** *for information on the other specializations.*

➤ *Cisco Certified Design Associate (CCDA)*—The CCDA is a basic certification aimed at designers of high-level internetworks. The CCDA consists of a single exam (640-441) that covers information from the Designing Cisco Networks (DCN) course. You must obtain CCDA and CCNA certifications before you can move up to the CCDP certification.

➤ *Cisco Certified Network Associate (CCNA)*—The CCNA is the first career certification. It consists of a single exam (640-507) that covers information from the basic-level class, primarily Interconnecting Cisco Network Devices (ICND). You must obtain CCNA certification before you can get your CCNP and CCDP certifications.

➤ *Cisco Certified Network Professional (CCNP)*—The CCNP is a more advanced certification that is not easy to obtain. To earn CCNP status, you must be a CCNA in good standing. There are two routes you can take to obtain your CCNP. For the first route, you must take four exams: Routing (640-503), Switching (640-504), Remote Access (640-505), and Support (640-506). For the second route, you must take the Foundation (640-509) and Support (640-506) exams.

Although it may seem more appealing on the surface, the second route is more difficult. The Foundation exam contains more than 130 questions and lasts almost 3 hours. In addition, it covers all the topics covered in the Routing, Switching, and Remote Access exams.

Whichever route you choose, there are four courses Cisco recommends that you take:

➤ *Building Scalable Cisco Networks (BSCN)*—This course corresponds to the Routing exam.

➤ *Building Cisco Multilayer Switched Networks (BCMSN)*—This course corresponds to the Switching exam.

➤ *Building Cisco Remote Access Networks (BCRAN)*—This course corresponds to the Remote Access exam.

➤ *Cisco Internetworking Troubleshooting (CIT)*—This course corresponds to the Support exam.

Once you have completed the CCNP certification, you can further your career (not to mention beef up your resume) by branching out and passing one of the CCNP specialization exams. These include:

➤ *Security*—Requires you to pass the Managing Cisco Network Security exam (640-442).

➤ *LAN ATM*—Requires you to pass the Cisco Campus ATM Solutions exam (640-446).

➤ *Voice Access*—Requires you to pass the Cisco Voice over Frame Relay, ATM, and IP exam (640-647).

➤ *SNA/IP Integration*—Requires you to pass the SNA Configuration for Multiprotocol Administrators (640-445) and the SNA Foundation (640-456) exams.

➤ *Network Management*—Requires you to pass either the Managing Cisco Routed Internetworks—MCRI (640-443)—or the Managing Cisco Switched Internetworks—MCSI (640-444) exam.

➤ *Cisco Certified Design Professional (CCDP)*—The CCDP is another advanced certification. It's aimed at high-level internetwork designers who must understand the intricate facets of putting together a well-laid-out network. The first step in the certification process is to obtain the CCDA and CCNA certifications (yes, both). As with the CCNP, you must pass the Foundation exam or pass the Routing, Switching, and Remote Access exams individually. Once you meet those objectives, you must pass the Cisco Internetwork Design exam (640-025) to complete the certification.

➤ *Cisco Certified Internetwork Expert (CCIE)*—The CCIE is possibly the most influential certification in the internetworking industry today. It is famous (or infamous) for its difficulty and for how easily it holds its seekers at bay. The certification requires only one written exam (350-001); passing that exam qualifies you to schedule time at a Cisco campus to demonstrate your knowledge in a two-day practical laboratory setting. You must pass the lab with a score of at least 80 percent to become a CCIE. Recent statistics have put the passing rates at roughly 20 percent for first attempts and 35 through 50 percent overall. Once you achieve CCIE certification, you must recertify every two years by passing a written exam administered by Cisco.

➤ *Certified Cisco Systems Instructor (CCSI)*—To obtain status as a CCSI, you must be employed (either permanently or by contract) by a Cisco Training Partner in good standing, such as Information Management Systems (IMS) Corporation. That training partner must sponsor you through Cisco's Instructor Certification Program, and you must pass the two-day program that Cisco administers at a Cisco campus. You can build on CCSI certification on a class-by-class basis. Instructors must demonstrate competency with each class they are to teach by completing the written exam that goes with each class. Cisco also requires that instructors maintain a high customer satisfaction rating, or they will face decertification.

Tracking Cisco Certification Status

As soon as you pass any Cisco exam (congratulations!), you must complete a certification agreement. You can do so online at the Certification Tracking Web site (**www.galton.com/~cisco/**), or you can mail a hard copy of the agreement to Cisco's certification authority. You will not be certified until you complete a certification agreement and Cisco receives it in one of these forms.

The Certification Tracking Web site also allows you to view your certification information. Cisco will contact you via email and explain it and its use. Once you are registered into one of the career certification tracks, you will be given a login on this site, which is administered by Galton, a third-party company that has no in-depth affiliation with Cisco or its products. Galton's information comes directly from Sylvan Prometric, the exam-administration company for much of the computing industry.

Once you pass the necessary exam(s) for a particular certification and complete the certification agreement, you'll be certified. Official certification normally takes anywhere from four to six weeks, so don't expect to get your credentials overnight. When the package arrives, it will include a Welcome Kit that contains a number of elements, including:

➤ A Cisco certificate, suitable for framing, stating that you have completed the certification requirements, along with a laminated Cisco Career Certification identification card with your certification number on it

➤ Promotional items, which vary based on the certification.

Many people believe that the benefits of the Cisco career certifications go well beyond the perks that Cisco provides to newly anointed members of this elite group. There seem to be more and more job listings that request or require applicants to have a CCNA, CCDA, CCNP, CCDP, and so on, and many individuals who complete the program can qualify for increases in pay or responsibility. In fact, Cisco has started to implement requirements for its Value Added Resellers: To attain and keep silver, gold, or higher status, they must maintain a certain number of CCNA, CCDA, CCNP, CCDP, and CCIE employees on staff. There's a very high demand and low supply of Cisco talent in the industry overall. As an official recognition of hard work and broad knowledge, a Cisco career certification credential is a badge of honor in many IT organizations.

About the Book

To aid you in fully understanding the internetworking concepts required for CCNP certification, there are many features in this book designed to improve its value:

➤ *Chapter objectives*—Each chapter in this book begins with a detailed list of the topics to be mastered within that chapter. This list provides you with a quick reference to the contents of that chapter, as well as a useful study aid.

➤ *Illustrations and tables*—Numerous illustrations of screenshots and components aid you in the visualization of common setup steps, theories, and concepts. In addition, many tables provide details and comparisons of both practical and theoretical information.

➤ *Notes, tips, and warnings*—Notes present additional helpful material related to the subject being described. Tips from the author's experience provide extra information about how to attack a problem, or what to do in certain real-world situations. Warnings are included to help you anticipate potential mistakes or problems so you can prevent them from happening.

➤ *Real-world projects*—Although it is important to understand the theory behind Cisco internetworking technology, nothing can improve upon real-world experience. To this end, along with theoretical explanations, each chapter provides numerous projects aimed at providing you with real-world implementation experience.

➤ *Chapter summaries*—Each chapter's text is followed by a summary of the concepts it has introduced. These summaries provide a helpful way to recap and revisit the ideas covered in each chapter.

➤ *Review questions*—End-of-chapter assessment begins with a set of review questions that reinforce the ideas introduced in each chapter. These questions not only ensure that you have mastered the concepts, but are written to help prepare you for the Cisco certification examination. Answers to these questions are found in Appendix A.

➤ *Sample tests*—Use the sample test and answer key in Chapters 15 and 16 to test yourself. Then, move on to the interactive practice exams found on the CD-ROM. The testing engine offers a variety of testing formats to choose from.

Where Should You Start?

This book is intended to be read in sequence, from beginning to end. Each chapter builds upon those that precede it, to provide a solid understanding of CCNP Remote Access topics. After completing the chapters, you may find it useful to go back through the book and use the review questions and projects to prepare for the CCNP Remote Access test (Exam 640-505). Readers are also encouraged to investigate the many pointers to online and printed sources of additional information that are cited throughout this book.

Please share your feedback on the book with us, especially if you have ideas about how we can improve it for future readers. We'll consider everything you say carefully, and we'll respond to all suggestions. Send your questions or comments to us at **learn@examcram.com**. Please remember to include the title of the book in your message; otherwise, we'll be forced to guess which book you're writing about. And we don't like to guess—we want to *know*! Also, be sure to check out the Web pages at **www.examcram.com**, where you'll find information updates, commentary, and certification information. Thanks, and enjoy the book!

Self-Assessment

The reason we included a Self-Assessment in this *Exam Prep* is to help you evaluate your readiness to tackle CCNP certification. It should also help you understand what you need to master the topic of this book—namely, Exam 640-505, "Remote Access." But before you tackle this Self-Assessment, let's talk about concerns you may face when pursuing a CCNP, and what an ideal CCNP candidate might look like.

CCNPs in the Real World

In the next section, we describe an ideal CCNP candidate, knowing full well that only a few real candidates will meet this ideal. In fact, the description of that ideal candidate might seem downright scary. But take heart: Although the requirements to obtain a CCNP may seem pretty formidable, they are by no means impossible to meet. However, you should be keenly aware that it does take time and requires some expense and substantial effort to get through the process.

The first thing to understand is that the CCNP is an attainable goal. You can get all the real-world motivation you need from knowing that many others have gone before, so you will be able to follow in their footsteps. If you're willing to tackle the process seriously and do what it takes to obtain the necessary experience and knowledge, you can take—and pass—all the certification tests involved in obtaining an CCNP. In fact, we've designed these *Exam Preps*, and the companion *Exam Crams*, to make it as easy on you as possible to prepare for these exams. But prepare you must!

The same, of course, is true for other Cisco career certifications, including:

➤ CCNA, which is the first step on the road to the CCNP certification. It is a single exam that covers information from Cisco's Interconnecting Cisco Network Devices (ICND) class.

➤ CCDA, which is the first step on the road to the CCDP certification. It is a single exam that covers the basics of design theory. To prepare for it, you should attend the Designing Cisco Networks (DCN) class.

➤ CCNP, which is an advanced certification regarding internetwork engineering, implementation, and troubleshooting. It consists of multiple exams. There are two ways to go about attaining the CCNP. You could pass the individual exams for BSCN, BCMSN, BCRAN, and CIT. However, if you're not one for taking a lot of exams, you can take the Foundation Routing/Switching exam and the CIT exam. Either combination will complete the requirements.

➤ CCDP, which is an advanced certification regarding internetwork design. It consists of multiple exams. There are two ways to go about attaining the CCDP. You could pass the individual exams for BSCN, BCMSN, BCRAN, and CID. However, if you're not one for taking a lot of exams, you can take the Foundation Routing/Switching exam and the CID exam. Either combination will complete the requirements.

➤ CCIE, which is commonly referred to as the "black belt" of internetworking. It is considered the single most difficult certification to attain in the internetworking industry. First you must take a qualification exam. Once you pass the exam, the real fun begins. You will need to schedule a two-day practical lab exam to be held at a Cisco campus, where you will undergo a "trial by fire" of sorts. Your ability to configure, document, and troubleshoot Cisco equipment will be tested to its limits. Do not underestimate this lab exam.

The Ideal CCNP Candidate

Just to give you some idea of what an ideal CCNP candidate is like, here are some relevant statistics about the background and experience such an individual might have. Don't worry if you don't meet these qualifications, or don't come that close—this is a far from ideal world, and where you fall short is simply where you'll have more work to do.

➤ Academic or professional training in network theory, concepts, and operations. This includes everything from networking media and transmission techniques through network operating systems, services, and applications.

➤ Three-plus years of professional networking experience, including experience with Ethernet, token ring, modems, and other networking media. This must include installation, configuration, upgrade, and troubleshooting experience.

➤ Two-plus years in a networked environment that includes hands-on experience with Cisco routers, switches, and other related equipment. A solid understanding of each system's architecture, installation, configuration, maintenance, and troubleshooting is also essential.

➤ A thorough understanding of key networking protocols, addressing, and name resolution, including TCP/IP, IPX/SPX, and AppleTalk.

➤ Familiarity with key TCP/IP-based services, including ARP, BOOTP, DNS, FTP, SNMP, SMTP, Telnet, TFTP, and other relevant services for your internetwork deployment.

Fundamentally, this boils down to a bachelor's degree in computer science, plus three years of work experience in a technical position involving network design, installation, configuration, and maintenance. We believe that well under half of all certification candidates meet these requirements; in fact, most meet less than half of these requirements—at least, when they begin the certification process. But because thousands of people have survived this ordeal, you can survive it too—especially if you heed what our Self-Assessment can tell you about what you already know and what you need to learn.

Put Yourself to the Test

The following series of questions and observations is designed to help you figure out how much work you must do to pursue Cisco career certification and what kinds of resources you should consult on your quest. Be absolutely honest in your answers, or you'll end up wasting money on exams you're not yet ready to take. There are no right or wrong answers, only steps along the path to certification. Only you can decide where you really belong in the broad spectrum of aspiring candidates.

Two things should be clear from the outset, however:

➤ Even a modest background in computer science will be helpful.

➤ Extensive hands-on experience with Cisco products and technologies is an essential ingredient to certification success.

Educational Background

1. Have you ever taken any computer-related classes? [Yes or No]

   If Yes, proceed to question 2; if No, proceed to question 4.

2. Have you taken any classes included in Cisco's curriculum? [Yes or No]

   If Yes, you will probably be able to handle Cisco's architecture and system component discussions. If you're rusty, brush up on basic router operating system concepts, such as RAM, NVRAM, and flash memory. You'll also want to brush up on the basics of internetworking, especially IP subnetting, access lists, and WAN technologies such as X.25, frame relay, ISDN, and dial-up.

   If No, consider some extensive reading in this area. We strongly recommend instructor-led training offered by a Cisco Training Partner. However, you may want to check out a good general advanced routing technology book, such as *Cisco CCIE Fundamentals: Network Design and Case Studies* by Andrea Cheek, H. Kim Lew, and Kathleen Wallace (Cisco Press, Indianapolis, IN, 1998, ISBN: 1-57870-066-3). If this title doesn't appeal to you, check out reviews for other, similar titles at your favorite online bookstore.

3. Have you taken any networking concepts or technologies classes? [Yes or No]

If Yes, you will probably be able to handle Cisco's internetworking terminology, concepts, and technologies. If you're rusty, brush up on basic internetworking concepts and terminology, especially networking media, transmission types, the OSI Reference model, and networking technologies such as Ethernet, token ring, FDDI, and WAN links.

If No, you might want to read one or two books in this topic area. Check out Appendix C, the Study Resources appendix, for a selection of resources that will give you additional background on the topics covered in this book.

4. Have you done any reading on routing protocols and/or routed protocols (IP, IPX, AppleTalk, etc.)? [Yes or No]

If Yes, review the requirements stated in the first paragraphs after Questions 2 and 3. If you meet those requirements, move on to the next question.

If No, consult the recommended reading for both topics. A strong background will help you prepare for the Cisco exams better than just about anything else.

Hands-on Experience

The most important key to success on all of the Cisco tests is hands-on experience with Cisco routers and related equipment. If we leave you with only one realization after taking this Self-Assessment, it should be that there's no substitute for time spent installing, configuring, and using the various Cisco products upon which you'll be tested repeatedly and in depth. It cannot be stressed enough that quality instructor-led training will benefit you greatly and give you additional hands-on configuration experience with the technologies upon which you are to be tested.

5. Have you installed, configured, and worked with Cisco routers? [Yes or No]

If Yes, make sure you understand basic concepts as covered in the Interconnecting Cisco Network Devices (ICND), Building Scalable Cisco Networks (BSCN), Building Cisco Multilayer Switched Networks (BCMSN), and Building Cisco Remote Access Networks (BCRAN), before progressing into the materials covered here, because this book expands on the basic topics taught there.

Tip: You can download objectives and other information about Cisco exams from the company's Training and Certification page on the Web at **www.cisco.com/training**.

If No, you will need to find a way to get a good amount of instruction on the intricacies of configuring Cisco equipment. You need a broad background to get through any of Cisco's career certification. You will also need to have hands-on experience with the equipment and technologies on which you'll be tested.

Tip: If you have the funds, or your employer will pay your way, consider taking a class at a Cisco Training Partner (preferably one with "distinguished" status for the highest quality possible). In addition to classroom exposure to the topic of your choice, you get a good view of the technologies being widely deployed and will be able to take part in hands-on lab scenarios with those technologies.

Before you even think about taking any Cisco exam, make sure you've spent enough time with the related software to understand how it may be installed and configured, how to maintain such an installation, and how to troubleshoot that software when things go wrong. This will help you in the exam, and in real life!

Testing Your Exam-Readiness

Whether you attend a formal class on a specific topic to get ready for an exam or use written materials to study on your own, some preparation for the Cisco career certification exams is essential. At $100 to $200 (depending on the exam) a try, pass or fail, you want to do everything you can to pass on your first try. That's where studying comes in.

6. Have you taken a practice exam on your chosen test subject? [Yes or No]

If Yes, and you scored 80 percent or better, you're probably ready to tackle the real thing. If your score isn't above that crucial threshold, keep at it until you break that barrier.

If No, obtain all the free and low-budget practice tests you can find and get to work. Keep at it until you can break the passing threshold comfortably.

We have included a practice exam in this book, so you can test yourself on the information and techniques you've learned. If you don't hit a score of at least 80 percent after this test, you'll want to investigate the other practice test resources we mention in this section.

For any given subject, consider taking a class if you've tackled self-study materials, taken the test, and failed anyway. The opportunity to interact with an instructor and fellow students can make all the difference in the world, if you can afford that privilege. For information about Cisco classes, visit the Training and Certification page at **www.cisco.com/training** or **www.imsinc.com** (use the "Locate a Course" link).

If you can't afford to take a class, visit the Training and Certification page anyway, because it also includes pointers to additional resources and self-study tools. And even if you can't afford to spend much at all, you should still invest in some low-cost practice exams from commercial vendors, because they can help you assess your readiness to pass a test better than any other tool. The following Web sites offer some practice exams online:

➤ CCPrep.com at **www.ccprep.com** (requires membership)

➤ Network Study Guides at **www.networkstudyguides.com** (pay as you go)

Tip: When it comes to assessing your test readiness, there is no better way than to take a good-quality practice exam and pass with a score of 80 percent or better. When we're preparing ourselves, we shoot for 85-plus percent, just to leave room for the "weirdness factor" that sometimes shows up on Cisco exams.

Assessing Readiness for Exam 640-505

In addition to the general exam-readiness information in the previous section, there are several things you can do to prepare for the Remote Access exam. You will find a great source of questions and related information at the CCprep Web site at **www.ccprep.com**. This is a good place to ask questions and get good answers, or simply to watch the questions that others ask (along with the answers, of course).

You should also cruise the Web looking for "braindumps" (recollections of test topics and experiences recorded by others) to help you anticipate topics you're likely to encounter on the test.

Tip: When using any braindump, it's OK to pay attention to information about questions. But you can't always be sure that a braindump's author will also be able to provide correct answers. Thus, use the questions to guide your studies, but don't rely on the answers in a braindump to lead you to the truth. Double-check everything you find in any braindump.

For Remote Access preparation in particular, we'd also like to recommend that you check out one or more of these resources as you prepare to take Exam 640-505:

➤ Cisco Connection Online (CCO) Documentation (**www.cisco.com/univercd/home/home.htm**). From the CCO Documentation home page you can select a variety of topics, including but not limited to WAN technologies and implementation guides, as well as Internetwork Technologies Overviews and Design Guides.

Stop by the Cisco home page, your favorite bookstore, or an online bookseller to check out one or more of these resources. We believe CCO Documentation provides a wealth of great material.

One last note: Hopefully, it makes sense to stress the importance of hands-on experience in the context of the Remote Access exam. As you review the material for that exam, you'll realize that hands-on experience with the Cisco IOS with various technologies and configurations is invaluable.

Onward, through the Fog!

Once you've assessed your readiness, undertaken the right background studies, obtained the hands-on experience that will help you understand the products and technologies at work, and reviewed the many sources of information to help you prepare for a test, you'll be ready to take a round of practice tests. When your scores come back positive enough to get you through the exam, you're ready to go after the real thing. If you follow our assessment regime, you'll not only know what you need to study, but when you're ready to make a test date at Sylvan Prometric. Good luck!

CHAPTER ONE

Determining Remote Access Needs

After completing this chapter, you will be able to:

✓ Describe various wide area network (WAN) services

✓ List different kinds of circuit-switching connections

✓ List different kinds of packet-switching connections

✓ Describe various WAN encapsulation types

✓ List the signaling standards used with serial connections

✓ Explain the difference between synchronous and asynchronous serial communications

✓ Describe site considerations to use in selecting remote access services and equipment

This chapter examines remote access services and the reasons to use such services. Wide area network (WAN) communication occurs between geographically separated areas. In enterprise internetworks, WANs connect the central office to remote branch offices. When one branch office wants to communicate with another remote branch office, information must be sent over one or more WAN links. You need to examine the needs of the branch and central offices, so that you can determine what kind of WAN services and WAN encapsulation protocols should be selected, and what routers and router interfaces need to be purchased. Routers within enterprise internetworks represent the local area network (LAN)/WAN junction points of an internetwork. This chapter will define these junction points by describing the WAN services they use.

WAN Services

WAN communication is often called a service because the network provider often charges users for the services provided by the WAN. These charges are known as tariffs. WAN services are provided primarily through the following three technologies:

➤ Dedicated lines (sometimes referred to as leased lines)

➤ Circuit switching

➤ Packet switching

Dedicated Lines (Leased Lines)

Dedicated lines are fixed connections, which do not involve establishing a new connection each time the link is used. They are permanent end-to-end connections. The telecommunications company provides a dedicated high-speed connection between the two desired locations, at speeds ranging from as low as 9600bps to as high as 45Mbps. The higher the speed, the greater the monthly fixed cost of the line. The connection is available 24 hours a day, 7 days a week, and is thus suited to companies that want permanent connections between their office branches, or perhaps to a company that wants a permanent connection to the Internet. One big advantage of dedicated lines is that you, the customer, own all the bandwidth on the connection, giving you a lot of flexibility for your WAN needs.

The basic unit of measurement for dedicated lines is a T1 connection, which supports 1.544Mbps. A T3 connection supports 45Mbps. Fractional T1 circuits are available in units of 64Kbps, with connections of 384Kbps, 512Kbps, and 768Kbps being common.

The connection is implemented with two units:

➤ *Channel Service Unit (CSU)*—This unit provides the interface to the dedicated line.

➤ *Data Service Unit (DSU)*—This unit interfaces between the CSU and the customer's equipment, using RS-232 for low speeds up to 56Kbps, and V.35

(RS-422/499) for higher speeds. It is common to have the units as a single component. Several modular Cisco routers can include CSU/DSUs as add-on modules.

Dedicated lines use synchronous communication links. Synchronous communication is usually much more efficient in use of bandwidth than asynchronous. With synchronous communications, the two devices initially synchronize themselves to each other, and then continually send characters to stay in sync. Even when data is not really being sent, a constant flow of bits allows each device to know where the other is at any given time. That is, each character that is sent is either actual data or an idle character. Synchronous communications allows faster data transfer rates than asynchronous methods because additional bits to mark the beginning and end of each data byte are not required. A 56Kbps synchronous line can be expected to carry close to 7000 bytes per second (that is, 56000/8), whereas the async data rate would be 56000/10. Another advantage of synchronous communications is that the frame structure allows for easy handling of control information. There is a natural position (usually at the start of the frame) for any special codes that are needed by the communication protocol.

Synchronous connections must always be in sync even if they have to make adjustments. The accurate decoding of the data at the remote end is dependent on the sender and receiver maintaining synchronization during decoding. The receiver must sample the signal in phase with the sender. If the sender and receiver were both supplied by exactly the same clock source, transmission could take place forever with the assurance that signal sampling at the receiver was always in perfect synchronization with the transmitter. This is seldom the case, so in practice the receiver is periodically brought into sync with the transmitter. It is left to the internal clocking accuracy of the transmitter and receiver to maintain sampling integrity between synchronization pulses.

Signaling Standards

A number of different standards define signaling over a serial cable, including EIA/TIA-232, X.21, V.35, EIA/TIA-449, EIA-530, and V.25bis. Each standard defines the signals on the cable and specifies the connector at the end of the cable.

Circuit Switching

Circuit switching is a WAN switching method in which a dedicated physical circuit is established, maintained, and terminated through a carrier network for each communication session. Circuit switching accommodates two types of transmissions: datagram transmissions and data-stream transmissions. Used extensively in telephone company networks, circuit switching operates much like a normal telephone call. Circuit switching moves data between two points by setting up a physical link, or circuit, between them. Data flows in a stream along a circuit that lasts as long as necessary, at which time the switches and lines used to build the circuit are freed for another connection.

The usual example of a circuit-switched network is the plain old telephone system (POTS) network. When you dial a phone number, the phone company's switching equipment sets up a direct circuit between your telephone and the destination. The chief advantage of circuit switching is that the flow of data (for example, your voice) is not subject to delays introduced by the network, and the recipient receives data exactly as it was sent. The big disadvantage is that much of the connection's available bandwidth may be wasted due to the bursty nature of data traffic, which will rarely saturate the link's capacity. Figure 1.1 illustrates how a laptop can dial into an access server using POTS.

There are two commonly used circuit-switching methods:

➤ *Asynchronous serial*—Dial-up using modems

➤ *Integrated Services Digital Network (ISDN)*—Two types: Basic Rate Interface (BRI) and Primary Rate Interface (PRI)

Asychronous Serial Communication

Asynchronous serial communication uses the existing telephone network with its associated low cost. Asynchronous communication happens when using the existing dial-up telephone network and when a connection is made between the two modems by dialing the number assigned to the other modem. Generally, connections are established for limited durations. This suits remote access users who might want to dial into their network after hours, or small offices that dial into their Internet Service Provider at regular intervals during the day to exchange email.

To allow an asynchronous serial call, a Cisco router needs to have an asynchronous serial interface attached to a modem. If the router uses an external modem, the interface on the modem will need the EIA/TIA-232 signal standard, and the interface to the telephone company will need the standard RJ-11 adapter.

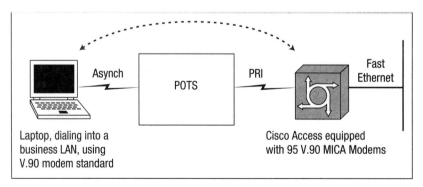

Figure 1.1 Circuit-switched network.

Types of Serial Communications

There are two basic types of serial communications, synchronous and asynchronous. Asynchronous means "no synchronization," and thus does not require sending and receiving idle characters. However, the beginning and end of each byte of data must be identified by start and stop bits. The start bit indicates when the data byte is about to begin, and the stop bit signals when it ends. The requirement to send these additional two bits causes asynchronous communications to be slightly slower than synchronous; however, it has the advantage that the processor does not have to deal with the additional idle characters. The serial ports on IBM-style PCs are asynchronous devices and therefore support only asynchronous serial communications.

An asynchronous line that is idle is identified with a value of 1 (also called a mark state). By using this value to indicate that no data is currently being sent, the devices are able to distinguish between an idle state and a disconnected line. When a character is about to be transmitted, a start bit is sent. A start bit has a value of 0 (also called a space state). Thus, when the line switches from a value of 1 to a value of 0, the receiver is alerted that a data character is about to come down the line.

ISDN

ISDN connections, like asynchronous serial connections, are circuit-switching connections. They are intended to compete with POTS by providing voice, data, and other traffic across a telephone network. Logically, ISDN consists of two types of communications channels: bearer service B channels, which carry data and services at 64Kbps; and a single D channel, which carries signaling and control information that is used to set up and tear down calls. The transmission speed of the D channel depends on the type of ISDN service you've subscribed to. ISDN services can be divided into two categories: Basic Rate Interface (BRI) service and Primary Rate Interface (PRI). Both services will be described in the following sections. ISDN configuration will be discussed in greater detail later in Chapter 6.

Basic Rate Interface (BRI)

ISDN BRI is the most basic ISDN interface. ISDN BRI provides the customer with two 64Kbps B channels and one 16Kbps D channel, all of which may be shared by numerous ISDN devices. It is the ideal service for homes and small offices, which, in the interest of controlling expenses, require a service that can integrate multiple communications needs. By bundling the two B channels together and using 2:1 data compression, an ISDN BRI link can achieve data throughput of over 250Kbps. You can have up to eight ISDN devices connected on a single bus because signals on the D channel automatically take care of contention issues as they route calls and services to the appropriate ISDN device. This allows you to have a router, phone, fax machine, and video conferencing equipment all sharing the same ISDN line. Although only two B channels are available to be used at any point in time, numerous other calls may be put "on hold" via D-channel signaling (a feature referred to as multiple call appearances). The D channel uses Link Access Procedure (LAPD), which is a data link protocol.

ISDN Primary Rate Interface (PRI)

Packet-switching ISDN PRI includes one 64Kbps D channel and 23 64Kbps B channels in North America, and 30 64Kbps B channels in Europe. The number of B channels is limited by the size of the standard trunk line used in the region; T1 in North America and E1 Europe. Unlike BRI, PRI does not support a bus configuration, and only one device can be connected to a PRI line. A PBX, however, can reallocate ISDN PRI resources onto multiple BRI buses.

Note: Routers that provide BRI services will need a BRI interface, which may have a built-in terminal adapter. The BRI interface with a built-in terminal adapter is described as a "U" interface. The BRI interface without a built-in terminal adapter is described as an "S/T" interface. Routers that provide PRI service will need a T1/PRI interface.

Dial-on-Demand Routing

One of the most attractive features for both asynchronous serial dial-up and ISDN connections is Dial-on-Demand Routing (DDR). Dial-on-Demand Routing provides session control for wide area connectivity over circuit-switched networks, which in turn provides on-demand services and decreased network costs. DDR starts and stops connections based on "interesting traffic" or data that needs to be sent. DDR also starts a connection when a backup connection is needed to supplement the main line.

DDR can also be used over synchronous serial interfaces such as over Integrated Services Digital Network (ISDN) interfaces and asynchronous serial interfaces. V.25bis and DTR dialing are used for Switched 56 CSU/DSUs and other synchronous serial connections. Asynchronous serial lines are available on the auxiliary port on Cisco routers and on Cisco communication servers with asynchronous interfaces. DDR is supported over ISDN using BRI and PRI interfaces. DDR is established and maintained using PPP or other WAN encapsulation techniques (such as High-Level Data Link Control [HDLC], X.25, and Serial Line IP [SLIP]).

Packet Switching

Instead of moving as a continuous, orderly stream, data on a *packet-switched* network is segmented into discrete units, or packets. Each packet contains a piece of the original data, plus information about the sender, recipient, and where that packet fits in with the others. Packet-switching networks simply forward these packets from one switch to another until they arrive at their destination. No direct, dedicated connection is ever formed. Consequently, individual data packets may travel different routes to the same destination.

Another feature of packet switching is multiplexing. Packet switching is a WAN switching method in which network devices share a single point-to-point link to transport packets from a source to a destination across a carrier network. This means that statistical multiplexing can be used to enable devices to share these circuits.

Packet–switching networks use synchronous serial connections. Packet–switching connections usually share bandwidth and are therefore less costly than leased lines.

There are four main packet-switching methods:

➤ Frame relay

➤ X.25

➤ Switched Multimegabit Data Service (SMDS)

➤ Asynchronous Transfer Mode (ATM)

Note: Unlike Frame Relay and X.25, which use variable-length packets to transport data, SMDS and ATM use fixed-length cells. Therefore, ATM and SMDS are actually considered cell-switching technologies.

A true circuit is an end-to-end, direct connection between two sources. Since packet switching uses multiple paths and allows different senders and receivers to share a connection during multiplexing, packet switching is considered a virtual circuit. A *virtual circuit* is a logical circuit created to ensure reliable communication between two network devices. Two types of virtual circuits exist: switched virtual circuits (SVCs) and permanent virtual circuits (PVCs). SVCs are virtual circuits that are dynamically established on demand and terminated when transmission is complete. Communication over an SVC consists of three phases: circuit establishment, data transfer, and circuit termination. A PVC is a permanently established virtual circuit that consists of one mode: data transfer. PVCs are used in situations in which data transfer between devices is constant. PVCs decrease the bandwidth use associated with the establishment and termination of virtual circuits, but they increase costs due to constant virtual circuit availability.

The advantage of packet switching is that short messages can be transferred with little latency because no end-to-end link needs to be set up. Moreover, carrier bandwidth can be shared by a large number of customers, resulting in lower costs. The disadvantage is that the data transfer rate varies from one packet to the next, limiting the usefulness of packet switching for voice or video applications that cannot tolerate variability.

Note: Each switching technique has advantages and disadvantages. For example, circuit-switched networks offer users dedicated bandwidth that cannot be infringed upon by other users. In contrast, packet-switched networks have traditionally offered more flexibility and used network bandwidth more efficiently than circuit-switched networks.

X.25

The International Telecommunication Union X.25 standard defines how connections between data terminal equipment (DTE) and data circuit-terminating equipment (DCE) are maintained for remote terminal access and computer communications.

The X.25 specification operates at the data link layer *and* the network layer of the OSI reference model. The data link layer protocol defined is LAPB. The network layer is sometimes called the packet layer protocol (PLP) but is commonly (although less correctly) referred to as "the X.25 protocol." More reliability is built into X.25 than frame relay because it is older, and at the time X.25 was created, central office telephone equipment was less reliable.

Frame Relay

Frame relay is a data service, specified in International Telecommunications Union-Telecommunication Standardization Sector (ITU-T) Recommendations I.122 and Q.922, for interconnecting data terminal equipment (DTE) across a public switched network. Frame relay provides a packet-switching data communications capability that is used across the interface between user devices such as routers, bridges, host machines, and network equipment, such as switching nodes. User devices are often referred to as data terminal equipment (DTE), whereas network equipment that interfaces to DTE is often referred to as data circuit-terminating equipment (DCE). The network providing the frame relay interface can be either a carrier-provided public network or a network of privately owned equipment serving a single enterprise.

Frame relay is a layer 2 protocol in the OSI model, and has been designed to be simple and effective. It is based on the core aspects of the link access procedure for the D channel (LAPD), in which error detection is carried out in the network, but no acknowledgment frames are exchanged between nodes in the network. If a frame is erroneous, it is discarded; the retransmission is done by the end-system. This reduces processing at the nodes and thus provides a higher speed than the X.25 network. Frame relay has no control fields and, therefore, has no frame types; it treats all frames alike as something to be delivered if possible.

Frame relay differs significantly from X.25 in its functionality and format. In particular, frame relay is a more streamlined protocol, facilitating higher performance and greater efficiency. The frame relay network is a digital network. To connect to the network, the device either uses RS-232, V.35, X.21, RS-449 to connect to an external DSU/CSU and then to the digital circuit supplied by the carrier, or uses a built-in DSU/CSU to connect directly to the carrier network.

WAN Encapsulation Protocols

No matter which WAN service type you use (dedicated leased line, circuit switching, or packet switching), your serial connection will be using a WAN encapsulation protocol. Most serial links use HDLC or some variant of it. Many variants of HDLC have been developed. Both Point-to-Point Protocol (PPP) and Serial Line IP (SLIP) use a subset of HDLC's functionality. ISDN's D channel uses a slightly modified version of HDLC. Cisco routers' default serial link encapsulation is HDLC.

Note: Remote access networks will make considerable use of PPP, because PPP is an open standard. HDLC, like PPP, is an open standard. Cisco, however, has added some extensions to it, making their implementation proprietary. So, Cisco's HDLC will work only on a connection where both devices are Cisco devices.

SLIP

Serial Line IP (SLIP), documented in RFC 1055, was the first protocol for relaying IP packets over dial-up lines. It defines an encapsulation mechanism, but little else. There is no support for dynamic address assignment, link testing, security, compression, or multiplexing different protocols over a single link. SLIP has been largely supplanted by PPP.

PPP

Point-to-Point Protocol (PPP), documented in RFC 1661, is the best solution for dial-up Internet connections, including ISDN. Dial-up modem lines first used SLIP, but PPP is now preferred. Both are HDLC-based, but PPP is more elaborate, supporting dynamic address assignment, on-the-fly data compression, and multiple network-layer protocols. In addition to data compression, header compression is also supported.

PPP is a layered protocol, starting with a Link Control Protocol (LCP) for link establishment, configuration, and testing. Once the LCP is initialized, one or many of several Network Control Protocols (NCPs) can be used to transport traffic for a particular protocol suite. The IP Control Protocol (IPCP), documented in RFC 1332, permits the transport of IP packets over a PPP link. Other NCPs exist for AppleTalk (RFC 1378), OSI (RFC 1377), DECnet Phase IV (RFC 1762), Vines (RFC 1763), Xerox Network System (XNS, RFC 1764), and transparent Ethernet bridging (RFC 1638).

The following PPP features are lacking in SLIP:

➤ *Dynamic IP addressing*—Allows a server to inform a dial-up client of its IP address for that link, but the mechanism is powerful enough for clients to request IP addresses, and it supports fallback configurations. SLIP required the user to configure this information manually. PPP options have also been specified (RFC 1877) for notification of name server addresses, both Internet and NetBIOS.

➤ *Authentication*—Available as an option, either with the Password Authentication Protocol (PAP), or the Challenge Handshake Authentication Protocol (CHAP). Both are documented in RFC 1334. Authentication includes the option callback for proper identification.

➤ *Multiple protocols*—Can interoperate on the same link, simply by running additional NCPs. For example, both IP and Internetwork Packet Exchange (IPX) traffic can share a PPP link.

➤ *Link monitoring*—Facilities include a link-level echo facility, which can periodically check link operation.

➤ *Multilink*—Allows for the combining of channels into one message-sending connection.

➤ *Compression*—Allows for higher data throughput across a link.

Selecting WAN Configuration Types

Remote access is generally used to define those instances where someone on a PC in a branch office can access the entire central office network as if he or she were actually in that central office. This has increased the pressure to find solutions that allow the remote user to connect to corporate information systems with the same capabilities as those in the corporate headquarters. These solutions try to offer high performance, scalability, flexibility, and reliability.

Remote access usage varies from file sharing, to dedicated applications, to email. Users need access to host computers for information processing purposes. Sometimes this takes the form of a communications session with a remote host where the local computer does nothing more than echo the screen data to the user. This can be done with remote control software that allows users to control a network-connected computer. In other cases, it may require a Telnet or some other communications session where the user's computer becomes a remote terminal to a host computer.

Note: For larger enterprises or mission-critical remote access services, a new technology has emerged in the last few years, which loses all the disadvantages of the traditional methods. This new technology is based on something called intelligent console architecture (ICA), developed by Citrix and sold as an original equipment manufacturer (OEM) item to many major terminal and software manufacturers. ICA currently leads as the core technology in what are known as "thin clients" and offers performance that is unbeatable for remote access to Windows GUI applications.

WAN Considerations

Understanding a company's needs is a critical aspect of selecting a WAN solution. The geographical composition of any company, when analyzed, can be broken down into three major categories: central site, remote site, and the telecommuter site. Determining which site category or offices fit into a company's plan will help you determine the appropriate remote access solution for that company. There are certain considerations for each category that will help you select services and equipment for each office. The following is a list of general considerations. In the next section, specific considerations will be described for each office type.

General factors a business should consider when choosing a solution for remote access sites are described in the following list:

➤ *Security*—Security is always a major factor in any component of a network. Your users are your customers, and you must design your network to minimize your security risks, yet still make it functional. Finding the right mix of security, performance, and cost can be very difficult.

➤ *Cost*—As with any technology, there is a cost/benefit relationship. As the technology becomes more beneficial, it becomes more expensive. In order to minimize costs, you can utilize circuit-switched networks, and you can bring up a network connection when it's needed and tear it down when you don't need it. Cost isn't always the same in all geographic locations for the same service. Tariffs differ from state to state; WAN circuits cost differing amounts from vendor to vendor, and personnel should always be factored into your cost analysis.

Note: Costs can be broken into two categories: fixed and recurring. Fixed costs are costs associated with the purchase of your equipment, such as a router and CSU/DSU, and the installation of the circuit. Recurring costs are costs that you must pay on an ongoing basis, such as maintenance, salaries, and the cost of the circuit. Both of these costs must be considered when choosing an appropriate WAN solution.

➤ *Scalability and flexibility*—Businesses can no longer afford to discard technology as they expand. Scalability and modularity are key requirements so that as a company grows, it can leverage its investment in existing equipment. For telecommuting and remote access solutions, it is critical that the central office solution allow system administrators to scale their network capacities.

➤ *Bandwidth needs and availability*—WAN bandwidth is one of the most critical aspects of selecting a WAN solution. Because bandwidth is expensive, it is important to make sure that you don't select too much capacity, thereby wasting precious resources. You will also need to forecast future bandwidth needs to keep up with expected business growth. The kinds of traffic expected on the WAN link should be taken into consideration. If you have small-sized, time-sensitive packets, your needs are much different than if you need to move large blocks of data for file transfers.

When selecting a WAN service, you will want to find all of the solutions that are available within your geographic region. Although asynchronous connections are available throughout the world, frame relay is not. If a service isn't offered at both ends of your connection, you may not be able to use it.

➤ *Manageability*—The ability to manage the WAN service should also play a key role in your selection. In many cases, the remote offices will may not have access to local IT support. Thus it is important to be able to control and administer the remote sites from the central office with solutions that are all designed to facilitate easy management from the central office. Many solutions have built-in monitoring and reporting, which makes it easy to monitor the levels and the nature of the remote access traffic.

➤ *Reliability*—If your business requires a connection to your remote site at all times, reliability will be a very important factor when determining the appropriate service. It may be necessary to design a backup solution in case the primary WAN service goes down.

Central Sites

The central site in any remote access application has to effectively address a number of key issues. For example, it will need to accommodate different types of remote access—from modems to ISDN, from permanent locations to mobile staff.

When choosing the best central site solution for its category, a business should consider the following:

➤ *Security*—Security is always important when permitting remote access to a central site. All of your standard network security should remain in place when anyone tries to log on. A security system should validate users with passwords to protect network-attached resources from unauthorized access. Added security measures can grant users access only to certain resources and protect the network communications link itself from eavesdropping. The more levels of security provided, the more secure the network resources and information become. By using access lists, you can filter out unwanted traffic (FTP, Telnet, WWW, and so on). In addition, you need to use authentication mechanisms such as Password Authentication Protocol (PAP) and Challenge Handshake Authentication Protocol (CHAP), and Caller ID and callback procedures to identify the user.

➤ *Cost*—One of the most important aspects of any network engineer's job is to maintain costs, while providing adequate service for the remote sites and telecommuters. Because some WAN charges, such as for ISDN, are based on usage, it is important for companies to have a solution that can implement features that will optimize your bandwidth and minimize WAN costs. Features such as bandwidth on demand (BOD), Dial-on-Demand Routing (DDR), snapshot routing, IPX spoofing, and compression ensure that WAN costs are kept to a minimum. Another way to keep costs down is to introduce Quality of Service (QoS) functionality. Using QoS, you can prioritize one type of traffic over another. For example, video conferencing could be routed before large FTP file transfers. This allows you to use a slower WAN connection that may not have been an option without QoS.

1

Note: If you are working in a remote office but need to be connected to the central network for email, access to databases, and so on, you may only need to send or receive data every 30 minutes or so. You could keep call charges down by logging in and out each time. But it takes time. Spoofing, on the other hand, fools the network into believing that the connection is still there. So you only incur call costs when actually sending data, while seeming to be connected all the time.

➤ *Scalability and flexibility*—The central site solution should have a modular design that can accommodate many different types of WAN connections coming in from remote locations including the telecommuter and the less mobile branch office. Many different remote sites can all connect to a single larger access server. It is important for a central site solution for telecommuting to have a modular design that can accommodate all types of connections from a single device. The most popular WAN service options for branch connectivity include: modem dial-up, Integrated Services Digital Network (ISDN), leased lines, frame relay, and X.25. The service for any one central office should meet the bandwidth and usage connection time requirements. ISDN provides a high-bandwidth, cost-effective solution for companies requiring light or sporadic high-speed access to either a central or branch office. Companies needing more permanent connections should choose between a dedicated leased-line connection and a packet-based service, such as frame relay or X.25. As a general rule, higher connect times and shorter distances make leased-line solutions more cost-effective. Branch office LANs with ISDN routers and single telecommuters with ISDN terminal adapters will link to an access server.

Central site scalability means that as more remote sites or users start to access the central site, the service can handle the added multiple simultaneous connections. Scalability also refers to provisions in place to accommodate fluctuating bandwidth usage without extra excessive costs. To accommodate fluctuating bandwidth, the central site could incorporate Multilink PPP to enable multiple bandwidth-on-demand connections per link at mixed speeds, providing a cost-effective method of supporting peak traffic requirements. Bandwidth on demand is another important feature that allows ISDN users to dynamically aggregate multiple B channels for high bandwidth when required.

➤ *Bandwidth needs and availability*—Bandwidth needs are determined by the kinds of traffic, the number of branch offices and telecommuter sites, and ultimately the total number of remote client computers. The implementation of different WAN types and the amount of bandwidth purchase for each type will be determined by the requirements of the branch and telecommuter sites. Central offices must accommodate the needs of all remote access sites and users. Products are needed to enable the central site to provide all remote users with high quality, high-speed access. Network managers need to consolidate and transport different traffic types while providing for different WAN connections such as analog dial-up, frame relay, ISDN, and leased lines.

➤ *Manageability*—Large central-site servers pose few problems for enterprise network managers. Configuration is relatively simple because it can be performed in one place. Such management issues as security and link utilization rates also are easier to monitor with a single locus of control.

In many cases, the remote offices may not have access to local IT support. Thus it is important to be able to control and administer the remote sites from the central office. Central-site solutions and products need to facilitate easy management from the central office. With built-in monitoring and reporting, it is easy to monitor the levels and the nature of the remote access traffic.

➤ *Reliability*—Despite the many advances technology is making, you can't count on technology to operate flawlessly in a 24/7/365 environment. A good network design lends itself to creating a more reliable network. By providing a backup link, you can provide an alternate connection to keep the office up and running while the primary WAN link is repaired. The central site will often have a backup WAN solution to support a faster primary WAN.

Remote Branch Sites

The branch site is a smaller office that houses employees in a specific location to fill a need in that geographic location. Communication becomes challenging for small- and medium-sized companies with customers, warehouses, or business partners located in various geographical areas. They frequently need to share customer information, check inventory, look up sales data, transfer files, process invoices, and exchange email. Yet a dispersed organization cannot communicate effectively and efficiently without the right technology.

When choosing the best branch office solution for its category, a business should consider the following:

➤ *Security*—All your standard network security still remains in place when anyone tries to log on from a branch office. In addition, added security features like Caller ID mean that only calls from recognized members would be accepted. The remote office bridge/routers can even be administered from the head office. So everything is simple to administer, simple to support, and simple to use.

Products are needed not only to let you connect to your corporate LAN; they also enable you to connect to the Internet as well. In a branch-office-to-central-site situation, you must make sure when you connect two LANs together that the central site authenticates users. For example, widely available ISDN and affordable remote access servers allow local networks that can communicate only through a central office to be linked into LAN-to-LAN internetworks. Branch-to-branch links can bypass the central office entirely in some cases.

➤ *Cost*—Cost is an issue no matter what type of site you are dealing with. Using DDR and compression techniques, you can ensure that you minimize your WAN costs. On the other hand, there is a large saving when implementing branch offices. The greatest challenge for any organization with multiple locations is how to avoid costly duplication of effort. Almost everything that is created in an office is generated electronically from memos to invoices, letters to reports; so it makes sense and saves money to connect branches to the main office.

➤ *Scalability and flexibility*—Because the branches are now effectively part of your head office LAN, they have access to all the central information they need. They can work on central databases and applications, and they can use the same e-mail system. Duplication is eliminated, information sharing is automatic, and communication is dramatically enhanced. People in the branch office don't need their own network and server; instead, they can simply connect an inexpensive hub to the router, which gives everyone immediate access to the head office network.

Similar to the central site, the remote site must be concerned about providing connections to other remote offices or to their telecommuters. In addition, they must make sure they connect to the central site. This requires that you consider devices that can provide multiple interfaces for your access solution. The branch office should be concerned about providing Quality of Service that can prioritize network traffic.

➤ *Bandwidth needs and availability*—Although WAN connections may vary considerably, you will find that the typical connections used in remote site locations revolve around the following: leased lines, ISDN (BRI and PRI), analog dial-up, X.25, and frame relay. Each branch office will have different bandwidth needs based on the amount of connection time that is needed and the size of files being transferred. These needs are related to the following applications: terminal emulation, email, client/server, file transfer, and delay-sensitive transfers such as video. As you move further from terminal emulation to delay-sensitive transfers, your bandwidth needs increase, and you are more likely to purchase WAN types that provide greater bandwidth. As bandwidth needs increase, you move from asynchronous dial-up, to ISDN, to frame relay, and ultimately to leased lines. All types of WAN services are not available in every geographic location in the world. You need to make sure that you inquire about the WAN services available in all of your remote locations as well as any possible locations that may be set up in the near future.

➤ *Manageability*—Like home offices, branch offices are less likely to grow than the central office. When the company grows, it is more likely to add more branch offices than to enlarge the existing ones. This means that many branch offices may never have their own MIS staff, and the most important feature a branch-office device can offer is management from a remote location. The ultimate challenge will be to allow access to multiple users and partners while receiving security assistance from the central office.

➤ *Reliability*—Link failures can occur at any time, and you must be prepared to handle those failures. In addition, you can use those secondary links to provide additional bandwidth when needed.

Telecommuter and SOHO Sites

More and more organizations are either outsourcing or using staff that are based at home. All the office costs are avoided, and staff can be more flexible over working hours. IT staff, from programmers to support staff, can then choose their own hours of work. Their requirement is usually for occasional access to the corporate system, rather than a permanent link. Teleworkers can be anyone, for example, senior managers, executives, and professionals who telework for one or two days a week to get work done without interruption. The needs of the telecommuter/SOHO site are different than those of the branch office and central site.

When choosing the best telecommuting solution for telecommuters and SOHO environments, a business should consider the following:

➤ *Security*—As with branch office sites, all standard network security remains in place when anyone tries to log on.

➤ *Cost*—Telecommuter and SOHO sites are very inexpensive to set up per user. Typically it will cost less than the cost of a PC. For example, all you need is the ISDN line, a router like the Cisco 700 series, and a standard network interface card to connect the PC to the router. Because most ISDN charges are based on usage, it is important that ISDN telecommuting users have a solution that can execute Dial-on-Demand Routing (DDR), which allows the user to start a WAN connection only when there is network traffic approaching a remote location. Bandwidth on demand (BOD) is another important feature that allows ISDN users to gather multiple B channels for high bandwidth when needed. Analog dial-up is also used for the telecommuter site.

➤ *Scalability and flexibility*—Typical access solutions for the telecommuter generally revolve around one of the following three connections: asynchronous dial-up, ISDN BRI, and frame relay. However, the two most popular WAN services for telecommuters are asynchronous dial-up and ISDN BRI. Asynchronous dial-up is a cost-effective solution for users who need occasional access to the corporate network to transfer relatively small amounts of data. ISDN offers an attractive alternative for users who need high-speed access to network resources and large files. In addition, frame relay is growing in popularity as a WAN service for full-time telecommuters. It is important that the equipment selected for the telecommuter site can be upgraded from modem dial-up to ISDN BRI to frame relay as easily as possible. It is also important for your central site solution for telecommuting to have a modular design that can accommodate all three types of connections from a single device.

➤ *Bandwidth needs and availability*—The primary objective of telecommuting is to set up an environment in a worker's home that is analogous to the environment that he or she finds in the office. Typically, that means a computer connected to the corporate network, along with a telephone and some form of fax service. Telecommuters should not only be able to connect to the corporate LAN; they should also be enabled to connect to the Internet as well. The telecommuting and SOHO environment will need the following: possible mainframe access, dial-up access to email, access to file sharing and client/server applications, Internet access, answering machine or service, and fax machines. Therefore, when designing a comprehensive telecommuting solution, careful attention has to be given to networking, voice, and fax. In many cases, this means that an ISDN line should be used. ISDN BRI links are around four times faster than a traditional modem link. Modems are influenced by the telephone infrastructure and can therefore sometimes be very slow. ISDN BRI, on the other hand provides guaranteed bandwidth.

➤ *Manageability*—Just as the branch may not have access to local IT support, the SOHO/Telecommuter site will be mostly isolated, constantly roving, and removed from any possible physical intervention by the company's IT staff. The Central site will need to monitor the SOHO/Telecommuter site usage and administer WAN operations for these sites, such as maintaining dynamic IP addressing.

➤ *Reliability*—Since we usually equate reliability with redundancy and the ability to provide a backup WAN connection, this is one area that is obviously lacking at the SOHO/Telecommuter site. It is unlikely that SOHO sites would have multiple ISDN lines or multiple routers, and Telecommuters would have multiple adapter cards or modems for PCs. However, with the right Cisco router or adapter card you can switch from ISDN to analog if the ISDN service fails.

Chapter Summary

WAN services consist of three categories: dedicated lines, circuit switching, and packet switching. Remote access connections are typically asynchronous dial-up and ISDN, which are both circuit-switching connection types. As connection time increases for users within a site, other more costly WAN services can be considered, such as X.25 and frame relay. These are classified as packet-switching connection types. Finally, if bandwidth needs are still not met, the site will need a dedicated leased line such as a T1 or T3. You can have a T1 deliver ISDN PRI, this would be considered circuit switching.

There are two kinds of ISDN services: Basic Rate Interface (BRI) and Primary Rate Interface (PRI). BRI ISDN includes two B channels, each having 64Kbps and one D channel with 16Kbps. PRI ISDN includes a T1 carrier service (T1/PRI), which includes 23 B channels each having 64Kbps and one D channel with 64Kbps. The ISDN D channel uses the data link layer LAPD protocol for signaling and control.

PPP is the most widely used encapsulation protocol for most remote access connections, especially those connections that use asynchronous dial-up or ISDN services. PPP provides many functions such as dynamic IP addressing, Multilink, compression, and authentication. The IPCP permits the transport of IP packets over a PPP link.

Frame relay uses virtual circuits including switched virtual circuits (SVCs) and permanent virtual circuits (PVCs). Most frame relay connections are forced to use PVCs where the connection is always up and data transfer is the only variable. This is different from circuit switching, which needs call setup and call tear-down.

Remote access connections that use dial-up procedures such as asynchronous dial-up and ISDN can reduce their costs by using Dial-on-Demand Routing (DDR) and bandwidth on demand (BOD). DDR uses "interesting traffic" to start sending data through a WAN connection and stops sending when that particular type of traffic ceases.

Asynchronous serial connections are normally slower than synchronous serial connections. Asynchronous serial connections use stop and start bits to delimit the beginning and ending points of packets, whereas synchronous serial connections use idle characters to determine packet boundaries.

The following standards define signaling over a serial cable: EIA/TIA-232, X.21, V.35, EIA/TIA-449, EIA-530, and V.25bis. Each standard defines the signals on the cable and specifies the connector at the end of the cable.

Business sites that use remote access connections are classified into three categories: telecommuter/SOHO, branch office, and central site. Each type of site has its own remote access needs. These needs are classified into the following categories: security, cost, scalability and flexibility, bandwidth and availability, manageability, and reliability. The needs of any one site are merged with the needs of the other site types.

Review Questions

1

1. What framing protocol is used on the ISDN D channel?

    a. LAPB

    b. LAPD

    c. SDLC

    d. PPP

2. Which of the following choices identify T1 ISDN PRI? [Choose the two best answers]

    a. Two B channels at 64Kbps

    b. Twenty-three B channels at 64Kbps

    c. Twenty-three D channels at 64Kbps

    d. One D channel at 16Kbps

    e. One D channel at 64Kbps

3. Which of the following WAN connection types are considered circuit-switching services? [Choose the two best answers]

    a. Frame relay

    b. ISDN BRI

    c. Asynchronous serial dial-up

    d. X.25

    e. Dedicated leased T1

4. Which of the following WAN connection types are considered packet-switching services? [Choose the two best answers]

    a. Frame relay

    b. ISDN BRI

    c. Asynchronous serial dial-up

    d. X.25

    e. Dedicated leased T1

5. Which of the following are characteristics of synchronous serial connections? [Choose the three best answers]

    a. Idle characters or bits

    b. Start bits

    c. Stop bits

    d. Signal sampling

    e. Clocking transmissions

6. Which of the following are characteristics of asynchronous serial connections? [Choose the two best answers]

    a. Idle characters or bits

    b. Start bits

    c. Stop bits

    d. Signal sampling

    e. Clocking transmissions

7. Dial-on-Demand (DDR) provides services for wide-area connections, which can decrease network costs. Which of the following are related to DDR services? [Choose the two best answers]

    a. Quality of service

    b. Traffic shaping

    c. Interesting traffic

    d. Backup connections

    e. Multilink PPP

8. WAN services are priced for the most part according to the overall amount of bandwidth they can provide. Which answer shows the correct price and bandwidth order for the following four WAN services where the cheapest service is at the left and the most expensive is at the right?

    a. Frame relay, analog dial-up, ISDN BRI, T1 leased line

    b. ISDN BRI, analog dial-up, Frame-Relay, T1 leased line

    c. Analog dial-up, ISDN BRI, T1 leased line, frame relay

    d. Analog dial-up, ISDN BRI, frame relay, T1 leased line

9. The LAPB protocol is used at the data link layer. Which WAN service uses LAPB?

    a. X.25

    b. Frame relay

    c. T1

    d. Analog dial-up

10. The PPP encapsulation protocol can provide many more services than SLIP. Which of the following services is provided by SLIP as well as PPP?

    a. Multilink

    b. Dynamic IP addressing

    c. Relaying IP packets

    d. Authentication

    e. Compression

11. Typically, users at branch offices will log on to a server at which remote access site?

    a. The same branch office

    b. Another branch office

    c. Central site

    d. SOHO

12. What is the most important part of any security system at any of the remote access site types?

    a. CHAP

    b. Caller ID

    c. Callback

    d. PAP

    e. User accounts and passwords

13. At which site type is it more important to have remote access equipment that is scalable in terms of needed interfaces that can be added in the future?

    a. Telecommuter

    b. SOHO

    c. Branch office

    d. Central office

14. Which set of dial-up connections is a more accurate statement that describes remote access among the three site types: telecommuter, branch office, and central office?

    a. Telecommuters and branch office users log in to the central office and are authenticated at the central office.

    b. Telecommuters log in to the branch office, which in turn sends their logon request to the central office to be authenticated by the central office.

    c. Telecommuters and branch office users log in to their branch office and are validated by the branch office, which gives them permissions to the central office.

    d. Telecommuters log in to the central office for validation, whereas branch office users log in to the branch office for validation.

15. Which WAN service can handle data, telephones, and faxes?

    a. Frame relay

    b. ISDN

    c. Analog dial-up

    d. X.25

    e. Switch 56K

16. Which remote access site type needs to more flexible for handling different kinds of services and needs to be equipped with different interfaces?

    a. Telecommuter

    b. SOHO

    c. Branch office

    d. Central office

17. A central office is more likely to have what kind of ISDN service?

    a. One BRI line

    b. One PRI line

    c. Two BRI lines

    d. Four BRI lines

Real-World Projects

Remote access solutions are being used across a vast spectrum of businesses today. Consider that you are a network engineer working for a consulting company that has contracted to design remote access solutions for three different companies. The following three scenarios and their resulting projects primarily use bandwidth needs and networking costs to determine a solution. The two costs are WAN tariffs and equipment costs. (These projects mention material that will be covered in depth in later chapters.)

Project 1.1

The Springfield Hospital Group has recently bought or merged with several well-known hospitals in the Baltimore City area. Now SHG has links to over 20 different clinics and hospitals in its region. In addition, SHG uses several database applications. Your company was asked to provide a complete audit of all local and wide-area connectivity and make any recommendations that would improve the overall performance of the systems.

To improve the overall performance of the local and wide-area connectivity, you recommend they take the following steps:

1. As the main component of the WAN, use a Cisco 3640 router that uses frame relay over a T1 line to its various clinics.

2. Set up the various clinics with a slower 56K leased line.

3. Create two other main WAN links to bigger hospitals that use dedicated leased lines over T1.

4. Set up the central office with traffic shaping to ensure the reliable performance of critical database applications across low-speed network connections.

Project 1.2

The National Children's Charity, based in Philadelphia, asked you, its top network engineer, to plan and install a network using their existing PCs and connect eight remote sites to the central site. The eight remote sites were very small and only included two to four employees in each. They also wanted an email and Web browsing facility for all staff. The plan had to keep costs down because their funding was strictly allocated for research and not administrative or infrastructure expenses.

You take the following steps to plan and install this network:

1. Install a new Category 5 structured cable system along with two Compaq 2500 servers.

2. Utilize an existing PC as a firewall and proxy server. Use one of the Compaq servers for File/Print services and the other for the Exchange Server v5.0 with the Internet Mail Service.

3. Because the branch offices don't need a local server, set them up with peer-to-peer networking, using Windows 98 or Windows NT Workstation, to share some information and printers.

4. Once the new network is installed, connect the eight regional offices to the Philadelphia office. Do this by using a Cisco 4500 router in Philadelphia and Cisco 700 series routers in each of the regional offices. The Cisco 700 series and not the Cisco 1600 series will be selected to facilitate the required connectivity, and yet keep the communication equipment costs to a minimum. The 700 series costs less than the 1600 series.

5. Connect all the routers via ISDN connections to try to minimize connection costs. Fit the Cisco 4500 router with an ISDN T1/PRI interface.

6. Configure the 700 series routers to open the ISDN line only when "interesting" packets are sent. These "interesting" packets would normally originate from the branch offices and would be requests for file or email synchronization.

Project 1.3

As part of its plan to expand the investment and financing profile, the Export-Import Bank of Princeton, New Jersey wants to upgrade its operations by adding four offices that will need to be connected through a wide area network (WAN). At present the bank has seven offices in the country. "We will soon have 11 WAN-linked offices with the head office in New York," said Fernando Cabrera, the bank's managing director. That's what the newspaper article said. Now it is time for the company to design a plan that would accommodate the anticipated future growth.

You need to recommend the following solution for the above scenario:

1. Because the plan requires high-bandwidth communications between sites, implement ISDN PRI at the central office.

2. Implement ISDN BRI at the remote branch offices.

3. Instruct branch office users to log on to the server at the central office, so that the central office will provide the point of security.

4. Install local servers in the branch offices, knowing that they will still rely on important information from the central office.

CHAPTER TWO

Selecting the Appropriate Cisco Remote Access Product

After completing this chapter, you will be able to:

✓ List the different Cisco series routers for each remote access environment

✓ Know the ISDN and analog service capabilities for each access server

✓ Understand the differences between WAN Interface Cards (WICs), Network Modules (NMs), and Network Processor Modules (NPMs)

✓ Describe various Cisco cables used for interface conversions

✓ List various signal standards used by Cisco access routers

✓ Know the interface configurations for popular Cisco access servers

✓ Understand the importance of light-emitting diodes (LEDs) on a Cisco router

✓ Design remote access connections and select the appropriate Cisco products for them

This chapter describes the various Cisco routers that are used for remote access connections. The chapter is organized by categorizing remote access routers into one of three groups: telecommuter, branch office, and central office. Chapter 1 explained the three environments, their relationships to each other, and the needs generated by each one. This chapter takes the next step by providing some recommended solutions for the needs created by each environment. These solutions include the selection of recommended access servers and network modules for each remote access setting.

This chapter describes several variants within each Cisco series and thus discusses many router features. You need to focus on each router's capability for providing ISDN and asynchronous services. The descriptions will include the Cisco product number assigned to each Cisco product that is mentioned, so that you can begin to recognize Cisco products as they are listed in major vendor catalogs. It is not necessary to memorize every remote access product number. Rather, just observe the patterns used within each line of products and recognize the major series numbers for the Cisco product line. For example, "NM" is found in the product number of every network module, and the major categories of routers include the 700, 1000, 1600, 2500, 2600, 3600, 5000, and AS5X00 series.

The Trio of Cisco Access Routers

You can categorize Cisco routers that are used for remote access according to their function within the telecommuter–branch office–central office trio. At the same time, you need to know whether a Cisco router series uses a fixed design with permanent interfaces or modular design where interfaces can be inserted or exchanged. Also, you need to be able to describe the variants within each series. Members within each series can vary according to their physical aspects, such as the number and type of interfaces and the amount of memory. First, let's look at the major divisions of remote access routers according to their function as shown in Tables 2.1 though 2.3. Notice that the telecommuter group is also called the small office/home office or SOHO group. Following these tables are descriptions of each series and its purpose in a LAN-WAN environment.

Cisco Solutions for the Telecommuter and SOHO

The telecommuter and SOHO group of routers includes the following series: Cisco 760, Cisco 770, and the Cisco 1000.

Table 2.1 Telecommuter and SOHO dial-up access routers.

Product Name	Data Type	Product Description
Cisco 760	ISDN/Analog	Small office multiprotocol router
Cisco 770	ISDN/Analog with integrated hub	Small office multiprotocol router
Cisco 1000	ISDN/Serial	Fixed configuration, desktop router

Table 2.2   Remote branch office access servers.

Product Name	LAN Technology	Configuration Design
Cisco 1000, 1600, 2500	Ethernet	Fixed configuration
Cisco 1600	Ethernet	Modular
Cisco 1600, 2500, 2600	Ethernet or Token Ring	Modular, Fixed configuration
Cisco 3620, 3640, 4500/4700	Ethernet, Fast Ethernet, Token Ring, Fiber Distributed Data Interface (FDDI)	Modular

Table 2.3   Central site access servers.

Product Name	Simultaneous ISDN Users	Simultaneous Analog Users	Type
Cisco 2509, 2511	0	8 or 16	Analog only
Cisco 3620	$\leq$20	32	ISDN and async via separate lines
Cisco 3640	$\leq$52	96	ISDN and async via separate lines
Cisco 3660	$\leq$48 (T1), $\leq$60 (E1)	8 (T1), 60 (E1)	ISDN and async via same lines
Cisco AS5200	$\leq$48 (T1), $\leq$60 (E1)	48 (T1), 60 (E1)	ISDN and async via same line
Cisco AS5300	$\leq$96 (T1), $\leq$120 (E1)	96 (T1), 120 (E1)	ISDN and async via same line

700 Series Routers

Cisco offers a variety of solutions for the home office. The Cisco 700 series ISDN access routers offer a cost-effective solution for telecommuters. The Cisco 760 and 770 series contains two analog telephone interfaces that allow devices such as standard telephones, fax machines, and modems to share one ISDN BRI line. This eliminates the need for multiple telephone lines or other expensive ISDN telephones.

The Cisco 700 series of routers has three main families: the 750, 760, and 770. The 750 family has been discontinued and was bought by Cisco from a company called Combinet. The Cisco 770 family added the option of a built-in 4-port hub instead of a single Ethernet port, giving SOHO users a single piece of equipment to supply all their phone and networking needs. The 760 and 770 family of routers is available in the variants shown in Table 2.4.

Note: POTS stands for plain old telephone service, which is another term for analog dial-up. Another name for analog dial-up is Public Telephone Switched Network (PTSN).

The Cisco 700 series does not run the Internetwork Operating System (IOS). Instead, it uses special software Feature Sets. Two packages are available for the Cisco 760 and 770 family of routers: the Internet-Ready Feature Set and Remote Office Feature Set. The Internet-Ready Feature Set is designed for a SOHO environment connecting to the Internet or a corporate WAN using only the TCP/IP protocol. It supports a maximum of four devices on the network, such as PCs and network printers connected to the Ethernet LAN. The Remote Office Feature Set is designed for

Table 2.4 Cisco 700 family description and model numbers.

Description	Model Number
Cisco 760-M Series	
ISDN BRI Router without Network Termination 1 (NT-1), without POTS	761
ISDN BRI Router with NT-1, without POTS	762
ISDN BRI Router with 2 POTS, without POTS	765
IDSN BRI Router with NT-1, with 2 POTS	766
Cisco 770 Series	
ISDN BRI Router with 4-port hub, without NT-1, without POTS	771
ISDN BRI Router with 4-port hub and with NT-1, without POTS	772
ISDN BRI Router with 4-port hub, 2 POTS, without NT-1	775
ISDN BRI Router with 4-port hub, NT-1, 2 POTS	776

remote offices. It adds the Novell IPX/SPX protocol, on-the-fly data compression, and support for 1,500 devices on the network.

1000 Series Routers

The Cisco 1000 series of compact, easily installed and managed, fixed-configuration desktop routers provide low-cost, high-speed connectivity for small offices as well as telecommuters. The Cisco 1000 series routers are the lowest cost IOS-based routers available. Only three variants are available: the 1003, 1004, and 1005. The 1000 series can include the following features and is available in the three variants as shown in Table 2.5. All 1000 models contain an RJ-45 console port and one Ethernet 10Base-T (RJ-45) port. The 1003 and 1004 use ISDN BRI for their WAN connection, whereas the 1005 uses a serial port capable of both synchronous and asynchronous communications. In order to make an ISDN connection, the 1003 requires an external Network Termination 1 (NT-1), whereas the 1004 has one built in. Neither the 1003 nor the 1004 has the POTS ports that are available on the 700 series routers. The ISDN service provider supplies the NT-1 connection worldwide except in North America, where the NT-1 is supplied by the customer. Therefore, the Cisco 1004 router is for use in North America, and the Cisco 1003 router is applicable worldwide. Designed for use with external serial-device WAN connections, the 1005's singular WAN port (DB-60) supports asynchronous serial communications at speeds up to 115.2Kbps. Also supported are synchronous connections such as leased lines, frame relay, switched 56Kbps, Switched Multimegabit Data Services (SMDS), and X.25 at speeds up to 2.048Mbps.

Table 2.5 Variations in the Cisco 1000 series.

Model Number	WAN Connections
Cisco 1003	ISDN BRI
Cisco 1004	ISDN BRI with NT-1
Cisco 1005	EIA/TIA-232, EIA/TIA-449, V.35, X.21, EIA-530

One of the most intriguing parts of this series of routers is a Personal Computer Memory Card International Association (PCMCIA) slot for a flash memory card. You can readily swap the PCMCIA flash memory card loaded with your IOS software in and out, making IOS upgrades amazingly easy.

Modular Components: NMs, WICs, and NPMs

Before proceeding with the descriptions of branch office and central office equipment, we need to cover the basic ingredients of modular design. Many of the routers used within branch and central site environments contain slots for adding interfaces. The interfaces can be added using simple WAN Interface Cards or by inserting one of the more elaborate network modules or network processor modules.

With respect to the number and kind of interfaces included in a Cisco router, the router can have either a fixed interface configuration, a completely modular configuration, or the router can be partially modular, that is, the router can have both fixed interfaces and some slots for modular components. Fixed routers are available with predetermined fixed LAN and WAN interface options. Modular or partially modular routers and access servers, such as the 2600 series, are built with one or more slots for customized network modules and/or WAN Interface Cards. This makes modular routers more scalable than fixed configuration routers. When you are selecting a router, either fixed or modular, it should have the interfaces that are necessary for your WAN connection(s). The following are the typical interfaces that are found on a Cisco router and the typical connections supported:

➤ *Asynchronous serial*—Asynchronous serial interfaces use modems and support asynchronous dial-up connections.

➤ *Synchronous serial*—Synchronous serial supports serial connections, such as leased lines, frame relay, and X.25.

➤ *Asynchronous/synchronous serial*—This interface support both asynchronous and synchronous serial connections, which are available for the 2600 series.

➤ *ISDN BRI*—This interface supports ISDN BRI connections.

➤ *Channelized T1 or E1*—This interface supports connections such as leased lines, dial-up, ISDN PRI, and frame relay.

➤ *Unchannelized T1 or E1*

➤ *High-Speed Serial Interface (HSSI)*

T1/E1: Channelized vs. Unchannelized

T1 and E1 connections come in different forms—there is no one type of T1 connection. If the T1 or E1 line connected to an access server acts as a trunk for several incoming connections at the same time, the line is channelized. A *channelized* T1 or

E1 service is divided into individual 64Kbps channels (or channels that are multiples of 64Kbps such as a 256Kbps channel made from four 64Kbps channels), as opposed to unchannelized service, which uses the entire bandwidth of the T1 (1.544Mbps) or E1 (2.048Mbps). Unchannelized T1 carriers can be used to support bandwidth-intensive services that do not lend themselves to 64Kbps channelization and standard framing conventions. In other words, the traditional convention of 64Kbps channels can be abandoned in favor of carving the T1 pipe into any segments of bandwidth of any usable size or increment.

Channelized T1 or E1 lines can consist of switched lines with in-band signaling or leased lines. Additionally, leased lines may be channelized, for example, when a leased line runs from the central office to the corporate headquarters as a single T1 or E1 line, but then branches into channels to remote sites from the corporate headquarters. A line can have three types of channels:

➤ *DS0*—A 64Kbps channel on a line using in-band signaling.

➤ *B channel*—56Kbps or 64Kbps channel that carries user data on a line using signaling.

➤ *D channel*—Carries WAN synchronization information on a line using ISDN D-channel signaling.

The term *channelized* has a different meaning than the term *fractional*. A fractional T1 line is a service aimed at customers who don't need all 24 channels of a full T1 line. Fractional T1 service offers the use of one or more channels. The customers, then, pay only for the channels they use. Fractional refers to the number of channels being purchased, whereas channelized refers to the way you use the number of channels already purchased.

Modular Routers and Partially Modular Routers

When determining which routers are needed for a particular LAN-WAN implementation, you need to examine each router's capability for adding interface components. Three basic types of components can be added to a modular router: WAN Interface Cards (WICs), network modules (NM), and network processor modules (NPM). A WIC is a small card containing one or two WAN ports, and it is inserted into a WAN slot found in the chassis of certain modular routers or in the WAN slot found on certain network modules. That's right: A few network modules have slots themselves for additional WICs, as shown in Figure 2.1. A network module is also inserted into its available slot, and it is larger and can contain more interfaces than a WIC. A network processor module is much like a network module but includes more circuitry, which is used for supplementary processing power that assists the router's central processing unit (CPU).

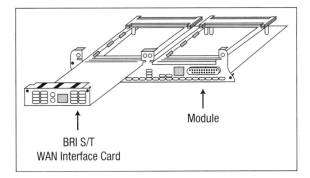

Figure 2.1 A WAN Interface Card being inserted into a network module.

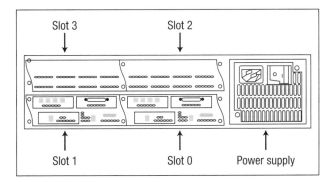

Figure 2.2 The four slots of the Cisco 3640.

One example of a modular router is the Cisco 3600 series. The Cisco 3660 has six network module slots; the Cisco 3640, as shown in Figure 2.2, has four network module slots, and the Cisco 3620 has two slots. Each network module slot accepts a variety of network module interface cards, including LAN and WAN mixed media cards supporting Ethernet, Fast Ethernet, Token Ring, and a variety of WAN technologies. These cards provide the foundation of LAN and WAN connectivity on a single, modular, network module. Additional applications are supported with a series of network module cards offering digital modems, asynchronous and synchronous serial, ISDN PRI, and ISDN BRI interfaces. In addition to the six network module slots, the Cisco 3660 has two internal Advanced Integration Module (AIM) slots for applications such as hardware-accelerated compression.

The Cisco 3600 series shares network modules and some WAN Interface Cards with the Cisco 2600, 1700, and 1600 series.

The following network modules are available for the Cisco 3660, Cisco 3640, and Cisco 3620 routers:

➤ LAN with modular WAN (WAN Interface Cards)

➤ 8- and 16-port analog modem network modules

➤ Channelized T1, ISDN PRI, and E1 ISDN PRI network modules

➤ Combined Fast Ethernet and PRI network modules

➤ 4- and 8-port ISDN BRI network modules

➤ 16- and 32-port asynchronous network modules

➤ 4- and 8-port synchronous/asynchronous network modules

➤ 1- and 4-port Ethernet network modules

➤ 1-port Fast Ethernet (10/100) network modules

➤ 8- and 16-port analog modem modules

➤ 4-port serial network module

➤ Analog and digital (T1) Voice Network Modules

➤ Single-port High-Speed Serial Interface (HSSI)

➤ ATM 25Mbps Network Module

➤ ATM OC3 155Mbps Network Module

➤ 6-, 12-, 18-, 24-, and 30-digital modem network modules

Certain network modules have slots for WAN Interface Cards like the NM-1E2W.

The most common WIC is the serial WAN Interface Card. The 1-port serial WAN Interface Card and the 2-port serial WAN Interface Card provide an EIA/TIA-232, EIA/TIA-449, V.35, X.21, or EIA-530 DTE serial interface to a Cisco modular router. In Cisco 3600 and Cisco 2600 series routers, the 2-port serial WAN Interface Card supports both asynchronous (up to 115.2Kbps) and synchronous (up to 2.048Mbps) data rates. The 1-port serial WAN Interface Card supports only synchronous data rates up to 2.048Mbps. In the Cisco 1720 router, the 1-port and 2-port serial WAN Interface Cards support both asynchronous (up to 115.2Kbps) and synchronous (up to 2.048Mbps) data rates. In Cisco 1600 series routers, the 1-port serial WAN Interface Card supports asynchronous data rates up to 115.2Kbps, and synchronous data rates up to 2.048Mbps. The 2-port serial WAN Interface Card is not supported on this platform.

Another interesting pair of WIC cards is the channelized T1/PRI card that comes either without a Channel Service Unit (CSU) (Figure 2.3) or with one (Figure 2.4). To connect a channelized T1/PRI module to the network, use a DB-15-to-DB-15 T1 serial cable to connect the channelized T1/PRI port to a T1 CSU. To connect a channelized T1/PRI with a built-in CSU to the network, use a straight-through RJ-48C-to-RJ-48C cable to connect the RJ-48C port to an RJ-48C jack at the demarc.

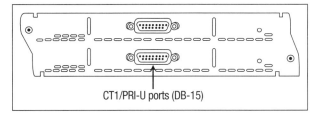

Figure 2.3   PRI port without a CSU.

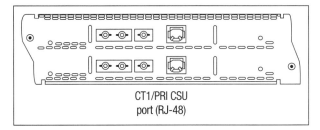

Figure 2.4   PRI port with a CSU.

Cisco Solutions for Branch Offices

Branch office routers include the Cisco 1600, 1700, 2500, 2600, and 4000 series routers. The 3600 will be described under central site access routers, but it too can be considered a branch office access server at times. Likewise, the entire list of branch office routers can be used in a central site. Obviously, there are no hard rules, especially if a router is placed in one particular site for supplementary or backup reasons. But you should try to keep your router selection based on the primary function of each router as listed in this chapter and section.

1600 Series Routers

The Cisco 1600 series represents a class of routers optimized for branch offices. With a WAN Interface Card slot and support for multiple WAN technologies, you can change cards when different services are required. The Cisco 1600 is at the low end of an extremely flexible class of routers that also includes the 2600 and 3600. Most variants come with one Ethernet and one WAN interface, whereas the 1601–R through 1605-R have two Ethernet ports. The 1601-R through 1605-R routers have a "run-from–RAM" architecture; the "R" suffix designates "run from RAM." The Cisco IOS software image is stored in flash memory in compressed form, but is loaded into RAM before being executed by the router.

All 1600 routers come with one WAN Interface Card slot to add optional WAN Interface Cards (WICs). The WAN Interface Cards used in the 1600 series are interchangeable with 2600 and 3600 routers as well. Table 2.6 describes the fixed interfaces and lists the number of WIC slots available for each 1600 model. Table 2.7 lists the available WICs for all 1600 models.

Table 2.6   Comparison of the 1600 series models.

Model	Base Configuration	Interface Slot
Cisco 1601	1 Ethernet, 1 serial sync/async	1
Cisco 1602	1 Ethernet, 1 56Kbps	1
Cisco 1603	4-wire DSU/CSU,1 Ethernet,1 ISDN BRI S/T	1
Cisco 1604	1 Ethernet, 1 ISDN BRI U (with NT-1)	1
Cisco 1605-R	2 EthernetWAN	1

Table 2.7   WAN Interface Card options for Cisco 1600 series routers.

Interface Type	Product Number
1-port Serial	WIC-1T
1-port ISDN BRI U	WIC-1B-U
1-port ISDN BRI S/T	WIC-1B-S/T
1-port ISDN BRI S/T Leased Line	WIC-1B-S/T-LL
1-port 56/64Kbps CSU/DSU	WIC-1DSU-56K4
1-port T1/FT1	WIC-1DSU-T1

> *Note: The BRI U module does not require an external NT-1. Some ISDN service providers require an external Network Termination 1 (NT-1) device to connect an ISDN S/T port to the ISDN line.*

Not all of these WICs can be used with each model. There are certain limitations as to which WICs can be used with which 1600 routers. The 1-Port ISDN BRI U card and the 1-Port ISDN BRI S/T card are not available with Cisco 1603 or Cisco 1604 routers, because they already have fixed ISDN ports. The 1-Port ISDN BRI S/T Leased-line card is available only with Cisco 1603 or Cisco 1604 routers.

Cisco 2500 Series

The Cisco 2500 series of access routers is the world's most popular line of branch office routers. Its broad range of models provides a wide variety of connectivity alternatives. For the most part, the Cisco 2500 series routers are fixed-configuration routers. They are one of the oldest products in Cisco's product line, and the number of variants has grown due to low price and high popularity. The 2500 series can be broken up into several families based on these features: LAN/WAN, Access Server, Dual LAN/WAN, Hub, Frame Relay Access Devices (FRAD), and Modular.

The LAN/WAN family consists of the 2501 through 2504 routers. These offer one Ethernet or Token Ring port, two high-speed serial ports, and (in the 2503 and 2504) an ISDN BRI port. The Access Server family consists of the 2509 through 2512 routers. These offer one Ethernet or Token Ring port, two high-speed serial ports, and either 8 or 16 low-speed serial ports (typically for modems or dumb terminals). The Cisco 2509 and 2511 and the AS2509-RJ and AS2511-RJ access server models are dial-up remote access servers with integrated routing. They provide high-speed synchronous and asynchronous serial line connections—perfect remote access solutions to the corporate LAN from a single platform. These fixed-configuration access server models provide Ethernet or Token Ring LAN connections for 8 or 16 simultaneous dialup users.

The Dual LAN/WAN family (consisting of the 2513 through 2515 routers) offers two Ethernet or Token Ring ports, or one of each and two high speed serial ports. The Hub Series consists of the 2505, 2507, and 2516 through 2519 routers. These offer dual high-speed serial and either 8, 14, 16, or 23 Ethernet, or 14 or 23 Token Ring ports. The Frame Relay Access Devices (FRAD) family has only four variants: 2520 through 2523. Each of these can come configured with a single Ethernet or a Token Ring and two high-speed serial, one ISDN BRI, and 2 or 8 low-speed asynchronous serial ports.

The Modular family consists of the 2524 and 2525 routers. These routers offer one Ethernet or Token Ring port, and three optional WAN module slots. The three WAN slots are not identical: two are for serial WAN connections and one is for ISDN. By eliminating multiple standalone network devices, clumsy cabling, and complicated installations, these versatile routers are ideal for deployment in remote office locations. WAN modules are available in the following modules:

➤ 2-Wire Switched 56Kbps with built-in DSU/CSU

➤ 4-Wire 56Kbps/64Kbps with built-in DSU/CSU

➤ Fractional/Full T1 with built-in DSU/CSU

➤ Synchronous Serial Five-in-One high-speed serial port

➤ ISDN BRI with S and T reference points

➤ ISDN BRI with built-in NT-1 and U reference point

Summary of the 2500 Series

All series 2500 routers come with a console and an auxiliary port. Both are low-speed asynchronous serial ports with RJ-45 connectors. The Cisco 2500 series of routers are available in the variants shown in Table 2.8.

Table 2.8 Summary of Cisco 2500 series routers.

Model	Ethernet	Token Ring	Low-Speed Serial	High-Speed Serial	ISDN BRI	Hub Ports
2501	1	0	0	2	0	0
2502	0	1	0	2	0	0
2503	1	0	0	2	1	0
2504	0	1	0	2	1	0
2505	0	0	0	2	0	8 Ethernet
2507	0	0	0	2	0	16 Ethernet

(continued)

Table 2.8   Summary of Cisco 2500 series routers *(continued)*.

Model	Ethernet	Token Ring	Low-Speed Serial	High-Speed Serial	ISDN BRI	Hub Ports
2509	1	0	8	2	0	0
2510	0	1	8	2	0	0
2511	1	0	16	2	0	0
2512	0	1	16	2	0	0
2513	1	1	0	2	0	0
2514	2	0	0	2	0	0
2515	0	2	0	2	0	0
2516	0	0	0	2	1	14 Ethernet
2517	0	0	0	2	1	14 Token Ring
2518	0	0	0	2	1	23 Ethernet
2519	0	0	0	2	1	23 Token Ring
2520	1	0	2	2	1	0
2521	0	1	2	2	1	0
2522	1	0	8	2	1	0
2523	0	1	8	2	1	0
2524	1	0	0	0	0	0
2525	0	1	0	0	0	0

Cisco 2600 Series

The Cisco 2600 series combines dial access, routing, LAN-to-LAN services, and multiservice integration of voice, video, and data in the same device. There are six variants of the 2600 series, the Cisco 2610 with one Ethernet port, the Cisco 2611 with two Ethernet ports, the Cisco 2612 with one Ethernet port and one Token Ring port, the Cisco 2613 with one Token Ring port, the Cisco 2620 with one 10/100 Mbps auto-sensing Ethernet port, and the Cisco 2621 with two 10/100 Mbps auto-sensing Ethernet ports. Each 2600 series router comes with two WAN Interface Card (WIC) slots, and one network module slot. These routers also come with one AIM slot, and console/auxiliary ports capable of running at 115.2Kbps. The 2600 series supports a wide variety of WIC and NM cards. Because most of these cards are compatible with the 1600 and 3600 series routers, you reduce your costs for maintaining inventory, and gain greater flexibility in your network design and evolution. The optional network modules for the 2600 series are listed in Table 2.9, and the available WICs are listed in Table 2.10.

4000 Series Routers

Although the Cisco 4000 series could also be used for a central office site, it is mostly considered a branch office router. The Cisco 4000 series consists of the 4000-M, 4500-M, and 4700-M, and their modular design allows easy reconfiguration as needs

2

Table 2.9   Network module options for Cisco 2600 series routers.

Product Number	Network Module
NM-1E	1-port Ethernet
NM-4E	4-port Ethernet
NM-4A/S	4-port Asynchronous/Synchronous Serial
NM-8A/S	8-port Asynchronous/Synchronous Serial
NM-16A	16-port Asynchronous Serial
NM-32A	32-port Asynchronous Serial
NM-4B-S/T	4-port ISDN BRI S/T
NM-8B-S/T	8-port ISDN BRI S/T
NM-4B-U	4-Port ISDN BRI with NT-1
NM-8B-U	8-port ISDN BRI with NT-1
NM-1CT1	1-port Channelized T1/ISDN PRI
NM-2CT1	2-port Channelized T1/ISDN PRI
NM-1CT1-CSU	1-port Channelized T1/ISDN PRI with CSU
NM-2CT1-CSU	2-port Channelized T1/ISDN PRI with CSU
NM-1CE1U	1-port Channelized E1/ISDN PRI Unbalanced
NM-2CE1U	2-port Channelized E1/ISDN PRI Unbalanced
NM-1CE1B	1-port Channelized E1/ISDN PRI Balanced
NM-2CE1B	2-port Channelized E1/ISDN PRI Balanced
NM-8AM	8-port Analog Modem
NM-16AM	16-port Analog Modem

Table 2.10   WAN Interface Card options for Cisco 2600 series routers.

Cisco Product Number	WAN Interface Card
WIC-1DSU-T1	T1/fractional T1 CSU/DSU
WIC-1DSU-56K4	One-port 4-wire 56Kbps CSU/DSU
WIC-1T	One-port high-speed serial
WIC-1B-S/T	One-port ISDN BRI
WIC-1B-U	One-port ISDN BRI with NT-1
Cisco 2600-specific WICs	
WIC 2T	Dual high-speed serial
WIC-2A/S	Two-port async/sync serial

Note: WICs with two ports are not compatible with Cisco 1600 series routers.

change. They are completely modular routers containing no LAN or WAN ports by default. The Cisco 4500 and 4700 series access routers are high-performance routers that support the most comprehensive set of LAN and WAN technologies including ATM (Asynchronous Transfer Mode), FDDI (Fiber Distributed Data Interface), DS-3, E3, and HSSI (High-Speed Serial Interface) at speeds of 12, 45, 52, 100, and 155Mbps.

The 4000 series routers have three Network Processor Module (NPM) slots. Table 2.11 displays NPMs available for the 4000 series. The 4000 series has many of the same types of media available to it as the modular series 3600. However, there are no available external communications devices like a DSU/CSU, modem, or an NT-1 in this product series. All ISDN BRI ports requires external NT-1s. All serial ports require modems or DSU/CSUs, and the channelized T1/E1/PRI cards require external CSUs. Note that an external CSU is not the same as a CSU/DSU. The channelized T1 cards act as the DSU; therefore, you only need a CSU.

Cisco Solutions for the Central Site

Cisco Systems offers a range of central site products ideal for telecommuting and remote user solutions. All of the following series of products are scalable and modular, and they offer the utmost in configuration flexibility.

3600 Series Routers

Although the Cisco 3600 series could also be used for a branch office site, it is generally considered a central office router. The Cisco 3600 series access servers provide amazing versatility to support branch/central site dial access applications, LAN-to-LAN or routing applications, and multiservice applications in a single router. The Cisco 3640 has four network module slots, and the Cisco 3620 access router is equipped with two slots that accept a variety of mixed-media or WAN network modules, including one slot that supports dual Ethernet and dual WAN ports; multi-service applications are supported by integrated voice network modules.

Table 2.11   Network processor modules configurable in 4000 series routers.

Product Number	Description
NP-1RV2=	1-port Token Ring module
NP-2R=	2-port Token Ring module
NP-2E=	2-port Ethernet module
NP-6E=	6-port Ethernet module
NP-1F-S-M=	1-port FDDI multimode single-attached module
NP-1F-D-MM=	1-port FDDI multimode dual-attached module
NP-1F-D-SS=	1-port FDDI single-mode dual-attached module
NP-1FE=	1-port Fast Ethernet module
NP-4B=	4-port ISDN BRI module
NP-8B=	8-port BRI module
NP-2T=	2-port serial module
NP-4T=	4-port serial module
NP-CE1B=	1-port channelized E1/ISDN-PRI network module, balanced
NP-CE1U=	1-port channelized E1/ISDN-PRI network module, unbalanced
NP-CT1=	Channelized T1/ISDN PRI module

A profusion of NM and WIC cards are available, making the 3600 the ultimate in configurable routers. Although only NM card slots are available, mixed media cards allow you one or two Ethernet and/or Token Ring ports and two WIC slots. WAN connections are available in just about every possible variation including: high-speed sync serial, ISDN BRI, Channelized T1/ISDN Primary Rate Interface (PRI), low-speed sync/async serial, low-speed async serial, 2- and 4-wire 56/64Kbps leased line, and full/fractional T1. Access server configurations can support up to 60 digital modems.

Table 2.12 lists most of the available network modules for the 3600 series. Notice that the three NMs that have slots for WICs are displayed in bold. Table 2.13 contains those WICs that can be inserted into the available NM slots. Included in Table 2.12 is the maximum number of NM cards that can be installed in each 3600 model.

Table 2.12   Network module cards for the Cisco 3600 series router.

Part Number	Description	Max per 3640	Max per 3620
NM-1E	1-port Ethernet	4	2
NM-1FE-FX	1-port Fast Ethernet, FX Only	3	2
NM-1FE-TX	1-port Fast Ethernet, TX Only	3	2
NM-1E2W	**1 Ethernet 2 WAN Card Slot**	**4**	**2**
NM-1E1R2W	**1 Ethernet 1 Token Ring 2 WAN Card Slot**	**4**	**2**
NM-2E2W	**2 Ethernet 2 WAN Card Slot**	**4**	**2**
NM-4A/S	4-port Async/Sync Serial	3	1
NM-4B-S/T	4-port ISDN-BRI	3	1
NM-4B-U	4-port ISDN-BRI with NT-1	3	1
NM-8A/S	8-port Async/Sync Serial	3	1
NM-8B-S/T	8-port ISDN-BRI	3	1
NM-8B-U	8-port ISDN-BRI with NT-1	3	1
NM-1CT1	1-port Channelized T1/ISDN-PRI	3	1
NM-1CT1-CSU	1-port Channelized T1/ISDN-PRI with CSU	3	1
NM-2CT1	2-port Channelized T1/ISDN-PRI	3	1
NM-2CT1-CSU	2-port Channelized T1/ISDN-PRI with CSU	3	1
NM-1CE1B	1-port Channelized E1/ISDN-PRI Balanced	3	1
NM-1CE1U	1-port Channelized E1/ISDN-PRI Unbalanced	3	1
NM-2CE1B	2-port Channelized E1/ISDN-PRI Balanced	3	1
NM-2CE1U	2-port Channelized E1/ISDN-PRI Unbalanced	3	1
NM-4E	4-port Ethernet	3	2
NM-4T	4-port Serial	4	2
NM-16A	16-port Asynchronous Module	3	1
NM-32A	32-port Asynchronous Module	3	1
NM-6DM	6-port Digital Modem	2	0
NM-12DM	12-port Digital Modem	2	0

(continued)

Table 2.12   Network module cards for the Cisco 3600 series router *(continued)*.

Part Number	Description	Max per 3640	Max per 3620
NM-18DM	18-port Digital Modem	2	0
NM-24DM	24-port Digital Modem	2	0
NM-30DM	30-port Digital Modem	2	0

Table 2.13   WAN Interface Cards (WICs) for the Cisco 3600 series routers.

Part Number	Description
WIC-1T	1-port high-speed serial
WIC 2T	Dual high-speed serial
WIC-1B-S/T	1-port ISDN BRI
WIC-1B-U	1-port ISDN BRI with NT-1
WIC-1DSU-T1	T1/fractional T1 CSU/DSU
WIC-1DSU-56K4	1-port 4-wire 56Kbps CSU/DSU
Cisco 3600-specific WICs	
WIC36-1B-U	One ISDN BRI port (U interface, includes NT-1)
WIC36-1B-S/T	One ISDN BRI port (S/T interface, requires external NT-1).
WIC-2A/S	2-port Asynchronous/Synchronous

Note: The WIC-2A/S is not supported in the 1600 or 2600 series. Also, if the WIC name includes "36", that particular model is not compatible with the 1600 or 2600 series and can only be installed in the 3600 series.

Access Servers AS5x00

The Cisco AS5x00 family of universal integrated access servers provides superior density and price/performance to accommodate the needs of general remote access users and high-bandwidth telecommuters. The AS5x00 series is extremely popular because it integrates the functions of standalone Channel Service Units (CSUs), channel banks, modems, communication servers, switches, and routers into a single chassis. By terminating both analog modem and ISDN calls on the same chassis from the same trunk line, the AS5x00 meets traditional analog dial-in needs, while supporting the growing demands for high-speed ISDN access.

All Cisco access servers can provide both modem and ISDN connections. Support for ISDN connections requires only a channelized T1 or E1/ISDN PRI card. If you are not using external modem banks as with the 2600 series, modem support requires the addition of modem carrier cards and modem modules as with the AS5x00 series. The modem carrier cards exist only to provide a frame for modem modules. Modem modules contain 6 or 12 modems each; however, the AS5200 does not support modem modules with 12 ports on each. These modems are not the typical end-user product, but rather digital modems on an integrated circuit. This technology allows access servers to decrease the size needed for large numbers of modems.

Both the AS5200 and AS5300 are three-slot access servers. Modem carrier cards can occupy any two available slots. The third slot is for the channelized T1 or E1/ISDN PRI card. This terminates the digital leased lines from the phone company. The AS5200 card supports two digital leased lines, and the AS5300 supports four. The AS5300 ships with standard console ports and two Ethernet LAN ports: one 10Base-T and the other configurable as either 10Base-T or 100Base-T. Three slots are available for modems and channelized T1/E1 cards.

Cisco uses Microcom and MICA modem technology in their access servers. Microcom modem modules are the older technology and hold 12 modems each. In both the AS5200 and AS5300, two modem modules can fit in a carrier card with a maximum of two carrier cards per access server. Simple arithmetic shows a maximum of 48 Microcom modems when using T1 and 60 modems when using E1. The channelized dual E1 card for the AS5200 adds an additional slot for a Microcom modem module. This is not true of the AS5300, which can support only 48 Microcom modems.

Both access servers can use the MICA modem modules, but the AS5200 has some limitations. The carrier cards for the AS5200 support 5 MICA modem modules with 6 modems each, while those for the AS5300 support 10 modem modules with 12 modem ports each. Both the AS5200 and AS5300 can hold two MICA carrier cards. An AS5200 using MICA modems has the same number of maximum connections as one using Microcom modems (60). However, the AS5300 is able to support 120 MICA modems, far outstripping the 48 available with Microcom technology. These numbers are for countries with E1. In countries with T1 lines, the AS5200 supports a maximum of 48 modems and the AS5300 supports 96.

Cabling

One of the most complicated parts of setting up a router is the selection of the serial cables to connect the router to the serial devices in your network. Many different serial cables with seemingly similar features are available, and finding the correct cable can be a challenge. The information that follows will quickly and easily guide you through the process of selecting the right serial cables for your network. Basically, all Cisco cables can be divided into two groups: synchronous serial and asynchronous serial. Before you connect a device to one of the serial ports, you will need to know the answers to the following questions:

➤ Is the router being connected to a DTE or DCE device?

➤ What signaling standard does the device require?

➤ Is a male or female connector required on the cable?

DTE or DCE

Devices that communicate over a serial interface are divided into two modes: DTE and DCE. The most important difference between these types of devices is that the DCE device supplies the clock signal that paces the communications on the line. The documentation that came with the device should indicate whether it is DTE or DCE (some devices have a jumper to select either mode). Table 2.14 summarizes the difference.

Signaling Standards

A number of different standards define signaling over a serial cable, including EIA/TIA-232, X.21, V.35, EIA/TIA-449, EIA-530, and EIA-613 HSSI. Each standard defines the signals on the cable and specifies the connector at the end of the cable. One end of a cable might have a DB-60 connector, which connects to one of the serial ports on your Cisco router, and the other end has the connector required for the signaling standard being used. For example, your external equipment may be a T1 Channel Service Unit/Data Service Unit (CSU/DSU), which converts the High-Level Data Link Control (HDLC) synchronous serial data stream into a T1 data stream. Several T1 CSU/DSU devices are available, which provide a V.35, EIA/TIA-449, or EIA-530 signal interface. Depending on the exact CSU/DSU you are using, the cable you select must have the correct signaling standard and pins at the device end.

The cable you select to connect the Cisco router to the device will be constructed to convert one signal interface type to another, and these cables are called interface converters. The interface converters are bidirectional with each port being DCE or DTE selectable. The interface converters are convenient because of the internal switch selectable configuration for RS-232 DTE to V.35, X.21 or RS-530 DCE or V.35, X.21 or RS-530 DTE to RS-232 DCE conversions. This allows the user to have one unit that can satisfy either interface conversion requirement without using two different products. The following are some of the more common interface conversion cables:

➤ *EIA/TIA-232 connections*—The EIA/TIA-232 standard supports unbalanced circuits at signal speeds up to 64Kbps. The EIA/TIA-232 serial transition cable, as shown in Figure 2.5, has a DB-60 connector for connection to a Cisco serial port. The opposite end has a DB-25 connector. The DB-25 connector can be male for DTE or female for DCE.

Table 2.14   DTE or DCE determination.

DTE	DCE	Selectable DTE or DCE Device
Terminals, computers	Modems, CSU/DSU, multiplexers	Hubs, routers

Note: All serial ports configured as DTE require external clocking from a CSU/DSU or other DCE device.

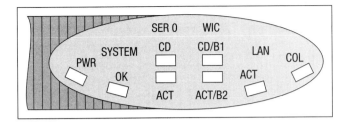

Figure 2.5 EIA/TIA-232 serial transition cable connectors.

➤ *EIA/TIA-449 connection*—The EIA/TIA-449 standard, which supports balanced and unbalanced transmissions, is a faster (up to 2Mbps) version of the EIA/TIA-232 standard that provides more functions and supports transmission over greater distances. The EIA/TIA-449 standard was intended to replace the EIA/TIA-232 standard, but it was not widely adopted primarily because of the large installed base of DB-25 hardware and because of the larger size of the 37-pin EIA/TIA-449 connectors, which limited the number of connections possible (fewer than are possible with the smaller, 25-pin EIA/TIA-232 connector).

➤ *V.35 connection*—The V.35 standard is recommended for speeds up to 48Kbps, although in practice it is used successfully at 4Mbps. The Cisco MC3810 supports speeds up to 2.048Mbps. The V.35 serial transition cable has a DB-60 connector for connection to a Cisco serial port. The opposite end has a standard 34-pin Winchester-type connector. The 34-pin Winchester-type connector can be male for DTE or female for DCE.

➤ *X.21 connection*—The X.21 connector uses a 15-pin connector for balanced circuits and is commonly used in the United Kingdom to connect to the public data network. X.21 relocates some of the logic functions to the DTE and DCE interfaces and, as a result, requires fewer circuits and a smaller connector than EIA/TIA-232. The X.21 serial transition cable has a DB-60 connector for connection to a Cisco serial port. The opposite end has a DB-15 connector. The DB-15 connector can be male for DTE or female for DCE.

➤ *EIA-530 connections*—The EIA-530 standard, which supports balanced transmission, provides the increased functionality, speed, and distance of EIA/TIA-449 on the smaller, DB-25 connector used for EIA/TIA-232. Like EIA/TIA-449, EIA-530 refers to the electrical specifications of EIA/TIA-422 and EIA/TIA-423. Although the specification recommends a maximum speed of 2Mbps, EIA-530 is used successfully at 4Mbps or faster speeds over short distances. The EIA-530 serial transition cable has a DB-60 connector for connection to a Cisco serial port. The opposite end has a DB-25 connector. The DB-25 connector can be male for DTE or female for DCE.

➤ *RS-422 connections*—The RS-422 is an electrical specification that allows communications speeds of up to 10Mbps at distances up to 40 ft (12 m) or communications speeds of 100Kbps at distances up to 4000 ft (1222 m). These speeds are possible because RS-422 specified balanced circuits.

Special Asynchronous Cables

Special cables are available for connecting asynchronous or async/sync serial interfaces. The following is a list of asynchronous cables for the 4000 series:

➤ *CAB-OCT-V.35-MT*—A 200-pin female to eight V.35 male connector cable. Used with the PA-8T-V35 port adapter for the Cisco 7000 family, and in Cisco 4000 series systems with the NP-2T16S-V.35 network processor module. This cable has a female 200-pin, Molex connector on the Cisco end and eight 34-pin Winchester block-type V.35 male connectors on the network end.

➤ *CAB-OCT-232-MT*—A 200-pin female to eight 25-pin EIA/TIA-232 male connector cable. Used with the PA-8T-232 port adapter for the Cisco 7000 family, and in Cisco 4000 series systems with the NP-2T16S-RS232 network processor module. This cable has a female 200-pin, Molex connector on the Cisco end and eight 25-pin Winchester block-type EIA/TIA-232 male connectors on the network end.

The following cables are used for 2509 through 2512 series Cisco routers:

➤ *CAB-OCTAL-6*—The Octal or "Octopus" cables for Cisco 2509 through 2512 series of routers. A male DB-68 SCSI II connector on the Cisco end to eight R-J45 connectors, six feet long. The 16-line Access Servers 2511 and 2512 will need two of these cables.

➤ *CAB-OCTAL-10*—The Octal or "Octopus" cables for Cisco 2509 through 2512 series of routers. A male DB-68 SCSI II to eight RJ-45 connectors, 10 feet long. The 16-line Access Servers 2511 and 2512 will need two of these cables.

➤ *CAB-OCTAL-15*—The Octal or "Octopus" cables for Cisco 2509 through 2512 series of routers. A male DB-68 SCSI II to eight RJ-45 connectors, 15 feet long. The 16-line Access Servers 2511 and 2512 will need two of these cables.

➤ *CAB-OCTAL-KIT*—The CAB-OCTAL-KIT includes a single CAB-OCTAL-6 and eight CAB-25AS-MMOD adapters, which is an RJ-45 to DB-25 male adapter. The MMOD type is a modified male DCE type. The 16-line Access Server 2511 and 2512 would require two CAB-OCTAL-ASYNC cables and 16 CAB-25AS-MMOD adapters to be used with 16 modems.

Table 2.15   Summary of interface signal standards.

Interface Name	Application (Often Used Frame Types)	Physical Connector
RS-232-C	Asynchronous, SDLC, HDLC	DB-25, DB-9 asynchronous only
V.35	SDLC, HDLC	MS-34
RS-449, RS-530	HDLC , SDLC, Frame Relay	DB-37 for RS-449, DB-25 for RS-530
RS-48	SDLC, HDLC 5	Usually DB-9 or DB-25
X.21	HDLC, SDLC, Frame Relay	DB-15
HSSI	E3 34Mbps, T3 = DS-3 45Mbps, SONET OC-1 52Mbps, SMDS, ATM	50-pin (SCSI-2)
BRI	HDLC, SDLC, Async. (V.110 or V.120), X.31 (= X.25 in the D-channel–LAPD)	4-wire-bus 100 ohms
PRI	G.704, vendor specific frame-formats (for leased lines only)	4-wire 120 ohms (often RJ-45)

The key is to make an association between signaling types or interfaces and their related cable connectors. Table 2.15 summarizes common cable connectors and their correlated signaling types or interfaces. The table also lists the frame types commonly used with each interface.

LEDs on a Cisco Router

Verification and Front Panel LEDs on the back or on the front panel of certain remote access routers can help verify router operation and assist in troubleshooting. In most cases, LEDs indicate system status and states in the startup sequence. By checking these LEDs, you can determine when and where the system failed. You should become familiar with all the LEDs found on the various 1600 models. This section is a good start for learning what LEDS indicate and how useful they can be. Table 2.16 shows the front panel LEDs, as shown in Figure 2.6, and their meaning for the Cisco 1601 and 1602. Table 2.17 lists the LEDs and their functions for the models 1603 and 1604.

Table 2.16   Front panel LEDs and their functions for Cisco 1601 and Cisco 1602.

LED	Color	Description
SYSTEM PWR	Green	The router is on, and DC power is being supplied.
SYSTEM OK	Green	The router has successfully booted. Blinks during the boot cycle.
LAN ACT	Green	Data is being sent to or received from the local Ethernet LAN.
LAN COL	Yellow	Flashing indicates packet collisions on the local Ethernet LAN.
SER 0 CD	Green	Cisco 1601 has an active connection on the serial port. Cisco 1602 has an active connection on the DSU/CSU port.
SER 0 ACT	Green	Cisco 1601 serial port is sending or receiving data. Cisco 1602 DSU/CSU port is sending or receiving data.
WIC CD/B1	Green	Serial WAN Interface Card has an active connection on the serial port ISDN WAN Interface Card has an ISDN connection on B-channel 1.
WIC ACT/B2	Green	WAN Interface Card serial port is sending or receiving data. WAN Interface Card ISDN port has a connection on B-channel 2.

Table 2.17 Front panel LED functions for Cisco 1603 and Cisco 1604.

LED	Color	Description
SYSTEM PWR	Green	The router is turned on, and DC power is being supplied.
SYSTEM OK	Green	The router has successfully booted. Blinks during the boot cycle.
LAN ACT	Green	Data is being sent to or received from the local Ethernet LAN.
LAN COL	Yellow	Flashing indicates packet collisions on the local Ethernet LAN.
BRI 0 B1	Green	An ISDN connection on B-channel 1. For the 1604, if an ISDN device connected to the ISDN S/T port is using B-channel 1, the LED turns on.
BRI 0 B and 2	Green	An ISDN connection on B-channel 2. For the 1604, if an ISDN device connected to the ISDN S/T port is using B-channel 2, the LED turns on.
WIC CD	Green	Active connection on the WAN Interface Card serial port.
WIC ACT	Green	Data is being sent over the WAN Interface Card serial port.

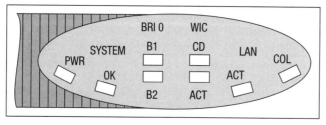

Figure 2.6 Cisco 1601 front panel.

Chapter Summary

Access servers are divided into three categories: telecommuter and SOHO, branch office, and central office. Because these categories relate to the size and function of remote access sites, routers are placed in each category according to the router's capabilities for providing varying amounts of ISDN and analog services. For example, a router that does not have a PRI interface for receiving multiple ISDN calls would not have the capability to be a central site access server.

The Cisco 1600 series router has five models. The 1601 and 1602 can use a modular ISDN interface, but they do not have a built-in ISDN interface. The 1603 and 1604 come with a built-in ISDN interface, but they can't use the ISDN module. The 1604 has a built-in NT-1 with U point of reference. Many of the same WICs used with the 1600 series can also be used with 2600 and 3600 series.

The Cisco 700 series is used for the telecommuter site and does not use the regular IOS software. Instead, the 700 series uses the Remote Office Feature Set. These routers are BRI routers because they all come with an ISDN BRI interface, and some even have a built-in NT-1. The 770 series includes a built-in 4-port hub.

The Cisco 1000 series router is a small inexpensive router used for small offices needing ISDN service. These routers have no analog capability. One of the Cisco 1000 features is the external PCMCIA flash card.

When it comes to selecting additional interfaces that can be added to an access server, there are WAN Interface Cards (WICs), network modules (NM), network modules with WICs, and network processor modules (NPM). The 3600 and 4000 series are modular routers. The 4000 series uses NPMs. The 2600 and 3600 series use NMs. The 2600 series uses WAN Interface Cards in one of two ways—the card can be placed in a WAN slot on the chassis or in the WAN slot of a network module. The 3600 series can use WICs in the appropriate WAN slot on a network module, but has no WAN slots on the chassis.

The Cisco 2500 series routers contain a few variants that are ideal for branch office access servers. The 2503 and 2504 include a built-in ISDN interface. The models 2509 to 2512 include built-in analog interfaces that divide into multiple analog connections and use an Octal cable. The models 2524 and 2525 are modular routers that can accept an ISDN WIC.

The Cisco 3600 series is completely modular. The Cisco 3620 has two modular slots and the Cisco 3640 has four modular slots. Both models can use digital modem cards. The Cisco 4000 series router includes no internal communication devices. So, in many cases the 3600 series router may be a better choice.

The AS5200 and AS5300 include network module slots for modem carriers and modem cards, which are made by either Microcom or MICA. When using a MICA card with 6 modem ports and an E1 line, you can have a maximum of 60 modems on the AS5200 and 120 on the AS5300. The MICA card with 12 modem ports can be used with AS5300 only and allows for a maximum of 240 modem ports per chassis. When using MICA and T1 lines, you can have a maximum of 48 modems on the AS5200 and 96 on the AS5300 with the 6-port card. When using MICA 12-port modems, T1 lines, and the AS5300, you can have a maximum of 192 per chassis.

Various interface conversion cables use various signal standards at the Cisco end and at the other end that attaches to either a communication device or the actual service. There are several cables that can be attached to serial WAN interfaces on a Cisco router that has a DB-60 pin port. Examples are the V.35 transitional cable that has a 34-pin Winchester-type connector for connecting to a CSU/DSU, or the EIA/TIA-232 transitional cable that has a DB-25 connector to connect a Cisco async/sync serial interface to an analog modem.

LEDS on the back and front panels of many Cisco routers are helpful for verifying the successful operation of the product. One example is the front panel LED of the Cisco 1600 series router. Most often when the LED indicator for a particular router's property shows the color green, that property is functioning normally.

Review Questions

1. The Cisco 1600 series router is an optimal router for small branch offices. Which two models in the 1600 series contain a built-in ISDN interface?

    a. 1601

    b. 1602

    c. 1603

    d. 1604

    e. 1605-R

2. The Cisco 1600 series router is an optimal router for small branch offices. Which three models in the 1600 series can have an ISDN WAN Interface Card?

    a. 1601

    b. 1602

    c. 1603

    d. 1604

    e. 1605-R

3. The Cisco 2500 series router is the most popular line of branch office routers. Which 2500 variants contain fixed low-speed asynchronous interfaces for 8 or 16 dial-up connections?

    a. 2501 to 2504

    b. 2509 to 2512

    c. 2520 to 2523

    d. 2516 to 2519

4. The Cisco 1600 series router has a slot for a WAN Interface Card (WIC). Most of the WICs used with the 1600 series can be used with other routers. Which set of Cisco routers can use most of the WICs that are used with the 1600 series?

    a. 4000 series and 700 series

    b. AS5200 and series AS5300

    c. 2600 series and 3600 series

    d. 2500 series and 700 series

5. Cisco routers either have fixed configurations where all interfaces are built into the chassis, or they have one or more slots for network modules and/or WAN Interface Cards. Which Cisco series router uses a special network module called a network processor module (NPM)?

    a. 4000

    b. AS5200

2

   c. 2600

   d. 1600

6. When you are selecting a WAN Interface Card for the Cisco 1601 series, the available WICs will have to be compatible with the 1600 series. Certain WICs are not compatible with the 1600 series because these WICs contain

   _____.

   a. Two ports

   b. A 56Kbps CSU/SDU

   c. ISDN port with NT-1

   d. T1 CSU/DSU

7. There are distinct differences between the telecommuter, branch office, and central office environments and their router requirements. Although some routers can be used in more than one of these settings, which of the following groups of Cisco series routers would be considered central office routers?

   a. 1600, 2600

   b. 3600, 2600

   c. 4000, 2600

   d. 3600, AS5200

   e. 700, 1000

8. If a T1/PRI network module contains a built-in CSU, what type of port and interface would the NM have in order to connect to the T1 service?

   a. DB-60

   b. DB-15

   c. EIA/TIA 232-25 pin

   d. RJ-45

   e. RJ-48

9. Which statement is true and matches the exact configuration for one of the Cisco 3600 series routers?

   a. The 3620 has two network module slots and one fixed Ethernet interface.

   b. The 3640 has four network module slots and one fixed Ethernet interface.

   c. The 3640 has four network module slots, one fixed Ethernet interface, and one Token Ring interface.

   d. The 3640 has four network module slots.

   e. The 3620 has four network module slots.

10. If you need a Cisco with a T1/PRI interface, which of the different router series would you select? [Choose all that apply]

    a. 1600

    b. 1000

    c. 2500

    d. 2600

    e. 3600

    f. 4000

    g. AS5200

11. The Cisco 1600 series router is a partially modular router with fixed interfaces and one WAN Interface Card slot. Which 1600 router contains a built-in serial async/sync interface?

    a. 1601

    b. 1602

    c. 1603

    d. 1604

    e. 1605-R

12. The Cisco 2509 through 2512 uses a large asynchronous port with a Small Computer System Interface (SCSI) II connector at the Cisco router end. The cable that connects to this port is called an Octal connector. What is the signal standard at the other end of this cable?

    a. V.35

    b. EIA-530

    c. EIA/TIA-232

    d. X.21

    e. EIA/TIA-449

13. When the LAN COL LED is flashing yellow on a Cisco 1603, this is providing you with information about the router. What does this mean?

    a. There are a certain number of packet collisions on the Ethernet LAN.

    b. Data is being sent and received with no problems.

    c. The router has successfully booted and all operations are OK.

    d. The power is on.

2

14. When describing telco communication equipment, we can use the terms DTE and DCE. Select the correct set of equipment where all items can qualify as DTE equipment.

    a. Computer, modem, CSU/DSU

    b. Computer, router, modem

    c. Computer, router, telephone

    d. Router, switch, modem

15. The Cisco 700 series router is appropriate for which kind of remote access site?

    a. Central office

    b. Telecommuter and SOHO

    c. Branch office

    d. Both central and branch offices

16. What type of connection point does an ISDN interface have if it also contains an internal NT-1?

    a. S/T

    b. U

    c. PRI

    d. RJ-48

17. Which pair of routers are real Cisco 2600 series routers?

    a. 2620 and 2640

    b. 2601 and 2603

    c. 2609 and 2611

    d. 2610 and 2611

18. Which Cisco 1600 series router comes with two fixed Ethernet ports?

    a. 1601

    b. 1602

    c. 1603

    d. 1604

    e. 1605-R

19. Which Cisco series router is completely modular and comes with no built-in interfaces?

    a. 3600

    b. 4000

    c. 1000

    d. AS5200

20. Which term describes a line that can allow the multiplexing of several connections into one T1 carrier or a portion of a T1 carrier?

    a. Channelized

    b. Unchannelized

    c. Fractional

    d. Dedicated

21. Which modular Cisco series router does not include any network modules with built-in DCE devices such as an NT-1 or CSU/DSU?

    a. 2600

    b. 3600

    c. 4000

    d. AS5200

22. Which Cisco series router can use a network module that has slots for WICs on the module itself?

    a. 2600

    b. 3600

    c. 4000

    d. AS5300

23. Which Cisco series router does not use the regular IOS software?

    a. 1000

    b. AS5200

    c. AS5300

    d. 3600

    e. 700

24. Which Cisco 700 series router contains a built-in interface?

    a. 750

    b. 760

    c. 770

    d. 780

Real-World Projects

Many IT consulting companies offer comprehensive remote access design and implementation services. They sometimes specialize in Public Switched Telephone Network (PSTN) dial-up (modems and access servers), ISDN, Terminal Servers,

Security and Authentication services, and their technicians specialize in network connections using Cisco products that integrate a secure reliable solution for their customers. Larry is a consultant for such a company, CGG Consultants.

Recently, Larry was assigned the task of installing a simple access server for a very small ISP company. Many small- to medium-sized Internet Service Providers (ISPs) configure one or two access servers to provide dial-in access for their customers, and most of these dial-in customers use individual remote PCs that are not connected to local-area networks (LANs). Larry was told that some customers are using Windows 98 and analog modems, whereas other customers use ISDN with internal or external terminal adapters. However, the ISP indicated that there are more customers using analog modems. Larry needs to select the right Cisco remote access equipment that would satisfy these needs.

Project 2.1

To select the right Cisco remote access equipment to satisfy the needs described above, perform the following steps:

1. Purchase a Cisco 2511 and Cisco AS5200 as the two access servers.

2. Configure a single Cisco 2511 connected to external modems to receive analog calls from remote PCs connected to modems.

3. Configure the single AS5200 to receive both ISDN and analog calls. A single Cisco AS5200 can support both types of remote clients.

4. Purchase the necessary cables and the required attached devices. In order to outfit the 2511, order two Octal cables with 8 RJ-45 extenders on each, which totals 16 analog extensions.

5. The 16 extensions require 16 modems, so purchase 16 U.S. Robotics Sportster V.90 modems.

6. The AS5200 needs a CSU/DSU, a channelized T1/PRI network module, and ten 6-port MICA modem cards. The channelized T1/PRI allows for 23 simultaneous ISDN connections, and the MICA cards allow for 48 simultaneous analog connections. Between the 2511 and the AS5200, you will be able to achieve a total of 64 simultaneous analog connections.

After Larry finished his work with the ISP company, he was assigned a new contract for outfitting one branch site that needed to connect to a central site for the Lenex Porcelain company. They felt that their connections were too slow with their present analog system. Larry decided to implement an ISDN solution.

Project 2.2

To implement an ISDN solution for this scenario, perform the following steps:

1. Use a Cisco 1604 router and a Cisco 760 router at the branch office, which would dial into a Cisco 3620 router at the central site. It would be best to use only ISDN digital calls and no analog dial-up for this scenario.

2. All calls need to be initiated by the remote routers on an as-needed basis.

3. The Cisco 3620 was not set up to dial out to the Cisco 1604 or the 760.

4. The 3620 will be set up to support an ISDN T1/PRI line; therefore, the correct network module has to be ordered. Select the NM-2CT1-CSU, which contains two ports with channelized T1/ISDN-PRI and a built-in CSU. The channelized ports will handle multiple incoming calls from the 1604 and 760.

5. The other network module slot on the 3620 was used for a backup serial connection and a local Ethernet port, so the central site router could point back to the remote LAN.

6. The configurations for both the Cisco 1604 and Cisco 3620 were to use Multi-link PPP, and the dial-load threshold feature, which brings up the second B channel when the first B channel exceeds a certain limit.

Project 2.3

BACA operates and maintains the Technical Manuals Integrated Management Program System (TMIMPS), which contains the Army's complete field and repair manuals, technical drawings, and all weaponry revision histories. Because of office consolidation, BACA's 30-member branch office site in Philadelphia, Pennsylvania was closing, and its staff would need immediate remote access to TMIMPS. BACA could neither afford to relocate its Philadelphia personnel nor rewrite its legacy application. So, many of its employees would become telecommuters. BACA needed a temporary solution, because the company was still going through reorganization. BACA contacted CCG, which directed Larry to design a solution. From the very beginning both Larry and BACA did not want to use ISDN, because the new group of telecommuters might not be a permanent condition.

To implement remote access without using ISDN, perform the following steps:

1. Upgrade an existing Cisco 3640 router by installing the necessary network module with digital modems that would give the company an additional 30 POTS connections.

2. Purchase the NM-30DM, which is a network module with digital modems that is compatible with the 3640 and has 30 modem ports.

3. Advise telecommuters to use their existing laptops and dial in to the central site using the 1–800 number.

2

CHAPTER THREE

Configuring Modems for Remote Access

After completing this chapter, you will be able to:

✓ Understand how modem standards help provide compatible communication equipment

✓ Describe modem modulation, modem compression, and modem error-checking standards

✓ Explain the function of the EIA/TIA-232 signal pins between a DTE device and DCE device

✓ Configure an asynchronous interface for analog dial-up connections

✓ Describe the various cables used for connecting different Cisco routers to a modem

✓ Describe the differences between rolled (crossover) and straight-through cables and adapters

✓ Perform a reverse Telnet session from a router to a modem

✓ Perform modem initialization and modem dialing from various methods

✓ Use chat scripts, reverse Telnet, and autoconfiguration commands

✓ Verify modem initialization and autoconfiguration using the **show line** command

✓ Connect two modems using an RS-232 null modem

✓ Using async interfaces, have one router dial up and connect to another router

In this chapter, you will learn about asynchronous communication and asynchronous router interfaces. You will learn how to attach and configure an asynchronous modem to a router's AUX port. After initializing the modem, you will learn how to create chat scripts that dial a modem that is connected to a router. In Chapter 5, we will discuss how a PC can connect to a router.

Modem Standards

A modem converts digital signals from your computer into analog signals, which can be transmitted over ordinary analog phone lines. This process is called *modulation*. On the receiving end, a modem demodulates the analog signals arriving over the phone line into electrical signals, which are then fed to the computer. MOdulation and DEModulation describe what modems do.

Generally, communications technology has developed a complex set of standards, technical terms, and jargon to describe specific features, problems, and aspects of transferring data. Various communication terms describe how modulation is conducted, how data is compressed, and how data travels with a certain amount of error control. Modem standards help to clarify these communication functions, as well as create a commonality for interconnecting equipment among vendors.

Modem standards address the following:

➤ Data signaling

➤ Data compression

➤ Error control

Data Signaling Standards

Signaling refers to the act of using electrical signals to transmit data between devices. One device sends data within a generated signal, and the other device receives the signal. Modulation refers to the shapes and frequencies involved within these electrical signals and the changes they need to go through in order for the receiving device to understand the contained data from the sending device. This implies that modulation techniques need to be standardized. The International Telecommunication Union (ITU) has defined and introduced several modem modulation standards over the years. In addition, various manufacturers have from time to time marketed their own proprietary versions of modems. Sometimes proprietary versions are forerunners to organizational standards. An example of a proprietary version becoming an ITU standard is the new V.90 standard.

The V.90 Standard

The 56Kbps technology was a new technology, which was released as a faster solution for end users and SOHO. After this technology was originally introduced, two technologies emerged—X2, which was developed by U.S. Robotics, and Lucent and

Rockwell's K56flex. Unfortunately, however, having two types of technologies with the lack of a standard created a problem for end users and Internet Service Providers. For example, if an end user had an X2 modem, but the Internet Service Provider only had Kflex modems, the end user would be unable to achieve optimal performance. Because of this dilemma, the V.90 standard was developed. This standard took both the X2 and Kflex technologies and merged them into one standard. This allowed end users to achieve maximum performance.

3

Traditional modem standards assume that both ends of a modem session have an analog connection to the public switched telephone network (PSTN). Data signals are converted from digital to analog and back again, limiting transmission speeds to 33.6Kbps with current V.34 modems. Due to limitations of the public telephone network, the theoretical maximum is 35Kbps. Now, with V.90 technology, a different assumption is made. The assumption is that one end of the modem session has a pure-digital connection to the phone network and takes advantage of that high-speed digital connection. By viewing the public switched telephone network as a digital network, V.90 technology is able to accelerate data downstream from the Internet to your computer at speeds of up to 56Kbps. In this way, V.90 technology is different because it digitally encodes downstream data instead of modulating it as analog modems do. The data transfer is an asymmetrical method, so upstream transmissions from your computer to the central site continue to flow at the conventional rates of up to 33.6Kbps. Upstream data from your modem is sent as an analog transmission that mirrors the V.34 standard. Only the downstream data transfer takes advantage of the high-speed V.90 rates.

Modems can receive data at speeds of up to 56Kbps; however, due to FCC (Federal Communications Commission) rulings on maximum permissible transmit power levels during download transmissions, speeds of 54Kbps are the practical maximum. Actual data speeds will vary depending on line conditions.

Note: There may be some confusion between the modulation speed from the DCE-to-DCE (modem-to-modem) and the DTE-to-DCE (router-to-modem) modulation speed. The speed between DCE-to-DCE is usually faster than the speed between the router and the modem. If the modem is allowed to set the speed between the router and the modem to match the speed between the two modems, there may be problems. This is why we lock the speed between the router and modem. Remember, a router will be a DTE in most cases. We will discuss DCE and DTE connections later in this chapter.

Other Modulation Standards

Several older modulation standards are still used. The following list contains brief descriptions of several of these standards. You can download descriptions of the various modem standards from the ITU-T and the CCITT at **http://www.itu.int/**.

➤ *V34*—The V.34 protocol is the standard for 33.6Kbps connections. This standard was initially ratified as 28.8Kbps but was updated to include 33.6Kbps in 1996.

➤ *V.32bis*—V.32bis is the standard for 14.4Kbps modems. A V.32bis modem can also fall back to 12Kbps and then to 9.6Kbps, 7.2Kbps, and 4.8Kbps Therefore, V.32bis is downward compatible with V.32.

➤ *V.32*—V.32 is the standard for 9.6Kbps communications. It also supports the fallback speed of 4.8Kbps.

➤ *V.23*—V.23 is the standard for 1.2Kbps communications. This protocol was developed with terminal operators in mind. It had a download speed of 1.2Kbps, but an upload speed of only 7.5bps. The upload speed was considered adequate for typing.

➤ *V.22 and V.22bis*—V.22 and V.22bis are standard modulation protocols for 1.2Kbps and 2.4Kbps modems receptively. They do not have fallback speeds, but they can adjust to the lower modulation speed for poor line conditions.

➤ *V.21*—V.21 is the standard for 300bps communications. It is very rarely used anymore.

Data Compression Protocols

Data compression and error control are closely related because each saves bandwidth. Bandwidth on WAN connections is limited. Using data compression techniques, you can reduce the size of the data that actually needs to be sent. Additionally, error detection and correction mechanisms can use bandwidth more efficiently. If you can avoid having to resend the data, you've just saved that much bandwidth.

All current high-speed modems support data compression protocols. That means that the sending modem will compress the data on the fly, and the receiving modem will decompress the data to its original form. There are two standards for data compression protocols, MNP-5 and CCITT V.42bis. Some modems also use proprietary data compression protocols. A modem cannot support data compression without utilizing an error control protocol. It is possible, however, to have a modem that supports an error control protocol, but does not support data compression protocol. An MNP-5 modem requires the MNP-4 error control protocol, and a V.42bis modem requires the V.42 error control protocol. Also note that although V.42 includes MNP-4, V.42bis does not include MNP-5. However, virtually all high-speed modems that support CCITT V.42bis also incorporate MNP-5. The maximum compression ratio that an MNP-5 modem can achieve is 2:1. The maximum compression ratio for a V.42bis modem is 4:1.

Microcom, a maker of modems, designed error-checking protocols and compression protocols that many modems support. Microcom Networking Protocols (MNP) 1–4 are error-checking protocols, whereas MNP-5 is a compression protocol. MNP-5 modems include at least some of the MNP-1–4 error-checking protocols (usually 4). Some of these protocols are included in the ITU standards.

In addition to hardware compression offered by modems, software compression is another alternative. Often, groups of files are compressed using software. These compressed files are meant to be decompressed by using similar software on the other side. This compression can be very efficient. In fact, compressed files can actually expand when going through a compressing modem unless the modem is smart enough to recognize that it is expanding the file and leaves it alone. MNP-5 modems don't recognize compressed files, but ITU V.42bis modems can. Compression by software may be faster and more efficient than either MNP-5 or V.42bis.

Error Control Protocols

Error correction is an important feature in the fastest modems. It allows fast and reliable connections over standard phone lines. All phone lines have noise, which degrades the data connection. Therefore, error correction is necessary.

All modems in a network must be using the same error-correction protocols for it to work. Fortunately, most modems use the same protocol, V.42. With it, modems can detect damaged data streams, and the data will be resent. The V.42bis protocol is just like V.42, but it incorporates data compression. Data compression allows modems to use higher bps levels. A 14.4 modem, with data compression, can boast transmission rates of 57,600bps. A 28.8 modem will boast transmissions of 115,200bps.

UART (8250, 16450, 16550) and Flow Control

The Universal Asynchronous Receiver/Transmitter (UART), which is a component in a PC, is a significant part of the communication process between a dial-up computer and remote router. The UART controls the process of breaking parallel data from the PC down into serial data that can be transmitted, and vice versa for receiving data. The type of UART chip you have will be the determining factor on how fast you can transmit and receive data for such devices as modems. A UART chip is an electronic circuit that transmits and receives data through the PC's serial port. It converts bytes into serial bits for transmission, and vice versa. It also generates and strips the start and stop bits appended to each character. The original PC serial interface specification utilized the 8250 Programmable Communications Interface, or UART. This device converts data from the microprocessor into a format that is easily transmittable via a single-wire connection. To accomplish this task, the UART takes data from the computer in a parallel format (that is, the bits are presented side by side) and shifts them out via a single pin in a serial (one bit directly after another, daisy-chain fashion) data stream. Various extra bits are added such as the start, parity, and stop bits to provide the UART on the other end of the serial data connection with an accurate means for the re-assembly of the original data format.

The new 16550 UART incorporates a buffer directly in the chip itself. This buffer is designed to hold up to 16 bytes before an overrun occurs. The buffer is arranged in a FIFO (First In, First Out). In programming terminology, this is known as a queue. The 16550 UART also has improved circuitry, which enables it to transmit data some four times faster than the old 8250. This high-speed circuitry helps in the PC environment mainly in interrupt timing, though the time saved is rather marginal. Of more importance is the FIFO buffer. By having a "reserve" storage area on the chip, if the processor is momentarily busy (say, executing an ANSII graphic sequence) the data is not lost, but held until the processor is free to receive it.

Asynchronous Communication: Lines and Interfaces

In this section, we will discuss how you configure an asynchronous interface (either TTY or AUX) for an analog dial-up connection, what needs to be configured within the async interface, and what needs to be configured within the line mode. In order to perform these configurations, you need to understand how absolute lines are numbered.

Configuring Lines and Interfaces

Remote clients dial in to the network through asynchronous ports, which can be on the back of an access server (for example, the Cisco 2511) or inside an access server (for example, the Cisco AS5300). To enable clients to dial in, you configure two components of each asynchronous port: lines and interfaces. Asynchronous interfaces correspond to physical terminal (TTY) lines. For example, asynchronous interface 1 corresponds to TTY line 1. Generally, commands entered in asynchronous interface mode enable you to configure protocol-specific parameters for asynchronous interfaces, whereas commands entered in line configuration mode let you configure the physical aspects for the same port. An asynchronous interface on an access server or router can be configured to support the following protocol functions:

➤ Network protocol support (such as IP, IPX, or AppleTalk)

➤ Encapsulation support (such as PPP)

➤ IP client addressing options (default and/or dynamic)

➤ IPX network addressing options

➤ PPP authentication

➤ ISDN BRI and PRI configuration

In contrast to functions performed by the interface, the asynchronous line and its configuration perform the following options:

➤ Physical layer options (such as modem configuration)

➤ Security for EXEC mode

➤ AppleTalk Remote Access (ARA) protocol configuration (PPP is configured in interface configuration mode)

➤ Autoselect to detect incoming protocols (ARA and PPP)

The following is an example of configuring IP resources to dial into a network. The first step configures the lines, and the second step configures the asynchronous interfaces:

1. Configure the physical aspect of a line that leads to a port. You might enter the following commands to configure lines 1 through 16 (asynchronous TTY lines on a Cisco 2511 access server). Notice that the **autoselect** command configures the line to autosense PPP:

```
line 1 16
login local
modem inout
speed 115200
flowcontrol hardware
autoselect ppp
```

2. On asynchronous interface 1, you configure your protocol-specific commands. You might enter the following commands:

```
interface async 1
encapsulation ppp
async mode interactive
async dynamic address
async dynamic routing
async default ip address 198.192.16.132
ppp authentication chap
```

Line Types and Numbering

Cisco devices have four types of lines: console, auxiliary, asynchronous, and virtual terminal lines. Different routers have different numbers of these line types. There are two kinds of numbering systems, as listed below:

➤ The relative line numbering within each set of line types

➤ The absolute line number for the entire router

Each relative set starts at zero. For example, the first Async interface has the line number of zero, and the first VTY line has the number of zero. You need to know the way each line type is numbered and when to use absolute line numbering, so you can make accurate reference to every line that is used in a router's configuration. The following is a list of line types, their command abbreviations, and their functions:

➤ *CON or CTY Console*—Typically used to log in to the router for configuration purposes. This line is numbered as line 0.

➤ *AUX Auxiliary*—This is a RS-232 DTE port used as a backup asynchronous port (TTY). This port should not be used as a second console port. This port is numbered such that its absolute line number is equal to the last TTY line number plus 1. So, if a router has eight asynchronous ports, the AUX has an absolute line numbered equal to 9. On a 2501 router, which has no asynchronous ports, the AUX is numbered as absolute line 1 (0+1=1).

➤ *TTY Asynchronous*—This line type refers to an asynchronous interface. Used typically for remote-node dial-in sessions that use such protocols as SLIP, PPP, and XRemote. The numbering varies widely between platforms.

➤ *VTY Virtual Terminal*—The VTY line is used for incoming Telnet, LAT, X.25 Packet Assembler/Disassembler (PAD), and protocol translation connections into synchronous ports (such as Ethernet and serial interfaces) on the router. The absolute line numbers for VTY lines start at the last TTY line number plus 2 through the maximum number of VTY lines specified. Relative line numbers, of course, start at VTY 0 and go to the maximum number of VTY lines for that particular router model.

Synchronous Interfaces and VTY Lines

Virtual terminal (VTY) lines provide access to the router through an interface. VTY lines do not correspond to interfaces in the same way that TTY lines correspond to asynchronous interfaces. VTY lines are created dynami-cally on the router, whereas TTY lines are static physical ports. When a user connects to the router on a VTY line, that user is connecting into a *virtual* port on an inter-face. You can have multiple virtual ports for each interface. For example, several Telnet connections can be made to an interface (such as an Ethernet or serial interface). The number of VTY lines available on a router are defined using the **line vty** *number-of-lines* global configuration command. Increase the number of VTY lines on a router using the **line vty** command. Delete VTY lines with the **no line vty** *line-number* global configuration command. The **line vty** command accepts any line number larger than 5 up to the maximum number of lines supported by your router with its current configuration.

Absolute vs. Relative Line Numbers

When you enter the line configuration mode, you can either designate an *absolute line number* or a *relative line number*. For example, in a Cisco 2511 router, the absolute line number 20 is VTY2 (line 18 is VTY0). See the printout below. It is easier to refer to lines in a relative format than to try to remember the absolute number of a line on a large system. The router uses absolute line numbers internally. You can view all of the absolute and relative line numbers with the **show users all** EXEC command. In the following sample display, absolute line numbers are listed at the far left. Relative line numbers are not shown. In this example, the first virtual terminal line has an absolute line number of 18, but its relative line number is VTY 0. Interface and line numbering schemes vary between access servers and routers and the type of assembled hardware configuration.

```
RouterA> show line
Tty   Typ  Tx/Rx              A  Modem  Roty  ACCO    ACCI  Uses  Noise  Overruns
*  0  CTY  -                  -         -     -       -     0     0      0/0
*  1  TTY  115200/115200      -  inout  -     4       -     31    26     0/0
*  2  TTY  115200/115200      -  inout  -     21630   -     37    23     0/0
A  3  TTY  115200/115200      -  inout  -     25      -     10    24     1/0
*  4  TTY  115200/115200      -  inout  -     4       -     20    63     1/0
*  5  TTY  115200/115200      -  inout  -     32445   -     18    325    22/0
A  6  TTY  115200/115200      -  inout  -     25      -     7     0      0/0
I  7  TTY  115200/115200      -  inout  -     6       -     6     36     1/0
I  8  TTY  115200/115200      -  inout  -     -       -     3     25     3/0
*  9  TTY  115200/115200      -  inout  -     4       -     2     0      0/0
A 10  TTY  115200/115200      -  inout  -     56      -     2     470    216/0
I 11  TTY  115200/115200      -  inout  -     4       -     31    26     0/0
I 12  TTY  115200/115200      -  inout  -     4       -     31    26     0/0
I 13  TTY  115200/115200      -  inout  -     4       -     31    26     0/0
I 14  TTY  115200/115200      -  inout  -     4       -     31    26     0/0
I 15  TTY  115200/115200      -  inout  -     4       -     31    26     0/0
I 16  TTY  115200/115200      -  inout  -     4       -     31    26     0/0
  17  AUX  9600/9600          -  -      -     -       -     2     1      2/104800
  18  VTY  9600/9600          -  -      -     -       -     103   0      0/0
  19  VTY  9600/9600          -  -      -     -       -     6     0      0/0
  20  VTY  9600/9600          -  -      -     -       -     1     0      0/0
  21  VTY  9600/9600          -  -      -     -       -     0     0      0/0
  22  VTY  9600/9600          -  -      -     -       -     0     0      0/0
  23  VTY  9600/9600          -  -      -     -       -     0     0      0/0
  24  VTY  9600/9600          -  -      -     -       -     0     0      0/0
  25  VTY  9600/9600          -  -      -     -       -     0     0      0/0
```

Modem-to-Router Signaling

Devices that communicate over a serial interface are divided into two modes: Data Terminating Equipment (DTE) and Data Circuit-terminating Equipment (DCE). The most important difference between these types of devices is that the DCE device supplies the clock signal that paces the communications on the interface.

The definitions for DCE and DTE here are slightly different than the ones used to describe DTE and DCE equipment when just talking about how modems are connected to PCs. Yes, modems, CSU/DSU, and multiplexers are typically DCE devices and terminals and computers are typical DTE devices. However, interfaces on routers can be either DTE or DCE, and both the console and auxiliary ports on most routers are usually DTE devices. So, when you configure and attach a TTY port on a 2511 or an AUX port to a modem, you can think of the router performing like a PC in the traditional modem-PC model. That is, both the computer and the router are DTE devices, and the one thing that remains the same is the signaling function of the pins associated with each terminating type.

Connecting the Router (DTE) to the Modem (DCE)

In Chapter 2, when we discussed signaling and interface types, we looked at the EIA/TIA-232 interface. Let's look again at a typical EIA/TIA-232 set of DTE and DCE signals. The EIA/TIA-232 standard supports two types of connectors: a 25-pin D-type connector (DB-25), and a 9-pin D-type connector (DB-9).

*Note: Although EIA-232 is still the most common standard for serial communication, the EIA has recently defined successors to EIA-232 called RS-422 and RS-423. The new standards are backward compatible so that RS-232 devices can connect to an RS-422 port. For more information go to the EIA-TIA web site at **http://www.tiaonline.org/**.*

The EIA/TIA-232 connector uses only 8 pins whether it's a DB-9 or DB-25 connector. The following is a list of common EIA/TIA-232 signals. DB-9s provide the eight most common serial signals, whose pin assignments are shown in Table 3.1 and followed by a brief explanation of each signal. Signal names that imply a direction, such as Transmit Data and Receive Data, are named from the point of view of the DTE device.

Table 3.1 DB-9 pin assignments.

DB-9 Pin	Corresponding DB-25 Pin	Signal	DTE to DCE	Function
2	3	RD	←	Received data
3	2	TD	→	Transmitted data
8	4	RTS	→	Request to send
7	5	CTS	←	Clear to send
6	6	DSR	←	Data set ready
5	7	SG	—	Signal ground
4	8	DCD	←	Data carrier detect
1	20	DTR	→	Data terminal ready

Note: These pins are divided into three functional groups that worked together when creating a successful connection. Each group of pins will help to provide either flow control, modem control, or data transfer.

Flow Control Pair

Pins 4 and 5 form the hardware control group that is activated when the DTE and DCE are ready to send data:

➤ *Request To Send (RTS)*—This signal line is asserted by the computer (DTE) to inform the modem (DCE) that it wants to transmit data. If the modem decides this is okay, it will assert the CTS line. When CTS is asserted by the modem, the computer will begin to transmit data. The DCE will receive data from the DTE and transmit it on to the communication link.

➤ *Clear To Send (CTS)*—Asserted by the modem after receiving a RTS signal, indicating that the computer can now transmit. When this signal is active, it tells the DTE that it can now start transmitting (on Transmitted Data line). When this signal is "On" and the Request To Send, Data Set Ready, and Data Terminal Ready are all "On," the DTE is assured that its data will be sent to the communications link. When "Off," it is an indication to the DTE that the DCE is not ready, and therefore data should not be sent.

Modem Control Threesome

Pins 20, 8, and 6 initiate, close, and monitor the status of the connection:

➤ *Data Terminal Ready (DTR)*—This signal line is asserted by the computer or router, and informs the modem that the computer or router is ready to receive data. This signal must be "On" before the DCE can turn Data Set Ready "On," thereby indicating that it is connected to the communications link. The Data Terminal Ready and Data Set Ready signals deal with the readiness of the equipment, as opposed to the Clear To Send and Request To Send signals that deal with the readiness of the communication channel. When "Off," it causes the DCE to finish any transmission in progress and to be removed from the communication channel.

➤ *Data Set Ready (DSR)*—This signal line is asserted by the modem in response to a DTR signal from the computer. The computer will monitor the state of this line after asserting DTR to detect if the modem is turned on.

➤ *Data Carrier Detect (DCD or CD)*—This control line is asserted by the modem, informing the computer that it has established a physical connection to another modem. It is sometimes known as *Carrier Detect (CD)*. The DCE uses this line to signal the DTE that a good signal is being received (a "good signal" means a good analog carrier, that can ensure demodulation of received data). DCD and DSR work together.

Data Transfer Pair

Pins 3 and 2 are responsible for the payload and actually move the data:

➤ *Transmit Data (TD)*—The line where the data is transmitted, a bit at a time.

➤ *Receive Data (RD)*—The line where data is received, a bit at a time.

Note: The interface transfers data between the computer and the modem via the TD and RD lines. The other signals are essentially used for flow control, in that they either grant or deny requests for the transfer of information between a DTE and a DCE. Data cannot be transferred unless the appropriate flow control lines are first asserted.

Let's follow the steps of an actual connection between a router and an attached modem. When the router (or PC) wants to send data, it sets the data terminal ready line. This DTR signal goes into the DTR line of the DCE, the modem. The DCE recognizes that the DTE is requesting a connection. If an open phone line exists for the DCE, it sets the DSR and Data Carrier Detected (DCD). When the router sees the DSR input line, it sets the request to send line—which says that the router has data to send to the DCE. If the DCE is clear to accept data, it sets the clear to send (CTS) line—which tells the router that the DCE is free to receive, and the router begins transmitting data over the TD line where it is received on the corresponding line on the DCE. Remember that the first thing that needs to happen is for the modem to detect a carrier, that is, the modem needs to connect to another modem before anything else can happen.

The last line of the **show line** command is the modem hardware state. CTS and DSR are signals supplied by the modem. DTR and RTS are signals provided by the router. When waiting for a call, the router will have DTR and RTS high. The modem will have CTS high. DSR is not supplied until there is a valid connection. When there is a valid connection, the modem will raise its DCD signal, which the router sees as DSR. Once DSR is raised, the line is activated and the connection process starts.

You can verify a connection with the **show line** command. Listings 3.1 and 3.2 show the results of two **show line** displays. The first display from **show line** con-tains the signal status for a reverse Telnet, and the second display shows the signal status for an up and running connection between two modems. Notice that both have CTS, DTR, and RTS up, whereas the connection between two modems has an additional DSR up. When the DSR is up, this clearly indicates that the modem has detected a carrier from another modem.

Listing 3.1   Display for successful reverse Telnet:

```
RouterA#sho line aux 0
Tty Typ Tx/Rx A Modem Roty AccO AccI Uses Noise Overruns9 AUX 38400/38400...
  - inout - - - 0 2 0/0
Modem hardware state: CTS* noDSR DTR RTS
```

Listing 3.2   Display for successful modem-to-modem connection:

```
RouterA#sho line aux 0
Tty Typ Tx/Rx A Modem Roty AccO AccI Uses Noise Overruns9 AUX 38400/38400...
 - inout - - - 0 2 0/0
Modem hardware state: CTS* DSR DTR RTS
```

Cisco Cables for Asynchronous Connections

When describing cables used for asynchronous connections between routers and modems, we are really referring to the signal standards found at a serial interface on a particular router and the conversion to EIA-232 signal standard found at the modem end of the cable. There are various instances of conversion cables, and you need to know the cables that are typically used when constructing remote networks.

RJ-45 for Cisco Console and Auxiliary Ports

The console and auxiliary ports on Cisco IOS routers are asynchronous serial ports. The console port is configured as Data Communications Equipment (DCE), and the auxiliary port is configured as Data Terminal Equipment (DTE). For Cisco 1000, 1600, 2500, 2600, and 3600 series routers, the console and auxiliary ports both use RJ-45 connectors. You can connect either a terminal (DTE) or a modem (DCE) to these ports. Either way, you'll need two components, an RJ-45 cable and an RJ-45-to-DB-25 connector. Adapters are available for connections to PC terminals, modems, or other external communications equipment.

RJ-45 connectors are a little bigger than the standard telephone connectors. They contain eight wires instead of the four wires in a telephone connector. Terminal servers are a good example of devices that often use RJ-45 connectors. There are two types of RJ-45 cabling, straight through and crossover (otherwise known as rolled). If you hold the two ends of an RJ-45 cable side by side, you'll see eight colored strips, or pins, at each end. If the order of the colored pins is the same at each end, the cable is straight. If the order of the colors is reversed at each end, the cable is rolled. In the previous section on signaling, we discussed DCE-to-DTE communication. However, there are times when two DTE devices need to communicate, such as a computer and a Cisco router. Cisco has defined the RJ-45 console and auxiliary ports on their access servers as DTE devices. This means that if you used the same cable for DTE-to-DTE communications as you did for DTE-to-DCE communications, the pin from one device would transmit data to the wrong pin of the receiving device. Instead of sending data to a receiving pin, the data is sent to another transmitting pin. Data can't travel with this setup. In order for two DTE devices to communicate, you need to use a null modem cable. A null modem cable reverses the TD and RD pins, the RTS and CTS pins, and the DTR and DSR pins.

In order to reverse the pinouts on the connectors, you can change the pins in one of two locations: in the cable, or in the physical interface. When the pins have been changed through the cable, it is called a "rolled cable." When it is implemented in the adapter, it is called a "rolled adapter." Because most Cisco products come with a cable with RJ-45 connectors at both ends and either a RJ-45 to DB25 or RJ-45 to DB9 adapter, you need to be careful that you don't mix a rolled cable with a rolled adapter. Two rolled devices equal a straight device, and you would end up with what you started with, a DTE-to-DCE cable. Also, when connecting a DTE to a DCE, you do not use rolled cables or adapters. So, you need to be careful of which adapter you use. The RJ-45 to DB-25 adapter can be straight through or rolled. A male adapter DTE called MDTE or female DTE adapter called FDTE is straight. A special male DCE adapter named MMOD is rolled and is only used for modems. Previously, in your Cisco Certified Network Associate (CCNA) and Building Scalable Cisco Networks (BSCN) classes, you needed to know about the null connection between a router's console port and the serial port of a terminal or PC. Here are two ways to enable a null connection between them for connecting DTE to DTE:

➤ DTE to a rolled RJ-45 cable to a straight DB-25 adapter to DTE

➤ DTE to a straight RJ-45 cable to a rolled DB-25 adapter to DTE

When connecting a DTE (router) to a DCE (modem), you will need to create a straight-through situation by either having a straight-through RJ-45 cable and straight-through DB-25 adapter or using both a rolled RJ-45 cable and a rolled DB-25 adapter. So, you could use a rolled RJ-45 cable connected to rolled MMOD for the purpose of connecting a modem to the AUX port of a Cisco 2501 router. This second method is suggested by Cisco. Connecting a router to a modem using other types of router interfaces and cables is covered in the next section.

Table 3.2 and Table 3.3 show the pinouts for RJ-45 console and AUX ports. The console port does not use RTS/CTS. The console and auxiliary ports are DTE connections with an RJ-45 female connector at the Cisco routers and an RJ-45 male connector at the terminal.

Table 3.2   Console port (DTE) pinouts (RJ-45).

Pin	Signal	Input/Output
1	-	-
2	DTR	Output
3	TxD	Output
4	GND	-
5	GND	-
6	RxD	Input
7	DSR	Input
8	-	-

Table 3.3   Auxiliary port (DTE) pinouts (RJ-45).

Pin	Signal	Input/Output
1	RTS	Output
2	DTR	Output
3	TXD	Output
4	GND	-
5	GND	-
6	RXD	Input
7	DSR	Input
8	CTS	Input

Cables for Connecting Modems

In the previous discussion, we used the AUX port of a 2501 when describing a cable/adapter combination for connecting a router to a modem. In this section, we will describe other Cisco router interfaces and their cables needed to connect to a modem.

You need to connect the modem to the router before configuring the modem to verify that communication between them is established. If it is the wrong cable, the rest of the process will fail. Most often, external modems are built with a female DCE DB-25 port for connection to a controlling device such as a PC or a router. Table 3.4 will help you select the appropriate cables to make the connection between the router and the modem. The table also includes information on the required cabling and the types of physical ports on Cisco routers to which a modem can be connected.

Table 3.4   Cables used for connecting external modems to routers.

Router Port	Examples of Where Found	Cabling Required
DB-25 DTE	Male DB-25 AUX on the Cisco 4000, 7000, 7200, and 7500.	Straight-through DB-25 Female to DB25 Male RS-232 cable.
DB-25 DCE	Female DB-25 console port on the Cisco 4000 and 7000 series.	Null-modem DB-25 Male—DB25 Male RS232 cable. A rolled RJ-45—RJ-45 with CAB-25AS-MMOD adapters on both ends.
DB-60-Sync/async interfaces.	Cisco 1005, 1600s, and 2520-2523; network modules on the Cisco 2600, 3600, and 4000.	CAB-232MT,cable with a male DB-60 connector on the Cisco end and a male DB-25 connector on the network end
RJ-45	AUX or CON on the Cisco 2500s, 2600, 3600, AS5200, and AS5300.	Rolled RJ-45—RJ-45 cable with adapter marked "MODEM" (part number CAB-25AS-MMOD).
68-pin	Cisco 2509-2512; network modules on the Cisco 2600 and 3600.	Cisco parts CAB-OCTAL-ASYNC (with connectors marked "MODEM") and CAB-OCTAL-MODEM

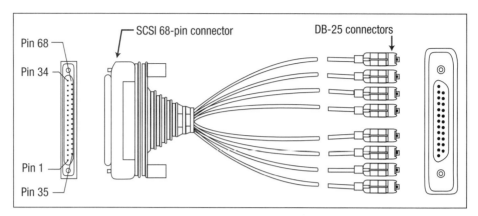

Figure 3.1 CAB-OCTAL-KIT.

When using the Cisco 2509-2512, 3600 16/32 Asynchronous Network Module, and 4000 2 Serial 16 Async/Sync Network Processor Module, there are two cables available for connection to the modems. The first is the CAB-OCTAL-MODEM (product number CAB-OCTAL-MODEM) as shown in Figure 3.1. This cable has a male DB-68 (SCSI II) connector on the Cisco end and eight RJ-45 connectors on the network end that are hard-wired into eight DB-25 modular adapters. The second cable is the CAB-OCTAL-KIT (product number CAB-OCTAL-KIT). This cable has a male DB-68 (SCSI II) connector on the Cisco end and eight RJ-45 connectors on the network end that are connected into eight DB-25 modular adapters (CAB-25AS-MMOD). The RJ-45 connectors are not hard-wired into the DB-25 modular adapters.

When connecting to a DB-60 sync/async port on a 2520-2523, 1005, 1600, 3600, or 4000 series router, use CAB-232MT. This cable has a male DB-60 connector on the Cisco end and a male DB-25 connector on the network end. When connecting to the DB-25 AUX port on a 4000 series router, use a straight DB-25 to DB-25 cable. Table 3.4 summarizes the cable types needed for connecting routers to external modems.

Getting Routers to Talk to Modems

Whether you are attaching an external modem to the AUX port or async port of a router for remote management or Dial-on-Demand Routing (DDR), the same steps must be followed for modem configuration.

Though cables come in a variety of connector types on the router's end of the connection, the modem end of the cable must be a male DTE 25-pin EIA/TIA-232 connector, with pins 2 through 5, 7, 8, and 20 present. The AUX ports on Cisco routers are either DB-25 or RJ-45. For the DB-25 type of AUX port, a straight-through EIA/TIA-232 cable is used. Routers equipped with an RJ-45 AUX port use a rolled RJ-45-to-RJ-45 cable. When you are using cables that terminate in an RJ-45, such as the AUX port cable or the octal cable used with a Cisco 2511, the 25-pin modem adapter is required.

Configuring Modems Attached to Routers

When configuring modems attached to routers, you need to configure the router's interface and the modem. The modem is accessed and configured by way of the router and not directly at the modem.

When routers are configured to talk to each other using asynchronous lines and modems, you will need to configure each router's asynchronous line by configuring it as a physical interface and as a line. In addition, you will need to initialize the modem for both outgoing and incoming calls. There are three methods to configure the modem as follows:

➤ Reverse Telnet session

➤ Chat scripts

➤ Autoconfiguration

Basically, you need to do two things when working with modems: initialize the modem and then get the modem to dial out. Reverse Telnet and autoconfiguration are typically used to initialize and reset a modem attached to a router. Autoconfiguration is typically used on access servers to initialize modems. Although you could reverse Telnet to a modem and give AT commands to allow the modem to dial another modem, the best way to get a router's modem to dial out is to use chat scripts. A typical configuration for an access server would be to use the autoconfiguration for initializing the modem and then a chat script for allowing the router/modem to dial out. This section will cover the steps needed to perform reverse Telnet, autoconfiguration, and chat scripts.

Basic Router Configuration

Before you can perform reverse Telnet, autoconfiguration, or chat scripts, it is essential that the TTY line be configured. You need to configure the TTY line for protocols using the interface mode and set certain physical attributes for the line using the line mode. The following is an example of one asynchronous line configuration on a Cisco router that is used in an asynchronous backup DDR.

The protocol settings are:

```
RouterA(config)# interface async 1
RouterA(config-if)# encapsulation ppp
RouterA(config-if)# async dynamic address
RouterA(config-if)# peer default ip address 10.3.3.5
RouterA(config-if)# async mode interactive
Router(config-if) physical-layer async
```

If the interface supports both synchronous and asynchronous communications, the default is synchronous. When connecting this interface to a modem, you need to execute **physical-layer async** on the interface.

The physical settings are:

```
RouterA(config)# line 1
RouterA(config-line)# modem InOut
RouterA(config-line)# speed 115200
RouterA(config-line)# transport input all
RouterA(config-line)# flowcontrol hardware
```

The following is a list of descriptions for the above commands entered in the line mode. The list contains the possible commands and parameters for the physical settings:

➤ **line *x***—AUX port is line 1 on the router, last_tty+1 on the access server, line 65 on the Cisco 2600s and 3620, and line 129 on the Cisco 3640.

➤ **modem inout**—Drop connection on loss of DCD (DSR). Cycle DTR for connection close. This command also allows outbound connections to the modem.

➤ **speed *xxxxx***—This is not the speed of a dial-up connection, DCE-DCE, but the speed of the DTE-to-DCE communications or router to modem (also known as clock speed). It is important to keep in mind that in order for any effective compression to take place, you need to keep the line speed higher than the dial-up connection; otherwise, you will starve the modem for data and potentially waste bandwidth.

The port speed should be set to the highest speed in common between the modem and the port. This value is usually 115200 baud. However, on some older routers, the top speed on the AUX port is 38400.

➤ **transport input all | telnet**—Allow outbound connections to this line. Needed in order to allow reverse Telnet to the modem.

➤ **stopbits 1**—Improve throughput by reducing async framing overhead (default is **stopbits 2**). Because the preceding example uses the default for stopbits, this parameter is not shown in the example.

➤ **flowcontrol hardware**—The typical flow control method for asynchronous ports is hardware. It is the equivalent of the RTS and CTS as described in Table 3.2, which controls the flow of data. The modem tells the router when its buffers are full and to back off from sending any more data.

The Reverse Telnet Method

To establish a reverse Telnet connection, issue the following command:

```
Telnet x.x.x.x 200y
```

The **x.x.x.x** represents the IP address of any interface on the Cisco router. The loopback is a good choice because the interface needs to be up/up. The **y** is the line number of the line to which you want to connect. If the TTY line has already been configured, you can issue the **telnet** command from anywhere on the network that can ping the *x.x.x.x* interface. Keep in mind that the AUX port of any router is the last async line number + 1. You can use the **show line** or **show line aux 0** command to see which line number this is.

Suppose you want to reverse Telnet from the router's AUX port at the EXEC prompt to a valid IP address on the router + 200x, where 2000 represents the TCP port type (telnet) and *x* is the absolute line number for the router that is added to 2000 . For example, if you are using a 2509 router, 2001 would be the first physical line, 2005 would be the fifth physical line, and 2009 would be the AUX port. This command will connect to the AUX port on a 2509:

```
RouterA#telnet 10.1.1.1 2009
```

*Note: The 3600 series uses a unique line nomenclature. This router assumes that each slot has 32 lines (whether they are there or not). Therefore, on a 3640 router, the line number for the AUX port is **129**.*

Once connected via a reverse Telnet, communication is possible via standard AT commands. After entering the above command, you will see [trying x.x.x.x, 200y.....open]. Do not wait for a prompt because you won't get one. Just type **AT** and press the Enter key, and you should see an OK right away. From here, you can enter other AT commands. Send the appropriate AT initialization string to the modem, and then save the initialization string to modem's Non-Volatile Random Access Memory (NVRAM). To terminate the reverse Telnet session, issue the escape sequence Ctrl+Shift+6 to suspend the session and then **x** to return to the EXEC prompt; then issue **disc** to terminate the session.

*Note: You can use the **IP host** command in the global configuration mode to associate the IP address, the port number, and the line number to one name that can be used with the reverse Telnet command.*

AT Commands

The most basic commands used to configure and troubleshoot a modem are from the AT command set. The AT command set was originally developed by Hayes to work with their Smartmodem 300. The AT command set can be broken down into two different kinds of instructions: configuration commands and operation commands (usually called the S-Registers). Configuration commands include how to define flow control and set data compression, whereas the operations commands include commands like how to dial a phone number or hang up the phone.

Always issue the command strings to the modem starting with AT, and issue them at the speed at which you want the modem to talk to the Cisco device. This ensures that the modem will always talk to the Cisco device at the expected speed regardless of the speed of any incoming modem connection. You need to set the modem to lock on the DTE speed, which is required. To send commands to most modems, you must start with the AT command. Then you can configure different attributes about the modem using a series of commands appended to each other. Table 3.5 lists what is required for all modem strings.

When several commands are placed together, the combination is called an initialization string. Although many of the commands used to configure the initialization strings are similar, they aren't identical from vendor to vendor, even from model to model. To know the commands used to configure a particular modem, you will have to refer to the documentation that came with the modem. The following are a few common modem initialization strings:

➤ Hayes: AT&FS0=1&C1&D3&K3&Q9&W

➤ Motorola: AT&FS0=1&C1&D3\Q3\J0\N3%C1&W

➤ U.S. Robotics: AT&FS0=1&C1&D3&H1&R2&B1&K1&M4&W

Tip: One of the important things to do when creating a modem script is to set the modem back to the factory defaults (see line 2 in Table 3.5). Many different modem variables can be set. It is important to ensure that you start from a known state.

Troubleshooting Reverse Telnet

Remember that when you reverse Telnet to a modem, you are only talking to the modem, and this action does not include using the modem for sending or receiving

Table 3.5 Required AT commands.

Function	Command String
"Attention" command	AT
Factory Defaults	&F
Auto-Answer	S0=1
Follow CD	&C1
Modem Resets on DTR Cycle	&D3
Hardware Flowcontrol [CTS/RTS]	*FL3
Lock DTE Speed	*SC1

of data, at least up to this point. To get a successful reverse Telnet, you must see the following display after entering the **show line** command at the router's EXEC prompt:

```
Modem state: Idle
Modem hardware state: CTS* noDSR DTR RTS
```

If you are unable to reverse Telnet, the first indication that there is a problem will be when the Telnet line does not say "open" and you are unable to receive an "OK" after pressing the Enter key. If this happens, and you do not see the above **show line** status, you need to check some of the more common causes. First check for the following:

1. The line must have "modem InOut" configured.

2. A valid IP address must be available.

3. The line must have a speed set to accommodate both DTE and DCE.

4. The line must set the **transport** command to allow all types of communication to be sent.

5. The line must have **flowcontrol** set for **hardware**.

6. The TCP port type 2000 is used at the EXEC prompt.

After correcting any of the possible problems, if the modem still does not respond to AT commands, try typing **ATE1Q0**. This will enable echo and result codes on the modem. Try displaying the configuration of the modem with an **AT&V** or **ATI4** command. Even if the modem is set to echo off and no result codes, it will still display the configuration if you are communicating correctly. If there is still no response, verify that the DTE speed is set correctly. The modem may be locked in at a specific DTE rate different than the one specified under the line setting. Terminate the reverse Telnet session. Reset the line speed and clear the line. Attempt the reverse Telnet again. Try different speeds if the modem will not respond. If the modem still will not respond after trying different line speeds, connect it directly to a PC running a terminal program and verify that the modem is operational.

If the router returns the error "Connection refused by remote host", verify that the line is not in use. Clear the line with the command **clear line *x*** and try again. Verify that the modem is not forcing DSR/DCD high by using the **show line** command to view the modem hardware state. If DSR is present, the modem is forcing DSR/DCD high. This means that there is already a connection to that port, or there is an EXEC (prompt) running on that port, or the cause could be that the modem failed to lower CD after a call disconnected. Turn off the modem and then reverse Telnet to the port. Once you're connected, turn the modem back on and try sending the AT initialization string. If it still fails, make sure that you have set the **modem inout** and **transport input all | telnet** commands for that line.

Chat Script Method

When you are using a modem attached to a router to connect to another modem that is attached to a second router, the router needs to be able to send commands to the modem. When using Cisco routers, you can use chat scripts to accomplish this type of communication. Chat scripts are strings of text used to send commands for initializing modems, modem dialing, and logging on to remote systems. Each script is defined for a different event. The chat script is used by the router to send commands to the modem. It can send initialization strings each time the modem hangs up. It can send login information that a called system may require. The chat script is primarily used to send dialing commands to the modem.

A chat script functions by waiting for a response from the modem, and then issuing a command. This is called an *expect-send* pair. This type of handshaking event can take place between two DTE devices or, as in this case, between a DTE device (the router) and DCE device (the modem). You can also set abort conditions in your chat script as well. These conditions are either responses received from the modem or a timeout period set in seconds.

To use a chat script, perform the following steps:

1. Define the chat script in global configuration mode using the chat-script command.

2. Configure the line so that a chat script is activated when a specific event occurs (using the **script** line configuration command), or start a chat script manually (using the **start-chat** privileged EXEC command).

Using Chat Scripts to Initialize a Modem

You can use a chat script to send the appropriate AT initialization string. To configure a chat script for configuring a modem, use the global configuration command:

```
RouterA(config)# chat-script usrv32bis "" "AT&F1S0=1&d2" "OK" ""
```

The chat script can be invoked manually for a single line with the following command. This command can only be used on the auxiliary port of the switch:

```
RouterA#start-chat usrv32bis aux 0
```

The chat script can also be invoked automatically by adding the following command to the line configuration. The chat script will be invoked every time the system reloads or the line resets at the termination of a session, or if the line is cleared manually.

```
RouterA(config-line)#script startup usrv32bis (initializing the modem)
RouterA(config-line)#script reset usrv32bis (resetting the modem)
```

The most typical method for starting a chat script is from within a **dialer map** command. In the example below, the chat script named *dialing* was created in the global configuration mode and it is activated when the **dialer map** command is activated. The **dialer map** command and other DDR commands will be covered in Chapters 6 and 7.

```
username CPA2520 password 7 02050D480809
chat-script dialing "" atdt\T TIMEOUT 60 CONNECT

interface Ethernet0
ip address 193.191.1.1 255.255.255.0

interface Async1
ip address 193.191.100.1 255.255.255.0
encapsulation ppp
keepalive 10
async default routing
async mode dedicated
dialer in-band
dialer map ip 193.191.100.2 name CPA2511-1 modem-script dialing
broadcast 5553735
dialer-group 1
```

You can also use the **script reset** *name* command to reinitialize a modem after it hangs up where *name* is the name of the reinitializing chat script. The command is entered within the line and not the interface. Cisco does not recommend reinitializing chat scripts.

Using Chat Scripts to Log On to a System

Chats scripts can contain user names and passwords for logging in to a secure system, and if they do, they are considered logon chat scripts. When a chat script is used to log in to a system and start PPP, the chat script would look like this:

```
chat-script login "login:" "username" "password:"
"password" "logged in" "ppp"
```

The script acts like this: First, the router waits for the system to prompt with [login], and then the script sends the username; second, the router waits for the system to prompt with [password], and then the script sends the password. Finally, the router waits for the system to prompt with [logged in], and then the router sends "ppp", starting the PPP session. These prompts and commands will change from system to system. You must know exactly how the router will be prompted by the system to make this work. You must manually log in to the remote system to find out what prompts it will be sending. You must then use those prompts in the chat script. You will also need to confirm the command needed to start PPP, SLIP, or any other protocol that will be running on this connection. You will also need to add the name of the login chat script to your **dialer map** command: **system-script** *login* where login is the name of your chat script. See the example in the next section.

Using Chat Scripts—An Example

The following example shows a modem chat script called *dial* and a system login chat script called *login*. The **dialer in-band** command enables DDR on asynchronous interface 10, and the **dialer map** command dials 6667777 after finding the specified dialing and system login scripts. The example below shows the following configuration:

➤ The configuration is on Router A.

➤ The modem chat script *dial* is used to dial out to Router B's modem.

➤ The system login chat script *login* is used to log in to Router B.

➤ The phone number is the number of the modem attached to Router B.

➤ The IP address in the **dialer map** command is the address of Router B.

Listing 3.3   Example of modem chat script and system login chat script.

```
chat-script dial ABORT ERROR "" "AT Z" OK "ATDT \T" TIMEOUT 30 CONNECT \c
chat-script   login ABORT invalid TIMEOUT 15   name: billw word: mypassword
">" "slip default"
interface async 10
 dialer in-band
 dialer map ip 10.55.0.1 modem-script dial system-script login 6667777
```

When a packet is received for 10.55.0.1, the first thing that happens is that the modem script is implemented. Table 3.6 shows the functions that are implemented with each *expect-send* pair in the modem script called *dialing*.

After the modem script is successfully executed, the system login script is executed.

Table 3.6   Example of a modem script execution.

Expect and Send Pair	Implementation
ABORT ERROR	Possible command options will end the attempt if the modem reports busy, end the attempt if the modem reports an error, or end the attempt if the modem reports that the other modem isn't answering.
" " "AT Z"	Without expecting anything, send an "AT Z" command to the modem. (Note the use of quotation marks to allow a space in the send string.)
OK "ATDT \T	Wait to see "OK." Send "ATDT 6667777."
TIMEOUT 30	Wait up to 30 seconds for next expect string.
CONNECT \c	Expect "connect," but do not send anything. (Note that \c is effectively nothing; " " would have indicated nothing followed by a carriage return.)

Table 3.7 Example system script execution.

Expect and Send Pair	Implementation
ABORT invalid	End the script execution if the message "invalid username or password" is displayed.
TIMEOUT 15	Wait up to 15 seconds.
name: myname	Look for "name:" and send "billw." (Using just "name:" will help avoid any capitalization issues.)
word: mypassword	Wait for "word:" and send "password."
">" "slip default"	Wait for the prompt and put the line into SLIP mode with its default address.

Table 3.7 shows the functions that are executed with each *expect-send* pair in the system script called *login*.

Making the Call and Debugging the Chat Script

Use this debug to see what the chat script is doing:

```
CHAT9: Attempting async line dialer script
CHAT9: Dialing using Modem script: dialout & System script: none
CHAT9: process started
CHAT9: Asserting DTR
CHAT9: Chat script dialout started
CHAT9: Sending string: ATDT\T
CHAT9: Expecting string: CONNECT.....
CHAT9: Completed match for expect: CONNECT
CHAT9: Chat script dialout finished, status = Success
```

To verify that the chat script is functioning properly, use the **debug chat** command. For this method to work, the modem must be configured with echo and response codes turned on. Modems usually come from the factory with these values set, but you may need to manually reverse Telnet to the modem and issue the command to turn on echo and response. The usual command to do this is **ATE1Q0**.

Modem Autoconfiguration Method

Modem autoconfiguration is used to automate the configuration of modems attached to a Cisco Access Server. Cisco Access Servers come with a number of preconfigured initialization strings for some of the most commonly used modems. These preconfigured initialization strings are stored in the modemcap database. You can use the modem command **autoconfigure type** *modemcap_name* to configure modems attached to async lines. If you are using a version of Cisco IOS earlier than 11.1, **script startup** and **script reset** can be used to configure the modems via a chat script. The Cisco IOS maintains a set of built-in modemcaps for various internal and external modems. Using the command **show modemcap** (without a specific modemcap name) will list the entries in the modemcap database. Here is an example from a router running Cisco IOS version 11.3:

```
router#show modemcap
default
codex_3260
usr_courier
usr_sportster
hayes_optima
global_village
viva
telebit_t3000
microcom_hdms
microcom_server
nec_v34
nec_v110
nec_piafs
cisco_v110
mica
```

Each modemcap database entry uses the specific vendor's own unique set of commands that are represented within a set of attributes. If you want to view the value settings for a particular modemcap, you can use the command **show modemcap modemcap_name**. This command will show you a list of configuration parameters that a particular modem uses. Table 3.8 contains a list of possible attributes for any

Table 3.8 Modem attributes used in modemcaps for modem initialization.

Attribute Symbol	Attribute
AA	Autoanswer
BCP	Best compression
BER	Best error control
CID	Caller ID
CD	Carrier detect
DTR	Drops the connection if DTR signal drops
FD	Factory default
HFL	Hardware flowcontrol
MSC	Miscellaneous commands
NCP	No compression
NEC	No echo
NER	No error control
NRS	No results
SFL	Software flowcontrol
SPD	Lock modem speed
FD	Factory default
TPL	Template entry – referencing the values to another modem type

Table 3.9   Modemcap entries for supported modems.

Modem Type	Output
Hayes_Optima	FD=&F:AA=S0=1:DTR=&D2:CD=&C1:TPL=default
Codex_3260	FD=&F:AA=S0=1:CD=&C1:DTR=&D2:HFL=*FL3:SPD=*SC1:BER=*SM3:BCP= *DC1:NER=*SM1:NCP=*DC0:NEC=E0:NRS=Q1:CID=&S1
usr_courier	HFL=&H1&R2:SPD=&B1:BER=&M4:BCP=&K1:NER=&M0:NCP=&K0:TPL=default.
usr_sportster	TPL=usr_courier
hayes_optima	HFL=&K3:BER=&Q5:BCP=&Q9:NER=&Q0:NCP=&Q0:TPL=default
Viva	HFL=&K3:BER=&Q5:BCP=%C1:NER=&Q6:NCP=%C0:TPL=default
telebit_t3000	HFL=S58=2:BER=S180=3:BCP=S190=1:NER=S180=0:NCP=S190=0:TPL=default

one modemcap that can be listed using this command. Table 3.9 lists entire attributes and values for certain modemcaps. The translation for each attribute value is beyond the scope of this book, but if you think one of these built-in modemcaps might be suitable, you can use the command **modem autoconfigure type** *modem-name*. If you know the name of the modem and the modemcap, you can apply the modemcap to the line configuration with the following command:

```
modem autoconfigure type modemcap_name

RouterA(config)#line 1
RouterA(config-line)#modem autoconfigure type usr_sportster
```

If you are not sure whether the modem you are using is in the modem capabilities database, you can use the command **modem autoconfigure discover**y. By using the **debug confmodem** command, you can see the results of the autodiscovery process. The command instructs the access server to send the AT string at various baud rates until it receives an OK. Then it tells the router to send a variety of AT commands to receive the identification of the modem and match that with the modem capabilities database.

```
RouterA(config)#debug confmodem
Modem Configuration Database debugging is on

RouterA(config)#line 1
RouterA(config-line)#modem autoconfigure discovery

*Mar  3 03:02:19.535: TTY1: detection speed (38400) response --OK--
*Mar  3 03:02:24.727: TTY1: Modem type is default
*Mar  3 03:02:24.731: TTY1: Modem command:   --AT&F&C1&D2S0=1H0--
*Mar  3 03:02:25.259: TTY1: Modem configuration succeeded
*Mar  3 03:02:25.259: TTY1: Detected modem speed 38400
*Mar  3 03:02:25.259: TTY1: Done with modem configuration
```

Creating Your Own Modemcap

So far you have learned that you can use the autoconfiguration method instead of an initialization chat script. The need to create your own initialization strings means you do not want to use any of the modems listed in the modemcap database. Another way to modify initialization strings is to create your own modemcap. You can't modify any of the predefined modemcap entries, so you must either create a new modemcap from scratch or create a modemcap entry similar to the one that is already defined.

When creating a modemcap from scratch, you need to know that there are two parts to creating a new entry; the attributes that need to be modified and their corresponding command and the name of the new modem entry. Using the command **modemcap edit**, you can create and edit new modemcap entries. When using your own modemcap, use the **modem autoconfigure type** command:

```
RouterA #debug confmodem
Modem Configuration Database debugging is on

RouterA #configure terminal
Enter configuration commands, one per line. End with CNTL/Z.
RouterA (config)#modemcap edit Mycap misc &FS0=1
RouterA (config)#line 1
RouterA (config-line)#modem autoconfigure type Mycap

*Mar  3 03:06:30.931: TTY1: detection speed (38400) response --OK--
*Mar  3 03:06:30.963: TTY1: Modem command: --AT&FS0=1--
*Mar  3 03:06:31.483: TTY1: Modem configuration succeeded
*Mar  3 03:06:31.487: TTY1: Detected modem speed 38400
*Mar  3 03:06:31.487: TTY1: Done with modem configuration
```

The preceding example creates a new modemcap called *mycap*, and at the same time it edits the modemcap, where the miscellaneous attribute will have a value of (&F) and (SO=1). The new modemcap name should not be the same as one of the predefined entries listed by the **show modemcap** command. The initialization string should begin with the command to reset to defaults (typically **&F** or **&F1**). For this method to work, the modem must be configured with echo and response codes turned on. Modems usually come from the factory with these values set, but you may need to manually reverse Telnet to the modem and issue the command to turn on echo and response. The usual command to do this is **ATE1Q0**.

Copying a predefined modemcap to a newly created modemcap is much easier than the above method of creating one from scratch. Cisco provides a way to use a predefined modemcap entry as a template for creating a new modemcap entry. You copy any predefined modemcap to a newly created modemcap with the name of your choice. This will allow you to cut down on the number of errors possible because you are creating an entry from a working source. The command to copy a predefined modemcap entry is:

```
Router (config)# modemcap edit new-modemcap template
predefined-modemcap
```

This command needs to be executed from the global configuration mode. From here you can modify your new modemcap entry using the **modemcap edit** command.

3

Chapter Summary

The ITU-T V.90 standard defines 56Kbps modem technology, which combines both X2 and Kflex proprietary standards.

Most high-speed modems support both of the standards for data compression protocols: MNP-5 and CCITT V.42bis. MNP stands for Microcom Networking Protocols, and the MNP-4 is an error-checking protocol, whereas the MNP-5 is a compression protocol. V.42 is an error-checking protocol, and the V.42bis is a compression protocol.

The Universal Asynchronous Receiver/Transmitter (UART) is a component found in a PC that converts parallel data into serial data.

Asynchronous interfaces correspond to physical terminal (TTY) lines, and Telnet connections correspond to virtual terminal (VTY) lines. When configuring an asynchronous interface, you configure protocol-specific parameters for asynchronous interfaces, and then you enter into the line configuration mode to configure the physical aspects for the same port.

The auxiliary port (AUX) is numbered where its absolute line number is equal to the last TTY line number plus 1. It is referred to as "interface async 1" and "Line 1" on a Cisco 2501 router because a 2501 has no async ports (other than the AUX port). The first VTY (Telnet) port is numbered where its absolute line number is equal to the last TTY line number plus 2.

The CTS and RTS signals from the EIA/TIA-232 standard are used for flow control. The DTR, DCD, and DSR signals are used for modem control. TD and RD are used for moving data.

When connecting a DTE (router) to a DCE (modem), you will need to create a straight situation by either having a straight-through RJ-45 cable and straight-through DB-25 adapter, or, as Cisco recommends, using both a rolled RJ-45 cable and a rolled DB-25 adapter.

When connecting a cable to the async port of a Cisco 2509 or 2511, the cable you use has a male DB-68 (SCSI II) connector on the Cisco end and eight RJ-45 connectors on the network side.

There are three methods for getting routers to talk to modems: create a reverse Telnet session, create chat scripts, or perform one of two autoconfiguration commands.

To perform a reverse Telnet on an AUX port, you need to have the following settings: **transport input all, modem InOut, speed 38400,** and **flowcontrol hardware.** You need to reference an IP address from one interface on the router in the Telnet command, preferably a loopback address. You need to use the Telnet port and the line number together, for example: Telnet 10.10.1.1 2001. Once you are in a reverse Telnet session, you can enter AT commands and initialize the modem.

You can escape a reverse Telnet session without disconnecting by entering Ctrl+Shift+6 followed by an **x.** This places you in the regular EXEC prompt. To terminate a session, you need to enter the **clear line _x_** command where **_x_** is the line number conducting the session.

Chat scripts are used for the following purposes: to send init strings to initiate a call and each time the modem hangs up, to send login information such as passwords, and to send dialing commands to the modem. Most often, a dialing chat script is enough to initialize a modem.

The command that calls a dialing chat script is **modem-script _name_** where **_name_** is the name of the dialing chat script. The command that calls a login chat script is **system-script _name_** where **_name_** is the name of your system chat script. The command that calls a reinitializing chat script is **script-reset _name_** where name is the name of the reinitializing chat script. The **modem-script** command and the **system-script** command are entered within the async interface, whereas the **script-reset** command is entered within the line.

The autoconfiguration method uses the router's modem capabilities database or modemcap database. This database contains the initializing strings for several common modems such as U.S. Robotics Sportster. You use **show modemcap** to see a list of these built-in strings listed by modem model. You can see the values of each built-in modem string by using the **show modemcap** command with a particular modem, such as **show modemcap usr_sportster**.

There are times when you need to initialize a modem before dialing. When this is the case, you can use the autoconfiguration method instead of a manually entered initialization string in a chat script. You can enter **modem autoconfigure type _modemcap_name_** where **_modemcap_name_** is the name of an entry in the modem capability database. Example: **modem autoconfigure type usr_sportster**. If you are not sure which modemcap to use, you could enter **modem autoconfigure discovery**. This command will instruct the router to investigate and then determine which modemcap you are to use. Both commands are entered within the line.

You can't add or change values in a built-in modem cap, but you can create your own by using a built-in one. You can create your own modemcap with the command **modemcap edit _new-modemcap_ template _predefined-modemcap_** where *new-modemcap* is the name of your newly created modem cap. This command copies a built-in modemcap to your modemcap and with this new modem cap, you add or change values in the initialization string using **modemcap edit *new-modemcap* attribute *new-value***. Example: **modemcap edit Mycap misc &FS0=1**. In this example, *misc* is one attribute found in the initialization string, which takes on the new value of (&FS0=1).

3

Review Questions

1. Which of the following are good reasons for using the **modem autoconfigure discovery** command? [Choose the two best answers]

   a. You need to troubleshoot an attempt to perform a reverse Telnet that gives you the message "connection refused by remote host".

   b. You need to present a user name and password for logging in to a router.

   c. You need to initialize a modem.

   d. You need to determine which TTY line is logically associated with the modem.

   e. You are not sure about the exact init string your modem uses.

2. What is the maximum speed an AUX port on a Cisco router can support?

   a. 115000

   b. 38400

   c. 9600

   d. 56000

3. What device translates digital transmissions to analog transmissions?

   a. ISDN adapter

   b. Rolled cable

   c. Modem

   d. UART

4. Why would you use the modem autoconfiguration command **modem autoconfigure type usr_sportster**? [Choose all that apply]

   a. You want to eliminate the need to create an initialization chat script.

   b. You want to keep the modem from hanging up, which may result from a DDR timeout.

   c. You forgot how to perform a reverse Telnet for the purpose of initializing your modem.

   d. You are sure that your modem is compatible with the Sportster init string.

   e. You don't have a rolled cable and you need to cross the DTE's TD with the modem's RD.

5. What command do you use to show the status of line and its parameters, and information about the asynchronous port configuration?

   a. **show interface**

   b. **show line**

   c. **debug modem**

   d. **debug chat**

   c. **debug confmodem**

6. Write the command that would find out what kind of modem you are using and initialize that modem at the same time:

   _____

7. Which sequence of commands would permit you to perform a reverse Telnet using line 1?

   a. **IP host mymodem 2001 10.1.1.1, Telnet mymodem**

   b. **IP host 2001 10.1.1.1 mymodem, Telnet mymodem**

   c. **IP host mymodem 10.1.1.1 2001, Telnet mymodem**

   d. **IP host mymodem 2001 10.1.1.1, Telnet mymodem 2001**

8. Which standard is used for in-band signaling to bit synchronous DCE devices?

   a. V.21

   b. V.90

   c. V.25

   d. V.42

   e. V.42bis

9. From the following choices, which EIA/TIA 232 DTE signal indicates that it is ready to accept data?

   a. DSR up

   b. TD

   c. DCD up

   d. RTS up

   e. DTR up

10. What command do you use to make an async/sync serial interface work as an async interface?

   a. **async–serial**

   b. **physical-layer async**

   c. **async–layer serial**

   d. **physical-async layer**

11. Which signal pairs are responsible for flow control?

    a. RTS/CTS

    b. DTR/DSR

    c. DTR/DCD

    d. TD/RD

    e. DCD/CTS

3

12. The formula for figuring the absolute AUX port line number is equal to:

    a. The last TTY line plus 1

    b. The last TTY line plus 2

    c. The last TTY line plus 4

    d. The Con line plus 1

13. Which command calls to a chat script named dialme that enables the modem to dial out?

    a. **system–script dialme**

    b. **modem script dialme**

    c. **modem–script dialme**

    d. **system script dialme**

14. Which Cisco router series can have an async/sync serial interface?

    a. 1600s, 2520-2523; network modules on the Cisco 2600, 3600, and 4000

    b. 1600s, 2509-2512; network modules on the Cisco 2600, 3600, and 4000

    c. 1600s, 2520-2523; network modules on the Cisco 7000, 7200, and 7500

    d. 2520-2523; network modules on the Cisco 2600, 3600, and 4000

15. Which statements are true about 56Kbps modem technology and the V.90 standard? [Choose all that apply]

    a. V.90 technologies are the result of a merge between X2, which was developed by U.S. Robotics, and Lucent and Rockwell's K56flex.

    b. V.90 technologies are the result of a merge between V.32 modulation standard and the V.42bis compression standard.

    c. With V.90 downstream, data from the Internet to your computer is digital and not analog, causing higher download speeds than upload speeds.

    d. With V.90 upstream, data from your computer to the Internet is digital and not analog, causing higher upload speeds than download speeds.

16. To use modem compression effectively, the line speed between the DTE device and the DCE device should be _____ the speed that connects the two DCEs (modems).

    a. The same as

    b. Lower than

    c. Higher than

    d. One half of

17. If you are using a TTY line, what type of connection are you using?

    a. Telnet

    b. Synchronous

    c. High-speed serial

    d. Asynchronous

    e. Async/sync

18. Reverse Telnet is used to _____?

    a. Transfer data between routers

    b. Update routing tables between routers

    c. Connect to a host

    d. Configure a modem

    e. Connect to the console port of a router

19. Which two modem standards specify data compression techniques?

    a. MNP-5 and CCITT V.42bis

    b. MNP-5 and CCITT V.42

    c. MNP- 4 and CCITT V.42bis

    d. MNP-4 and CCITT V.42

20. Which two modem standards specify error-checking techniques and not compression? [Choose the two best answers]

    a. V.42bis

    b. V.42

    c. MNP-4

    d. MNP-5

21. When connecting and configuring two routers at different locations by using modems, what is the order of device types for the following physical sequence?

    RouterA—modem—modem—RouterB

    a. DCE-DCE-DTE-DTE

    b. DTE-DTE-DCE-DCE

    c. DTE-DCE-DCE-DTE

    d. DCE-DTE-DTE-DCE

22. Which two statements are correct when comparing the number of EIA/TIA-232 pins used by the console and auxiliary ports?

    a. The console port uses more pins than the auxiliary port.

    b. The auxiliary port uses more pins than the console port.

    c. The console port is a DTE device, whereas the auxiliary port is a DCE.

    d. Both the console port and the auxiliary ports are DTE.

    e. Both the console port and the auxiliary ports are DCE.

    f. The auxiliary port is a DTE device and the console port is a DCE.

23. The CAB-OCTAL-KIT is a cable kit used for asynchronous connections to an async interface on Cisco routers, such as the 2509 and the 2511. What is the physical interface type that the cable attaches to at the router end?

    a. DB-60 pin

    b. DB-25 (SCSI II)

    c. DB-60 (SCSI II)

    d. DB-25

    e. RJ-45

    f. DB-68 (SCSI II)

24. Which set of Cisco series routers uses an RJ-45 interface for the auxiliary port?

    a. 2500, 2600, 3600, AS5200, and AS5300

    b. 4000, 7000, 7200, and 7500

    c. 2500, 2600

    d. 2500, 2600, 4000, 7000

Real-World Projects

Gloria was just hired by the OCRA pharmaceutical company as an assistant network administrator. She has been assigned the task of installing and configuring two remote branch sites that will connect to the central site in Albany. The two branch offices are in Boston and Philadelphia. Because Gloria just received her CCNP certification and is fairly new at working with Cisco routers, she decided to work on the configurations first in a lab setting. This would allow her to make sure the equipment and configurations would be correct before installing them in their intended locations. The company decided to use a Cisco 2509 at the central location and in each branch office to use a 2501.

To begin with, Gloria wanted to see if she could get the two Cisco 2501 routers to communicate with each other by way of their AUX ports and without a modem. This was a start to see if she could correctly configure asynchronous interfaces. She wanted to eliminate any problems that might arise from trying to configure modems. In this example, you will do what Gloria did and connect two async AUX ports back-to-back using no modems. This configuration has Cisco 2500-series routers back-to-back using the async AUX port. The Cisco AUX port is connected to another Cisco AUX port running Point-to-Point Protocol (PPP).

Project 3.1

Configure the connection to allow IP for a permanent connection.

Note: The example uses a null modem cable and RJ-45-to-DB-25 adapter converters.

1. Position two 2501 routers near each other and call one router RouterA and the other RouterB.

2. Connect the two 2501 routers by attaching a null modem RS-232 cable and an RJ-45-to-DB-25 adapter converted to each router's AUX port.

3. At RouterA, perform the following configuration:

```
hostname RouterA

interface Ethernet0
 ip address 172.16.1.1 255.255.0.0
!
interface Serial0
 no ip address
 shutdown
!
interface Serial1
 no ip address
 shutdown
!
interface Async1
 ip address 192.168.10.1 255.255.255.0
 encapsulation ppp
 async dynamic routing
 async mode dedicated
 dialer-group 1
```

```
 no cdp enable
 dialer-group 1
!
ip route 0.0.0.0 0.0.0.0 Async1
!
dialer-list 1 protocol ip permit
!
line con 0
 exec-timeout 0 0
line aux 0
 modem InOut
 transport input all
 rxspeed 38400
 txspeed 38400
 flowcontrol hardware
line vty 0 4
 exec-timeout 0 0
 password bar
 login
!
end
```

4. At RouterB, perform the following configuration:

```
!
hostname RouterB
!
interface Ethernet0
 ip address 10.0.3.4 255.255.255.0
!
interface Serial0
 no ip address
 shutdown
!
interface Serial1
 no ip address
 shutdown
!
interface Async1
 ip address 198.168.10.2 255.255.255.0
 encapsulation ppp
 async dynamic routing
 async mode dedicated
 no cdp enable
!
ip route 0.0.0.0 0.0.0.0 async1
!
```

```
dialer-list 1 protocol ip permit
!
line con 0
 exec-timeout 0 0
line aux 0
 modem InOut
 transport input all
 rxspeed 38400
 txspeed 38400
 flowcontrol hardware
line vty 0 4
 exec-timeout 0 0
 password foo
 login
!
end
```

5. At RouterB, ping RouterA by entering **ping 192.168.10.1** at the EXEC prompt.

6. At RouterA, ping RouterB by entering **ping 192.168.10.2** at the EXEC prompt.

After Gloria was successful in getting the two routers to communicate using an asynchronous line and without modems, she decided the next step was to get the same routers to communicate using modems, but still in a lab setting. However, before she tried attaching the two modems/routers together, she decided to test one modem at a time by using reverse Telnet. Gloria wanted to experiment with reverse Telnet even though she didn't need to, because the Sportster modem she was using is included in the router's modemcap database.

Gloria wanted to first create a direct Telnet or connection session to the modem and then send an initialization string to the modem. She could have used **AT&F** as a basic modem initialization string for most cases, but instead she decided to use the modem initialization string for a U.S. Robotics Sportster modem: **FS0=1&C1&D2&H1&R2&N14&B1**

Project 3.2

Create a direct Telnet or connection session to the modem, and then send an initialization string to the modem by performing the following:

1. Enable RouterA to perform a simple reverse Telnet by adding the loopback interface to existing configuration:

```
!interface Loopback0 ip address 1.1.1.1 255.255.255.255
!
```

2. After adding the loopback interface to RouterA's configuration, enter the Telnet command: **RouterA# Telnet 1.1.1.1 2001**. (Receive an OPEN message.)

3. Type **AT** and press Enter. (Receive an OK message.)

4. Press Ctrl+Shift+6 followed by x. (Temporarily exit from the modem session in order to enter commands at the EXEC prompt.)

5. RouterA# **Show sessions** (Receive the following results:)

```
Conn Host     Address     Byte    Idle    Conn Name
1.1.1.1       1.1.1.1     92      0       1.1.1.1
```

6. RouterA# **Show line 1** (Receive the following results:)

```
Modem hardware state: CTS* noDSR  DTR  RTS, Modem Configured
```

7. RouterA# Press the Enter key. (Receive an OK. If you press the Enter key at the next EXEC prompt, this places you back in the Telnet session.)

8. Enter **AT&FS0=1&C1&D2&H1&R2&N14&B1** (U.S. Robotics Sportster 28800 [V.34])

9. Enter **AT&w** (Stores the modem settings in NVRAM on the modem.) (Receive an OK.)

10. Repeat steps 1 through 9 for RouterB. You can use the same loopback IP address for both routers.

After performing reverse Telnet, Gloria was sure that her modems were working. The next step for Gloria was to connect the two routers with one modem attached to each router's AUX port and then attach both modems to the same analog phone line. To perform this configuration, she used a Teltone Telephone Line simulator. The simulator gave her the necessary POTS lines she needed. Gloria decided to connect the AUX port of one 2501 to the AUX port of the other 2501. Gloria decided to use chat scripts for having the two routers communicate with their modems. She decided to use a chat script for reinitializing the modem and another chat script for modem dialing. She also used the autoconfiguration command to initialize the modem in the beginning of the connection. Gloria was smart enough to use a modem with a built-in modemcap like the U.S. Robotics Sportster. This allows the router to recognize the modem easily. The use of the **script reset** command and the autoconfiguration command together may have been more than she needed because both methods initialize a modem. However, Gloria wanted to make sure this lab example worked. Later on, she will attempt to remove one of the commands and see if the new configuration still works.

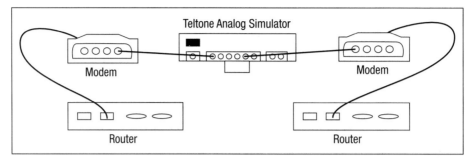

Figure 3.2 Diagram of Teletone Simulator and two attached modems with routers.

Gloria first tested the simulator with regular audible phones to make sure the simulator was working properly. She then attached a rolled RJ-45-R-J45 cable to a rolled modem adapter. Although this combination actually yields a straight-through connection, this is the combination of cable and adapter used for attaching a router's AUX port to a modem, as suggested by Cisco. The R-11 wire for each modem was then attached to the simulator and to the modem. Now everything was in place as shown in Figure 3.2, and Gloria was ready to write her configurations.

Project 3.3

Perform the following steps to configure the router:

1. Setup one 2501 as the dialing router and call it RouterA. Setup the other 2501 as the router to dial in to and name it RouterB.

2. Using Dial-on-Demand Routing (DDR) with the **dialer map** command, create the following configuration on RouterA. The two routers will not need static routes because of the use of the **dialer map** command from DDR.

Note: DDR will be covered in Chapters 6 and 7. I had to use a few DDR commands here in order to get this project to work. At the end of the project, several necessary DDR commands used in the following configurations are explained.

```
hostname RouterA
!
enable password test
!
username RouterB
chat-script dialnum "" "atdt\T" TIMEOUT 60 CONNECT \c
chat-script rstusr "" "at&fs0=1e0&r2&d2&c1&b1&h1&m0&k0" "OK"
!
interface Ethernet0
ip address 172.16.1.1 255.255.0.0
no shutdown
!
```

```
interface Serial0
no ip address
shutdown
!
interface Serial1
no ip address
shutdown
!
interface Async1
ip address 192.168.10.1 255.255.255.0
encapsulation ppp
async dynamic routing
async mode dedicated
dialer in-band
dialer idle-timeout 300
dialer map ip 192.168.10.2 name RouterB modem-script dialnum
broadcast 103
dialer-group 1
!
dialer-list 1 protocol ip permit
!
line con 0
line aux 0
script reset rstusr
modem inout
modem autoconfiguration type usr_sportster
transport input all
rxspeed 38400
txspeed 38400
flowcontrol hardware
line vty 0 4
password cisco
!
end
```

3. At RouterB, create the following configuration. No chat scripts are needed for RouterB because this router is not dialing.

```
hostname RouterB
!
username RouterA
!
interface Ethernet0
no ip address
shutdown
!
```

```
interface Serial0
no ip address
shutdown
!
interface Serial1
no ip address
shutdown
!
interface Async1
encapsulation ppp
ip address 192.168.10.2 255.255.255.0
async dynamic routing
async mode dedicated
dialer-group 1
!
dialer-list 1 list 100
access-list 100 permit ip any any

line con 0
line aux 0
modem InOut
modem autoconfiguration type usr_sportster
transport input all
rxspeed 38400
txspeed 38400
flowcontrol hardware
line vty 0 4
password test
login
!
end
```

4. Ping RouterB's Async IP address 192.168.10.2 from RouterA. The first ping will bring up the line as RouterA's modem starts to dial RouterB's modem, but the first ping will not be successful and will indicate a zero success rate.

5. Ping again. This second ping will send packets between the routers with the resulting success rate of 100 percent. Here's an explanation of configuration elements:

➤ **hostname RouterA**—RouterA is the name of this router. This name will be passed by this router in a PPP authentication process. It is case-sensitive. The opposite router, RouterB, must have a username RouterA defined.

➤ **username RouterB**—The username RouterB is the hostname of the opposite router and is referenced in the **dialer map** command for authentication purposes. The username is case-sensitive and must match the opposite router's hostname exactly. Because Gloria did not use PPP authentication, a password was not needed.

➤ **chat-script dialnum "" "atdt\T"TIMEOUT 60 CONNECT \c**—
A chat script can be used to send commands to the modem. Chat scripts are case-sensitive. This script is named dialnum and when called upon, it sends the atdt string to the modem. The **\T** causes the script to send the phone num-ber that appears in the dialer map statement.

➤ **chat-script rstusr "" "at&fs0=1e0&r2&d2&c1&b1&h1&m0&k0"
"OK"**—When rstusr is called upon, the modem string at&fs0=1e0&r2&d2&c1&b1 &h1&m0&k0 will be sent. This string is the appropriate modem configuration setting for a U.S. Robotics Sportster modem. Other modems will require similar settings, but different syntax. In this example this script is executed by the command **script reset rstusr** that follows. The reset string will ensure that the modem is always set with the same settings.

➤ **async dynamic routing**—This command allows routing protocols to be run over the async interface to resolve IP routes dynamically. If the command is omitted, static routes can still be used.

➤ **async mode dedicated**—This command enables the configured session type to start automatically when the DDR link comes up. In this example, PPP encapsulation is defined. A PPP session will be automatically used by the router for this interface. Note that with this command, an interactive login is not possible.

➤ **dialer in-band**—The dialer in-band command specifies that DDR is to be supported on the interface.

➤ **dialer idle-timeout 300**—This command sets the number of seconds the connection will remain open if no interesting traffic is being routed across this link. The timer is reset each time an interesting packet is forwarded across the DDR connection. The idle-timeout should be set to the same value on both routers. In this example, the line will drop after five consecutive minutes without interesting traffic.

➤ **dialer map ip 192.168.10.2 name RouterB modem-script dialnum broadcast 103**—With this command, the name "RouterB" will be used to authenticate the dial in user. If authentication is successful, the IP address 192.168.10.2 will be mapped to the remote user. The command **modem-script** starts the chat script named dialnum, which dials out to other modems. The phone number in this simulation example is 103.

➤ **dialer-group 1**—The dialer-group 1 command associates this interface with the dialer-list 1 definition. The interface will now consider anything defined in dialer-list 1 as interesting traffic.

➤ **dialer-list 1 protocol ip permit**—This command references the filter that allows all IP traffic to become interesting traffic for a DDR interface belong-ing to dialer-group 1.

Gloria's task for installing an analog dial-up service between two remote branch offices and one central office is not finished. At this point, Gloria will need to know more about Dial-on-Demand Routing (DDR) before going any further. You will meet Gloria again in Chapters 6 and see how she finishes her installations and configurations.

CHAPTER FOUR

Point-to-Point Protocol (PPP) Features and Configuration

After completing this chapter, you will be able to:

✓ Understand the architecture of Point-to-Point Protocol (PPP)

✓ Describe the components of Link Control Protocol (LCP) and Network Control Protocols (NCP)

✓ Compare Password Authentication Protocol (PAP) to Challenge Handshake Authentication Protocol (CHAP) authentication methods

✓ Configure a router to provide Internet Protocol (IP) addresses to dial-up client PCs

✓ Configure a router to provide Multilink, Compression, and Callback

✓ Configure aysnc interfaces into a group for easier configurations

✓ Use various debug and show commands to verify and troubleshoot PPP

✓ Configure a router for incoming calls and outgoing calls

n this chapter you will learn about the various protocols within the Point-to-Point Protocol (PPP) protocol suite. The chapter explains the operations of a PPP connection, and the configuration tasks applied to a router or PC making a PPP connection to a second router. Because a router can either accept incoming calls or dial out, the chapter uses the term "client router" to refer to the router making a call, and the term "server router" refers to the router accepting the initial call.

PPP Architecture

The Point-to-Point Protocol (PPP) originally emerged as an encapsulation protocol for transporting IP traffic over point-to-point links. PPP also established a standard for the assignment and management of IP addresses, asynchronous (start/stop) and bit-oriented synchronous encapsulation, network protocol multiplexing, link configuration, link quality testing, error detection, and option negotiation for such capabilities as network layer address negotiation and data-compression negotiation. PPP supports these functions by providing an extensible Link Control Protocol (LCP) and a family of Network Control Protocols (NCPs) to negotiate optional configuration parameters and facilities.

PPP is based on the High-Level Data Link Control (HDLC) protocol and provides a standard for sending data over data terminal equipment (DTE) and data communications equipment (DCE) interfaces such as V.35, T1, E1, HSSI, EIA-232-D, and EIA-449. PPP can also simultaneously transmit multiple protocols across a single serial link, eliminating the need to set up a separate link for each protocol. PPP is also ideal for interconnecting dissimilar devices such as hosts, bridges, and routers over serial links. For example, a standalone TCP/IP host can communicate with a router across a serial PPP link.

As a universal standard, PPP enables multivendor interoperability across serial links, dedicated links, dial-up links and/or switched ISDN links, traditionally restricted to equipment supplied by the same manufacturer. PPP was first proposed as a standard in 1990 to replace an older de facto standard known as SLIP (Serial Line Internet Protocol) that requires links to be established and torn down manually. However, unlike SLIP, which only supports IP, PPP is not limited in protocol support. PPP provides the flexibility to add support for other protocols through software upgrades. In addition to IP, PPP supports other protocols, including Novell's Internetwork Packet Exchange (IPX) and DECnet.

Point-to-Point Protocol (PPP) is a complete specification for transmitting datagrams between data communications equipment from different manufacturers over dial-up and dedicated serial point-to-point links. It is a recommended standard of the Internet Advisory Board (IAB) and is represented by a number of RFCs (Request for Comments) produced by the Point-to-Point Protocol Working Group. A list of the more common RFCs follows:

➤ *RFC 1332*—PPP Internet Protocol Control Protocol (IPCP)

➤ *RFC 1333*—PPP Link Quality Monitoring

➤ *RFC 1334*—PPP Authentication Protocols (PAP and CHAP)

➤ *RFC 1471*—Managed Objects for the LCP of the PPP

➤ *RFC 1472*—Managed Objects for the Security Protocols of the PPP

➤ *RFC 1473*—Managed Objects for the IPCP of the PPP

➤ *RFC 1552*—PPP Internetwork Packet Exchange Control Protocol (IPXCP)

➤ *RFC 1570*—PPP LCP Extensions

➤ *RFC 1618*—PPP over ISDN

➤ *RFC 1717*—PPP Multilink Protocol (MP)

PPP is really a protocol suite. Table 4.1 lists several common PPP protocols. The protocols with an asterisk are discussed in this chapter.

Table 4.1   The Point-to-Point Protocol (PPP) suite of protocols.

Protocol	Full Name
PPP Multilink*	Point-to-Point Multilink
LCP*	Link Control Protocol
LQR	Link Quality Report
PAP*	Password Authentication Protocol
CHAP*	Challenge Handshake Authentication Protocol
IPCP*	IP Control Protocol
IPXCP	IPX Control Protocol
ATCP	AppleTalk Control Protocol
BAP	Bandwidth Allocation Protocol
BCP	Bridging Control Protocol
CCP	Compression Control Protocol
L2F	Layer 2 Forwarding Protocol
L2TP	Layer 2 Tunneling Protocol
PPTP	Point-to-Point Tunneling Protocol

PPP Components

The three main components of PPP and their purposes are:

➤ Encapsulation—Creates the mainframe

➤ Link Control Protocol—Controls the link

➤ Network Control Protocol—Manages the network layer protocol

Encapsulation

Standard encapsulation schemes exist for the transmission of datagrams over most Local Area Networks (LANs), such as Ethernet, Token Ring, and Fiber Distributed Data Interface (FDDI). In the past, the only Wide Area Network (WAN) encapsulation scheme that provided a standard for the transmission of datagrams was X.25. The introduction of new WAN schemes such as frame relay expanded the variety of encapsulation schemes. However, the majority of LAN-to-LAN traffic is still carried over dedicated leased lines. The introduction of PPP allows these existing proprietary leased lines the opportunity to convert to a new encapsulation scheme that gives the user the true interoperability that traditionally could only be found on LANs. In addition, PPP has become the standard for LAN transmission over switched ISDN networks or via dial modem connections.

PPP is a full-duplex, bit-oriented protocol that can run over synchronous or asynchronous links. PPP uses a variant of High Speed Data Link Control (HDLC) as the basis for encapsulation. Links may be dedicated or circuit-switched, and PPP can work over copper, fiber optic, microwave, or satellite connections. PPP provides data error detection, whereas higher layer protocols are responsible for error recovery.

PPP has certain physical layer requirements. PPP is capable of operating across any DTE/DCE interface. Examples include EIA/TIA-232-C (formerly RS-232-C), EIA/TIA-422 (formerly RS-422), EIA/TIA-423 (formerly RS-423), and International Telecommunication Union Telecommunication Standardization Sector (ITU-T, formerly CCITT) V.35. The only absolute requirement imposed by PPP is the provision of a duplex circuit, either dedicated or switched, that can operate in either an asynchronous or synchronous bit-serial mode, transparent to PPP link-layer frames. PPP does not impose any restrictions regarding transmission rate other than those imposed by the particular DTE/DCE interface in use.

The descriptions in Table 4.2 summarize the PPP frame fields illustrated in Figure 4.1.

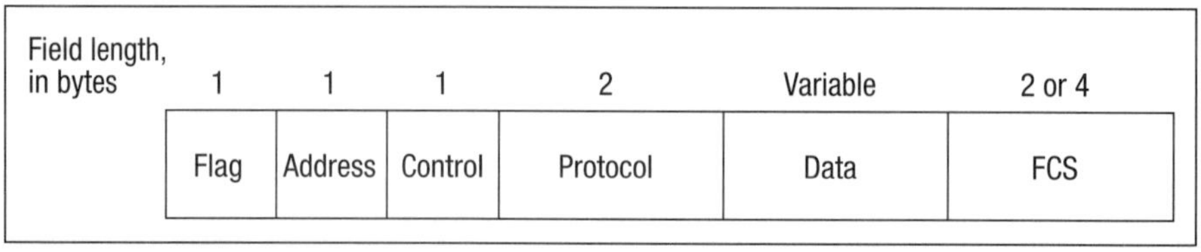

Field length, in bytes	1	1	1	2	Variable	2 or 4
	Flag	Address	Control	Protocol	Data	FCS

Figure 4.1   PPP frame.

Table 4.2   PPP frame fields.

Field	Description
Flag	A single byte that indicates the beginning or end of a frame. The flag field consists of the binary sequence 01111110.
Address	A single byte that contains the binary sequence 11111111, the standard broadcast address. PPP does not assign individual station addresses.
Control	A single byte that contains the binary sequence 00000011, which calls for transmission of user data in an unsequenced frame.
Protocol	Two bytes that identify the protocol encapsulated in the information field of the frame.
Data or Information	Zero or more bytes that contain the datagram for the protocol specified in the protocol field. The end of the information field is found by locating the closing flag sequence and allowing 2 bytes for the FCS field. The default maximum length of the information field is 1,500 bytes The IP packet is contained in this field.
Frame Check Sequence (FCS)	Normally 16 bits (2 bytes). By prior agreement, consenting PPP implementations can use a 32-bit (4-byte) FCS for improved error detection.

4

Link Control Protocol (LCP)

In this section we will describe management functions within the LCP. In order to be portable to a wide variety of environments, PPP provides the Link Control Protocol (LCP) for establishing, configuring, and testing the data link connection. LCP is used to automatically agree upon the encapsulation format options, handle varying limits on sizes of packets, detect common misconfiguration errors, and terminate the link. Other optional facilities provided are authentication of the identity of its peer on the link, and determination of when a link is functioning properly and when it is failing. LCP is responsible for opening, configuring, and terminating the link.

In addition to providing procedures for establishing, configuring, testing, and terminating data link connections, LCP also negotiates other non-default LCP options such as Maximum Receive Unit (MRU), Magic Number, Link Quality Monitoring (LQM), and authentication. MRU defines the optimal packet size for both ends of the serial link, which increases the transmission efficiency of the link. Magic Number identifies each peer so that loopback conditions can be recognized and corrected. Additionally, Link Quality Monitoring (LQM) can be configured along with Password Authentication Protocol (PAP) or Challenge Handshake Authentication Protocol (CHAP). The peer may be authenticated after the link has been established, using the authentication protocol decided on. If authentication is used, it must take place prior to starting the network layer protocol phase.

Let's summarize the LCP management functions as follows:

1. Determine encapsulation format options.

2. Negotiate optimal packet size.

3. Authenticate the identity of the peer on the link (optional).

4. Perform data compression (optional)

5. Perform link quality monitoring (optional)

6. Terminate the link

Network Control Protocols

The last key component of PPP is the Network Control Protocols (NCPs). After the link has been established and optional facilities have been negotiated as needed by the LCP, PPP must send NCP packets to choose and configure one or more network layer protocols. NCPs are a series of independently defined protocols that encapsulate network layer protocols such as TCP/IP, DECnet, AppleTalk, IPX, and XNS. Each NCP has individual requirements for addressing and advertising connectivity for its network layer protocol. Each NCP is defined in a separate RFC. Future protocols can be supported by defining new NCPs.

NCP opens, configures, and terminates network layer protocol communication, for example, IP, IPX, AppleTalk, and DECnet. Both LCP and NCP operate at layer 2. There is an extension to PPP to cater for multiple links, which is called Multilink PPP (MPPP) and uses the Multilink Protocol (MLP) to link the LCP and NCP layers. PPP is designed to allow the simultaneous use of multiple network layer protocols.

IP Control Protocol (IPCP)

The IP Control Protocol (IPCP) is responsible for configuring the IP protocol parameters on both ends of the point-to-point link. IPCP uses the same packet exchange mechanism as the Link Control Protocol (LCP). IPCP packets may not be exchanged until PPP has reached the network layer protocol phase. Any IPCP packets received before this phase is reached are discarded. IPCP offers certain options, including IP address negotiation and IP compression protocol determination.

PPP IOS Commands and Cisco Router Configuration

In this section we will discuss the various IOS commands that implement PPP connections between two Cisco routers or between a PC and a Cisco router. In the following subsections we will discuss the IOS commands listed in Table 4.3. They are grouped according to purpose. Authentication and Multilink PPP are not covered here. They will be discussed in the following section, "Selecting Encapsulation Types," which includes commands used to establish the PPP Link Control Protocol.

Table 4.3 IOS commands for PPP.

Selecting an Encapsulation Type	
encapsulation (ppp I slip)	Turns on PPP or SLIP
autoselect (arap I ppp I slip I during-login)	Automatically senses the encapsulation selection made by the user.
User Control	
async mode-interactive	Allows user to make selections; need to do this before autoselect
async mode-dedicated	Provides automatic connection; the user cannot change the encapsulation method, or IP address
Providing IP Addresses	
peer default ip address	The router directly assigns an IP address to the user.
async dynamic address	The user enters his own IP address at the EXEC line.
ip local pool *poolname*	The router directly assigns an IP address to the user from a group of available IP addresses found on the router.
ip address-pool dhcp-proxy-client	The router directly assigns an IP address to the user from a group of available IP addresses found on a DHCP server.
Enable Routing at the User End	
async default routing	Turns on the routing protocols at the user that are included in the configuration of the server router.

Selecting Encapsulation Types

Both the **encapsulation (ppp I slip)** command and the **autoselect {arap I ppp I slip I during login}** command are needed in a typical PPP connection. The **encapsulation** command is entered in the interface mode, whereas **autoselect** is added to the line mode. It is not an either/or condition.

Encapsulation (ppp I slip)

The **encapsulation** command is used to change the layer 2 encapsulation of a serial interface. Cisco's default WAN encapsulation is HDLC. Other options include **frame-relay**, **ietf**, and **x25**. But for remote access connections involving async or ISDN, you need to use either **ppp** or **slip**. The following is an example of **ppp** used as the option in the **encapsulation** command. Listing 4.1 shows an example of encapsulation PPP.

Listing 4.1   Example—Encapsulation PPP.

```
interface async 4
encapsulation ppp
ppp authentication chap
```

Autoselect

The **autoselect** command eliminates the need for users to enter an EXEC command to start a PPP or SLIP session. The **autoselect** command configures the router to identify the type of connection being requested. For example, when a user on a Macintosh running ARA selects the Connect button, the router automatically starts an ARA protocol session. If, on the other hand, the user is running SLIP or PPP and uses the **autoselect ppp** or **autoselect slip** command, the router automatically starts a PPP or SLIP session, respectively. This command is appropriate for *lines* used to make different types of connections. A line that does not have **autoselect** configured regards an attempt to open a connection as noise. Then when the router does not respond, the user client times out. The following example enables PPP on a line. Listing 4.2 shows an example of the **autoselect** command. Table 4.4 lists the options for the command.

Listing 4.2   Example—autoselect.

```
line con 0
line aux 0
transport input noneline 1 24
autoselect during-login
autoselect ppp
modem InOut

line vty 0 4
password XX
!end
```

User Control

You can configure the router to provide a prompt for entering encapsulation information and an IP address, or you can take the prompt away and assign everything by the router.

async mode dedicated

By using the dedicated asynchronous network mode, the interface will use either SLIP or PPP encapsulation as configured by the network engineer. The EXEC prompt does not appear, which makes the router unavailable for normal interactive

Table 4.4   Autoselect options.

Option	Description
arap	Configures the router to allow an ARA session to start up automatically.
ppp	Configures the router to allow a PPP session to start up automatically.
slip	Configures the router to allow a SLIP session to start up automatically.
during-login	The user receives a username and/or password prompt without pressing the Enter key. After the user logs in, the autoselect function begins.

use. If you configure a line for dedicated mode, you will not be able to use the **async dynamic address** command, because there is no user prompt. See Listing 4.3 for an example of the dedicated asynchronous network mode.

Listing 4.3   Example—dedicated.

```
interface async 4
async default ip address 172.31.7.51
async mode dedicated
encapsulation slip

line 20
location Joe's computer
stopbits 1
speed 115200
```

async mode interactive

The **async mode interactive** command allows SLIP and PPP EXEC commands for the user. Listing 4.4 gives an example of this command.

Listing 4.4   Example—interactive.

```
interface async 6
 async default ip address 172.31.7.51
 async mode interactive
 ip unnumbered ethernet 0
```

Providing IP Addresses

When a client router dials a server router and the protocol in use is TCP/IP, the dialing party must have an IP address to complete the connection. Basically, there are two methods for acquiring an IP address; the client router can supply its own previously assigned IP address, or the server router can deliver an IP address to the client router or client PC.

async dynamic address

With async lines, you can let the client enter an IP address using the **async dynamic address** command. The term "dynamic" used in the command may seem to be a contradiction to the normal use of the term "dynamic addressing," which refers to the delivery process of a random IP address to a PC. Cisco uses the term a little differently to show that a router is allowing a client to enter its own IP address. If you specify dynamic addressing, the communication server must be in the interactive mode and the user will enter the address at the EXEC level on his laptop. Listing 4.5 shows a simple configuration that allows routing and dynamic addressing. With this configuration, if the user specifies /routing in the EXEC **ppp** command, routing protocols will be sent and received.

Listing 4.5   Example—dynamic address.

```
interface async 6
async dynamic routing
async dynamic address
```

It is common to configure an asynchronous interface to have a default address and to allow dynamic addressing. With this configuration, the choice between the default address or a dynamic addressing is made by the user when he or she enters the **slip** or **ppp** EXEC command. If the user enters an address, it is used, and if the user enters the default keyword, the default address is used.

async default ip address or peer default ip address

By using the command **peer default ip address**, shown in Listing 4.6, you are implementing default IP addressing. Default IP addressing occurs when the server router gives an IP address to the client PC or client router. The client does not enter its own IP address; the router does it for the client. Before IOS 11.1, the Cisco router could only work with remote clients with permanently allocated IP addresses that were fixed to the PC prior to any connection as in dynamic addressing.

*Note: The **peer default ip address** command replaces the **async default ip address** command.*

Listing 4.6   Example—peer default ip address (async).

```
Router(config)# interface async 1
Router(config-if)# peer default ip-address 172.16.42.26
```

Pooling Local

One approach to giving the user a fixed IP address is the use of IP address pools. In IOS 11.1, Cisco released a new feature that allowed the Cisco router to have a pool of IP addresses that could be automatically allocated to remote clients at connection time. This is the simplest mechanism for assigning IP addresses to dial-in clients and is most useful when there is only one access server providing access to the network. A set of IP addresses is defined in a database that exists inside the access server. If there is more than one access server providing access to the network, you should provide IP address pooling using a DHCP server, which is explained in the next section. The allocation of IP addresses is done as part of the options of the IPCP (IP Control Protocol) negotiation that is done by PPP, and this is automatically handled by Windows 95 Dial-Up Networking. See Listing 4.7 for an example of an address pool.

Listing 4.7   Example—address pool.

```
Router(config)# ip address-pool local
Router(config)# ip local pool pool1 172.16.80.1 172.16.80.16
```

In the preceding example, the address pool named **pool1** is entered at the global configuration mode and is applied automatically to each asynchronous interface configured for point-to-point access, so you do not have to apply it manually. If you need to apply this pool manually to asynchronous interfaces, you will need to issue the **peer default ip-address pool pool1** interface configuration command, as in Listing 4.8.

Listing 4.8   ISDN example—address pool.

```
username bill password bailey
isdn switch-type basic-net3
ip local-pool isdnpool 192.1.170.2 192.1.170.9
ip address-pool local
:
interface BRI0
encapsulation ppp
ip address 192.1.170.1 255.255.255.0
peer default ip address pool isdnpool
dialer-group 1
ppp authentication chap
isdn answer1 01815110001

access-list 101 permit ip any any
dialer-list 1 list 101
```

The **username** statement defines the username (**bill**) and password (**bailey**) that the workstation will use on the Dial-up Networking logon panel. The **ip local-pool** and **ip address-pool** statements define a pool of IP addresses that can be used by remote workstations when they dial in. The **peer default** statement instructs the Cisco router to allocate IP addresses dynamically from the pool called "isdnpool" (defined earlier). The **ppp authentication** statement decides whether PAP or CHAP authentication will be used—the workstation automatically uses the mode requested by the Cisco router, and does not need to be configured for PAP/CHAP. The **isdn answer1** statement tells the Cisco router to bring up the phone connection for the specified phone number on the first ISDN channel. This is useful when there is another ISDN device sharing the connection that the Cisco router is plugged into.

When the Cisco router is using fixed IP addresses for clients (with the **dialer map** statement), it needs to know the ISDN numbers of the remote clients. When the Cisco router uses the dynamic IP pool, it no longer cares about the ISDN numbers of clients, and these are not needed in the Cisco configuration.

Pool-DHCP

The next method of IP address assignment is most useful for a medium- to large-sized pool of dial-in clients. A pool of IP addresses is defined inside a centralized IP address server, called a Dynamic Host Configuration Protocol (DHCP) server. This central database can serve addresses to several different access servers at the same time. Although this method provides long-term flexibility, it requires that you configure a third-party host (such as a UNIX computer) as a DHCP server.

You can enable DHCP address pooling on an access server by performing the following commands:

➤ Specify that the access server uses the DHCP client-proxy on all asynchronous interfaces by using the command **ip address-pool dhcp-proxy-client**.

➤ (Optional) Specify the IP address of at least one and up to ten DHCP servers for the proxy-client (the Cisco access server) to use. DHCP servers provide temporary IP addresses by using the command **ip dhcp-server [*ip-address* | *name*]**.

Then configure the appropriate interfaces by using the command **peer default ip-address dhcp**. Listing 4.9 gives an example of DHCP pooling.

Listing 4.9 Example—DHCP pooling.

```
Router(config)# ip address-pool dhcp-proxy-client
Router(config)# interface group-async 1
encapsulation ppp
Router(config-if)# peer default ip-address dhcp
```

You also must configure the client software on client PCs to obtain IP addresses from a DHCP server.

async default routing

Async default routing permits Routing Information Protocol (RIP), Open Shortest Path First (OSPF), and Interior Gateway Routing Protocol (IGRP) routing protocols on an asynchronous interface when using the **/routing** argument with the **ppp** and **slip** EXEC commands. When using asynchronous interfaces in interactive mode, the **async default routing** command causes the **ppp** and **slip** EXEC commands to act as though they included the **/route** argument in the command. When using asynchronous interfaces in dedicated mode, the **async default routing** command turns on the routing protocols included in the configuration of the server router. Without the **async default routing** command, there is no way to enable the use of routing protocols automatically on a dedicated *asynchronous* interface. See Listing 4.10 for an example of default routing.

Listing 4.10   Example—default routing.

```
interface async 4
encapsulation ppp
 ip address 191.191.191.191 255.255.255.0
 async default routing
 async mode dedicated
```

async dynamic routing

When you use the **async dynamic routing** interface configuration command, you are allowing the use of routing protocols on an interface as determined by the client PC in the interactive mode. The client has the option of not using them. This command uses the term dynamic differently than the way it is used in "dynamic routing." Dynamic routing refers to the automatic creation of routing tables by dynamic routing protocols as compared to static routing, which requires manually entered routing paths. In the **async dynamic routing** command, the term dynamic really means interactive. If the client wants to use the routing protocols offered by the router, the user enters **/routing** after the keyword **ppp** at the **EXEC** command. Listing 4.11 provides an example of the **async dynamic routing** command.

Listing 4.11   Example of **async dynamic routing** command.

```
interface async 6
encapsulation ppp
 async dynamic routing
 async dynamic address
 async default ip address 10.11.14.2

 ip unnumbered ethernet 0
```

Group Asynchronous Interfaces

Many times it is more convenient to gather asynchronous interfaces into a group interface and configure only the group interface to eliminate manual configuration duplication. The following example shows how to create an asynchronous group interface 0 with group interface members 2 through 7, starting in global configuration mode:

```
interface group-async 0
 group-range 2 7
```

This example includes async interfaces 2 through 7 in the group interface.

The following example shows how you need to configure asynchronous interfaces 1, 2, and 3 separately if you do not have a group interface configured:

```
interface Async1
 ip unnumbered Ethernet0
 encapsulation ppp
 async default ip address 172.30.1.1
 async mode interactive
 async dynamic routing
!
interface Async2
 ip unnumbered Ethernet0
 encapsulation ppp
 async default ip address 172.30.1.2
 async mode interactive
 async dynamic routing
!
interface Async3
 ip unnumbered Ethernet0
!
 encapsulation ppp
 async default ip address 172.30.1.3
 async mode interactive
 async dynamic routing
```

The following example configures the same interfaces, but from a single group asynchronous interface:

```
interface group-async 0
 ip unnumbered Ethernet0
 encapsulation ppp
 async mode interactive
 async dynamic routing
 group-range 1 3
 member 1 async default ip address 172.30.1.1
 member 2 async default ip address 172.30.1.2
 member 3 async default ip address 172.30.1.3
```

Link Control Protocol Options and Cisco Router Configuration

The PPP Link Control Protocol includes the following options, which will be described in the following sections.

➤ Authentication

➤ Callback

➤ Compression

➤ Multilink PPP

Authentication: PAP and CHAP

PPP supports two authentication protocols, PAP and CHAP. The PPP authentication option has three settings: PAP, CHAP, and PAP CHAP. The last setting, PAP CHAP, allows the client router or PC to determine which setting to use.

Password Authentication Protocol (PAP)

PAP provides a simple method for a remote node to establish its identity using a two-way handshake. This is done only upon initial link establishment. After the PPP link establishment phase is complete, a username/password pair is repeatedly sent by the remote node across the link until authentication is acknowledged, or the connection is terminated. Passwords are sent across the link in clear text, and there is no protection from playback or trial-and-error attacks. The remote node is in control of the frequency and timing of the login attempts. When a connection is established, each end can request the other to authenticate itself, regardless of whether it is the caller or the callee. A PPP device can ask its peer for authentication by sending yet another LCP configuration request identifying the desired authentication protocol.

PAP works basically the same way as the normal login procedure. The client authenticates itself by sending a user name and a password to the server, which the server compares to its secrets database. This technique is vulnerable to eavesdroppers who may try to obtain the password by listening in on the serial line, and to repeated trial-and-error attacks. CHAP does not have these deficiencies. PAP protocol details can be found in RFC 1334. The PAP packet is encapsulated in the Information field of a PPP data link layer frame where the protocol field indicates type hex c023.

Challenge Handshake Authentication Protocol (CHAP)

CHAP is used to verify the identity of the peer using a three-way handshake. This is done upon initial link establishment and may be repeated any time after the link has been established. With CHAP, the authenticator (that is, the server) sends a randomly generated "challenge" string to the client, along with its hostname. The client uses the hostname to look up the appropriate secret, combines it with the challenge, and encrypts the string using a one-way hashing function. The result is returned to the server along with the client's hostname. The server now performs the same computation, and acknowledges the client if it arrives at the same result. Exactly one CHAP packet is encapsulated in the Information field of a PPP data link layer frame where the protocol field indicates type hex c223. CHAP is more commonly used rather than PAP because it can encrypt the password as well as the data.

Each end of the link shares the same CHAP secret, and each end is given its own local name. The secret is used as an input variable to a "hashing" algorithm, which produces a "hash value," which is sent across the link in an initial Type 1 authentication packet. This algorithm is called Message Digest 5 (MD5). The other end uses the hash value to calculate a secret and compares it to its own secret; on success, the other end sends back a new hash value, in a Type 2 authentication reply. Once this has been successful, the authentication phase is complete. Type 3 packets mean that the authenticated link is still "legal," whereas the Type 4 packet indicates that the authentication is incorrect. Hashing is different from encryption because it is not reversible.

PPP CallBack

Callback allows a router to initiate a circuit-switched WAN link to a second device and request that device to call back. This can be configured for async as well as ISDN. The second device, such as a central site router, responds to the callback request by calling the device that made the initial call. Besides being used as an added security feature, callback is useful for minimizing costs. Callback provides centralized billing for synchronous dial-up services. It also allows you to take advantage of tariff disparities on both a national and an international basis. Because callback requires a circuit-switched connection to be established before the callback request can be passed, a small charge is always incurred by the router initiating the call that requests a callback. Ideally, for maximum security, the callback should occur on a different modem at the server end from the line used by the incoming call. When using ISDN, callback can use the D channel, which usually incurs no charge at all, whereas callback using modems will always incur a small charge while the authentication process occurs. ISDN callback will be discussed in Chapter 6.

Below are the processes that occur during a PPP callback connection:

1. Initiation of a call by a client. The client requests callback as one of the options during the LCP negotiation phase (the Callback Option Message Field defined in RFC 1570).

2. Callback request is acknowledged by the server, and the server checks its configuration to see if the call is allowed.

3. User authentication occurs, and the client username is used in the **dialer map** command to identify the dial string to be used in the return call.

4. If authentication is successful but there is no callback option, the call continues and the client pays for the call; otherwise, the call is disconnected by server.

5. Client is called by the server using the dial string.

6. Authentication occurs again.

7. The connection continues.

Table 4.5 lists the various IOS commands used for establishing a PPP callback connection, and following the table, Listing 4.12 provides two examples.

Listing 4.12   Example—ISDN PPP callback.

```
RouterA Calling Client
hostname RouterA
!
enable password ww
!
username RouterB password 7 140005
no ip domain-lookup
isdn switch-type basic-net3
!
```

Table 4.5   PPP callback commands for ISDN and async.

Callback Command	Description
dialer callback-secure	To enable callback security.
dialer callback-server [username dialstring]	To enable an interface to make return calls when callback is successfully negotiated, use the **dialer callback-server** interface configuration command.
username	(Optional) Identifies the return call by looking up the authenticated host name in a **dialer map** command. This is the default.
dialstring	(Optional) Identifies the return call during callback negotiation.
map-class dialer classname	To define a class of shared configuration parameters for PPP callback, use the **map-class dialer** global configuration command. **classname** is a unique class identifier.
ppp callback {accept I request}	To enable a dialer interface that is not a data terminal ready (DTR) interface to function either as a callback client that requests callback or as a callback server that accepts callback requests, use the **ppp callback** interface configuration command. **accept** enables this dialer interface to accept PPP callback requests (and function as the PPP callback server). **request** enables this dialer interface to request PPP callback (and function as the PPP callback client).

4

```
interface BRIO
ip address 193.10.12.1 255.255.255.0
encapsulation ppp
bandwidth 64
dialer map ip 193.10.12.2 name RouterB broadcast 208
dialer-group 1
ppp callback request
dialer hold-queue 100 timeout 20
ppp authentication chap

ip host RouterA 199.92.60.161
ip host RouterB 200.0.2.1
ip host wiske 200.0.3.1
ip route 200.0.2.0 255.255.255.0 193.10.12.2 200
ip route 200.0.3.0 255.255.255.0 193.10.12.3 200

dialer-list 1 protocol ip permit
!
line con 0
exec-timeout 0 0
line aux 0
transport input all
line vty 0 4
password ww
login
!
end

Router B—Callback Server
hostname RouterB
!
enable password ww
!
username RouterA password 7 10591E
no ip domain-lookup
isdn switch-type basic-net3
!
interface BRIO
ip address 193.10.12.2 255.255.255.0
encapsulation ppp
bandwidth 64
dialer map ip 193.10.12.1 name RouterA class dialer1 broadcast 206
dialer-group 1
ppp callback accept
dialer callback-secure
dialer enable-timeout 1
dialer hold-queue 10
```

```
ppp authentication chap
!
ip host STRANGE-BREW 192.135.243.130
ip host RouterA 200.0.1.1
ip host RouterB 200.0.2.1
ip route 200.0.1.0 255.255.255.0 193.10.12.1 200
!
map-class dialer dialer1
dialer callback-server username
!
dialer-list 1 protocol ip permit
!
line con 0
exec-timeout 0 0
line aux 0
transport input all
line vty 0 4
password ww
login
!
end
```

In this configuration, RouterA is the client router that calls RouterB, the server router. RouterA brings up a circuit-switched con-nection to RouterB. Routers A and B negotiate PPP Link Control Protocol (LCP). RouterA can request a callback, and RouterB can initiate the callback process. In this case, Router A configuration includes callback request. RouterA authenticates itself to RouterB using PPP Challenge Handshake Authentication Protocol (CHAP). RouterB can optionally authenticate itself to RouterA. Both routers drop the circuit-switched connection. RouterB brings up a circuit-switched connection to RouterA. The **dialer map** command for the server includes the server's hostname. The **dialer hold-queue** interface configuration command specifies that up to 100 packets can be held in a queue until the server router returns the call. If the server site router does not return the call within 20 seconds plus the length of the enable timeout configured on the server site router, the packets are dropped.

RouterB's configuration uses a **map-class dialer <*name*>**, which was entered at the global configuration prompt. This includes **dialer callback-server username**. The **map-class** global configuration command establishes parameters that are to be associated with the **dialer map** command. In this case, the dialer1 name is a user-defined value that creates a map class to which subsequent encapsulation specific commands apply. The **dialer map** interface configuration command has been modified to include the class keyword and the name of the class (dialer1), as specified in the **map-class** command. The *name* keyword is required so that, when the client router dials in, the interface can locate this **dialer map** statement and obtain the dial string for calling back the server router.

The BRI interface on the server router includes callback accept, which enables the router to accept all calls coming into that interface that request callback. The **dialer map** command includes the dial string, and RouterA's phone number and IP address. The use of **dialer callback-secure** at the global configuration makes the callback server always disconnect the initial call and only call back if the server has a complete configuration for the remote end (that is, **dialer map** with class and class defined). The default is **no dialer callback-secure**, which will keep up the initial call if the server does not have a complete configuration for the remote.

When using DDR to access the server from the client, you should see the BRI line go up, then down very quickly, and then up again. The enable timeout of the callback server determines how long to wait after disconnecting the initial call before making the return call. The **dialer enable-timeout** interface configuration command specifies that the interface is to wait one second after disconnecting the initial call before making the return call. Hold queues have been extended when callback is configured. Both the client and server can have hold queues, which will hold packets destined for the remote destination until the return call is connected or the holdq timer expires. The time entered in the timeout option of the **dialer hold-queue** command is added to the enable time for the same interface. The sum is used to determine the actual timeout. The default for the timeout option is 45 sec. [(**dialer holdq <XX>**) plus (**timeout <XX>**)]. An example of async-PPP callback is shown in Listing 4.13.

Listing 4.13   Example—async-PPP callback.

```
Router 1 Callback Server
hostname Router1
!
username Callman callback-dialstring 5551234 password foo
chat-script callback ABORT ERROR ABORT BUSY "" "ATDT\T"
TIMEOUT 30 "CONNECT" \c
!
interface Ethernet0
ip address 172.16.1.1 255.255.255.0
!
interface Async7
ip unnumbered Ethernet0
encapsulation ppp
async default ip address 172.16.1.2
async mode interactive
ppp callback accept
ppp authentication pap
!
interface Async8
ip unnumbered Ethernet0
encapsulation ppp
async default ip address 172.16.1.3
```

```
async mode interactive
ppp callback accept
ppp authentication pap
!
interface Async9
ip unnumbered Ethernet0
encapsulation ppp
async default ip address 172.16.1.4
async mode interactive
ppp callback accept
ppp authentication pap
!
line 7 9
 login local
 modem InOut
 speed 115200
 transport input all
 flowcontrol hardware
 script callback callback
 autoselect ppp
 autoselect during-login
```

In this configuration, a user from a Windows 95 PC dials into an access server, authenticates, and then the router disconnects the call. The access server then dials the phone number for calling the client. The client software needs to support RFC 1570 for Point-to-Point Protocol (PPP) callback. You need Cisco IOS release 11.3(2)T or later for Windows 95 callback to work. The authentication option is PAP, the remote PPP client username is "Callman", and the callback number is "5551234" (for user-specified callback number, use a callback-dialstring). In this example, the callback will be on the same line that received the call:

```
Session as seen by client:
ats0=1&d3\q3\j0\n3%c1&w
OK
atdt1244
CONNECT 38400

Username: Callman
Password:
Callback initiated - line is disconnected
NO CARRIER

RING

CONNECT 38400

Router1>
```

Multilink PPP (MLP)

The Multilink PPP Protocol (RFC 1717) is a standardized extension of the PPP (Point-to-Point Protocol) standard. It allows you to combine channels into a "Multi-link bundle" so that data can be sent at higher rates and to use packet sequencing to order packets and ensure compatibility between manufacturers of internetworking equipment. You may also enable a feature known as "packet fragmentation" where larger individual packets are chopped into smaller fragments. MLP works by splitting and re-assembling upper-layer protocol data units (PDUs) between the participating devices. That is, datagrams are split, sequenced, transmitted, and reassembled. The multiple links used are referred to as a bundle. To configure MLP, set up a standard Dial-on-Demand Routing (DDR) configuration, and then add the multilink commands.

PPP Multilink is advantageous because it ensures packet ordering. It also guarantees compatibility with other vendors' equipment because it is an open standard. Packet fragmentation over a number of links is beneficial because it reduces latency (the length of time a packet waits to receive an acknowledgement from the other end of the link), which decreases transit times and so speeds up transmission. Listing 4.14 provides an example of PPP Multilink.

Listing 4.14   Example—PPP Multilink.

```
interface bri 0
ip address 1.2.3.4 255.255.255.0
encapsulation ppp
ppp multilink
ppp authentication chap
no ip route-cache
dialer map ip 1.2.3.5 name mlpPeer 5551212
dialer-group 1
dialer load-threshold 128 either
username mlpPeer password sharedSecret
```

The line **dialer load-threshold 128 either:** specifies that when load hits 128 of 255, another call should be placed to the PPP peer. The keyword "either" specifies this should happen based on either inbound or outbound traffic. Note that multilink rotary groups dialing the same destination will combine into one large bundle, based on the CHAP authentication name (**mlpPeer** in the example).

PPP Compression

When you configure a Cisco router for **ppp** compression, you perform the **ppp compress predictor**, the **ppp compress stacker**, or the **ip tcp header-compression** commands on both sides of a link. The compression commands are slightly different when using asynchronous connections as compared to synchronous connections. Synchronous connection commands drops off the **ppp** in the command (example: **compress stacker**).

Cisco uses two main forms of compression: stacker and predictor. Stacker examines the data and sends each data type only once and sends information indicating to the other end where each type occurs within the data stream. The other end reassembles the data into the various data types from the data stream. Stacker tends to be more CPU-intensive and less memory-intensive. Predictor examines the data to see if it is already compressed and sends it. It does not waste time compressing data that is already compressed. Predictor tends to be more memory-intensive and less CPU-intensive. Listing 4.15 provides an example of PPP compression.

Listing 4.15   Example—PPP compression.

```
interface serial 0
encapsulation ppp
ppp compress predictor
```

Cisco also uses the Van Jacobson TCP header compression. The following example configures async interface 7 with a default IP address, allowing header compression if it is specified in the **slip** or **ppp** connection command entered by the user or if the connecting system sends compressed packets. The command **ip tcp header-compression passive** allows the router to accept packets that have been compressed, but the router does not perform its own compression by default. If we left off the word **passive** and replaced it with **on** as in **ip tcp header-compression on**, the router would also perform its own compression. Refer to Listing 4.16 for an example of TCP header compression.

Listing 4.16   Example TCP header compression.

```
interface async 7
ip address 150.136.79.1
async default ip address 150.136.79.2
ip tcp header-compression passive
```

Verifying and Troubleshooting

If the call is being initiated correctly and received by the remote side, but connectivity is not established at the higher layer protocols (that is, IP, IPX, and so forth), there might be a problem with authentication. To diagnose, issue the commands **debug ppp negotiation** and **debug ppp chap | pap**. If the CHAP or PAP username and password are correct, the message "remote passed CHAP authentication" or "remote passed PAP authentication" will be seen. If not, then the message "failed CHAP authentication with remote" or "failed PAP authentication with remote" will be displayed. In this event, the situation can be verified by removing authentication from the interface (that is, **no ppp authentication chap** on both routers) and retesting. If this remedies the problem, verify that the username and passwords on both routers are exact matches, including case.

Tables 4.6 and 4.7 include some of the more common **debug** commands used to troubleshoot dial-up connections.

Table 4.6   ISDN debug and show commands used for verifying and troubleshooting.

IOS Command	Description
debug dialer (most important debug)	Shows what packets trigger dialing and why. Used with DDR.
debug ppp negotiation	To see if a client is passing PPP negotiation; this is when you check for address negotiation.
debug ppp authentication	To see if a client is passing authentication. If you are using a Cisco IOS Software Release prior to 11.2, use the **debug ppp chap** command instead.
debug callback	To display callback events when the router is using a modem and a chat script to call back on a terminal line.
show dialer	Shows successful calls; shows you the state associated with each IP interface.
debug isdn q931	To see the ISDN Q.931 call setup and teardown messages and debugs.
debug isdn events	To see ISDN events occurring on the user side (router).

Table 4.7   Async debug and show commands used for verifying and troubleshooting.

IOS Command	Description
debug modem	To check to see if the router is getting the right signals from the modem.
debug ppp negotiation	To see if a client is passing PPP negotiation; this is when you check for address negotiation.
debug ppp authentication	To see if a client is passing authentication. If you are using a Cisco IOS Software Release prior to 11.2, use the **debug ppp chap** command instead.
debug ppp error	To display protocol errors and error statistics associated with PPP connection negotiation and operation.
debug callback	To display callback events when the router is using a modem and a chat script to call back on a terminal line.
debug ppp multilink	To see PPP multilink events.
show ppp multilink	To see the members of the multilink bundle.
show line [# tty line]	To look for the modem hardware state
show ip local pool	Verifies that the IP address pool was created.

Chapter Summary

The three main components of PPP are the encapsulation scheme, the Link Control Protocol, and the Network Control Protocols. These components are responsible for creating the frame, controlling the link, and managing the network layer protocol respectively.

LCP determines encapsulation format options, negotiates optimal packet size, authenticates the identity of the peer on the link, performs data compression, performs link quality monitoring, and terminates the link.

NCP opens, configures, and terminates network layer protocol communication. NCP is really a family of protocols that includes IPCP. IPCP configures IP at the network layer and can negotiate IP addresses such as using DHCP. Multilink Protocol (MLP) links the LCP and NCP layers.

The **autoselect** command eliminates the need for users to enter an EXEC command to start a PPP session. The **autoselect** command can also provide an automatic prompt for a password without the user pressing the Enter key.

If you want the user to enter an IP address for a client PC, you need to configure the interface on the router with **async mode-interactive** and **async dynamic address**. If you want to assign an IP address to a client without the user entering the IP address, use **async mode-dedicated** along with **peer default ip address xxx.xxx.xxx.xxx** or **peer default ip address pool** *poolname* or **peer default ip address dhcp**. If you are using pooling or DHCP, the pool or DHCP reference had to have been made in the global configuration mode with **ip local pool** *poolname* **x.x.x.x.y.y.y.y.** or **ip address pool dhcp-proxy-client**.

You can gather async interface into groups using the **interface group** command and the **group-range** command. This is a more efficient way for configuring multiple interfaces that will have the same configurations.

CHAP uses encryption, secret strings, and hashing values during a three-way handshake that authenticates a user. PAP uses clear text and a two-way handshake. Both the client router and the server router can authenticate each other using either PAP or CHAP. It doesn't matter which initiates the call; they both can authenticate each other.

Callback is used to increase security and minimize costs. When a router or PC requests a callback, the server router disconnects the originating call and makes a second call on the same or different line. When using async connections and modems, the callback number is added to the username/password line with the parameter **callback-dialstring**. When using ISDN connections, the callback number is added to the **dialer map** command. The callback process can include certain hold timers that allow for enough time for the second call to be completed before packets from the initiating call are dropped.

4

Cisco uses stacker and predictor compression for data and Van Jackobson TCP header-compression. The command **ip tcp header-compression passive** allows a router to use packets that have been compressed. The command **ppp compress stacker** can be entered in the interface mode.

There are several debug and show commands for verifying and troubleshooting PPP connections, but **debug ppp negotiation** would be the most useful as it shows the progress in each of the three PPP stages. In particular, you can see address negotiation happening.

Review Questions

1. Which command is used for making a local pool of IP addresses?

   a. **IP local pool** *poolname*

   b. **IP address local pool** *poolname*

   c. **IP address-pool dhcp-proxy-client**

   d. **IP pool dhcp-proxy-client**

2. Which are Cisco compression methods?

   a. Stacker

   b. Downstream

   c. Predictor

   d. TCP header compression

   e. MNP-5

3. From the following configuration lines, which one would identify DHCP as the IP address source for an interface?

   a. **peer ip address pool dhcp**

   b. **peer default ip address dhcp**

   c. **peer default ip address pool dhcp**

   d. **default ip address pool dhcp**

4. From the following configuration lines, which one would identify a specific IP address to be assigned to all dial-in clients on an interface?

   a. **peer default ip address 10.2.2.2**

   b. **peer ip address 10.2.2.2**

   c. **async dynamic address**

   d. **async dynamic IP address**

5. From the following pairs of configuration lines, which would identify a specific default address pool for giving IP addresses to clients on an interface?

   a. `Router(config)#ip local pool mypool 172.1.1.1 ...172.1.1.100`

      `Router(config-if)# peer default ip pool mypool`

   b. `Router(config)#ip local pool mypool 172.1.1.1 172.1.1.100`

      `Router(config-if)#default ip address pool mypool`

   c. `Router(config)#ip address local pool mypool 172.1.1.1 172.1.1.100`

      `Router(config-if)# peer default ip address pool mypool`

   d. `Router(config)#ip local pool mypool 172.1.1.1 172.1.1.100`

      `Router(config-if)# peer default ip address pool mypool`

6. Write the command for enabling MLP.

   _____

7. If you want to permit a remote client to specify his own IP address when asking for a connection to a router, which of the following commands would you use?

   a. **async dynamic address**

   b. **peer default ip address**

   c. **peer default ip address pool dhcp**

   d. **async dynamic routing**

8. Which command would you use to enable a PPP client to dial in to an interface and request a callback?

   a. **ppp callback request**

   b. **ppp callback accept**

   c. **ppp callback require**

   d. **ppp callback apply**

9. Which is the correct configuration line for configuring a username and password that can be used for PAP or CHAP authentication?

   a. **password *(password)* username *(name)***

   b. **host *(name)* password *(password)***

   c. **hostname *(name)* password *(password)***

   d. **username *(name)* password *(password)***

10. You can gather async interfaces into groups to avoid making the same repeated configuration for each individual interface. Which set of configuration lines is the correct method for creating async grouped interfaces?

    a. **router(config)# interface group-async 1**
       router(config)group-range 1 8

    b. **router(config)# interface group async 1**
       router(config-if)group range 1 8

    c. **router(config)# interface group-async 1 8**
       router(config-if)group-range 1

    d. **router(config)# interface group-async 1**
       router(config-if)group-range 1 8

11. You want to enable PPP encapsulation on a virtual interface. Which command would you choose?

    a. **ppp encapsulation**

    b. **no encapsulation slip**

    c. **encapsulation ppp**

    d. **encapsulation ppp 1**

12. Which ppp authentication method uses "clear text"?

    a. PAP

    b. CHAP

    c. TACACS

    d. MS-CHAP

13. The command **ppp authentication chap pap** has what effect?

    a. It enables the client router to use CHAP and the server router to use PAP.

    b. It enables the server router to use CHAP and the client router to use PAP.

    c. It enables either router to use both CHAP and PAP, but it will perform PAP before CHAP.

    d. It enables either router to use both CHAP and PAP, but it will perform CHAP before PAP.

14. Which statement(s) are important reason(s) for using CHAP over PAP?

    a. Only CHAP can be used with PPP. Only PAP can be used with SLIP. So, if you want to use PPP you must use CHAP.

    b. Only CHAP can be used with Multilink PPP.

    c. CHAP uses encryption.

    d. Only CHAP can be used with Callback.

15. The IP Control Protocol (IPCP) is responsible for configuring the IP protocol parameters on both ends of the point-to-point link. Which PPP process level contains IPCP?

    a. NCP

    b. LCP

    c. Encapsulation

    d. All three

16. If you examined a PPP packet for a DHCP request, which PPP protocol field would contain the information?

    a. Flag

    b. FCS

    c. LCP

    d. IPCP

17. Which statement best describes Challenge Handshake Authentication Protocol (CHAP)?

    a. CHAP verifies the identity of the peer using a two-way handshake by sending a randomly generated string to the client. The secret string is used as an input variable to a "hashing" value.

    b. CHAP verifies the identity of the peer using a three-way handshake by sending a randomly generated string to the client. The secret string is used as an input variable to a "hashing" value.

    c. CHAP verifies the identity of the peer using a three-way handshake by sending a randomly generated string to the client. No hashing algorithm is used; hashing is used with PAP.

    d. CHAP verifies the identity of the peer using a two-way handshake by having the peer send a password in "clear text."

18. Authentication is an optional PPP process. You can configure a connection to use CHAP or PAP or no authentication at all. If you choose to use authentication, at which PPP process level is it operating?

    a. Encapsulation

    b. LCP

    c. NCP

    d. Encapsulation and NCP

19. When configuring two connecting routers to perform callback, what is the function of the command **dialer callback-secure**?

    a. To require the client router to use PPP CHAP

    b. To require the server router to use a second interface for the callback

    c. To drop the connection if the name of the client router and its dial string are not present

    d. To continue the connection if the name of the client router and its dial string are not present

20. When using the command **async dynamic address**, which of the following statements are true?

    a. The router must also be configured for the interactive mode.

    b. The router must also be configured for the dedicated mode.

    c. The user will receive an EXEC prompt.

    d. The user gets to enter an IP address.

21. Which debug command would display the earliest connection information?

    a. **debug ppp authentication**

    b. **debug ppp negotiation**

    c. **debug callback**

    d. **debug ppp chap**

22. The Multilink PPP Protocol is a standardized extension of the PPP standard. Which statements accurately describe Multilink PPP?

    a. MLP is not dependent on having an Dial-on-Demand Routing (DDR) configuration.

    b. MLP can further fragment packets when needed.

    c. MLP works by splitting and re-assembling upper-layer PDUs (protocol data units).

    d. MLP splits, sequences, transmits, and reassembles datagrams.

23. You have configured a router server to accept callback requests. You entered the hold queue as **dialer hold-queue 10**, and the default timeout happens to be 45 seconds. How much time is allowed before a connection will timeout?

    a. 450 seconds

    b. 100 seconds

    c. 45 seconds

    d. 55 seconds

Real-World Projects

Lonzo Campbell is the head network engineer for ARMAT, a food and cafeteria company. Several salespeople in the northeast section negotiate and contract with other large companies and universities to have ARMAT provide their cafeteria needs. These salespeople need timely database information and must send in their clients' contractual information as new accounts are created. Lonzo decided to have the salespeople communicate with the branch office in New Haven, Connecticut. He decided that the branch office should have a Cisco 2509 access server that could handle both analog and ISDN incoming calls.

Lonzo knew that the Cisco 2509 will provide all control and management functions for remote access. He also decided to purchase the MP/8 I-modem made by 3Com's U.S. Robotics. This modem pool will provide the required modem ports, which are not internal to the Cisco 2509. Together, support is provided for dial-in and dial-out using V.34 analog, 56 Kbps, and ISDN connections. Each I-modem port automatically switches to the appropriate connection type for a specific call, allowing the remote access server to terminate or originate any combination of supported call types without reconfiguration.

Lonzo began by organizing the hardware components and making the necessary physical attachments.

Project 4.1

To prepare for the configuration of the Cisco 2509, you need to set up the following hardware components:

1. To configure the Cisco 2509, you will need a terminal or a PC with terminal emulation software and available serial port. Use the provided adapters and cable to connect the Cisco 2509 console line to your PC serial port.

2. Because the Cisco 2509 is brand new, it is unconfigured. This means it does not have an assigned IP address, which means you must enter the console port because you cannot Telnet.

3. To configure the MP/8 I-modem, you will need a Windows PC with an available serial port and floppy drive.

4. You will also need several details about your network (which may be obtained from your system administrator), including network address, network netmask, available IP addresses, and DNS server and gateway addresses.

5. Cisco cable (part #CAB-OCTAL- KIT) must be purchased separately.

6. Plug the two "four-connector octopus wires" into the ports labeled Channels 1-4 (first cable) and Channels 5-8 (second cable) on the MP/8 rear panel.

7. Plug the Cisco cable (part #CAB-OCTAL-KIT) into the port labeled Async 1-8 on the rear panel of the Cisco.

8. Connect the serial DB-25 connectors on the cables shown in Table 4.8.

Table 4.8   Cisco MP/8.

DB-25 Connector	Router Cable Extender
Port 1	Port 1 (first cable)
Port 2	Port 2 (first cable)
Port 3	Port 3 (first cable)
Port 4	Port 4 (first cable)
Port 5	Port 1 (second cable)
Port 6	Port 2 (second cable)
Port 7	Port 3 (second cable)
Port 8	Port 4 (second cable)

Next, Lonzo needed to configure the Cisco 2509 router for accepting calls. Configuration of the Cisco 2509 for use with the MP/8 I-modem is divided into two sections: generate a basic configuration and modify the general configuration for use with the MP/8 I-modem.

Project 4.2

To configure the Cisco 2509 router for incoming calls, perform the following:

1. Connect the adapter cable from your terminal or emulator to the console port on the Cisco 2509.

2. Configure the terminal for 9600 BPS, 8 data bits, 1 stop bit, No parity, and no flow control.

3. You will be prompted to answer a series of questions. The results will be used to generate the Cisco 2509's default configuration.

4. After the configuration is built, you will be prompted to press Enter; the Cisco 2509 will restart.

5. Now, you will modify the configuration for dial-in.

6. Telnet to the Cisco 2509 from any PC on the same network (using the IP address previously assigned).

7. When prompted, enter your password.

8. Type **enable** and press Enter.

9. When prompted, type your privilege password.

10. Type **config terminal** and press Enter to enter configuration mode.

11. Type the following commands to delete the default async settings:

```
no int async1 [ENTER]
no int async2 [ENTER]
no int async3 [ENTER]
no int async4 [ENTER]
no int async5 [ENTER]
no int async6 [ENTER]
no int async7 [ENTER]
no int async8 [ENTER]
```

12. Create an IP address pool to assign to dial-up users by typing the following (substitute your network's IP addresses):

```
ip local pool ip-pool1 10.10.10.10 10.10.10.17 [ENTER]
```

13. Create a chat script by typing the following:

```
chat-script I-Modem "" "atV1&b1&h1&r2&c1&d2&m4&k1s0=1" "OK" "" [ENTER]
```

14. Configure all of the async line with the following:

```
line 1 8 [ENTER]
autoselect during-login
autoselect PPP
login
script reset I-Modem [ENTER]
modem InOut [ENTER]
speed 115200 [ENTER]
flowcontrol hardware [ENTER]
```

15. Create and configure a new async interface group by typing the following:

```
interface Group-Async1 [ENTER] {you must create this group if not
   already present}
ip unnumbered Ethernet0 [ENTER]
ip tcp header-compression passive [ENTER]
no ip mroute-cache [ENTER]
encapsulation ppp [ENTER]
async dynamic routing [ENTER]
async mode interactive [ENTER]
```

```
peer default ip address pool ip-pool1 [ENTER]
no fair-queue [ENTER]
compress stac [ENTER]
no cdp enable [ENTER]
ppp authentication pap [ENTER]
ppp multilink [ENTER]
group-range 1 8 [ENTER] {sets this group to use async ports 1-8}
```

16. Type **show run** and press Enter to review your configuration.

17. Type **copy run star** and press Enter to save your configuration.

Dial-in configuration is complete. Now, Lonzo needs to configure the Cisco 2509 router for dialing out.

Project 4.3

To modify the configuration for dial-out, perform the following steps:

1. Telnet to the Cisco 2509 (using the IP address previously assigned).

2. When prompted, enter your password.

3. Type **enable** and press Enter.

4. When prompted, type your privilege password.

5. Type **config terminal** and press Enter to enter configuration mode.

6. Create two chat scripts by typing the following:

```
chat-script call-out "" "atdt5551234" TIMEOUT 60 "CONNECT"
chat-script I-modem "" "atv1&b1&h1&r2&c1&d2&m4&k1&s0=1" "OK" ""
```

7. Create a needed static route, by typing the following:

```
ip route 192.168.2.0 255.255.255.0 Async5
```

8. Create the filter for determining interesting traffic that turns on DDR:

```
dialer-list 1 protocol ip permit
```

9. You need a singular async interface for dialing out, so type the following:

```
interface Async5
ip unnumbered Ethernet0
ip tcp header-compression passive
no ip mroute-cache
encapsulation ppp
async dynamic routing
async mode interactive
peer default ip address 192.168.2.3
dialer in-band
dialer idle-timeout 300
dialer string 5551234
dialer group 1
no fair-queue
compress stac
no cdp enable
ppp multilink
pulse-time 1
```

10. Now configure the associated line by typing the following:

```
line 5
script dialer call-out
script reset I-modem
modem InOut
transport input all
speed 115200
flowcontrol hardware
```

11. Press Ctrl+Z.

12. Type **show run** and press Enter

13. Type **copy run star**

Dial–out configuration is complete.

CHAPTER FIVE

Configuring Windows 95/98 for Remote Access

After completing this chapter, you will be able to:

✓ Configure Windows 95/98 for POTS dial-up into a router

✓ Configure Windows 95/98 for an ISDN dial-up into a router

✓ Describe the various adapters included in the Cisco 200 series

✓ Explain how to create a dial-up script for Windows 95/98

This chapter discusses two methods for dialing into a branch or central office router from a Windows 95/98 workstation. One method uses regular POTS and an analog modem attached to the Windows 95/98 workstation. The second method uses an ISDN adapter card attached to the Windows 95/98 workstation. Both methods use the PPP protocol and many of the PPP options including PAP or CHAP and Multilink PPP. The chapter discusses many IOS features used to configure a Cisco router that are directly related to the workstation's configuration.

Windows 95/98 Connections Using POTS

The Windows 95/98 subsystem that connects to remote computers is called Dial-Up Networking. This fulfills the role played by Remote Access Services in Windows NT and Windows 2000. Dial-Up Networking is implemented by a layer of software caller the Dial-Up Adapter, which binds or connects the network protocols to the modem. In Windows 3.x, each communications application was responsible for initializing the attached modem, setting up the call, and managing the online session. This is in marked contrast with the application independence provided by other Windows components in the areas of printer and graphics support, where output on printers and screens is handled by Windows itself rather than the application. Windows 95/98 provides a device-independent interface to modems and telephony equipment called the Telephony Applications Programming Interface (TAPI). Communications software written to use TAPI will work with whatever modem is attached to a Windows 95/98 system.

Connecting a Windows 95/98 Workstation to a Cisco Router Using an Analog Modem

Connecting a Windows 95/98 workstation to a Cisco router through the use of an analog modem is similar to making a connection to an ISP. In order to perform a successful POTS connection between a Windows 95/98 computer and a Cisco router, you need to perform the following tasks, which will be explained in the following sections:

➤ Installing a modem

➤ Setting up the Dial-Up Adapter

➤ Configuring the Dial-Up Adapter

➤ Configuring basic TCP/IP properties

➤ Installing Dial-Up Networking

➤ Creating a dial-up connection icon

➤ Using the connection icon: manual login

➤ Using the connection icon: automatic login

Installing a Modem

Before you start the installation, you will need to physically connect a working modem to your machine. You will also need to have the installation media for Windows 95/98. Dial-Up Networking uses TAPI. To use Dial-Up Networking, you need to "tell" Windows about your modem. If Windows was able to detect your modem during setup, the necessary driver will already be installed. To check this, open the Control Panel folder and double-click on the Modems icon. If your modem is installed, you will see a property sheet with a list of installed modems. If not, the Install New Modem Wizard program will start up and will attempt to detect the modem. Make sure the modem is connected to the computer and switched on before proceeding. If Windows 95/98 fails to identify the modem correctly, you will be prompted to select your modem from a list. If the modem manufacturer is shown in the left-hand pane, select the manufacturer's name and choose the model, or nearest similar model, from the right-hand list. If your modem manufacturer is not on the manufacturer list, choose the first entry, Standard Modem Types, and in the right-hand pane select "Standard $<n>$ Modem" where $<n>$ is the baud rate indicated by your modem's name or documentation.

Next, select the communications port to which the modem is connected, which is usually either COM1 or COM2. The port will normally be identified on the back of the computer by name or number. TAPI needs to know about the location you will normally be calling from. The correct country should already be selected, but you will need to enter the area code. If you are on a switchboard line, you will need to enter the network access number (usually 9) in the field "If you dial a number…" Click on Next to complete installation of the modem.

Setting Up Dial-Up Adapter for Windows 95/98

The next thing you need for configuring the Windows 95/98 connection is to install the Dial-Up Adapter. The default Windows 95/98 installation does not install Dial-Up Adapter or Dial-Up Networking automatically, so you will have to install the program separately. From the Desktop, double-click on My Computer and then double-click on the Control Panel icon. You will see the Control Panel window. Double-click on the Network icon, and then click on the Configuration tab near the top of the Network window. This will bring up the configuration portion of the Network window, which you use to add and remove network components of your operating system.

If you have some networking components already installed, they may appear in the configuration window. If you see Dial-Up Adapter and TCP/IP or TCP/IP|Dial-Up Adapter on the list of installed components, the Dial-Up Adapter is already installed, and you can skip to Configuring The Dial-Up Adapter. If it isn't already installed, click on Add, and the Select Network Component Type window should appear. In this window, click on Adapter, and then click on Add. This should bring up the Select Network Adapters window. Now, click on Microsoft, then click Dial-Up Adapter. The results should be a window that looks like Figure 5.1.

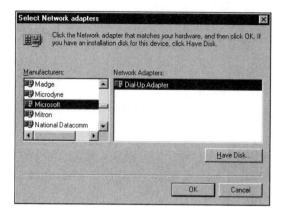

Figure 5.1   The Select Network Adapters window.

Click OK and follow the prompts, and insert your Windows 95/98 installation disk if necessary. When the Dial-Up Adapter has finished installing, you should be returned to the Network window, which should look something like Figure 5.2. Again, you may need to scroll down to see everything if you have other network components installed.

Note: If you have an Ethernet card on your machine, you may see two versions of TCP/IP—one for the Dial-Up Adapter, and one for the Ethernet card. This is normal.

If the computer is used by a mobile user who moves his or her PC between a branch office, and home, he or she can work without having to reconfigure Network protocols each time, because the network card and the Dial-Up Adapter will

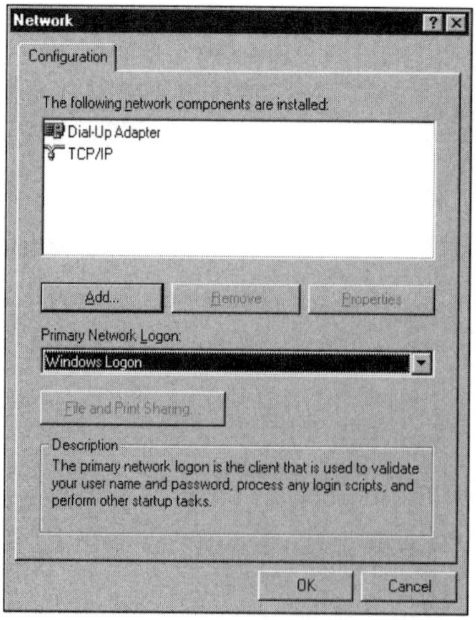

Figure 5.2   The Network window.

have different TCP/IP stacks. A PC connected to a work network will contain an entry for a network card adapter in the Network option of the Control Panel. This should remain untouched. If the PC is relocated to home, an entry for a Dial-Up Adapter can be added in addition to the network card adapter and configured separately. Notice in Figure 5.3 the presence of a Network adapter along with the Dial-Up Adapter.

If you don't see either TCP/IP or TCP/IP | Dial-Up Adapter, you will need to install the TCP/IP protocol. To do so, click on Add from the Network screen, click on Protocol, and then on Add. The Select Network Protocol screen should open, as shown in Figure 5.4.

5

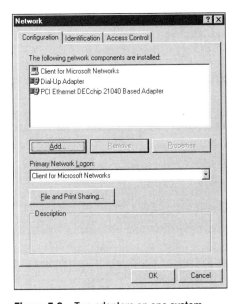

Figure 5.3   Two adapters on one system.

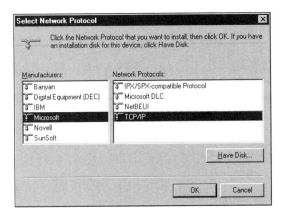

Figure 5.4   The Select Network Protocol screen.

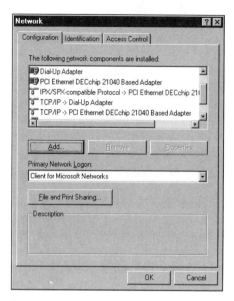

Figure 5.5 The Network screen.

Now you need to click on Microsoft, and then on TCP/IP, then on OK. This should install the TCP/IP protocol and return you to the Network screen as shown in Figure 5.5.

Multiple ISP Connections

Users who need to connect to multiple branch offices or Internet Service Providers may create a dial-up connection icon for each office or provider. Configuring dial-up connection icons is covered in the following section. Users can create and configure additional connection icons for each additional branch office. If each branch office requires TCP/IP settings different from the first connection, these changes should be entered in the TCP/IP entry provided within each dial-up connection icon and *not* in the global TCP/IP entry accessed through the Network Control Panel. The entry in the Control Panel is a global setting that affects all dial-up connections.

Configuring the Dial-Up Adapter's TCP/IP Properties

Now that the Dial-Up Adapter is installed, you need to configure TCP/IP. In the Control Panel, double-click on the Network icon and select TCP/IP or TCP/IP|Dial-Up Adapter by scrolling through the window of installed network components and clicking on TCP/IP or TCP/IP|Dial-Up Adapter. Do not choose the option Dial-Up Adapter without TCP/IP. Click on Properties to bring up the TCP/IP Properties window. You will need to enter information in the IP Address, Gateway, and DNS Configuration portions of the TCP/IP Properties window. To call up each portion, click on the appropriate tab. Click on the IP Address tab of the TCP/IP Properties dialog box. Check the radio button for Obtain An IP

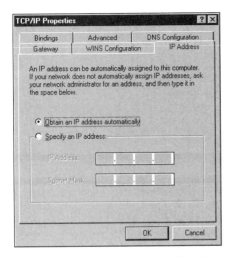

Figure 5.6   The TCP/IP Properties dialog box.

5

Address Automatically, as shown in Figure 5.6, if the routers you are going to dial up are configured to handout IP addresses. Enter a DNS address if your connection takes you out to the Internet. Also, select the Bindings tab and ensure that Client for Microsoft Network is listed and selected. Exit the Network window and restart the computer.

Enter a one-word name for your computer in the Host box, and enter a domain name in the Domain box. If you have domains on your network, you would put the name of the domain you are part of in this field. If you only have workgroups, you would put the name of the workgroup you are part of in this field. In simple terms, this field is used identically for Workgroup or Domain.

Your TCP/IP protocol should now be configured properly. Click on OK at the bottom right of the TCP/IP Properties window, and then click on OK at the bottom right of the Network window. At this point you should be asked if you want to restart your system in order for the changes to take effect. Restart your computer by clicking on Restart.

Installing Dial-Up Networking

After you have installed and configured the Dial-Up Adapter and the global TCP/IP settings, you need to install the Dial-Up Networking program. Go to the Desktop and double-click on My Computer. If you see a Dial-Up Networking icon here, it is already installed, and you can go directly to the next step. If not, double-click on Control Panel and continue. Double-click on Add/Remove Programs, and then click on the Windows Setup tab near the top of the Add/Remove Programs window. This should bring up the Windows Setup screen, which you use to install the optional components of Windows 95/98. Click on the Communications option, which should appear in the middle of the Windows Setup window, and then click on the Details box. This should bring up a window that shows which communication options, if any, you have installed. The option necessary for PPP is Dial-Up Networking, so select this option by clicking the checkbox just to the left of the Dial-Up Networking option as in Figure 5.7, and then click OK.

Follow the prompts and insert your Windows 95/98 installation disk if necessary. When Dial-Up Networking has finished installing, you should be returned to the Add/Remove Programs Properties window. Click OK and you are now ready to go on to the next step, which is to create a dial-up connection icon for each branch office.

Creating a Dial-Up Connection Icon

The Dial-Up Connection icon is what you will eventually double-click on to initiate the PPP connection. Double-click on Dial-Up Networking In My Computer. If this is the first time you have opened Dial-Up Networking, the Make New Connection screen should appear automatically. If it does not appear, double-click on the Make New Connection icon in the Dial-Up Networking window. If you haven't yet installed your modem, you should also see the Install New Modem screen. If so, Windows 95/98 will temporarily break away from the creating the dial-up connection to install a modem. If you need to install a modem, follow the on-screen instructions, and keep entering the requested information and clicking Next until you get back to the Make New Connection window.

In the first screen of the Make A New Connection wizard, you need to enter a name for the connection icon (for example, Router1). If your modem has been set up properly, it should already be selected in the Select A Modem window as in Figure 5.8, and you should not have to click on Configure.

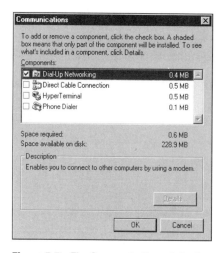

Figure 5.7 The Communications dialog box.

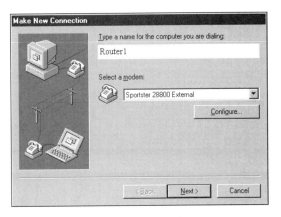

Figure 5.8   The Make New Connection screen.

Click on Next, and the phone number screen should appear. Enter the number of the router you are calling and then click on Next. You should get a "success" screen indicating that your new connection has been successfully created. Click on Finish. However, you will have to go back and configure the connection icon some more.

You should now see the new improved Dial-Up Networking window, which should now include an icon for Router1. Click on this icon, and then select Properties from the File menu. You should see a window entitled Router1 or whatever it was you called your connection. Then click on Server Type. Make sure PPP: Windows 95 Windows NT 3.5 Internet is selected as the Type of Dial-Up Server. The option Log Onto Network will be checked by default. Click once to deselect it. The option Enable Software Compression will be checked by default. You can leave it checked if you intend not to use PPP compression. The option Require Encrypted Password will be unchecked by default. This option *must* be left unchecked (deselected) or PAP authentication will not work; make sure this box is deselected before you proceed. If you are using CHAP, you need to select it. Look in the section Allowed Network Protocols. If either NetBEUI or IPX/SPX Compatible is checked, click in the check box for those protocols to clear them. If the TCP/IP box is not checked, click it to select it. Finally, the Server Types configuration window should look like Figure 5.9.

Click OK to return to the Router1 screen, and again click OK to close the Router1 PPP window. Your PPP connection should now be configured properly.

Click on the TCP/IP Settings button. Here you have a chance to set different TCP/IP settings than those that take effect in the set of global TCP/IP settings. The boxes that should be checked are Server Assigned IP Address, Server Assigned Name Server Address, Use IP Header Compression, and Use Default Gateway on Remote Network. Server Assigned IP Address is used if the server is providing your workstation the dial-in IP address such as IP pooling or DHCP. This setting was configured

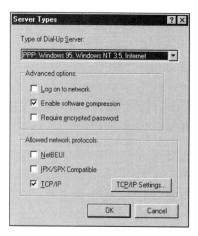

Figure 5.9   PPP settings.

globally, but you need to do it again if there are multiple connection icons. Specify that an IP address is used if you already have a static IP address predefined on your workstation. Server Assigned Name Server Address is used if the server is providing your workstation the IP addresses for your primary and secondary DNS and WINS servers. Specify Name Server Addresses is used to define which DNS/WINS server you want to connect to upon dial-up. Figure 5.10 shows the typical settings for the TCP/IP configuration. Click OK to close the TCP/IP Settings dialog box.

Click on the General tab and then click on the Configure button. Select the Communication COM port your modem is connected to, COM2 or COM1. Select the Port Speed of your modem. Because PPP uses compression, 14400 modems can

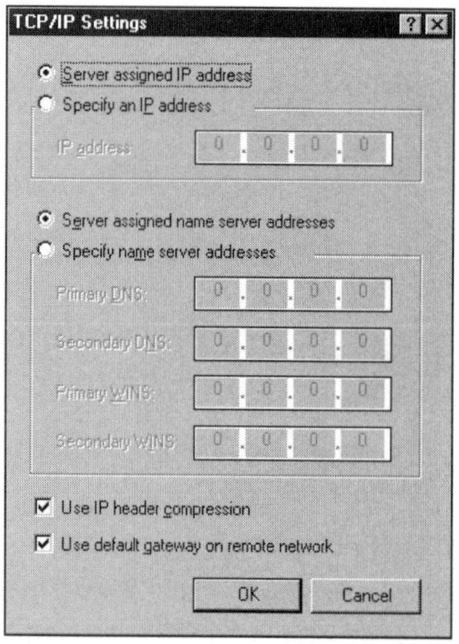

Figure 5.10   A typical configuration.

utilize 38400 and 28800 modems can utilize 57600. Ignore the Connection tab and select the Options tab. Select Bring Up a Terminal Window After Dialing by checking its box. You will want to do this for logging in with the workstation name and password, and for starting PPP if the router is configured for the interactive mode with autoselect turned off. Make sure that Display Modem Status is selected and select OK. Make sure that the entries for Area Code, Telephone No., and Country Code are correct. Click OK. You are now ready to make a connection.

Using the Connection Icon: Manual Login

There are two techniques for dialing in to a router from a Windows 95/98 computer that uses POTS: manual login and automatic login. Manual login is used when there is no Windows 95/98 dial-up script and you need to enter the account and password by typing after the associated prompts in the terminal window, which can be configured to come up after a connection is made. Automatic login uses a dial-up script to enter the account and password instead of typing. How to create and use dial-up scripts is covered in the next section. When using the manual login method, you need to open up Dial-Up Networking from the Start menu or from My Computer and select the icon Router1, which was created earlier. When the dialog box Connect comes up, remove any entries in the Username and Password boxes. Windows will place entries in here automatically if you have a Windows Login procedure. After removing these entries, select Connect in order to have the software dial the modem for you. The modem should dial and connect to the router. After a phone connection has been established, a terminal window will appear.

If you successfully connected to the router, you should be presented with a window to log in. Press Enter a couple of times to get the router's attention. A username prompt should appear, and you will need to enter a remote access account user-name. After you enter the name and press Enter, a second prompt should ask for a password. At the password prompt, enter the corresponding password and press Enter. There may be a short delay before the next router prompt appears. After the next router prompt appears, you should then enter **PPP** if the router was not configured for autoselect. You should then click on the Continue button or press F7. After a short wait, you should be presented with an alert message stating that you are connected to Router1, showing details of your connection speed and the duration of your connection. Now you should be able to use your client software and email programs. Remember, most routers will be configured with **autoselect ppp**, so all you need to do is to click on Continue without typing PPP. In the example in Figure 5.11, the workstation's name is the same as the user.

Automatic Login Using Scripts

Setting up the connection icon for automatic login is the same as manual login except that when you select the Options tab, you need to ensure that neither Bring Up A Terminal Window Before Dialing or Bring Up A Terminal Window After

Figure 5.11 The Post-Dial Terminal screen.

Dialing is selected. If it works correctly, you don't need the terminal window. To create a script, you will need to install the Dial-Up Scripting Tool. From the Start menu, select Programs | Accessories | Dial-Up Scripting Tool. If Dial-Up Scripting Tool does not appear on the menu, proceed with the following to add it. The Dial-Up Scripting Tool is located on the Windows 95/98 CD-ROM. Open the Control Panel and select Add/Remove Programs. Select the Windows Setup tab and click on the Have Disk button. Either enter the following path to the application, or select the Browse button and navigate to /Admin/Apptools/dscript/rnaplus.inf. Select OK, and Scripting for Dial-Up Networking is now listed in the Components box to install (see Figure 5.12). Finally, select Install.

Once you have completed the installation, you will be returned to the Add/Remove Program Properties window. There should now be an entry for SLIP and Scripting

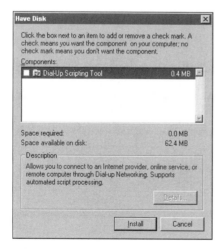

Figure 5.12 The Have Disk screen.

for Dial-Up Networking. Click on the OK button. The Dial-Up Scripting tool will now be listed in the Accessories group. Start it and continue with the following steps. From the Start menu, choose Programs | Accessories | Dial-Up Scripting Tool. The Dial-Up Scripting Tool dialog box (see Figure 5.13) allows you to assign a script to a Connection name (for example, Router1). A list of current dial-up connections will be shown. On the left, select the connection you have just made. Now in the File name box on the right, enter a file name for the script. Scripts usually have .scp extensions, such as C:\windows\cwruppp.scp. If you enter a script name that has not been created, you will be prompted to start a new file. Next, click the Edit button. Choose Yes to create the new file. You will be placed in a new Notepad file. Enter the following code as it appears in Figure 5.14.

5

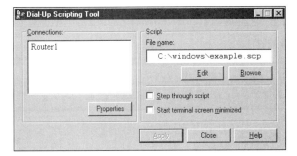

Figure 5.13   The Dial-Up Scripting Tool dialog box.

```
proc main

    ; Wait a second and allow host time
    ; to send initial chars

    delay 1
    transmit "^M^M"

    ; Log into terminal server

    waitfor "Username:"
    transmit $USERID
    transmit "^M"

    waitfor "Password:"
    transmit $PASSWORD
    transmit "^M"

    ; Enter PPP mode

    waitfor ">"

    transmit "ppp^M"

    ;We're done! Get our IP Address from the server

    set ipaddr getip 1

endproc
```

Figure 5.14   Entering the script in Notepad.

Now save the script by choosing File | Save in the editor. Then exit Notepad choosing File | Exit. Click the Apply button and then choose Close. This script should automatically execute when you run the connection that it is associated with.

Multilink PPP

There are add-ons to Dial-Up Networking that allow for Multink PPP. The following is a list of the necessary upgrades in order to perform Multilink with Microsoft Windows:

➤ Windows NT supports Multilink PPP with a maximum of four modems. Service Pack 4 should be installed for better performance.

➤ Windows 98 supports Multilink PPP with a maximum of four modems. The Dial-Up Networking Security upgrade should be installed for better performance.

➤ Windows 95 will support Multilink PPP with a maximum of two modems if the Dial-Up Networking 1.3 upgrade is installed.

The Multilink PPP dialog box for Windows 98 is displayed in Figure 5.15. Notice the addition of the Multilink tab.

Windows 95/98 and ISDN

Windows 95/98 can be configured to use internal or external ISDN adapters. These adapters either have a built-in or external NT1. It is possible to have an internal ISDN adapter card with a built-in NT1 or an external ISDN adapter with its own

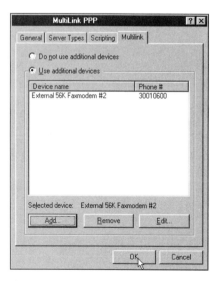

Figure 5.15   The Multilink PPP dialog box.

NT1. Internal ISDN adapters go inside your PC. Internal adapters require you to open your PC to install the card. To install an internal adapter, you need a slot free in your PC that supports the same type of bus (for example, Industry Standard Architecture [ISA], Extended Industry Standard Architecture [EISA], or Peripheral Component Interconnect [PCI]), as the card you want to install. Look for ISDN adapters with the Windows 95/98 logo, which support Plug and Play, so that Windows 95/98 can automatically detect and configure the adapter for you. Cisco makes a set of plug-and-play ISDN adapter cards called the Cisco 200 series, which will be covered in the next section.

External ISDN adapters are easier to install than internal ISDN adapters. External ISDN adapters look similar to a modem. Some manufacturers even call them "ISDN modems." Communication programs control the external ISDN modem the same way they control an analog modem, typically with AT commands. An external ISDN adapter plugs into a PC's serial, parallel port, or USB port.

Certain limitations are imposed by these ports. Most PC serial ports will not transmit information faster than 115 kilobits/second, which is less than ISDN's maximum data speed of 128 kilobits/second. These serial ports impose overhead on the transfer of information between the PC and the external adapter, further slowing data speeds. To reduce this effect, you can install Microsoft's ISDN Accelerator Pack 1.1, which supports the full advantage of Multilink PPP.

Cisco 200 ISDN Adapter Card

Cisco 200 series remote node access solutions combine software and an adapter in a complete package that delivers high-speed ISDN connectivity for individual PC users. The Cisco 200 for Windows 95/98 is a remote-node product designed to provide a single desktop PC with transparent access to LAN resources such as databases, hosts, printers, and email through a high-performance ISDN connection. In addition to support for traditional DOS and ISA platforms, the Cisco 200 series remote node access includes native Network Driver Interface Specification (NDIS) support for Windows 95/98 PCs. The series also has a model for a PC card adapter for notebook computers.

The Cisco 200 software features provide performance and usability benefits for remote node users. Whereas many ISDN cards from other manufacturers use the same Dial-Up Networking program as analog modems, the Cisco 200 series remote node access software features the ISDN Connection Manager. This is a user-friendly connection monitoring tool that can also be used to modify session configurations or create new ones. ISDN connection status can be monitored, and call logs viewed.

Components of the Cisco 200 for Windows 95/98

The Cisco 200 for Windows 95/98 contains two main components: software and hardware. The software for the Cisco 200 for Windows 95/98 software includes two disks, which include the ISDN Connection Manager. The hardware feature consists of three hardware options that are available for Windows 95/98: Cisco 201, Cisco 202, and Cisco 250. The Cisco 201 requires an external NT1 and is used primarily outside North America. The Cisco 201 may be used within North America when another ISDN device, such as an ISDN telephone, shares the ISDN connection with the Cisco 201. Outside North America, the NT1 is often included with the ISDN service by the ISDN service provider. The Cisco 202 includes an integrated NT1 and is available only in North America. In North America, the NT1 is not provided by the ISDN service provider and would have to be purchased separately if not included in the package. The Cisco 250 includes a PCMCIA card for a laptop computer.

The Cisco 200 for Windows 95/98 includes the following features:

➤ An optional built-in Network Termination 1 (NT1) interface, which eliminates the need for a separate NT1 device and power supply. One ISDN Basic Rate Interface (BRI) port using an S/T or U interface.

➤ Support for all major ISDN switch protocols and security features for compatibility with ISDN services.

➤ Dial-on-demand communications to help control costs when you connect to the WAN.

➤ A Windows 95/98 Network Driver Interface Specification (NDIS) driver for state-of-the-art Windows 95/98 connectivity.

➤ IP address negotiation, which allows for pooling of IP addresses and simplifies network maintenance.

➤ Software compression for faster data transfer.

➤ PPP support for compatibility with the Internet and other networks. PPP multilink support to enable additional bandwidth on demand. 128Kbps over two B channels (with PPP multilink). PPP callback support to control access and toll costs.

➤ Support for Password Authentication Protocol (PAP) authentication and Challenge Handshake Authentication Protocol (CHAP) two-way and one-way authentication.

➤ An installation utility that runs in Windows 95/98 to simplify hardware and software setup and initial configuration. An ISDN Connection Manager to monitor, manage, and reconfigure network connections.

➤ Call logging that allows for statistics and data collection for connection troubleshooting and maintenance.

Hardware Installation

As you install the ISDN Adapter in your PC, you must configure it with appropriate IRQ and I/O settings. In most cases, you should use the following default settings:

➤ Default I/O port address (I/O)—390

➤ Default interrupt request (IRQ)—11

If there are other devices in this PC that conflict with the default I/O port address and interrupt, you can change the settings for the other device or change the jumpers on the ISDN Adapter. If you change the jumpers on the ISDN Adapter to select an alternative I/O port address and interrupt, make sure you indicate these new settings in the software configuration program.

5

Software Installation

The software installation for the Cisco 200 series is fairly simple. You do need to create a MAC address and assign it to the Cisco 200 ISDN Adapter. A MAC address is required for the Cisco 200 software to function. The address must be no more than 12 hexadecimal characters. It can include a combination of numbers (1-9, 0) and letters (A-F). Each node MAC address must be unique. The first two characters should be 00 to avoid confusion with a broadcast address. You will need to have the name of your Windows 95/98 workstation. If connected to a router that uses authentication, this name must be identical to the "username" configured on the router. If connected to a router using authentication, the Cisco 200 for Windows 95/98 will have to include the connecting router's hostname, which must be identical to the hostname configured on that router. The authentication password must be identical to the password entered on the router after the username. You will need to include all digits necessary to connect to the router (country code, area code, international access, long distance access, public access, and so on). The D-channel protocol configuration will need to be entered. A second SPID is left blank unless you are using PPP multilink on the NT1 protocol that will run on a DMS100 switch. In this case, the second SPID and directory are required.

Let's take a look at how you would actually configure the Cisco 200. First, you need to start the Setup.exe file on the disk that contains the Cisco 200 for Windows 95/98 Setup program. You will be prompted for the following information:

1. You will need to select the desktop protocol(s) you will be using. Click the boxes to choose TCP/IP.

2. You must choose an Internet Protocol (IP) addressing scheme. The first choice, Specify An IP Address, allows you to specify an IP address, dedicated to the PC in which you have installed the Cisco 200. If you have been assigned an IP address, select this option. The other choice is Obtain An IP Address Automatically. This will set up the Cisco 200 to obtain an IP address when it connects

to the network. If your connecting router has been configured to provide IP addresses automatically, select this option.

3. You will need to specify the IP address and/or Domain Name Service (DNS) information for the PC in which you have installed the Cisco 200.

4. You can now specify a default gateway IP address. This is the IP address of the ISDN port of your connecting router.

5. You will need to enter the node MAC address assigned to your Cisco 200 ISDN Adapter. This consists of 12 hexadecimal characters (1–9, 0, A–F). It must be a unique address. If you are not sure what your node MAC address is, consult your system administrator. You could use "000113446788" as the example node MAC address.

6. You will need to enter the user name assigned to the local system (the PC in which you have installed the Cisco 200). The user name consists of up to 30 alphanumeric characters. It is case-sensitive. You could use "MyHomeOffice" as the example user name.

7. You will need to enter the hostname, password, and dialnumber of the connecting router. Use the Tab key or the mouse to move from one field to another. The connecting router hostname is case-sensitive and can include up to 12 characters in any combination of numbers (1–9, 0) and letters (A–Z, a–z). It cannot include underscores (_), hyphens (-), asterisks (*), or spaces. In this document, we will use "Headquarters" as an example connecting router hostname. The authentication password is case-sensitive and must match exactly the password on the connecting router. Otherwise, authentication will fail. In this document, we will use "Secret" as an example authentication password. The number should include in a single string all numbers necessary to dial the connecting router. Do not separate the numbers with spaces, hyphens, or any non-numeric character. In this document, we will use "914085553000" as an example connecting router telephone number.

8. When the Select ISDN Service dialog box appears, select the appropriate data transfer rate for your ISDN connection. Click one of the following: Data rate 56Kbps (per B channel) or Data rate 64Kbps (per B channel).

9. Next, the PPP Configuration dialog box appears. Select PPP Multilink and/or PPP Callback if you want to use these features. PPP Multilink dynamically adds the second B channel when necessary. This increases ISDN bandwidth, but can result in increased line charges. PPP Callback configures the Cisco 200 to be called back from the connecting router.

10. Next, the ISDN Adapter Resource Configuration dialog box appears. Select the interrupt request (IRQ) for which the ISDN Adapter was configured. The choices include the following: 11 (default), 10, 5, 2/9.

11. Next, another ISDN Adapter Resource Configuration dialog box appears. Select the port I/O base address for which the ISDN Adapter was configured. The choices include the following: 390 (default), 398, 3A0, 3A8.

12. Next, the Select D-Channel Protocol dialog box appears. Select the appropriate D-channel protocol for your ISDN connection. Click one of the following:

   ➤ *DSS1 (Euro-ISDN, NET3)*

   ➤ *NI1 (North American National ISDN-1)*

   ➤ *5ESS (AT&T Custom—both point-to-point and multipoint)*

Other Manufacturers of ISDN Adapter Cards

The Cisco 200 series is not a typical ISDN adapter card and does not use the usual method for communicating with the PC. Other manufacturers of ISDN adapters provide drivers much like the drivers for analog modems, which show up in Dial-Up Networking under modem selection. For example Diva's DIVA Pro 2.0 ISA/PCI/ PC Card called "EICON Channel 0 and 1" will show up in Dial-Up Networking. Once the necessary drivers are installed, you can configure a new connection in Dial-Up Networking.

In Dial-Up Networking, double-click on Make New Connection. Next, set the name to Router (or some other suitable name) and select the device type, for example Eicon Channel 0, which is the interface and represents one 64Kbps channel. (see Figure 5.16). Click on Next.

Next, enter the telephone number of the router's BRI port (see Figure 5.17). Click on Next and then click on Finish. Now go back and right-click on the Router icon and click on Properties.

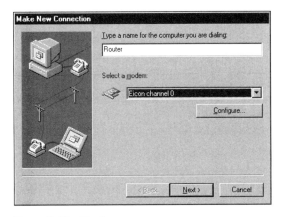

Figure 5.16   Diva1.

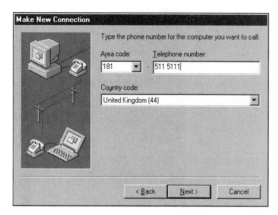

Figure 5.17 Diva2.

Many routers will support Multilink PPP (that is, two B channels connected), giving a 128Kbps connection. The DIVA for Windows 95/98 also supports this when using Microsoft's ISDN Accelerator Pack version 1.1, which is shipped with the DIVA for Windows 95/98. On the router, you need to enable the Multilink mode on the ISDN interface. For example, on a Cisco router from the configure mode, you would type:

```
interface bri0
ppp multilink
```

Next, select the General tab. You should see the first phone number you previously entered, as shown in Figure 5.18.

Click on the Settings button. Then click on Use Additional Devices and click on Add. Figure 5.19 shows the Edit Extra Device dialog box. From the Device List, select Eicon Channel 1; this is the second B channel available through the Eicon WAN Miniport interface. In the Phone Number field, put the ISDN number of the router BRI interface, and click OK.

Now, click OK to leave Set Additional Devices, and then OK to save the changes. Now when you click on Router, the DIVA card will make two ISDN calls to the router, and the channels are "bundled" together so that the applications just see a single 128Kbps connection to the router.

Select the Server Types tab. The Type Of Dial-Up Server field should say "PPP: Windows 95, Windows NT 3.5, Internet". Now click the TCP/IP Settings button. Now you need to enter a fixed IP address or leave the default for Dial-Up Networking as dynamic IP addresses. You also need to disable unwanted protocols. On the new panel, select Specify An IP Address, and fill in the field with the IP address for your workstation

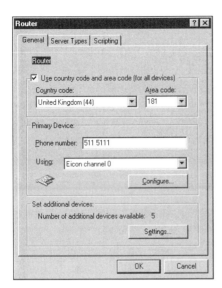

Figure 5.18   The General tab.

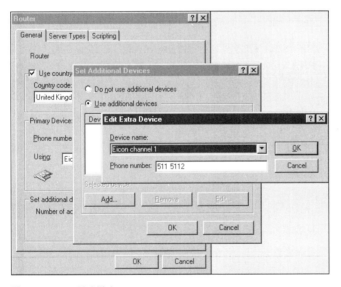

Figure 5.19   Multilink.

Chapter Summary

Three Windows 95/98 programs need to be configured for making analog connections to a router: Modem icon, Dial-Up Adapter, and Dial-Up Networking. The Dial-Up Adapter and the Dial-Up Networking programs are not installed automatically when Windows 95/98 is installed. Because these programs support PPP, they provide for PAP and CHAP, callback, and Multilink PPP.

The Dial-Up Adapter should be installed and configured before the Dial-Up Networking program. The Dial-Up Adapter contains global settings for all analog connections including TCP/IP settings. Each connection to a separate router or ISP will need its own Dial-Up Networking connection icon, which will have to be configured separately to accept the services provided by that particular router or ISP. Each connection icon can contain different customized TCP/IP settings other than the global TCP/IP settings found in the Dial-Up Adapter. However, only the Dial-Up Adapter communicates directly with the TAPI drivers in the PC; Dial-Up Networking does not.

The TCP/IP protocol for Dial-Up Adapter and Dial-Up Networking are not associated with the TCP/IP protocol installed for any LAN adapter cards on the PC. They do not share things like IP addresses.

When making a connection to a router, you usually configure the connection icon to bring up the terminal screen after the initial connection is made. This allows you to log on to the router with the workstation name and password. These two items must be listed in the router's configuration in order for logon to happen. If you do not use the **autoselect** command on the router, you will need to type "PPP" at the next prompt after the password.

When you choose to Obtain An IP Address Automatically in Dial-Up Networking, the router should be set to handout IP addresses, such as by using the command **peer default ip-address**.

Besides using manual logins, you can configure Windows 95/98 with a script that includes the workstation's name and password, and the EXEC command **PPP** if needed. Using scripts eliminates the need to bring up a terminal screen after the initial connection.

Microsoft has upgraded its DUN (Dial-Up Networking) for better performance and to be able to handle Multilink PPP.

Most manufacturers of ISDN adapter cards provide drivers that work with the Dial-Up Networking program much like analog modems. This is not true for Cisco. Cisco's 200 series ISDN adapter cards use a proprietary software program for installing the card and making connections. The Cisco 202 includes a built-in NT1 and the Cisco 201 needs an external NT1.

Review Questions

1. When performing a regular POTS connection using an analog modem, the Dial-Up Networking program uses which Windows 95 independent device?

   a. UART

   b. TAPI

    c. NDIS

    d. Redirector

2. What Windows 95 program binds or connects the network protocols to the modem?

    a. Dial-Up Networking

    b. Dial-Up Adapter

    c. Device Manager

    d. Network Neighborhood

3. To configure a Dial-Up Networking connection to use CHAP, you must do which one of the following setup tasks?

    a. Check the option Require Encrypted Password.

    b. Uncheck the option Require Encrypted Password.

    c. Check the option Enable Software Compression.

    d. Uncheck the option Enable Software Compression.

4. When making a connection between a Windows 95/98 and a branch office router what is the last software program or hardware device that needs to be configured?

    a. Modem

    b. Dial-Up Adapter

    c. Dial-Up Networking

    d. TAPI

5. Which statement best describes the configuration tasks needed when there are two or more different branch offices that need to be connected to?

    a. Each branch office will have its own Dial-Up Adapter. Each Dial-Up Adapter will have its own TCP/IP settings.

    b. Each branch office will have its own Dial-Up Networking Connection icon, but they will all have the same TCP/IP settings that utilize the global TCP/IP settings.

    c. Each branch office will have its own Dial-Up Adapter, but they will all have the same TCP/IP settings.

    d. Each branch office will have its own Dial-Up Networking Connection icon and can have its own TCP/IP settings.

5

6. What happens if you install Dial-Up Networking on a PC that has not been configured for a modem?

    a. The Dial-Up Networking installation will stop and you must install a modem.

    b. The Dial-Up Networking installation will temporarily break away and install the modem.

    c. The Dial-Up Networking installation will finish and then you will be prompted to install a modem.

    d. The Dial-Up Networking installation will work without a modem installed.

7. Which tab do you select when you choose PPP for use with a Dial-Up Networking connection?

    a. Server Type

    b. General

    c. TCP/IP Settings

    d. Options

8. Which tab do you select to choose TCP Header compression?

    a. Server Type

    b. General

    c. TCP/IP Settings

    d. Options

9. When performing a manual connection to a router, what do you do after you enter PPP at the prompt?

    a. Manually close the terminal window

    b. Run Telnet or FTP

    c. Click on the Continue button or press F10

    d. Click on the Continue button or press F7

10. What subdirectory on the Windows 95 installation disk contains the files for installing the Scripting Tool?

    a. /Admin/Apps/

    b. /Admin/Tools/

    c. /Apptools/Admin/

    d. /Admin/Apptools/

11. What does the Dial-Up Networking 1.3 upgrade do that the previous version of Dial-Up Networking could not do?

    a. Multilink PPP for analog modems

    b. CHAP

    c. Run scripts

    d. TCP header compression

12. What software program do you need to install on a Windows 95 computer to take full advantage of the 128Kbps bandwidth derived from using both B channels?

    a. Dial-Up Networking 1.3 upgrade

    b. Microsoft's ISDN Accelerator Pack version 1.1

    c. Microsoft Service Pack for Windows 95

    d. Windows 95 C version

13. Which Cisco 200 series ISDN adapter card contains a built-in NT1 device?

    a. 201

    b. 202

    c. 250

    d. 260

14. Above all, a Cisco 200 ISDN adapter card must be configured with which of the following addresses or it will not work?

    a. IP

    b. IPX

    c. NetBIOS name

    d. MAC

15. From a Windows 95 point of reference, what speed can 28800 modems utilize?

    a. 38400

    b. 57600

    c. 14400

    d. 28800

Real-World Projects

Rachel is an associate controller for the Santos Credit Card company in Northbridge, Alaska. She is the head of the marketing department for the company and doesn't go to her branch office that much during the winter months. Because of extremely poor weather conditions, Rachel often spends many days at home completing her responsibilities. Frequently, she needs to connect to the central office for recent inventory items and current prices. Rachel just received a new desktop computer for her SOHO site and she needs to configure the computer for making dial-up connections to the company's router at the central site. John, one of the company's network engineers, gave Rachel a set of detailed directions that would help her configure her computer and her Sportster internal modem for making this connection. Rachel will try to follow John's directions, but John expects Rachel at some point to call him for assistance.

Project 5.1

To insert a modem into a laptop and select a new modem:

1. Open the computer, insert the Sportster 28.8 interior modem into an ISA slot, and close the computer.

2. Start the computer.

3. Double-click on My Computer and double-click on Control Panel.

4. Double-click on Modems and click the Add button.

5. Check Don't Detect My Modem and click on the Next button.

6. Scroll down the Manufacturers until you find US Robotics and select it.

7. Scroll down the Models until you see Sportster 28800 Internal and select it.

8. Click on Next and select Com1.

9. Click on Finish. Windows is now finished installing the modem.

Well, that went OK for Rachel—now her modem is listed when she clicks the Modem icon in the Control Panel. Now she will have to install the Dial-Up Adapter and configure the global TCP/IP.

Project 5.2

To install Dial-Up Adapter and configure TCP/IP Protocol:

1. Double-click on My Computer and double-click on Control Panel.

2. Double-click on Network and click on the Configuration tab.

3. Click on the Add button and select Adapter.

4. Click on the Add button and select Microsoft from the manufacturer list.

5. Select Dial-Up Adapter from the Microsoft options, click on the OK button, and click on the Add button.

6. Select Protocol and click on the Add button.

7. Select Microsoft from the manufacturer list and select Microsoft TCP/IP from the network protocol list.

8. Click on the OK button and click the next OK button.

9. Wait while the PC reboots.

10 Double-click on My Computer and double-click on Control Panel.

11. Double-click on Network and click on TCP/IP.

12. Click on the Properties button and click on the IP Address tab.

13. Select Obtain An IP Address Automatically.

14. Click on the WINS Configuration tab and select Disable WINS Resolution.

15. Click on the Gateway tab and enter "0.0.0.0" in the New Gateway box.

16. Click on the Add button. (PPP will negotiate the Gateway address.)

17. Click on the DNS Configuration tab and select Enable DNS.

18. Enter the Host Name of Workstation and enter the Domain Name of **goodconnection.edu**.

19. Enter "128.240.229.18" in the DNS Search Order box and click on the Add button.

20. Enter "128.240.229.34" in the DNS Search Order box and click on the Add button.

21. Enter "128.240.2.80" in the DNS Search Order box and click on the Add button.

22. Enter "goodconnection.edu" in the Domain Suffix Search Order box and click on the Add button.

23. Click on the Advanced tab and select Set This Protocol To Be The Default.

24. Click on Bindings tab and click on any network component required (none is acceptable).

25. Click on the OK button and click on the next OK button.

26. Confirm that you want the computer to be shut down and restarted.

Now that the Dial-Up Adapter is installed and the global TCP/IP configured, Rachel's next task is to enable Dial-Up Networking and create a new Dial-Up Connection icon.

5

Project 5.3

To enable Dial-Up Networking, create a New Dial-Up Connection, and set the Dial-Up properties:

1. Double-click on My Computer and double-click on Control Panel.

2. Double-click on Add/Remove Programs and click on the Windows Setup tab.

3. Select Communications and click on the Details button.

4. Check that Dial-Up Networking is ticked, click on the OK button, and click on the OK button.

5. Double-click on My Computer and double-click on Dial-Up Networking.

6. Double-click on Make New Connection and type the name "Router2".

7. Select the Sportster 28.8 modem.

8. Configure and make sure the port is COM1.

9. Click on Next and enter "2024600" as the telephone number.

10. Click on the Next button and click on the Finish button.

11. Double-click on My Computer and double-click on Dial-Up Networking

12. Click on your connection icon (for example, the "Router2" icon).

13. Click on File and click on Properties.

14. Click on the General tab and click Configure.

15. Click on the Options tab and deselect Bring Up Terminal Window Before Dialing.

16. Deselect Bring Up Terminal Window After Dialing.

17. Deselect Operator Assisted Or Manual Dial.

18. Select Display Modem Status and click OK.

19. Click on the Server Type tab and select PPP: Windows 95, Windows NT, Internet.

In Advanced options:

20. Deselect Log On To The Network and deselect Enable Software Compression.

21. Deselect Require Encrypted Password.

22. In Allowed Network Protocols, deselect NetBEUI, deselect IPX/SPX Compatible, and select TCP/IP.

23. Click OK to close the Dial-Up Networking General dialog.

Finally, after all the necessary software and hardware components are installed and configured, Rachel will attempt to make the connection.

Project 5.4

To use the Dial-Up Connection and make a dial-up connection:

1. Double-click on My Computer and double-click on Dial-Up Networking.

2. Double-click on "Router2".

3. Do not enter anything in the User name and Password sections.

4. Check to see if the phone number is correctly entered.

5. Click on the Connect button to have the software dial the modem for you. The modem should dial and connect to Router2.

6. If you connect successfully, you should be presented with a window to log in. Press Enter a couple of times to get the Router2's attention.

7. At the username: prompt, enter your remote access account username and press Enter.

8. At the password: prompt, enter the corresponding password and press Enter.

9. There may be a short delay before the Router2> prompt appears. You should then enter "ppp".

10. Click on the Continue button.

11. After a short wait, you should be presented with an alert stating that you are Connected to *<whatever you named the connection>*, showing details of your connection speed and the duration of your connection.

CHAPTER SIX

Configuring Integrated Subscriber Digital Network (ISDN) for Remote Access

After completing this chapter, you will be able to:

✓ Understand the Integrated Subscriber Digital Network (ISDN) architecture and protocols

✓ Describe ISDN reference points and functional devices

✓ Describe the steps involved when an ISDN device makes a call setup and call teardown

✓ Know how to configure ISDN connections between BRI-to-BRI and BRI-to-PRI interfaces

✓ Configure dial-on-demand routing (DDR) methods within ISDN configurations

✓ Know how to apply static routes and snapshot routing to ISDN connections

✓ Verify ISDN connections and protocols

This chapter is important for understanding ISDN connections. The chapter details ISDN architecture components and outlines ISDN configurations for Basic Rate Interfaces (BRI) and Primary Rate Interfaces (PRI). The chapter attempts to sequentially explain what you need to know about ISDN service and Cisco routers. We will begin with a comprehensive discussion on ISDN architecture.

ISDN Architecture

ISDN stands for Integrated Services Digital Network. The term represents a telecommunications service package, consisting of digital facilities from end to end. In most cases, analog dial-up service providers will not guarantee support for specific data rates even if users purchase analog modems capable of handling up to 56Kbps transmission rates. Little or no diagnostic information is available from the service provider other than normal testing performed on residential and business lines. Also, line quality varies widely, and the amount of noise on a line has a direct bearing on the maximum data transmission rate. ISDN is completely digital. Digital circuits are typically characterized by very low error rates and high reliability. ISDN can support voice, video, and data transmissions. ISDN uses a circuit-switching network. Individual channels can transmit at speeds up to 64Kbps, and these channels can sometimes be combined to support even higher speeds.

In general, ISDN has been more rapidly deployed and accepted in countries such as Australia, France, and Japan, with the United States lagging somewhat behind. ISDN is now available in essentially all major metropolitan areas in the United States, but not in some outlying areas.

ISDN BRI and PRI Components

In Chapter 1, we discussed WAN technologies including ISDN, where you learned about the differences between Basic Rate Interface (BRI) and Primary Rate Interface (PRI) ISDN. In the following section, we will discuss the two services in terms of channel make-up.

B Channels

B channels are logical digital pipes that exist on a single ISDN line. B channels each provide a 64Kbps clear channel. The term *clear* means that the entire bandwidth is available for data because call setup and other signaling is done through a separate D channel. B channels typically form circuit-switched connections. Just like a regular telephone connection, a B-channel connection is an end-to-end physical circuit that is temporarily dedicated to transferring data between two devices. The circuit-switched nature of B-channel connections, combined with their reliability and relatively high bandwidth, is what makes ISDN suitable for a range of applications including voice, video, fax, and data. They can be used to transfer any layer 2 or higher protocols across a link. B channels are normally used for dial-on-demand connections, taking full-advantage of the circuit-switched networks upon which they are based.

D Channels

The D channel is used mostly for administrative signaling, such as instructing the ISDN carrier to set up or tear down a call along a B channel, to ensure that a B channel is available to receive an incoming call, or to provide the signaling information that is required for such features as caller identification. Depending on ISDN service subscription, the D channel transmits at either 16Kbps (for BRI service) or 64Kbps (for PRI service). Unlike the B channel, which can function as a simple pipe, the D channel is associated with higher level protocols at layers 2 and 3 of the OSI model, which form the packet-switched connections. The ITU layer 3 protocol specifications for use on the D channel are described within the *Digital Subscriber Signaling System No. 1 (DSS1)* network layer definition.

Note: Digital Subscriber Signaling System No. 1 is the network access signaling protocol for users connecting to ISDN. It includes the ITU Q.931 and Q.932 standards.

Q.931 is the call-control protocol component of this definition. This layer 3 signaling protocol is transferred on the D channel using Link Access Procedure-D channel (LAPD), a layer 2 HDLC-like protocol. We will further discuss Q.931 in the next section.

Primary Rate Interface (PRI)

ISDN Primary Rate Interface (PRI) service offers 23 B channels and one D channel in North America, yielding a total bit rate of 1.544Mbps (the PRI D channel runs at 64Kbps). ISDN PRI in Europe, Australia, and other parts of the world provides 30 B channels plus one 64Kbps D channel and a total interface rate of 2.048Mbps. PRIs are dedicated trunks that connect medium and large locations to a telephone company central office. Virtually all modern telephone and computing systems can be connected to ISDN through a PRI, including PBXs, mainframe and distributed systems, LANs and WANs, multiplexers and ISDN controllers, videoconferencing units, and more. PRIs are designed to maximize the use of these systems by allocating dynamically, or call by call, the number and type of channels (for example, data, voice in, voice out) required for each application.

ISDN Explained Using Protocol Layers

The standards used to define ISDN make use of the OSI reference model. This is simply a generic standard of how protocols are defined. This modular approach allows work to be performed on various levels of the model knowing what is required from the lower level and the requirements of the next higher level. In ISDN, we are concerned with the first three layers of the OSI reference model. Figure 6.1 shows how these layers are applied to the actual ISDN connection segments.

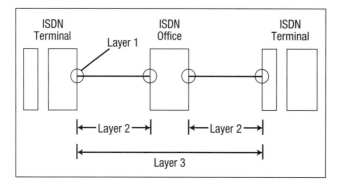

Figure 6.1 The first three layers of the OSI model.

Layer 1: Physical Layer

The physical layer of the OSI model defines the physical properties of an ISDN circuit, which include the connector type, how many leads are in a cable, how many volts in a pulse, what is on pin 1 through pin 8, and so on. All of these parameters make up the layer 1 specifics of the ISDN line. The technical specifics are contained in the ITU-T documents. The specification for a Basic Rate Interface is document I.430, and for the Primary Rate Interface it is document I.431. To specify the electrical standard, there has to be agreement on where to measure these requirements. This question was answered by the ITU. The ITU I.430 describes the physical layer and lower data link layers of the ISDN BRI interface. The specification defines a number of ISDN reference points between the telco switch and the end system. The protocol also contains descriptions of the devices at the end system, which are called ISDN *functional devices*. The interfaces and devices for an ISDN Basic Rate Interface are as follows.

ISDN Functional Devices

Functional devices are definitions for specific tasks performed in an ISDN connection. These functional devices reside on the user side of the connection. Actual ISDN equipment often embodies multiple functional devices, but may include only one. The following sections explain the functional devices in an ISDN connection, which are diagrammed in Figure 6.2.

➤ *Network Termination 1 (NT1)*—The NT1 represents the boundary of the ISDN network from the end-user side. An NT1 is a device that physically connects the customer site to the telephone company local loop. Because the ISDN line doesn't provide power as the analog line does, NT1 also includes the power function for operating the ISDN line. Each BRI access has only one NT1 device. An NT1 can be embodied in a standalone device or included in a specific device. For PRI access, the NT1 is a CSU/DSU device, whereas for BRI access the device is simply called by its reference name, NT1. It provides a 4-wire connection to the customer site and a 2-wire connection

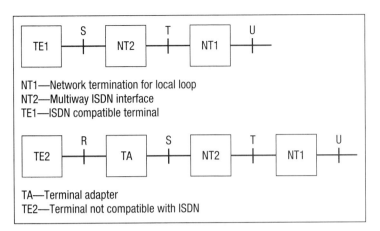

NT1—Network termination for local loop
NT2—Multiway ISDN interface
TE1—ISDN compatible terminal

TA—Terminal adapter
TE2—Terminal not compatible with ISDN

Figure 6.2   ISDN reference points.

6

to the network. In Europe, the NT1 is owned by the telecommunications carrier and considered part of the network. In North America, the NT1 is located on the customer premises and is usually the customer's responsibility to provide it.

➤ *Network Termination 2 (NT2)*—An NT2 device provides customer site switching, multiplexing, and concentration, such as a PBX for voice and data switching. An NT2 device is not needed in every installation and will most likely be used with PRIs rather than BRIs. NT2s are needed for PRI multiplexing. The NT2 works with the NT1 and is on the customer side of the NT1.

➤ *Terminal Equipment (TE)*—Terminal Equipment (TE) refers to any end-user device connected to an ISDN line, both TE1 and TE2. This is the general class of equipment that covers both ISDN-ready equipment and non-ISDN equipment such as analog telephones, faxes, and modems. The encompassing term for any equipment on the customer side of the ISDN connection is customer premise equipment (CPE). ISDN can support up to eight pieces of CPE to perform multiple tasks using a single line.

➤ *Terminal Equipment 1 (TE1)*—Terminal Equipment 1 (TE1) refers to ISDN devices that support the standard ISDN interface directly, including digital phones, digital faxes, and integrated voice/data terminal devices. These TE1 devices provide direct access to an ISDN connection without adapters. Currently, most ISDN-ready equipment is too expensive to be practical, but expect to see low-cost ISDN telephones and other devices in the near future.

➤ *Terminal Equipment 2 (TE2)*—The Terminal Equipment 2 (TE2) includes any device that isn't ISDN-ready. This category includes the equipment you now use for analog communications. Any device in this class, such as a modem, requires an adapter to work with ISDN. A growing number of ISDN equipment vendors offer products that consolidate TE2 adapter and NT1 devices into a single unit.

➤ *Terminal Adapter (TA)*—TAs translate signaling from non-ISDN TE2 devices into a format compatible with ISDN. TAs are usually standalone physical devices. The TA device is a protocol converter that adapts equipment that's not designed for ISDN. ISDN equipment vendors market terminal adapter devices that include the NT1 function as well as support other devices. For example, using a terminal adapter, you can plug an analog telephone, a fax, and an ISDN adapter into your PC. This type of product, which controls the traffic from different devices sharing the same ISDN line, is called an NT1 Plus device.

ISDN reference points define the communication between the different devices and the parameters for the functional devices. The four protocol reference points that are commonly defined for ISDN are called R, S, T, and U. Understanding ISDN reference points is important because most CPE vendors refer to their equipment in terms of the reference points they embody. The ISDN reference points are described below and diagrammed in Figure 6.2.

➤ *The S and T Reference Points*—The S reference point lies between ISDN user equipment (TE1 or TE2 with a TA) and the NT1 device. The T reference point lies between customer site switching equipment (NT2) and the local loops termination (NT1). The user-network reference point is usually the S/T reference point. The S/T reference point is one of two reference points that most ISDN equipment vendors incorporate in their devices. An S/T device requires a standalone NT1 device to work with your ISDN connection. The most important of these are S/T and U. The U interface is the local loop between the telephone company and the customer premises. At the customer site, the 2-wire U interface is converted to a 4-wire S/T interface by an NT1. Originally, the T interface was point-to-point and could be converted to a point-to-multipoint S interface by an NT2. However, the electrical specifications of the S and T interfaces were almost identical, so most modern NT1s include built-in NT2 functionality and can support either single or multiple ISDN devices on what is now called the S/T interface.

➤ *The U Reference Point*—The U reference point is where the telephone company's network arrives at your doorstep up to the NT1 device. The U interface is also called the U-Loop because it represents the loop between your premises and the telephone company. ISDN devices made for the U interface include a built-in NT1 function.

➤ *The R Reference Point*—The R reference point lies between the terminal equipment 2 (TE2) device and a terminal adapter. There are no specific standards for the R reference point, so the TA manufacturer determines and specifies how a TE2 and TA communicate with each other.

In Europe and Japan, the telco owns the NT1 and provides the S/T interface to the customer. In North America, however, the U interface is provided to the customer, who owns the NT1. This effectively produces two incompatible variants of ISDN, which some manufacturers have attempted to remedy with devices, such as the Cisco 760, containing both S/T and U jacks. Normal ISDN devices plug into the S/T interface, an RJ-45 jack carrying two pairs of wires, each pair a current loop. As current flows into the positive line, it flows out of the negative line, maintaining a net balance between the two. The two lines should be grouped together on a single twisted pair, minimizing crosstalk between signals. One pair carries signal from the TE to the NT (user to network), and the other pair carries signal from the NT to the TE (network to user).

Contained within the layer 1 specifications are descriptions of framing and line coding. These specifications describe the variations in voltage and the pulse timing of bits during transmission You will need to know about these specifications especially for PRI. If an ISDN PRI circuit is carried on a T1 circuit, it uses Extended Super Frame (ESF) framing and Bipolar Eight Zero Substitution (B8ZS) or Alternate Mark Inversion (AMI) for line coding as standards. If an ISDN PRI circuit is carried on an E1 circuit, the line coding protocol is high-density bipolar 3 (HDB3), and the framing type is typically CRC-4. Line coding is defined in ITU Recommendation G.703 and G.704.

6

Layer 2: Q.921

The ISDN data link layer is specified by the ITU Q-series documents Q.920 through Q.923. All of the signaling on the D channel is defined in the Q.921 protocol specification. The Q.921 recommendation defines layer 2 for ISDN lines. In the OSI reference model, layer 2 provides for procedures established to maintain communication between two network components. In the case of ISDN, the two components are the ISDN terminal, such as a router, and the ISDN switch. This means that ISDN terminals are in constant communication with the ISDN switch. An example of this is that when an ISDN router is plugged in, a red light-emitting diode (LED) will illuminate. This LED is an indication that layer 2 is established with the ISDN switch.

Q.921 defines the frame structure of the data packets, the format of the fields in the frame, and procedures known as Link Access Procedures D Channel (LAPD). The LAPD procedures describe such things as flags, sequence control, flow control, and retransmission. So, Q.921 can also be referred to as LAPD. Also, LAPD is almost identical to the X.25 LAP-B protocol. We need to examine some of the fields in the LAPD frame. Figure 6.3 shows the structure of an LAPD frame.

The 16 bits of address contain a command/response (C/R) field, a SAPI (Service Access Point Identifier), and a TEI (Terminal Endpoint Identifier). TEIs are used to distinguish between several different devices using the same ISDN links. TEIs are unique IDs given to each device (TE) on an ISDN S/T bus. These numbers can be preassigned (TEIs 0-63), or dynamically assigned (TEIs 64-126). TEI 127 is broadcast. Before any higher level (Q.931) functions can be performed, each ISDN device

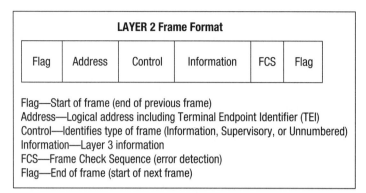

LAYER 2 Frame Format

Flag	Address	Control	Information	FCS	Flag

Flag—Start of frame (end of previous frame)
Address—Logical address including Terminal Endpoint Identifier (TEI)
Control—Identifies type of frame (Information, Supervisory, or Unnumbered)
Information—Layer 3 information
FCS—Frame Check Sequence (error detection)
Flag—End of frame (start of next frame)

Figure 6.3 Structure of an LAPD frame.

must be assigned at least one unique TEI value. Most TEI assignment is done dynamically, using the TEI management protocol. The user broadcasts an Identity request and the network (the telco switch) responds with an Identity assigned containing the TEI value. Functions are also provided to verify and release TEI assignments. All TEI management functions are performed using TEI 127 (broadcast), SAPI 63, and 5-byte UI frame. So, what is a SAPI?

SAPIs play the role of a protocol or port number, and identify the higher layer protocol being used in the data field. The *Service Access Point Identifier (SAPI)* is a 6-bit field that identifies the point where layer 2 provides a service to layer 3. Q.931 messages are sent using SAPI 0, SAPI 16 means X.25, and SAPI 63 is used for TEI assignment procedures. These are usually the only SAPI values used.

The control field specifies how the frame will be used by indicating the frame type. There are three frame types (Information, Supervisory, or Unnumbered). Data transfer can occur in one of two formats: Information (I) frames or Unnumbered Information (UI) frames. UI, offering unreliable delivery, is the simplest of the two because no sequence numbering, acknowledgements, or retransmissions are involved.

The information field contains layer 3 protocol information and user data, which will be discussed below.

Establishing the Link Layer (Layer 2)

Let's now examine the steps in making a layer 2 link, which is the first step in establishing an ISDN connection. The layer 2 establishment process is very similar to the X.25 Link Access Procedure B-Channel (LAPB) setup. Here are the steps:

1. The TE (Terminal Endpoint) and the telco office initially exchange Receive Ready (RR) frames, listening for someone to initiate a connection.

2. The TE sends an Unnumbered Information (UI) frame with a SAPI of 63 (management procedure, query network) and TEI of 127 (broadcast).

3. The telco office assigns an available TEI (in the range 64-126).

4. The TE sends a Set Asynchronous Balanced Mode (SABME) frame with a SAPI of 0 (call control, used to initiate a SETUP) and a TEI of the value assigned by the network.

5. The telco office responds with an Unnumbered Acknowledgement (UA), SAPI=0, TEI=assigned.

6. At this point, the connection is ready for a layer 3 setup.

Switch Types

In the preceding list of steps, any procedure that refers to the "telco office" really means communication with a switch. The "engines" of the ISDN phone network are the complex network switches that deliver the service. Telephone companies have several different kinds of switches that handle calls, validate SPIDs, assign TEIs, create connections, and participate in call teardown. Cisco routers *must* be able to be configured to interface with the particular switch used by a particular local telephone company. Table 6.1 displays the common switch types and their associated Cisco keyword for use when configuring a router to select particular switch types.

Table 6.1   ISDN switch types and their Cisco keyword.

Cisco Keyword	Switch Type
North America:	
basic-5ess	AT&T basic rate switches
basic-dms100	NT DMS-100 basic rate switches
basic-ni1	National ISDN-1 switches
primary-4ess	AT&T 4ESS switch type for the U.S. (ISDN PRI only)
primary-5ess	AT&T 5ESS switch type for the U.S. (ISDN PRI only)
primary-dms100	NT DMS-100 switch type for the U.S. (ISDN PRI only)
New Zealand:	
basic-nznet3	New Zealand Net3 switches
Japan:	
Ntt	Japanese NTT ISDN switches
primary-ntt	Japanese ISDN PRI switches
Europe:	
basic-1tr6	German 1TR6 ISDN switches
basic-nwnet3	Norway NET3 switches (phase 1)
basic-net3	NET3 ISDN switches (UK and others)
primary-net5	European ISDN PRI switches
vn2	French VN2 ISDN switches
vn3	French VN3 ISDN switches
Australia:	
basic-ts013	Australian TS013 switches
none	No switch defined

6

Service Profile IDs

When we talk about switch types, we immediately think of SPIDs. Service Profile IDs (SPIDs) are used to identify what services and features the telco switch provides to the attached ISDN device. SPIDs are not always required, SPIDs are optional. When they are used, they are only accessed at device initialization time, before the call is set up. The format of the SPID is usually the 10-digit phone number of the ISDN line, plus an optional 7-digit local directory number (LDD). Service providers may use different numbering schemes, but it all amounts to one large telephone-like number. If an ISDN line requires a SPID, but it is not correctly supplied, then layer 2 initialization will take place, but layer 3 will not, and the device will not be able to place or accept calls.

When a company acquires ISDN services, the service provider may assign each ISDN device one or more SPIDs. The use of SPIDs defines the ISDN service that is supplied by the provider and act as links to information delivered by the provider's switch. The assigned SPIDs must be included in the router's configuration when accessing the service provider's switch to initiate the connection. Only National ISDN-1 (NI-1) and DMS-100 switch types require SPIDs. You may use SPIDs with the AT&T switch type, but Cisco recommends that you do not use SPIDs with this switch type. SPIDs are important within the local connection between the router and the switch and are not sent to the remote router.

Layer 3: Q.931

The layer 3 protocol is responsible for the actual setup and teardown of ISDN calls. The Q.931 defines the layer 3 specifications for ISDN. Actually, the ISDN network layer is specified by the ITU Q-series documents Q.930 through Q.939. Layer 3 is used for the establishment, maintenance, and termination of logical network connections between two devices. The emphasis here is on the word logical. The network layer provides procedures to make end-to-end connections on the network. Remember that the ISDN connections established are for circuit-switched voice and circuit-switched data connections. Connections that involve Q.931 procedures use packetized messages to initiate, monitor, and release circuit-switched connections. These call control messages are relayed between the ISDN terminal and the ISDN switch as the "information" part of the Q.921 information frame. Each message can be identified by type. The Message Type is a single byte (octet) that indicates what type of message is being sent/received. There are four general categories of messages that might be present: Call Establishment, Call Information, Call Clearing, and Miscellaneous. Generally, the most useful messages to understand are the Call Establishment and Call Clearing messages. The following is a list of message types:

➤ Call Establishment:

   ➤ Alerting

   ➤ Call Proceeding

- ➤ Connect
- ➤ Connect ACK
- ➤ Progress
- ➤ Setup
- ➤ Setup ACK
- ➤ Call Information:
  - ➤ Resume
  - ➤ Resume ACK
  - ➤ Resume REJ
  - ➤ Suspend
  - ➤ Suspend ACK
  - ➤ Suspend REJ
- ➤ Call clearing
  - ➤ Disconnect
  - ➤ Release
  - ➤ Release Complete
  - ➤ Restart
  - ➤ Restart ACK
- ➤ Miscellaneous:
  - ➤ Segment
  - ➤ Congestion Control
  - ➤ Information
  - ➤ Facility
  - ➤ Notify
  - ➤ Status
  - ➤ Status Enquiry

6

Layer 3 Call Setup

Let's see how these messages are used during an actual call setup at layer 3. Do not be confused between this call setup and the connection links that preceded it at layer 1 and layer 2. As displayed in Figure 6.4, the following steps occur when an ISDN call is established. In the following call setup, there are three points where messages are sent and received: 1) the Caller, 2) the ISDN Switch, and 3) the Receiver.

These are the call setup steps:

1. Caller sends a SETUP to the Switch.

2. If the SETUP is OK, the switch sends a CALL PROCEEDING to the Caller, and then a SETUP to the Receiver.

3. The Receiver gets the SETUP and the Receiver sends an ALERTING message to the Switch.

4. The Switch forwards the ALERTING message to the Caller.

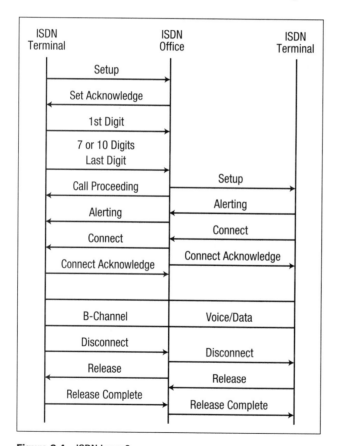

Figure 6.4 ISDN layer 3.

5. When the receiver answers the call, it sends a CONNECT message to the Switch.

6. The Switch forwards the CONNECT message to the Caller.

7. The Caller sends a CONNECT ACK message to the Switch.

8. The Switch forwards the CONNECT ACK message to the Receiver.

9. Done. The connection is now up.

These are the call teardown steps:

1. Caller sends a DISCONNECT to the Switch.

2. The Switch sends a DISCONNECT to the Receiver.

3. The Switch sends a RELEASE to the Sender.

4. The Receiver sends a RELEASE to the Switch.

5. The Sender sends a RELEASE COMPLETE to the Switch.

6. The Switch sends a RELEASE COMPLETE to the Receiver.

SS7 Protocol

The ISDN office in Figure 6.4 actually represents several switches connected to each other. When the ISDN router sends a Q.931 instruction to a carrier network's switch to complete a call setup with another ISDN router, the carrier's network uses a different signaling system between its switches. Signaling between remote ISDN devices and the public voice and data network switches occurs using D-channel protocols such as Q.931, which in turn is converted into Signaling System No. 7 (SS7) signals within the carrier's digital voice and data networks. With SS7, carriers are able to maintain clear channel 64Kbps connections by communicating signaling information in a distinct channel. The switch at the destination side of the network then communicates with the remote ISDN device using its D-channel protocol. Any ISDN call that passes through at least one network lacking full SS7 signaling must limit its B-channel traffic to 56Kbps. In such cases, the ISDN equipment on both ends must be configured to put only 56Kbps of data onto their 64Kbps link. In order to do so, the communications equipment at both ends must support a rate adaptation scheme that pads bandwidth above 56Kbps with blank information, using such schemes as V.110 or V.120 rate adaptation.

Configuring Cisco Routers for ISDN with DDR

There are three tasks you need to perform when configuring a basic BRI ISDN connection between two routers. The tasks are listed here, and the individual steps for each task will be discussed below:

1. Configure global properties for ISDN BRI

2. Configure interface properties for an ISDN BRI

3. Provide for routing for the ISDN BRI

Configure Global Properties for ISDN BRI

To configure the ISDN global properties, you need to configure the switch type and configure TEI Negotiation Timing. Although you usually set the switch type globally, you can deviate from the global setting and change the switch type for any individual interface, as explained in the section "Configure Interface Properties for an ISDN BRI."

When you select the switch type, you are actually selecting the service provider's switch type. The various switch types and their Cisco keyword values are listed in Table 6.2. To configure the switch type, use one of the following keywords in the ISDN switch type command in the global configuration mode:

```
isdn switch-type switch-type
```

At certain times, you can configure TEI Negotiation Timing. TEI negotiation is useful for switches that may deactivate layers 1 or 2 when there are no active calls. Typically, this setting is used for ISDN service offerings in Europe and connections to DMS-100 switches that are designed to initiate TEI negotiation. You can specify when layer 2 ISDN terminal endpoint identifier (TEI) negotiation occurs. TEI negotiation is useful in Europe and also useful for switches that might deactivate layer 2 when no calls are active. By default, TEI negotiation occurs when the router is powered on, or it can be delayed until "first-call". To define when TEI negotiation will occur, use the following command in global configuration mode:

```
isdn tei [first-call | powerup]
```

Table 6.2   Keywords for ISDN switch types.

Keyword	Switch Type
none	No switch defined
basic-ts013	Australian TS013 switches
basic-1tr6	Europe 1TR6 ISDN switches
basic-net3	NET3 ISDN, Norway NET3, and New Zealand NET3 switches (covers the Euro-ISDN E-DSS1 signaling system and is ETSI-compliant)
vn3	French VN3 and VN4 ISDN BRI switches
ntt	Japanese NTT ISDN switches
basic-5ess	North America AT&T basic rate switches
basic-dms100	Northern Telecom DMS-100 basic rate switches
basic-ni	National ISDN switches

Configure Interface Properties for an ISDN BRI

You will need to perform the following tasks, which are described below, to set interface characteristics for an ISDN BRI:

1. Specify the interface and its IP address

2. Configure encapsulation

3. Configure network addressing

In addition, you can configure the following optional interface characteristics on the BRI:

4. Configure the Service Provider Switch Type for an interface

5. Configure TEI Negotiation Timing

6. Specify ISDN Service Profile Identifiers (SPIDs)

7. Configure Calling Line Identification Screening

8. Configure Called Party Number Verification

9. Configure ISDN Calling Number Identification

Specify the Interface and Its IP Address

To specify an ISDN Basic Rate Interface (BRI) and enter interface configuration mode, use the following command in global configuration mode:

```
interface bri [number]
```

or

```
interface bri [slot/port]
```

Configure Encapsulation

PPP encapsulation is configured for most ISDN communication. Each ISDN B channel is treated as a synchronous serial line and supports HDLC and PPP encapsulation. The default serial encapsulation is HDLC. To configure PPP encapsulation, use the following command in interface configuration mode:

```
encapsulation ppp
```

The router might need to communicate with devices that require a different encapsulation protocol, or the router might send traffic over a frame relay or X.25 network.

Configure Network Addressing

Network addressing involves the use of DDR. Cisco routers employ dial-on-demand routing (DDR) for ISDN networks. With DDR, the router opens the ISDN connection only when there is traffic that needs to be transmitted. The context for using DDR involves infrequent or intermittent traffic to and from remote sites, or when ISDN line usage is tariffed, usually per B channel. You will need to determine which packets are *interesting*, which will cause the router to make an outgoing call. You need to indicate whether broadcast messages will be sent and the dialing string to use in the call.

To configure network addressing, use the following commands beginning in interface configuration mode. These steps use shared argument values that tie the host identification and dial string to the interesting packets to be transmitted to that host.

Commands for configuring network addressing:

1. Determine the remote host where the calls are going. Define the remote recipient's protocol address, host name, and phone number; optionally, provide the ISDN subaddress; set the dialer speed to 56 or 64Kbps, as needed.

   ```
   dialer map protocol next-hop-address name hostname speed 56|64
                       phone-number[:isdn-subaddress]
   ```

   For example: **dialer map ip 10.1.1.1 name cisco speed 56 broadcast 4155551212**. This command is executed on the BRI interface.

2. Assign the interface to a **dialer-group** to control access to the interface.

   ```
   dialer-group group-number
   ```

3. Create what constitutes interesting traffic using the **dialer-list** and associate the **dialer-group** number with the **dialer-list**, identify protocol permission, and reference any optional **access-list** numbers.

   ```
   dialer-list dialer-group-number protocol protocol-name
                       permit|deny list access-list-number
   ```

   For example, the command: **dialer-list 1 protocol ipx permit**

4. Define an **access-list** permitting or denying access to specified protocols, sources, or destinations. Permitted packets cause the router to place a call to the destination protocol address.

```
access-list access-list-number deny|permit protocol
                    source-address source-mask
                    destination-address destination-mask
```

This is an example of an extended IP **access-list**.

5. Define an optional call parameter that specifies the time that a line can remain idle before it is disconnected. The default time is 120 seconds.

```
dialer idle-time seconds
```

6. Define an optional call parameter that specifies the time a line remains idle before the current call is disconnected to allow another call that is waiting to use the line. The default is 20 seconds.

```
dialer fast-idle seconds
```

7. Define an optional parameter where the interface initiates a second channel. Specify the maximum load before the dialer places another call to a destination. The number value represents a calculated weighted average based on the percentage of bandwidth utilization; it is a number between 1 and 255, where 255 is 100 percent.

```
dialer load-threshold load [outbound | inbound | either]
```

*Note: Although the **dialer map** command includes a speed setting and a call might originate at a speed of 56Kbps, the network or internetworking networks might improperly deliver the call to the user at a speed of 64Kbps. This creates a speed mismatch and causes the data to be garbled. Enabling the command **isdn not-end-to-end {56 | 64}** makes the router look more closely at the information elements of the incoming call to determine a speed.*

Configure the Service Provider Switch Type for Individual Interfaces—Optional

A global ISDN switch type is required and must be configured on the router before you can configure a switch type on an interface. You must ensure that both global and interface level ISDN switch types are valid for the ISDN interfaces on the router. Because global commands are processed before interface level commands, the command parser will not accept the ISDN switch-type command on an interface unless a switch type is first added globally. If an ISDN switch type is configured globally, but not at the interface level, the global switch type value is applied to all ISDN interfaces. If an ISDN switch type is configured globally and on an interface, the interface level switch type supersedes the global switch type at initial configuration.

For example, if the global BRI switch type defined is basic-net3, and the interface level BRI switch type is basic-ni, the basic-ni switch type is the value applied to that BRI interface. If you reconfigure the global ISDN switch type, the new value is not applied to subsequent interfaces. Therefore, if you require a new switch type for a specific interface, you must configure that interface with the desired ISDN switch type. If an ISDN global switch type is not compatible with the interface type you are using, or you change the global switch type and it is not propagated to the interface level, as a safety mechanism, the router will apply a default value to the interface level.

There are times when the global switch type results in a different switch type when applied to the interface. If, for example, you reconfigure the router to use global switch type basic-net3, the router will apply a primary-net5 switch type to PRI interfaces and basic-net3 to any BRI interfaces. You can override the default switch assignment by configuring a different ISDN switch type on the associated interface. Table 6.3 contains a list of global switch types and their automatic effect of issuing switch types on individual interfaces.

Configure TEI Negotiation Timing—Optional

You can configure ISDN terminal endpoint identifier (TEI) negotiation on individual ISDN interfaces. TEI negotiation is useful for switches that may deactivate layers 1 or 2 when there are no active calls. Typically, this setting is used for ISDN service offerings in Europe and connections to DMS-100 switches that are designed to initiate TEI negotiation. By default, TEI negotiation occurs when the router is powered on. The TEI negotiation value configured on an interface overrides the default or global TEI value. For example, if you configure ISDN TEI first-call globally and ISDN TEI powerup on BRI interface 0, then TEI negotiation powerup is the value applied to BRI interface 0. It is not necessary to configure TEI negotiation unless you want to override the default value (**isdn tei powerup**). On PRI interfaces connecting to DMS-100 switches, the router will change the default TEI setting to **isdn tei first-call**. To apply TEI negotiation to a specific BRI interface, use the following command in interface configuration mode:

```
isdn tei [first-call | powerup]
```

Specify ISDN Service Profile Identifiers (SPIDs)—Optional

Some service providers use service profile identifiers (SPIDs) to define the services subscribed to by the ISDN device that is accessing the ISDN service provider. The

Table 6.3   Global switch types and related default interface switch types.

Global Switch	Resulting Switch Type for BRI Interface	Resulting Switch Type for PRI Interface
basic-net3	basic-net3	primary-net5
primary-ts014	basic-ts013	primary-ts014
primary-ni	basic-ni	primary-ni

service provider assigns the ISDN device one or more SPIDs when you first sub-scribe to the service. If you are using a service provider that requires SPIDs, your ISDN device cannot place or receive calls until it sends a valid, assigned SPID to the service provider when accessing the switch to initialize the connection. Currently, only the DMS-100 and NI-1 switch types require SPIDs. It is optional for the AT&T 5ESS switch type. In addition, SPIDs have significance at the local access ISDN interface only. Remote routers are never sent the SPID. Switch types in this docu-ment refer to the ISDN software that runs on the switches, not the manufacturer or the model. For the DMS-100 switch type, two SPIDs are assigned, one for each B channel. The LDN is optional but might be necessary if the router is to answer calls made to the second directory number. To define the SPIDs and the local directory number (LDN) on the router, use the following commands in interface configura-tion mode:

```
isdn spid1 spid-number [ldn]
isdn spid2 spid-number [ldn]
```

spid1 is for the first B channel and **spid2** is for the second.

Configure Calling Line Identification Screening—Optional

This task applies only to Cisco 2500 series, Cisco 3000 series, and Cisco 4000 series routers that have a BRI. Calling line identification (CLI, also called caller ID) screening adds a level of security by allowing you to screen incoming calls. You can verify that the calling line ID is from an expected origin. CLI screening requires a local switch that is capable of delivering the CLI to the router. If caller ID screening is configured and the local switch does not deliver caller IDs, the router rejects all calls. To configure caller ID screening, use the following command in interface configuration mode:

```
isdn caller number
```

Configure Called Party Number Verification—Optional

When multiple devices are attached to an ISDN BRI, you can ensure that only a single device answers an incoming call by verifying the number or subaddress in the incoming call against the device's configured number or subaddress or both. You can specify that the router verify a called-party number or subaddress number in the incoming setup message for ISDN BRI calls, if the number is delivered by the switch. You can do so by configuring the number that is allowed. To configure verification, use the following command in interface configuration mode:

```
isdn answer1 [called-party-number][:subaddress]
```

Verifying the called-party number ensures that only the desired router responds to an incoming call. If you want to allow an additional number for the router, you can configure it, too. To configure a second number to be allowed, use the following command in interface configuration mode:

```
isdn answer2 [called-party-number][:subaddress]
```

Configure ISDN Calling Number Identification—Optional

A router with an ISDN BRI interface might need to supply the ISDN network with a billing number for outgoing calls. Some networks offer better pricing on calls in which the number is presented. When configured, this information is included in the outgoing call Setup message. To configure the interface to identify the billing number, use the following command in interface configuration mode:

```
isdn calling-number calling-number
```

Provide Routing for ISDN Connections

There is a problem with dynamic routing and DDR. Because the purpose of DDR is to use the ISDN connection for interesting traffic only, constant routing updates can interfere with this objective by bringing up the connection too often. Therefore, we look to alternative ways for providing the necessary routes between routers. These routing methods include the use of static routing, snapshot routing, and passive interfaces.

Static Routing

With static routes, network protocol routes are entered manually, eliminating the need for a routing protocol to broadcast routing updates across the DDR connection. Static routes can be effective in small networks that do not change often. Routing protocols can generate traffic that causes connections to be made unnecessarily. The command is as follows:

```
ip route network subnet-mask {next-hop-address | outgoing-interface}
```

Here are some examples:

```
ip route 0.0.0.0 0.0.0.0 10.1.1.1
ip route 10.1.1.1 255.255.255.255 BRI0
```

This command defines a static IP route. The first and second fields define the destination network number and subnet mask. The third field defines the next hop and can either be specified as an IP address or an interface. Under most circumstances, the third field contains the IP address of the next hop. However, for routes over unnumbered point-to-point interfaces, specify the interface used to reach the destination. In some statically routed examples, a static IP route is used. In other examples, a static IP default route is defined using 0.0.0.0 as both the destination network number and subnet mask. The default route is used if the router does not already have an explicit routing table entry for a destination network. For instance, in the ISP examples, **ip route 0.0.0.0 0.0.0.0 BRI0** defines a static IP default route to the ISP. In these cases, the router forwards all packets not destined for its local network onto the ISP using interface BRI0.

Snapshot Routing

If snapshot routing is used, you can still use dynamic routing with DDR. When using distance vector protocols you can use snapshot routing. Snapshot routing uses the client-server design model. When snapshot routing is configured, one router is designated as the snapshot server, and one or more routers are designated as snapshot clients. The server and clients exchange routing information during an active period. At the beginning of the active period, the client router dials the server router to exchange routing information. At the end of the active period, each router takes a snapshot of the entries in its routing table. These entries remain frozen during a quiet period. At the end of the quiet period, another active period begins, and the client router dials the server router to obtain the latest routing information. The client router determines the frequency at which it calls the server router. The quiet period can be as long as 100,000 minutes (approximately 69 days).

The sample configuration below dynamically routes IP between two Cisco IOS routers using snapshot RIP, and PPP with CHAP authentication over ISDN. With snapshot RIP, routing updates are exchanged between routers during a user-configured interval rather than the constant periodic exchange required of normal RIP. Aside from this snapshot interval, the ISDN line activates only when traffic demands. This is known as dial-on-demand routing (DDR). In contrast, the periodic exchange of normal RIP would force the ISDN line to be permanently active, potentially resulting in high ISDN costs. Here is the sample configuration:

```
interface Dialer0
ip unnumbered Ethernet0
encapsulation ppp
dialer in-band
dialer idle-timeout 300
dialer map snapshot 1 name Boston speed 56
dialer map ip 20.1.1.1 name Boston speed 56 broadcast 16175553333
dialer map ip 20.1.1.1 name Boston speed 56 broadcast 16175554444
dialer hold-queue 10
dialer load-threshold 200 either
dialer-group 1
snapshot server 15
no fair-queue
no cdp enable
ppp authentication chap
ppp multilink
```

For smaller networks, static routes may suffice. However, for larger networks, manually maintaining static routing tables on every router can be an administrative chore. Fortunately, the duration and frequency of the snapshot routing interval can be configured such that any ISDN costs due to dynamic routing are relatively negligible compared with the benefits of simplified network administration.

Passive Interfaces

Interfaces that are tagged as passive will not send routing updates. To prevent routing updates from establishing DDR connections on dialer interfaces that do not rely on dynamic routing information, configure DDR interfaces with the **passive-interface** command or use access lists. Using either the **passive-interface** command or an **access-list** prevents routing updates from triggering a call.

BRI Configuration Examples

An ISDN configuration example will be helpful to understand how the various ISDN commands relate to each other. The following example shows the configuration for a Cisco 2503 connected to Cisco 4000 using ISDN BRI. The configurations for the Cisco 2503 and the Cisco 4000 are presented below.

2503 Router Code

Here's the code for the 2503 router:

```
Router(config)# hostname ROUTER2503
ROUTER2503(config)# enable password test
ROUTER2503(config)# username ROUTER4000 password cisco
ROUTER2503(config)# isdn switch-type basic-dms100
ROUTER2503(config)#
ROUTER2503(config)# interface Ethernet0
ROUTER2503(config-if)# ip address 166.16.10.1 255.255.255.0
ROUTER2503(config-if)# no shutdown
ROUTER2503(config-if)# exit
ROUTER2503(config)# interface Serial0
ROUTER2503(config-if)# no ip address
ROUTER2503(config-if)# shutdown
ROUTER2503(config-if)# exit
ROUTER2503(config)# interface Serial1
ROUTER2503(config-if)# no ip address
ROUTER2503(config-if)# shutdown
ROUTER2503(config-if)# exit
ROUTER2503(config)#
ROUTER2503(config)# interface BRI0
ROUTER2503(config-if)# ip address 166.16.20.1 255.255.255.0
ROUTER2503(config-if)# encapsulation ppp
ROUTER2503(config-if)# bandwidth 56
ROUTER2503(config-if)#
```

```
ROUTER2503(config-if)# dialer idle-timeout 300
ROUTER2503(config-if)# dialer map ip 166.16.20.2 name ROUTER4000
                       speed 56 broadcast 14122221234
ROUTER2503(config-if)# dialer map ip 166.16.20.2 name ROUTER4000
                       speed 56 broadcast 14122226789
ROUTER2503(config-if)# dialer hold-queue 5
ROUTER2503(config-if)# dialer load-threshold 100
ROUTER2503(config-if)# dialer-group 1
ROUTER2503(config-if)#
ROUTER2503(config-if)# isdn spid1 408555432101 5554321
ROUTER2503(config-if)# isdn spid2 408555987601 5559876
ROUTER2503(config-if)#
ROUTER2503(config-if)# ppp authentication chap
ROUTER2503(config-if)# exit
ROUTER2503(config)#
ROUTER2503(config)# router igrp 1
ROUTER2503(config-router)# network 166.16.0.0
ROUTER2503(config-router)# exit
ROUTER2503(config)#
ROUTER2503(config)# ip route 192.168.24.0 255.255.255.0 166.16.20.2
ROUTER2503(config)# access-list 100 deny ip 0.0.0.0 255.255.255.255
                       255.255.255.255 0.0.0.0
ROUTER2503(config)# access-list 100 permit ip any any
ROUTER2503(config)#
ROUTER2503(config)# dialer-list 1 list 100
ROUTER2503(config)#
ROUTER2503(config)# line con 0
ROUTER2503(config)# line aux 0
ROUTER2503(config)# line vty 0 4
ROUTER2503(config-line)# password test
ROUTER2503(config-line)# login
```

Let's explain some of the commands that were used in the above example. The **username ROUTER4000** is the hostname of the remote router and is used by the **dialer map** command below. The username is case sensitive and must match the remote router's hostname exactly. The password, which is used by the CHAP authentication process, is case-sensitive and must match the remote router's password exactly.

The ISDN switch type, specified by the **isdn switch–type basic–dms100** command, must match your carrier's equipment. If you change the switch-type, you must reload the router for the new switch type to take effect. The **isdn spid1** and **spid2** commands are used if your carrier assigns spids to your ISDN lines.

PPP encapsulation, specified by the **encapsulation ppp** command, is recommended over HDLC in order to allow the use of CHAP authentication and the **ppp authentication chap** command enables CHAP authentication.

The default bandwidth setting for a BRI interface is 64K. If you configured your dialer map statements with the speed 56 option, you should include the **bandwidth** command to reflect this change. Note that this command does not control the speed of your ISDN line. It sets the correct reference point for the BRI port's show interface statistics, for the dialer load-threshold command, and for IGRP/EIGRP routing metrics.

The **dialer idle-timeout 300** command sets the number of seconds the ISDN connection will remain open if no interesting traffic is being routed. The timer is reset each time an interesting packet is forwarded.

The **dialer map** command(s) is used with CHAP authentication to place the initial call to the remote router when interesting traffic is forwarded to the BRI interface. Once the connection is active, the **dialer idle-timeout** command determines how long it will remain active. A **dialer map** statement is required for each ISDN phone number that will be called: **166.16.20.2** is the IP address of the remote router's BRI interface. **name ROUTER4000** represents the hostname of the remote router. The name is case-sensitive and should match the name configured for the username command above. **speed 56** sets the dialer speed to 56K for ISDN circuits that are not 64K end-to-end, and should be included in both routers' **dialer map** statements. Most installations in North America must be configured for 56K. **broadcast** allows the forwarding of broadcast packets. Unless broadcast packets are specified as interesting packets by the **dialer-list** command, they will only be forwarded when the ISDN link is active. **14122221234** and **14122226789** are the remote router's ISDN telephone numbers.

The **dialer hold-queue 5** command allows interesting packets to be queued until the ISDN connection is established. In this example, five interesting packets will be queued.

The **dialer load-threshold 100** command is used to configure bandwidth on demand by setting the maximum load before the dialer places another call through the second B channel. In this example, the second B channel will be activated when the load reaches 39 percent of maximum utilization, which is 100 divided by 255.

The **dialer-group 1** command enables the **dialer-list 1** on the BRI interface, which determines which packets will be interesting and activate the ISDN connection.

The **ip route** command creates a static route to the remote router's network via the remote router's BRI interface. This is required because dynamic routes are lost when the ISDN link is down. Note that the command parameters for this example are: **192.168.24.0** (the target network) and **255.255.255.0** (the target network mask). A 255 in an octet's position specifies that an exact match for that octet is required, and a 0 in an octet's position specifies that any value will match. **166.16.20.2** is the address of the next hop that can be used to reach the target network.

The **access-list** command determines which IP packets will be interesting and activate the ISDN link. The access-list you should create depends on your particular network design. Note: The command parameters for this example are: **access-list 100 deny ip 0.0.0.0 255.255.255.255 255.255.255.255 0.0.0.0,** which defines all broadcast packets as uninteresting, and **access-list 100 permit ip any any,** which defines all other IP packets as interesting.

The **dialer-list 1 list 100** command points to **access-list 100**, which determines which IP packets will be interesting.

4000 Router Code

Here's the code for the 4000 series router:

```
Router(config)# hostname ROUTER4000
ROUTER4000(config)# enable password test
ROUTER4000(config)# username ROUTER2503 password cisco
ROUTER4000(config)# isdn switch-type basic-dms100
ROUTER4000(config)#
ROUTER4000(config)# interface Ethernet0
ROUTER4000(config-if)# ip address 192.168.24.65 255.255.255.0
ROUTER4000(config-if)# exit
ROUTER4000(config)# interface Serial0
ROUTER4000(config-if)# no ip address
ROUTER4000(config-if)# shutdown
ROUTER40C0(config-if)# exit
ROUTER4000(config)# interface Serial1
ROUTER4000(config-if)# no ip address
ROUTER4000(config-if)# shutdown
ROUTER4000(config-if)# exit
ROUTER4000(config)#
ROUTER4000(config)# interface BRI0
ROUTER4000(config-if)# ip address 166.16.20.2 255.255.255.0
ROUTER4000(config-if)# encapsulation ppp
ROUTER4000(config-if)# bandwidth 56
ROUTER4000(config-if)#
ROUTER4000(config-if)# dialer idle-timeout 300
ROUTER4000(config-if)# dialer map ip 166.16.20.1 name ROUTER2503
                       speed 56 broadcast 14082224321
ROUTER4000(config-if)# dialer map ip 166.16.20.1 name ROUTER2503
                       speed 56 broadcast
ROUTER4000(config-if)# dialer hold-queue 5
ROUTER4000(config-if)# dialer load-threshold 100
ROUTER4000(config-if)# dialer-group 1
ROUTER4000(config-if)#
ROUTER4000(config-if)# isdn spid1 415555123401 5551234
ROUTER4000(config-if)# isdn spid2 415555678901 5556789
```

6

```
ROUTER4000(config-if)# ppp authentication chap
ROUTER4000(config-if)# exit
ROUTER4000(config)#
ROUTER4000(config)# router igrp 1
ROUTER4000(config-router)# network 166.16.0.0
ROUTER4000(config-router)# network 192.168.24.0
ROUTER4000(config-router)# exit
ROUTER4000(config)#
ROUTER4000(config)#ip route 166.16.10.0 255.255.255.0 166.16.20.1
ROUTER4000(config)#
ROUTER4000(config)# access-list 100 deny ip 0.0.0.0 255.255.255.255
                        255.255.255.255 0.0.0.0
ROUTER4000(config)# access-list 100 permit ip any any
ROUTER4000(config)#
ROUTER4000(config)# dialer-list 1 list 100
ROUTER4000(config)#
ROUTER4000(config)# line con 0
ROUTER4000(config)# line aux 0
ROUTER4000(config)# line vty 0 4
ROUTER4000(config-line)# password test
ROUTER4000(config-line)# login
ROUTER4000(config-line)# exit
```

Let's explain some of the code that was used on the 4000 router. The **username ROUTER2503** is the hostname of the remote router and is used by the **dialer map** command below. The username is case-sensitive and must match the remote router's hostname exactly. The password, which is used by the CHAP authentication process, is case-sensitive and must match the remote router's password exactly.

The dialer map commands, **dialer map ip 166.16.20.1 name ROUTER2503 speed 56 broadcast 14082224321** and **dialer map ip 166.16.20.1 name ROUTER2503 speed 56 broadcast 14082229876** are used with CHAP authentication to place the initial call to the remote router when interesting traffic is forwarded to the BRI interface. After the connection is active, the **dialer idle-timeout** command determines how long it will remain active. A **dialer map** statement is required for each ISDN phone number that will be called: **166.16.20.1** is the IP address of the remote router's BRI interface. **name ROUTER2503** represents the hostname of the remote router. The name is case-sensitive and should match the name configured for the username command above. **speed 56** sets the dialer speed to 56K for ISDN circuits that are not 64K end-to-end, and should be included in both routers' **dialer map** statements. Most installations in North America must be configured for 56K. **broadcast** allows the forwarding of broadcast packets. Unless broadcast packets are specified as *interesting* packets by the **dialer-list** command, they will be forwarded only when the ISDN link is active. **14082224321** and **14082229876** are the remote router's ISDN telephone numbers.

The **dialer-group 1** command enables the **dialer-list 1** on the BRI interface, which determines which packets will be interesting and activate the ISDN connection. The **dialer-list 1 list 100** command points to **access-list 100**, which determines which IP packets will be interesting.

The **ip route** command, **ip route 166.16.10.0 255.255.255.0 166.16.20.1**, creates a static route to the remote router's network via the remote router's BRI interface. This is required because dynamic routes are lost when the ISDN link is down. Note that the command parameters for this example are **166.16.0.0** (the target network) and **255.255.0.0** (the target network mask). A 255 in an octet's position specifies an exact match for that octet is required, and a 0 in an octet's position specifies any value will match. **166.16.20.1** is the address of the next hop that can be used to reach the target network.

PRI Configuration

PRI ports can use either E1 or T1 connections. Each network module card has two like interfaces. Each Cisco AS5200 access server has one dual T1/PRI card installed in the chassis, which provides the channelized interface necessary to handle digital and analog calls that are terminated in the unit. You can configure the card so that both ports are channelized T1, or both ports are ISDN PRI, but you cannot configure one of each. If the card is configured to support ISDN PRI, it can terminate analog modem calls and ISDN calls. The card resolves which type of call is coming in by reading the Q.931 signaling in the ISDN D channel associated with each PRI line. In dual PRI mode, the card can handle 23 B channels plus one D channel on each line, for a total of 46 B channels and two D channels. The Cisco AS5200 access server supports E1/PRI configuration. Channelized E1/PRI offers 30 B channels on each controller. The dual E1/PRI card enables up to 60 remote connections to network resources at any given time.

The terms *in-band* and *out-of-band* indicate whether various signals, which are used to set up, control, and terminate calls, travel in the same channel with voice calls or data made by the user, or whether those signals travel a separate channel. ISDN, which uses the D channel for signaling and the B channels for user data, fits into the out-of-band signaling category. Robbed-bit signaling, which uses bits from specified frames in the user data channel for signaling, fits into the in-band signaling category.

You can configure the Cisco AS5000 series access servers in the following ways:

➤ All channels can be configured to support ISDN PRI.

➤ All channels can be configured to support robbed-bit signaling, which enables a Cisco AS5200 modem to receive and send analog calls.

➤ All channels can be configured in a single channel group.

You can mix and match channels supporting ISDN PRI, robbed-bit signaling, and channel grouping across the same T1 line. For example, on the same channelized T1 line, you can create two different groups by using the **pri-group timeslots 1–10** command and **channel-group 11 timeslots 11–16** command.

ISDN PRI is supported on the Cisco 7200 series and 7500 series routers using T1 or E1 versions of the Multichannel Interface Processor (MIP) card and on the Cisco 4000 series channelized E1/T1/PRI network processor module (NPM).

If you want to configure ISDN PRI, you need to perform the following necessary tasks:

➤ Request a PRI line and switch configuration from a Telco service provider (required)

➤ Configure channelized E1 ISDN PRI

or

➤ Configure channelized T1 ISDN PRI

➤ Configure the serial interface

Configuring Channelized E1 or T1 ISDN PRI

The following steps are used to configure the controller on a Cisco 5200 router with a dual T1 or E1 network module card for ISDN PRI.

1. Enter your telco's switch type.

```
5200(config)# isdn switch-type (primary-4ess | primary-5ess
                      | primary-dms100 | primary-net5
                      | primary-ntt
                      | primary-ts014)
```

2. Enter controller configuration mode to configure your controller port. The controller ports are labeled 0 through 1 on the dual T1/PRI and dual E1/PRI cards.

```
5200(config)# controller (t1 | e1) (0 | 1)
5200(config-controller)#
```

3. Enter your telco's framing type.

```
5200(config-controller)# framing ( esf | sf | crc4 | nocrc4)
```

4. Enter your telco's line code type.

```
5200(config-controller)# linecode (ami | b8zs | hdb3)
```

Note: ISDN PRI T1 circuit uses Extended Super Frame (ESF) framing and Bipolar Eight Zero Substitution (B8ZS) or Alternate Mark Inversion for line coding. ISDN PRI E1 uses high-density bipolar 3 HDB3) for line coding, and the framing type is CRC4.

5. Enter the clock source for the line. Configure other lines as clock source secondary or clock source internal. Note that only one PRI can be clock source primary and only one PRI can be clock source secondary.

```
5200(config-controller)# clock source line primary
```

Configure all channels for ISDN.

6. Enter **pri-group timeslots 1–24** for T1. If E1, enter **pri-group timeslots 1–31**.

```
5200(config-controller)# pri-group timeslots (1-24 | 1-31)
```

The resulting configuration for T1/PRI:

```
5200(config-controller)# controller t1 1
5200(config-controller)# framing esf
5200(config-controller)# linecode b8zs
5200(config-controller)# clock source line secondary
5200(config-controller)# pri-group timeslots 1-24
```

Configuring the Serial Interface

The channelized E1 or channelized T1 controller is a logical serial interface that corresponds to the PRI group time slots. After you create the logical serial interface by configuring the controller, you must configure the D-channel serial interface. The configuration applies to all the PRI B channels (time slots). To configure the D-channel serial interface, perform the following tasks:

1. Designate a D channel on the serial interface for channelized T1.

```
interface serial slot/port:23
interface serial number:23
```

Or designate a D channel on the serial interface for channelized E1.

```
interface serial slot/port:15
interface serial number:15
```

Note that these are logical interfaces where your data link and network configurations are defined, such as the IP address and encapsulation type. The **23** and **15** refer to the timeslot that is used for ISDN signaling.

2. Specify an IP address for the interface.

```
ip address ip-address subnet-mask
```

3. Configure PPP encapsulation. Each ISDN B channel is treated as a serial line and supports HDLC and PPP encapsulation. The default serial encapsulation is HDLC.

```
encapsulation ppp
```

Other PRI configuration steps, such as configuring network addressing, overriding the default TEI Value, and configuring ISDN calling number identification, remain the same as when you configured them for BRI.

PRI Configuration Example

The following sections describe the configurations of the central site and the branch site routers. In this case study, both the central site and the home sites can place calls. The central site uses a Cisco 7000 router that connects to a NorTel DMS-100 central office ISDN switch. One remote site router (Ricardo) connects to the same central office switch that the central site router uses. Connections from the other remote site router (Monica) pass through two central office switches to reach the central site router.

Central Site

Two remote site users, Monica and Ricardo, dial from their branches into the central site router that is configured as follows. The configuration for the central site router is presented in the following code example with followed by their explanations.

```
Router(config)# hostname central-isdn
central-isdn(config)# username Monica password 7 130318111D
central-isdn(config)# username Ricardo password 7 08274D02A02
central-isdn(config)#
central-isdn(config)# isdn switch-type primary-dms100
central-isdn(config)#
central-isdn(config)# interface ethernet 0
central-isdn(config-if)# ip address 11.134.40.53 255.255.255.0
central-isdn(config-if)# exit
central-isdn(config)#
central-isdn(config)# controller t1 1/0
central-isdn(config-controller)# framing esf
```

```
central-isdn(config-controller)# linecode b8zs
central-isdn(config-controller)# pri-group timeslots 3-8
central-isdn(config-controller)# exit
central-isdn(config)#
central-isdn(config)# interface serial 1/0:23
central-isdn(config-if)# ip address 11.134.90.53 255.255.255.0
central-isdn(config-if)# encapsulation ppp
central-isdn(config-if)#
central-isdn(config-if)# dialer idle-timeout 300
central-isdn(config-if)# dialer map ip 11.134.90.1 name Monica
                        speed 56 14085553680
central-isdn(config-if)# dialer map ip 11.134.90.7 name Ricardo 8376
central-isdn(config-if)# dialer-group 1
central-isdn(config-if)#
central-isdn(config-if)# ppp authentication chap
central-isdn(config-if)# exit
central-isdn(config)#
central-isdn(config)#router igrp 10
central-isdn(config-router)# network 11.134.0.0
central-isdn(config-router)# redistribute static
central-isdn(config-router)# exit
central-isdn(config)#
central-isdn(config)# ip route 11.134.137.0 255.255.255.0
                        11.134.90.7
central-isdn(config)# ip route 11.134.147.0 255.255.255.0
                        11.134.90.1
central-isdn(config)#
central-isdn(config)# access-list 101 deny igrp any any
central-isdn(config)# access-list 101 deny udp any any eq 123
central-isdn(config)# access-list 101 deny udp any any eq 161
central-isdn(config)# access-list 101 permit ip any any
central-isdn(config)#
central-isdn(config)# dialer-list 1 list 101
```

The following paragraphs explain the commands in the above code example.

The configuration begins by establishing the host name of the router with the
hostname central–isdn command. The two **username** commands for the two
destination routers **Monica** and **Ricardo** establish the names of the routers that
are allowed to dial up this router. The **isdn switch-type** command global configuration command specifies that the central site router connects to a NorTel DMS-100
switch.

The controller global configuration command, **controller t1 1/0**, uses T1 to specify
a T1 controller interface. The "1" indicates that the controller card is located in backplane slot number 1. The "0" indicates port 0. All physical layer configuration tasks

are performed on the controller interface, like the framing, linecoding, and the timeslots that you will be using on the T1 or E1. The framing controller configuration command, **framing esf**, selects the frame type for the T1 data line. In this case, the **framing** command uses the **esf** keyword to indicate the extended super frame (ESF) frame type. The framing types are **sf**, **esf**, or **crc4**. The linecode controller configuration command, **linecode b8zs**, defines the line-code type for the T1 data line. In this case, the **linecode** command uses the b8zs keyword to indicate that the line-code type is bipolar 8 zero substitution (B8ZS). The service provider determines which line-code type, either alternate mark inversion (AMI) or B8ZS, is required for your T1/E1 circuit. The pri-group controller configuration command, **pri-group timeslots 3-8**, specifies an ISDN PRI on a channelized T1 card in a Cisco 7000 series router. The timeslots keyword establishes the B channels. In this example, only six B channels (channels 3 through 8) are in use on this controller.

All of the data link and network layer configurations are done on the logical serial interface, **interface serial 1/0:23**, which is associated with the physical controller interface. The **ip address** interface configuration command establishes the IP address of the interface, and the **encapsulation ppp** command establishes the Point-to-Point protocol (PPP) as the encapsulation method and the **ppp authentication chap** interface configuration command enables CHAP authentication.

All of your dial-up configurations is also performed on the logical serial interface. **The dialer idle-timeout** interface configuration command, **dialer idle-timeout 300**, sets the idle timeout to five minutes. The **dialer map** interface configuration commands, **dialer map ip 11.134.90.1 name Monica speed 56 14085553680** and **dialer map ip 11.134.90.7 name Ricardo 8376**, establish the remote sites that the router can call. Because Monica's router connects to a central office switch that does not use Signaling System 7, the **dialer map** command for calling Monica's router uses the **speed** keyword, which is valid for native ISDN interfaces only. The native ISDN interface on the Cisco 2503 operates at either 64 or 56Kbps. If the calling party and the called party use the same ISDN switch, they can communicate at 64Kbps. Otherwise, they must communicate at 56Kbps. Because Ricardo's ISDN line connects to the same central office as the line that the central site router uses, the telephone number in the **dialer map** command for connecting to Ricardo's router does not have to include the three-digit prefix. The **dialer-group 1** interface configuration command associates the BRI with **dialer-group 1**.

ip route 11.134.137.0 255.255.255.0 11.134.90.7 defines the static route to Monica and **ip route 11.134.147.0 255.255.255.0 11.134.90.1** defines the static route to Ricardo. The **router igrp 10** global configuration command enables the Interior Gateway Routing Protocol (IGRP) and sets the autonomous system number to 10. The redistribute command sends the static route information as defined with the **ip route** global configuration commands to other routers in the same IGRP area. This is needed for other routers connected to the central site so that they will have routes to the remote routers. DDR needs to use static routes because routing updates are not received when the dial-up connection is not active.

DDR uses **access-lists** to determine whether a packet is *interesting or uninteresting*. Interesting packets cause a call to be placed if a call is not active or cause a call that has already been placed to be maintained as active. The first extended **access-list** global configuration command states that IGRP updates are uninteresting. The second extended **access-list** command states that Network Time Protocol (NTP) packets are uninteresting. The third extended **access-list** command specifies that Simple Network Management Protocol (SNMP) packets are uninteresting, and the final extended **access-list** command states that all other IP packets are interesting and therefore should trigger an ISDN phone call. The **dialer-list** global configuration command, **dialer-list 1 list 101**, assigns the set of **access-lists** to dialer access group 1.

Verifying BRI and PRI ISDN

BRI or PRI problems can be diagnosed by using **show** commands and **debug** commands. You can categorize verification commands by OSI layers. Table 6.4 lists the various ISDN **show** and **debug** commands, as related to their associated layer, and their explanations. Figure 6.5 displays those links that make up the ISDN connection.

Show Commands to Verify and Troubleshoot ISDN

The following **show** commands can be used for both BRI and PRI ISDN verification and troubleshooting.

show isdn status

The **show** commands are helpful in solving ISDN problems. The **show** commands can tell you whether you are connected to the local ISDN switch: **show isdn status**,

Table 6.4   ISDN show and debug commands.

Command	Function
show controllers bri *number* **show interfaces bri** *slot/port* (Cisco 7200 series)	Check Layer 1 (physical layer) of the BRI.
show dialer interface bri *number*	Obtain general diagnostic information about the specified interface.
debug q921	Check Layer 2 (data link layer).
**show isdn {active	history	memory	status	timers}** **debug isdn events** **debug q931** **debug dialer** **show dialer**	Display information about calls, history, memory, status, and Layer 2 and Layer 3 timers.
show ppp multilink	Check Layer 3 (network layer).

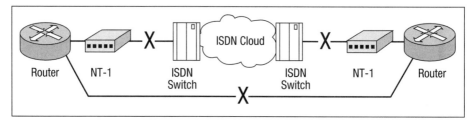

Figure 6.5 ISDN links with potential problems.

or whether you have successfully made a call: **show dialer**. Upon getting the ISDN line provisioned by the telco, the only parameters that are required for the router to synchronize with the switch are the switch type and the SPID(s). After proper configuration, output from the **show isdn status** EXEC command should look like the following screen print. This command displays the ISDN status of layers 1, 2, and 3. You can see from the following screen print that layer 1 is active on the circuit, which means that the router senses the line coding of the BRI circuit. Layer 2 status indicates that a TEI has been assigned for both B channels. You also see that the SPIDs for both B channels have been sent to the switch and are valid.

```
The current ISDN Switchtype = basic-ni1
ISDN BRI0 interface
    Layer 1 Status:
        ACTIVE
    Layer 2 Status:
        TEI = 64, State = MULTIPLE_FRAME_ESTABLISHED
        TEI = 65, State = MULTIPLE_FRAME_ESTABLISHED
    Spid status
TEI 64, ces = 1, state = 8 (established)
    Spid1 configured, spid1 sent, spid1 valid
Endpoint ID Info: epsf = 0, usid = 70, tid = 1
TEI 65, ces = 2, state = 8 (established)
    Spid1 configured, spid1 sent, spid1 valid
Endpoint ID Info: epsf = 0, usid = 70, tid = 2
    Layer 3 Status:
        No Active Layer 3 Call(s)
    Activated dsl 0 CCBs = 0
    Total Allocated ISDN CCBs = 0
```

Failure of the Cisco router to synchronize properly with the ISDN switch would yield the following display:

```
ISDN BRI0 interface
    Layer 1 Status:
        DEACTIVATED
    Layer 2 Status:
        Layer 2 NOT Activated
```

```
Layer 3 Status:
    No Active Layer 3 Call(s)
Activated dsl 0 CCBs = 0
Total Allocated ISDN CCBs = 0
```

If you receive this output, you might have a faulty cable. Another reason might be that you configured the wrong switch type or incorrect SPID(s). In this case you would need to contact the telco and confirm the switch type and SPID(s). Another possibility is a faulty ISDN line. Confirm that the current ISDN switch type matches the actual switch type that you are using. If you are having problems, do the following: Make sure that any external NT1 is functioning correctly. Refer to the documentation that came with the NT1. Make sure that the ISDN line is correctly configured by checking with the ISDN service provider. The following is a check-list for detecting layer 1 and layer 2 problems.

1. Check layer 1

   If active, proceed.

   If inactive:

   ➤ *Check switch type*

   ➤ *Check cable: should be straight-through*

   ➤ *Check interface by using* **show int bri0** *and make sure it is not administratively shut down.*

   ➤ *Check with the telco to make sure the line is live.*

2. Check layer 2

   If TEIs assigned with multiple frames established, proceed.

   If no TEIs assigned or TEI assigned awaiting establishment:

   ➤ *Check switch type*

   ➤ *Check with Telco*

   ➤ *Check SPID status: only available on IOS 11.2.9 or higher*

   ➤ *If SPIDs are sent and valid and LDNs set, proceed.*

   ➤ *If SPIDs are sent and valid and LDNs not set:*

      ➤ *Add 7-digit directory number to SPID configs*

      ➤ *If SPID sent invalid:*

      ➤ *Check SPID numbers*

      ➤ *Check switch type*

show dialer

The **show dialer** command displays numbers dialed and the reasons for the calls. After getting successful connection with the local ISDN switch and after having entered the basic Dial-On-Demand Routing configuration into the router, you should be able to initiate a test call by issuing interesting traffic to the next hop address. Even if full PPP connectivity has not been established, you can determine whether a physical call was made by issuing the **show dialer** EXEC command. The following screen print displays the output from the **show dialer** command. The command shows that router will drop a B channel after five minutes, but no calls have been made. If a call were made, more information would appear under each B channel stating that the physical layer is up and stating the reason for the call. Reasons include the listing of IP addresses used during pinging that created a call for the B1 channel and "multilink bundle overload" message that indicates a multilink call was created for the B2 channel.

```
Dial String       Successes    Failures    Last called    Last status
4155551212            1           0         00:00:00       successful
4155551213            1           0         00:00:00       successful
0 incoming call(s) have been screened.
BRI0: B-Channel 1
Idle timer (300 secs), Fast idle timer (20 secs)
Wait for carrier (30 secs), Re-enable (15 secs)
BRI0: B-Channel 2
Idle timer (300 secs), Fast idle timer (20 secs)
Wait for carrier (30 secs), Re-enable (15 secs)
```

show ppp multilink

The **show ppp multilink** command can confirm Multilink PPP configuration for the B1 and B2 channels. In the following screen print, you can see that the message "Master link is Virtual-Access1" appears in the command output and that we have an MLPPP bundle consisting of two members. The two members are BRI 0 1 and BRI 0 2.

```
router# show ppp multilink
Bundle HQ, 2 members, Master link is Virtual-Access1
Dialer Interface is BRI0
0 lost fragments, 0 reordered, 0 unassigned,
        sequence 0x0/0x0 rcvd/sent
0 discarded, 0 lost received, 1/255 load
Member Links: 2
BRI0:1
BRI0:2
```

show interface BRI 0 (1 and 2)

From the privileged EXEC command mode, you can enter the **show interface** command. The **show interface** command can confirm that the ISDN line is up and connected to the other router. Notice in the following screen print that the "LCP Open, multilink Open" message appears in the command output. This confirms the Multilink PPP configuration for the B2 Channel. The two B channels will be in the down state until a call is made.

```
Router# show interface bri 0 1 2
BRI0:1 is up, line protocol is up
Hardware is BRI with U interface and external S bus interface
MTU 1500 bytes, BW 64 Kbit, DLY 20000 usec, rely 255/255,
        load 3/255
Encapsulation PPP, loopback not set, keepalive set (10 sec)
LCP Open, multilink Open
Last input 00:00:00, output 00:00:00, output hang never
Last clearing of "show interface" counters never
```

show ip route

The **show ip route** command can confirm the IP static route and confirm basic connectivity to the other router. Use the IP address of the other router's ISDN interface for the IP address shown in the example. As in the following screen print, you should see that the other router's IP address is accessible through this router's BRI 0 interface as indicated by the message "directly connected via BRI".

```
Router# show ip route 192.168.37.40
Routing entry for 192.168.37.40/32
Known via "connected", distance 0, metric 0 (connected)
Routing Descriptor Blocks:
* directly connected, via BRI0
```

ping

You can verify your configuration to this point by testing connectivity to the central-site router, as follows: From the privileged EXEC command mode, enter the **ping** command followed by the IP address of the central-site route to have the router dial the central-site router. Wait for the "ISDN-6-CONNECT" message. If the success rate is 100 percent on the second attempt, this verification step is successful. If you are having problems, do the following: Make sure the router is configured with the correct IP address. Make sure the router is configured with the correct static routes.

```
Router# ping 192.168.37.40

Type escape sequence to abort.
Sending 5, 100-byte ICMP Echos to 192.168.37.40,
        timeout is 2 seconds:
```

```
.!!!!
Success rate is 80 percent (4/5), round-trip
        min/avg/max = 40/43/48 ms
Router#
*Mar 1 03:37:46.526: %LINK-3-UPDOWN: Interface BRIO:1,
        changed state to up
*Mar 1 03:37:46.923: %LINEPROTO-5-UPDOWN: Line protocol
        on Interface BRIO:1, changed state to up

*Mar 1 03:37:46.939: %LINK-3-UPDOWN: Interface Virtual-Access1,
        changed state to up
*Mar 1 03:37:47.923: %LINEPROTO-5-UPDOWN: Line protocol on
        Interface Virtual-Access1, changed state to up
*Mar 1 03:35:57.217: %ISDN-6-CONNECT: Interface BRIO:1 is
        now connected to 5552053 HQ
```

Enter the **ping** command followed by the IP address of the other router again:

```
router# ping 192.168.37.40

Type escape sequence to abort.
Sending 5, 100-byte ICMP Echos to 192.168.37.40,
        timeout is 2 seconds:
.!!!!
Success rate is 100 percent (5/5), round-trip min/avg/max = 40/43/48 ms
1700#
*Mar 1 03:37:46.526: %LINK-3-UPDOWN: Interface BRIO:1, changed state to up
*Mar 1 03:37:46.923: %LINEPROTO-5-UPDOWN: Line protocol on Interface
BRIO:1, changed
state to up
*Mar 1 03:37:46.939: %LINK-3-UPDOWN: Interface Virtual-Access1, changed
state to up
*Mar 1 03:37:47.923: %LINEPROTO-5-UPDOWN: Line protocol on Interface Vir-
tual-Access1,
changed state to up
*Mar 1 03:35:57.217: %ISDN-6-CONNECT: Interface BRIO:1 is now
        connected to 5552053
HQ
```

Using **Debug** Commands to Troubleshoot ISDN Networks

When the **show** commands are inadequate in providing details regarding the ISDN failure, **debug** commands can be helpful. Table 6.5 shows the **debug** commands that are applicable to ISDN troubleshooting.

Here are some examples of ISDN **debug** commands:

➤ **Debug isdn event**—The **debug ISDN event** can indicate a SPID problem, which will show an invalid SPID and TE1 assignment as in the following screen

Table 6.5   ISDN debugging commands.

Command	Explanation
Debug isdn event	ISDN activity occurring on the user side of the ISDN interface; similar to **debug isdn q931**.
Debug dialer	Dial-on-demand routing information
Debug isdn q921	Data link layer (Layer 2) access procedures that are taking place at the router on the D-channel (LAPD) of its ISDN interface.
Debug isdn q931	Information about call setup and teardown of ISDN network connections (Layer 3) between the local router (user side) and the network.
Debug ppp negotiation	Negotiation of Point-to-Point Protocol (PPP) options and Network Control Protocol (NCP) parameters.
Debug ppp authentication	Exchange of Challenge Authentication Protocol (CHAP) and (Password Authentication Protocol (PAP) packets.

6

print. If you get this output, you will need to verify that the TEI is assigned by trying show ISDN status. Layer 2 information will tell if TEI is assigned. You will need to check to see if the SPIDS are configured correctly. You may need to have the service provider verify SPIDs, if necessary, and have them track the SPIDs.

```
BRIO: ISDN Event: incoming ces value = 1 BRIO:
received HOST_TERM_REGISTER_NACK -
invalid EID/SPID or TEI not assigned Cause i = 0x8082 -
No route to specified network
```

➤ **Debug dialer**—The **debug dialer** command can show that dialing cannot occur. If it says no **dialer string**, as displayed below, check the configuration for your **dialer string**, **dial-list**, **dialer-group**, **map statement** and **routing** commands. If the attempted connection dials but the carrier times out, try using **Debug ISDN Q931**.

```
BRIO: Dialing cause: BRIO: ip PERMIT BRIO: No dialer string defined.
Dialing cannot occur.. BRIO: Dialing cause: BRIO: ip PERMIT BRIO:
No dialer string defined. Dialing cannot occur.. BRIO: Dialing cause:
BRIO: ip PERMIT BRIO: No dialer string defined. Dialing cannot occur..
BRIO: Dialing cause: BRIO: ip PERMIT BRIO: No dialer string defined.
Dialing cannot occur.. BRIO: Dialing cause: BRIO: ip PERMIT BRIO:
No dialer string defined. Dialing cannot occur.
```

➤ **Debug isdn q921**—The **debug isdn q921** command output is limited to commands and responses exchanged during peer-to-peer communication carried over the D channel. This debug information does not include data transmitted over the B channels. The peers (data link layer entities and layer management entities on the routers) communicate with each other via an ISDN switch over the D channel.

A router can be the calling or called party of the ISDN Q.921 data link layer access procedures. If the router is the calling party, the command displays information about an outgoing call. If the router is the called party, the command displays information about an incoming call and the keepalives. In the first example, the call is made and the switch has responded. In the second example below, the router is sending Identification Requests (IDREQ) to the ISDN switch, but does not get a response from the switch. When this happens, you should check the configuration of SPIDs, verify SPIDs with telco, and if necessary, have telco track the SPIDs.

The following is a sample of the output of this **debug** command:

```
Jan  3 14:49:22.507: ISDN BR0: TX ->  RRp sapi = 0  tei = 64 nr = 0
Jan  3 14:49:22.523: ISDN BR0: RX <-  RRf sapi = 0  tei = 64  nr = 2
Jan  3 14:49:32.527: ISDN BR0: TX ->  RRp sapi = 0  tei = 64 nr = 0
Jan  3 14:49:32.543: ISDN BR0: RX <-  RRf sapi = 0  tei = 64  nr = 2
Jan  3 14:49:42.067: ISDN BR0: RX <-  RRp sapi = 0  tei = 64 nr = 2
Jan  3 14:49:42.071: ISDN BR0: TX ->  RRf sapi = 0  tei = 64  nr = 0
```

Here is another example of the output of this command:

```
19:27:31: TX ->  IDREQ  ri = 19354  ai = 127 dsl = 0
19:27:33: TX ->  IDREQ  ri = 1339   ai = 127 dsl = 0
19:27:35: TX ->  IDREQ  ri = 22764  ai = 127 dsl = 0
19:27:37: TX ->  IDREQ  ri = 59309  ai = 127 dsl = 0
19:27:39: TX ->  IDREQ  ri = 25214  ai = 127 dsl = 0
19:27:41: TX ->  IDREQ  ri = 35423  ai = 127 dsl = 0
19:27:43: TX ->  IDREQ  ri = 12368  ai = 127 dsl = 0
19:27:45: TX ->  IDREQ  ri = 13649  ai = 127 dsl = 0
```

➤ **Debug isdn q931**—The display information **debug isdn q931** command output is limited to commands and responses exchanged during peer-to-peer communication carried over the D channel. This debug information does not include data transmitted over the B channels. The peers (network layers) communicate with each other via an ISDN switch over the D channel. The **debug isdn event, debug isdn q931** command can show that the call is connected or torn down. If you see that the call is not connected, you can try turning on **debug ppp negotiation** and **debug ppp chap** to see if ppp negotiation and ppp authentication are good.

Listing 6.1   Call Setup Procedure for an Outgoing Call.

```
router# debug isdn q931
TX -> SETUP pd = 8 callref = 0x04
  Bearer Capability i = 0x8890
```

```
Channel ID i = 0x83
Called Party Number i = 0x80, '415555121202'
RX <- CALL_PROC pd = 8 callref = 0x84
Channel ID i = 0x89
RX <- CONNECT pd = 8 callref = 0x84
TX -> CONNECT_ACK pd = 8 callref = 0x04....
Success rate is 0 percent (0/5)
```

Listing 6.2   Call Setup Procedure for an Incoming Call.

```
router# debug isdn q931
RX <- SETUP pd = 8 callref = 0x06
 Bearer Capability i = 0x8890
 Channel ID i = 0x89
 Calling Party Number i = 0x0083, '81012345678902'
TX -> CONNECT pd = 8 callref = 0x86
RX <- CONNECT_ACK pd = 8 callref = 0x06
```

Listing 6.3   Call Teardown Procedure from the Network.

```
router# debug isdn q931
RX <- DISCONNECT pd = 8 callref = 0x84
 Cause i = 0x8790
 Looking Shift to Codeset 6
 Codeset 6 IE 0x1 1 0x82 '10'
TX -> RELEASE pd = 8 callref = 0x04
 Cause i = 0x8090
RX <- RELEASE_COMP pd = 8 callref = 0x84
```

Listing 6.4   Call Teardown Procedure from the Router.

```
router# debug isdn q931
TX -> DISCONNECT pd = 8 callref = 0x05
 Cause i = 0x879081
RX <- RELEASE pd = 8 callref = 0x85
 Looking Shift to Codeset 6
 Codeset 6 IE 0x1 1 0x82 '10'
TX <- RELEASE_COMP pd = 8 callref = 0x05
```

In Listing 6.5, the **debug ISDN q931** shows a failed call. You will need to verify the telephone number and SPIDs. Look for a disconnect message with a cause code. The code can tell you a possible cause. The code can indicate that you have not included your LDNs with your SPIDS, or that the speed you have set does not match what the line will do. If the cause comes from the remote location, check with the far side router. If the cause is coming from the switch and you have checked everything above, refer to the telco. In this example there are at least two cause codes (0xC48A and 0x8492) indicating that the problem exists at the remote location.

Listing 6.5   Ouput from **debug ISDN q931**.

```
ISDN BR0: TX -> SETUP pd = 8 callref = 0x1C
Bearer Capability i = 0x8890
Channel ID i = 0x83
Called Party Number i = 0x80, '2691725'
ISDN BR0: RX <- CALL_PROC pd = 8 callref = 0x9C
Channel ID i = 0x89
ISDN BR0: RX <- PROGRESS pd = 8 callref = 0x9C
Progress Ind i = 0xC48A - Delay in response at called interface
Signal i = 0x01 - Ring back tone on
ISDN BR0: RX <- DISCONNECT pd = 8 callref = 0x9C
Cause i = 0x8492 - No user responding
Signal i = 0x01 - Ring back tone on
ISDN BR0: TX -> RELEASE pd = 8 callref = 0x1C
```

Debug ppp negotiation, Debug ppp authentication—Both of these **debug ppp** commands need to be used in combination with a command that will cause a connection attempt, such as the **ping** command. The commands **debug ppp negotiation** and **debug ppp authentication** can show that CHAP authentication failed. You will need to check username and passwords for correct spelling and use of lower- and uppercase letters. Check **dialer map** command for name keyword and correct hostname. Check username global configuration command entries. Make sure that username statements use the host name of the remote router. Make sure that the passwords on both the local and remote router are identical. Use the username command to add or alter username entries. These commands can also indicate that the remote device does not authenticate itself. This can be seen usually with non-Cisco devices, for example, Ascend and Livingston. You will need to use the commands **ppp authentication chap callin**, or **ppp authentication pap callin**. The following is a screen print from performing both the **debug ppp negotiation** command and **ping**. In this particular case, CHAP authentication failed.

```
router#debug ppp negotiation
router#ping 192.9.198.1
Type escape sequence to abort.
Sending 5, 100-byte ICMP Echos to 192.9.198.1, timeout is 2 seconds:
%LINK-3-UPDOWN: Interface BRIO: B-Channel 1, changed state to up
%LINK-5-CHANGED: Interface BRIO: B-Channel 1, changed state to up
ppp: sending CONFREQ, type = 3 (CI_AUTHTYPE), value = C223/5
ppp: sending CONFREQ, type = 5 (CI_MAGICNUMBER), value = 28CEEF99
ppp: received config for type = 3
(AUTHTYPE) value = C223 value = 5 acked
ppp: received config for type = 5 (MAGICNUMBER) value = 1E23F5C acked
PPP BRIO: B-Channel 1: state = ACKSENT fsm_rconfack(C021): rcvd id E4
ppp: config ACK received, type. = 3 (CI_AUTHTYPE), value = C223
ppp: config ACK received, type = 5 (CI_MAGICNUMBER), value = 28CEEF99
```

```
BRIO: B-Channel 1: PPP AUTH CHAP input code = 1 id = 82 len = 16
BRIO: B-Channel 1: PPP AUTH CHAP input code = 2 id = 95 len = 28
BRIO: B-Channel 1: PPP AUTH CHAP input code = 4 id = 82 len = 21
BRIO: B-Channel 1: Failed CHAP authentication with remote.
Remote message is: MD compare failed
```

Verify ISDN PRI

The **show** and **debug** commands shown in the preceding section are applicable to PRI ISDN. The **show controller** command is one of the only unique verification commands for PRI.

You can use the **show controllers t1** privileged EXEC command on the Cisco 7000 to display information about the T1 links supported by the Multichannel Interface Processor (MIP), as shown below. This command displays controller status information that is specific to the controller hardware. Enter the **show controller t1** or **show controller e1** command and specify the port number.

```
show controllers t1 [slot/port]
```

slot is the backplane slot number, which can be 0, 1, 2, 3, or 4. *port* is the port number of the controller, which can be 0, 1, 2, or 3.

There are no errors were reported in the following two screen prints.

```
5200# show controller t1 0
T1 0 is up.
  No alarms detected.
  Framing is ESF, Line Code is B8ZS, Clock Source is Line Primary.
  Version info of slot 2:  HW: 2, Firmware: 14, NEAT PLD: 13,
        NR Bus PLD: 19
  Data in current interval (476 seconds elapsed):
     0 Line Code Violations, 0 Path Code Violations
     0 Slip Secs, 0 Fr Loss Secs, 0 Line Err Secs, 0 Degraded Mins
     0 Errored Secs, 0 Bursty Err Secs, 0 Severely Err Secs,
        0 Unavail Secs
  Total Data (last 24 hours)
     0 Line Code Violations, 0 Path Code Violations,
     0 Slip Secs, 0 Fr Loss Secs, 0 Line Err Secs, 0 Degraded Mins,
     0 Errored Secs, 0 Bursty Err Secs, 0 Severely Err Secs,
        0 Unavail Secs

5200# sh cont e1 2
  E1 2 is up.
    Applique type is Channelized E1 - balanced
    No alarms detected.
    Version info of Slot 0:  HW: 2, Firmware: 4, PLD Rev: 0
```

Chapter Summary

BRI ISDN includes 2 B channels with 64K each and one D channel with 16K. PRI (using T1) includes 23 B channels with 64K each and one D channel at 64K. PRI (using E1) includes 30 B channels with 64K each and one D channel at 64K.

ISDN works at the first three layers of the OSI model. At the physical layer, the specification for a BRI is documented by I.430 and for the PRI is documented by I.431. At the data link layer, the D channel is defined in the Q.921 protocol specification. At the network layer, the D channel uses Q.931 to define call setup and call teardown.

The address field of the ISDN frame includes SAPIs, which identify the higher layer protocol being used in the data field, and TEIs (Terminal Endpoint Identifier) that are used to tag ISDN devices. TEIs are distributed to the customer's ISDN devices by the telco switch during layer 2 links.

You need to specify the switch type used by the telco and configure associated SPIDS if necessary.

Call setup and call teardown occur at layer 3. Both procedures include several messages that are sent from the sending ISDN device to the telco switch, from the telco switch to the receiving ISDN switch, and back again. The messages include: Alerting, Call Proceeding, Connect, Connect ACK, Progress Setup, Setup ACK, Disconnect, Release, and Release Complete.

When configuring a router for ISDN BRI, you need to perform three tasks: configure global properties, configure Interface Properties, and provide for routing. In the global mode, you need to set the switch type and optionally set TEI negotiation timing. In the interface mode, you need to specify the Interface and its IP Address, configure encapsulation, configure the dial string, specify what is interesting traffic, enter the hostname, and configure optional SPIDs associated with the specified switch. You will also need to configure routing in the global configuration by using static routes or snapshot routing.

When configuring a router for ISDN PRI, you need to perform two tasks: configure the channelized E1 or T1 ISDN PRI controller and configure the serial interface. When configuring the controller, you need to configure the line coding type and the framing type, and specify the number of timeslots to be used. When configuring the serial interface for the D channel, you need to configure the **dialer map** with the **dial string** and determine what is interesting traffic. Various **show** and **debug** commands can be used to verify and troubleshoot ISDN connections during the link stages that take place at each layer. For layer 1 diagnosis, you can use **show interface bri**. For layer 2 diagnosis, you can use **show isdn status** and **debug q921**. For layer 3 diagnosis, you can use **show isdn status, debug isdn events, debug q931, debug dialer, show dialer**, and **show ppp multilink**.

Review Questions

1. Which reference point has two wires?

   a. R

   b. U

   c. S

   d. T

   e. TA

2. What is a route configured with a high administrative distance that can be overridden by dynamically learned routes?

   a. IGRP routing table

   b. Floating static route

   c. Passive interface

   d. Dynamic

3. You need to configure a PRI interface. Which of the following are valid line coding types if your PRI is an E1?

   a. B8ZS

   b. ESF

   c. SF

   d. Ami

   e. HDB3

4. You need to configure a PRI interface. Which of the following are valid line coding types if your PRI is a T1?

   a. B8ZS

   b. ESF

   c. SF

   d. Bipolar Ami

   e. HDB3

5. Incoming data may be corrupted when calls are made at 56Kbps but delivered by the ISDN network at 64Kbps. How do you set the speed for incoming calls to ensure the proper speed?

   a. Dialer map

   b. ISDN not-end-to-end (56|64)

   c. Dialer-group

   d. Bandwidth 56

6. What is the method where a router can automatically start and close a circuit-switched connection when needed?

    a. Dial-on-demand

    b. Bandwidth-on-demand

    c. In-band signaling

    d. Robbed-bit

7. What is the correct bandwidth-on-demand command and parameters to initiate another call to the destination and maintain that second call if the load on a particular interface exceeds one fourth of the bandwidth?

    a. **dialer load-threshold 65**

    b. **dialer load-threshold 25**

    c. **dialer load-threshold 200**

    d. **dialer load-threshold 250**

8. Which type of switch would not be used in North America?

    a. Basic-5ess

    b. Basic-nil

    c. Basic-dms100

    d. Basic-net3-ans

9. Which statement is true regarding snapshot routing?

    a. Snapshot routing can be configured with link-state routing protocols only.

    b. Snapshot routing can be configured with distance-vector routing protocols only.

    c. Snapshot routing updates the routing table with constant periodic updates.

    d. Snapshot routing only works with ISDN BRI and not PRI.

10. Which single command is used to display both B channels' information?

    a. **show interface BRI 0 1 2**

    b. **show interface BRI 0 1 BRI0 2**

    c. **show isdn event**

    d. **show dialer**

11. How do you configure an ISDN BRI to identify the billing number?

    a. **ISDN billing-number**

    b. **ISDN caller-number**

    c. **ISDN calling-number**

    d. **ISDN answer1**

12. How many B channels does a T1 version of PRI support?

    a. 25

    b. 29

    c. 23

    d. 24

13. What are the characteristics of ISDN BRI? [Choose the two best answers]

    a. 64K D channel

    b. 2B+1 D

    c. 16Kb D channel

    d. 2D+1B

    e. 64K D channel

14. ISDN uses which form of signaling?

    a. Out-of-band

    b. In-band

    c. Robbed-bit

    d. RS 232

15. Which statements are true relating to ISDN SPIDS? [Choose the two best answers]

    a. SPIDS are required only for AT&T 5ESS switch type.

    b. SPIDS are required only for DMS-100 and NI-1 switch types and for BRI only.

    c. SPIDS are user-defined but must stay within an assigned limited number of digits.

    d. SPIDS have significance at the local ISDN interface only.

16. Which command is used to examine if data is interesting or not?

    a. **dialer-list**

    b. **dial-list**

    c. **dialer map**

    d. **dialer-group**

17. What reference point is between a non–ISDN device (TE2) and the TA adapter?

    a. R

    b. U

    c. S

    d. T

    e. TA

18. What is the valid frame type for PRI interface used with E1?

    a. ESF

    b. CRC-4

    c. B8ZS

    d. AMI

19. When an ISDN connection completes a call teardown, which message types are sent? [Choose the three best answers]

    a. Release

    b. Alerting

    c. Call Proceeding

    d. Connect

    e. Release Complete

    f. Disconnect

20. You are diagnosing a data link layer problem in an ISDN connection. Which command would give you the most information?

    a. **debug isdn q921**

    b. **debug isdn q931**

    c. **show isdn event**

    d. **show dialer**

21. How can you reduce routing updates and still provide routing for an ISDN connection? [Choose all that apply]

    a. Distance-vector routing

    b. Snapshot routing

    c. Link-state routing

    d. Static routes

    e. Static default routes

22. During the ISDN call setup, which entity initiates the ALERTING message?

    a. Sender

    b. Sender's switch

    c. Receiver

    d. Receiver's switch

23. What ISDN command makes the actual call to the receiving site?

    a. **dialer-list**

    b. **dialer-dial**

    c. **dialer map**

    d. **dialer-group**

24. What is the protocol used between and among switches at the telco office?

    a. LAPD

    b. LAPB

    c. SS7

    d. ATM

6

Real-World Projects

Gloria is still working for the OCRA pharmaceutical company as an assistant network administrator. Now, she has another assignment. The company wants to install ISDN BRI at the two branch offices in Boston and Philadelphia and implement ISDN PRI at the central site in Albany. Gloria was asked to head the implementation team, which consisted of herself and two consultants. This would be the first time Gloria has attempted to configure Cisco routers for ISDN connections. Gloria decided that she should first test her ISDN configurations in a lab setting. She needed to configure two newly purchased Cisco 2503 routers each with a BRI interface and a newly purchased Cisco AS5200 with a dual T1/PRI interface. After the testing is successful, Gloria will install the routers in their intended locations. To begin, Gloria decided to test the ISDN BRI connection between the two Cisco 2503 routers. To do this is a lab setting, she acquired a Teltone ISDN Simulator, which gave the necessary BRI services.

Project 6.1

You need to configure two Cisco 2503 routers for ISDN BRI service and have them successfully communicate with each other using ping.

1. Set up the Cisco 2503s and Teltone ISDN simulator as shown in Figure 6.6.

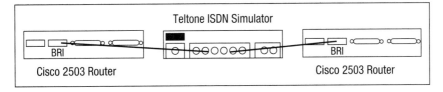

Figure 6.6   Cisco routers connected to a Teltone ISDN simulator.

2. At RouterA, enter the privilege Exec mode to get the prompt RouterA#

3. Enter **Router# config t**

4. Enter **Router(config)# hostname RouterA**

5. Enter **RouterA(config)# username RouterB password 7 030752180500**

6. Enter **RouterA(config)# isdn switch-type basic-ni1**

7. Enter **RouterA(config)# interface Serial0/0**

8. Enter **RouterA(config-if) no ip address**

9. Press Ctrl+Z.

10. Enter **Router(config)# interface BRI0/0**

11. Enter **Router(config-if)# ip address 196.1.1.1 255.255.255.0**

12. Enter **Router(config-if)# encapsulation ppp**

13. Enter **Router(config-if)# isdn spid1 5101 8995101**

14. Enter **Router(config-if)# isdn spid2 5102 8995102**

15. Enter **Router(config-if)# dialer idle-timeout 90**

16. Enter **Router(config-if)# dialer map ip 196.1.1.2 name RouterB broadcast 8995201**

17. Enter **Router(config-if)# dialer load-threshold 1**

18. Enter **Router(config-if)# dialer-group 1**

19. Enter **Router(config-if)# no fair-queue**

20. Enter **Router(config-if)# ppp authentication chap**

21. Enter **Router(config-if)# ppp multilink**

22. Press Ctrl+Z.

23. Enter **Router(config)# no ip classless**

24. Enter **Router(config)# dialer-list 1 protocol ip permit**

25. At RouterB, enter the privilege Exec mode to get the prompt RouterB#

26. Enter **RouterB# config t**

27. Enter **RouterB(config)# hostname RouterB**

28. Enter **RouterB(config)# username RouterA password 7 030752180500**

29. Enter **RouterB(config)# isdn switch-type basic-ni1**

30. Enter **RouterB(config)# interface BRI0/0**

31. Enter **RouterB(config-if)# ip address 196.1.1.2 255.255.255.0**

32. Enter **RouterB(config-if)# encapsulation ppp**

33. Enter **RouterB(config-if)# isdn spid1 5201 8995201**

34. Enter **RouterB(config-if)# isdn spid2 5202 8995202**

35. Enter **RouterB(config-if)# dialer idle-timeout 90**

36. Enter **RouterB(config-if)# dialer map ip 196.1.1.1 name RouterA**

Note: Because the second router is not initiating calls, it does not need the dial string.

37. Enter **RouterB(config-if)# dialer-group 1**

38. Enter **RouterB(config-if)# no fair-queue**

39. Enter **RouterB(config-if)# ppp authentication chap**

40. Enter **RouterB(config-if)# ppp multilink**

41. Press Ctrl+Z.

42. Enter **RouterB(config)# no ip classless**

43. Enter **RouterB(config)# dialer-list 1 protocol ip permit**

44. Press Ctrl+Z.

Verify ISDN BRI connection:

45. Enter **RouterB#ping 196.1.1.1**

46. Enter **RouterB#show isdn status**

47. Enter **RouterB#show interface bri0**

48. Enter **RouterB#show interface bri0 1**

49. Enter **RouterB#show dialer**

50. Enter **RouterB#show ppp multilink**

Now that Gloria successfully connected two Cisco 2503 routers with an ISDN connection and verified that connection, her next task was to connect one Cisco 2503 (BRI) to the new central site, AS5200 router (PRI). In order to produce an ISDN BRI-to-PRI connection, Gloria acquired an Adtran 800 ISDN Simulator.

6

Project 6.2

You need to configure one Cisco 2503 to connect to one Cisco AS5200 using BRI to PRI ISDN. You will be changing the configuration on RouterA, one of the Cisco 2503 routers, and some of RouterA configuration commands will be entered a second time.

1. Set up the Cisco 2505 router, the Cisco AS5200, and the Adtran 800 as shown in Figure 6.7.

2. At RouterA, enter the privilege Exec mode to get the prompt RouterA#

3. Enter **Router(config)# hostname RouterA**

4. Enter **Router(config)# username AS5200 password cisco**

5. Enter **Router(config)# isdn switch-type basic-ni1**

6. Enter **Router(config)# interface BRI0/0**

7. Enter **Router(config-if)# ip address 196.1.1.1 255.255.255.0**

8. Enter **Router(config-if)# encapsulation ppp**

9. Enter **Router(config-if)# isdn spid1 8995101 5101**

10. Enter **Router(config-if)# isdn spid2 8995102 5102**

11. Enter **Router(config-if)# dialer idle-timeout 30**

12. Enter **Router(config-if)# dialer map ip 196.1.1.7 name RouterB broadcast 8991000**

13. Enter **Router(config-if)# dialer load-threshold 1**

14. Enter **Router(config-if)# dialer-group 1**

15. Enter **Router(config-if)# no fair-queue**

16. Enter **Router(config-if)# ppp authentication chap**

17. Enter **Router(config-if)# ppp multilink**

18. Press Ctrl+Z.

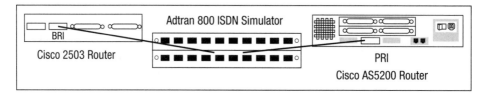

Figure 6.7 Cisco routers connected to Adtran 800 ISDN simulator.

19. Enter **Router(config)# no ip classless**

20. Enter **Router(config)# dialer-list 1 protocol ip permit**

21. At the Cisco AS5200, enter the privilege EXEC mode to get to the Router5200# prompt.

22. Enter **Router5200# config t**

23. Enter **Router5200(config)# hostname Router5200**

24. Enter **Router5200(config)# username RouterA password cisco2**

25. Enter **Router5200(config)# isdn switch-type primary-5ess**

26. Enter **Router5200(config)# controller T1 0**

27. Enter **Router5200(config-if)# framing esf**

28. Enter **Router5200(config-if)# linecode b8zs**

29. Enter **Router5200(config-if)# pri-group timeslots 1–24**

30. Press Ctrl+Z.

31. Enter **Router5200(config)# interface Serial0:23**

32. Enter **Router5200(config-if)# ip address 196.1.1.7 255.255.255.0**

33. Enter **Router5200(config-if)# encapsulation ppp**

34. Enter **Router5200(config-if)# no ip mroute-cache**

35. Enter **Router5200(config-if)# isdn incoming-voice modem**

36. Enter **Router5200(config-if)# dialer idle-timeout 900**

37. Enter **Router5200(config-if)# dialer-group 1**

38. Enter **Router5200(config-if)# no fair-queue**

39. Enter **Router5200(config-if)# no cdp enable**

40. Enter **Router5200(config-if)# ppp authentication chap**

41. Enter **Router5200(config-if)# ppp multilink**

42. Press Ctrl+Z.

43. Enter **Router5200(config)# interface Dialer1**

44. Enter **Router5200(config-if)# no ip address**

45. Enter **Router5200(config-if)# encapsulation ppp**

46. Enter **Router5200(config-if)# dialer in-band**

47. Enter **Router5200(config-if)# dialer idle-timeout 900**

48. Enter **Router5200(config-if)# dialer-group 1**

49. Enter **Router5200(config-if)# no fair-queue**

50. Enter **Router5200(config-if)# ppp authentication chap**

51. Press Ctrl+Z.

52. Enter **Router5200(config)# no ip classless**

53. Enter **Router5200(config)# ip route 192.1.5.0 255.255.255.0 196.1.1.1**

54. Enter **Router5200(config)# dialer-list 1 protocol ip permit**

55. Press Ctrl+Z.

Verify the ISDN BRI to PRI connection:

56. Enter **RouterA#ping 196.1.1.7**

57. Enter **Router5200show isdn status**

58. Enter **Router5200#show interface bri0**

59. Enter **Router5200#show interface bri0 1**

60. Enter **Router5200#show dialer**

61. Enter **Router5200#show isdn service**

62. Enter **Router5200#show controller t0**

63 Enter **Router5200#show ppp multilink**

CHAPTER SEVEN

Configuring Dialer Profiles and Rotary Groups for DDR

After completing this chapter, you will be able to:

✓ Explain the purpose of and describe the components of dialer profiles

✓ Explain the purpose of and describe the components of rotary groups

✓ Compare dialer profiles to rotary groups

✓ Configure rotary groups for ISDN and asynchronous connections

✓ Configure dialer profiles for ISDN and asynchronous connections

In this chapter, you will learn how dialer profile groups and dialer rotary groups can enhance Integrated Services Digital Network (ISDN) and dial-on-demand routing (DDR). Up to now, you have learned how to configure ISDN and DDR on an access server where only one identified physical interface can call a single destination or multiple locations using a **dialer-map** command for each destination. This means that each physical interface is reserved for certain calls and cannot be used for others. This is not as efficient as dialer rotary groups and dialer profile groups, which allocate physical interfaces in a flexible manner.

Before discussing dialer rotary groups and dialer profile groups, let's review the **dialer-map** command. The **dialer map** statements actually attach the next hop address to the telephone number. If a match is not found between a packet's next hop address and the **dialer map** statement as defined for an interface, the packet is dropped. The next hop address for a packet is determined based on routing information. In the following example, packets received for a host on network 142.252.49.0 are routed to a next hop address of 140.224.15.2 and mapped to telephone number 555-1212:

```
dialer map ip 140.224.15.2 name longdist speed 56 1415551212
```

Each **dialer-map** command includes its own dial string and next hop address. In one physical interface, you can have several **dialer-map** statements, and each statement is used for a different destination. However, the single physical interface cannot be configured to handle different communication parameters such as authentication settings like PAP or CHAP, and different idle-timeout settings. All of the destinations that are handled by the single physical interface would have to use the same communication parameters.

Dialer Interface

Now it's time for you to be introduced to the dialer interface, which is used for both dialer rotary groups and dialer profile groups. In order to have a separate set of parameters associated with a particular called destination, you will need to configure a logical interface called the *dialer interface*, which is written as **interface dialer** as a command. The dialer interface will contain the communication parameters, whereas associated physical interfaces will no longer include them. Instead, the physical interface will be connected to a logical interface and receive the necessary parameters on a call-by-call basis. Using the dialer interface allows you to specify one set of **dialer maps** that can be applied to multiple physical lines. The dialer interface can be created using one of two methods for associating physical interfaces (that have no communication parameters) to logical interfaces (where each logical interface has a different set of communication parameters).

The two methods for connecting physical interfaces to a logical interface are rotary groups and dialer profiles. Rotary groups use the **dialer rotary-group** statement to combine several physical interfaces to one dialer interface, and dialer profiles use the **dialer pool-member** statement to combine several interfaces to one dialer interface. These two statements are equivalent. Both methods are similar, but used in different ways. Both the rotary group and the dialer profile allow you to group multiple physical interfaces into a single pool or group and apply a configuration to each pool or group. When you use rotary groups, a physical interface is committed to only one logical interface. However, with dialer profiles, each physical interface can reside in multiple pools. Dialer profiles are best used when you have multiple physical interfaces like multiple BRIs on a Cisco 4000 and need to apply different configurations on a per-call basis for incoming and outgoing calls. Although rotary groups can be used for incoming calls, it is used mostly for dialing out.

Both methods can use the **map-class** to apply configurations on a per-group basis, such as different idle time-outs for different groups. The **map-class** command is used mostly for dialing out. The **map-class** command, which is applied at the global configuration mode, is used to define a class of shared configuration parameters for outgoing calls from an ISDN interface.

Dialer Rotary Groups

When you use a single interface with multiple **dialer maps**, competition for the interface can occur. This conflict starts a fast-idle timer that causes lines to remain connected for a shorter idle time than usual, allowing other destinations to shut down the first call and use the interface. Dialer rotary groups prevent contention by creating a set of interfaces to draw from to be used for dialing out. Instead of statically assigning an interface to a destination, dialer rotary groups allow dynamic allocation of interfaces to telephone numbers. When a call is placed, the rotary group is searched for an interface that is not in use to place the call. It is not until all of the interfaces in the rotary group are in use that the fast-idle timer is started.

Rotary groups can be used in a hub-and-spoke topology, in which a central site is connected to two or more remote sites. In this design, the remote sites communicate only with the central site directly and do not call any of the other remote sites. The central site has several interfaces that map to the remote sites. These interfaces are placed into a rotary group. A rotary group allows several sites to share several interfaces without dedicating an interface to each site. When a rotary group is used for placing calls, a free interface is selected out of all of the physical interfaces in the rotary group. When a rotary group is used for incoming calls, the incoming call can be received by any of the physical interfaces, and packets will still be routed correctly. If an interface is already connected, incoming or outgoing calls can be received or placed by the next available interface in the rotary group.

Creating Rotary Groups

Creating a dialer interface is the first step in defining a dialer rotary group. Although a dialer interface is not a physical interface, all of the configuration commands that can be specified for a physical interface can be used for a dialer interface. The commands used under the **interface dialer** command are identical to those used for a physical serial interface when configuring a single interface. When configuring a rotary group, you will place each BRI interface in a rotary group. You do this by entering **interface dialer** with a group number at the global configuration mode. For example, **interface dialer1** creates a rotary group with 1 for a group number. Next, you use the **dialer rotary-group** command in the physical interface to include that physical interface in the rotary group. For example, Listing 7.2 shows a configuration for a Cisco 3620. This configuration makes the PRIs a member of the rotary group 0 by using the **dialer rotary-group** command.

Besides the **dialer map** statement, you can use the **dialer-string** command to specify the phone number to dial when placing a call from an interface to a specific destination. If the **dialer-string** command is specified without a dialer group command with access lists defined, dialing will never happen.

Before a packet is sent out to the dialer interface, DDR checks to determine whether the packet is "interesting" or "uninteresting." DDR then checks the dialer map. Next, all of the physical interfaces in the rotary group are checked to determine whether they are connected to the telephone number. If an appropriate interface is found, the packet is sent out to that physical interface. If an interface is not found and the packet is deemed interesting, the rotary group is scanned for an available physical interface. The first available interface found is used to place a call to the telephone number.

The routing section for a configuration using rotary groups has not changed from how you would configure static routing for a single interface. If you could examine the routing table using the **show ip route** command, you would see that the output interface for packets sent to this subnet is **interface dialer 0**. If you use dynamic routing, in which two of the remote sites communicate with each other via the central site, the **no ip split-horizon** command is required and the **passive-interface** command must be removed.

Dialer Rotary Group Applications

Dialer rotary groups can be used with ISDN and asynchronous calls for either outgoing or incoming calls. However, they are more likely to be used for making outgoing calls. The following sections describe four different scenarios in which dialer rotary groups are used.

ISDN Rotary Group Used for Incoming Calls (Dialing in)

Listing 7.1 displays a common configuration for a Cisco 1604 remote office router dialing in to a Cisco 3620 access router located at a central site. The Cisco 3620 is not set up to dial out to the Cisco 1604. The dialer rotary groups used in this example belong to Cisco 3620 and are used for incoming calls. ISDN digital calls are supported in this scenario, and no analog modem calls are supported. All calls are initiated by the remote router on an as-needed basis. The following configurations for the Cisco 1604 and Cisco 3620 (in Listing 7.2) use the IP unnumbered address configuration and Multilink PPP. The dial-load threshold feature brings up the second B channel when the first B channel exceeds a certain limit. Static routes are used and no routing protocol is configured. A default static route is configured on the Cisco 1604, which points back to the central site. The central site also has a static route that points back to the remote LAN. Static route configurations assume that you have only one LAN segment at each remote office. The Cisco 3620 access router has one 2-port PRI network module installed in slot 1 and one 1-port Ethernet network module installed in slot 0.

These listings contain a few statements that need to be explained. The statement **isdn incoming-voice modem** within the Cisco 3620 configuration is used to configure the D channel to switch incoming analog calls to the modem, where incoming voice calls are forwarded to the devices connected to the telephone ports.

The statement **dialer load-threshold 100 either** on the 1604 router allows both incoming and out-going calls to activate the second B channel. The statements **ppp authentication chap pap callin** and **ppp authentication chap pap dialin** enable PAP or CHAP on incoming calls only.

Listing 7.1   Cisco 1604.

```
hostname remotelan1
enable secret cisco
username NAS password dialpass
username admin password cisco
isdn switch-type basic-5ess
interface Ethernet0
 ip address 10.2.1.1 255.255.255.0
interface BRI0
 ip unnumbered Ethernet0
 encapsulation ppp
 dialer map ip 10.1.1.10 name NAS 5551234
 dialer load-threshold 100 either
 dialer-group 1
 no fair-queue
 ppp authentication chap pap callin
 ppp multilink
```

```
ip classless
ip route 0.0.0.0 0.0.0.0 10.1.1.10
dialer-list 1 protocol ip permit
line con 0
line vty 0 4
 login local
end
```

Listing 7.2 Cisco 3620.

```
hostname NAS
aaa new-model
aaa authentication login default local
aaa authentication login console enable
aaa authentication login vty local
aaa authentication login dialin local
aaa authentication ppp default local
aaa authentication ppp dialin if-needed local
enable secret cisco
username admin password cisco
username remotelan1 password dialpass
async-bootp dns-server 10.1.3.1 10.1.3.2
isdn switch-type primary-5ess
controller T1 1/0
 framing esf
 clock source line
 linecode b8zs
 pri-group timeslots 1-24
controller T1 1/1
 framing esf
 clock source line
 linecode b8zs
 pri-group timeslots 1-24
interface Loopback0
 ip address 10.1.2.254 255.255.255.0
interface Ethernet 0/0
 ip address 10.1.1.10 255.255.255.0
 ip summary address eigrp 10 10.1.2.0 255.255.255.0
interface Serial 1/0:23
 no ip address
 encapsulation ppp
 isdn incoming-voice modem
 dialer rotary-group 0
 no fair-queue
 no cdp enable
interface Serial 1/1:23
 no ip address
 encapsulation ppp
```

```
 isdn incoming-voice modem
 dialer rotary-group 0
 no fair-queue
 no cdp enable
interface Dialer0
 ip unnumbered Loopback0
 no ip mroute-cache
 encapsulation ppp
 peer default ip address pool dialin_pool
 dialer in-band
 dialer group 1
 no fair-queue
 no cdp enable
 ppp authentication chap pap dialin
 ppp multilink
router eigrp 10
 network 10.0.0.0
 passive-interface Dialer0
 default-metric 64 100 250 100 1500
 redistribute static
 no auto-summary
ip local pool dialin_pool 10.1.2.1 10.1.2.50
ip default-gateway 10.1.1.1
ip route 10.2.1.1 255.255.255.255 Dialer0
ip route 10.2.1.0 255.255.255.0 10.2.1.1
ip classless
dialer-list 1 protocol ip permit
line con 0
 login authentication console
line aux 0
 login authentication console
line vty 0 4
 login authentication vty
 transport input telnet rlogin
end
```

ISDN Rotary Group Dialing Out

The following is a sample configuration for three BRIs in a rotary group, which are involved in making outgoing calls. The dialer interface, called Dialer2, contains four **dialer map** statements, which can initiate calls if interesting traffic is directed towards one of the listed IP address destinations. When interesting traffic turns on DDR, the dialer interface hunts for an interface that is not in use.

```
interface BRI0
no ip address
encapsulation ppp
dialer rotary-group 2
```

```
interface BRI1
no ip address
encapsulation ppp
dialer rotary-group 2
interface BRI2
no ip address
encapsulation ppp
dialer rotary-group 2
interface Dialer2
ip address 6.1.1.3 255.255.255.0
encapsulation ppp
dialer in-band
dialer map ip 6.1.1.1 name dallas 1890
dialer map ip 6.1.1.2 name austin 1885
dialer map ip 6.1.1.4 name raleigh 1886
dialer map ip 6.1.1.19 1889
dialer-group 1
ppp authentication chap

dialer-list 1 protocol ip permit
```

Asynchronous Rotary Group Used for Outgoing Calls

The configuration of this central site access router includes the following commands for configuring dialer rotary group 2. Below the configuration are explanations for several significant statements.

```
hostname CENTRAL_A
enable-password as5100
username RouterB password 7 071C2D4359
username RouterC password 7 0448070918
chat-script CALL666 ABORT ERROR ABORT BUSY TIMEOUT 30
  "" "ATDT\T" "CONNECT" \c
chat-script Romio TIMEOUT 40 "name:" "CENTRAL" "word:" "secret"
chat-script usrv32bis "" "AT&F1S0=1&d2" "OK" ""
interface loopback 0
 ip address 172.16.254.3 255.255.255.255
 interface loopback 1
 ip address 172.16.1.1 255.255.255.0
 interface ethernet 0
 ip address 172.19.1.8 255.255.0.0
 interface serial 0
 no ip address
 shutdown
 interface async 1
 ip unnumbered loopback 1
 encapsulation ppp
```

```
   async dynamic address
   async dynamic routing
   async mode interactive
   dialer in-band
   dialer rotary-group 2
...
interface async 16
 ip unnumbered loopback 1
 encapsulation ppp
 async dynamic address
 async dynamic routing
 async mode interactive
 dialer in-band
 dialer rotary-group 2
interface dialer 2
 ip unnumbered loopback 1
 encapsulation ppp
 dialer in-band
 dialer idle-timeout 60
 dialer map ip 172.16.2.1 name RouterB modem-script
                     CALL666 system-script Romio 5551234
 dialer map ip 172.16.121.1 name RouterC modem-script
                     CALL666 system-script Romio 5555678
 dialer-group 3
 dialer wait-for-carrier 60

ip route 172.16.0.0 255.255.0.0 Dialer2
ip route 172.16.2.0 255.255.255.0 172.16.2.1 200
ip route 172.16.2.1 255.255.255.255 Dialer2
ip route 172.16.121.0 255.255.255.0 172.16.121.1 200
ip route 172.16.121.1 255.255.255.255 Dialer2

dialer-list 3 list 101
access-list 101 deny udp 0.0.0.0 255.255.255.255 0.0.0.0
                     255.255.255.255 eq 520
access-list 101 permit ip 0.0.0.0 255.255.255.255 0.0.0.0
                     255.255.255.255
```

The interface dialer global configuration command defines dialer rotary group 2. Any interface configuration commands that are applied to a dialer rotary group apply to the physical interfaces that are its members. When the router's configuration includes multiple destinations, any of the interfaces in the dialer rotary group can be used to place outgoing calls. The **ip unnumbered** interface configuration command specifies that the IP address of loopback interface 1 is to be used as the source address for any IP packets that dialer rotary group 2 might generate. The **dialer idle-timeout** interface configuration command causes a disconnect if 60 seconds elapse without any interesting traffic.

7

The configuration includes a **dialer map** interface configuration command for each remote router that the central site access router might dial. The IP address is the next-hop address of the destination that is to be called, and the **name** keyword specifies the hostname of the remote router that is to be called. The **modem-script** keyword specifies that the CALL666 chat script is to be used, and the **system-script** keyword specifies that the Romio chat script is to be used. The last value specified by the **dialer map** command is the telephone number for the remote router. Because the **dialer map** command does not specify the **broadcast** keyword, Routing Information Protocol (RIP) updates are not sent to the remote sites.

Within the interface dialer 2, the **dialer-group** interface configuration command defines "interesting" packets to be those packets defined by the corresponding **dial-list** command. In this case, access list 101 defines RIP as uninteresting. (RIP uses User Datagram Protocol [UDP] port 520.) All other packets are defined as interesting. Static routes are used to the remote sites. The first **ip route** global configuration command creates a static route for major network 172.16.0.0 and assigns it to the dialer interface 2. The first **ip route** command is followed by pairs of static routes, one pair for each remote site. In unnumbered IP environments, two static routes are required for each remote site. One static route points to the next hop on the **dialer map**. This static route is required for unnumbered interfaces. Note that there is no need to make this a floating static route.

The configuration of the individual interfaces and Internet Protocol (IP) addresses is straightforward. The IP address for each interface is provided. The **dialer in-band** command enables DDR and V.25bis dialing on a serial interface. You need to use the **in-band** statement when using a serial interface with DDR. V.25bis is an ITU-T standard for in-band signaling to bit-synchronous data communications equipment (DCE) devices. The **dialer wait-for-carrier-time** command is set to 60 seconds. When using V.25bis, the router does not parse any responses it receives from the DCE. Instead, the router depends on the modem's Carrier Detect (CD) signal to indicate that a call has been connected. If the modem's CD signal is not activated before the time allotted with the **dialer wait-for-carrier-time** command, the router assumes that the call has failed and disconnects the line. Because the calls are international, and thus take longer to connect than local calls, the **wait-for-carrier-time** is set to 60 seconds. Even for local calls, analog modems can take 20 to 30 seconds to synchronize to each other, including the time to dial and answer. The **dialer-group** command is used to identify each interface with a dialer list set. The **dialer-list** command associates each interface with access lists that determine which packets are "interesting" versus "uninteresting" for an interface.

Asynchronous Rotary Group Used for Dialing Out

In the following example, we have a modem PPP link between a Cisco 2610 router and Cisco 2509 router via asynchronous ports. The 2610 dials into the 2509, and brings up the link.

```
Cisco 2610
hostname notthill
chat-script brooklyn ABORT ERROR ABORT BUSY ABORT
"NO ANSWER" "" "ATDT\T" TIMEOUT 60 CONNECT \c
modemcap entry netcomm:FD=&F:AA=S0=0:CD=&C1:DTR=&D3:NEC=E0:NRS=Q1
interface Ethernet0/0
 ip address 192.168.3.1 255.255.255.0
 ip broadcast-address 192.168.3.255
 no cdp enable
interface Serial1/0                          ! ISDN link - ignore this
 ip address 192.168.2.2 255.255.255.0
 encapsulation ppp
 no ip mroute-cache
 no fair-queue
 ppp authentication pap callin
interface Serial1/2
 physical-layer async
 description connected to brooklyn
 no ip address
 ip tcp header-compression passive
 encapsulation ppp
 keepalive 10
 dialer in-band
 dialer rotary-group 1
 async default routing
 async mode dedicated
interface Dialer1
 ip unnumbered Ethernet0/0
 ip tcp header-compression passive
 encapsulation ppp
 dialer in-band
 dialer idle-timeout 2147483
 dialer map snapshot 1 name brooklyn modem-script
 brooklyn broadcast 91234567
 dialer map ip 192.168.6.1 name brooklyn modem-script
brooklyn broadcast 91234567
 dialer hold-queue 10
 dialer-group 1
 snapshot client 15 360 suppress-statechange-update dialer
 pulse-time 3
router rip
 network 192.168.2.0
 network 192.168.3.0
ip default-gateway 192.168.2.1
ip classless
dialer-list 1 protocol ip permit
```

7

```
line 35
 modem InOut
 modem autoconfigure type netcomm
 transport input all
 speed 115200
 flowcontrol hardware
no scheduler allocate
end


Cisco 2509
hostname brooklyn
chat-script default ABORT ERROR ABORT BUSY ABORT
"NO ANSWER" "" "ATDT\T" TIMEOUT 60 CONNECT \c
modemcap entry netcomm:FD=&F:AA=S0=1:CD=&C1:DTR=&D3:NEC=E0:NRS=Q1
interface Loopback0
 ip address 192.168.6.1 255.255.255.0
 ip broadcast-address 192.168.6.255
interface Async1
 description connected to notthill
 ip unnumbered Dialer1
 ip tcp header-compression passive
 encapsulation ppp
 keepalive 10
 async default routing
 async mode dedicated
 dialer in-band
 dialer rotary-group 1
interface Dialer1
 ip unnumbered Loopback0
 ip tcp header-compression passive
 encapsulation ppp
 dialer in-band
 dialer idle-timeout 2147483
 dialer map snapshot 1 name notthill broadcast
 dialer map ip 192.168.3.1 name notthill modem-script default broadcast
 dialer-group 1
 snapshot server 15 dialer
 pulse-time 3
router rip
 network 192.168.6.0
ip default-gateway 192.168.3.1
ip classless
dialer-list 1 protocol ip permit
line 1
 modem InOut
 modem autoconfigure type default
 transport input all
```

```
stopbits 1
speed 38400
flowcontrol hardware
end
```

Rotary Groups Using **Map-Class**

The **map-class** configuration portion of DDR can be used with both rotary groups and dialer profiles. Although the map class configuration is optional, you can specify special characteristics for different types of calls on a per-call-destination basis. For example, you can specify a different speed for some ISDN calls than for other ISDN calls. A particular map class is tied to a specific call destination by the use of the **map-class** name in the **dialer-string** command or **dialer map** command with the **class** keyword. You can use the **map-class dialer** *class-name* command to specify a **map-class** and enter the **map-class** configuration mode. Most often used is the **dialer isdn speed 56** command, which specifies an ISDN bit rate of 56Kbps for use in the **map-class**. You can set the speed to 56; 64 is the default value.

To create a map class and define its optional characteristics, complete the following tasks beginning in global configuration mode:

1. Define a map class and enter **map-class** configuration mode: **map-class dialer** *class-name*

2. Define the accepting speed: **isdn speed [56|64]**

3. Define the fast idle timer value: **dialer fast-idle** *seconds*

4. Define the idle time before the calls in this map class are disconnected: **dialer idle-timeout** *seconds*

5. Define the length of time to wait for a carrier when dialing out to the dial string associated with the map class: **dialer wait-for-carrier-time** *seconds*

6. Define the length of time an interface stays down after a call has completed or failed before it is available to dial again: **dialer enable-timeout**

7. Specify the bit rate used on the B channel associated with a specified map class: **dialer isdn [speed** *speed***]**

*Note: The **speed** parameter is used only with 56Kbps line speed; 64 is not a valid option.*

Here is a configuration example with **map-class**:

```
hostname Atlanta
enable secret cisco
isdn switch-type basic-ni1
interface Ethernet0
 ip address 200.200.200.1 255.255.255.0
interface BRI0
```

```
      no ip address
      encapsulation ppp
      dialer rotary-group 0
      isdn spid1 014045551111000 5551111
      isdn spid2 014045552222000 5552222
      no fair-queue
      no cdp enable
     interface Dialer0
      ip unnumbered Ethernet0
      encapsulation ppp
      dialer in-band
      dialer idle-timeout 300
      dialer string 14085553333 class 56K
      dialer hold-queue 10
      dialer load-threshold 200 either
      dialer-group 1
      no fair-queue
      no cdp enable
      ppp authentication pap callin
      ppp pap sent-username Atlanta password gocisco1
      ppp multilink
     ip classless
     ip route 0.0.0.0 0.0.0.0 Dialer0
     ip http server

     map-class dialer 56K
      dialer isdn speed 56
      dialer idle-timeout 180
      dialer fast-idle 30
      dialer enable-timeout 10
      dialer wait-for-carrier-time 60

     dialer-list 1 protocol ip permit
     line con 0
      password console
      login
     line aux 0
     line vty 0 4
      password telnet
      login
```

Dialer Profiles

As with rotary groups, you can use dialer profiles to configure the router's physical interfaces apart from the logical configuration with parameters needed for making a call. In addition, these logical and physical configurations can be dynamically bound together on a per-call basis. The dialer profile becomes the recognized interface by the destination and not the serial or asynchronous interface, and all calls going to or from a destination subnetwork use the same dialer profile.

A dialer profile consists of the following elements:

➤ A dialer interface configuration with one or more dial strings, each used to reach a specific destination subnetwork.

➤ A dialer map class defining all the characteristics for any call to the specified dial string (telephone number). Although it is optional, it is typically used to specify ISDN speeds. The dialer map class can also be used with rotary groups, but is more often used with dialer profiles. You can use the **map-class dialer** *class-name* command to specify a map-class and enter the map-class configuration mode. In the example under "Dialer Profile Example 1" in this chapter, the **dialer isdn speed 56** command specifies an ISDN bit rate of 56Kbps for use in the map-class. You can set the speed to 56; 64 is the default value. Several other map-class commands are available as well.

➤ A dialer pool of physical interfaces to be used by the dialer interface. This is how the dialer interface goes out to collect physical interfaces as members. The physical interfaces in a dialer pool are ordered according to priority. A dialer pool can also have more than one dialer interface, but this is an advanced feature.

As displayed in Figure 7.1, the dialer interface uses one group of physical interfaces called a *dialer pool*. However, one physical interface can belong to multiple dialer pools. If you use dialer profiles to configure dial-on-demand routing (DDR), physical interfaces are configured only for encapsulation and the identification of the dialer pool or dialer pools to which the interface belongs. The other characteristics used for making calls, which would have been configured under the physical interface if there were no dialer interfaces, are defined in the dialer map of the dialer interface. If needed there is a method for adding additional parameters in an extended optional **map-class**. The **map-class** acts as an extension to the dialer map containing further call parameters.

A dialer interface configuration is a group of settings the router uses to connect to a remote network. One dialer interface can use multiple dial strings (telephone numbers). Each dial string can be associated with its own dialer map-class. The dialer **map-class** defines all the characteristics for any call to the specified dial string. For example, the dialer **map-class** for one destination might specify the amount of idle time as 4 seconds before calls are disconnected, and the **map-class** for a different destination might specify 12 seconds.

Dialer Profiles Illustrated

All configuration settings specific to the destination go into the dialer interface configuration. Multiple dial strings can be specified for the same dialer interface.

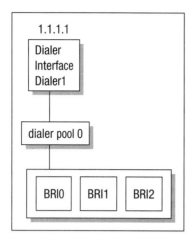

Figure 7.1 Dialer pool connected to dialer interface.

A dialer string can be associated with different per-call parameters defined with each dialer **map-class**. As mentioned before, the dialer **map-class** defines specific characteristics for any call to the specified dial string. Another example would be the **map-class** for one destination might specify ISDN speed 56Kbps. The **map-class** for a different destination might specify ISDN speed 64Kbps. Each dialer interface uses a dialer pool. A dialer pool is a group of one or more physical interfaces. A physical interface can belong to multiple dialer pools. Contention for a specific physical interface is resolved with a configurable priority.

Note: The biggest difference between dialer profiles and rotary groups is that a physical interface can be associated with only one rotary group, but can be associated with multiple dialer interfaces.

Dialer profiles currently support PPP and HDLC encapsulation on the physical interface. All other settings are part of a logical configuration applied to the physical interface as needed for specific calls. When dialer profiles are used to configure DDR, a physical interface has no configuration settings except encapsulation and the dialer pools to which the interface belongs.

In order to avert contention within a dialer pool, you can prioritize the dialer pool's physical interfaces. In Figure 7.2, the BRI1 interface is a member of all three dialer pools, but it has a lesser priority than BRI0 in dialer pool 1.

The **dialer pool-member** *number* command is used to assign a physical interface to a dialer pool. An interface can be assigned to multiple dialer pools by using this interface configuration command to specify several dialer pool numbers. In addition, you can use the priority option of this command to set the interface's priority within a dialer pool.

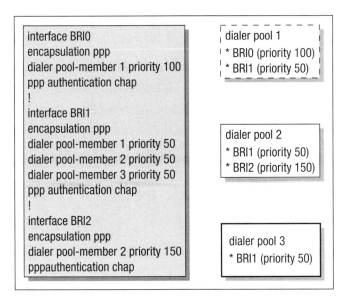

Figure 7.2   Physical interfaces with multiple dialer pool memberships.

You can configure any number of dialer interfaces for a router. Each dialer interface is the complete configuration for a destination. Use the **dialer remote-name** *user-name* command to specify the remote destination. This is the remote router name passed for authentication. The **dialer string** command has been modified to support map classes. Use the **dialer pool** *number* command to bind a dialer interface to a dialer pool that has been configured with the **dialer remote-name** command. The **dialer-group** command is used to reference a **dialer-list**. The **dialer list** *protocol* command specifies an **access-list** number or a protocol that defines "interesting" packets to trigger a call.

Just the dialer interfaces are visible to the upper layer protocols, not the physical interfaces making up the dialing pool. Because one dialer interface maps to one destination, addressing, **access-lists**, and static routes can be utilized on a per-destination basis, regardless of which interface actually makes the call.

Configuring Dialer Profiles

To configure a dialer interface, complete the following tasks beginning in global configuration mode with the first command:

1. Create a dialer interface: (**interface dialer** *number*)

2. Configure the IP address and mask of the dialer interface as a node in the destination network to be called: (**ip address** *address mask*)

3. Configure PPP encapsulation: (**encapsulation ppp**)

4. Configure the remote router CHAP authentication name: (**dialer remote-name** *name*)

5. Configure the remote destination to call and the map class that defines characteristics for calls to this destination: (**dialer string** *string* **class** *class-name*)

6. Configure the dialing pool to use for calls to this destination (**dialer pool** *number*)

7. Assign the dialer interface to a dialer group (**dialer-group** *number*)

8. Configure an **access-list** by list number or by protocol and list number to define the "interesting" packets that can trigger a call (**dialer-list** *dialer-group* **protocol** *protocol-name* {**permit** | **deny** | **list** *access-list-number*})

Configure the physical interfaces:

9. Configure the physical interface: **interface** *type number*

10. Enable PPP encapsulation: **encapsulation ppp**

11. Configure PPP CHAP authentication if you also want to receive calls on this interface: **ppp authentication chap**

12. Put the interface in a dialing pool and, optionally, assign the interface a priority. For ISDN interfaces, you can also optionally specify the minimum number of channels reserved and maximum number of channels that can be for this dialing pool: **dialer pool-member** *number* **[priority** *priority*]

```
dialer pool-member number [priority priority]
  [min-link minimum] [max-link maximum]1
```

13. If you want to put the interface in additional dialing pools: **dialer pool-member** *number* **[priority** *priority*] or **dialer pool-member** *number* **[priority** *priority*] **[min-link** *minimum*] **[max-link** *maximum*]

You can use a combination of synchronous, serial, BRIs, or PRIs with dialer pools. The **dialer pool-member** optional command parameters include:

➤ **dialer pool-member** *number*—Sets the dialer pooling number. This is a decimal value from 1 to 255.

➤ **priority** *priority*—Sets the priority of the physical interface within the dialer pool. Interfaces with a priority number are selected first for dial out. This is a decimal value from 1 to 255.

➤ **mix-link** *minimum*—Sets the minimum number of ISDN B channels on an interface reserved for this dialer pool. This is a number from 1 to 255.

➤ **max-link** *maximum*—Sets the maximum number of ISDN B channels on an interface reserved for this dialer pool. This is a number from 1 to 255.

Dialer Profile Example 1

The dialer profile can be used for making and receiving calls. In the following example, a central site router will be communicating with remote site routers. This central site can place or receive calls from three remote sites over four ISDN BRI lines. Because each remote site is on a different IP subnet and has different bandwidth requirements, the central site configuration will need three dialer interfaces and three dialer pools.

Notice that BRI 0 has a higher priority than BRI 1 when they are both in dialer pool 1, BRI 2 has a higher priority than BRI 1 when they are both in dialer pool 2, and BRI 3 has the highest priority in dialer pool 2. BRI 1, which uses the **min-link** parameter, has a reserved channel in dialer pool 3; the channel remains inactive until BRI 1 uses it to place calls.

```
interface Dialer1
 ip address 10.6.6.6 255.255.255.0
 encapsulation ppp
 dialer remote-name Smalluser
 dialer string 4540
 dialer pool 3
 dialer-group 1
interface Dialer2
 ip address 10.7.7.7 255.255.255.0
 encapsulation ppp
 dialer remote-name Mediumuser
 dialer string 5264540 class Eng
 dialer load-threshold 50 either
 dialer pool 1
 dialer-group 2
interface Dialer3
 ip address 10.8.8.8 255.255.255.0
 encapsulation ppp
 dialer remote-name Poweruser
 dialer string 4156884540 class Eng
 dialer hold-queue 10
 dialer load-threshold 80
 dialer pool 2
 dialer-group 2
map-class dialer Eng (makes calls use an ISDN speed of 56 kbps)
 isdn speed 56
interface BRI0
 encapsulation PPP
```

7

```
  dialer pool-member 1 priority 100
  ppp authentication chap
 interface BRI1
  encapsulation ppp
  dialer pool-member 1 priority 50
  dialer pool-member 2 priority 50
  dialer pool-member 3 min-link 1
  ppp authentication chap
 interface BRI2
  encapsulation ppp
  dialer pool-member 2 priority 100
  ppp authentication chap
 interface BRI3
  encapsulation ppp
  dialer pool-member 2 priority 150
  ppp authentication chap
```

Dialer Profile Example 2

The following bidirectional dial configuration runs on a Cisco AS5200. This configuration enables calls to be sent to the SOHO router and received from remote hosts
and clients.

```
hostname 5200
enable secret cisco
username async1 password cisco
username async2 password cisco

username isdn1 password cisco
username isdn2 password cisco
username DialupAdmin password cisco
isdn switch-type primary-dms100
chat-script cisco-default ABORT ERROR "" "AT" OK
"ATDT\T" TIMEOUT 60 CONNECT
controller T1 0
 framing esf
 clock source line primary
 linecode b8zs
 pri-group timeslots 1-24
controller T1 1
 framing esf
 clock source line secondary
 linecode b8zs
 pri-group timeslots 1-24
interface loopback 1
 ip address 131.108.38.40 255.255.255.128
```

```
interface loopback 2
 ip address 131.108.38.130 255.255.255.128
interface Ethernet0
 ip address 131.108.39.40 255.255.255.0
 no ip mroute-cache
 ip ospf priority 0
interface Serial0:23
 no ip address
 no ip mroute-cache
 encapsulation ppp
 isdn incoming-voice modem
 dialer pool-member 2
interface Serial1:23
 no ip address
 no ip mroute-cache
 encapsulation ppp
 isdn incoming-voice modem
 dialer pool-member 2
interface Group-Async1
 no ip address
 no ip mroute-cache
 encapsulation ppp
 async mode interactive
 dialer in-band
 dialer pool-member 1
 ppp authentication chap pap
 group-range 1 48
interface Dialer10
 ip unnumbered loopback 1
 encapsulation ppp
 peer default ip address dialin_pool
 dialer remote-name async1
 dialer string 14085268983
 dialer hold-queue 10
 dialer pool 1
 dialer-group 1
 ppp authentication pap chap callin
 ppp pap sent-username DialupAdmin password 7 07063D11542
interface Dialer11
 ip unnumbered loopback 1
 encapsulation ppp
 no peer default ip address pool
 dialer remote-name async2
 dialer string 14085262012
 dialer hold-queue 10
 dialer pool 1
```

7

```
      dialer-group 1
      ppp authentication pap chap callin
      ppp pap sent-username DialupAdmin password 7 07063D11542
      ....
   interface Dialer18
    ip unnumbered loopback 2
    encapsulation ppp
    no peer default ip address pool
    dialer remote-name isdn1
    dialer string 14085267887
    dialer hold-queue 10
    dialer pool 2
    dialer-group 1
    ppp authentication chap pap
   interface Dialer19
    ip unnumbered loopback 2
    encapsulation ppp
    no peer default ip address pool
    dialer remote-name isdn2
    dialer string 14085261591
    dialer hold-queue 10
    dialer pool 2
    dialer-group 1
    ppp authentication chap pap
      ......
   router ospf 1
    redistribute static subnets
    passive-interface Dialer1
    passive-interface Dialer2
    network 131.108.0.0 0.0.255.255 area 0
   ip local pool dialin_pool 10.1.2.1 10.1.2.50
   ip domain-name cisco.com
   ip classless
   dialer-list 1 protocol ip permit
   line con 0
    exec-timeout 0 0
   line 1 24
    no exec
    exec-timeout 0 0
    autoselect during-login
    autoselect ppp
    script dialer cisco-default
    login local
    modem InOut
    modem autoconfigure type microcom_hdms
```

```
 transport input telnet
line aux 0
line vty 0 4
 exec-timeout 60 0
 password cisco
 login
end
```

Verifying Dialer Profile Operations

You can use the **show dialer interface bri (*number*)** command for DDR statistics. Below is the output from the **show dialer interface bri0** command, which displays information in the same format as the DDR statistics on incoming and outgoing calls for a single physical interface configuration without dialer profiles or rotary groups. The fast idle timer and the wait for carrier time are displayed in the same way they would appear if the router configuration had no interface dialers. The statement "interface bound to profile Dialer2" indicates that BRI1 is a member of the dialer pool for interface dialer2. The "Dialer state is data link layer up" line in the output means that the dialer came up properly. The "physical layer up" message in the output means that the Link Control Protocol (LCP) came up, but the Network Control Program (NCP) did not. The "Dial reason" line of the output shows the source and destination address of the packet that initiated the dialing.

```
Router #show dialer interface bri 1
BRIO - dialer type = ISDN
DIAL String     Successess     Failures    Last called    Last status
0 incoming call(s) have been screened.
BRIO: B-Channel 1
Idle timer (120 secs), Fast idle timer (20 secs)
Wait for carrier (30 secs), Re-enable (15 secs)
Dialer state is data link layer up
Dial reason: ip (s=10.1.1.8, d=10.1.1.1)

Interface bound to profile Dialer2

Time until disconnect 102 secs
Current call connected 00:00:19
Connected to 5773872 (system1)

BRI1: B-Channel 2
Idle timer (120 secs), Fast idle timer (20 secs)
Wait for carrier (30 secs), Re-enable (15 secs)
Dialer state is idle
```

Chapter Summary

Both dialer profiles and rotary groups use dialer interfaces. A separate set of parameters associated with a particular called destination can be configured to a logical interface called the dialer interface. The dialer interface will contain the communication parameters once configured under the physical interfaces.

The dialer rotary group method uses the **interface dialer** statement to create a dialer interface, and the **dialer rotary-group** statement to assign a physical interface to a dialer interface. Rotary groups only allow a physical interface to join one dialer interface. The dialer profile group method uses the **interface dialer** statement to create a dialer interface. The dialer interface uses the **dialer pool** *number* command to assign the dialer interface to dialer pool. The **dialer pool-member** command assigns the physical interface to the dialer pool.

Review Questions

1. When describing dialer profiles, what is the purpose of the interface dialer?

    a. An order pool of physical interfaces

    b. A logical entity that uses a per-destination dialer profile

    c. A parameter that defines specific characteristics for a call to a specified dial string

    d. A physical entity that uses a per-destination dialer profile

2. When describing dialer profiles, what is the purpose of the dialer map class?

    a. A logical entity that uses a per-destination dialer profile

    b. A parameter that defines specific characteristics for a call to a specified dial string.

    c. An order pool of physical interfaces

    d. A physical entity that uses a per-destination dialer profile

3. When describing dialer profiles, what is the purpose of the dialer pool?

    a. A logical entity that uses a per-destination dialer profile

    b. A parameter that defines specific characteristics for a call to a specified dial string

    c. A pool of physical interfaces

    d. A physical entity that uses a per-destination dialer profile

4. Which statement best describes the permitted usage of the **map-class** statement?

   a. You can only use the **map-class** statement when using rotary groups with asynchronous physical interfaces.

   b. You can only use the **map-class** statement when using dialer profile groups with asynchronous physical interfaces.

   c. You can only use the **map-class** statement when using rotary groups with ISDN physical interfaces.

   d. You can only use the **map-class** statement when using dialer groups with asynchronous physical interfaces or ISDN interfaces.

   e. You can use the **map-class** statement when using rotary groups or dialer profile groups with asynchronous physical interfaces or ISDN interfaces.

5. When describing dialer rotary groups, what is the purpose of the **dialer rotary-group 0** statement?

   a. Assigns a particular physical interface to a particular logical interface.

   b. Creates a logical interface.

   c. The statement points to a particular **dialer-list** that determines interesting traffic.

   d. It enhances the **dialer map** statement with characteristics such as 56K speed acceptance.

6. When describing dialer rotary groups, what is the purpose of the **dialer-group 1** statement?

   a. The statement points to a particular **dialer-list** that determines interesting traffic.

   b. Assigns a particular physical interface to a particular logical interface.

   c. Creates a logical interface.

   d. It enhances the **dialer map** statement with characteristics such as 56K speed acceptance.

7. When describing dialer rotary groups, what is the purpose of the **interface dialer0** statement?

   a. The statement points to a particular **dialer-list** that determines interesting traffic.

   b. Assigns a particular physical interface to a particular logical interface.

   c. Creates a logical interface.

   d. It enhances the **dialer map** statement with characteristics such as 56K speed acceptance.

7

8. Which statement is true when comparing dialer rotary groups with dialer profile groups?

   a. Rotary groups allow you to assign a physical interface to multiple dialer interfaces.

   b. Dialer profile groups allow you to assign a physical interface to multiple dialer interfaces and dialer pools.

   c. Rotary groups are used for dialing out only, whereas dialer profile groups are used for both outgoing calls and incoming calls.

   d. Rotary groups can use static routes, whereas dialer profiles must use a dynamic routing protocol.

9. From within the **map-class** mode, identify all of the possible map-call statements that you use. [Choose the four best answers]

   a. **dialer idle-timeout**

   b. **dialer fast-idle**

   c. **dialer wait-for-carrier-time**

   d. **dialer hold-queue**

   e. **dialer isdn speed**

10. Which statements are true describing how physical interfaces are assigned to dialer pools when using dialer profile groups? [Choose the two best answers]

    a. One physical interface can belong to multiple dialer pools.

    b. More than one dialer interface can operate one dialer pool.

    c. Only one physical interface can belong to one dialer pool.

    d. Several dialer interfaces can operate the same dialer pool.

11. Which two commands can be duplicated and appear under both the physical interface and logical interface configurations? [Choose the two best answers]

    a. **dialer-group**

    b. **encapsulation ppp**

    c. **dialer string**

    d. **ppp authentication pap chap**

    e. **dialer map**

12. What is the correct order of entries for creating a dialer profile configuration on a router?

    A. Configure the physical interface (**interface type number**).

    B. Put the physical interface in a dialing pool and, optionally, assign the interface a priority.

    C. Assign the dialer interface to a dialer group.

    D. Configure the dialing pool to use for calls to a destination (**dialer pool number**).

    E. Create a dialer interface (**Interface dialer number**).

    a. A, C, D, E, B

    b. E, D, C, A, B

    c. C, D, E, A, B

    d. C, E, A, B, D

    e. A, B, C, D, E

13. What is the significance of the following **dialer pool** statements? Select all of the interpretations below that are true. [Choose the two best answers]

```
interface BRI1
  encapsulation ppp
  dialer pool-member 1 priority 100
  dialer pool-member 2 priority 50
  dialer pool-member 3 min-link 1
```

    a. The interface BRI1 can only use one B channel when it is used with the dialer pool 3.

    b. The interface BRI1 would be used before BRI0 for a call being made by dialer pool 2 if BRI0 has a priority of 100.

    c. The interface BRI1 would not be used before BRI0 for a call being made by dialer pool 2 if BRI0 has a priority of 100.

    d. The interface BRI1 would be used for making the call needed for dialer pool 1 before it would be used to make a call for dialer pool 2.

14. When using the **map–class**, which is the best description below used to describe the following statement: **dialer string 14085553333 class 56K**

    a. The required speed 56K setting is selected in this statement.

    b. The **dialer string** contains the SPID and makes a call only if the destination uses Cisco routers.

    c. The above statement is invalid because you should only use the **dialer map** statement and not the **dialer string** statement..

    d. The **dialer string** refers to a map class named 56K.

15. Which statements are accurate when describing the use and purpose of the **dialer in-band** statement and V.25bis? [Choose the three best answers]

   a. The **dialer in-band** statement is needed when using a BRI interface.

   b. The **dialer in-band** statement and V.25bis are needed when using a serial interface for DDR.

   c. When using DDR and V.25bis modems, the router disconnects calls by deactivating DTR.

   d. V.25bis can be used with a variety of devices, including synchronous modems, ISDN terminal adapters, and Switched 56 Data Service Units/Channel Service units (DSU/CSUs).

Real-World Projects

Chung is the head network engineer for a small department store company called City Blues located in the South. The company maintains eight locations and all the locations are franchised. Each location includes a department store and adjoining offices. The offices maintain inventory and receipts for their respective store. Because each office has its own manager and maintains almost complete autonomy, there is no central site. Rather, all of the offices are considered equal branch offices. The branch offices need to communicate with each other and share marketing statistics and other database items.

The company decided to implement a Cisco 1604-R router at each branch office. Chung decided to perform trial runs with dialer rotary groups and dialer profile groups. At one site Chung used rotary groups, and at another site he used dialer profiles.

Project 7.1

Complete the following tasks to configure a Cisco 1604-R to use dialer rotary-groups with DDR.

To begin:

1. Configure RouterB as the router name:
   router (config)# hostname RouterB

2. Configure an encrypted password:
   RouterB (config)# enable secret Cisco Router 1234

3. Disable the router from translating unfamiliar words entered during a console session into IP addresses: **RouterB (config)# no ip domain-lookup**

Configure the LAN interface by performing the following steps:

1. Enter the Ethernet interface: **RouterB (config)#interface e0**

2. Configure parameters for the LAN interface:
   RouterB (config-if)# ip address 10.1.1.1 255.0.0.0

Configure the WAN interface by performing the following steps:

1. Change to global configuration mode: **RouterB (config-if)# exit**

2. Configure parameters for the WAN interface:
   RouterB (config)# interface bri 0

3. Enable PPP: **RouterB (config-if)# encapsulation ppp**

4. Create a dialer rotary group: **RouterB (config-if)# dialer rotary-group 1**

5. Enter the SPIDs: **RouterB (config-if)# isdn spid1 0 4085551111
   4085552222, RouterB (config-if)# isdn spid2 0 4085553333 4085554444**

6. Enable the automatic detection of ISDN SPID numbers and switch type:
   RouterB (config-if)# isdn autodetect

7. Disable CDP: **RouterB (config-if)# no cdp enable**

To configure characteristics of the dialer rotary groups that were created earlier:

1. Change to global configuration mode: **RouterB (config-if)# exit**

2. Create a dialer rotary group leader: **RouterB (config)#interface dialer 1**

3. Set the IP address and subnet mask to 10.1.1.1 and 255.0.0.0, respectively:
   RouterB (config-if)# ip address 10.1.1.1 255.0.0.0

4. Enable PPP: **RouterB (config-if)# encapsulation ppp**

5. Enable dial-on-demand routing (DDR):
   RouterB (config-if)# dialer in-band

6. Configure the amount of time that the line can be idle before it is disconnected
   as 300 seconds: **RouterB (config-if)# dialer idle-timeout 300**

7. Configure the telephone number to be called for interfaces calling a single site:
   RouterB (config-if)# dialer string 14085553333

8. Set the number of packets to be held in the outgoing queue to 10:
   RouterB (config-if)# dialer hold-queue 10

9. Define the load level that must be exceeded on the first ISDN B channel
   before the second B channel is brought up for either outbound or inbound:
   dialer load-threshold 100 either

10. Assign this interface to dialer access group 1 for later DDR interesting traffic:
    RouterB (config-if)# dialer-group 1

11. Configure PAP and specify authentication on incoming calls only:
    RouterB (config-if)# ppp authentication pap callin

12. Enable Multilink PPP: **RouterB (config-if)# ppp multilink**

Configure how the IP routing protocol learns routes:

1. Change to global configuration mode: **RouterB (config-if)# exit**

2. Set up a best route for packets destined for networks unknown by the router:
   RouterB (config)# ip classless

3. Set up static routes: **RouterB (config)# ip route 0.0.0.0 0.0.0.0 192.168.1.1,**
   RouterB (config)# ip route 192.168.1.1 255.255.255.255 dialer0

4. Configure that dialer-list 1, which was defined earlier, permits dialing by the IP
   routing protocol: **RouterB (config)# dialer-list 1 protocol ip permit**

Perform the next two steps only if ISDN calls at 64Kbps are not supported:

5. Define a class of shared configuration parameters for outgoing calls from an
   ISDN interface: **RouterB (config)# map-class dialer 56K**

6. Create the unique identifier that identifies the class as 56K and specifies 56Kbps
   as the B-channel speed: **RouterB (config-map-class)# dialer isdn speed 56**

7. Exit and save your configuration:
   RouterB (config-map-class)# exit, RouterB (config)#copy run star

Project 7.2

Complete the following tasks to configure dialer profiles for ISDN.

To configure global parameters:

1. Enter configuration mode: **Router#configure terminal**

2. Configure the type of central office switch being used on the ISDN interface:
   Router(config)#isdn switch-type basic-ni

3. Verify your configuration by checking the ISDN line status as follows. From
   the privileged EXEC command mode, enter the **show isdn status** command.
   You should see command output similar to the following:

```
RouterC# show isdn status
The current ISDN Switchtype = basic-5ess
ISDN BRI0 interface
Layer 1 Status:
ACTIVE
```

```
Layer 2 Status:
TEI = 80, State = MULTIPLE_FRAME_ESTABLISHED
Layer 3 Status:
No Active Layer 3 Call(s)
Activated dsl 0 CCBs = 0
Total Allocated ISDN CCBs =
```

4. Confirm that the current ISDN switch type matches the actual switch type that you are using.

5. Confirm that the "Layer 1 status: ACTIVE" message (shown in bold in the example) appears in the command output.

6. Confirm that the "State = MULTIPLE_FRAME_ESTABLISHED" message (shown in bold in the example) appears in the command output. You might see a "State = TEI_ASSIGNED" message instead of the "State = MULTIPLE_FRAME_ESTABLISHED" message. This message also means that the ISDN line is correctly configured.

To configure security:

1. Configure the router with a host name, which is used in prompts and default configuration file names: **Router(config)#hostname RouterC**

2. Configure a password to prevent unauthorized access to the router: **RouterC(config)# enable password cisco**

3. Configure the password that will be used during CHAP caller identification and PAP, which must match the hostname of the central site router: **RouterC(config)# username HQ password <guessme>**

To configure the Fast Ethernet interface:

1. Enter configuration mode for the Fast Ethernet interface: **RouterC(config)#interface fastethernet0**

2. Configure this interface with an IP address and a subnet mask: **RouterC(config-if)# ip address 172.16.25.42 255.255.255.224**

3. Enable the interface and the configuration changes you have just made on the interface: **RouterC(config-if)# no shutdown**

4. Exit configuration mode for this interface: **RouterC(config-if)# exit**

To configure the ISDN interface:

1. Enter configuration mode for the ISDN interface: **RouterC(config)# interface BRI0**

2. Add a description of the ISDN interface to help you remember what is attached to it: **router(config-if)# description ISDN connectivity**

3. Enter the service profile identifier (SPID) number that has been assigned by the ISDN service provider for the B1 channel. This step is required only when the service provider has assigned a SPID to your ISDN line:
RouterC(config)# isdn spid1 555987601

4. Define the SPID number that has been assigned by the ISDN service provider for the B2 channel. This step is required only when the service provider has assigned a SPID to your ISDN line: **RouterC(config)# isdn spid2 555987602**

5. Disable IP routing on this interface: **RouterC(config-if)# no ip address**

6. Put this interface in a dialing pool. As an option, you can also assign a priority to the interface with this command:
RouterC(config-if)# dialer pool-member 1

7. Set the encapsulation method on this interface to PPP:
RouterC(config-if)# encapsulation ppp

8. Enable CHAP and PAP authentication on this interface. CHAP authentication is attempted first. If the central site router does not support CHAP, PAP is used for authentication: **RouterC(config-if)# ppp authentication chap pap**

9. Enable Multilink PPP on this interface: **RouterC(config-if)# ppp multilink**

10. Enable the interface and the configuration changes you have just made on the interface: **RouterC(config-if)# no shutdown**

11. Exit configuration mode for this interface: **RouterC(config-if)# exit**

To configure the dialer interface:

1. Create a dialer interface: **RouterC(config)# interface Dialer10**

2. Enable IP routing on this interface without assigning an IP address:
RouterC(config-if)# ip unnumbered fastethernet0

3. Configure the central site router CHAP authentication name:
RouterC(config-if)#dialer remote-name HQ

4. Configure the string (telephone number) to be called for this interface when calling a single site: **RouterC(config-if)# dialer string 5552053**

5. Put this interface in a dialing pool. As an option, you can also assign a priority to the interface with this command: **RouterC(config-if)# dialer pool 1**

6. Assign the dialer interface to a dialer group:
RouterC(config-if)# dialer-group 1

7. Set the encapsulation method on this interface to PPP:
RouterC(config-if)# encapsulation ppp

8. Enable CHAP and PAP authentication on this interface. CHAP authentication is attempted first. If the central site router does not support CHAP, PAP is used for authentication: **RouterC(config-if)# ppp authentication chap pap**

9. Enable Multilink PPP on this interface: **RouterC(config-if)# ppp multilink**

10. Enable the interface and the configuration changes you have just made on the interface: **RouterC(config-if)# no shutdown**

11. Exit configuration mode for this interface: **RouterC(config-if)exit**

To verify your configuration:

1. Confirm Multilink PPP configuration for the B1 channel.

2. Confirm that the ISDN is up and connected to the central site router.

3. From the privileged EXEC command mode, enter the **show ppp multilink** command.

4. Confirm that the "Master link is Virtual–Access1" message (shown in bold in the example) appears in the command output.

```
RouterC# show ppp multilink
Bundle HQ, 1 member, Master link is Virtual-Access1
Dialer Interface is BRI0
0 lost fragments, 0 reordered, 0 unassigned, sequence 0x0/0x0 rcvd/sent
0 discarded, 0 lost received, 1/255 load
Member Link: 1
BRI0:1
```

To confirm Multilink PPP configuration for the B1 channel:

1. Confirm that the ISDN is up and connected to the central site router.

2. From the privileged EXEC command mode, enter the **show interface** command.

3. Confirm that the "LCP Open, multilink Open" message (shown in bold in the example) appears in the command output:

```
RouterC# show interface bri 0 1 2
BRI0:1 is up, line protocol is up
Hardware is BRI with U interface and external S bus interface
MTU 1500 bytes, BW 64 Kbit, DLY 20000 usec, rely 255/255, load 3/255
Encapsulation PPP, loopback not set, keepalive set (10 sec)
LCP Open, multilink Open
Last input 00:00:00, output 00:00:00, output hang never
Last clearing of "show interface" counters never
Queueing strategy: fifo...
```

To confirm when the router dials out:

1. Establish a static IP route to the remote network:
   RouterC(config)# ip route 192.168.37.0 255.255.255.0 192.168.37.40

2. Establish a static IP route to the remote network through the router BRI interface:
   RouterC(config)# ip route 192.168.37.40 255.255.255.255 BRI0

3. Define a standard access list based on your network:
   RouterC(config)# access-list 101 permit icmp any any

4. Configure an access list by list number and protocol (IP) to define the "interesting" packets that can trigger a call to the destination:
   RouterC(config)# dialer-list 1 protocol ip list 101

5. Confirm the IP Static Route by entering **show ip route 192.168.37.40**. Confirm that the "directly connected via BRI" message appears in the command output:

```
RouterC# show ip route 192.168.37.40
Routing entry for 192.168.37.40/32
Known via "connected", distance 0, metric 0 (connected)
Routing Descriptor Blocks:
* directly connected, via BRI0
```

6. Confirm connectivity to the central site router by entering **ping 192.168.37.40** twice. The second time, you should see 100 percent success.

To configure command-line access to the router:

1. Configure the console terminal line: **RouterC(config)# line console 0**

2. Set the interval that the EXEC command interpreter waits until user input is detected: **RouterC(config-line)# exec-timeout 5**

3. Configure a virtual terminal for remote console access:
   RouterC(config-line)# line vty 0 4

4. Configure a password on the line:
   RouterC(config-line)# password <lineaccess>

5. Enable password checking at terminal session login:
   RouterC(config-line)# login

6. Exit configuration mode: **RouterC(config-line)# end, RouterC (config)#copy run star**

CHAPTER EIGHT

Cisco's 700 Series Routers

After completing this chaptor, you will bc ablc to:

✓ Become familiar with the different 700 series models

✓ Understand the supported software features

✓ Become comfortable with the CLI and the basic management commands

✓ Understand the use and implementation of profiles

✓ Configure the 700 series routers for ISDN dial-up

An Overview

The Cisco 700 series of routers provides a very flexible, cost-effective solution for small office/home office (SOHO) environments. Cisco recommends the product for environments with fewer than six people. With a single BRI ISDN line, it can easily support access to the Internet and the corporate office while supporting two optional analog telephone ports for phone and fax connections. The 700 series routers include everything a SOHO environment would need for fast WAN access without requiring any additional hardware or software on your desktop PCs—all you need is an Ethernet NIC in your PC, which is connected to a hub that, in turn, is connected to the 700 series router. Alternatively, some of the 700 series have a four-port hub built right into them.

700 Series Features

Cisco designed the product knowing that the person installing the router would have little, if any, networking expertise. All the cables are color coded to match the ports on the router that one needs to connect them to. Cisco includes the Fast Step CD-ROM, which contains the easy-to-use ClickStart software, to provide a quick-and-easy method for configuring the software of the router: It allows you to configure your ISP's information, ISDN connectivity, and other information and have your router up and running in less than 30 minutes. Plus, once the router is operational, you can use the included ClickStart software, which uses a standard browser interface, to monitor your router's connections and statistics.

Hardware Features

The 700 series comes in a variety of models to meet a SOHO's individual needs. The routers are of a fixed configuration and are not hardware upgradeable. Table 8.1 lists the different models and features of the 700 series routers.

Note: Some 700 series have an "M" after their model number. This denotes that the router has 1.5MB of RAM. The standard amount of RAM on a 700 series router is 1MB.

Table 8.1   The 700 series platform.

Model	Ethernet Port	Hub	Integrated NT1 (U port)	Telephone Services	RJ-11 Interfaces
761	1		N	N	
762	1		Y	N	
765	1		N	Y	2
766	1		Y	Y	2
772		four-port	Y	N	
775		four-port	N	Y	
776		four-port	Y	Y	

All the routers support Ethernet. The 760 series has a single Ethernet port that you can connect to a single PC or to an Ethernet hub. The 770 series has a four-port integrated hub, reducing the number of networking devices you will have to deal with in a SOHO environment. All the 700 series routers also have an S/T BRI interface for ISDN connectivity. Some of the routers in the 700 series have an additional U BRI interface with the NT1 integrated into the chassis of the router. This option can be used for users located in North America, where the ISDN carrier does not typically provide the NT1 device but rather requires the customer to furnish it.

The 700 series is compatible with almost all ISDN switch types; however, not all switch types are available within a given software set. Table 8.2 is a list of switch types supported by the 700 series routers and where they are more commonly found.

When ordering the 700 series, you will need to specify what ISDN switch type you will be connecting to so that Cisco will ship you the software with the required switch type. Note that your switch type is usually based on where you will be connecting to your provider. In Europe, this is typically I-CTR3, or in Australia, its TPH. If you forget, it is a very simple matter to download the appropriate software from Cisco and upgrade the router either via TFTP or from a console connection.

Some of the 700 series routers support enhanced telephone services, as noted in Table 8.1. These services include:

➤ Three-way calling

➤ Call waiting

➤ Call forwarding

➤ Call transfer

➤ Call hold

For routers with analog support for phones or fax machines, calls can be prioritized such that a current call can be disconnected to have the router make a more important

Table 8.2   ISDN switch types supported by the 700 series.

Location	Switch Type
North America	AT&T 5ess
North America	NorTel DMS 100
North America	NI-1
Europe	I-CTR3 (or NET3)
Germany	1TR6
France	VN3
Australia	TPH
Japan	INS HSD64 and 128

phone connection. This is useful when both B channels are currently being used for data connections and an incoming phone or fax connection is signaled to the 700 series router from the carrier or when you need to make an outgoing phone connection. In this case, the router can bring down one (or even both) B channel(s) to handle the voice or fax connection(s).

Software Features

The 700 series routers use a unique operating system that is different from the IOS on Cisco's higher-end routers, such as the 1600, 3600, and 7500 series routers. The biggest difference is in the CLI; however, the 700 series is completely interoperable and compatible with its bigger brothers. With Ethernet and BRI ISDN connectivity, the 700 series routers can handle bridged traffic and routed IP and IPX traffic.

Note: Cisco has replaced the 700 series routers with the 800 series. The two routers are the same hardware platform. The major difference between the two router series is that the 800 series uses the IOS CLI while the 700 does not. For the purpose of the Remote Access test, only the 700 is covered in this book.

IP Features

The following are IP features supported by the 700 series routers:

➤ Dynamic Host Configuration Protocol (DHCP) relay agent and server

➤ Port Address Translation (PAT)

➤ IP RIP version 1 and 2

DHCP, defined in RFC 2132, is a mechanism that details how clients can dynamically obtain their IP addressing information (including BOOTP client requests). A 700 series router acting as a DHCP *relay agent* takes all DHCP client requests for addressing information and changes the destination address from a local broadcast to either a destination unicast address or a directed broadcast, which it will then forward appropriately to a destination DHCP server to handle the addressing request. This is similar to the IP Helper feature of the IOS-based routers. As a DHCP server, the 700 series router will handle all client requests for IP addressing information, including the client's IP address, subnet mask, default gateway, DNS server(s), and WINS server(s).

PAT is a feature that allows the 700 series router to use a single public IP address for its Internet connection to your ISP while using private addresses for your networked computers. From the outside world's perspective (including the ISP), all communication occurs with the 700 series router. PAT is a process that will translate your private addresses to a single public IP address, keeping each connection unique by assigning different port numbers. This process will be discussed in more depth in Chapter 13.

IPX Features

The following are IPX features supported by the 700 series routers:

➤ **Access-lists** for filtering

➤ IPX RIP

➤ IPX spoofing of Watchdog and SPX keepalives

General Network Features

The following are general network features of the 700 series routers:

➤ Static IP and IPX routes and static IPX SAPs

➤ Dial-on-Demand Routing (DDR)

➤ Bandwidth on demand (BOD) for meeting increased bandwidth needs

➤ **Access-lists** for filtering traffic

➤ Snapshot routing for IP RIP and IPX RIP

PPP Features

For WAN connectivity, the 700 series router support the standards-based PPP protocol stack. The following are some additional features that are integrated into PPP on the 700 series routers:

➤ Multilink

➤ 4:1 compression using Stacker (this is a purchasable option)

➤ PAP and CHAP authentication

➤ Dial callback

➤ Caller-ID screening

---

700 Series Configuration

Most of the configuration tasks for the 700 series routers are easy and straightforward. The command-line interface supports context-sensitive help as well as command and parameter abbreviations. For most ISDN WAN connections, little configuration is required.

Command-Line Interface (CLI)

The CLI of the 700 series routers is very different from that of the IOS-based routers. It is more similar to a Unix shell prompt than the IOS. The prompt will contain the ">" sign. In the router's default configuration (when you receive the router directly from Cisco), this is all you will see; once you assign a name to the router, you will see the router's hostname followed by the ">" sign, as shown in the following example:

```
Home700>
```

Help

No matter where you're at in the CLI, you can always use the **?** command to bring up help. The following is a truncated view of the output of this command:

```
?
CAll [ C# | L# | # | C#/L# | C#/# | #/# ] [ P# | CH# | P#/CH# ]
                        [<number>] where
 C#              indicates a Connection number
 # or L#         indicates a Link number
 C#/L# or #/#  indicates Link of a Connection
 P#              indicates Port
 CH#             indicates Channel
 P#/CH#          indicates Channel of a Port
CD [<username>]
DEmand [<link>] [THreshold=kb/s] [DUration=<seconds>]
                        [SOurce= WAN | LAn | BOth]
DIsconnect [ C# | L# | # | C#/L# | C#/# #/# | P# | CH# |
                        P#/CH# | AL1 ] where
 C#              indicates a Connection number
 # or L#         indicates a Link number
 C#/L# or #/#  indicates Link of a Connection
 P#              indicates Port
 CH#             indicates Channel
 P#/CH#          indicates Channel of a Port
EStablish [<spid id>]
<Q> and <enter> to Quit or <enter> for MORE

<...Output truncated...>
```

Each command is listed with a brief explanation of what it does. Note that the commands are listed in mixed case—the beginning of the command starts with capital letters and the command ends with lowercase letters. The router CLI supports abbreviated commands: You only have to enter the letters listed in the capital case.

If there is more information than will fit on the screen, the CLI will tell you to press the Enter key for the display of the next screen of information. If you want to quit the help text, just type the letter "q".

Basic Commands

Most of the commands you will use to configure the 700 series routers will be **set** commands. These commands are used to change a parameter's configuration. To change it back to the factory default, use the **reset** command. One example of a **set** command is **set default**, which, when executed, will erase the router's existing configuration (stored in NVRAM) and perform a "soft reboot" of the router. The following is an example of this command:

```
Home700> set default
01/02/1995 22:55:36  Connection 1 Closed
Home700> 01/02/1995 22:55:36  Connection 2 Closed
Home700>

Boot version 2.1(1) 11/04/96 17:33
Copyright (c) 1993-1996.  All rights reserved.

POST ............ OK (1.5MB).
Validating FLASH ... OK.
Waiting ...
Booting up ..........................
01/01/1995 00:00:00  Connection 1 Opened
> 01/01/1995 00:00:00  LO1  0                Started Operation
>
```

Note that the prompt changed from "Home700>" to ">", the default prompt. The **set default** command is similar to executing **erase start/write erase** and **reload** on an IOS router.

*Note: All changes made to the 700 series routers are automatically saved to NVRAM—you do not need to execute **copy running-config startup-config** or **write memory**, as you must do on the IOS-based routers.*

If you want to examine the router's configuration or the settings of different parameters, you will use the **show** commands. For example, the **show config** command is used to display the general settings of the 700 series router:

```
Home700> show config
System Parameters
    Environment
        Screen Length         24
        Echo Mode             ON
        CountryGroup          1
    Bridging Parameters
        LAN Forward Mode      ANY
        WAN Forward Mode      ONLY
        Address Age Time      OFF
    Call Startup Parameters
        Multidestination      OFF
    Line Parameters
        Switch Type           5ESS
```

```
        Call Parameters          Link 1          Link 2
           Retry Delay           30              30


Profile Parameters
    Bridging Parameters
        Bridging             ON
        Routed Protocols
        Learn Mode           ON
        Passthru             OFF
    Call Startup Parameters
        Encapsulation PPP
    Line Parameters
        Line Speed           AUTO
        Numbering Plan       NORMAL
    Call Parameters          Link 1          Link 2
        Auto                 ON              ON
        Called Number
        Ringback Number
```

Once you have made changes to your router's configuration, you can use the **upload** command to examine your changes:

```
Home700> upload
CD
SET SCREENLENGTH 24
SET COUNTRYGROUP 1
SET LAN MODE ANY
SET WAN MODE ONLY
SET AGE OFF
SET MULTIDESTINATION OFF
SET SWITCH 5ESS
SET AUTODETECTION  OFF
SET 1 DELAY 30
SET 2 DELAY 30
SET BRIDGING ON
SET LEARN ON
SET PASSTHRU OFF
SET SPEED AUTO
SET PLAN NORMAL
SET 1 AUTO ON
SET 2 AUTO ON
SET 1 NUMBER
SET 2 NUMBER
SET 1 BACKUPNUMBER
SET 2 BACKUPNUMBER
SET 1 RINGBACK
```

```
SET 2 RINGBACK
SET CLICALLBACK OFF
SET SYSTEMNAME Home700
LOG CALLS TIME VERBOSE
SET UNICASTFILTER OFF
DEMAND 1 THRESHOLD 0
DEMAND 2 THRESHOLD 48
DEMAND 1 DURATION 1
DEMAND 2 DURATION 1
DEMAND 1 SOURCE LAN
DEMAND 2 SOURCE BOTH
TIMEOUT 1 THRESHOLD 0
TIMEOUT 2 THRESHOLD 48
TIMEOUT 1 DURATION 0
TIMEOUT 2 DURATION 0
TIMEOUT 1 SOURCE LAN
TIMEOUT 2 SOURCE BOTH
SET REMOTEACCESS PROTECTED
SET LOCALACCESS ON
SET LOGOUT 5
SET CALLERID OFF
SET PPP AUTHENTICATION IN CHAP  PAP
SET PPP AUTHENTICATION OUT NONE
SET PPP CALLBACK REQUEST OFF
SET PPP CALLBACK REPLY OFF
SET PPP NEGOTIATION INTEGRITY 10
SET PPP NEGOTIATION COUNT 10
SET PPP NEGOTIATION RETRY  3000
SET PPP TERMREQ COUNT 2
SET PPP MULTILINK ON
SET COMPRESSION OFF
SET PPP BACP ON
SET PPP ADDRESS NEGOTIATION LOCAL OFF
SET IP PAT UDPTIMEOUT 5
SET IP PAT TCPTIMEOUT 30
SET SNMP CONTACT ""
SET SNMP LOCATION ""
SET SNMP TRAP COLDSTART OFF
SET SNMP TRAP WARMSTART OFF
SET SNMP TRAP LINKDOWN OFF
SET SNMP TRAP LINKUP OFF
SET SNMP TRAP AUTHENTICATIONFAIL OFF
SET DHCP OFF
SET DHCP DOMAIN
SET DHCP NETBIOS_SCOPE
SET VOICEPRIORITY INCOMING INTERFACE PHONE1 ALWAYS
```

8

```
SET VOICEPRIORITY OUTGOING INTERFACE PHONE1 ALWAYS
SET CALLWAITING INTERFACE PHONE1 ON
SET VOICEPRIORITY INCOMING INTERFACE PHONE2 ALWAYS
SET VOICEPRIORITY OUTGOING INTERFACE PHONE2 ALWAYS
SET CALLWAITING INTERFACE PHONE2 ON
SET USER LAN
SET IP ROUTING OFF
SET IP FRAMING ETHERNET_II
SET USER Internal
SET IP FRAMING ETHERNET_II
SET USER Standard
SET PROFILE ID 000000000000
SET PROFILE POWERUP ACTIVATE
SET PROFILE DISCONNECT KEEP
SET IP ROUTING ON
SET IP ADDRESS 0.0.0.0
SET IP NETMASK 0.0.0.0
SET IP FRAMING NONE
SET IP RIP RECEIVE V1
SET IP RIP UPDATE OFF
SET IP RIP VERSION 1
CD
Home700>
```

To back up the configuration to a TFTP server, add the **tftp** parameter to the **upload** command. Use the following syntax to backup your configuration:

```
> UPload tFtP server's_ip_address config_file_name
```

To reload a configuration file back into the router, use the **swl** command:

```
> SWL CONFIG server's_ip_address config_file_name
```

If you need to upgrade your router, you'll also use the **swl** command, except you will use the **tftp** parameter:

```
> SWL TFTP server's_ip_address config_file_name
```

Note: You will always want to read the release notes before performing an upgrade, because the upgrade process might differ based on the software release you are currently running. Some software releases have the 700 series act as a TFTP server, and you must use TFTP client software to push the software to the 700 router. In all cases, however, you can upgrade the router through the serial console port.

To examine the version of the operating system you are currently running, use the **version** command:

```
Home700> version
Software Version c760-i.b.US 4.3(1) - Feb 22 1999 19:34:14
Cisco 776
ISDN Stack Revision US 2.10 (5ESS/DMS/NI-1)
Copyright (c) 1993-1999 by Cisco Systems, Inc. All rights reserved.
Software is used subject to software license agreement contained
with this product. By using this product you agree to accept the
terms of the software license.
Hardware Configuration:
   DRAM:  1.5MB
   Flash: 1.0MB
   POTS:  Type 0 (Rev. 73-1797-05-C0)
   NT1:   Installed
   ROM:   2.1(2)
Home700>
```

700 Series Profiles

The 700 series uses profiles to perform configuration tasks that are necessary to pass traffic between the Ethernet LAN interface and the ISDN WAN interface. Profiles are grouped sets of commands that allow you to customize your connections to different destinations. There are four different types of profiles, with a possible total of 20 different profiles in the 700 series routers:

➤ *LAN profile*—Defines how information is passed to and from the Ethernet interface. There is only one LAN profile (even for the 700 series routers that sport a four-port hub).

➤ *Internal profile*—Used to pass traffic through the bridge/route engine between the LAN and ISDN BRI interface. There is only one internal profile.

➤ *System profile*—Defines system-level configurations that affect the router as a whole. There is only one system profile.

➤ *Standard profile*—Defines a default configuration connection for ISDN dial-up, which does not support routing. There is only one standard profile.

➤ *User profile*—Defines a user-configured connection for ISDN dial-up. You can have up to 16 user profiles.

A better way to view profiles and their usage is to examine how the router processes information between the LAN and WAN interfaces. The LAN profile is used to handle all traffic to/from the Ethernet port. All changes performed on this profile affect only the LAN interface. The standard and user profiles are used to handle all traffic to/from the ISDN BRI WAN interface. If traffic meets the criteria for a destination specified by a user profile, the router uses the user profile to process the traffic; otherwise, it uses the standard profile. To move traffic between the LAN and WAN profiles, the internal profile is used. It handles all routing and/or bridging functions between these two sets of profiles.

Profile Characteristics

The system profile affects all components of the system, including other profiles. Profiles, such as user profiles, get all their default configurations from a template. The template is created within the system profile. All profiles then take their default configurations from this template.

User profiles are used when you will be dialing to different destinations. By default, user profiles get all their configurations from the system template. You can override the default by making custom changes to a user profile. This provides you with greater flexibility in your configuration because you can specify different configurations—such as PPP passwords, compression, multilink, phone numbers, filters, and so on—based on the destination you are connecting to.

Entering into a Profile

Profiles are similar to the different configuration modes that the IOS routers use. Global Configuration mode on the IOS routers is similar to the system profile of the 700 series. Any changes made in the system profile affect the router globally. You know you are at the system level by examining the prompt. If you see the ">" sign or the name of the router and ">", this means you are in the system profile. To make changes to the LAN, standard, or user profile, you use the **cd** command. This is similar to the Unix **cd** command. When you enter one of these profiles, it affects only that specific profile. This is like the interface Configuration mode of the IOS-based routers. When you are in an interface on an IOS-based router, the commands you execute affect only that specific interface. When you are in a profile, the name of the profile appears after the name of the router when looking at the CLI prompt:

```
Router_name:profile_name>
```

Any changes made to any profile are automatically stored in NVRAM, unlike changes done on an IOS-based router. Of the 20 profiles, four cannot be deleted, but only modified: LAN, internal, system, and standard.

If you wish to leave a profile and return to the system profile, use the **cd** command, as follows:

```
Home700:Chicago> cd
Home700>
```

Creating, Verifying, and Deleting a User Profile

To create a user profile, use the **set user** system command:

```
> set user profile_name
:profile_name>
```

Note that in this example, when you create a profile, you are automatically placed in it. At this point, all changes you make affect only this individual profile.

Items that are typically set within a profile include IP information, such as the IP address, subnet mask, and default gateway; PPP information, such as the authentication type (PAP or CHAP), password, and multilink; and caller information, such as the phone number.

If you are within a profile and execute a **show** command, you will be shown the parameters for that specific profile only. If you are not happy with a specific value and want to set it back to the system default—the value defined in the system profile template—use the **unset** command. What's more, if you want to remove the whole profile, use the following **reset** command:

```
> reset user profile_name
```

To view the configured parameters for a specific profile, use the **show profile** command.

Activating Profiles

Profiles are in one of two states: active or inactive. Active profiles have a virtual connection to a remote destination. This means that, even though the router does not have a physical ISDN connection to the destination, the router can use DDR to establish one. Another way of looking at virtual and physical connections is that the router cannot forward packets across a virtual connection but can use DDR to establish a physical one, which the router can then forward packets across.

An inactive profile does not have any type of connection—physical or virtual—to a destination. In this state, the router cannot use the profile to initiate a phone call to the destination using the profile.

A profile can be activated in one of two ways: physically, using the **set active** command, or dynamically, being triggered by a phone call. To manually activate a profile, use the **set active** command:

```
> cd profile_name
:profile_name> set active
```

8

To change a profile back to the inactive state, use the **set inactive** profile command within the profile you wish to deactivate.

For the router to initiate a phone call using DDR, the profile it wishes to use must be active. However, this is not true for an incoming phone call. Whenever the router receives an incoming phone call (where the connection is using PAP or CHAP for authentication), the router looks for the incoming connection's name in its list of profiles. If it finds a match and the profile is active, it uses this profile. If the profile is inactive, the router will activate it for the connection and then deactivate it once the connection is broken. Inactive profiles, therefore, are very useful for situations where you want your 700 series router to handle incoming connections from various destinations but do not want your router to make phone calls to these destinations (for example, for cost reasons you might want your central site router to call your 700 series router).

System Profile Commands

The follow sections cover some of the more common commands you will use to configure your 700 series router to handle your LAN and WAN connectivity. You will look at some typical commands used within the system, LAN, and user profiles.

First, you will want to assign the router a name using the **set systemname** command:

```
> set systemname router_name
```

The name of the router is then used in the authentication of PAP or CHAP—the 700 sends this name to the router to which it wants to connect. If connecting to an IOS-based router, you will need a matching router name in the username database.

You will also need to specify the type of ISDN switch you are connected to by using the **set switch** command:

```
> set switch switch_type
```

Some popular switch types in the U.S. are 5ess, dms, and ni-1. Some ISDN carriers, most commonly in the U.S., sometimes require SPID numbers. Use the following commands to set these for your two bearer channels:

```
> set 1 spid spid_for_channel_1
> set 2 spid spid_for_channel_2
```

Your provider will give these to you if they are necessary. Also, you will want to configure the phone numbers that your provider has assigned you for your bearer channels—these can be used for caller-ID purposes when connecting to remote sites:

```
> set 1 directorynumber phone_number_for_channel_1[:sub_address]
> set 2 directorynumber phone_number_for_channel_2[:sub_address]
```

To verify your configuration to your provider's ISDN switch, use the following **show** command:

```
> show status
Status
LineStatus
LineActivated
TerminalIdentifierAssigned
>
```

The output should look like the preceding text. To test whether your router can place phone calls, use the **call** command to manually place an ISDN call:

```
> call phone_number
```

Note that this command can be executed either at the system profile or user profile level. To disconnect an active phone call, use the **disconnect** command:

```
> disconnect 1|2|all
```

The **1** or **2** parameter disconnects the specified bearer channel, whereas the **all** parameter disconnects both bearer channels.

LAN Profile Commands

To allow your desktop users to move data through the 700 series router and out of its ISDN interface, you will need to configure the Ethernet port. Note that some of the 700 series routers have a four-port hub. In this case, the hub is treated as one logical Ethernet port. The following are some of the necessary commands for configuring the LAN interface:

```
> cd LAN
:LAN> set ip address ip_address
:LAN> set ip netmask subnet_mask
:LAN> set ip routing on
:LAN> set bridging off
:LAN> cd
>
```

First, you must change to the LAN profile using the **cd** command. The next two commands assign an IP address and subnet mask to the Ethernet interface. By default, bridging is enabled. You will probably (at least in most situations) want to enable routing and disable bridging on your 700 series routers. The **set ip routing** and **set bridging** commands accomplish this.

User Profile Commands

Remember that you will first have to create your user profile with the **set user** command, and, when finished with your configuration, activate it with the **set active** user profile command (if you will be using it for dial-out purposes).

PPP Configuration

By default, PPP is enabled on 700 series routers running software version 4.1 and later. For earlier routers, you will need to enable it by executing the following user profile command:

```
> cd profile_name
:profile_name> set encapsulation ppp
```

Note: The 700 series routers have multilink enabled by default—it is not necessary to enable this.

To configure PAP authentication, use the following commands:

```
> cd profile_name
:profile_name> set ppp authentication pap
:profile_name> set ppp password
Enter new Password: pap_password_is_entered_here
Re-Type new Password: enter_pap_password_again
Enter User Name: enter_the_username_to_send_to_the_remote_device
```

For CHAP configuration, use the following commands for two-way authentication:

```
> set ppp authentication incoming chap
> set ppp authentication outgoing chap
>
> cd profile_name
:profile_name>
:profile_name> set ppp secret client
Enter new Password: chap_password_is_entered_here
Re-Type new Password: enter_chap_password_again
:profile_name>
:profile_name> set ppp secret host
Enter new Password: chap_password_is_entered_here
Re-Type new Password: enter_chap_password_again
:profile_name>
```

The first two commands are required if you will be performing two-way authentication for CHAP. Note that the two parameters, **incoming** and **outgoing**, refer to the direction of the request for the challenge.

*Note: The **incoming** parameter sets the 700 router as a client, where the remote router (usually your corporate router) will initiate the challenge. The **outgoing** parameter, on the other hand, has the 700 router sending the challenge to the connecting router.*

The next two commands set the passwords. The **set ppp secret client** command assigns the password that the 700 router will use to authenticate to the destination router. The **set ppp secret host** command assigns the password that the 700 router will use to authenticate the incoming connection.

If you are only performing one-way authentication, you only need the **set ppp auth incoming chap** and **set ppp secret client** commands if the 700 series is requesting the challenge from the central site or the **set ppp auth outgoing chap** and **set ppp secret host** commands if the 700 series router will be generating the challenge.

If you want to configure dial callback using PPP, you must first enter the respective user profile. If you want the 700 series to request its remote router to call back the 700 series, use the following PPP command:

```
> cd profile_name
:profile_name> set ppp callback request on phone_number_to_call_back
```

The phone number that you list is the phone number you want the remote router to use when calling back. If you want the 700 series router to perform the callback function, use the following PPP command:

```
> cd profile_name
:profile_name> set ppp callback reply on
```

Typically, you will use the first command and have your central site router (with its cheaper phone rates) call back to your 700 series router.

Configuring Phone Information

To specify the phone number of the destination, enter the user profile and execute the following command:

```
> cd profile_name
:profile_name> set number phone_number_to_dial
```

If you wish to configure caller ID, use the following two system profile commands:

```
> set caller id on
> set callidreceive phone_number_allowed_to_connect_to_the_700
```

The first command activates caller ID, whereas the second command lists the phone number that is allowed to connect to this 700 series router.

Configuring IP Routing

If you want to have your router dynamically acquire an IP address from the ISDN router that it is connecting to as well as use a default router, you will need to use the following user profile command:

```
> cd profile_name
:profile_name> set ip route destination 0.0.0.0/0
                        gateway default_gateway's IP address
```

When the preceding command is used in this form, the 700 series router will dynamically acquire its IP address and subnet mask. Use this form of the command if the 700 series router is performing the dial-up connectivity. If, however, the destination router is initiating the phone call, specify "0.0.0.0" as the default gateway. In this instance, the 700 series router will also dynamically acquire the IP address of the default gateway router.

If you want to run a dynamic routing protocol (RIP, for example) just on the LAN segment and default or static routes on the WAN side, use the following configuration:

```
> cd LAN
:LAN> set ip address ethernet_IP_address
:LAN> set ip netmask ethernet_subnet_mask
:LAN> set ip routing on
:LAN> set ip rip update periodic
:LAN> cd
> cd profile_name
:profile_name> set ip routing on
:profile_name> set rip update off
:profile_name> set bridging off
:profile_name> set ip route destination 0.0.0.0/0
                        gateway default_gateway's_IP address
:profile_name> cd
>
```

In this example, you will have to configure both the LAN and user profiles. In the LAN profile, you have to assign an IP address and mask as well as enable routing and RIP. In the user profile, you will need to enable routing and RIP as well as disable bridging (remember that bridging is enabled by default on your profiles). You will also need a default route.

If you want to run a dynamic routing protocol across the WAN link, use the following configuration for your user profile:

```
> cd profile_name
:profile_name> set ip address WAN_IP_address
:profile_name> set ip netmask WAN_subnet_mask
:profile_name> set ip routing on
:profile_name> set ip rip update periodic
:profile_name> set bridging off
```

Typically, these two examples would be very rare—your 700 would be connected to a single segment and therefore would not require a dynamic routing protocol such as RIP. Instead, you would use a default route on your WAN interface and a static route at your central site pointing to the single segment off of the 700 series router.

To verify your configuration, you can use different **show ip** commands:

```
> show ip configuration all
Profile    Routing    Frame   IPAddress    Netmask
---------------------------------------------------
Internal   ON           ETH2   172.16.1.1  255.255.255.0
Corporate  ON           IPCP   172.16.2.1  255.255.255.0


Profile    PAT     Multicast  Summarization
-----------------------------------------------
Internal   OFF     OFF        OFF
Corporate  OFF     OFF        OFF
```

The **show ip configuration all** command gives you an overview of the assigned IP addresses your profiles are using. To examine your router's routing information (for example, default routes), use the **show ip route all** command:

```
> show ip route all
Profile    Type   Destination  Bits   Gateway
----------------------------------------------
Internal   NET    172.16.1.0    24     DIRECT
Corporate  WAN    172.16.2.1    24     DIRECT
Corporate  WAN    0.0.0.0        0     172.16.2.2
```

In this example, "NET" refers to the Ethernet profile and "WAN" to the user profile.

DHCP Configuration

As mentioned earlier, a 700 series router can perform the function of a DHCP server or relay agent if it has at least software version 4.1 running. To configure a 700 series router as a relay agent, use the following system profile command:

```
> set dhcp relay destination_IP_address
```

For the destination IP address, you can list a DHCP server's specific IP address or the directed broadcast address of a specific segment.

Note: *The DHCP relay agent performs the same function as the IP Helper feature of IOS-based routers.*

Configuring a 700 series router as a DHCP server requires a bit more configuration than as a relay agent. All the commands are executed in the system profile:

```
> set dhcp server
> set dhcp address starting_IP_address_in_pool
                    total_number_of_addresses
> set dhcp netmask subnet_mask
> set dhcp gateway primary|secondary default_gateway_address
> set dhcp dns primary|secondary DNS_server's_IP_address
> set dhcp wins primary|secondary WINS'_server's_IP_address
> set dhcp domain domain_name_to_assign
```

The **set dhcp server** command allows the router to perform the function of a DHCP server. The **set dhcp address** command lists the beginning IP address in the clients' address pool and then the total addresses that are in this pool, including the starting address. The **set dhcp gateway** command allows you to assign clients a primary and secondary default gateway address(es). The last three commands allow you to assign the DNS servers, WINS servers, and the domain name that the clients will use, respectively.

To verify your DHCP configuration, use the following **show** command:

```
> show dhcp config
Environment
DHCPServer          ON
DHCPRelay           OFF

IPAddressPool
StartIPAddress      172.16.1.2
Count               253
LeaseTime(minutes)  Infinite
SubnetMask          255.255.255.0
```

```
DNSConfiguration
PrimaryDNSServer          10.17.5.2
SecondaryDNSServer        NONE
Domain                    "thedealgroup.com"

Gateways
PrimaryGateway            172.16.1.1
SecondaryGateway          NONE

WINSConfiguration
PrimaryWINSServer         NONE
SecondaryWINSServer       NONE
NetBiosScopeId            ""

AddressInUse
IPAddressMacAddressLeaseExpiration
172.16.2.2                00000ce01fa2   Infinite
172.16.2.3                00000cd017ed   Infinite
2  Ipaddresses allocated, 251 free
```

8

Chapter Summary

The 700 series routers represent Cisco's entry-level routers in their router line. Primarily developed for SOHO use, the 700 series presents a very economical solution for small offices that require a mixture of data and voice needs—and with its ClickStart software, the initial installation of the router is simple even for novices.

The 700 series platform comes in a mixture of different models. These models include support for a four-port Ethernet hub, an integrated NT1, RJ-11 telephone interfaces, and enhanced telephony features, such as three-way calling, call waiting, and call forwarding. For WAN connectivity, the 700 series only supports ISDN. It supports all the standard switch types, even those used in Europe, Asia, and Australia.

The rich set of software features will meet any SOHO's needs: Support for both IP and IPX are included. For IP environments, the routers support the function of a DHCP server and relay agent, static routes and the RIP routing protocol (version 1 and 2), and Port Address Translation. For IPX environments, the routers can perform IPX spoofing and support static routes and SAPs as well as IPX's RIP routing protocol. For WAN features, the routers support DDR and bandwidth on demand as well as snapshot routing. With its standards-compliant PPP, the 700 series supports PAP and CHAP authentication as well as multilink, dial callback, compression, and caller ID.

The 700 series CLI is similar to the Unix shell prompt. The prompt will always display which profile you are currently configuring. If you only see a ">" sign or the router's name and ">", you are in the system profile. Otherwise, you are in the standard, LAN, internal, or user profile. If you are stuck and are not sure what command to enter, the 700 series routers support a limited form of context-sensitive help, which works the same way as it does on the IOS-based routers. The **set** commands allow you to make changes to parameters, whereas the **show** commands allow you to view these changes. The **set default** command will erase the configuration on the router and reboot it.

The configuration tasks you will be performing will affect the different profiles on the 700 series router. The router supports 20 different profiles. There is one LAN profile that is used to define parameters for the Ethernet port (or hub), an internal profile that is used to pass traffic between the LAN and WAN interfaces, a system profile for commands that affect the whole router (such as the router's name), and a standard profile and 16 user profiles that are used to define DDR functions for the ISDN interface. With the exception of the system profile, commands executed in a profile affect only that profile. To enter a profile, use the **cd** command followed by the profile name. The prompt will change, including the name of the profile in it. To return to the system profile, execute the **cd** command by itself.

Review Questions

1. A 700 series router that has an "M" after its model number has how much RAM?

   a. 0.5MB

   b. 1MB

   c. 1.5MB

   d. 15MB

2. Which of the following 700 series routers have an integrated NT1 interface? [Choose the two best answers]

   a. 761

   b. 762

   c. 765

   d. 766

3. Which of the following is not a standard software feature of the 700 series routers?

   a. PAT

   b. DHCP relay agent

   c. IPX spoofing

   d. Stacker compression

4. Which of the following is not a software feature of the 700 series routers?

   a. IP spoofing

   b. Access-lists

   c. PAT

   d. DHCP relay agent

5. Which of the following is not a PPP feature of the 700 series routers?

   a. Caller-ID screening

   b. 4:1 compression using Predictor

   c. Dial callback

   d. Multilink

6. _____ brings up the CLI context-sensitive help.

7. The _____ command sets the router back to its factory defaults and reboots the router. This is equivalent to **erase start/write erase** and **reload** on the IOS-based routers.

8. What command saves the configuration on a 700 series router?

   a. **copy running-config startup-config**

   b. **copy startup-config running-config**

   c. **upload**

   d. None

9. What command do you use to view the commands configured on the 700 series router?

   a. **show config**

   b. **write terminal**

   c. **show running-config**

   d. **upload**

10. What is the command to back up the 700 series' configuration file to a TFTP server: _____

11. How many profiles does a 700 series router support?

    a. None

    b. 10

    c. 15

    d. 20

8

12. Which profile type, when you're performing changes, affects the whole router?

    a. Internal

    b. System

    c. LAN

    d. User

13. The _____ command returns you from a profile to the system profile.

14. The _____ command creates a user profile.

15. An incoming phone call can be processed by a profile that is inactive.

    a. True

    b. False

16. Which command changes the name of the router?

    a. **set systemname**

    b. **set name**

    c. **set hostname**

    d. **hostname**

17. What commands are necessary to appropriately assign an IP address? [Choose the two best answers]

    a. **ip address** *IP_address subnet_mask*

    b. **set ip address** *IP_address*

    c. **set ip netmask** *subnet_mask*

    d. **set ip address** *IP_address subnet_mask*

18. To have the central site router challenge the 700 series router in one-way authentication, which PPP authentication command should you use on the 700 series router?

    a. **set ppp auth incoming**

    b. **set ppp auth outgoing**

19. What command should you use to assign the CHAP password if the 700 series router will be initiating the challenge?

    a. **set ppp secret client**

    b. **set ppp secret host**

20. The _____ command assigns a phone number to a user profile.

21. What command do you use on a user profile for the router's ISDN interface to dynamically acquire its IP addressing information?

    a. **set ip address 0.0.0.0**

    b. **set ip netmask 0.0.0.0**

    c. **set ip route destination 0.0.0.0/0 gateway** *remote_IP_address*

    d. **set ip acquire**

22. What command is not required to enable routing on a user profile?

    a. **set ip address**

    b. **set ip routing on**

    c. **set ip rip update periodic**

    d. **set bridging off**

    e. None of the above

23. The _____ command sets up the router as a DHCP relay agent.

24. Which of the following items can the 700 series router not assign a DHCP client?

    a. Domain name

    b. Hostname

    c. IP address

    d. WINS server

    e. None of the above

Real-World Projects

Brainstorm Computers, a company located in Orlando, FL, has just won a big programming contract from a company located in Oviedo, a suburb of Orlando. The management at Brainstorm Computers has decided to add a branch office in Oviedo to better serve this large customer. They currently have two employees there who need intermittent access to the corporate office, which is located in the downtown area of Orlando. At most, they expect the office size to remain under five or six employees.

The IT manager, Cecilia Anderson, has decided to place a Cisco 762 router at the Oviedo location and use ISDN to connect it to the corporate office router, a Cisco 3640, which already has an ISDN PRI controller card. The 762 router was previously used by one of the network administrators for his home use to connect to the corporate office. When the network administrator left the company, the router was

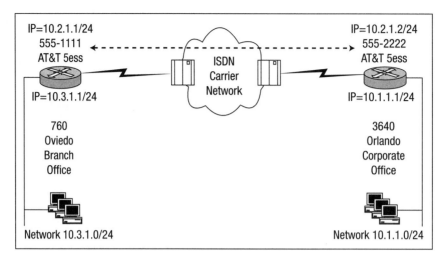

Figure 8.1   Brainstorm Computer's network layout.

returned and has remained on the shelf. The 762 router has an integrated NT1 as well as a single Ethernet port. The PRI on the 3640 router is currently being used for the company's other dial-up needs—ISDN and analog. Brainstorm Computer's planned network layout is shown in Figure 8.1.

Cecilia wants the configuration to remain as simple as possible, so everyone will be using static routes—this way, the ISDN line will not be tying up channels on the PRI 24 hours a day to handle the Oviedo office's intermittent daily traffic. She has entrusted the task of setting up the 762 router and configuration as well as the 3640 router's configuration to get the connection up and running to you, her junior network administrator.

Project 8.1

You will need to complete the following tasks to configure the 762 router to connect to the 3640 corporate office router:

➤ Prepare the 762 router for ISDN connectivity

➤ Prepare the 3640 router for a DDR connection to the Oviedo router

➤ Verify that the dial-up configuration works from the Oviedo router

Preparing the 762 router for ISDN connectivity:

1. Reset the router's current configuration back to the factory defaults:

```
Net762> set default
Net762>
```

```
Boot version 2.1(1) 11/04/96 17:33
Copyright (c) 1993-1996.  All rights reserved.

POST ........... OK (1.5MB).
Validating FLASH ... OK.
Waiting ...
Booting up .........................
12/17/2000 00:00:00  Connection 1 Opened
> 12/17/2000 00:00:00  L01  0                    Started Operation
>
```

Make sure the prompt displays ">".

2. Assign a name to the router. Use the name "Oviedo762":

```
> set systemname Oviedo762
Oviedo762>
```

Make sure the prompt changes from ">" to "Oviedo762>".

3. Set up ISDN connectivity to the carrier's network and verify connectivity. The switch type that the carrier is using is an AT&T 5ess switch:

```
Oviedo762> set switch 5ess
```

Now verify connectivity to the carrier:

```
Oviedo762> show status
Status
LineStatus
LineActivated
TerminalIdentifierAssigned
Oviedo762>
```

Make sure the line has been activated and the TEI (terminal identifier) has been assigned.

4. Configure the Ethernet interface. You will need to enter the LAN profile to perform this task, which includes the assignment of the IP address and subnet mask. You will be routing IP, so enable this and disable bridging:

```
Oviedo762> cd LAN
Oviedo762:LAN> set ip address 10.3.1.1
Oviedo762:LAN> set ip netmask 255.255.255.0
```

```
Oviedo762:LAN> set ip routing on
Oviedo762:LAN> set bridging off
Oviedo762:LAN> cd
Oviedo762>
```

5. Configure a user profile for the 3640 connection. The profile's name will be "Orlando3640". Set up your IP addressing, including the subnet mask. Configure your routing using a static route to access the corporate site. Next, define the 3640's phone number. Finally, you will need to activate this new profile:

```
Oviedo762> set user Orlando3640
Oviedo762:Orlando3640> set ip address 10.2.1.1
Oviedo762:Orlando3640> set ip netmask 255.255.255.0
Oviedo762:Orlando3640>
Oviedo762:Orlando3640> set ip routing on
Oviedo762:Orlando3640> set bridging off
Oviedo762:Orlando3640> set ip route destination 0.0.0.0/0 gateway
                          10.2.1.2
Oviedo762:Orlando3640>
Oviedo762:Orlando3640> set number 555-2222
Oviedo762:Orlando3640>
Oviedo762:Orlando3640> set active
Oviedo762:Orlando3640> cd
Oviedo762>
```

6. Verify your configuration. Use the **upload** command to print out your configuration:

```
Oviedo762> upload
CD
SET SCREENLENGTH 24
SET COUNTRYGROUP 1
SET LAN MODE ANY
SET WAN MODE ONLY
SET AGE OFF
SET MULTIDESTINATION OFF
SET SWITCH 5ESS
SET AUTODETECTION  OFF
SET 1 DELAY 30
SET 2 DELAY 30
SET BRIDGING ON
SET LEARN ON
SET PASSTHRU OFF
SET SPEED AUTO
```

```
SET PLAN NORMAL
SET 1 AUTO ON
SET 2 AUTO ON
SET 1 NUMBER
SET 2 NUMBER
SET 1 BACKUPNUMBER
SET 2 BACKUPNUMBER
SET 1 RINGBACK
SET 2 RINGBACK
SET CLICALLBACK OFF
SET SYSTEMNAME Oviedo762
LOG CALLS TIME VERBOSE
SET UNICASTFILTER OFF
DEMAND 1 THRESHOLD 0
DEMAND 2 THRESHOLD 48
DEMAND 1 DURATION 1
DEMAND 2 DURATION 1
DEMAND 1 SOURCE LAN
DEMAND 2 SOURCE BOTH
TIMEOUT 1 THRESHOLD 0
TIMEOUT 2 THRESHOLD 48
TIMEOUT 1 DURATION 0
TIMEOUT 2 DURATION 0
TIMEOUT 1 SOURCE LAN
TIMEOUT 2 SOURCE BOTH
SET REMOTEACCESS PROTECTED
SET LOCALACCESS ON
SET LOGOUT 5
SET CALLERID OFF
SET PPP AUTHENTICATION IN CHAP  PAP
SET PPP AUTHENTICATION OUT NONE
SET PPP CALLBACK REQUEST OFF
SET PPP CALLBACK REPLY OFF
SET PPP NEGOTIATION INTEGRITY 10
SET PPP NEGOTIATION COUNT 10
SET PPP NEGOTIATION RETRY  3000
SET PPP TERMREQ COUNT 2
SET PPP MULTILINK ON
SET COMPRESSION OFF
SET PPP BACP ON
SET PPP ADDRESS NEGOTIATION LOCAL OFF
SET IP PAT UDPTIMEOUT 5
SET IP PAT TCPTIMEOUT 30
SET SNMP CONTACT ""
SET SNMP LOCATION ""
SET SNMP TRAP COLDSTART OFF
```

8

```
SET SNMP TRAP WARMSTART OFF
SET SNMP TRAP LINKDOWN OFF
SET SNMP TRAP LINKUP OFF
SET SNMP TRAP AUTHENTICATIONFAIL OFF
SET DHCP OFF
SET DHCP DOMAIN
SET DHCP NETBIOS_SCOPE
SET VOICEPRIORITY INCOMING INTERFACE PHONE1 ALWAYS
SET VOICEPRIORITY OUTGOING INTERFACE PHONE1 ALWAYS
SET CALLWAITING INTERFACE PHONE1 ON
SET VOICEPRIORITY INCOMING INTERFACE PHONE2 ALWAYS
SET VOICEPRIORITY OUTGOING INTERFACE PHONE2 ALWAYS
SET CALLWAITING INTERFACE PHONE2 ON
SET USER LAN
SET BRIDGING OFF
SET IP ROUTING ON
SET IP ADDRESS 10.3.1.1
SET IP NETMASK 255.255.255.0
SET IP FRAMING ETHERNET_II
SET IP PROPAGATE ON
SET IP COST 1
SET IP RIP RECEIVE V1
SET IP RIP UPDATE OFF
SET USER Internal
SET IP FRAMING ETHERNET_II
SET USER Standard
SET PROFILE ID 000000000000
SET PROFILE POWERUP ACTIVATE
SET PROFILE DISCONNECT KEEP
SET IP ROUTING ON
SET IP ADDRESS 0.0.0.0
SET IP NETMASK 0.0.0.0
SET IP FRAMING NONE
SET IP RIP RECEIVE V1
SET IP RIP UPDATE OFF
SET IP RIP VERSION 1
SET USER Orlando3640
SET PROFILE ID 000000000000
SET PROFILE POWERUP ACTIVE
SET PROFILE DISCONNECT KEEP
SET BRIDGING OFF
SET 1 NUMBER 5552222
SET 2 NUMBER 5552222
SET IP ROUTING ON
SET IP ADDRESS 10.2.1.1
SET IP NETMASK 255.255.255.0
```

```
SET IP FRAMING NONE
SET IP PROPAGATE ON
SET IP COST 1
SET IP RIP RECEIVE V1
SET IP RIP UPDATE OFF
SET IP RIP VERSION 1
SET IP ROUTE DEST 0.0.0.0/0 GATEWAY 10.2.1.2 PROPAGATE OFF COST 1
CD
LOGOUT
Oviedo762>
```

7. Test the connection by placing a manual call to the 3640 router. Make sure the call at least connects—it may disconnect because of authentication problems on the 3640, however:

```
Oviedo762> cd Orlando3640
Oviedo762:Orlando3640> call 5552222
```

8. Configure PPP CHAP authentication. The authentication will be "two way." Use "stormBRAIN" as the password in both directions:

```
Oviedo762> set ppp authentication incoming chap
Oviedo762> set ppp authentication outgoing chap
Oviedo762> cd Orlando3640
Oviedo762:Orlando3640> set ppp secret client
Enter new Password: stormBRAIN
Re-Type new Password: stormBRAIN
Oviedo762:Orlando3640>
Oviedo762:Orlando3640> set ppp secret host
Enter new Password: stormBRAIN
Re-Type new Password: stormBRAIN
Oviedo762:Orlando3640>
```

Prepare the 3640 router for a DDR connection to the Oviedo router:

1. Examine the configuration of the 3640 router. Pay close attention to the configuration of the PRI interface (controller t1/0) and the serial interface associated with it (serial 1/0:23):

```
Orlando3640# show running-config
Building configuration...

Current configuration:
!
version 12.0
```

```
no service password encryption
!
hostname Orlando3640
!
enable password storming
username homeuser password 0 letmein
no ip domain-lookup
isdn switch-type primary-5ess
!
controller t1/0
 framing esf
 linecode b8zs
 pri-group timeslots 1-24
!
interface Ethernet0/0
 ip address 10.1.1.1 255.255.255.0
!
interface Serial0/0
no ip address
 shutdown
!
interface Serial1/0:23
 no ip address
 encapsulation ppp
 dialer pool-member 1
 isdn switch-type primary-5ess
 isdn incoming-voice modem
 no fair-queue
 ppp authentication chap
 ppp multilink
!
interface Group-Async1
 ip unnumbered Ethernet0/0
 encapsulation ppp
 dialer in-band
 dialer-group 1
 async mode interactive
 peer default ip address pool homeusers
 no cdp enable
 ppp authentication chap
 group-range 65 76
!
router igrp 1
 network 10.0.0.0
```

```
!
ip local pool homeusers 10.1.1.200 10.1.1.254
ip classless
!
line con 0
!
line 65 76
 autoselect during-login
 autoselct ppp
 login local
 modem InOut
 modem autoconfigure type mica
 transport input all
 stopbits 1
 flowcontrol hardware
!
line aux 0
!
line vty 0 4
 login local
!
end

Orlando3640#
```

Currently, administrators from home are dialing into the network using analog modems. To efficiently accommodate them, Brainstorm has installed a PRI connection and interface into the router and a bank of 12 mica modems in one of the slots of the 3640. This can be seen by examining the group-async1 interface as well as the configuration for lines 65 through 76.

2. Add a username entry for the Oviedo router. When doing this, make sure you use the same password the Oviedo 762 router has configured (stormBRAIN):

```
Orlando3640# conf t
Orlando3640(config)# username Oviedo762 password stormBRAIN
Orlando3640(config)# end
Orlando3640# copy run start
Building configuration...

Orlando3640#
```

3. Configure a dialer interface for the Oviedo router. On the dialer interface, you will need to configure your IP addressing, PPP information (the encapsulation,

multilink, and CHAP), the name and phone number of the 762 router, and the interface (PRI) to use for dial-out connections (this is a **dialer pool** command):

```
Orlando3640# conf t
Orlando3640(config)# interface Dialer762
Orlando3640(config-if)# dialer inband
Orlando3640(config-if)# ip address 10.2.1.2 255.255.255.0
Orlando3640(config-if)#
Orlando3640(config-if)# encapsulation ppp
Orlando3640(config-if)# ppp multilink
Orlando3640(config-if)# ppp authentication chap
Orlando3640(config-if)#
Orlando3640(config-if)# dialer remote-name Oviedo762
Orlando3640(config-if)# dialer string 5551111
Orlando3640(config-if)#
Orlando3640(config-if)# dialer pool 1
Orlando3640(config)# end
Orlando3640# copy run start
Building configuration...

Orlando3640#
```

4. Ensure that no routing information is being propagated out of the new dialer interface and set up a static route to the Oviedo router. Enter IGRP and set up the dialer interface as passive and then set up a static route to reach the 10.3.1.0 network at the Oviedo location:

```
Orlando3640# conf t
Orlando3640(config)# router igrp 1
Orlando3640(config-router)# passive-interface dialer762
Orlando3640(config-router)# exit
Orlando3640(config)#
Orlando3640(config)# ip route 10.3.1.0 255.255.255.0 dialer762
Orlando3640(config)# end
Orlando3640# copy run start
Building configuration...

Orlando3640#
```

5. Set up a dialer-list that allows any type of IP traffic to trigger a phone call and apply it to the dialer interface:

```
Orlando3640# conf t
Orlando3640(config)# dialer-list 1 protocol ip permit
```

```
Orlando3640(config)#
Orlando3640(config)# interface dialer762
Orlando3640(config-if)# dialer-group 1
Orlando3640(config-if)# end
Orlando3640# copy run start
Building configuration...

Orlando3640#
```

Verify that the dial-up configuration works from the Oviedo router:

1. Call the Orlando router from the "Orlando3640" profile:

```
Oviedo762> cd Orlando3640
Oviedo762:Orlando3640> call
    01/01/1998 00:04:50 L05 0 5552222 Outgoing Call Initiated
    01/01/1998 00:04:53 L08 1 5552222 Call Connected
    01/01/1998 00:04:53 Connection 1 Add Link 1 Channel 1
Oviedo762:Orlando3640> call
```

2. Ping the Orlando router:

```
Oviedo762:Orlando3640> ping 10.2.1.2
    Start sending: round trip time is 76 msec.
```

3. Verify the connection:

```
Oviedo762:Orlando3640> show connection
    Connections 12/17/2000 00:09:23
    Start Date & Time # Name # Ethernet
        1 12/17/2000 00:01:02 # Orlando3640 #
        2 12/17/2000 00:00:00 # # 00 00 00 00 00 00
Link: 1 Channel: 1 Phone: 5552222
```

8

CHAPTER NINE

Configuring X.25 for Remote Access

After completing this chapter, you will be able to:

✓ Describe the characteristics of X.25 for providing remote access solutions

✓ Describe the X.25 protocol stack, including LAPB

✓ Differentiate between an X.25 DTE and DCE

✓ Distinguish the differences between PVC and SVC circuits used for X.25

✓ Understand the fields of the X.121 address and their purpose

✓ Configure Cisco routers for X.25 remote access

An Overview of X.25

X.25 is based on a set of standards that the International Telecommunication Union-Telecommunication Standardization Sector (ITU-T) is responsible for. Developed in the early 1970s, X.25 was designed to cope with the unreliable, high-latency analog connections in WAN environments in a cost-effective manner. It gave telephone companies and carriers a standards-based mechanism to allow the reliable flow of data across their analog networks.

X.25 was the first packet-switched network (PSN) for WAN environments. Packet-switched networks operate under the guise of logical connections, called *virtual circuits* (VCs). VCs provide connectivity between all the edge devices. One of the main reasons this was very popular at the time—and still is today with services such as frame relay and ATM—is that the cost of deployment is greatly reduced over traditional leased-line implementations. With leased lines, for every destination that you wish to connect to, you need a separate line and a separate interface on your edge device. With packet-switched services, such as X.25, you create the illusion of many physical connections by using VCs. On one physical connection on an edge device, many VCs can exist to a multitude of destinations, providing a very cost-effective WAN solution for large WAN networks.

Public vs. Private Networks

Typically, you do not build your own private X.25 network because of the cost associated with all the physical wiring you would have to run between all your remote locations. Instead, you provision your X.25 services from a telephone company or carrier. The advantage of this approach is that your upfront deployment costs are greatly reduced because you are using a common network that many other companies are connected to. However, the downside of this approach is that there are limited guarantees of service because your data is traversing the same network and connections as other companies' data. The tradeoff is cost versus Quality of Service (QoS): You are somewhat sacrificing QoS for a decrease in cost. If you are very concerned about QoS, leased lines are a much better solution because you own all the bandwidth on the connection. For most companies that only require the transmission of traditional data, this is not that important.

Reliability of X.25

Of course, administrators had concerns about using these new PSN networks. For applications that needed reliability, such as SNA, concerns arose about using an unreliable analog medium. Analog connections have a much higher error ratio than today's digital services (such as ISDN, frame relay, and ATM). If information was dropped because of errors, customers did not want to have to retransmit a lot of information. The X.25 protocol stack tackles this task very effectively by providing connection-oriented reliability between each device in the X.25 network as well as a connection-oriented reliability between the two endpoints connected to the X.25 network.

The obvious advantage of this approach is that if information is dropped because of errors, it will be retransmitted by the X.25 devices, not the actual source of the information, which may be a LAN device. With most X.25 networks, carriers can guarantee at least a 99-percent delivery of information across their PSN backbones, thus providing a high level of reliability. The downside, however, is that a lot of latency is introduced into the flow of data—each X.25 device must perform extensive error checking and flow control to maintain a high level of reliability. This is not to say that X.25 is a good solution for only analog connections, because X.25 will also run across a digital circuit. However, because of its built-in reliability mechanisms, it is less efficient than other packet-switched services such as frame relay and ATM.

X.25 was not built as an all-encompassing solution for a company's WAN needs. If you need to transport voice across a WAN, X.25 would be a poor solution because of the increased latency it introduces in the traffic flow. This would cause problems with undesirable echo in the voice conversations. One of its biggest strengths, however, is that because X.25 has been around for almost 30 years, you can use it practically anywhere in the world. This is probably its biggest advantage in WAN environments today. No matter where you need to establish a connection, you can almost bet that X.25 will be available as a service. It is a very stable, reliable protocol that is easy to configure, administer, and troubleshoot.

X.25 Protocol Stack

X.25 is somewhat of a misnomer in that it defines the Network layer connectivity for WAN environments. Link Access Procedure, Balanced (LAPB) defines the Data Link layer, and a variety of standards, such as X.21 and X.32, define the Physical layer. However, in the industry, the composite of these protocols is generally referred to as *X.25*. Figure 9.1 shows a comparison between the OSI reference model and the X.25 protocol stack.

As you can see, the bottom three layers of the OSI Reference Model match up with the only three layers of the X.25 protocol suite. In the ITU–T standard, X.25 is referred to as the *Packet Layer Protocol* (PLP), because it handles layer-3 packet information.

Network Layer: X.25

The X.25 (or PLP) layer is responsible for managing circuits between the two DTEs at layer 3 of the OSI reference model. It is responsible for five different modes:

➤ Call setup

➤ Data transfer

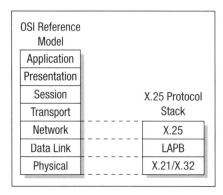

Figure 9.1 The OSI reference model and X.25 protocol stack.

➤ Idle

➤ Call clearing

➤ Restarting

Call Setup Mode

Call setup is only necessary when dealing with Switched Virtual Circuits (SVCs). In this mode, the PLP is responsible for setting up a VC to the destination DTE. It does this by using the destination's address, defined by the X.121 standard, discussed later in this chapter.

Data Transfer Mode

Whenever a virtual circuit is established—after call setup with an SVC or manually created with a Permanent Virtual Circuit (PVC)—data can then be transferred across the circuit. The PLP handles the *data transfer* mode by performing any necessary segmentation of information into X.25 packets and reassembly of X.25 payload information back into the original packet format. Another of its functions is to handle layer-3 error and flow control. If any errors are seen in the X.25 packet, the DTE will acknowledge this to the source and cause the source to resend the information. To remove any chance of overrunning each other's buffers, the PLP implements windowing as a flow-control mechanism. Based on the window size the two devices are using, the source can send as many frames to the destination as specified by the window size. Once sending the maximum number, it will wait for the destination to acknowledge the receipt of the frames. Also, the acknowledgement is used for error checking—if a packet is lost between the two, the destination acknowledges back to the source the *next* packet that it is expecting (that is, the lost one). The source then starts resending packets starting from this point forward. Also, to prevent the loss of large amounts of information, PLP supports different packet sizes that you can adjust for your specific environment. These are similar mechanisms to what TCP employs in the IP protocol suite.

Other Modes

The *idle* mode is only used for SVCs. This is used by PLP when there is no information being transferred between the two devices, but the VC has already been set up. Once the user is finished transferring his information, the PLP will tear down the SVC in the *call-clearing* mode. The last mode that the PLP is responsible for is the *restarting* mode. This mode is used on a user's interface connected to the carrier's X.25 switch. Whenever the interface of the user comes up, a synchronization will occur between the two connected devices.

PLP Packet

The PLP packet contains four fields, as shown in Figure 9.2.

The GFI (General Format Identifier) defines whether this packet contains data from the user or is control information between the two X.25 end-user devices. If it is the latter, other information is included in this header, such as the sequence number used for flow control and windowing and the acknowledgment number.

The LCI (Logical Channel Identifier) is the address of the VC—it uniquely identifies the circuit on a connection. Note that the VC address is locally significant—it only has meaning on the segment between the two directly connected physical devices, such as the user's router and the carrier's switch, or between two of the carrier's switches. In other words, the LCI value of a circuit could change on a segment-by-segment basis—it is up to the X.25 switches to maintain this information in their switching tables and to update the PLP headers correctly when switching packets. In this sense, the LCI is functioning like the Data Link Connection Identifier (DLCI) in frame relay.

The PTI (Packet Type Identifier) identifies the contents contained in the payload. Some possible types are IP, IPX, and AppleTalk.

The User Data portion of the PLP contains data information. If this information is from the user, the contents would contain information such as IP and IPX packets. Otherwise, control information can be contained here.

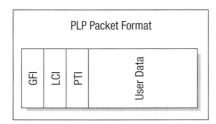

Figure 9.2   PLP packet format.

Data Link Layer: LAPB

The X.25 protocol stack uses Link Access Procedure Balanced (LAPB) as its Data Link layer protocol. This is used to provide communication between two directly connected devices, such as a router and a carrier's X.25 switch. LAPB also defines the frame type to use, which it heavily borrows from ISO's HDLC frame format. Like PLP, LAPB provides a reliable connection—it uses error and flow control to maintain the integrity of the information between the two connected devices.

One advantage of this approach is that each segment can be tuned with different window and packet sizes, allowing a high degree of optimization and efficiency. If one segment is somewhat susceptible to errors, you can lower the window and packet sizes, reducing the amount of information that needs to be transmitted when errors do occur. However, for reliable links, you can create larger window and packet sizes, thus using the bandwidth on the segment more efficiently.

Physical Layer

The two initial standards that defined connectivity between two X.25 devices were X.21 and X.32. X.21 is a Physical layer protocol that defines the physical properties for a dedicated synchronous connection between two devices. X.32 defines a synchronous modem connection between two devices. One shortcoming of these two standards is that they only support speeds up to 19.2Kbps, which is slow by today's standards. Other physical medium types are supported. For instance, Cisco supports the following additional standards:

➤ EIA/TIA-232

➤ EIA/TIA-449

➤ EIA-530

➤ G.703

X.25 DTE and DCE

When employing X.25 for your WAN services, you will find two types of devices: data terminal equipment (DTE) and data circuit-terminating equipment (DCE). If you remember, these two terms were discussed in Chapter 2. In Chapter 2, these terms were used to describe Physical layer properties. X.25, however, uses these terms differently. An X.25 DTE terminates a VC from the carrier, whereas an X.25 DCE is responsible for switching X.25 packets across those circuits. DTE and DCE, in this sense, are not describing a Physical layer process, but a Data Link and Network layer one.

Examples of DTEs would be routers and front-end processors (FEPs), whereas DCEs would be X.25 carrier switches (which can also be Cisco routers, because Cisco

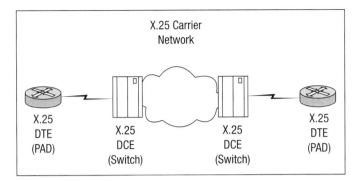

Figure 9.3   X.25 DTE and DCE connectivity.

supports X.25 switching in its router line). Figure 9.3 gives an example of this type of interconnection.

X.25 PAD

The X.25 DTE is called a *packet assembler/disassembler* (PAD). This name defines the basic function of the X.25 DTE. One issue in the early days of networking, before such devices as routers, was that the devices that needed to transfer information across the network did not have the intelligence or capability of handling the extra overhead of the X.25 process. A special device was developed to handle the integration of non-X.25 devices to an X.25 network: the PAD. The PAD performs three basic functions: First, when a user has data to send, it segments that data to fit into X.25 packets—the disassembler part. Second, as X.25 packets are coming in, the PAD needs to extract the contents from the packets and place them into a buffer. Third, once it has received all the original packets (be they IP, IPX, and so on), the PAD must then reassemble all the pieces back into the original user packet. In today's world, the function of the PAD is usually built into the end-user device. In Cisco's case, the PAD functionality is part of the IOS of the router.

Throughout this whole process, the PAD is responsible for sending and retrieving information from the VCs that connect it to the DCE and, ultimately, the X.25 switched network. Whenever an X.25 DTE sends out X.25 packets to a destination device, it expects an acknowledgment from the destination DTE upon receipt of the packets. The X.25 layer supports windowing as a flow-control mechanism to ensure that a destination's buffer does not overflow, thus causing the retransmittal of information.

It is important to note that the PAD functions at the X.25 layer, or layer 3. Therefore, all flow control happens between the source and destination PADs, not between the PAD and the switch, or between the switches themselves. The switches are unaware of this specific flow-control mechanism. Later, you'll learn how flow control is handled when traffic is sent between two directly connected devices, such as a DTE and a DCE or two DCEs.

X.25 Switch

The X.25 DCE is the X.25 switch. Its main function is to pull in X.25 packets from the DTE and switch them out the correct destination port based on VC information inside the X.25 packet header. When X.25 DCEs interoperate with other DCEs or a PAD, the switch operates at two levels. First, the DCE must look at the X.25 packet to make a switching decision to get the packet to the correct destination. Second, the DCE is responsible for flow control. This is slightly different than the flow control employed by the DTE-to-DTE connection, because this process is handled by the X.25 layer. With the DCE, LAPB handles all flow control between the switch and either its connected DTE or DCE. Therefore, if a LAPB frame becomes corrupted between two devices—for instance, two DCEs—the frame is resent from the source DCE. This works out very well because the DTE at the edge of the X.25 network does not have to be involved in the resending process. Actually, it is completely unaware of the fact that something became corrupted and had to be resent.

You would think that this is a very big advantage, and it is in many cases; however, the downside to this process is that there is flow control happening at two layers: the network layer between the two DTEs and the Data Link Layer between two connected devices. This lower layer of flow control adds additional overhead in the form of extra acknowledgements. This is examined in more depth in the "Configuring X.25" section, later in this chapter.

X.25 Virtual Circuits

X.25 is a connection-oriented protocol. This means that a connection must exist between the source and destination before any information can be transmitted. To provide the connection, X.25 uses a virtual circuit (VC). A VC is a bidirectional, full-duplexed, logical connection between two devices. Note that a physical connection between two devices can hold many VCs. A VC is not bound to a specific physical connection—it can traverse many segments between the source and destination X.25 DTEs.

Basically, VCs provide a multiplexing function—on one interface you can connect to a multitude of destinations. Of course, something must uniquely identify the circuit so that the source knows which VC to use when sending information to a particular destination; likewise, the destination must know how to process the information correctly when it performs a demultiplexing function.

Types of VCs

X.25 supports two types of VCs: switched (SVCs) and permanent (PVCs). SVCs are temporary connections, similar to the circuit-switched connections that a carrier's telephone network uses. When a user has information to send, the X.25 DTE requests an SVC to be set up. Once the SVC is operational, the user sends his information and, when finished, requests the SVC to be torn down. Typically this is thought of as a Session layer function, but all packet-switched WAN protocols, such as X.25, frame relay, and ATM, do not have the luxury of having additional layers in their protocol suites, so they implement them appropriately.

PVCs, on the other hand, are permanent VCs between the two PADs. This is similar to a dedicated leased line. Because the circuit already exists, the transfer of data can occur at any time. One disadvantage that SVCs have over PVCs is that they have additional latency because they must initially set up a VC before transferring data. However, PVCs usually cost more and therefore should be used only when you are constantly moving information between two sites.

PVC Addressing

In either case, a VC must have a unique address so that traffic from different sites can be differentiated by the PAD. This is a decimal number between 1 and 4,095. This information is placed in the X.25 PLP so that the switch can forward it to the correct destination. Your provider will assign this value to you for both ends of your circuits.

Note: This is locally significant, and the value could be different at the two endpoint PADs.

SVC Addressing

SVCs present a unique problem in that no VC initially exists between two devices. Somehow, the source PAD must have some type of addressing knowledge about the destination PAD. X.25 uses X.121 addresses to solve this problem. Unlike PVC virtual circuit numbers, which are locally significant, X.121 addresses must be unique through-out the network (and unique throughout the world if you are connected to a public X.25 network).

X.121 addresses are made up of two components:

➤ Data Network Identification Code (DNIC)

➤ National Terminal Number (NTN)

The DNIC, which is optional, identifies the country and carrier where the X.25 DTE resides. The DNIC is four decimal digits in length. There are reserved numbers for the assignment of addresses when connecting to a public X.25 network, some of which are listed in Table 9.1.

The DNIC is made of two subfields—one is the global region, and the other is the X.25 carrier's number within that region. For a more complete listing of reserved addresses, visit ITU-T's Web site at **www.itu.org**.

The NTN is the identifier used to uniquely identify your X.25 PAD in an X.25 carrier's network. When you connect to a provider's network, you will be assigned

Table 9.1   X.121 reserved addresses.

X.121 Address Range	Global Location
200s	Europe
300s	North America, including the U.S.
400s	Asia
500s	Pacific Islands
600s	Africa
700s	South America

a value to use for your PAD. The NTN can range from 8 to 10 or 11 decimal digits, depending on the providers' X.25 software on their switches.

Note: If you are building your own private X.25 network and plan on using SVCs, you will still need to come up with X.121 addresses. However, you do not need to follow the nomenclature of the X.121 format. The addresses can range anywhere from 1 to 15 digits in length.

As mentioned earlier, to set up an SVC to a destination, you will have to know the destination's X.121 address. When performing the call setup, your PAD will pass the X.121 address to the X.25 switch, which will go through the process of setting up the VC. When the switches are setting up the VC, they will be assigning a VC number between 1 and 4,095 on each segment that the VC traverses. Once the VC is set up, the two endpoint switches connected to the two PADs will share the local VC number so that the PADs can start transmitting their data. Once the SVC is set up, it operates no differently from a PVC. Based on your specific needs, you can use both PVCs and SVCs on the same interface of a PAD.

X.25 VCs and User Data

Once the VC is set up, you are now ready to move your data across it. X.25 allows a multitude of protocols to traverse a single X.25 VC. Cisco supports the following protocols:

➤ IP

➤ IP with compressed TCP headers

➤ IPX

➤ AppleTalk

➤ CLNS

➤ XNS

➤ VINES

➤ Bridged traffic

➤ DECnet

X.25 accomplishes this by encapsulating these different kinds of packets inside a PLP packet. This process, defined in RFC 1356, is sometimes called *tunneling*. Tunneling is defined as encapsulating traffic from either the same layer of the OSI reference model or lower into another protocol. An example of this would include one of X.25's supported protocols—IP. IP is layer 3, and X.25 is layer 3.

Address Resolution

Unfortunately, X.25 does not support inverse-ARP, as does frame relay. Inverse-ARP allows two connected devices to advertise their layer-3 address across the VC, thereby allowing the two sides to dynamically discover who resides at the other end of the circuit. In X.25, this process is done manually. On Cisco routers, as you will see in the "Configuring X.25" section, this is done with **x25 map** statements.

For each protocol that you want to send across the VC, you must map the corresponding destination layer-3 address to it. You can map up to nine protocols to one destination PAD. If you had two protocols—IP and IPX, for example—that you wanted to traverse a circuit, you would have to map the destination PAD's IP and IPX addresses to the local VC in order for them to use it. If you did not take this necessary step, no information would traverse the VC.

Usage of VCs

You must plan carefully when setting up your network, especially in the number of VCs that you will need to provision. You are allowed up to 4,095 VCs on a single interface of the PAD. How you use these VCs has a definite impact—positive or negative—on the efficiency of the transmission of your data traffic.

For instance, you could send all your information across one VC between two destinations: IP, IPX, and every other protocol would use the same VC. One advantage of this approach is that it simplifies your setup and maintenance. However, its downside is that one type of traffic, such as IP, could negatively affect your other traffic, such as DECnet and IPX. If this is your concern, you could set up a separate VC per protocol and use a Cisco feature called *Generic Traffic Shaping* to allot bandwidth appropriate to your protocols' needs.

One less-obvious reason for using multiple VCs is shown in Figure 9.4.

In this example, the access link speed is 28.8Kbps. If you set up only one VC between the two PADs, you would not get 28.8 throughput because there is a 9.6Kbps bottleneck between the two switches. At most, you would get 9.6Kbps throughput, no matter what bandwidth you had available on your DTE-DCE connection. To solve this problem, you could deploy three separate PVCs, each one traversing a different link between the two DCEs, thereby getting a full 28.8Kbps between the two PADs. Of course, you will have to work very closely with your X.25 provider to determine these kinds of limitations.

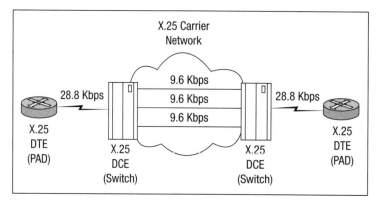

Figure 9.4 X.25 and the use of multiple VCs.

Imagine for the previous example that you needed to enforce bandwidth restrictions between different protocols, where each required a separate VC, and some of them needed more than 9.6Kbps worth of bandwidth to accommodate peaks in their traffic. Because of these types of issues—link speed limitations, multiple protocols, and address resolution—your configuration can become quite complex and involve hundreds of VCs to solve your remote access needs.

Note: Cisco allows eight SVCs per protocol for each destination that you wish to connect to.

Configuring X.25

All of the configuration of X.25 is done on your serial interfaces that connect to your X.25 provider. When configuring X.25 on a Cisco router, you must perform three required tasks in order for X.25 to work correctly:

➤ Set up your X.25 encapsulation.

➤ Define your X.121 address provided by your carrier.

➤ Set up your statements for resolution to destination PADs.

Required Configuration Tasks

First, configure your X.25 encapsulation on your serial interface:

```
Router(config)# interface serial [module_number/]port_number
Router(config-if)# encapsulation x25 [dte|dce]
```

If you omit the **dte** or **dce** parameter from the **encapsulation** command, it defaults to **dte**, which means that the interface will act as a PAD (**dce** means that the interface will act as a switch). If you decide to change the PAD/switch function, all the

X.25 configuration commands will disappear from the interface, requiring you to reenter them one by one.

After you have defined the interface, you will next need to specify your X.121 address. Even if you are using PVCs, you will need this statement (again, this is done on the interface):

```
Router(config)# interface serial [module_number/]port_number
Router(config-if)# x25 address x.121_address
```

The X.121 address can be between 1 and 15 decimal digits. If you are connected to a public carrier, they will assign this value to you.

The last required command is the resolution statement. There are two different commands, depending on whether you are configuring SVCs or PVCs. The following is the X.25 command for setting up an SVC:

```
Router(config)# interface serial [module_number/]port_number
Router(config-if)# x25 map protocol protocol_destination_address
                   [protocol2 protocol_destination_address2]...
                   destination_x.121_address
                   [broadcast]
```

The *protocol* parameter can include **ip, ipx, appletalk, xns, decnet, vines, clns, apollo, bridge**, and/or **compressed tcp**. The *protocol_destination_address* parameter is the protocol address of the destination PAD. You must also include the X.121 address of the destination PAD. There is an optional parameter, **broadcast**, that permits broadcasts to traverse the VC.

*Note: X.25 is a NBMA (Non-Broadcast Multiaccess) environment. This means that broadcasts, by default, do not work. The **broadcast** option overrides this behavior.*

If you are configuring PVCs, the syntax is slightly different:

```
Router(config-if)# x25 pvc circuit_number
                   protocol protocol_destination_address
                   [protocol2 protocol_destination_address2]...
                   destination_x.121_address
                   [broadcast]
```

The *circuit_number* parameter is the value that the switch is expecting for the PVC. All the other parameters are the same as those used for configuring the **map** statement for SVCs.

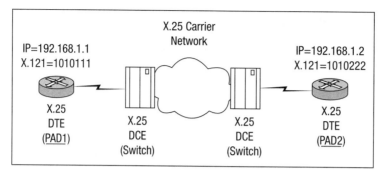

Figure 9.5 Simple X.25 network.

Examples

Figure 9.5 shows an example of a simple X.25 network with two PADs.

SVC Example

The first code example involves configuring SVCs on both PAD1 and PAD2. Here is the coding example for PAD1:

```
PAD1(config)# interface serial 0
PAD1(config-if)# encapsulation x25
PAD1(config-if)# ip address 192.168.1.1 255.255.255.0
PAD1(config-if)# x25 address 1010111
PAD1(config-if)# x25 map ip 192.168.1.2 1010222 broadcast
PAD1(config-if)# no shutdown
```

And here's the example for PAD2:

```
PAD2(config)# interface serial 0
PAD2(config-if)# encapsulation x25
PAD2(config-if)# ip address 192.168.1.2 255.255.255.0
PAD2(config-if)# x25 address 1010222
PAD2(config-if)# x25 map ip 192.168.1.1 1010111 broadcast
PAD2(config-if)# no shutdown
```

Notice that for the **encapsulation** command on both interfaces, neither **dte** nor **dce** was specified, which means the encapsulation defaults to **dte** (the interface will act as a PAD). The **broadcast** parameter is used in order to allow broadcast traffic to traverse the SVC.

PVC Example

This next example involves the same situation just described, but it uses PVCs instead. In this case, the provider has assigned a value of 5 for the PVC on PAD1 and 10 for the PVC on PAD2.

Here is the code example for PAD1:

```
PAD1(config)# interface serial 0
PAD1(config-if)# encapsulation x25
PAD1(config-if)# ip address 192.168.1.1 255.255.255.0
PAD1(config-if)# x25 address 1010111
PAD1(config-if)# x25 pvc 5 ip 192.168.1.2 1010222 broadcast
PAD1(config-if)# no shutdown
```

And here's the code example for PAD2:

```
PAD2(config)# interface serial 0
PAD2(config-if)# encapsulation x25
PAD2(config-if)# ip address 192.168.1.2 255.255.255.0
PAD2(config-if)# x25 address 1010222
PAD2(config-if)# x25 pvc 10 192.168.1.1 1010111 broadcast
PAD2(config-if)# no shutdown
```

Other than using the **pvc** parameter with the VC number instead of the **map** parameter, the configurations are exactly the same.

Optional Configuration Tasks

As you have seen in the overview of the protocol, X.25 is over-engineered compared to today's reliable digital circuits. Because of the high probability of errors occurring in analog connections, both X.25 and LAPB use error checking and windowing (flow control) to deal with these problems. When you compare this technology with newer technologies such as frame relay and ATM, you'll note that the newer technologies do not employ these techniques because of the inherent reliability in the digital circuits that they use: They rely on upper layers to provide error checking and correction mechanisms. That is not to say that X.25 is an obsolete protocol, because not every destination that you wish to connect to will support digital circuits. This is true of many second- and third-world countries, especially in Africa and Asia.

One of the concerns in X.25 is the retransmission of traffic when errors occur. Many X.25 networks typically bill customers for every packet they transmit. Obviously, if you had to continuously retransmit packets, your price would go up. Therefore, an optimal window size is of utmost importance in the transmission of your data. You would think that you would want your window size to be large so that the number of acknowledgements that were generated were small in number, thereby reducing your overall cost.

However, a window size that is set too large could create a lot of retransmissions. Imagine a window size of 100 and the X.25 DTE sends 100 packets, but the very first one is discarded because of a bad CRC. Not just the first packet, but *all* 100 would be resent, which is bad if there are continuous errors in your packets. Of course, setting a window size too small is just as bad. Imagine a window size of 1—for each packet you send, you will get an acknowledgement back. The problem with this is that you have just doubled the price for your X.25 circuit.

With X.25, you have a lot of flexibility because you can adjust not just the window size, but also the packet size, to create an efficient and reliable data transfer.

Changing X.25 Packet Sizes

By default, Cisco uses a packet size of 128 bytes. You can change this with the following configuration commands:

```
Router(config)# interface serial [module_number/]port_number
Router(config-if)# x25 ips packet_size_in_bytes
Router(config-if)# x25 ops packet_size_in_bytes
```

Remember that X.25 uses bidirectional VCs. These two commands allow you to create different packet sizes in both directions. The **ips** parameter represents the packet size for incoming packets, and the **ops** parameter represents the packet size for outgoing packets. The incoming size on one PAD must match the outgoing size on the destination PAD, and vice versa. Normally, you would configure the values the same. Valid values for this command are 16, 32, 64, 128, 256, 512, 1024, 2048, and 4096.

Tip: Before you become ambitious and try to start tuning your network by changing these values, you should first check with your carrier, who might have a maximum packet size that is smaller than what you configured. If this is the case, all packets sent to the carrier that exceed this packet size will be dropped.

Changing X.25 Window Parameters

Besides changing the packet sizes for your VCs, you can also change the window sizes. Three commands affect the window sizes; these are shown in the following code example:

```
Router(config)# interface serial [module_number/]port_number
Router(config-if)# x25 win window_size
Router(config-if)# x25 wout window_size
Router(config-if)# x25 modulo window_modulus
```

The **win** and **wout** parameters define the window size in both directions on the VCs, just like the packet size parameters (that is, how many X.25 packets can be sent before the source PAD has to wait for an acknowledgement from the destination). However, you cannot change these values haphazardly, because they are dependent on the **modulo** value. By default, the modulus is set to 8. This means that you can have window sizes from 1 to 7. If you change the modulus to its only other value, 128, you can increase your window size from 8 to 127. The default window size for your VCs is 2. Based on the modulus, this value can be any value between 1 and 127.

Tip: For analog connections, it is highly recommended that you leave the modulus to its default, 8. Setting it to 128 and creating larger window sizes will create a lot of retransmissions and greatly decrease your efficiency and throughput.

Setting Restrictions for VC Circuit Numbers

For SVCs, you can set limits to the ranges of VC numbers that can be used to identify your VCs. It is preferred that your PVC circuit numbers be lower than the ones that you will employ for your SVCs. The following commands are used to implement this restriction:

```
Router(config)# interface serial [module_number/]port_number
Router(config-if)# x25 lic circuit_number
Router(config-if)# x25 hic circuit_number
Router(config-if)# x25 ltc circuit_number
Router(config-if)# x25 htc circuit_number
Router(config-if)# x25 loc circuit_number
Router(config-if)# x25 hoc circuit_number
```

For these parameters to function correctly, both the PAD and switch must have the same restrictions defined. The preceding commands are broken into three categories:

➤ Incoming SVC call setup requests by the switch (**lic** and **hic**)

➤ Two-way SVC call setup requests by either the PAD or switch (**ltc** and **htc**)

➤ Outgoing SVC call setup requests by the PAD (**loc** and **hoc**)

The **lxc** and **hxc** parameters are used to restrict the values the switch can use when setting up an SVC to this PAD. Here, "l" represents *lowest*, and "h" represents *highest*. Whatever values you specify, the lowest value must be lower than or equal to the highest value. Likewise, your range of values between the three categories cannot overlap.

Example

Building on the previous PVC example in the last section, using Figure 9.5, we will add to it some additional configuration commands—the default packet size will be changed to 256, and the window size will be changed to 5.

Here is the PVC code example for PAD1:

```
PAD1(config)# interface serial 0
PAD1(config-if)# encapsulation x25
PAD1(config-if)# ip address 192.168.1.1 255.255.255.0
PAD1(config-if)# x25 address 1010111
PAD1(config-if)# x25 pvc 5 ip 192.168.1.2 1010222 broadcast
PAD1(config-if)# x25 ips 256
PAD1(config-if)# x25 ops 256
PAD1(config-if)# x25 win 5
```

9

```
PAD1(config-if)# x25 wout 5
PAD1(config-if)# no shutdown
```

And here's the PVC code example for PAD2:

```
PAD2(config)# interface serial 0
PAD2(config-if)# encapsulation x25
PAD2(config-if)# ip address 192.168.1.2 255.255.255.0
PAD2(config-if)# x25 address 1010222
PAD2(config-if)# x25 pvc 10 192.168.1.1 1010111 broadcast
PAD2(config-if)# x25 ips 256
PAD2(config-if)# x25 ops 256
PAD2(config-if)# x25 win 5
PAD2(config-if)# x25 wout 5
PAD2(config-if)# no shutdown
```

Verifying X.25 Configuration

To verify your configuration, you will use the **show interfaces** command. Using the preceding example, here is some sample output from PAD1:

```
Router# show interfaces serial 0
Serial 0 is up, line protocol is up
    Hardware is MCI Serial
    Internet address is 192.168.1.1, subnet mask is 255.255.255.0
    MTU 1500 bytes, BW 1544 Kbit, DLY 20000 usec,
                        rely 255/255, load 1/255
    Encapsulation X25, loopback not set
    X.25 DTE, address 1010111, state R1, modulo 8, timer 0
    Defaults: idle VC timeout 0
    Cisco encapsulation
    Input/output window sizes 5/5, packet sizes 256/256
    Timers T20 180, T21 200, T22 180, T23 180
    Channels: Incoming-only none, Two-way 1-1024, Outgoing-only none
    RESTARTS 1/0 CALLS 0+0/0+0/0+0 DIAGS 0/0
    LAPB DTE, state CONNECT, modulo 8, k 7, N1 12056, N2 20
    T1 3000, T2 0, interface outage (partial T3) 0, T4 0
    VS 5, VR 3, tx NR 3, Remote VR 5, Retransmissions 0
    Queues: U/S frames 0, I frames 0, unack. 0, reTx 0
    IFRAMES 5/3 RNRs 0/0 REJs 0/0 SAMB/Es 0/1 FRMRs 0/0 DISCs 0/0
    Last input 0:00:21, output 0:00:21, output hang never
    Last clearing of "show interface" counters never
    Queueing strategy: fifo
    Output queue 0/40, 0 drops; input queue 0/75, 0 drops
    Five minute input rate 0 bits/sec, 0 packets/sec
    Five minute output rate 0 bits/sec, 0 packets/sec
        16263 packets input, 1347238 bytes, 0 no buffer
```

```
        Received 13983 broadcasts, 0 runts, 0 giants
        2 input errors, 0 CRC, 0 frame, 0 overrun, 0 ignored, 2 abort
<Output omitted>
```

When examining the output of this command, you want to pay special attention to the X.25 values. Make sure the encapsulation is "X25". On the line below this, verify that the router is a DTE and check its X.121 address. Remember that if a PAD does not have an X.121 address, X.25 will not function. The third parameter in this command, **state**, represents the state of the X.25 interface. The possible values are shown in Table 9.2.

Make sure that the state is "R1". Also, check the modulus value listed to the right of the state display.

The next line of output to examine is three lines down from this—verify your configured window and packet sizes.

To check whether or not you are receiving information, check the input and output rates at the bottom of the display.

Chapter Summary

X.25 is a protocol stack developed in the early 1970s to overcome the issues involved in moving data across a public switched network using unreliable analog lines. To deal with these issues, X.25, at layer 3, implements flow and error control as well as LAPB at layer 2.

The implementation of X.25 involves devices called DTEs and DCEs. A DTE, also known as a *PAD*, is responsible for taking user data and fragmenting and encapsulating it into X.25 packets, which it then forwards to the DCE, the carrier X.25 switch. The primary responsibility of the DCE is to switch the X.25 packets across the network to the correct destination.

For connectivity, X.25 uses VCs, which can be PVCs, SVCs, or a combination of the two, depending on your specific needs. Because X.25 is connection oriented, a VC must first be established before data can be transmitted into the network. Regardless of whether you are using PVCs or SVCs, there are three required steps that you must perform on the serial interface. First, you must specify the encapsulation type as a DTE for X.25 by using the **encapsulation x25** command.

Table 9.2   X.25 interface states.

State	Description
R1	The interface is in an operational state.
R2	The DTE is in the process of restarting.
R3	The DCE is in the process of restarting.

Second, you must specify the X.121 address for your PAD using the **x25 address** command. X.121 addresses are composed of two components: the Data Network Identification Code (DNIC) and the National Terminal Number (NTN). The DNIC is four digits in length and represents the global region and country as well as the X.25 carrier. The NTN uniquely defines your PAD within the carrier's network. The NTN can range from 8 to 11 digits. When you purchase X.25 services, your provider will assign you a unique number for communication in the public X.25 network. If, however, you will be building your own private X.25 network, the addressing scheme you use becomes much looser—the X.121 address can range from 1 to 15 digits. You only need to ensure that each of your PADs has a unique address.

Third, you must establish VC connectivity. You have two choices: Either use a PVC or an SVC. With PVCs, you predefine the VC number for each PVC that you have. To do this, use the **x25 pvc** command on the interface with the VC number that the switch expects. For an SVC, use the **x25 map** statement with the destination X.121 address that you wish to connect to. With either of these two commands, you will also have to specify the protocol that you wish to encapsulate in the X.25 packets and the destination layer-3 address. If you want broadcast traffic to traverse your VC, you will need to add the optional **broadcast** parameter.

To optimize your connectivity, you can perform some optional tasks. For example, you can manipulate the X.25 packet sizes, which default to 128 bytes, to create a more efficient payload size. These can range from 64 to 4,096 bytes in length. You can also change the default widow size from 2 to a value that works better in your environment. Remember that if you want to change the window size to a value greater than 7, you will first have to change the modulus from 8 to 128. Window sizes can span from 1 to 127. Finally, you can affect the VC numbers that SVCs can use—you will want to coordinate this with your X.25 carrier because the restrictions you place on your DTE must match the carrier's DCE configuration.

Review Questions

1. X.25 supports all the following features except which one?

   a. Error correction

   b. Connection oriented

   c. Flow control

   d. Low latency

2. X.25 uses what protocol at layer 2?

   a. LAPD

   b. HDLC

   c. LAPB

   d. LAPF

3. The PLP supports all the following modes except which one?

    a. Idle

    b. Restarting

    c. Call clearing

    d. Call cancel

4. Which field of the PLP packet identifies the VC number?

    a. GFI

    b. LCI

    c. PTI

    d. User data

5. LAPB is related to which protocol?

    a. HDLC

    b. SDLC

    c. LAPD

    d. LAPF

6. Which of the following is an X.25 DTE?

    a. DCE

    b. PAD

    c. DTR

    d. PDA

7. What does PAD stands for?

    a. Packetization and depacketization

    b. Protocol assembler/disassembler

    c. Payload and data

    d. Packet assembler/disassembler

8. Which device switches X.25 packets?

    a. DTE

    b. PAD

    c. DCE

    d. DTR

9. What type of circuit is temporary?

    a. PVC

    b. SVC

9

10. How many X.25 VCs can you configure on an interface on a Cisco router?

    a. Depends on the amount of RAM

    b. 1,024

    c. 2,048

    d. 4,095

    e. 4,096

11. X.121 addresses are made up of which two components? [Choose the two best answers]

    a. DNIC

    b. PAD

    c. NTN

    d. Country code

12. X.121 addresses have a maximum length of what?

    a. 4

    b. 8

    c. 11

    d. 15

13. Which of the following are mechanisms used by X.25 to perform address resolution? [Choose the two best answers]

    a. The **x25 map** command

    b. The **x25 pvc** command

    c. Inverse-ARP

    d. The **x25 address** command

14. How many X.25 SVCs can you configure per protocol per destination on an interface of the router?

    a. 1

    b. 4

    c. 8

    d. 9

15. Which is not a requirement when configuring X.25 on a router?

    a. Restricting the VC numbers that can be used

    b. Defining the X.25 encapsulation

    c. Configuring your resolution statements to destination PADs

    d. Assigning the X.121 address

16. What is the command to set up your router as an X.25 switch?

    a. `Router(config)# encapsulation x25 dce`

    b. `Router(config-if)# encapsulation x25`

    c. `Router(config-if)# encapsulation x25 dce`

    d. `Router(config-if)# x25 encapsulation dce`

17. You are given an X.121 address, 30017898015763, from your provider. Type in the command to assign it to your serial interface:

    _____

18. You are trying to get to a destination with an IPX address of 1301.1122.a579.89ef with an X.121 address of 30117123905891 using SVCs. What is the correct syntax of this X.25 command?

    a. `Router(config-if)# x25 map 1301.1122.a579.89ef 30117123905891`

    b. `Router(config)# x25 map ipx 1301.1122.a579.89ef 30117123905891`

    c. `Router(config-if)# x25 map ipx 30117123905891 1301.1122.a579.89ef`

    d. `Router(config-if)# x25 map ipx 1301.1122.a579.89ef 30117123905891`

19. What is the default packet size for a PLP packet?

    a. 64

    b. 128

    c. 256

    d. 1024

20. What command do you use to allow for very large window sizes?

    a. **x25 ips**

    b. **x25 win**

    c. **x25 modulo**

    d. **x25 wout**

21. Which command restricts the VCs that can be used for the call setup of two-way SVCs?

    a. **x25 pvc**

    b. **x25 ltc**

    c. **x25 hic**

    d. **x25 loc**

9

Real-World Projects

Sarah Davis is a recent CCNP working at WFY, a mid-sized medical research company in Oviedo, Florida. The company has just purchased a small pharmaceutical company in Tver, Russia that specializes in the development of medicines to treat lung cancer. Because the carrier in Tver does not currently have a digital infrastructure, and because of the constant traffic that will have to be sent back and forth between Oviedo and Tver, Sarah has decided that analog modems will not be cost beneficial. Therefore, she and WFY have decided to purchase X.25 services using SVCs to connect to their smaller holding in Tver. Based on traffic predictions, they are installing a 28.8Kbps access connection on both ends. Currently WFY has a 3640 series router. Besides having a 10/100 Ethernet connection in slot 0 and a dual T1/PRI card for slot 1 to handle their telecommuters and individuals who work at home, they have decided upon purchasing a four-port serial module for their X.25 connection to Tver. This will allow for future X.25 connections and also give them the option of easily migrating to frame relay from their ISDN and/or X.25 connectivity. This card is placed in slot 2. Currently, their Tver facility does not have a router. Sarah has decided upon purchasing a 2600 router with a one-port 10BaseT module and a two-port serial WIC.

Sarah has talked to a carrier based in the middle of Florida that will sell her SVC X.25 services and, after spending a lot of time on the phone with the Russian telephone company in Tver, was successful in provisioning X.25 SVC services for their local office there. From her CCNP training and studies, Sarah remembered that she needed to get X.121 addresses from the two providers. Also, she does not want routing updates to traverse the X.25 network, so she will have to set up static routes.

It has been a while since Sarah took the Remote Access class, and she had to go back to her books to figure out how to configure X.25. She came up with the diagram shown in Figure 9.6. She decided to use a private IP address space with a 30-bit

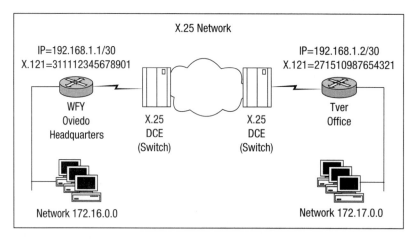

Figure 9.6   WFY X.25 WAN design.

subnet mask. She has decided to configure both routers in Florida and then ship the 2600 to Tver for the final installation.

Project 9.1

Complete the following tasks to configure the 3600 router (PAD) for the Oviedo facility as well as the 2600 router for the Tver location.

Follow these steps for the Oviedo router:

1. Enable the serial interface for the router:

   ```
   Oviedo(config)# interface serial 2/0
   Oviedo(config-if)# no shutdown
   ```

2. Configure the IP address, 192.168.1.1/30, for the router:

   ```
   Oviedo(config)# interface serial 2/0
   Oviedo(config-if)# ip address 192.168.1.1 255.255.255.252
   ```

3. Set the X.25 encapsulation for PAD functionality (note that you do not need to specify **dte** because this is the default):

   ```
   Oviedo(config)# interface serial 2/0
   Oviedo(config-if)# encapsulation x25
   ```

4. Define the X.121 address, 311112345678901, for the router:

   ```
   Oviedo(config)# interface serial 2/0
   Oviedo(config-if)# x25 address 311112345678901
   ```

5. Configure the X.25 map statement to connect to the Tver router:

   ```
   Oviedo(config)# interface serial 2/0
   Oviedo(config-if)# x25 map ip 192.168.1.2 271510987654321
   ```

6. Configure the static route to connect to the Tver network, 172.17.0.0:

   ```
   Oviedo(config)# ip route 172.17.0.0 255.255.0.0 192.168.1.2
   ```

Follow these steps for the Tver router:

1. Enable the serial interface for the router:

   ```
   Tver(config)# interface serial 0
   Tver(config-if)# no shutdown
   ```

9

2. Configure the IP address, 192.168.1.2/30, for the router:

```
Tver(config)# interface serial 0
Tver(config-if)# ip address 192.168.1.2 255.255.255.252
```

3. Set the X.25 encapsulation for PAD functionality (note that you do not need to specify **dte** because this is the default):

```
Tver(config)# interface serial 0
Tver(config-if)# encapsulation x25
```

4. Define the X.121 address, 271510987654321, for the router:

```
Tver(config)# interface serial 0
Tver(config-if)# x25 address 271510987654321
```

5. Configure the X.25 map statement to connect to the Oviedo router:

```
Tver(config)# interface serial 0
Tver(config-if)# x25 map ip 192.168.1.1 311112345678901
```

6. Configure the static route to connect to the Oviedo network, 172.16.0.0:

```
Tver(config)# ip route 172.16.0.0 255.255.0.0 192.168.1.1
```

Project 9.2

Now that Sarah has completed the router configuration and has shipped the 2600 to Tver and the local technician there has connected it up, she is ready to test the X.25 connection by verifying connectivity.

Follow these steps on both routers:

1. Examine the interface status on the Oviedo router:

```
Oviedo# show interface serial 2/0
Serial 0 is up, line protocol is up
    Hardware is MCI Serial
    Internet address is 192.168.1.1, subnet mask is 255.255.255.0
    MTU 1500 bytes, BW 1544 Kbit, DLY 20000 usec,
                        rely 255/255, load 1/255
    Encapsulation X25, loopback not set
    X.25 DTE, address 311112345678901, state R1, modulo 8, timer 0
    Defaults: idle VC timeout 0
```

```
Cisco encapsulation
Input/output window sizes 2/2, packet sizes 128/128
Timers T20 180, T21 200, T22 180, T23 180
Channels: Incoming-only none, Two-way 1-1024, Outgoing-only none
RESTARTS 1/0 CALLS 0+0/0+0/0+0 DIAGS 0/0
LAPB DTE, state CONNECT, modulo 8, k 7, N1 12056, N2 20
T1 3000, T2 0, interface outage (partial T3) 0, T4 0
VS 5, VR 3, tx NR 3, Remote VR 5, Retransmissions 0
Queues: U/S frames 0, I frames 0, unack. 0, reTx 0
IFRAMES 0/0 RNRs 0/0 REJs 0/0 SAMB/Es 0/1 FRMRs 0/0 DISCs 0/0
Last input 0:00:00, output 0:00:00, output hang never
Last clearing of "show interface" counters never
Queueing strategy: fifo
Output queue 0/40, 0 drops; input queue 0/75, 0 drops
Five minute input rate 0 bits/sec, 0 packets/sec
Five minute output rate 0 bits/sec, 0 packets/sec
    0 packets input, 0 bytes, 0 no buffer
    Received 0 broadcasts, 0 runts, 0 giants
    0 input errors, 0 CRC, 0 frame, 0 overrun, 0 ignored, 0 abort
<Output omitted>
```

Make sure that the interface is "up and up." Next, check the encapsulation type, your X.121 address, and the status, which should be "R1".

2. Examine the interface status on the Tver router—use the same **show** command and examine the same information.

3. Ping from the Oviedo router to the Tver router. It should be successful. Also, you can check the interface statistics to make sure that your "packets input" at the bottom of the display has increased by five—the five echo replies from your ping command.

Project 9.3

The X.25 connection has been up now for approximately one month, and Sarah has noticed that there are very few dropped packets, which is a pleasant surprise. Because some people have complained about the slowness of the connection, Sarah has decided to incrementally increase the packet and window sizes until she can fully optimize the connection while still keeping the same level of reliability. She will increase the window size to 5 and the packet size to 256.

Follow these steps on the Oviedo router:

1. Change the window sizes to 5 in both directions:

```
Oviedo(config)# interface serial 2/0
Oviedo(config-if)# x25 win 5
Oviedo(config-if)# x25 wout 5
```

2. Change the packet sizes to 256 in both directions:

```
Oviedo(config)# interface serial 2/0
Oviedo(config-if)# x25 ips 256
Oviedo(config-if)# x25 ops 256
```

Follow these steps on the Tver router:

1. Change the window sizes to 5 in both directions:

```
Tver(config)# interface serial 0
Tver(config-if)# x25 win 5
Tver(config-if)# x25 wout 5
```

2. Change the packet sizes to 256 in both directions:

```
Tver(config)# interface serial 0
Tver(config-if)# x25 ips 256
Tver(config-if)# x25 ops 256
```

Verify the changes on your routers:

1. Check the interface configuration from the Oviedo router:

```
Oviedo# show interface serial 2/0
Serial 0 is up, line protocol is up
    Hardware is MCI Serial
    Internet address is 192.168.1.1, subnet mask is 255.255.255.0
    MTU 1500 bytes, BW 1544 Kbit, DLY 20000 usec,
                        rely 255/255, load 1/255
    Encapsulation X25, loopback not set
    X.25 DTE, address 311112345678901, state R1, modulo 8, timer 0
    Defaults: idle VC timeout 0
    Cisco encapsulation
    Input/output window sizes 5/5, packet sizes 256/256
    Timers T20 180, T21 200, T22 180, T23 180
    Channels: Incoming-only none, Two-way 1-1024, Outgoing-only none
    RESTARTS 1/0 CALLS 0+0/0+0/0+0 DIAGS 0/0
    LAPB DTE, state CONNECT, modulo 8, k 7, N1 12056, N2 20
    T1 3000, T2 0, interface outage (partial T3) 0, T4 0
    VS 5, VR 3, tx NR 3, Remote VR 5, Retransmissions 0
    Queues: U/S frames 0, I frames 0, unack. 0, reTx 0
    IFRAMES 0/0 RNRs 0/0 REJs 0/0 SAMB/Es 0/1 FRMRs 0/0 DISCs 0/0
    Last input 0:00:00, output 0:00:00, output hang never
    Last clearing of "show interface" counters never
    Queueing strategy: fifo
```

```
    Output queue 0/40, 0 drops; input queue 0/75, 0 drops
    Five minute input rate 0 bits/sec, 0 packets/sec
    Five minute output rate 0 bits/sec, 0 packets/sec
        0 packets input, 0 bytes, 0 no buffer
        Received 0 broadcasts, 0 runts, 0 giants
        0 input errors, 0 CRC, 0 frame, 0 overrun, 0 ignored, 0 abort
<Output omitted>
```

Examine the ninth line of the display to verify that your changes were made. Use the same command on the Tver router and check the same display line.

2. Execute a ping from the Oviedo router to the Tver router to verify that connectivity still works. If you have a mismatch in packet sizes, you will see "input errors" increasing in your display.

9

CHAPTER TEN

Configuring Frame Relay for Remote Access

After completing this chapter, you will be able to:

✓ Describe the components of frame relay

✓ Describe the operation of frame relay

✓ Understand the function of Local Management Interface (LMI)

✓ Configure basic frame relay remote access

✓ Understand WAN topology issues

✓ Understand and configure traffic shaping

✓ Implement flow control

An Overview of Frame Relay

With the growth of private companies' WAN bandwidth needs, carriers were looking for a solution that could solve their customers' problems by providing an alternative, lower-cost solution than dedicated digital circuits. Previous to this, a company that needed a lot of bandwidth in the WAN had to purchase a dedicated digital circuit, which is obviously very expensive. To meet these new needs, carriers were looking for a solution that would provide a reliable public network that could be shared by many end users, but had less overhead and was more efficient than X.25.

In the mid-to-late 1980s, carriers and networking vendors were working separately, and sometimes together, to form a standard to solve this problem.

Note: Frame relay, unlike X.25, defines only the interaction between the DTE and DCE. How information is transferred between the different DCEs in the carriers' networks is left to the carriers themselves.

From the users' perspective, they send a frame relay frame into the provider's network, some magic happens, and a frame relay frame comes out the other side of the provider's network. Almost all carriers today deploy ATM as their backbone to transport the users' frames across their networks. The frame relay frame is segmented into small pieces and placed into the payload of ATM cells, and the ATM cells carry the frame to the destination switch, which reassembles it back into the original frame relay frame.

Data Link Connection Identifiers (DLCIs)

X.25 and frame relay do share some common characteristics. Like X.25, frame relay is connection-oriented, supporting both PVCs and SVCs.

Note: In this book, we will concentrate only on PVCs.

Frame relay has a DTE and a DCE, as shown in Figure 10.1.

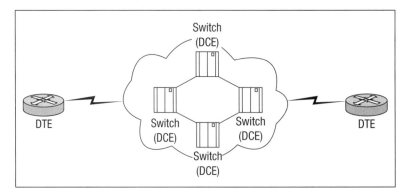

Figure 10.1 An example of a simple frame relay network.

A DTE is the edge-user device, such as a router; a DCE is a frame relay switch. The switch is responsible for switching frame relay frames.

Note: Each VC needs a unique address. In frame relay, this is called a Data Link Connection Identifier (DLCI). Like its sister protocol, X.25, the DLCI is locally significant. This means that the DLCI could be a different value on a segment-by-segment basis between the source and destination DTEs. It is the responsibility of the switch to handle this conversion of the DLCI number between the two segments. Your frame relay provider should tell you the DLCI numbers for your PVCs and the destination that they connect to.

On the lower end, DLCI numbers between 0 and 15 are reserved. At the upper end of the range, DLCIs 1008 through 1023 are also reserved.

Reliability

But beyond being connection-oriented and using VCs, the similarities between frame relay and X.25 diverge very quickly. Because digital circuits are much more reliable than their older analog cousins that X.25 typically deploys, frame relay implements no error correction or flow control through a windowing mechanism. Frame relay does have error detection, however. If a frame has a bad CRC, the frame is discarded. Frame relay relies on an upper-layer protocol such as TCP or SPX to resend the information. X.25 has three layers to its protocol stack, as was discussed in Chapter 9. Because frame relay only defines how two directly connected devices interact, it does away with layer 3, leaving only two layers in its protocol stack.

Signaling Protocols

Throughout this process of trying to develop a unified standard, three separate implementations of frame relay were created. The process as to how frame relay works is the same for all three implementations; however, the mechanics as to how it should work are slightly different. The signaling protocol is referred to as *Local Management Interface* (LMI). The three different standards for LMI are:

➤ *Cisco*—Developed jointly by Cisco, DEC, Nortel, and StrataCom (now owned by Cisco). This is sometimes referred to as the *gang of four* protocol.

➤ *Annex D*—Specified by ANSI's T1.617 standard.

➤ *Annex A*—Specified by ITU-T's Q.933 standard.

LMI serves two basic purposes. First, it is used to ensure that communication between the DTE and DCE is ongoing. In this sense, it functions as a keepalive. Second, it is used by the DTE to gather status information about the VCs that are connected to it.

10

LMI Interaction with the DTE and DCE

LMI operates on a special VC between the DTE and DCE. Depending on the LMI that you are running, the DLCI number used for this will either be 0 (for Annex A or Annex D) or 1023 (for Cisco). On a DTE-to-DCE connection, the DTE, by default, will be the one to initiate communication. It does this by generating a Status Enquiry (StEnq) frame. In the frame relay implementation in Cisco's routers, this is performed every 10 seconds. For every StEnq sent to the DCE, the DTE expects an acknowledgement back from the DCE.

Periodically, the DTE will ask for a status update of the VCs that terminate at its interface. This is called a *full status report*. Cisco routers do this on every sixth StEnq (60 seconds). When the DCE receives this, it responds with the statuses of the different PVCs connected between the DTE and the DCE. If a VC is added or deleted, or operational or nonoperational, the DCE passes on this information to the DTE. The switch will also pass information specific to the configuration of the VC, like *the Committed Information Rate* (CIR), which is discussed later in this chapter. Table 10.1 lists the different statuses for VCs in the full status report.

In this manner, the DTE will understand the status of each of its connected VCs.

Address Resolution

Once you bring up the interface on your frame relay DTE, somehow it must know about the VCs that it can use, the status of those VCs, and who is at the other end of the VCs. The DTE will learn about the VCs via one of two methods: Either you will tell your DTE by manually configuring them, or, if you don't like to do a lot of configuration, you can let the DCE tell you about them in its full status report. Once a minute your Cisco router receives this information (in the reply to its sixth StEnq). Besides seeing the DLCI numbers, the DCE also shares the statuses of the respective VCs. If the VC is in an *active* state, the DTE knows that it can start using the VCs.

Table 10.1   LMI PVC statuses.

Hexadecimal Value	Meaning
0x0	This is an existing VC that is inactive. This means that the VC is okay between the DTE and DCE, but there is a problem somewhere from the DCE to the destination DTE.
0x2	This is an existing VC that is active. This means that the VC is okay from the source DTE all the way to the destination DTE.
0x4	This is an existing VC that is deleted. This usually means that the carrier has either changed the VC's configuration or removed the VC from its configuration.
0x8	This is a new VC that is inactive. This means that the newly created VC is okay between the DTE and DCE, but there is a problem somewhere from the DCE to the destination DTE.
0xA	This is a new VC that is active. This means that the newly created VC is okay from the source DTE all the way to the destination DTE.

Before your DTE can start sending information across the VC, your DTE needs to know who it is connected to at the other end. If you remember from Chapter 9, X.25 requires manual resolution to perform this process. In frame relay, you have two options. The first is very similar to X.25: You use **map** statements to perform the resolution manually. When you are configuring your resolution statement, you define the protocol that will be carried across the circuit, the destination's layer-3 protocol address, and the DLCI to use. The only difference between this and X.25 is that you specify an X.121 address or PVC number for X.25 and a DLCI for frame relay.

However, there is a much simpler and easier method available to you than having to manually define all these resolution statements. In frame relay, this process is called *inverse-ARP*. When your DTE receives the full status report, for all VCs that are active, it will generate an inverse-ARP across those VCs. Inside the inverse-ARP it includes its layer-3 addressing information. When the destination DTE receives the inverse-ARP, it examines the VC that it came from—more specifically the DLCI number of the VC—and the layer-3 address of the source and adds this information to its resolution table.

This assumes, however, that both endpoints support inverse-ARP. If the destination DTE does not support inverse-ARP or doesn't support it for a specific protocol, you will have to employ static resolution. And in some instances, different releases of the software might cause a conflict between the two connected DTEs, requiring static resolution.

Configuring Basic Frame Relay Connectivity

Configuring frame relay remote access, as you will see, is even easier than configuring X.25 connectivity. Like X.25, your basic frame relay configuration is done on your serial interfaces. There are possibly three different items you'll have to configure:

➤ The encapsulation type

➤ The signaling protocol (LMI)

➤ The address resolution for your PVCs

Configuring the Frame Encapsulation

Out of the three possible items, the first one is required. To define the frame type, use the following command:

```
Router(config)# interface serial [module_number/]port_number
Router(config-if)# encapsulation frame-relay [cisco|ietf]
```

The default encapsulation method, if not specified, is **cisco**. When connecting to non-Cisco routers, use the RFC 1490-defined frame type by specifying **ietf**. This command defines the actual frame type that will be used to encapsulate your layer-3 packets. It is recommended to always use the RFC 1490 frame type because every frame relay device supports it, thus alleviating any mismatch of frame types; if the frame type does not match the device at the other end of the VC, connectivity will fail.

Configuring the Signaling Protocol

Prior to 11.2 of the IOS, you had to manually specify the LMI protocol that the carrier's switch had configured. The interface command to do this is:

```
Router(config)# interface serial [module_number/]port_number
Router(config-if)# frame-relay lmi-type ansi|q933I|cisco
```

Note: ansi is used for Annex D, *q933i* is used for Annex A, and *cisco* is used for the "gang of four" LMI implementation.

The carrier can give you this information when you order your circuit. However, one nice feature that Cisco included in IOS 11.2 is the ability of the router to auto-sense the LMI type. If you are running 11.2, you do not need this command—instead, the router will generate an LMI frame of each type and see which one the switch responds back to. The router will keep on performing this round-robin approach until it receives a response back from the switch. Therefore, depending on your version of the IOS, you might not need to configure this command.

Note: Cisco routers generate an LMI inquiry every ten seconds. On the sixth inquiry, or every sixty seconds, the router asks for a full status update of all the VCs connected to it.

Configuring Manual Address Resolution

One large advantage that frame relay has over its older protocol, X.25, is the support for dynamic address resolution. In frame relay, this is called *inverse-ARP*. However, not every frame relay DTE that your router is connected to will support inverse-ARP. If this is the case, you will have to perform manual resolution by configuring a **frame-relay map** statement(s) for each destination that you want to connect to (this is similar to the configuration of X.25):

```
Router(config)# interface serial [module_number/]port_number
Router(config-if)# frame-relay map protocol
                   destination_protocol_address dlci_number
                   [broadcast] [ictf]
```

As with the configuration for X.25, you must specify the protocol that will traverse the VC as well as the layer-3 address of the remote router. However, unlike X.25, where you specify the X.121 address, frame relay uses DLCIs for identifying VCs, which is the last required parameter. There are two optional parameters: **broadcast** allows broadcast traffic to traverse the VC, whereas **ietf** specifies the framing type. If you omit the framing type, it defaults to the frame type specified with the **encapsulation frame-relay** command.

There is one other instance when you may want to configure manual resolution even if inverse-ARP is functioning correctly. One problem with inverse-ARP is that a Cisco router only asks for a full-status update of its VCs every sixth keepalive. This means that when the router's interface comes up, it will have to wait one minute before receiving the status of the VCs, performing the inverse-ARP and receiving an inverse-ARP from its connected neighbor. By using manual resolution with **map** statements, you can dramatically speed up this process.

Examples of a Basic Configuration for Frame Relay

Let's take a look at a simple example of connecting two routers together via a frame relay PVC. The layout of the design is shown in Figure 10.2.

We'll make the assumption that both routers are running IOS 12.0. A stripped configuration for RouterA would look like the following:

```
RouterA(config)# interface serial 0
RouterA(config-if)# encapsulation frame-relay ietf
RouterA(config-if)# ip address 192.168.2.1 255.255.255.252
```

Here's the configuration for RouterB:

```
RouterB(config)# interface serial 1
RouterB(config-if)# encapsulation frame-relay ietf
RouterB(config-if)# ip address 192.168.2.2 255.255.255.252
```

Because both routers support auto-sensing of the LMI protocol and inverse-ARP, the configuration is very simple and straightforward. Notice, however, that the encapsulation type must match on both sides. In this case, the routers are using **ietf**.

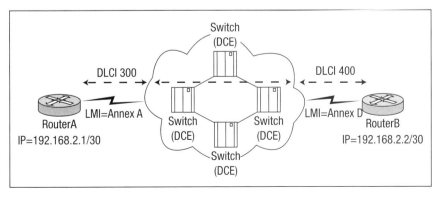

Figure 10.2 Simple frame relay configuration.

Let's change the criteria and assume that we are running 11.1 of the IOS on RouterA and 12.0 on RouterB and that there is a problem with inverse-ARP working between the two routers. The configuration for RouterA would look like this:

```
RouterA(config)# interface serial 0
RouterA(config-if)# encapsulation frame-relay ietf
RouterA(config-if)# ip address 192.168.2.1 255.255.255.252
RouterA(config-if)# frame-relay lmi-type q933I
RouterA(config-if)# frame-relay map ip 192.168.2.2 300 broadcast
```

Note the LMI type, which is Annex A, which is required in IOS 11.1 and earlier (because autosensing wasn't introduced until version 11.2) and the **frame-relay map** statement. The **map** statement performs the resolution for IP: To reach RouterB at 192.168.2.2, it will use the local DLCI of 300.

For RouterB, the configuration would look like this:

```
RouterB(config)# interface serial 1
RouterB(config-if)# encapsulation frame-relay ietf
RouterB(config-if)# ip address 192.168.2.2 255.255.255.252
RouterB(config-if)# frame-relay map ip 192.168.2.1 400 broadcast
```

There are two differences in this configuration compared to RouterA's. First, because RouterB is running IOS 12.0, it can auto-sense the LMI type, making the **frame-relay lmi-type** command unnecessary. The second difference is in the **frame-relay map** statement: RouterB is resolving RouterA's IP address to the local DLCI 400.

Verifying Connectivity

One of the first commands you will use in troubleshooting frame relay is the **show interfaces** command:

```
Router# show interfaces serial 0

Serial 0 is up, line protocol is up
   Hardware is MCI Serial
   Internet address is 192.168.2.1, subnet mask is 255.255.255.252
   MTU 1500 bytes, BW 1544 Kbit, DLY 20000 usec,
                      rely 255/255, load 1/255
   Encapsulation FRAME-RELAY, loopback not set, keepalive set
   LMI DLCI    0, LMI sent 10, LMI stat recvd 10
   LMI type is ANSI Annex D
   Last input 0:00:00, output 0:00:00, output hang never
   Output queue 0/40, 0 drops; input queue 0/75, 0 drops
```

```
Five minute input rate 1000 bits/sec, 1 packets/sec
Five minute output rate 1000 bits/sec, 1 packets/sec
    379 packets input, 18728 bytes, 0 no buffer
    Received 46 broadcasts, 0 runts, 0 giants
    0 input errors, 0 CRC, 0 frame, 0 overrun, 0 ignored, 0 abort
    392 packets output, 19138 bytes, 0 underruns
    0 output errors, 0 collisions, 0 interface resets, 0 restarts
```

You can use this command to verify the operation of LMI and that traffic is coming into and out of the interface. First, make sure the router has the correct frame type (the sixth line of the display). Next, examine the two lines after this. Make sure that the router has the right LMI type configured, or that it has auto-sensed an LMI type, and that the "LMI sent" and "LMI stat recvd" fields have numbers. Execute the **show interfaces** command again in ten seconds and make sure that the two LMI fields are *both* incrementing. If only the "LMI sent" field is incrementing, that means your router is functioning, but the switch is not responding back, indicating an LMI failure. Last, if LMI is functioning and your address resolution is correct for at least one of your VCs, you should see traffic statistics at the bottom of the display below the "Five minute" statements.

LMI Troubleshooting

Besides using the **show interfaces** command to display LMI information, you can use the **show frame-relay lmi** command to get more detailed information, as in the following example:

10

```
Router# show frame-relay lmi

LMI Statistics for interface Serial1 (Frame Relay DTE) LMI TYPE = ANSI
    Invalid Unnumbered info 0          Invalid Prot Disc 0
    Invalid dummy Call Ref 0           Invalid Msg Type 0
    Invalid Status Message 0           Invalid Lock Shift 0
    Invalid Information ID 0           Invalid Report IE Len 0
    Invalid Report Request 0           Invalid Keep IE Len 0
    Num Status Enq. Sent 8             Num Status msgs Rcvd 0
    Num Update Status Rcvd 0           Num Status Timeouts 8
```

The first line of the output shows the type of LMI that is being used on the interface. The "Invalid" entries displayed after this represent the LMI messages that are not understood by your router. This can happen if you have an LMI protocol configured on your router that is different from what the switch is attempting to use. A good example of this is when the router is using Annex A and the switch is using Annex D—both LMI protocols use DLCI 0 for their local address, which causes invalid messages to increment. At the bottom of the screen the "Num" entries refer to the exchange of LMI messages. The "Num Status Enq. Sent" entries are the LMI messages that your router generates every 10 seconds, and the "Num Status msgs Rcvd" entries are the replies coming back from the switch. The "Num Update Status Rcvd" entry is the number of full status reports your router has received from the switch. Remember that your router requests this only once every minute, by default. The last field, "Num Status Timeouts," indicates LMI failures. If this is incrementing every time you execute the command, your router is generating LMI messages but is not receiving a reply back from the switch. In the preceding example, you can see that there is an LMI problem based on the "Sent" and "Timeouts" fields.

VC Troubleshooting

Once your router receives the full status report from the switch, you can examine the status of your VCs with the **show frame-relay pvc** command:

```
Router# show frame-relay pvc

PVC Statistics for interface Serial0 (Frame Relay DTE)
DLCI = 112, DLCI USAGE = LOCAL, PVC STATUS = ACTIVE,
                    INTERFACE = Serial0
      input pkts 13          output pkts 21          in bytes 304
      out bytes 348          dropped pkts 1          in FECN pkts 0
      in BECN pkts 0         out FECN pkts 0         out BECN pkts 0
      in DE pkts 0           out DE pkts 0
      out bcast pkts 0       out bcast bytes 0
      pvc create time 00:35:11, last time pvc status changed 00:00:22

<output omitted>
```

In this display you will be shown each of the VCs that the switch shared with your router, including their DLCI numbers, their PVC status, and statistical information. You will want to check the status and make sure that is "ACTIVE" and that traffic is traversing the VC. Refer back to the "LMI Interaction with the DTE and DCE" section for the different statuses.

Address Resolution Troubleshooting

If you are using inverse-ARP, once your router knows that the VC is active, it will send an inverse-ARP across the VC. To see the address resolution table, use the **show frame-relay map** command:

```
Router# show frame-relay map
Serial0 (up): ip 192.168.4.1 dlci 112(0x70, 0x1C80), dynamic,
                    Broadcast, CISCO, status defined, active
```

In this example, the DTE at the other end of VC #112 is 192.168.4.1, and it was learned via inverse-ARP. This can be seen by the "dynamic" entry. If it had been "static," this would indicate that this entry was created with a **frame-relay map** command.

Detailed Troubleshooting

For more detailed troubleshooting of your frame relay service, Cisco offers many different **debug frame-relay** commands. The following is an example of trouble-shooting an LMI problem:

```
Router# debug frame-relay lmi
Serial0 (in): Status, myseq 290
RT IE 1, length 1, type 0
RT IE 3, length 2, yourseq 107, my seq 290
PVC IE 0x7, length 0x6, dlci 112, status 0x2 bw 0
Serial0 (out): StEnq, myseq 291, yourseq 107, DTE up
Datagramstart = 0x1959DF4, datagramsize = 13
FR encap = 0xFCF10309
00 75 01 01 01 03 02 D7 D4
```

In this example, an IE value of 1 (the second and third lines) indicates a reply received by your router from the switch. In this example, the switch's sequence number is 107 for its reply, and the sequence number that the router is expecting back from its original inquiry is 290. The 290 sequence number was the original sequence number in the router's StEnq. The information about DLCI 112 indicates that this is a full status report. The line with "Serial0 (out)" indicates that the router is generating a StEnq (an inquiry), and that it expects an acknowledgement back (with the router's sequence number) from the switch.

There are many other **debug** commands to assist you in troubleshooting frame relay problems such as the testing of inverse-ARP (**debug frame-relay events**).

Topology Issues and NBMA Environments

When you use VCs to provide connections to destinations, you are given a lot of flexibility in how you decide to lay out your WAN design. Based on your traffic patterns, you might decide to fully mesh your routers, as shown in Figure 10.3.

In a fully meshed environment, every device has a VC to every other device, providing full connectivity. Because most environments do not have traffic patterns that require a fully meshed network, a partially meshed network provides a better cost solution because you have fewer VCs. A partially meshed network is shown in Figure 10.4.

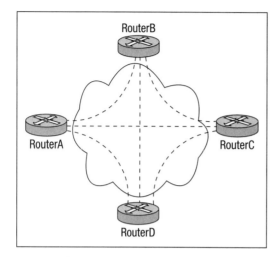

Figure 10.3 Fully meshed WAN network.

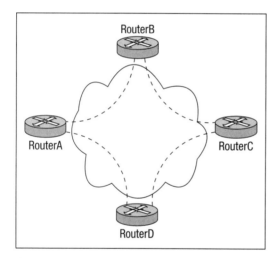

Figure 10.4 Partially meshed WAN network.

As you can see from this example, not every device is connected to every other device: RouterA and RouterC as well as RouterB and RouterD do not have a VC directly between them. Probably the most popular topology in WAN networks that deploy VCs is the star (or hub-and-spoke) topology, shown in Figure 10.5.

In this topology, a central router ties together all the other remote routers. This is very popular in most companies when they need to connect their corporate office to all their branch offices, because most of the traffic is between the central and remote sites, not remote to remote. However, if your traffic patterns change, it is very easy to provision an additional VC to accommodate this, which is a problem if you're using dedicated leased lines. When adding a dedicated leased line between

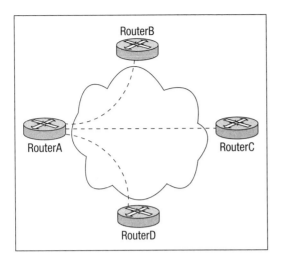

Figure 10.5 Hub-and-spoke WAN network.

two sites, it could take up to eight weeks for some carriers to actually install it. With VCs, some carriers can turn around this change in less than a day.

Split Horizon

One of the advantages of using services that deploy VCs is that they reduce the cost of your hardware—you need only a single WAN interface. However, using a single interface can create problems in Non-Broadcast Multi-Access (NBMA) environments—environments that deploy VCs.

If you examine a LAN segment, when a user generates a local broadcast on the wire, everyone in the broadcast domain sees the frame. This can be problematic in VC environments. First, let's assume that all the devices are fully meshed, as is the case in Figure 10.3. In this topology, we do not have a single wire connecting all the devices. Instead, we have a handful of VCs. If RouterA generates a broadcast, it cannot send it out its serial interface; it must replicate the broadcast across all its VCs. In this example, RouterB, RouterC, and RouterD would receive the broadcast. So you can see that, yes, everyone sees the broadcast, but how the broadcast is propagated is different from a LAN environment.

Let's look at a different example by examining Figure 10.5 again. In this example, not all the devices are connected to each other. If RouterA generates a broadcast, because it has a VC to all the destinations, the broadcast is received by all the other routers. However, if RouterB sends a broadcast, only RouterA would receive it—not RouterB and RouterC. This presents a large problem when dealing with routing protocols. Distance vector protocols, such as IP RIP, use local broadcasts to disseminate their routing information. If RouterB sends out its routing update, only RouterA would receive it. You might think that when RouterA sends out its update,

RouterC and RouterD would receive the routing information concerning RouterB's networks. However, distance vector protocols use a mechanism called *split horizon* to ensure that routing loops do not occur. Split horizon restricts how routing information is sent to other routers: If a router receives knowledge about a network on an interface, it will not propagate that network number back out the same interface.

In the example of Figure 10.5, even though RouterA has a *different* VC to each of the destinations, the VCs happen to be on the *same* interface. Therefore, when RouterA receives RouterB's networks, it cannot share them with RouterC and RouterD. There are three ways to solve this problem.

Configure Static Routes

First, you could configure static routes on all the spoke routers pointing to RouterA to reach destination networks at the other branch offices. The problem with this approach is that RouterB, RouterC, and RouterD might not be branch offices with just a handful of networks but instead be regional offices with dozens and dozens of networks. This means that you will be very, very busy configuring many static routes, which is prone to mistakes.

Disable Split Horizon

Another option is to disable split horizon on your router. This poses two problems, however. First, you might be accidentally creating routing loops in your WAN environment in times of instability, such as when some of your VCs fail. Another problem is that some routed protocols, such as IPX and AppleTalk, do not give you this option. With these protocols, split horizon is always enabled.

Use Subinterfaces

The last option is to use a feature called *subinterfaces* on your Cisco routers. A sub-interface is basically a logical interface that is associated with a physical one. You can have up to 256 subinterfaces associated with a single physical interface in version 11.x and earlier of the IOS, and up to 1,024 subinterfaces in version 12.x and later. The advantage of this approach is that you can assign a separate VC to each sub-interface. From the router's perspective, it treats the subinterface like any other physical interface in its chassis. If a routing update is received on one subinterface, the network numbers contained in this routing update can be propagated out any other interface, including other subinterfaces.

Note: This solves the routing problem but creates one additional problem. Because each sub-interface is treated as a separate interface on the router, each subinterface must be associated with a unique network number, thereby increasing your addressing needs and management of these addresses.

In Figure 10.3, where all the routers are fully meshed, you can place them all in one subnet, thereby reducing your address requirements. However, in Figure 10.4, where the network is partially meshed, you would have to use subinterfaces to solve the routing problem. In this example, the number of network numbers needed would be four—and in Figure 10.5, you would need three subnets.

Configuring Subinterfaces with Frame Relay

There are two types of subinterfaces you can create:

➤ Point-to-point subinterface

➤ Multipoint subinterface

A point-to-point subinterface is like a dedicated leased line—there are only two devices at the ends of the VC. Each point-to-point connection is a separate subnet, and each subinterface will only support *one* VC. This type of design is very good for partially meshed or hub-and-spoke topologies, but it requires a separate subnet for each point-to-point link. You can overcome this problem for IP traffic by using the **ip unnumbered** command on the subinterface. However, this can present problems when it comes to troubleshooting frame relay, because all your VCs will have the same IP address associated with them.

A multipoint subinterface is like the traditional multipoint physical WAN interface: On one subinterface there are many VCs (destinations). In this topology, there could be many devices off the multipoint interface; however, all these devices would be in the same subnet. This is a good topology to use when your network is fully meshed or if you have a shortage of network numbers to deploy in a point-to-point environment.

Creating Subinterfaces

When configuring frame relay, you will still need to specify the **encapsulation frame-relay** and the **frame-relay lmi-type** (if autosensing does not work) commands on the physical interface. All the rest of the commands, such as the layer-3 addressing and the optional **frame-relay map** commands, go on subinterfaces.

To create a subinterface, use the following global Configuration mode command:

```
Router(config)# interface serial
                [module_number/]port_number.subinterface_#
                multipoint|point-to-point
```

Subinterface numbers can range from 1 to 4,294,967,293; however, you are restricted to 256 or 1,024 on a physical interface, depending on your version of the IOS. The number you choose for your subinterface has no significance and has no relation to the DLCI(s) associated with the subinterface.

Once you've set up your subinterface, you need to associate it with its VC(s). You do this with the **frame-relay interface-dlci** command:

```
Router(config)# interface serial
                    [module_number/]port_number.subinterface_#
                    multipoint|point-to-point
Router(config-subif)# frame-relay interface-dlci dlci_number
```

Note that this command is not necessary on a multipoint interface (physical or subinterface) if you are using manual resolution with **frame-relay map** statements.

Example Using Subinterfaces for Point-to-Point Connections

Going back to the previous example in Figure 10.2, we will now set up a configuration between the two routers using point-to-point subinterfaces. We will make the assumption that both routers are running IOS 12.0. The configuration for RouterA looks like this:

```
RouterA(config)# interface serial 0
RouterA(config-if)# encapsulation frame-relay ietf
RouterA(config-if)# interface serial 0.1 point-to-point
RouterA(config-subif)# ip address 192.168.2.1 255.255.255.252
RouterA(config-subif)# frame-relay interface-dlci 300
```

And here's the configuration for RouterB:

```
RouterB(config)# interface serial 1
RouterB(config-if)# encapsulation frame-relay ietf
RouterB(config-if)# interface serial 0.1 point-to-point
RouterB(config-subif)# ip address 192.168.2.2 255.255.255.252
RouterB(config-subif)# frame-relay interface-dlci 400
```

Frame Relay Traffic Management

Besides using LMI to manage the connection between your router and switch, frame relay has additional mechanisms to help shape your traffic before transmission, as well as flow-control mechanisms. The shaping and managing of your traffic in frame relay can be accomplished with three different tools that your Cisco router provides:

➤ Standard frame relay rate algorithms

➤ Congestion notification

➤ Queuing

The first two items will be covered in the next few sections. The topic of queuing will be covered in Chapter 12. To implement the first two of these mechanisms, frame relay uses many terms that describe the components involved in the process. You will become acquainted with these throughout the remainder of this chapter.

Traffic Shaping

Before talking about traffic shaping and the effect it has on your traffic, let's first examine some frame relay terms used in traffic shaping. Table 10.2 defines some of these terms.

Data transfers are bursty by nature—from one second to the next, the amount of information sent is variable. Over a one-minute period, you might have no traffic for a small amount of time and then a high burst as a user starts and finishes a file transfer that lasts 30 seconds. *Traffic shaping* is the process of smoothing out bursts in your traffic flow. When traffic shaping is employed, the router will control how much traffic is sent and at what rate. Instead of sending the traffic into the frame relay network at the same rate that it arrives at the router from a LAN segment, the router will shape the traffic flow by sending it out at an *average* rate. In frame relay, this value is called the *committed information rate* (CIR). Figure 10.6 shows an example of this process.

Reasons for Traffic Shaping

Without traffic shaping, the data is sent at whatever rate the physical connection is clocked at (access rate). The problem with this is that the provider's network might not have enough bandwidth to allow everything into its network at the line speed of the user's connections. When provisioning VCs, you will have at least a CIR value associated with each of them, and sometimes a BC and/or BE value also. This is the "guarantee" that the provider is giving to you.

Of course, you could ignore these values and always send your traffic at the line rate into the carrier's network. However, the provider will enforce the configuration rules of the VC. In some cases, the provider may drop the nonconforming traffic. In

10

Table 10.2   Frame relay traffic shaping terms.

Term	Definition
Access rate	The clocked speed of the connection between the DTE and DCE (such as a T1)
Committed information rate (CIR)	The average rate over time that the provider guarantees for a VC
Committed burst rate (BC)	The average rate that a provider guarantees for a VC over a period of time that is smaller than that of CIR's measurement (a smaller, but higher, average rate)
Excessive burst rate (BE)	The fastest rate, at any given moment, that the provider will service the VC
Discard eligibility (DE)	Prioritizes the frame relay frame as a low-priority frame
Oversubscription	Occurs when the sum of the rates of all your VCs exceeds the access rate of the connection

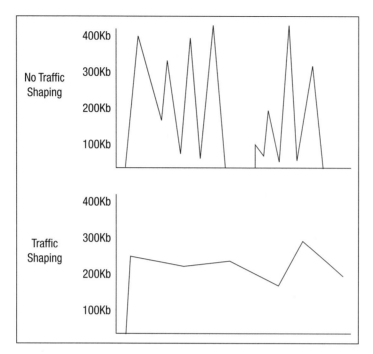

Figure 10.6 An example of traffic shaping.

most cases, assuming that the provider is not experiencing any current congestion problems, the carrier switch will mark the frame as discard eligible (a bit in the frame relay frame's header) and permit the frame into the network. This is true if you exceed the BC value on your VC. In most instances, if your VC rate exceeds BE, the service provider will drop the non-conforming frame(s). If, however, congestion occurs later in the provider's network, as the frame is making its way to the destination, the provider will start dropping these nonconforming frames first.

This creates a problem, because if the provider drops these frames, you must resend them. Therefore, it is better that you implement traffic shaping and send the traffic into the network at the prescribed rate—what you are paying for and what the provider is expecting. Sometimes this means buffering up your traffic for a short period of time to ensure that you are not exceeding the VC's rate values. The advantage of this is that you are not having the provider determine which frames should be low priority and then causing some of those frames to be dropped because of congestion issues. Therefore, it is very important to order your VCs with the correct rate values. If you order a VC with a rate value that is too low, you will be throttling your traffic, thus causing a lot of retransmissions and delays. If you order a VC with a rate value too high, you will be wasting bandwidth that is never being used—but that you are always paying for.

You might face another problem: a mismatch in access rates between two different DTEs. Imagine that a corporate office router has a T1 into the frame provider's network, whereas the branch offices have only a 64Kb connection. Obviously, if the corporate office router tried to send 1.5Mb worth of continuous data to a single branch office router, most of the traffic would end up being dropped at the destination frame relay switch because of the lack of bandwidth needed to support this traffic. Traffic shaping would fix this problem—you could customize your CIR to the destination's access rate.

Also, if you have multiple types of traffic sharing the same VC, there is a chance that one type of traffic could accidentally affect the other types by using up all, or most of, the bandwidth. If you have time-sensitive traffic such as voice, video, or SNA, you can give them their own VC(s) with their own guaranteed rates.

Sometimes you might hedge your bets and oversubscribe your access link—you provision your VCs where the sum of all the CIRs exceeds the physical speed of the link into the carrier's network. Here you are assuming that all your VCs will not, at the same time, be sending data at their CIR rates, but at a lower rate. The advantage of this approach is that it accommodates temporary bursts for a VC; however, the disadvantage is that if all the VCs *do* need to use all the bandwidth of their CIRs, you will not have enough bandwidth on your physical link to support their bandwidth needs. Therefore, this type of configuration takes careful planning and monitoring. A typical example of this is in a hub-and-spoke topology. For example, suppose you have 28 branches with 64Kb access links and a corporate router with a T1 link. Based on your traffic analysis, you notice that not all 28 branches simultaneously send 64Kb worth of traffic. This means that you can still use your single T1 connection without having to buy an additional one.

10

Note: Each VC has its own CIR, BC, and BE values, allowing you to optimally configure your frame relay connections based on your actual traffic patterns.

Configuring Traffic Shaping

Most of the configuration for the traffic shaping of your VCs is done with **map-class** statements. A **map-class** is a list of related commands that will affect the traffic for a VC(s). You will build your **map-class** first and then apply it to your frame relay serial interface. The name of the class is an arbitrary name that must be unique on the router. The following is a list of commands you can use to set up your map-class:

```
Router(config)# map-class frame-relay name_of_class
Router(config-map-class)# frame-relay traffic-rate
                        average_rate [peak_rate]
```

The first command takes you into a subconfiguration mode—this is where you place your traffic-shaping statements. The second command defines your traffic-shaping values. Here, *average_rate* is your CIR, and the optional *peak_rate* is your BE value. The rate is specified in bits per second.

Next, you need to apply your **map-class** to the interface or subinterface that has the VC that you wish to affect:

```
Router(config)# interface serial [module_number/]port_number
Router(config-if)# frame-relay traffic-shaping
Router(config-if)# frame-relay class name_of_class
```

The first interface command allows for traffic shaping for all the VCs associated with this interface. This command is always configured on the major interface. The second interface command applies the **map-class** traffic rate values to the interface. At this point, the VCs associated with this interface will have traffic shaping performed on them.

Note that you can apply one **map-class** to many interfaces. Also, if you have two different VCs on the same interface with different traffic-shaping values, you will have to do one of two things: You can configure two classes and create two (sub)interfaces—one interface for each VC and its respective class. However, a much cleaner solution is to use the following command:

```
Router(config)# interface serial [module_number/]port_number
Router(config-if)# frame-relay interface-dlci dlci_number
                      class name_of_class
```

With this command, you can apply a different **map-class** for each of your VCs on the same (sub)interface.

Flow Control

Frame relay has flow-control mechanisms to help deal with temporary bursts of congestion: FECN and BECN. These are special fields in the frame relay frame header that can be marked by either a carrier frame relay switch or the destination DTE to indicate that there is congestion. Table 10.3 describes these terms.

Let's look at an example to see how FECNs and BECNs work. If a source DTE is sending information into the network, and the network is experiencing congestion, the carrier switch can do one or both of the following. The carrier switch can set the FECN bit in the frame relay frame header in the user's frames that are going to

Table 10.3   Frame relay congestion terms.

Term	Definition
Forward Explicit Congestion Notification (FECN)	Set by the carrier switch to indicate congestion to the destination DTE
Backward Explicit Congestion Notification (BECN)	Set by the destination DTE to indicate congestion to the source DTE or set by the switch to indicate congestion back to the source

the destination DTE. The destination DTE, upon receiving the frame, will respond back with a frame relay frame with the BECN bit set. The carrier switch can also generate a frame relay frame with the BECN indicator set and send that back to the source DTE. You will have to verify with your carrier to determine whether FECN/BECN support has been enabled for your connections.

Based on receiving BECNs, the source DTE can then quench its traffic flow. Cisco supports this feature in IOS 11.2 and later. If no congestion is seen, the router can then increase its traffic output up to the maximum specified by the traffic shaping parameters. If no parameters are defined, the router can ramp up the VC to the access rate speed.

Configuring BECN Flow Control

Just like traffic shaping, BECN support is configured with a **map-class** statement:

```
Router(config)# map-class frame-relay name_of_class
Router(config-map-class)# frame-relay adaptive-shaping becn
Router(config-map-class)# frame-relay custom-queue-list list_number
Router(config-map-class)# frame-relay priority-group list_number
```

The first **map-class** command enables the router to adjust its output for a VC based on the BECNs, or lack thereof, it is receiving from either the switch or the DTE at the other end of the VC.

The second two commands in the **map-class** affect the prioritization of traffic before it leaves the router. Custom queuing and priority queuing will be discussed in Chapter 12.

Example of Traffic Shaping and Flow Control

Let's build on the previous example based on Figure 10.2. In this case, we want to set a CIR rate of 64Kbps and a peak rate of 96Kbps as well as enable BECN support. Here is the configuration for RouterA:

```
RouterA(config)# map-class frame-relay Vcshape1
RouterA(config-map-class)# frame-relay traffic-rate 64000 96000
RouterA(config-map-class)# frame-relay adaptive-shaping becn
RouterA(config)# interface serial 0
RouterA(config-if)# encapsulation frame-relay ietf
RouterA(config-if)# frame-relay traffic-shaping
RouterA(config-if)# interface serial 0.1 point-to-point
RouterA(config-subif)# ip address 192.168.2.1 255.255.255.252
RouterA(config-subif)# frame-relay interface-dlci 300
                 class Vcshape1
```

And here's the configuration for RouterB:

```
RouterB(config)# map-class frame-relay Vcshape2
RouterB(config-map-class)# frame-relay traffic-rate 64000 96000
RouterB(config-map-class)# frame-relay adaptive-shaping becn
RouterB(config)# interface serial 1
RouterB(config-if)# encapsulation frame-relay ietf
RouterB(config-if)# frame-relay traffic-shaping
RouterB(config-if)# interface serial 0.1 point-to-point
RouterB(config-subif)# ip address 192.168.2.2 255.255.255.252
RouterB(config-subif)# frame-relay interface-dlci 400
                              class Vcshape2
```

Chapter Summary

Frame relay is a protocol that was developed in the late 1980s to provide consumers with a low-cost, reliable, packet-switching solution as an alternative to X.25. Because it is a digital service, it provides no error correction, but it does provide error detection. If a frame has a bad CRC, the frame relay devices will discard it. Frame relay uses VCs for connectivity. Each VC is assigned a locally significant number called a *DLCI* to uniquely identify it.

Frame relay defines the Data Link layer process that occurs between the DTE and DCE and leaves it up to the carrier as to how this information will be sent across the backbone. To accomplish this, there are three different standards for a signaling protocol: Cisco's "gang of four," ITU-T's Annex A, and ANSI's Annex D. Cisco routers as of 11.2 of the IOS can auto-sense the LMI type.

When configuring frame relay, you must specify the **encapsulation frame-relay** command on the major serial interface (not a subinterface). If your router does not support auto-sensing, you will have to use the **frame-relay lmi-type** command to hard-code the protocol that the carrier switch is using. The rest of the configuration can be done on either the major interface or subinterfaces. Subinterfaces are typically used to overcome the problems of split horizon issues when dealing with distance-vector routing protocols. Subinterfaces can either be point to point or multipoint. If your router or the destination router does not support inverse-ARP, you will have to define **frame-relay map** statements.

You can optionally set up traffic shaping and flow control. The traffic-shaping parameters you can specify are CIR and BE. If you do not set up traffic shaping, your router will always attempt to transmit traffic at the access rate, which might cause a lot of frames to be dropped because of congestion issues or because of a smaller access rate at the destination side. Frame relay allows you to adapt the flow of the traffic based on congestion occurring in the carrier network using BECNs and

FECNs. Cisco routers, if enabled with this support, will slow down a VC if it sees congestion and then speed it back up when the congestion disappears. Both traffic shaping and flow control are defined with **map-class** statements, which are then applied to either an interface or to a specific VC.

Review Questions

1. The address of a frame relay VC is called which of the following?

   a. DLCI

   b. X.121 address

   c. E.164 address

   d. Data Link Connection Identity

2. Which of the following uses Annex D for LMI?

   a. Cisco

   b. ANSI

   c. ITU-T

   d. Gang of four

3. How often does a Cisco router generate a status enquiry?

   a. Once a second

   b. Ten times a second

   c. Once every ten seconds

   d. Once a minute

4. What are the two ways that frame relay performs address resolution? [Choose the two best answers]

   a. Via static routes

   b. Via inverse-ARP

   c. Via **map-class** statements

   d. Via **frame-relay map** statements

5. Which of the following commands is required when configuring frame relay on your Cisco router?

   a. **encapsulation frame-relay**

   b. **frame-relay lmi-type**

   c. **frame-relay map**

   d. All of the above

10

6. Which of the following commands will permit a Cisco router to talk to non-Cisco one?

 a. **encapsulation frame-relay**

 b. **frame-relay encapsulation ietf**

 c. **frame-relay encapsulation**

 d. **encapsulation frame-relay ietf**

7. Which of the following commands sets the LMI protocol to Annex A?

 a. **frame-relay lmi-type ansi**

 b. **frame-relay lmi-type q933i**

 c. **frame-relay lmi-type cisco**

8. What command do you use when inverse-ARP doesn't work for IP?

 a. **frame-relay map**

 b. **ip route**

 c. **map-class**

 d. **frame-relay lmi-type**

9. Which command will display the LMI type, the number of status enquires sent and the replies received, as well as the DLCI used by the LMI protocol?

 a. **show interfaces**

 b. **show frame-relay lmi**

 c. **show frame-relay pvc**

 d. **show frame-relay map**

10. Which of the following commands can you use to verify that the switch is sending full status reports for LMI?

 a. **show interfaces**

 b. **show frame-relay lmi**

 c. **show frame-relay pvc**

 d. **debug frame-relay lmi**

11. What command shows the status of a VC?

 a. **show interfaces**

 b. **show frame-relay lmi**

 c. **show frame-relay pvc**

 d. **show frame-relay map**

12. The **show frame-relay map** command will show all the following information for a VC except what?

    a. DLCI number

    b. Status of the interface

    c. Status of the circuit

    d. X.121 address

13. What can you do to solve split horizon problems for IPX? [Choose the two best answers]

    a. Turn off split horizon

    b. Use static routes

    c. Use subinterfaces

    d. Use **frame-relay map** commands

14. Which of the following statements are true concerning subinterfaces? [Choose the two best answers]

    a. You can have an unlimited number of them on a physical interface.

    b. They are used to solve split horizon problems.

    c. Subinterfaces are necessary in a fully meshed environment.

    d. Mulitpoint subinterfaces conserve layer-3 address space.

15. A _____ subinterface is like a dedicated leased line.

    a. point-to-multipoint

    b. multicast

    c. multipoint

    d. point-to-point

16. Which commands are used to assign the DLCI to a multipoint subinterface? [Choose the two best answers]

    a. **frame-relay map**

    b. **frame-relay pvc**

    c. **frame-relay interface-dlci**

    d. **frame-relay lmi-type**

17. What prioritizes frame relay traffic as either normal or low priority?

    a. CIR

    b. BC

    c. DE

    d. BECN

10

18. What command is used to enable traffic shaping on the router's interface?

    a. **map–class frame–relay**

    b. **frame–relay traffic–rate**

    c. **frame–relay traffic–shaping**

    d. **frame–relay interface–dlci**

19. Which flow-control mechanisms does the Cisco router support to slow its rate down? [Choose the two best answers]

    a. CIR

    b. FECN

    c. BECN

    d. DE

20. What command is used to allow the source router to adjust the rate of VCs based on the presence or absence of FECNs?

    a. Router(config)# **map–class frame–relay** *name_of_class*

    b. Router(config-map-class)# **frame–relay adaptive–shaping becn**

    c. Router(config-map-class)# **frame–relay priority–group** *list_number*

    d. None of the above

Real-World Projects

Sarah Davis has been working at WFY for a while now. WFY is a mid-sized medical research company in Oviedo, Florida. Their bandwidth requirements to their Tver office have steadily increased so much that their X.25 solution is not providing an adequate service. After some digging around, Sarah found out that there is a telco in Tver that will sell her company frame relay services through AT&T. Based on the two routers that she has—a 3640 and a 2600—she has an extra serial interface on each to deploy frame relay alongside their current X.25 configuration. This scenario has made management very happy, because it can run tests very easily without having to buy additional hardware (with the exception of a CSU for each site).

Sarah still does not want routing updates to traverse the WAN network, so she wants to continue to use her static routes. She will use another private-class address subnet for the frame relay connection as well as set up the additional static routes. She wants to hard-code the LMI type, just in case the provider makes a change. This will obviously break connectivity, but it will alert her to any problems—LMI and others—that the carrier has inadvertently created. Likewise, she has had some bad experiences with inverse-ARP and therefore wishes to use manual resolution. Use Figure 10.7 as a reference.

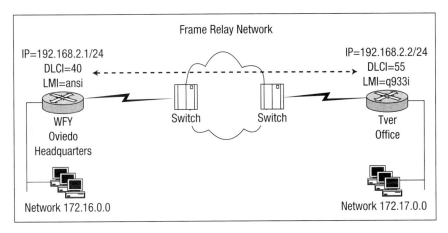

Figure 10.7   WFY WAN design.

Project 10.1

Follow these steps to configure the 3600 router for the Oviedo facility:

1. Enable the serial interface for the router:

```
Oviedo(config)# interface serial 2/1
Oviedo(config-if)# no shutdown
```

2. Configure the IP address, 192.168.2.1/24, for the router:

```
Oviedo(config)# interface serial 2/1
Oviedo(config-if)# ip address 192.168.2.1 255.255.255.0
```

3. Set the frame relay encapsulation (use the RFC 1490 standard):

```
Oviedo(config)# interface serial 2/1
Oviedo(config-if)# encapsulation frame-relay ietf
```

4. Define the LMI protocol for **ansi**:

```
Oviedo(config)# interface serial 2/1
Oviedo(config-if)# frame-relay lmi-type ansi
```

5. Configure the frame relay map statement to connect to the Tver router to use DLCI 40:

```
Oviedo(config)# interface serial 2/1
Oviedo(config-if)# frame-relay map ip 192.168.2.2 40
```

10

6. Configure the static route to connect to the Tver network (172.17.0.0):

```
Oviedo(config)# ip route 172.17.0.0 255.255.0.0 192.168.2.2
```

Note: If this were a real scenario, you would have created a second static route pointing to the same destination network number, 172.17.0.0. For testing purposes, you would want to assign a higher administrative distance to the static route using the frame relay circuit. Once testing was completed, you would remove the X.25 static route. Otherwise, the router would attempt to load balance across the two static routes: X.25 and frame relay.

Follow these steps to configure the 2600 router for the Tver facility:

1. Enable the serial interface for the router:

```
Tver(config)# interface serial 1
Tver(config-if)# no shutdown
```

2. Configure the IP address, 192.168.2.2/24, for the router:

```
Tver(config)# interface serial 1
Tver(config-if)# ip address 192.168.2.2 255.255.255.252
```

3. Set the frame relay encapsulation (use the RFC 1490 standard):

```
Tver(config)# interface serial 1
Tver(config-if)# encapsulation frame-relay ietf
```

4. Define the LMI protocol for ITU-T:

```
Tver(config)# interface serial 1
Tver(config-if)# frame-relay lmi-type q933i
```

5. Configure the frame relay map statement to connect to the Oviedo router to use DLCI 55:

```
Tver(config)# interface serial 1
Tver(config-if)# frame-relay map ip 192.168.2.1 55
```

Note that the **broadcast** parameter has been omitted from the **frame-relay map** statement, forcing you to use static routes.

6. Configure the static route to connect to the Oviedo network (172.16.0.0):

```
Tver(config)# ip route 172.16.0.0 255.255.0.0 192.168.2.1
```

Note: Remember the issues of the previous note and the use of static routes.

Project 10.2

Now that Sarah has completed the router configuration and activated the two interfaces—and things are working—she is experiencing a lot of dropped frames. She realizes that she forgot to configure traffic shaping to reflect the bandwidth that she purchased for the VC between the two sites. She has a CIR of 64Kbps and a BE of 72Kbps. She also wants to enable BECN traffic flow, because the carrier has been passing this information to her.

Follow these steps to configure the Oviedo router:

1. Set up your map-list:

```
Oviedo(config)# map-class frame-relay oviedo_VC_shaping
Oviedo(config-map-class)# frame-relay traffic-rate 64000 72000
Oviedo(config-map-class)# frame-relay adaptive-shaping becn
```

2. Apply the map-list to your interface:

```
Oviedo(config)# interface serial 2/1
Oviedo(config-if)# frame-relay traffic-shaping
Oviedo(config-if)# frame-relay class oviedo_VC_shaping
```

Follow these steps for the Tver router:

1. Set up your map-list:

```
Tver(config)# map-class frame-relay tver_VC_shaping
Tver(config-map-class)# frame-relay traffic-rate 64000 72000
Tver(config-map-class)# frame-relay adaptive-shaping becn
```

2. Apply the map-list to your interface:

```
Tver(config)# interface serial 1
Tver(config-if)# frame-relay traffic-shaping
Tver(config-if)# frame-relay class tver_VC_shaping
```

10

Project 10.3

WFY has just opened a branch office in New York and needs to set up a VC between New York and Oviedo. Sarah has decided to purchase a 2600 series router that has the same specs as the one being used in the Tver office. The New York office needs to implement ANSI LMI, and the VC needs traffic shaping for a CIR of 64Kbps and a BE of 96Kbps.

Complete the frame relay configuration to accomplish this. Refer to Figure 10.8 for assistance.

Follow these steps for the Oviedo router:

1. Configure the frame relay map statement to connect to the New York router to use DLCI 41:

```
Oviedo(config)# interface serial 2/1
Oviedo(config-if)# frame-relay map ip 192.168.2.3 41
```

2. Configure the static route to connect to the New York network (172.18.0.0):

```
Oviedo(config)# ip route 172.18.0.0 255.255.0.0 192.168.2.3
```

Complete the following task for the Tver router:

Configure the static route to connect to the New York network (172.17.0.0):

```
Tver(config)# ip route 172.18.0.0 255.255.0.0 192.168.2.1
```

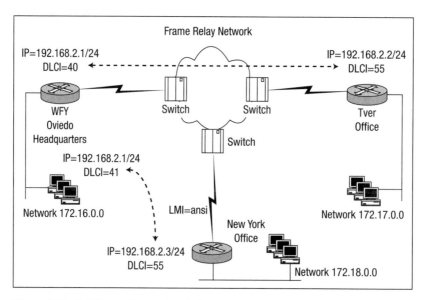

Figure 10.8 WFY's new frame relay design.

You must point the Tver office to the Oviedo router in order to reach the New York site because the Tver router does not have a VC directly between it and the New York router.

Follow these steps for the New York router:

1. Enable the serial interface for the router:

```
NewYork(config)# interface serial 1
NewYork(config-if)# no shutdown
```

2. Configure the IP address, 192.168.2.3/24, for the router:

```
NewYork(config)# interface serial 1
NewYork(config-if)# ip address 192.168.2.3 255.255.255.0
```

3. Set the frame relay encapsulation (use the RFC 1490 standard, because this is what the Oviedo router is using):

```
NewYork(config)# interface serial 1
NewYork(config-if)# encapsulation frame-relay ietf
```

4. Define the LMI protocol for ANSI:

```
NewYork(config)# interface serial 1
NewYork(config-if)# frame-relay lmi-type ansi
```

10

5. Configure the frame relay map statement to connect to the Oviedo router to use DLCI 55:

```
NewYork(config)# interface serial 1
NewYork(config-if)# frame-relay map ip 192.168.2.1 55
```

Note that the **broadcast** parameter has been omitted from the **frame-relay map** statement, forcing you to use static routes.

6. Configure the static route to connect to the Oviedo and Tver networks:

```
NewYork(config)# ip route 172.16.0.0 255.255.0.0 192.168.2.1
NewYork(config)# ip route 172.17.0.0 255.255.0.0 192.168.2.1
```

Configuring Dial Backup for WAN Redundancy

After completing this chapter, you will be able to:

✓ Compare and contrast the different methods of dial backup

✓ Understand how backup interfaces work

✓ Understand how floating static routes work

✓ Understand how Dialer Watch works

✓ Configure dial backup with backup interfaces, floating static routes, and Dialer Watch

An Overview of Dial Backup

As more and more companies deploy WAN technologies to meet their critical business needs, WAN redundancy has become very important to today's businesses. Unlike LAN environments where redundancy can be deployed at a very reasonable cost, WAN redundancy is much harder because you are relying on an external entity to provide your services to you—which comes at a cost much higher than LAN redundancy.

Issues with WAN Redundancy

You have many, many solutions available to you to provide redundancy in your network. The most costly would be to duplicate your current WAN environment. For instance, if you are using frame relay or leased lines as your WAN backbone, you might purchase separate services from two different carriers and deploy dual routers at each location, attempting to minimize the impact of a failure in one provider's network. You must be very careful when taking this approach because many carriers do not necessarily own all the equipment and cabling that your connection traverses. For instance, you might think that you have WAN redundancy by purchasing separate services from AT&T and Sprint. However, both of these carriers might be leasing part of their circuit path for you from some other third party. If that third party has a failure, both your primary and backup solutions would fail. Therefore, redundancy in this situation can cost you a lot of money and will require a lot of time on your part to ensure that these design issues are taken care of in the layout of your service.

Dial Backup Redundancy

Another solution is to use dialup as a redundant solution to your primary WAN solution. *Dial backup* is a process that can protect you from WAN downtime by allowing your Cisco router to monitor your critical serial connections—leased lines and frame relay, X.25, and ATM connections—and employ an alternative dialup interface as a backup. Dial backup supports both digital and analog technologies: ISDN and modems. However, because of the inherit delay in the call setup for analog connections and the randomness of connection rates, most companies deploy ISDN as a backup solution.

You will face many issues when considering redundancy in your network, with cost probably being at the top of your list. However, there are many others that can cause you a lot of headaches. One, for instance, is planning for a major failure. Take the example of when (not *if*) your frame relay network fails, causing your 50 branch offices to lose connectivity to your corporate site. If you were deploying dial backup, you would need to ensure that you had enough dialup lines (and bandwidth on them) to temporarily and efficiently take over until your frame relay service was restored. If your branch offices had 64Kb connections, this would require three ISDN

Primary Rate Interfaces (PRIs)s to handle the 50 connections. And if the branch offices had 128Kb requirements, you would need six PRIs. So, as you can see, careful planning is essential. You need to determine how much down time, if any, you can afford on a connection-by-connection basis and then use an appropriate technology to provide for your redundancy.

Implementing Dial Backup

Dial backup can be implemented in one of three ways:

➤ Backup interfaces

➤ Floating static routes

➤ Dialer Watch

Backup Interfaces

A *backup interface* is an interface that is reserved as a backup in case your primary serial interface fails or when the load on the primary interface exceeds a certain threshold. In this sense, it can serve two roles: It can provide for redundancy and can give you a bandwidth boost when your primary link becomes temporarily saturated.

Backup interfaces assume that you are using a dynamic routing protocol for all your routing needs. Note that routing must be able to function on the backup interface. This means that you will need to configure a layer-3 address on the interface as well as make any additional changes, such as include the appropriate **network** statement for your IP routing protocol.

11

Your backup interface will remain in a standby state while your primary interface is in an operational state or the traffic on the primary interface stays below your configured threshold. To determine whether the traffic load has exceeded your threshold, the router takes an average of your traffic rate over a five-minute interval.

Note: In a traditional configuration, a backup interface is in a reserved state—this means that once you configure it, the interface can be used only for backup purposes. In other words, interesting traffic for DDR will not trigger a phone call on a backup interface. If you need it for other purposes, you will want to configure your setup with a dialer profile, which removes this restriction. You could also use a floating static route with DDR as an alternative to backup interfaces.

Floating Static Routes

One issue with using backup interfaces is that they function based on the status of the line and line protocol of your primary connection: They monitor the Physical layer status as well as the keepalives and other mechanisms deployed at the Data

Link layer. If there is a failure at either of these two layers, a phone call is triggered and the backup interface is activated. However, issues could arise that dial backup would not detect and therefore would not deploy your backup interface. One example of this is found in frame relay. Your VC may be inactive, but the interface associated with it could be "up, line protocol is up," thereby causing the router to *not* use the backup interface. If you remember from Chapter 10, the bulk of the interaction in frame relay is between the DTE and DCE—on the local connection.

Floating static routes provide a solution to this problem. A floating static route is used in conjunction with a dynamic routing protocol. The floating static route is used only if the primary route fails. One advantage this provides over dial backup is that, in this situation, the router is monitoring layer-3 routing information. If your router loses sight of its WAN neighbor and its associated network numbers, your router can use a backup static route(s). Basically, a floating static route is a static route that has a lower preference. Cisco has a default ranking of routing protocols within a routed protocol suite. Each routing protocol is assigned an *administrative distance*, or ranking. This is used in situations where two routing protocols, perhaps a static route and IGRP, are telling your router information about the same network. The route will choose the routing protocol that has the lowest administrative distance value. Table 11.1 lists the administrative distances of various IP routing protocols.

You have the ability to change the administrative distances for the routing protocols. To create a floating static route, you would change its administrative distance to something higher than the dynamic routing protocol that you are running. A good number is 225. By doing this, you are ensuring that your router will always use the dynamic routing protocol, because it has a better administrative distance; it then will use the floating static route only when your primary path fails.

Table 11.1   Routing protocols and their administrative distances.

Routing Protocol	Administrative Distance
Connected interface	0
Static route	0/1
Summarized EIGRP route	5
External BGP	20
Internal EIGRP	90
IGRP	100
OSPF	110
IS-IS	115
RIP	120
EGP	140
Internal BGP	200
Unknown	255

In the example of the frame relay network with 50 branch offices, you could set up a floating static route at each of the branch office routers. If a branch router does not see routing updates coming from the corporate office router from the frame relay VC, it can use the interface that the floating static route points to. This can be any type of interface, including an ISDN or a serial interface with an analog modem on it. In this case, you would have to configure DDR, which was discussed in Chapters 6 and 7.

Dialer Watch

There are some problems with the prior two solutions. For dial backup, it may take some time before your backup interface is used when the primary fails. In frame relay, for example, this might mean a number of missed LMI keepalives. Or, because frame relay has problems with DTE-DTE status, your backup line might not ever be activated.

The advantage of a floating static route is that it works as intended when a failure occurs: after a missed number of routing updates or neighbor keepalives, an alternative interface is used. There is a problem, however, when the primary path is restored. In this situation the router will still use the floating static route as well as the primary path—load-balancing across the two. It will not bring down the backup interface that the floating static route uses until your DDR idle-timer expires for interesting traffic. This is not a very good situation if the backup solution requires you to make a long-distance telephone call: Your floating static route interface could be up for minutes, if not hours, after your primary service is restored.

Dialer Watch is a Cisco feature that builds upon dial backup by integrating it with special route-tracking capabilities that can overcome these two problems. Dialer Watch works hand-in-hand with your dynamic routing protocol. You will need to tell the router which routes are important to watch—those that are associated with your primary serial interface. Dialer Watch will then closely examine the contents of the routing table, keeping track of the "watched" routes that are deleted *and* added. If a watched route is deleted or does not exist in the routing table, Dialer Watch will activate your secondary interface. If your primary interface becomes active and your router relearns the original route from the primary interface, Dialer Watch will deactivate the secondary interface. This solution solves the problem that floating static routes have—the secondary interface remains up until the idle time period expires.

Dialer Watch is very flexible in that it works with your routing protocol—the faster the convergence of your routing protocol, the faster Dialer Watch can bring up your secondary link. Dialer Watch also allows you to employ any type of interface as a secondary interface—frame relay, ATM, X.25, and dial-up, as some examples. Another issue with floating static routes and backup interfaces is that they require you to use DDR. One problem with DDR is that if the router attempts to make a phone call and fails, it will retry it for only a set number of times before it gives up.

11

With Dialer Watch, the router will continually try to redial for secondary interfaces that use DDR.

There are, however, some restrictions for Dialer Watch:

➤ The only protocol stack supported is IP.

➤ The only routing protocols supported are IGRP and EIGRP.

➤ The router must be capable of dial backup and configured with DDR.

Configuring Backup Interfaces

Most of the configuration in this chapter builds upon the knowledge and commands that you learned from Chapters 2 through 7 concerning dialup on Cisco's routers. For example, in all the solutions that follow, you will need to configure DDR in either the traditional method or by using dialer profiles.

Legacy DDR Dial Backup

To configure basic redundancy for a primary interface, you will need to execute two commands on the *primary* serial interface:

```
Router(config)# interface serial [module_number/]port_number
Router(config-if)# backup interface type [module_number/]port_number
Router(config-if)# backup delay enable_time_value|never
                    disable_time_value|never
```

The first **backup** command specifies the interface you will use as your backup in case this interface fails. The second command defines how long to wait before activating the backup interface when the primary fails and how long to wait to deactivate the backup interface when the primary is reactivated. The time values are specified in seconds. If you specify **never** for the enable timer, the backup interface will *not* be activated when the primary interface fails. You probably want to put an actual time period here; otherwise, you're defeating the purpose of implementing dial backup. If you specify **never** for the disable timer, the backup interface will stay up forever after the primary is activated. The only time that you would want to specify this is if you have also configured load balancing—the backup interface could then be brought down if the load falls below a threshold that you define. You will want to give your backup interface a little bit of time before activating and deactivating; this will suppress small problems. If you bounce your frame relay interface, or it has a hiccup for a few seconds, you probably won't want to immediately bring up your backup interface; instead, you will want to make sure that the primary has failed first by giving the process a little bit of time.

Note: When you're configuring backup interfaces, do so only on one side of the WAN connection—do not do this on both sides. A interface that is specified as a backup interface can make a call only when the primary interface fails. It cannot make any other type of call, nor can it accept any incoming calls. If you configured backup interfaces on both sides, your backup solution would fail.

Backup Interface Redundancy Example

Figure 11.1 shows an example of a network that is using frame relay as its primary WAN service.

In this example, you will configure backup interfaces using a Basic Rate Interface (BRI) as the backup interface. You can assume that inverse–ARP is working for frame relay and that the routing protocol is IGRP. All the DDR commands required here were discussed in Chapters 6 and 7, and the frame relay commands were covered in Chapter 10.

The following is the configuration for RouterA:

```
RouterA(config)# router igrp 101
RouterA(config-router)# network 172.16.0.0
RouterA(config-router)# exit
RouterA(config)#
RouterA(config)# isdn switch-type basic-5ess
RouterA(config)#
RouterA(config)# dialer-list 1 protocol ip list 101
RouterA(config)# access-list 101 deny igrp any any
RouterA(config)# access-list 101 permit ip any any
RouterA(config)#
RouterA(config)# interface bri 0
RouterA(config-if)# ip address 172.16.2.1 255.255.255.0
RouterA(config-if)# encapsulation ppp
RouterA(config-if)# ppp multilink
RouterA(config-if)# dialer load-threshold 85 either
RouterA(config-if)# dialer map ip 172.16.2.2 name RouterB
                    broadcast 555-2222
RouterA(config-if)# dialer-group 1
RouterA(config-if)# no shutdown
RouterA(config-if)# exit
RouterA(config)#
RouterA(config)# interface serial 0
RouterA(config-if)# encapsulation frame-relay ietf
RouterA(config-if)# ip address 172.16.1.1 255.255.255.0
RouterA(config-if)# frame-relay lmi-type Cisco
RouterA(config-if)# backup interface bri0
RouterA(config-if)# backup delay 20 40
RouterA(config-if)# no shutdown
RouterA(config-if)# exit
RouterA(config)#
```

11

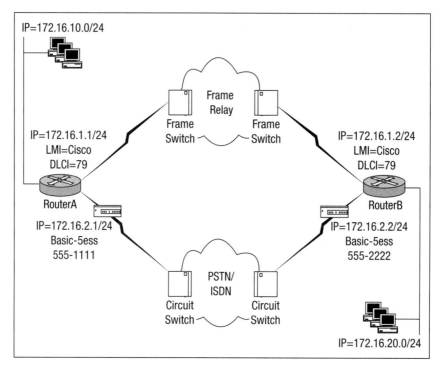

IP=172.16.10.0/24

Frame Relay

Frame Switch

Frame Switch

IP=172.16.1.1/24
LMI=Cisco
DLCI=79

IP=172.16.1.2/24
LMI=Cisco
DLCI=79

RouterA

RouterB

IP=172.16.2.1/24
Basic-5ess
555-1111

IP=172.16.2.2/24
Basic-5ess
555-2222

PSTN/
ISDN

Circuit Switch

Circuit Switch

IP=172.16.20.0/24

Figure 11.1 Backup interface example.

First, notice the extended **access–list** that is associated with the **dialer–list**. This ensures that no IGRP routing updates will inadvertently trigger a phone call on the backup interface—the only time updates should traverse this is if the frame relay connection fails. In that case, the **broadcast** parameter on the **dialer map** statement allows IGRP routing updates to occur on the ISDN interface. Last, you need your **backup** commands: The BRI0 interface is the backup, and there is a 20-second delay in activating the connection and a 40-second delay in deactivating it.

The following is the configuration for RouterB:

```
RouterB(config)# router igrp 101
RouterB(config-router)# network 172.16.0.0
RouterB(config-router)# exit
RouterB(config)#
RouterB(config)# isdn switch-type basic-5ess
RouterB(config)#
RouterB(config)# dialer-list 1 protocol ip list 101
RouterB(config)# access-list 101 deny igrp any any
RouterB(config)# access-list 101 permit ip any any
RouterB(config)#
RouterB(config)# interface bri 0
```

```
RouterB(config-if)# ip address 172.16.2.2 255.255.255.0
RouterB(config-if)# encapsulation ppp
RouterB(config-if)# ppp multilink
RouterB(config-if)# dialer map ip 172.16.2.1 name RouterB
                          broadcast 555-1111
RouterB(config-if)# dialer-group 1
RouterB(config-if)# no shutdown
RouterB(config-if)# exit
RouterB(config)#
RouterB(config)# interface serial 0
RouterB(config-if)# encapsulation frame-relay ietf
RouterB(config-if)# ip address 172.16.1.2 255.255.255.0
RouterB(config-if)# frame-relay lmi-type cisco
RouterB(config-if)# no shutdown
RouterB(config-if)# exit
RouterB(config)#
```

The configuration is fairly straightforward. The only major difference is the lack of **backup** interface commands. One important point to note regarding RouterB's configuration is the **access-list** and **dialer-list** statements, which are used to prevent IGRP from triggering a phone call on the BRI interface.

Configuring Load Balancing

Besides being used to handle redundancy, backup interfaces can also be used to lighten the load on your primary link by bringing up the backup interface and load-balancing across the two. You set this up like you would in the last example. However, instead of using the **backup delay** command to bring up the backup interface when the primary fails, you will use the **backup load** command. This is similar to the **dialer load-threshold** command. The one big difference is that the **dialer load-threshold** command is used for only dial-up links, whereas the **backup load** command is used with a mixture of links (dial-up and frame relay, for example). The following are the commands used to implement this feature on your primary interface:

```
Router(config)# interface serial [module_number/]port_number
Router(config-if)# backup interface type [module_number/]port_number
Router(config-if)# backup load enable_threshold_value|never
                        disable_threshold_value|never
```

Unlike the **dialer load-threshold** values of 1 to 255, the thresholds here are defined as percentages. The backup link will be enabled when the primary's bandwidth exceeds the first threshold value. The backup link will be disabled when the combined load of the two falls below the percentage threshold when compared to the primary's total bandwidth. Because load is calculated on an interface basis, this command can be used only on physical interfaces—not subinterfaces.

11

*Note: The **backup delay** and **backup load** commands are not mutually exclusive—you can use them on the same primary interface.*

It is important to remember that backup interfaces work with dynamic routing protocols. For the load balancing to work across the primary and backup interfaces, the metrics will have to be the same. For OSPF, this means you might have to change the bandwidth value on the backup interface with the **bandwidth** command to match that of the primary interface. For EIGRP and IGRP, you can use the **variance** and **traffic-share balance** routing protocol commands to load-balance across unequal metric paths. This topic is covered in a lot more depth in the Building Scalable Cisco Networks (BSCN) class.

Configuring Dial Backup with Dialer Profiles

Configuring backup interfaces can be done with dialer profiles, which were discussed in Chapter 7. You will have to set up your dialer interface and dialer pools following the steps outlined in Chapter 7. If you recall from that chapter, *dialer pools* allow you to associate a physical interface to many logical interfaces—called *dialer interfaces*. The advantage of this is that you are placing your physical interfaces into pools to get more efficient use out of them.

One problem with using a standard configuration employing a backup interface is that it precludes you from using the physical backup interface for other purposes. Plus, each primary connection you want to deploy redundancy for would require a separate backup interface.

The advantage of using a dialer profile configuration over a standard configuration is that with a dialer profile, you associate the backup interface with a dialer interface, not a physical one. The dialer interface is, in turn, tied to a pool of physical interfaces. This gives you much more flexibility—with a small number of physical interfaces, you can back up a larger number of primary interfaces.

Once you have configured your dialer interface and associated it with a dialer pool, you only need to specify your newly created dialer interface as the backup interface for your primary connection. It's as simple as that. The hardest part of the configuration, as you saw in Chapter 7, is the setup of the dialer profile—the **backup** commands are simple to configure.

Configuration with Dialer Profiles

Let's use the same example previously discussed in Figure 11.1, but instead of using a legacy DDR solution, you will implement backup with a dialer profile. In this example, you will remove the legacy commands and put in the profile commands.

Here's RouterA's configuration:

```
RouterA(config)# router igrp 101
RouterA(config-router)# network 172.16.0.0
```

```
RouterA(config-router)# exit
RouterA(config)#
RouterA(config)# isdn switch-type basic-5ess
RouterA(config)#
RouterA(config)# dialer-list 1 protocol ip list 101
RouterA(config)# access-list 101 deny igrp any any
RouterA(config)# access-list 101 permit ip any any
RouterA(config)#
RouterA(config)# interface bri 0
RouterA(config-if)# encapsulation ppp
RouterA(config-if)# ppp multilink
RouterA(config-if)# no ip address
RouterA(config-if)# no dialer map ip 172.16.2.2 name RouterB
                         broadcast 555-2222
RouterA(config-if)# no dialer-group 1
RouterA(config-if)# dialer pool-member 1
RouterA(config-if)# no shutdown
RouterA(config-if)# exit
RouterA(config)#
RouterA(config)# interface serial 0
RouterA(config-if)# encapsulation frame-relay ietf
RouterA(config-if)# ip address 172.16.1.1 255.255.255.0
RouterA(config-if)# frame-relay lmi-type Cisco
RouterA(config-if)# no backup interface bri0
RouterA(config-if)# no backup delay 20 40
RouterA(config-if)# no shutdown
RouterA(config-if)# exit
RouterA(config)#
```

First, you remove the dialer configuration from the BRI0 interface. Second, you remove the backup commands from the frame relay serial interface.

In the following section, you build the dialer interface with the appropriate **dialer** commands:

```
RouterA(config)# interface dialer 0
RouterA(config-if)# encapsulation ppp
RouterA(config-if)# ppp multilink
RouterA(config-if)# dialer load-threshold 85 either
RouterA(config-if)# ip address 172.16.2.1 255.255.255.0
RouterA(config-if)# dialer remote-name RouterB
RouterA(config-if)# dialer string 555-2222
RouterA(config-if)# dialer pool 1
RouterA(config-if)# dialer-group 1
RouterA(config-if)# no shutdown
RouterA(config-if)# exit
```

11

Then, set up the frame relay interface to reflect the dialer interface as the backup interface:

```
RouterA(config)# interface serial 0
RouterA(config-if)# encapsulation frame-relay ietf
RouterA(config-if)# ip address 172.16.1.1 255.255.255.0
RouterA(config-if)# frame-relay lmi-type Cisco
RouterA(config-if)# backup interface dialer 0
RouterA(config-if)# backup delay 20 40
RouterA(config-if)# no shutdown
RouterA(config-if)# exit
RouterA(config)#
```

As is, RouterB's configuration will work. However, if you are performing other types of dialup on it, you will want to configure a dialer profile on it to provide for a more flexible dialup design.

Verifying Your Dial Backup Solution

Now that you have configured dial backup, you will want to verify its configuration and operation. To verify that your backup interface is ready to perform its job, use the **show interfaces** command. In the following example, verify that the backup interface is in *standby* mode by examining the first output of the display:

```
RouterA# show interfaces dialer 0
Dialer 0 is standby mode, line protocol is down
 Hardware is Unknown
 Internet address is 172.16.2.1/24
 MTU 1500 bytes, BW 64Kbit, DLY 20000 usec,
                          rely 255/255, load 1/255
 Encapsulation PPP, loopback not set

<output omitted>
```

Before you perform your live test and disable the primary interface to check that the backup interface works, first look at the router's routing table. Again, referring to Figure 11.1, examine RouterA's routing table:

```
RouterA# show ip route
Codes: I - IGRP derived, R - RIP derived, O - OSPF derived
       C - connected, S - static, E - EGP derived, B - BGP derived
       i - IS-IS derived, * - candidate default route,
       IA - OSPF inter area route, E1 - OSPF external type 1 route,
       E2 - OSPF external type 2 route, L1 - IS-IS level-1 route,
       L2 - IS-IS level-2 route
```

```
Gateway of last resort is not set

     172.16.0.0 is subnetted (mask is 255.255.255.0), 4 subnets
C       172.16.10.0  255.255.255.0 is directly connected, Ethernet0
C       172.16.1.0   255.255.255.0 is directly connected, Serial0
C       172.16.2.0   255.255.255.0 is directly connected, Dialer0
I       172.16.20.0  [100/158350] via 172.16.1.2, 0:00:15, Serial0
```

Verify that the dynamic routes from the destination router are in the routing table—in this case, RouterB's route 172.16.20.0. Now it is time to test the configuration. To perform a quick test, shut down the frame relay interface. When this happens, the backup interface should come up and IGRP should share routes across it, which should show up in the routing table:

```
RouterA# config t
RouterA(config)# interface serial 0
RouterA(config-if)# shutdown
RouterA(config-if)# end
RouterA#
RouterA# show ip route
Codes: I - IGRP derived, R - RIP derived, O - OSPF derived
       C - connected, S - static, E - EGP derived, B - BGP derived
       i - IS-IS derived, * - candidate default route,
       IA - OSPF inter area route, E1 - OSPF external type 1 route,
       E2 - OSPF external type 2 route, L1 - IS-IS level-1 route,
       L2 - IS-IS level-2 route

Gateway of last resort is not set

     172.16.0.0 is subnetted (mask is 255.255.255.0), 4 subnets
C       172.16.10.0  255.255.255.0 is directly connected, Ethernet0
C       172.16.2.0   255.255.255.0 is directly connected, Dialer0
I       172.16.20.0  [100/180671] via 172.16.2.2, 0:00:15, Dialer0
```

In this example, it will take 20 seconds for the backup interface to come up. Note that the 172.16.20.0 route is being learned from the dialer interface.

Finally, to complete your test, re-enable the serial interface to make sure the backup interface deactivates itself after its 40-second delay timer expires.

Configuring Floating Static Routes

Floating static routes offer another alternative for creating redundancy in your WAN. They require that you run a dynamic routing protocol over your primary link. The floating static route, which has a worse administrative distance than the routing protocol, will not be used unless the primary path fails. You will need to configure DDR for your backup connection, making sure that routing traffic will not trigger a phone call on it. One way to ensure this is to use **deny** entries in your **access-list**, which your **dialer-list** then specifies. Another option is to make sure your backup interface is placed in a "passive" mode for your routing protocol. When the interface is configured this way, routing updates will not be sent out the interface, thus preventing the router from inadvertently making a DDR phone call triggered by a routing update. This is done within the routing protocol by using the **passive-interface** command.

The following command is used to create a static route for IP:

```
Router(config)# ip route destination_network destination_mask
                        next_hop_ip_address|outgoing_interface
                        administrative_distance
```

In the preceding command, you need to specify the route exactly the way it appears in your router's routing table—the one that is across the WAN on your primary serial interface. You specify the destination network and its subnet mask. Next, you must list the next-hop router that you will use to reach the destination network. This will be the router's interface address at the other end of your DDR connection. When configuring the administrative distance, make sure this number is *higher* (numerically speaking) than the distance used by your dynamic routing protocol. This will ensure that the static route will be used only when the dynamic route disappears from your router's routing table.

Floating Static Route Example

Using the same example that we have been using so far, let's change it to use floating static routes:

```
RouterA(config)# router igrp 101
RouterA(config-router)# network 172.16.0.0
RouterA(config-router)# passive-interface dialer 0
RouterA(config-router)# exit
RouterA(config)#
RouterA(config)# isdn switch-type basic-5ess
RouterA(config)# dialer-list 1 protocol ip list 101
RouterA(config)# access-list 101 deny igrp any any
RouterA(config)# access-list 101 permit ip any any
RouterA(config)#
RouterA(config)# interface bri 0
RouterA(config-if)# encapsulation ppp
RouterA(config-if)# ppp multilink
RouterA(config-if)# dialer pool-member 1
RouterA(config-if)# no shutdown
```

```
RouterA(config-if)# exit
RouterA(config)#
RouterA(config)# interface dialer 0
RouterA(config-if)# encapsulation ppp
RouterA(config-if)# ppp multilink
RouterA(config-if)# dialer load-threshold 85 either
RouterA(config-if)# ip address 172.16.2.1 255.255.255.0
RouterA(config-if)# dialer remote-name RouterB
RouterA(config-if)# dialer string 555-2222
RouterA(config-if)# dialer pool 1
RouterA(config-if)# dialer-group 1
RouterA(config-if)# no shutdown
RouterA(config-if)# exit
RouterA(config)#
RouterA(config)# interface serial 0
RouterA(config-if)# encapsulation frame-relay ietf
RouterA(config-if)# ip address 172.16.1.1 255.255.255.0
RouterA(config-if)# frame-relay lmi-type Cisco
RouterA(config-if)# no backup interface dialer 0
RouterA(config-if)# no backup delay 20 40
RouterA(config-if)# no shutdown
RouterA(config-if)# exit
RouterA(config)#
RouterA(config)# ip route 172.16.20.0 255.255.255.0 172.16.2.2 200
```

In this example, we first set the dialer interface in a passive state for IGRP. This prevents IGRP from sending out updates on it as well as triggering a phone call on it. Next, we remove the **backup** commands from the serial interface. And last, we add the floating static route to reach the Ethernet subnet off of RouterB. Note that you need to use RouterB's DDR IP address: 172.16.2.2.

You will also need to set up RouterB's BRI interface as passive for IGRP and add a floating static route on RouterB so that when the primary interface goes down, it knows of an alternative path across its dial-up link (this is necessary because IGRP is not running across it):

```
RouterA(config)# router igrp 101
RouterA(config-router)# network 172.16.0.0
RouterA(config-router)# passive-interface BRI 0
RouterA(config-router)# exit
RouterA(config)#
RouterB(config)# ip route 172.16.10.0 255.255.255.0 172.16.2.1 200
```

Again, to test this configuration, check your routing table first and then temporarily disable your frame relay interface and verify that the DDR works with the floating static route by issuing a ping.

Configuring Dialer Watch

One problem with floating static routes is that the floating static route will not disappear from the routing table once the primary comes back up; instead, the router will load-balance across the two connections (assuming that they are equal-cost paths). Only when there is no interesting traffic traversing the link for the idle period is the DDR link brought down. *Interesting* traffic, if you recall from Chapter 6, is traffic defined in your **access-list** and **dialer-list**. Dialer Watch fixes this problem by monitoring the routes in the routing table. You need to determine which routes you will want to monitor. You will also want to monitor the subnet (or subnets) that encompasses the WAN.

One of the interesting things about the Dialer Watch is that the router that is doing the "watching" does not have to have the primary WAN interface upon which the routes are arriving. Dialer Watch requires that you have a dial-up interface as well as some other connection to the router with the primary WAN connection. Figure 11.2 illustrates this. RouterA has the primary connection and RouterB has the backup analog link.

However, both the primary interface (where the routes are arriving from) and the DDR interface can be in the same router. If this is the case, you can instead monitor a specific address of the primary WAN interface instead of listing all the routes that are arriving from across the WAN—the address of your neighboring router that you are receiving updates from.

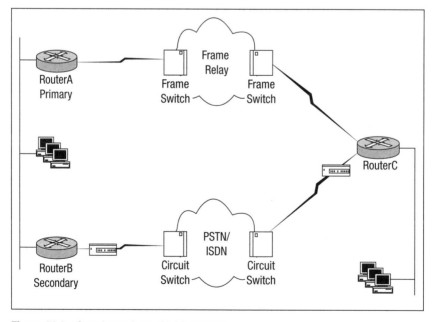

Figure 11.2   Sample topology with Dialer Watch.

The following are the commands you will need to execute in order to set up Dialer Watch. First, you must specify which routes or specific IP addresses you wish to monitor:

```
Router#(config)# dialer watch-list group_number
                    ip ip_network(or ip_address) subnet_mask
```

Here, *group_number* allows you to group your "watch" statements together. This is similar to the number used with **access-lists** and **dialer-lists**. You must also specify the IP network number (or IP address) and the corresponding subnet mask.

Once you have built your list of statements, you must apply the **dialer watch-list** configuration to the DDR interface (which could be a dialer profile interface) with the **dialer watch-group** command:

```
Router(config)# interface type [module_number/]port_number
Router(config-if)# dialer watch-group group_number
```

One optional interface command is to set a delay, in seconds, that determines how long the backup link will remain up once the primary WAN connection is back in action:

```
Router(config)# interface type [module_number/]port_number
Router(config-if)# dialer watch-disable delay_in_seconds
```

Use this command to ensure that a flapping interface does not create any stability problems with Dialer Watch.

Once you have performed these configuration tasks, you will still need to configure your primary WAN interface and your DDR commands on your backup interface.

Dialer Watch Example

Using the same topology in Figure 11.1, we will configure Dialer Watch on RouterA. This time we will start from scratch, ignoring the commands we have previously configured. We will use a dialer profile for the DDR connection.

Let's look at RouterA's configuration:

```
RouterA(config)# router igrp 101
RouterA(config-router)# network 172.16.0.0
RouterA(config-router)# exit
RouterA(config)#
RouterA(config)# isdn switch-type basic-5ess
RouterA(config)#
RouterA(config)# dialer-list 1 protocol ip list 101
```

```
RouterA(config)# access-list 101 deny igrp any any
RouterA(config)# access-list 101 permit ip any any
RouterA(config)#
RouterA(config)# interface bri 0
RouterA(config-if)# encapsulation ppp
RouterA(config-if)# ppp multilink
RouterA(config-if)# dialer pool-member 1
RouterA(config-if)# no shutdown
RouterA(config-if)# exit
RouterA(config)#
RouterA(config)# interface serial 0
RouterA(config-if)# encapsulation frame-relay ietf
RouterA(config-if)# ip address 172.16.1.1 255.255.255.0
RouterA(config-if)# frame-relay lmi-type Cisco
RouterA(config-if)# no shutdown
RouterA(config-if)# exit
RouterA(config)#
RouterA(config)# dialer watch-list 1 ip 172.16.1.0 255.255.255.0
RouterA(config)# dialer watch-list 1 ip 172.16.20.0 255.255.255.0
RouterA(config)#
RouterA(config)# interface dialer 0
RouterA(config-if)# encapsulation ppp
RouterA(config-if)# ppp multilink
RouterA(config-if)# dialer load-threshold 85 either
RouterA(config-if)# ip address 172.16.2.1 255.255.255.0
RouterA(config-if)# dialer remote-name RouterB
RouterA(config-if)# dialer string 555-2222
RouterA(config-if)# dialer pool 1
RouterA(config-if)# dialer-group 1
RouterA(config-if)# dialer watch-group 1
RouterA(config-if)# no shutdown
RouterA(config-if)# exit
```

In RouterA's configuration, the **dialer watch-list** is monitoring two different subnets, and it is applied to the dialer interface. If either of these disappears from the routing table, the dialer interface will bring up BRI0. RouterB's configuration would remain the same: DDR would be configured and IGRP would be defined as non-interesting traffic.

Chapter Summary

Because of the growing need to maintain a high service level for WAN networks, redundancy has become a key issue in a network administrator's network design. Using low-cost dialup services provides a very flexible option for lower-speed primary WAN connections. You have three different methods that you can use to provide for dial backup: backup interfaces, floating static routes, and Dialer Watch.

A *backup interface* is a reserved interface that has DDR configured on it. The router monitors your primary WAN circuit, and when that fails, it will make a phone call on the backup interface. You can implement legacy DDR or use dialer profiles to accomplish this. It is preferable to use dialer profiles because the legacy implementation forces you to dedicate your DDR interface explicitly to a backup role of a single physical interface. With a dialer profile, you are placing only the logical dialer interface in a reserved state—any physical interfaces associated to it via the dialer pool are still available for any DDR operations. To implement this, on the primary WAN interface you specify the **backup interface** and **backup delay** commands. Implementing the optional **backup load** command can help reduce the load on overcongested primary connections. To verify your configuration, use the **show interfaces** command.

Floating static routes are an alternative to backup interfaces. A *floating static route* is a route that is less desirable than others because it has a worse administrative distance (numerically higher). As with backup interfaces, you are required to run a dynamic routing protocol and implement DDR. However, floating static routes use the characteristics of a routing protocol to help with convergence and to detect failures. To configure an IP floating static route, use the **ip route** command—make sure you assign an administrative distance higher than your dynamic routing protocol. One problem with a floating static route is that when your primary link comes back, the floating static route is still used and the DDR interface remains active until interesting traffic is not seen over the period of the idle timeout.

A better solution than using floating static routes is to implement Dialer Watch. Dialer Watch monitors the routes in the routing table that you specify with a **dialer watch-list**. When one of these routes disappears in the routing table, the router will bring up the backup interface associated with your list of watched routes. You execute the **dialer watch-group** command on the interface that will be performing the backup function. Once the DDR interface has been activated, it will be brought back down once the network number (or numbers) being watched reappears in the routing table.

11

Review Questions

1. Which is not a method employed for dial backup?

    a. X.25

    b. Backup interfaces

    c. Floating static routes

    d. Dialer Watch

2. With legacy DDR and backup interfaces, can the backup interface be used for other dialing purposes?

   a. Yes

   b. No

3. Floating static routes require all the following except what? [Choose the two best answers]

   a. Low administrative distance

   b. Dynamic routing protocol

   c. DDR

   d. Backup interface

4. For a floating static route to work in a RIP environment, which of the following administrative distances will work?

   a. 1

   b. 110

   c. 120

   d. 125

5. What is the problem with floating static routes?

   a. They can only monitor layer-1 and layer-2 information and cannot track information from DTE to DTE.

   b. They cannot support load balancing.

   c. They only work with dialer profiles.

   d. They remain up even after the primary link becomes active.

6. Which solution monitors the router's routing table to perform dial backup?

   a. DDR

   b. Dialer Watch

   c. Floating static routes

   d. Backup interfaces

7. The Dialer Watch feature has all the following restrictions except which one?

   a. Only works with IP and IPX

   b. Only supports IGRP and EIGRP

   c. Only works with routers supporting DDR

8. Which commands are required when configuring backup interfaces? [Choose the two best answers]

   a. **backup load**

   b. **backup delay**

   c. **backup primary**

   d. **backup interface**

9. Backup interfaces can be configured on which of the following? [Choose the two best answers]

   a. Both source and destination routers

   b. Source router

   c. Destination router

   d. Neither

10. Which command is used for load balancing across multiple interfaces of any type?

    a. **backup interface**

    b. **backup delay**

    c. **backup load**

    d. **dialer load-threshold**

11. The load with the **backup load** command is specified as what?

    a. A number between 1 and 255

    b. A number between 1 and 200

    c. A percentage

    d. None of the above

12. Which commands are used with EIGRP to perform load balancing across unequal cost links? [Choose the two best answers]

    a. **bandwidth**

    b. **variance**

    c. **backup load**

    d. **traffic-share balance**

13. What advantage do dialer profiles have over legacy DDR when using backup interfaces?

    a. They allow the use of the backup interface for other purposes.

    b. They remove the limitation of using static routes.

    c. They require a dynamic routing protocol.

    d. They support load balancing.

14. What command is used to monitor the status of backup interfaces?

    a. **show ip route**

    b. **show ip protocol**

    c. **show interfaces**

    d. None of the above

15. You need to set up a floating static route. The administrative distance is 200. The dynamic routing protocol running on the router is RIP. The network is 172.16.10.0/24. The router that will receive the traffic is 192.168.1.1. The command to configure this correctly is _____.

16. All the following items should be used for implementing floating static routes except which one?

    a. DDR

    b. Passive interface

    c. Static route

    d. Dynamic routing protocol

    e. All should be used

    f. None should be used

17. The DDR portion of Dialer Watch can be implemented in a different router than the one with the primary WAN interface.

    a. True

    b. False

18. Which commands are necessary to implement Dialer Watch?

    a. **backup interface**

    b. **dialer watch-group**

    c. **dialer watch-list**

    d. **backup delay**

    e. **dialer watch-disable**

Real-World Projects

Sarah Davis has taken on some freelance consulting jobs. Currently, she is working with a company called Creative Widgets, which is experiencing some reliability problems with the frame relay connection between their Orlando and Tampa offices. Sarah has found out that she can get a BRI at both facilities for dial backup. She has decided to use backup interfaces with legacy DDR to solve her redundancy problem. Currently, both sites have a 2522 router with the following interfaces:

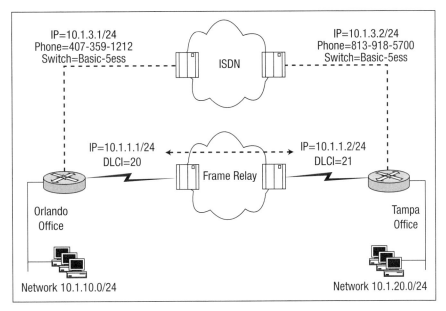

Figure 11.3   Creative Widgets network topology.

10 serial, one BRI, and one Ethernet. Refer to Figure 11.3 as a reference to her network topology.

Project 11.1

Sarah will need to complete the following tasks to configure the 2522 router for the Orlando facility as well as the router for the Tampa location. First, she will need to verify the frame relay configuration at both sites. After this, she is then ready to perform her configuration on the two 2522 routers. She will need to set up her ISDN configuration by specifying the telco's ISDN switch type that she will use on her BRI backup interface. She'll also need to create a **dialer-list** to make sure that IGRP routing updates don't trigger a phone call on the backup BRI interface, but make all other traffic "interesting." She'll next configure the BRI interface by specifying the encapsulation type and IP address, applying the **dialer-list**, specifying the phone number, and enabling the interface. Once this is done, she will need to specify, on the primary interface, that the BRI is the backup interface and verify that the backup solution is functioning correctly.

Configure dial backup for the Orlando router configuration:

1. Verify the frame relay configuration:

```
Orlando# show run
Building Configuration ...
```

11

```
hostname Orlando

router igrp 101
 network 10.0.0.0

interface ethernet 0
 ip address 10.1.10.1 255.255.255.0
 no shutdown

interface serial 0
 encapsulation frame-relay ietf
 ip address 10.1.1.1 255.255.255.0
 no shutdown

<output omitted>
```

2. Set the ISDN switch type:

```
Orlando(config)# isdn switch-type basic-5ess
```

3. Set up the **dialer-list** to deny IGRP updates for interesting traffic, but permit everything else:

```
Orlando(config)# dialer-list 1 protocol ip list 101
Orlando(config)# access-list 101 deny igrp any any
Orlando(config)# access-list 101 permit ip any any
```

4. Set up the encapsulation on the BRI interface:

```
Orlando(config)# interface bri 0
Orlando(config-if)# encapsulation ppp
```

5. Define the ISDN IP address:

```
Orlando(config)# interface bri 0
Orlando(config-if)# ip address 10.1.1.1 255.255.255.0
```

6. Assign the **dialer-list** to the BRI interface:

```
Orlando(config)# interface bri 0
Orlando(config-if)# dialer-group 1
```

7. Set up the phone number of the destination:

```
Orlando(config)# interface bri 0
Orlando(config-if)# dialer map ip 10.1.1.2 name Tampa
                          broadcast 1-813-918-5700
```

8. Enable the interface:

```
Orlando(config)# interface bri 0
Orlando(config-if)# no shutdown
```

9. Configure the backup interface feature (set a delay of 20 seconds to activate and 40 seconds to deactivate):

```
Orlando(config)# interface serial 0
Orlando(config-if)# backup interface bri 0
Orlando(config-if)# backup delay 20 40
```

10. Verify the status of the backup interface:

```
Orlando# show interfaces BRI 0
BRI 0 is standby mode, line protocol is down
 Hardware is Unknown
 Internet address is 10.1.1.1/24
 MTU 1500 bytes, BW 64Kbit, DLY 20000 usec,
                           rely 255/255, load 1/255
 Encapsulation PPP, loopback not set

<output omitted>
```

11

Configure DDR for the Tampa router configuration:

1. Verify the frame relay router:

```
Tampa# show run
Building Configuration ...

hostname Tampa

router igrp 101
 network 10.0.0.0

interface ethernet 0
 ip address 10.1.20.1 255.255.255.0
 no shutdown
```

```
interface serial 0
 encapsulation frame-relay ietf
 ip address 10.1.1.2 255.255.255.0
 no shutdown
```

```
<output omitted>
```

2. Set the ISDN switch type:

```
Tampa(config)# isdn switch-type basic-5ess
```

3. Set up the **dialer-list** to deny IGRP updates for interesting traffic, but permit everything else:

```
Tampa(config)# dialer-list 1 protocol ip list 101
Tampa(config)# access-list 101 deny igrp any any
Tampa(config)# access-list 101 permit ip any any
```

4. Set up the encapsulation on the BRI interface:

```
Tampa(config)# interface bri 0
Tampa(config-if)# encapsulation ppp
```

5. Define the ISDN IP address:

```
Tampa(config)# interface bri 0
Tampa(config-if)# ip address 10.1.1.2 255.255.255.0
```

6. Assign the **dialer-list** to the BRI interface:

```
Tampa(config)# interface bri 0
Tampa(config-if)# dialer-group 1
```

7. Set up the phone number of the destination:

```
Tampa(config)# interface bri 0
Tampa(config-if)# dialer map ip 10.1.1.1 name Orlando
                        broadcast 1-407-359-1212
```

8. Enable the interface:

```
Tampa(config)# interface bri 0
Tampa(config-if)# no shutdown
```

Test the backup interface operation on the Orlando router:

1. Verify the current routing table:

```
Orlando# show ip route
Codes: I - IGRP derived, R - RIP derived, O - OSPF derived
       C - connected, S - static, E - EGP derived, B - BGP derived
       i - IS-IS derived, * - candidate default route,
       IA - OSPF inter area route, E1 - OSPF external type 1 route,
       E2 - OSPF external type 2 route, L1 - IS-IS level-1 route,
       L2 - IS-IS level-2 route

Gateway of last resort is not set

     10.0.0.0 is subnetted (mask is 255.255.255.0), 3 subnets
C       10.1.10.0   255.255.255.0 is directly connected, Ethernet0
C       10.1.1.0    255.255.255.0 is directly connected, Serial0
I       10.1.20.0   [100/158350] via 10.1.1.2, 0:00:15, Serial0
```

Note that 10.1.20.0 is off of Serial0, the frame relay connection.

2. Shut down the frame relay interface:

```
Orlando(config)# interface bri 0
Orlando(config-if)# shutdown
```

3. Wait about 30 seconds and check the routing table—this will give the router enough time (20 seconds plus the call setup time) to establish the backup connection:

```
Orlando# show ip route
Codes: I - IGRP derived, R - RIP derived, O - OSPF derived
       C - connected, S - static, E - EGP derived, B - BGP derived
       i - IS-IS derived, * - candidate default route,
       IA - OSPF inter area route, E1 - OSPF external type 1 route,
       E2 - OSPF external type 2 route, L1 - IS-IS level-1 route,
       L2 - IS-IS level-2 route

Gateway of last resort is not set

     10.0.0.0 is subnetted (mask is 255.255.255.0), 3 subnets
C       10.1.10.0   255.255.255.0 is directly connected, Ethernet0
C       10.1.1.0    255.255.255.0 is directly connected, Serial0
I       10.1.20.0   [100/158350] via 10.1.3.2, 0:00:15, BRI0
```

Note that 10.1.20.0 is now off of BRI0, the ISDN interface.

11

4. Re-enable the serial interface:

```
Orlando(config)# interface bri 0
Orlando(config-if)# no shutdown
```

5. Recheck the routing table—this time, wait about a minute before rechecking:

```
Orlando# show ip route
Codes: I - IGRP derived, R - RIP derived, O - OSPF derived
       C - connected, S - static, E - EGP derived, B - BGP derived
       i - IS-IS derived, * - candidate default route,
       IA - OSPF inter area route, E1 - OSPF external type 1 route,
       E2 - OSPF external type 2 route, L1 - IS-IS level-1 route,
       L2 - IS-IS level-2 route

Gateway of last resort is not set

     10.0.0.0 is subnetted (mask is 255.255.255.0), 3 subnets
C       10.1.10.0   255.255.255.0 is directly connected, Ethernet0
C       10.1.1.0    255.255.255.0 is directly connected, Serial0
I       10.1.20.0   [100/158350] via 10.1.1.2, 0:00:15, Serial0
```

10.1.20.0 goes back to the original connection, the frame relay interface.

Project 11.2

Creative Widgets is complaining about intermittent problems, usually between 9 to 9:30 A.M. and 1:00 to 1:30 P.M., with slowness when sending information between the two offices. Sarah has decided to solve this problem by implementing the load feature for the backup interface: She will configure a load threshold of 85 percent to bring up the backup interface and a threshold of 65 percent to bring it back down.

Enter the following commands on the Orlando router:

```
Orlando(config)# interface serial 0
Orlando(config-if)# backup load   85 65
```

CHAPTER TWELVE

Bandwidth-Saving Strategies

After completing this chapter, you will be able to:

✓ Understand when to implement queuing and/or compression

✓ Implement Weighted Fair Queuing

✓ Implement Custom Queuing

✓ Implement Priority Queuing

✓ Configure compression on your WAN links

An Overview of Bandwidth-Saving Strategies

After implementing a WAN solution, your troubles are not over. You will be facing a constant battle between bandwidth and money—your users will always be clamoring for more bandwidth and faster access rates as your IT WAN budget keeps on getting smaller and smaller. There are some features that Cisco supports that can help alleviate some of your delay and bandwidth problems on your serial interfaces—namely, queuing and compression.

Queuing

Queuing allows you to reorder your packets before transmitting them out of your serial interface. This allows you to transfer delay-sensitive traffic, such as Telnet and SNA sessions, out of the serial interface before data-intensive protocols, such as FTP and network print requests. Note that queuing does *not* solve your congestion problems—it *reprioritizes* your traffic. Queuing works very well in environments where you have temporary bursts of congestion. If congestion is a continual problem, compression might provide a better solution.

Compression

Compression squeezes your data into a smaller size, allowing you to transfer more information across the same size WAN circuit. However, the downside of compression is that it is very CPU and/or memory intensive—if your router is already utilizing over 50 percent of its CPU cycles, implementing compression will probably make the performance of your router much worse.

Therefore, any time you implement a bandwidth-saving strategy, whether it be queuing or compression, you should always monitor your performance to determine whether the feature is helping your users or creating more problems for them.

Queuing

When managing enterprise networks, you will be faced with many problems, especially with the protocols that you must support across your WAN infrastructure. Each of your protocols will have certain needs. Your SNA sessions require little bandwidth but are sensitive to delay. At the opposite end of the spectrum, your desktop protocols, such as IPX and AppleTalk, have a lot of overhead in broadcast and/or multicast traffic. Add to this all the quirks of your other user applications and the impact of your Internet traffic. When you combine all of this, you can imagine the problems you will face in trying to carve up your WAN bandwidth. On one hand, you need to meet the needs of your mission-critical applications, but on the other hand, you still need to provide bandwidth to your remaining applications in a fair manner.

For instance, you may have SNA, IP, and IPX in your environment. For your SNA traffic, you need to guarantee a minimal amount of bandwidth to ensure that your users' mainframe sessions do not have timeout problems. Also, you need to make sure your IP and IPX traffic can happily coexist—that IP doesn't run rampant over your IPX traffic and vice versa—and that neither of these two has a negative impact on your critical SNA traffic. Sometimes this can be a difficult challenge.

Queuing Policies

Queuing is a mechanism that can assist you in this balancing process. Queuing affects the order in which information is sent *out* of your serial interface. Issues faced in queuing are:

➤ Which queuing mechanism to implement

➤ The number of queues employed

➤ The size of the queues

➤ How information is placed into the queues

➤ How information is taken out of the queues and forwarded out of the interface

Four different types of queuing are available to you: First In, First Out (FIFO), Weighted Fair Queuing (WFQ), Custom Queuing (CQ), and Priority Queuing (PQ). First, you must decide if queuing can help you with your bandwidth problems.

Determining If You Have a Congestion Problem

The first issue you must face is whether you even need queuing on your serial interfaces. Here are some questions you should examine when thinking about queuing as a congestion management solution:

➤ Do you have time-sensitive applications such as SNA, video conferencing, and voice traffic?

➤ Are users complaining about the slowness of their interactive applications, such as Telnet and SNA sessions?

➤ Are you experiencing high bursts of data traffic, causing temporary congestion problems?

➤ Are your current bandwidth connections running at T1/E1 speeds or less?

➤ Do you even have a congestion problem?

This last question is common sense. In other words, if you are not having a congestion problem, there is no reason to implement a queuing policy. To determine if you have a congestion problem, check your serial interfaces to see if you are dropping outbound traffic.

12

Queuing Considerations

If there is no congestion on the WAN link, there is no reason to implement traffic prioritization. If you have no congestion problem and you implement queuing, you could be making things worse by having your traffic incur more delay. The queuing solutions discussed here will reorder your traffic before transmitting it out the interface. To accomplish this, the router will have to buffer up its traffic, causing more delay and therefore possibly creating problems for you that did not exist before.

If you feel that queuing will help you with your temporary bursts of congestion, you will need to consider the following issues:

➤ Which application or network protocol is being negatively impacted?

➤ What kind of problem is this application or network protocol having in your WAN?

➤ What type of traffic is most critical to your business?

Note: Queuing is not going to solve your congestion problem. Queuing only reorders the transmission of your packets. If you had congestion before queuing, it will still exist after you implement a queuing strategy. Therefore, it is very important that after you implement a queuing strategy, you monitor the effectiveness of it to make sure it is solving your specific problem(s). Also, you will need to periodically reassess your queuing strategy because your company's business goals and traffic patterns can change over time. The queuing strategy that is currently in place might be inadvertently affecting your changing environment.

Comparison of Queuing Mechanisms

To choose an appropriate queuing strategy, you will need to carefully examine your traffic patterns and the problems that the users are experiencing. You will also need to assess which protocols or types of application traffic should be given preference over other types of traffic—that is, you must determine which are most important to the operation of your company. This will help you in choosing a queuing strategy that fits your environment.

Note: Queuing works best on T1/E1 links or less. If you have a serial connection that is clocked faster than this, queuing is a poor solution because it might reduce the amount of bandwidth available to you.

When you have decided to use queuing as a congestion-management strategy, you will need to choose a type of queuing to use. Many Cisco queuing options are available to you. This book, however, only discusses four of them: FIFO, WFQ, CQ, and PQ. Each of these queuing polices will have a different impact on the processing of traffic before it leaves your serial interface.

Some of these queuing mechanisms give you very specific control over this processing (CQ and PQ), whereas others are completely left to the router to decide (FIFO

Table 12.1   Cisco's queuing mechanisms.

	FIFO	WFQ	CQ	PQ
Configuration	None required	None required	Required	Required
Number of queues	1	Traffic dependent	4	17
Prioritization	None	Interactive traffic	User defined	User defined
Servicing of queues	FIFO	Interactive first	High queue first	Round-robin
When best used	No congestion exists.	A lot of bandwidth is available.	Router prioritization solves your problem.	Little bandwidth is available (64K or less).

and WFQ). With some of these queuing mechanisms, you will have to perform the configuration manually (CQ and PQ), whereas some are done automatically for you by the router (FIFO and WFQ). Table 12.1 compares these different queuing mechanisms.

Note: You can implement different queuing strategies on a single router; however, you are restricted to implementing only a single queuing strategy per interface.

You will need to decide which of these queuing mechanisms is most appropriate for your serial interface. To make your decision, use the following list:

1. If you are experiencing no congestion, use FIFO.

2. If you are experiencing congestion, implement one of the following queuing strategies:

    a. If you do not need to dictate the order of transmission for your packets, use WFQ.

    b. If you need to have control over the transmission of your traffic, use either CQ or PQ.

        i. If you can afford some delay or have a lot of bandwidth, use CQ.

        ii. Otherwise, if you are experiencing unacceptable delay for very important traffic, or you have very little bandwidth, use PQ.

FIFO Queuing

Whether you realize it or not, your router is performing queuing on its interfaces. It is either performing FIFO or WFQ, depending on the type of interface.

Note: WFQ is automatically used on all serial interfaces at T1/E1 speeds or less. FIFO is used on every other interface. If you configure a different queuing strategy, such as CQ or PQ, on a serial interface, this overrides any automatic queuing that the router was previously using.

FIFO queuing does not reprioritize any of your traffic. When traffic traverses the backplane of the router and reaches your serial interface, it is queued up in the order in which it arrives. In other words, the first packet that reaches the interface will be the first packet sent across your WAN. All packets are treated equally.

12

The problem with this approach is that misbehaving traffic can cause problems for your other applications and protocols, perhaps causing very annoying delays or timeouts. Likewise, if an application generates large amounts of bandwidth, it could inadvertently fill up the serial interface's queue, causing other types of traffic to be dropped. However, the one advantage that FIFO has is that it is the most efficient of the queuing mechanisms—it requires very few CPU cycles.

FIFO queuing should therefore be used when you have very few, if any, congestion problems—in other words, when your WAN connection is very large and you have a lot of bandwidth at your disposal.

FQ is the default queuing method enabled on all your serial interfaces. To disable it and have the router employ FIFO queuing on an interface, execute the following command on your serial interface:

```
Router(config)# interface serial [module-number/]port-number
Router(config)# no fair-que
```

Weighted Fair Queuing (WFQ)

WFQ is the default queuing mechanism on all of Cisco's serial interfaces: No configuration is required on your part to enable it. WFQ overcomes the problem of FIFO, where one packet stream can negatively impact all the traffic on an interface. WFQ will dynamically sort traffic into *conversations*. A conversation is uniquely identified by the following components inside the packet:

➤ Source and destination address (network layer or MAC)

➤ Protocol, such as IP

➤ Protocol type, such as TCP or UDP

➤ Application type determined by source and destination port numbers

➤ Quality of Service (QoS)

➤ Type of Service (ToS)

How WFQ Works

To allocate bandwidth, each conversation is assigned a weight that is used to differentiate between the low- and high-volume conversations. This is then used to determine how much bandwidth a conversation is allowed compared to other conversations that are using the serial interface.

There are two types of conversations. Interactive traffic, such as Telnet and SNA sessions, are considered low-volume conversations. File transfers are considered high-volume conversations. WFQ gives a higher preference to low-volume conversations over high-volume conversations; however, within the same conversation type, such as two Telnet sessions, the conversations are treated equally by the router. This ensures that interactive traffic is serviced first, giving the user the illusion that no congestion exists in the WAN.

Traffic is queued up based on low versus high priority. These queues have a threshold, where, once the queue is filled, traffic for the conversation is dropped. This is used to make sure that high-volume conversations, such as file transfers, do not use up all the queue space. Also, it ensures that two high-volume conversations are treated equally—each is given the same queue space and each is given an equal amount of bandwidth on the interface, thus preventing one file transfer from hogging all the queue space and bandwidth.

The queue space is processed a little bit differently from the FIFO mechanism. In WFQ, the router will send a packet out of the serial interface based on its arrival time in the queue. This is measured by the time of arrival of the last bit of the packet. Within a conversation type, this is used as a sorting mechanism.

Limitations of WFQ

WFQ will not work in all situations. If you employ tunnels or encryption, WFQ will not work. The reason for this is that tunnels and encryption alter the contents of the packet and packet headers—information that is necessary for differentiating traffic into different conversations. WFQ is also not supported for X.25/LAPB and SDLC encapsulations for your serial interfaces.

Configuring WFQ

As mentioned earlier, WFQ is enabled on all serial T1/E1 interfaces by default—barring any of the restrictions mentioned in the last section. One command is used for WFQ, which is executed on the serial interface:

```
Router(config)# interface serial [module_number/]port_number
Router(config-if)# fair-queue [congestive_discard_threshold]
```

If WFQ has been disabled on a serial interface, you can use this command to reenable it. The other function of this command is to define the maximum number of packets that a conversation can keep in the queue space. This is used to make sure one conversation does not use up all the queue space on the interface.

Note: This value defaults to 64 packets. You can set this from 1 to 512 messages.

Custom Queuing (CQ)

One of the issues with WFQ is that, even though it gives preference to lower-volume conversations over higher ones and adapts to the changing conditions of your network's traffic patterns, it does not allow you to rank conversations outside the low-versus-high-volume comparison. There might be certain cases where a specific file transfer should be given higher priority than other transfers, or when a specific connection between two machines should be given the highest priority. Unfortunately WFQ cannot implement such prioritizations.

Where WFQ falls short, CQ picks up. CQ allows *you* to allocate bandwidth based on traffic classifications—classifications that you have very strict control over. You determine what traffic is placed into a queue and then how the queue will be serviced. With this type of control, you can break up your allotted bandwidth, giving one type of traffic a certain amount of bandwidth compared to others. This allows you to give your traffic the bandwidth guarantees it needs. And when a specific type of traffic is not using its assigned bandwidth, this bandwidth can be temporarily reallocated to other traffic types, thereby ensuring that you can always maximize your bandwidth efficiency.

Limitations of Custom Queuing

One issue with CQ, however, is that it is a static configuration—it cannot adapt to changing patterns in your traffic. For instance, let's assume you have set up two queues—one for SNA and one for everything else. In this configuration, you have assigned SNA half of the serial interface's bandwidth, and all your other protocols get the remaining bandwidth. This works well for a few weeks until your SNA traffic patterns change, doubling the amount of bandwidth normally consumed. Unfortunately, custom queuing is still configured to split the traffic load on the interface.

In this case, your SNA traffic would suffer from delays and possibly dropped sessions. WFQ does not have this problem—SNA is always treated as a low-volume conversation and therefore gets a higher priority. Consequently, you should always monitor the operation of your queuing mechanism to ensure it's meeting your users' and company's needs.

How Custom Queuing Works

CQ employs 17 queues, 0 through 16. Queue 0 is a reserved queue and is always processed first. This queue is referred to as the *system queue*. High-priority information, such as signaling packets (LMI for frame relay), keepalives, and other system information, is placed in this queue. Queues 1 through 16 are used for user traffic.

Note: For the test, the answer Cisco will be looking for is a total of 16 queues; however, in reality, there are a total of 17.

In CQ, every queue is guaranteed to be serviced. The queues are processed in a round-robin fashion, starting with queue 0. After queue 0 is emptied, the router will then start processing queue 1. When processing a queue, the router will forward packets from the queue until the router reaches the queue's threshold. Once a queue has been processed, the router proceeds to the next queue. It will process all the queues in order and then return to the system queue. Note that the system queue does not have any thresholds assigned to it—guaranteeing that your high-priority system traffic will always get bandwidth.

CQ and Queue Thresholds

A router processes a queue until the queue's threshold has been exceeded. The *threshold* defines how much information is to be processed before the router moves on to the next queue.

Note: This value is specified in bytes and defaults to 1,500. One important point to note is that the route will process at least this much information from the queue (assuming that there is that much traffic in the queue). Care must be taken in defining this threshold because a misconfiguration of the threshold can negatively impact certain types of your traffic.

To give one queue more bandwidth than another queue, you assign it a higher threshold. The higher the threshold that you assign, the more information that can be sent out the serial interface when it is that queue's turn to be processed. Note that this is not an exact allocation of bandwidth because a queue might not have that much information in it, if any. This means that when the queue is processed, the traffic in it is getting less bandwidth than you specified. Likewise, the threshold does *not* define that a queue will *exactly* dispatch so many bytes at a time: If a queue has a packet in it where the beginning of the packet is under the threshold but the end of it is over the threshold, the *complete* packet is dispatched. In other words, the router will not fragment any packets. This means that the traffic in this queue is getting more bandwidth than the threshold you assigned it.

Problems with Thresholds

As an example, let's assume you have two packets in queue 1—one is 750 bytes in size and the other is 800 bytes, arriving at a total of 1,550 bytes. Assuming that the threshold is 1,500 bytes, the router will at least service this much information when it is processing queue 1. When servicing a queue, it will not stop at the threshold if there is still a portion of the packet currently being processed left in the queue. Instead, it will continue forwarding the remaining portion of the packet. This prevents the router from having to perform any type of fragmentation of the packet, thus allowing for a streamlined, efficient process.

If this is true all the time (the queue is always forwarding traffic a bit beyond its threshold), then the traffic associated with this queue could impact other traffic in other queues—it is constantly getting more bandwidth than you anticipated. Therefore, you should be careful when configuring a threshold value that is very small. To solve this problem, you might think that you should increase your thresholds to very large sizes—the exact opposite approach. However, this also creates a problem. If your threshold is a large size, the router will spend a long time in a single queue processing its traffic before proceeding to the next queue, thereby incurring lengthy delays for the traffic in the other queues.

12

Note: The challenge you face with queue thresholds is to balance bandwidth allocation with a timely processing of all the queues. The best way of handling this is to run IOS 12.1. In 12.1, the router remembers the extra bytes that it processed from a queue. The next time the router processes the queue, it reduces the threshold by this amount. This ensures that bandwidth is allocated on a fair basis.

Configuring Custom Queuing

There are two basic steps to configuring CQ. First, you need to define a set of allocations for your types of traffic by assigning them to different queues and then setting appropriate thresholds for these queues. These commands are global Configuration commands. Next, you need to assign the CQ list to your serial interface. As soon as you do this, the router is performing CQ on the interface.

Defining Your Queuing Policy

First, you need to define your queue policies with **queue-list** global Configuration mode commands. The following are the commands necessary to implement your queuing policies:

```
Router(config)# queue-list list_number protocol name_of_protocol
                queue_number queue_key_words_and_values
```

Here, *list_number* is the number of the CQ list. You can have up to 16 different sets of CQ configurations (different lists). The list number can be from 1 to 16. Next, you define the protocol that will be assigned to one of the 16 queues, specified by the *queue_number* parameter. Examples of protocols are AppleTalk, IPX, IP, DECnet, and many others. Remember that you have up to 16 different queues in which to implement your policies. The *queue_key_words_and_values* parameter defines what type of protocol traffic should be placed in this queue. Table 12.2 lists the possible key words and their associated values and meanings.

With these parameters, you can specify, by protocol, which type of traffic is placed in which queue. Optionally, instead of specifying traffic by protocol, you can place

Table 12.2   CQ queue-list key words and values.

Key Words	Values	Meaning
Fragments		Any packet fragments are placed in this queue.
gt	Number of bytes	Packets with a byte size greater than this are placed in this queue.
lt	Number of bytes	Packets with a byte size less than this are placed in this queue.
list	**Access-list** number	Packets meeting the criteria of this **access-list** are placed in this queue.
tcp	Port number	Packets matching this TCP port number (source or destination) are placed in this queue.
udp	Port number	Packets matching this UDP port number (source or destination) are placed in this queue.

all the traffic from a source router interface into a specific queue with the following command:

```
Router(config)# queue-list list_number interface interface_type
                         [module_number/]port_number
                         queue-number
```

Note: *These commands are processed top-down until a match is found—in which case the packet is placed in that specific queue. Therefore, the order of your **queue-list** statements does matter. If traffic is received by the router and none of the preceding **queue-list** commands match the contents of the packet, you will want to place the traffic in a default queue.*

Use the following command to place unmatched traffic in a default queue:

```
Router(config)# queue-list list_number default queue_number
```

If you do not specify a default queue, this traffic will be *dropped*. Even though you have 16 queues to implement your traffic policies, you are not required to use all of them.

The following commands allow you to implement your policies for the traffic you assigned to your queues:

```
Router(config)# queue-list list_number queue queue_number
                         limit maximum_number_of_packets
```

The default maximum number of packets that can be placed in a queue is 20. You can change this from 0 to 32,767. If you set it to 0, an unlimited number of packets can be placed in this specific queue. If the router tries to place a packet in the queue and the limit is exceeded, the packet is dropped. You will want to monitor this to ensure that you are not dropping packets—if you are, you will want to slowly increase the queue size.

To implement your queue thresholds, use the following command:

```
Router(config)# queue-list list_number queue queue_number
                         byte-count threshold_in_bytes
```

This command assigns the threshold value that defines the minimum number of bytes that will be processed from this queue when the router is forwarding packets from it. Remember that the router will not fragment packets—it always forwards complete packets, even if that means the router will exceed the queue's threshold value. The default value of the threshold is 1,500 bytes.

Activating Your Queuing Policy

Once you have created your CQ list, you will need to activate it on your serial interface with the following commands:

```
Router(config)# interface serial [module_number/]port_number
Router(config-if)# custom-queue-list list_number
```

Once you have performed this, the router will process your traffic using your CQ list.

Example of Using Custom Queuing

Let's take a look at an example to show you some of the functionality of a CQ. First, separate your traffic into different queues:

```
Router(config)# queue-list 1 interface tok 0 1
Router(config)# queue-list 1 protocol ip 2 list 1
Router(config)# queue-list 1 protocol ip 3 list 101
Router(config)# queue-list 1 protocol ip 4 tcp 23
Router(config)# queue-list 1 protocol ipx 5
Router(config)# queue-list 1 default 6
Router(config)#
Router(config)# access-list 1 permit 172.16.39.0 0.0.0.255
Router(config)#
Router(config)# access-list 101 permit icmp any any
```

Remember that the router processes the CQ top-down: As soon as a packet matches a **queue-list** statement, the packet is placed in the specified queue and the router does not process any further statements. The first **queue-list** statement places all traffic from interface token-ring 0 into queue #1. The second statement will take all traffic originating from network 172.16.39.0 and place it into queue #2. This queuing command references **access-list 1**. The third statement places all ICMP traffic in queue #3. This queuing command also references an **access-list**; in this case it is an extended **access-list**. Any Telnet sessions are placed in queue #4, and all IPX traffic is placed in queue #5. All remaining traffic is placed in queue #6, the default queue.

Next, you will need to define your queue sizes (if 20 is not sufficient) and your thresholds (which default to 1500 bytes):

```
Router(config)# queue-list 1 queue 5 limit 40
Router(config)# queue-limit 1 queue 6 limit 40
Router(config)# queue-limit 1 queue 2 byte-count 3000
Router(config)# queue-limit 1 queue 3 byte-count 500
```

The first two commands increase the queue size to 40 packets for IPX traffic and the default queue. The third command increases the threshold to 3,000—this give traffic from 172.16.39.0 twice as much bandwidth as the other queues. The last command reduces the traffic allocation by one-third for ICMP traffic. This ensures that someone does not flood the serial interface with pings.

Last, you will need to assign your CQ list to your serial interface (in this case, serial 0):

```
Router(config)# interface serial 0
Router(config-if)# custom-queue-list 1
```

Priority Queuing (PQ)

CQ works very well when you have more than 64Kb of bandwidth on your serial connection. When you have less, CQ is less effective because it cannot give an absolute guarantee for your critical traffic—your traffic may sit in a queue too long while the router tries to process all of the queues in its round-robin fashion. And with WFQ, you cannot tell the router which traffic type is critical—low-volume conversations are always given preference. In your specific situation, you might want to give a single file transfer the highest priority, or any traffic between two critical end stations. To do this, you will need to implement PQ. PQ guarantees that your highest-priority traffic will always be sent out the serial interface before any other type of traffic. For delay-sensitive traffic, such as SNA, interactive sessions, voice and video, this is important.

The problem, however, is that other types of traffic might get very little bandwidth, if any. But you are guaranteed that your critical traffic will get the bandwidth that it needs—with a maximum bandwidth guarantee equal to that of the serial interface. And just like CQ, PQ cannot adapt to changing traffic patterns in your network environment. Therefore, you will need to monitor PQ on an ongoing basis.

12

How Priority Queuing Works

PQ, like CQ, gives you control over how traffic is to be prioritized before it is sent out of your serial interfaces. You define a set of queuing policies that determines your traffic prioritization. With PQ, you are given four queues:

➤ High

➤ Medium

➤ Normal

➤ Low

The high queue has the highest priority, and your most critical and time-sensitive traffic should be placed here. The low queue has the lowest priority, and your least important and delay-insensitive traffic should be placed here.

You define a list, similar to a CQ list, that assigns each of your different traffic types to one of the four queues. Next, just like in CQ, you activate your PQ list on your serial interface. At this point, your router will begin using your PQ list to prioritize your traffic before forwarding it out of the serial interface.

Placing Packets in the Queues

When a packet arrives on a different interface and the router routes it to the serial interface, the router will place the packet into one of the four queues based on your queuing policy. When placing the packet in a queue, the router checks the queue limit first. Each queue has a limit that defines how many packets can be placed in it. If the queue is already full, the router will drop the packet; otherwise, the packet is placed in the queue.

Certain types of traffic are automatically assigned to the high- priority queue—for instance, keepalives and signaling are placed here. Other management traffic, such as routing traffic, is placed in one of the four queues based on your policies.

Emptying the Queues

When the router is processing the four queues to forward traffic out of the serial interface, it starts with the high priority queue first and empties it. It then checks the high-priority queue again for any more packets that might have just arrived. If there are no packets in the high queue, the router empties the medium queue. Once emptied, the router goes back and checks the high queue. The only time the normal queue will be processed is when the router checks both the high and medium queues and they contain no packets. Likewise, the only time the router will process the low priority queue is when the high, medium, and normal queues are empty.

Given this priority scheme, traffic in the high-priority queue is always guaranteed to get serviced. There are no guarantees for the other queues. In other words, if the high-priority queue always contains packets, the other queues do not get serviced. Therefore, care must be taken when setting up your priority scheme to ensure that you don't inadvertently starve some of your important traffic that might be placed in a lower queue. One method you can take to help with this is to assign lower-bandwidth traffic flows to the higher-priority queues while assigning the higher-bandwidth flows to the lower queues.

Configuring Priority Queuing

As with CQ, there are two basic steps to configuring PQ. First, you need to create your queuing policy by ranking your traffic into one of four priority categories: high, medium, normal, and low. These commands are global Configuration commands. Next, you need to assign the PQ list to your serial interface. As soon as you do this, the router will perform PQ on the interface.

Defining Your Queuing Policy

First, you need to define your queue policies with **priority–list** global Configuration mode commands. The following are the commands necessary to implement your queuing policies:

```
Router(config)# priority-list list_number protocol name_of_protocol
                      high|medium|normal|low
                      queue_key_words_and_values
```

Here, *list_number* is the number of the PQ list. You can have up to 16 different sets of PQ configurations. The list number can be from 1 to 16. Next, you define the protocol that will be assigned to one of the four queues, specified by either the **high**, **medium**, **normal**, or **low** queue parameter. Examples of protocols are AppleTalk, IPX, IP, DECnet, and many others. Remember that you have only four different queues in which to implement your policies. The *queue_key_words_and_values* parameter defines what type of protocol traffic should be placed in this queue. Refer back to Table 12.2 for the possible key words and their associated values and meanings that you can use here.

Just as with CQ lists, you can also place all the traffic from a source router interface into a specific queue with the following command:

```
Router(config)# priority-list list_number interface interface_type
                      [module_number/]port_number
                      high|medium|normal|low
```

*Note: These commands are processed top-down until a match is found—in which case the packet is placed in that specific queue. Therefore, the order of your **priority–list** statements does matter. If traffic is received by the router and none of the preceding **priority–list** commands match the contents of the packet, the packet will be placed into a default queue. The default queue is the normal queue, unless you change it.*

12

Use the following command to place "unspecified" traffic into the default queue:

```
Router(config)# priority-list list_number default
                      high|medium|normal|low
```

This is only necessary if you want to change the default queue to something other than the normal queue. Unlike CQ, PQ does have a default queue preconfigured.

The default sizes of the four queues are listed in Table 12.3.

Table 12.3 **Default queue sizes for PQ.**

Queue	Size in packets
High	20
Medium	40
Normal	60
Low	80

To change the sizes of the queues, use the following command:

```
Router(config)# priority-list list_number queue-limit
                    size_of_high_queue size_of_medium_queue
                    size_of_normal_queue size_of_low_queue
```

If the router tries to place a packet in a queue and the limit of the queue is exceeded, the packet is dropped. You will want to monitor this to ensure you are not dropping packets—if you are, you will want to slowly increase the queue size. Care must be taken, however, especially with the sizes of the higher-priority queues. If you set these too large, the lower-priority queues may never get serviced.

Activating Your Queuing Policy

Once you have created your PQ list, you will need to activate it on your serial interface with the following commands:

```
Router(config)# interface serial [module_number/]port_number
Router(config-if)# priority-group list_number
```

Once you have performed this, the router will process your traffic using your PQ list.

Example of Using Priority Queuing

Let's take a look at an example that displays some of the functionality of PQ. First, separate your traffic into different queues:

```
Router(config)# priority-list 1 interface tok 0 high
Router(config)# priority-list 1 protocol ip medium list 1
Router(config)# priority-list 1 protocol ip normal
Router(config)# priority-list 1 protocol ipx normal
Router(config)# priority-list 1 default low
Router(config)#
Router(config)# access-list 1 permit 172.16.39.0 0.0.0.255
```

Remember that the router processes the PQ top-down: As soon as a packet matches a **priority-list** statement, the packet is placed in the specified queue and the router does not process any further statements. The first **priority-list** statement places all traffic from interface token-ring 0 into the high-priority queue. This example assumes that the SNA sessions are originating from the token ring interface and therefore should be given the highest priority. The second statement will take all traffic originating from network 172.16.39.0 and place it in the medium queue. These might be client/server databases that have your second-most-critical traffic. The third and fourth statements place all other IP traffic as well as all IPX traffic in the normal queue. All other remaining traffic is placed in the default queue, which is changed to be the low queue.

Because you are concerned with the amount of IP and IPX traffic, it would be a good idea to increase the size of the normal queue to prevent inadvertent drops of your packets because the queue is filled up. Here's how:

```
Router(config)# priority-list 1 queue-limit 20 40 80 80
```

This command increases the size of the normal queue from 60 to 80 packets. Last, you will need to assign your PQ list to your serial interface (in this case, serial 0):

```
Router(config)# interface serial 0
Router(config-if)# priority-group 1
```

Once you have executed the above command, the router will use PQ on the serial interface.

Verifying Your Queuing Configuration and Operation

Once you have configured your queuing policy, you will want to verify its operation. To examine the configuration, use the following **show** command:

```
Router# show queueing [custom|fair|priority]
```

You can optionally qualify the output of the command by listing the type of queuing policies that you wish to see, using either **custom** for CQ, **fair** for WFQ, or **priority** for PQ. If you do not specify one of these, the router will display all your queuing policies.

The following is an example of the output of this command for your configuration for PQ:

```
Router# show queueing priority

Current priority queue configuration:
List    Queue   Args
1       high    interface tok 0
```

```
1       medium  list 1
1       normal  protocol ip
1       normal  protocol ipx
1       low     default
```

To verify your queuing operation on an interface, use the following **show** command:

```
Router# show queueing interface serial [module_number/]port_number
```

Note: *The parameter* **queueing** *is misspelled—this is the "correct" spelling to use to execute the command in Cisco's IOS.*

The following is an example of WFQ on a serial interface:

```
Router# show queueing interface serial 0

Interface Serial 0
  Input queue 0/75/0 (size/max/drops); Total output drops: 0
  Queueing strategy: weighted fair
  Output queue: 5/532/64/17 (size/max total/threshold/drops)
    Conversations  1/2/256 (active/max active/max total)
    Reserved Conversations 0/0 (allocated/max allocated)

  (depth/weight/discards/tail drops/interleaves) 5/4096/17/0/0
  Conversation 264, linktype: ip, length: 254
  source: 10.1.5.7, destination: 10.1.2.20, id: 0x0000, ttl: 37,
  TOS: 0 prot: 17, source port 23, destination port 1237
```

In the preceding output, there are five packets in the queue structure and one conversation. For the one active conversation, 17 packets were dropped. Below this, the details of the conversation are listed: The packets are originating from 10.1.5.7 and are from a Telnet connection. You will want to pay special attention to the number of "drops" in the "Output queue:" line of the display—if this is constantly increasing, you will want to increase your queue size(s).

Compression

Queuing is a mechanism that you can use to prioritize traffic—it does not solve your bandwidth problems. To help alleviate your bandwidth problems, you have two choices: You can implement compression or buy more bandwidth. Before you run out and give your carrier more money, you should take a careful look at compression to see if it can help with your congestion problem. And even if you decide you need to buy more bandwidth—that is, you determine that compression cannot help you—you might decide to implement compression as a *temporary* solution until you are able to install a larger circuit.

Types of Compression

By default, compression is not enabled on your serial interfaces. Cisco has a handful of compression options to help you with your congestion problems:

➤ Link compression can be used to compress all the information leaving an interface.

➤ Payload compression can be used to compress the payload of a frame—this is typically used in environments that use VCs, such as frame relay or X.25.

➤ Header compression is used to compress the headers of transport layer segments—this is very efficient for applications that have little data, such as Telnet. In this example, the Telnet data is very small, whereas the TCP segment header is very large.

Link Compression

Link compression is used on point-to-point links using either HDLC, LAPB, or PPP as an encapsulation type on your serial interfaces. With link compression, the entire frame—header, payload, and trailer—are compressed. This type of compression is not supported in WAN environments that use VCs. The reason for this is that these environments need to see the header to make switching decisions—frame relay switches need to see the DLCI number, and X.25 switches need to see the VC address. If you used link compression on this, the switch would drop the traffic because it wouldn't know how to switch it. Therefore, only point-to-point connections are supported.

Cisco supports three types of link compression algorithms:

➤ Stacker, developed by STAC Electronics, uses Lempel-Ziv, a compression algorithm based on a dictionary method.

➤ Predictor is a compression algorithm that is based on a dictionary method—Cisco implements this in a proprietary fashion.

➤ The Microsoft Point-to-Point Compression (MPPC) is used on dial-up (point-to-point) links between Cisco routers and Microsoft clients.

These algorithms use a dictionary process to perform their compression. This process examines a data string for repetitive patterns and replaces the pattern with a special code sequence, which is listed in a dictionary. When this information is sent to the destination, the compression algorithm at the other side seeks out these special codes in the incoming data and finds the appropriate match in its dictionary. When it finds the match in the dictionary, it then replaces the special codes with the information found in the dictionary, thus producing the original data stream.

Note: These types of compression are appropriate for leased lines and dial-up links, such as analog modems and ISDN.

12

Configuring Link Compression

To configure link-level compression, use the following serial interface command:

```
Router(config)# interface serial [module_number/]port_number
Router(config-if)# compress mppc|predictor|stac
```

You need to ensure that the compression type matches on both sides of the link. To verify your configuration, use the **show interfaces** command.

Payload Compression

Payload compression only compresses the payload of the frame—the header and trailer are left intact. This type of compression is most often used in VC switching environments such as X.25, frame relay, SMDS, and ATM. In these environments, the VC switches need to see the headers of the frames in order to make their switching decisions. They also need to see the trailer, which typically carries the checksum of the frame.

Configuring Payload Compression

To configure payload compression for frame relay, use the following interface Configuration mode command:

```
Router(config)# interface serial [module_number/]port_number
Router(config-if)# frame-relay payload-compress
                    packet-by-packet | frf9 stac
```

If you choose **packet-by-packet**, the router uses a variation of the stacker algorithm; **frf9 stac** uses the FRF.9 standard, which implements a variation of the Stacker algorithm. Again, to verify your configuration, use the **show interfaces** command.

Header Compression

Header compression uses the Van Jacobson algorithm defined in RFC 1144. Currently, only TCP is defined. TCP headers are typically 40 bytes in length, most of which is repetitive or predictable in nature. The Van Jacobson algorithm, using an intelligent prediction and pattern-finding process, can reduce the size of the header to 4 bytes in length in the most optimal of conditions. If most of your data involves low-bandwidth applications, such as Telnet, header compression can free up 50 to 90 percent of your bandwidth, providing a very cost-effective bandwidth-saving solution.

Cisco's current header-compression implementation supports PPP, HDLC, frame relay, ATM, and X.25 interfaces. To perform header compression, the router will have to look inside the IP packet for the segment header. Because of the additional processing that is required to perform header compression, Cisco recommends that it only be deployed for connections running at 64Kbps or less. For dial-up connections that support a lot of interactive traffic, header compression can work wonders.

Configuring Header Compression

To configure header compression, enter your interface and execute the following command:

```
Router(config)# interface serial [module_number/]port_number
Router(config-if)# ip tcp header compression [passive]
```

The **passive** option allows you to perform header compression only if the interface is receiving packets that have compressed headers inside them. Using this option allows you to specify header compression without having to worry about whether the other side matches your configuration. Therefore, it can easily be used in access server environments where you do not know whether an incoming dial-up client will perform header compression. On X.25 connections, specify **compressedtcp** as your protocol in your **x25 map** interface Configuration mode command. To verify your configuration, use the **show interfaces** command.

Concerns and Considerations for Compression

The preceding software solutions are implemented by the IOS on the router. One problem with software-based compression is that it utilizes valuable CPU and memory resources on your router. If your CPU utilization is above 40 percent, software compression will probably cause more problems than it will solve.

If your CPU cycles are high and you cannot afford to increase the size of your circuit, you may want to look into hardware-based compression. Cisco sells interface cards that will perform the compression in hardware, thereby not affecting the overall processing of your router. Of course, these interface cards can be expensive. The advantage of this type of card is that the cost is a one-time cost; the problem with buying more bandwidth is that bandwidth is a recurring cost.

12

If you have a modem connection (either analog or digital), you can employ modem compression. There are a couple of standards defined for this process: MNP5 and V.42bis. MNP5 is a compression standard developed by Microcom, whereas V.42bis is an ITU-T standard. For modem compression to work, both modems must use the same compression mechanism.

Note: Also, if you are using modem compression, do not use the IOS's software compression mechanisms. If you do this, the modem will not be able to compress the information any smaller. Actually, the information that your modem sends will end up being larger—not smaller—if your router first performs software compression on your data.

Another warning involves using encryption on your links, such as IPSec. Encryption removes all the patterns from your data, thus making it random. Unfortunately, compression looks for patterns to reduce the size of your data. If you try to use both of these mechanisms, then after encryption encrypts your information, there will be no patterns for your compression algorithm to use to reduce the size of your data. This creates a problem because compression won't work, but you are wasting valuable CPU cycles while the router tries to find any nonexistent patterns.

Chapter Summary

When you're faced with temporary congestion problems, Cisco offers some congestion-management features that you can use in order to put off (or avoid altogether) purchasing more bandwidth for your WAN network. Two easy solutions to implement are queuing and compression.

Queuing enables you to override the default FIFO queuing method and prioritize your traffic to meet your specific users' needs. For interactive traffic that is constantly suffering from delays, queuing is a very effective solution. However, queuing can only reorder your traffic flow—it does not solve your congestion problem. Cisco offers many queuing options, including First In, First Out (FIFO), Weighted Fair Queuing (WFQ), Custom Queuing (CQ), and Priority Queuing (PQ).

FIFO queuing processes traffic the same way it comes in—in other words, FIFO does not reprioritize any information. WFQ is the default queuing method on serial interfaces. It breaks traffic up into conversations based on source and destination information, including application type. Low-volume conversations, such as Telnet sessions, are given priority over high-volume conversations, such as FTP sessions. The router handles this prioritization automatically. The only change you may want to make for WFQ is to increase the size of your queues with the **fair-queue** command.

If you need to influence the prioritization process, you can override WFQ by implementing CQ or PQ. Custom Queuing uses 16 user queues, where you tell the router what queue your different traffic types should be placed in. This is done with **queue-list** commands, which are then applied to a serial interface with the **custom-queue-list** command. The router processes the queues in a round-robin fashion, where every queue is guaranteed at least some bandwidth. To give a traffic type more bandwidth, you assign a queue a higher traffic threshold than the other queues.

For critical traffic on slower-speed circuits, PQ is a better solution. PQ has four queues—high, medium, normal, and low—and guarantees that your critical traffic in the high queue will always get serviced. You assign traffic to a specific queue with **priority-list** commands. To activate your PQ policy, enter the **priority-group** command on your serial interface. One problem with PQ is that traffic in the other queues can be starved if the high queue always has traffic in it. Therefore, you should use this solution only for slow-speed circuits.

Queuing is a congestion-management feature that allows you to prioritize traffic— it does not solve your congestion problems. Compression, on the other hand, squeezes your traffic into a smaller size, thus freeing up bandwidth for other uses. Compression works well on slower-speeds circuits where bandwidth is a scarce commodity. Cisco offers different software compression solutions, including link compression, payload compression, and header compression. One issue with header compression is that it is very CPU and memory intensive. If your router is already overloaded, you may want to implement compression either with a Cisco add-on card or in your dial-up modems for circuit-switched networks.

As in any congestion management implementation, you should always periodically monitor your implemented solutions—whether they use compression or queuing— to verify that they are still effective.

Review Questions

1. What issues do you face when using queuing?
   a. Number of queues used
   b. Size of queues
   c. How information is placed into queues
   d. All of the above

2. When should you implement queuing?
   a. When you have many file transfers.
   b. When file transfers are taking too long.
   c. When your traffic rates are always high.
   d. When you have limited bandwidth.

3. Queuing will _____.
   a. Create less delay for all your traffic
   b. Solve your congestion problem
   c. Reorder the forwarding of traffic
   d. All of the above

4. Queuing works best on T1/E1 lines or faster.
   a. True
   b. False

12

5. Which queuing mechanisms allow you to prioritize traffic? [Choose the two best answers]

   a. FIFO Queuing

   b. Custom Queuing

   c. Priority Queuing

   d. Weighted Fair Queuing

6. What type of queuing processes all the queues in a round-robin fashion?

   a. FIFO Queuing

   b. Custom Queuing

   c. Priority Queuing

   d. Weighted Fair Queuing

7. Which of the following queuing mechanisms require configuration? [Choose the two best answers]

   a. Custom Queuing

   b. Priority Queuing

   c. Weighted Fair Queuing

   d. FIFO Queuing

8. Which type of queuing breaks traffic streams into conversations?

   a. Custom Queuing

   b. Priority Queuing

   c. FIFO Queuing

   d. Weighted Fair Queuing

9. What is the default congestive discard threshold for WFQ?

   a. 32

   b. 64

   c. 128

   d. 512

10. Custom Queuing has how many queues?

   a. 4

   b. 10

   c. 16

   d. 17

11. What command is used to build a Custom Queuing list?

    a. **custom-queue-list**

    b. **queue-list**

    c. **priority-list**

    d. **custom-list**

12. Which of the following commands is used to define a threshold for a queue when processing a CQ list?

    a. `Router(config)# queue-list list_number protocol name_of_protocol queue_number queue_key_words_and_values`

    b. `Router(config)# queue-list list_number default queue_number`

    c. `Router(config)# queue-list list_number queue queue_number limit maximum_number_of_packets`

    d. `Router(config)# queue-list list_number queue queue_number byte-count threshold_in_bytes`

13. Which type of queuing dynamically adapts to changes in your traffic?

    a. Weighted Fair Queuing

    b. Custom Queuing

    c. FIFO Queuing

    d. Priority Queuing

14. Which queue should you place Telnet traffic into for Priority Queuing?

    a. Low

    b. Medium

    c. Normal

    d. High

15. Which queues in Priority Queuing are not guaranteed to be serviced? [Choose all correct answers]

    a. High

    b. Medium

    c. Normal

    d. Low

16. What is the command to activate a priority queue list on an interface?

    a. **queue-group**

    b. **queue-list**

    c. **priority-list**

    d. **priority-group**

12

17. What is the default size for the medium priority queue?

   a. 20

   b. 40

   c. 80

   d. 160

18. What command is used to verify WFQ?

   a. **show queuing weighted**

   b. **show queueing priority**

   c. **show queueing fair**

   d. **show queueing weighted**

19. X.25 uses what type of compression? [Choose the two best answers]

   a. Payload

   b. Header

   c. Link

   d. All of the above

20. Link compression works on all the following except which one?

   a. HDLC

   b. SDLC

   c. LAPB

   d. PPP

21. Which of the following is not a supported link-compression algorithm?

   a. Stacker

   b. Predictor

   c. Van Jacobson

   d. MPPC

22. Header compression works with which of the following?

   a. PPP

   b. HDLC

   c. Frame relay

   d. X.25

   e. All of the above

23. Software compression does not work well with which of the following? [Choose the two best answers]

    a. Encryption

    b. Modem compression

    c. Low CPU utilization

Real-World Projects

Sarah Davis has been called by a friend who is having trouble with his point-to-point connection. He has two routers—one located in New York, and one in Boston. Each has a LAN, and they are tied together across a 64Kbps dedicated leased line. Examine Figure 12.1 for the layout of the network.

His New York router's configuration is shown here:

```
hostname NewYork

enable password san-fran
ipx routing 1111.1111.1111

ip classless
ip subnet-zero

interface ethernet 0
 ip address 10.10.2.1 255.255.254.0
 ipx network 20 encapsulation sap

interface serial 0
 encapsulation ppp
 ip address 10.10.0.1 255.255.254.0
 ipx network 10

router rip
 network 10.0.0.0

line console 0
 login
 password cisco

line aux 0

line vty 0 4
 login
 password Cisco
```

12

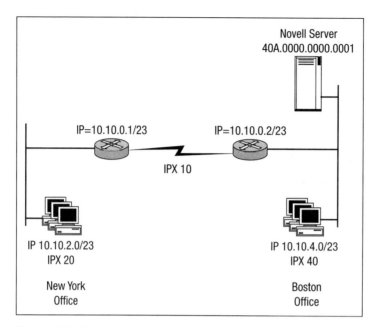

Figure 12.1 Network layout.

Here's the Boston router's configuration:

```
hostname Boston

enable password san-fran
ipx routing 2222.2222.2222

ip classless
ip subnet-zero

interface ethernet 0
 ip address 10.10.4.1 255.255.254.0
 ipx network 40 encapsulation sap

interface serial 0
 encapsulation ppp
 ip address 10.10.0.2 255.255.254.0
 ipx network 10

router rip
 network 10.0.0.0

line console 0
 login
 password cisco
```

```
line aux 0

line vty 0 4
 login
 password cisco
```

The routers' current problems are that Telnet sessions are very slow, and the traffic for IP and IPX is always causing problems for the other traffic types. Plus, there is one Novell file server—40A.0000.0000.0001—that is very important, and users from the New York office are always complaining about how slow their interactive sessions are to access this file server in the Boston office. Sarah explained the different kinds of queuing available and upon her recommendation, her friend has decided to use Priority Queuing to solve his problem.

Project 12.1

To solve these problems, you will need to perform the following tasks for setting up a priority queuing solution. First, you will need to place telnet traffic into the high queue to allow for minimal delay in the processing of this interactive traffic. Next, you will need to place traffic from the Novell file server (40A.0000.0000.0001) into the medium queue. IP and IPX traffic should be placed in the normal queue and any remaining traffic should be placed in the low queue. Also, to ensure that the normal queue does not run out of buffer space, you will need to double the size of the buffer space for the normal queue.

Create the priority queue list:

1. Build the list on the New York router first. Place the Telnet traffic in the high queue:

   ```
   NewYork(config)# priority-list 1 protocol ip high tcp 23
   ```

2. Place IPX traffic for the Novell file server (40A.0000.0000.0001) in the medium queue:

   ```
   NewYork(config)# access-list 800 permit 40A.0000.0000.0001 -1
   NewYork(config)# access-list 800 permit -1 40A.0000.0000.0001
   NewYork(config)# priority-list 1 protocol ipx medium list 800
   ```

   The **access-list** assigns any traffic from or to the Novell file server to the medium queue. Remember that, unlike standard IP **access-lists**, standard IPX **access-lists** allow you to specify both a source and a destination address.

12

3. Place IP and IPX traffic in the normal queue:

```
NewYork(config)# priority-list 1 protocol ip normal
NewYork(config)# priority-list 1 protocol ipx normal
```

4. Set the low queue to be the default queue:

```
NewYork(config)# priority-list 1 default low
```

5. Double the size of the normal queue:

```
NewYork(config)# priority-list 1 queue-limit 20 40 120 80
```

6. Verify the queuing configuration:

```
Router# show queueing priority

Current priority queue configuration:
List    Queue   Args
1       high    protocol ip tcp 23
1       medium  list 800
1       normal  protocol ip
1       normal  protocol ipx
1       low     default
```

7. Copy the queuing configuration, log into the Boston router, and paste the configuration into global Configuration mode.

Activate the priority queue list:

1. Log onto the New York router and activate the list:

```
NewYork(config)# interface serial 0
NewYork(config-if)# priority-group 1
```

2. Log onto the Boston router and activate the list:

```
Boston(config)# interface serial 0
Boston(config-if)# priority-group 1
```

Project 12.2

The previous solution worked for a while, but Sarah's friend realized that congestion was getting worse and the implemented priority queuing solution was causing more problems than it was solving. He decided to double the size of his circuit to

128Kbps. After doing this, some of his users complained about intermittent problems with their interactive sessions—specifically telnets and access to the Novell file server. To solve this, he decided to implement custom queuing. He placed telnets into one queue, file server access into a second queue, IP traffic into a third queue, and IPX traffic into a fourth queue. He also created a default queue for all other remaining traffic.

Remove the priority queue lists:

1. Remove the list on the New York router first:

```
NewYork(config)# no priority-list 1
NewYork(config)# interface serial 0
NewYork(config-if)# no priority-group 1
```

2. Remove the list on the Boston router next:

```
Boston(config)# no priority-list 1
Boston(config)# interface serial 0
Boston(config-if)# no priority-group 1
```

Create the custom queue list:

1. Build the list on the New York router first. Place the Telnet traffic into the first queue:

```
NewYork(config)# queue-list 1 protocol ip 1 tcp 23
```

2. Place IPX traffic for the Novell file server (40A.0000.0000.0001) in the second queue:

```
NewYork(config)# queue-list 1 protocol ipx 2 list 800
```

Remember that the **access-list** already exists from the previous configuration.

3. Place IP and IPX traffic into separate queues:

```
NewYork(config)# queue-list 1 protocol ip 3
NewYork(config)# queue-list 1 protocol ipx 4
```

4. Set the low queue to be the default queue:

```
NewYork(config)# queue-list 1 default 5
```

12

5. Verify the queuing configuration:

```
Router# show queueing custom

Current custom queue configuration:
List   Queue  Args
1      1      protocol ip tcp 23
1      2      list 800
1      3      protocol ip
1      4      protocol ipx
1      5      default
```

6. Copy the queuing configuration, log into the Boston router, and paste the configuration into global Configuration mode.

Activate the custom queue list:

1. Log onto the New York router and activate the list:

```
NewYork(config)# interface serial 0
NewYork(config-if)# custom-queue-list 1
```

2. Log onto the Boston router and activate the list:

```
Boston(config)# interface serial 0
Boston(config-if)# custom-queue-list 1
```

CHAPTER THIRTEEN

Network Address Translation and Remote Access

After completing this chapter, you will be able to:

✓ Use private addresses

✓ Understand how Network Address Translation is performed

✓ Understand how Port Address Translation is performed

✓ Understanding how traffic distribution can help redistribute your traffic loads among different servers

✓ Configure address translation for IOS routers

✓ Configure address translation for 700 series routers

When implementing a large enterprise network, you will be faced with many protocol issues when deploying IP. Broadcast issues, routing protocols, address allocation, and addressing assignment are just a few of the topics that you will have to deal with. One problem that every network faces is the assignment of IP addresses. With the shortage of public IP addresses for accessing the Internet and the need for every machine to have an IP address for communication, some type of solution was needed before the public address space ran out.

Private Addresses

RFC 1918 was developed to meet every company's growing address needs. RFC 1918 has set aside a range of addresses, called *private addresses*, for any company to use. Table 13.1 lists the three different private address spaces that have been set aside for use by anybody within a particular company.

With this range of addresses, any company's address needs can be met: Every machine can be given a unique IP address. Of course, these addresses work well when the machines using them only need to access resources inside their own network. However, when they're trying to access resources outside of the company, reachability issues arise.

For example, both Company A and Company B are using network 10.0.0.0 for their internal networks, as shown in Figure 13.1.

Table 13.1   RFC 1918 private address space.

Class	Addresses
A	10.0.0.0 to 10.255.255.255
B	172.16.0.0 to 172.31.255.255
C	192.168.0.0 to 192.168.255.255

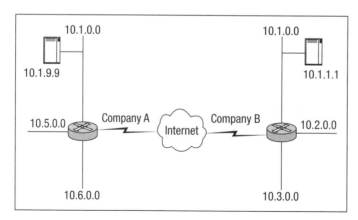

Figure 13.1   Addressing example.

A situation arises where both companies need to exchange information. Suppose a computer on segment 10.1.0.0 from Company A (10.1.9.9) needs to send some information to 10.1.1.1 on segment 10.1.0.0 on Company B's network. The problem in this situation is that 10.1.9.9 assumes that all machines with an IP address of 10.1.0.0 are on the same segment as itself, and therefore it will never be able to reach Company B's 10.1.0.0 segment. This is also true for all the other segments in Company A's network—they will always send information from machines such as 10.1.9.9 to Company A's 10.1.0.0 segment, based on routing metrics.

In most situations, this is not a problem, because most of the time the machines within a network only access each other; only a small percentage of the time do they access resources outside of their own network. In this situation, another solution is needed to accommodate intercompany communication, which RFC 1631 addresses. Any time a packet with a private address in either the source or destination field is destined to a public network, it must first be translated to a public IP address.

Network Address Translation (NAT)

RFC 1631 defines the process of translating private IP addresses to a public space address. This process is called *Network Address Translation*, or *NAT* for short. There are many reasons why you might want to, or need to, design a network with private addresses:

➤ Your ISP has not given you enough public addresses to assign to all your computers.

➤ You are merging two networks together that have an overlapping address space (perhaps the two companies are using the same private address space).

➤ You have changed ISPs, and your new ISP will not support your old public address space.

➤ Because of the growing demands for resources on a critical machine, you need to duplicate those resources on redundant computers and spread the access requests that are sent to the original machine to all these redundant machines.

Advantages of NAT

One of the obvious advantages of NAT is that it you no longer have to worry about your ISP assigning you enough public addresses. With one A class network, sixteen B class networks, and 256 C class networks, you have over 17,000,000 private addresses at your disposal, which is more than enough for your addressing needs. And if you have to change ISPs, you will only have to reconfigure your NAT device instead of having to readdress your entire network. Also, because it is illegal to propagate packets with private addresses into the Internet, using private addresses provides additional security—all traffic leaving or entering your network will have to pass through your NAT device, giving you tight control over traffic patterns.

13

Disadvantages of NAT

There are disadvantages to using NAT, however. By performing NAT, additional delay is introduced into your traffic streams—your NAT device will have to manipulate the addresses in the IP packet and possibly the port numbers in the TCP/UDP headers, as well as calculate a new CRC for the IP packet and, possibly, the TCP segment. Because NAT changes IP addresses, it becomes more difficult to troubleshoot problems—you really don't know whether the address you are examining is the real address of the machine. This, ironically, can create security problems. In some instances, certain applications may stop working when NAT is introduced into the data stream. Some applications use IP addresses instead of domain names, or some applications may embed IP addresses inside the data payload, which NAT does not translate. Sometimes the NAT device can handle this. Cisco's PIX firewall has the ability to change IP addresses embedded in the data of certain applications. In other instances, this can be overcome by static address mappings on the NAT device.

Operation of NAT

NAT can be performed by many types of devices, including file servers, firewalls, bastion hosts, and even routers. The NAT device translates private addresses to legal addresses as traffic traverses from the inside of the network to the outside world. It also translates legal addresses to private addresses as traffic flows from the outside world into the private network. Cisco's IOS 11.2 (and later) supports RFC 1631 NAT functionality.

NAT Terminology

To help in your understanding of how NAT works, Table 13.2 describes some of the more important NAT terms used to describe IP addressing for end stations.

Table 13.3 describes some of the different types of translations that a NAT device may perform.

Table 13.2   NAT terminology for addressing.

NAT Term	Definition
Inside	The networks that will have their addresses translated.
Outside	All networks that are seen as public addresses—usually machines on the Internet.
Inside local IP address	An end-station address located inside a private network with an address from the RFC 1918 address space.
Inside global IP address	An end-station address located inside a private network with a publicly registered IP address.
Outside global IP address	An end-station address located outside the private network with a publicly registered IP address.

Table 13.3   NAT device translation types.

NAT Translation Type	Definition
Simple	One IP address is mapped to another address.
Extended	One IP address and port are mapped to another address and port.
Static	Manual translation between two addresses (and ports).
Dynamic	Dynamic translation between two addresses (and ports).
Port Address Translation (PAT)	All inside devices are translated to one public IP address, where each inside machine is given a different source port number for uniqueness.

Translation of Addresses

Different types of translation can be performed by an address-translation device. Let's take a look at the simplest type of address translation: NAT. With Network Address Translation, the IP address of either the source or destination IP address is changed from one value to another. Figure 13.2 shows a network that requires NAT.

In this example, the network on the left is using a private address space: 10.0.0.0. Device 10.0.0.1 wants to send information to 201.17.39.55, a machine with a public address that is located across the Internet. Circle 1 denotes the IP packet that 10.0.0.1 generates. In Figure 13.3, the router on the left receives 10.0.0.1's packet, indicated by circle 2.

Typically, the NAT router will perform a dynamic address translation. It will take the inside local IP address, 10.0.0.1, and map it to a public address space (called an *inside global IP address*) that it has in a local pool. In this situation, each machine inside the 10.0.0.0 network will be mapped to a unique address in the pool. If a small number of machines are communicating to machines out on the Internet, the

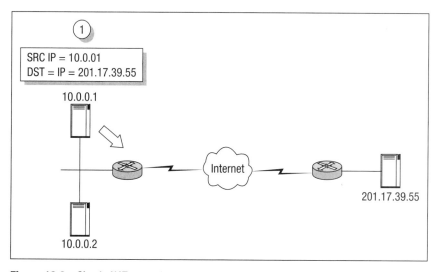

13

Figure 13.2   Simple NAT example.

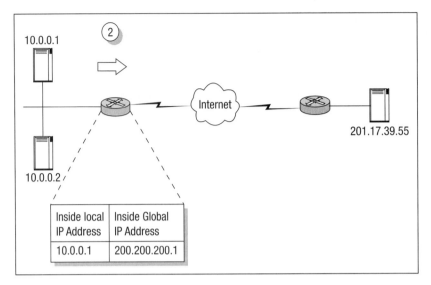

Figure 13.3 The NAT router receives the IP packet from 10.0.0.1.

size of the pool can be small. If, however, a large number of machines are sending traffic out to the Internet, the pool must be large. In this type of translation, for every private address that you have that passes through the NAT router, you will need a separate unique public address. In the example, the NAT router is mapping the 10.0.0.1 address to 200.200.200.1 and putting this entry into its pool.

The NAT router updates the IP packet and then forwards the packet out to the Internet, as shown by circle 3 in Figure 13.4.

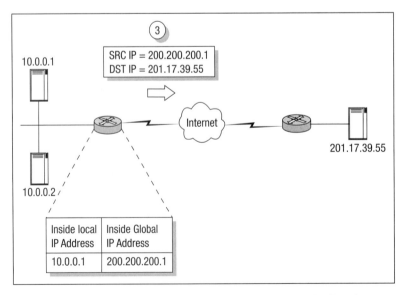

Figure 13.4 The NAT router translates the address and forwards the IP packet.

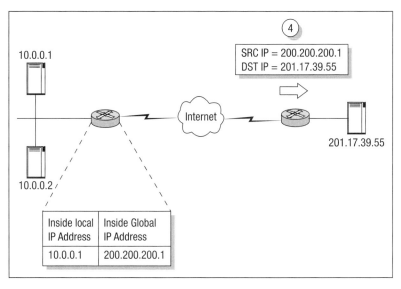

Figure 13.5   The destination receives the translated packet.

In circle 4 (shown in Figure 13.5), 201.17.39.55 (the destination) receives the IP packet.

From the destination's perspective, it looks like the actual source address is 200.200.200.1, when in fact this is not true. As mentioned earlier, one disadvantage of NAT is that the source is anonymous—the destination has no idea who the real source is. When 201.17.39.55 responds back, it sends its packet to 200.200.200.1, which it assumes is the real destination of the information. This can be seen in circle 5 of Figure 13.6.

This traffic is forwarded out to the Internet and makes its way back to the NAT router on the left side of Figure 13.7.

When the NAT router receives the packet, the router consults its translation table and looks for the inside global IP address of 200.200.200.1. If it does not find a match, it performs no translation and forwards the packet in a normal fashion. In this case, however, it finds 200.200.200.1 and the corresponding local IP address of 10.0.0.1. It reverses the address translation and changes 200.200.200.1 back to 10.0.0.1, as shown in circle 6 of Figure 13.7. This is then forwarded to 10.0.0.1.

 If 10.0.0.2 had traffic to send out, another entry would have to either exist (if you are using static translations) or be created by the NAT router (if you are using dynamic translations). This table can be seen in Figure 13.8.

As mentioned earlier, each device needs a unique inside global address (inside the NAT device) if it wishes to access outside networks.

13

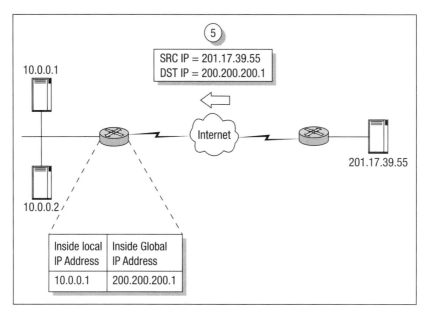

Figure 13.6 201.17.39.55 responds.

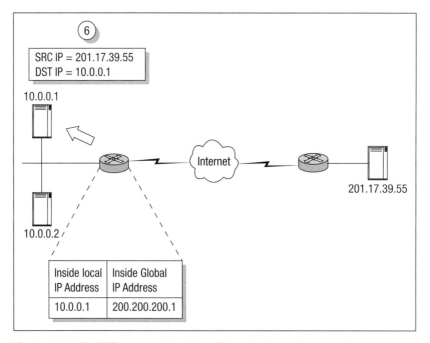

Figure 13.7 The NAT router receives the traffic and performs its translation.

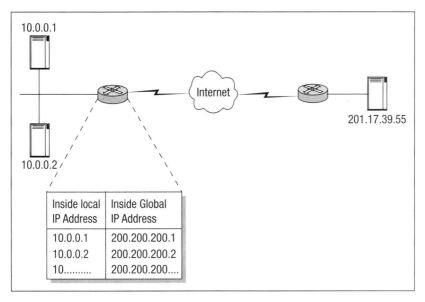

Figure 13.8   The NAT router is performing multiple translations for inside devices.

Overlapping Address Space

You might also run into situations where two networks merge and are using the same private address space. In this case, you can use NAT as a solution to provide uniqueness to each set of addresses. Not only will NAT perform its traditional address translation of IP addresses, it will also intercept DNS replies and change the IP address that the DNS server is responding with. Take the example of two networks represented by the same private address space, 10.0.0.0. With this ability, you could represent one network with 172.16.0.0 and the other with 172.17.0.0. When a device from one network tries to access a device in the other network, and the DNS server from the second network responds back with a 10.0.0.0 address, the translation router will intercept the DNS reply and change the address to a 172.17.0.0 address and then use this address for subsequent communication between the two devices across their network boundaries. One restriction with address overloading is that the NAT router must see all DNS queries for traffic that must cross between the two networks.

Address Overloading or Port Address Translation (PAT)

For large networks, the use of NAT can pose a problem, especially when accessing the Internet—you probably do not have enough public addresses to handle all your internal machines that need to access the Internet. To solve this problem, your Cisco NAT router can use a process called *address overloading*, sometimes referred to as *Port*

13

Address Translation, or *PAT* for short. PAT allows all the inside local IP addresses to share a single inside global IP address. With this ability, the translation router can handle thousands of machines with a single global IP address.

Of course, the translation router must have some means of uniquely identifying each of the inside machines when traffic returns from the outside to be forwarded back into the network. To accomplish this, the translation device assigns a unique source port number for each outgoing connection from each inside device. This allows the translation device to uniquely identify each connection from each inside machine, even though their IP address will be the same when the translation is performed.

Note: *NAT and PAT are different in the types of translation they perform. However, in the industry, the term NAT is commonly used to refer to both Network and Port Address Translation.*

To better understand how this process works, take a look at the example shown in Figure 13.9.

The address-translation router in Figure 13.9 has three entries in its address table: two for 10.0.0.1 and one for 10.0.0.2. Note that in case of all three entries, they are assigned an inside global IP address of 200.200.200.1. To uniquely identify each connection, the inside source port numbers are reassigned by the PAT router to a unique number: each connection is different, with port values of 1024, 1025, and 1026. Note the first connection for 10.0.0.1 and the connection for 10.0.0.2: their inside local port numbers are both 1024. However, when the PAT router performs

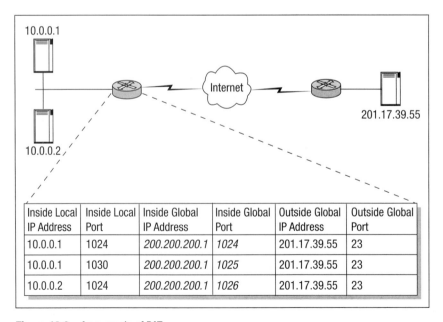

Inside Local IP Address	Inside Local Port	Inside Global IP Address	Inside Global Port	Outside Global IP Address	Outside Global Port
10.0.0.1	1024	200.200.200.1	1024	201.17.39.55	23
10.0.0.1	1030	200.200.200.1	1025	201.17.39.55	23
10.0.0.2	1024	200.200.200.1	1026	201.17.39.55	23

Figure 13.9   An example of PAT.

its translation, they are assigned 1024 and 1026 respectively, ensuring that each connection has a unique inside global port number. Therefore, when traffic is returned from the Internet, the PAT router can redirect it to the correct inside machine.

Note that NAT and PAT are not mutually exclusive. PAT is used for handling traffic that originates on the inside of your network and is destined to the Internet. If traffic originates on the Internet and is trying to access services on the inside of your network, PAT is not very flexible. Each of your services will need unique global IP addresses. For the outside world to access these internal machines, these machines will have to be represented with unique inside global IP addresses—that is, addresses from the public address space. To efficiently handle this, NAT is more appropriate. You would statically assign each inside local IP address (a private address) to its own inside global IP address (a public address). Your DNS server(s), email server(s), Web server(s), FTP server(s), and any other public access servers would have a static mapping, and they would use private, not public addresses, in their configurations. With an address-translation device performing NAT and PAT, you can easily see why individuals use a single term, NAT, to describe address translation.

Traffic Distribution for Load Balancing

Address-translation devices can also help out with an overloaded server that computers on the Internet are accessing inside your network. Most people would assume that when your server becomes overloaded, you would have to upgrade it to handle the new load that Internet users are placing on it. Address translation provides an alternate and more flexible solution.

Using traffic distribution, users on the Internet send their traffic to a single inside global IP address. This single inside global IP address is represented by a group of inside machines, each with a unique inside local IP address. Sometimes this inside global IP address is referred to as a *virtual IP address*—no computer actually has this configured on any of its NICs. Figure 13.10 shows an example of a translation router's address table.

In this example, the Web servers 10.0.0.1 and 10.0.0.2 are represented by the global IP address of 200.200.200.5. When machines on the Internet want to access the Web service offered by this company, they send their traffic to 200.200.200.5. When the translation router receives this traffic, it distributes the load between the two different internal services. It does this on a connection-by-connection basis: Each connection is represented by a separate entry in the address-translation table. To maintain a connection-oriented process, all traffic from one connection will be directed to a single inside server.

Advantages of Traffic Distribution

Given this ability, you do not have to upgrade a server to handle additional loads placed on it. Instead, you can add additional servers and distribute the incoming

13

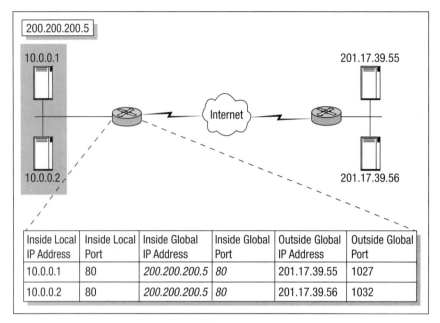

Figure 13.10 An example of traffic distribution.

traffic load between these servers. This advantage also provides redundancy—if a single server fails, you already have backup devices in place.

Disadvantages of Traffic Distribution

One concern, however, is that some translation devices, such as Cisco's routers, do not have the ability to detect whether a server is active. If a server is down, the router will *still* forward traffic to it. Another limitation of this feature on Cisco routers is that they cannot detect the load of a server and distribute the traffic load accordingly. If these are concerns, you will probably want to use a different device to perform traffic distribution. Cisco has a product, called LocalDirector, that can perform this critical function.

Restrictions of NAT

As mentioned earlier, NAT will not work with all types of IP communication. Some applications embed IP addresses in their data, which may cause problems when this information passes through the translation device, which, by default, is not looking for these types of situations. Many vendors know of such applications and therefore look for specific places in the data payload for IP addresses and then do the appropriate translation; but not all of these applications may be known to the vendor of the NAT device. Likewise, if the end station adds encryption to its data, where IP addresses are embedded inside, it becomes impossible for the NAT device to perform the translation for these encrypted addresses.

ICMP traffic can also be problematic for NAT, because it may require changes to two different addresses. ICMP messages (the payload) contain part of the IP packet header itself, including the addresses. Because of the duplication of addresses, the NAT device will have to perform its translation twice—for the real IP header and for the IP header embedded in the ICMP message payload. Sometimes this dual modification is not necessary because the end station receiving the message may or may not use the IP address in the ICMP message. SNMP has an even worse issue with these types of embedded IP addresses, because SNMP is notorious for embedding IP addresses in its data. This usually makes it impractical to carry SNMP traffic through NAT devices, because each vendor implements this process for SNMP differently.

Because of these types of problems, you need to be aware of the limitations of NAT and the traffic types that it can handle. The following is a list of the types of traffic *not* supported for address translation by Cisco's IOS:

➤ TCP traffic with embedded addresses in the payload

➤ UDP traffic with embedded addresses in the payload

➤ SNMP traffic

➤ Multicast traffic

➤ Routing table updates

➤ Zone transfers for DNS

➤ BOOTP and DHCP

➤ NetShow application traffic

➤ Talk and ntalk application traffic

Typical types of traffic supported are DNS, NTP, TFTP, FTP, telnet, HTTP, and other common UDP and TCP applications.

13

Configuration of Address Translation for IOS Routers

The configuration of address translation—whether it be NAT, PAT, or traffic distribution—is a simple, straightforward process. Some of the configuration is done in the interface Configuration mode, and some is done in the global Configuration mode.

Configuration of NAT

The standard configuration of NAT can be done either statically or dynamically. The configurations for both are very similar, using the same basic commands. The hardest part of the configuration is understanding the difference between *inside* and *outside*. If you are having difficulties, refer back to Table 13.2.

Static NAT

For static NAT, two sets of commands are required. First, you must manually create the static mappings of inside local IP addresses to inside global IP addresses. This is done with the **ip nat inside | outside source static** commands. The syntax of these commands are as follows:

```
Router(config)# ip nat inside source static inside_local_IP_address
                        inside_global_IP_address
Router(config)# ip nat outside source static outside_global_IP_address
                        outside_local_IP_address
```

The **inside** and **outside** parameters specify the direction of the translation. When you're using the **inside** parameter, source local IP addresses on the inside are translated to global addresses when sent to the outside. This is used for traffic originating on the inside of your network. When you're using the **outside** parameter, destination global IP addresses coming from the outside are changed to local IP addresses when forwarded to the inside network. This is used for traffic originating on the outside of your network that is trying to reach resources, such as Web, DNS, and email servers, on the inside of your network.

Next, you must specify which interface(s) is on the inside of the network and which interface(s) is on the outside of the network—the interface connected to the Internet. This is done with the **ip nat inside** and **ip nat outside** interface Configuration mode commands, as shown with the following code:

```
Router(config)# interface type [module_number/]port_number
Router(config-if)# ip nat inside|outside
```

The following is an example of static NAT, translating addresses for two machines—10.0.0.1 and 10.0.0.2—to a public address space when they access the outside world (you can view a picture of this network by referring back to Figure 13.8):

```
Router(config)# ip nat inside source static 10.0.0.1 200.200.200.1
Router(config)# ip nat inside source static 10.0.0.2 200.200.200.2
Router(config)#
Router(config)# interface ethernet 0
Router(config-if)# ip address 10.0.0.254 255.255.255.0
Router(config-if)# ip nat inside
Router(config-if)# exit
Router(config)#
Router(config)# interface serial 0
Router(config-if)# ip address 192.168.1.1 255.255.255.0
Router(config-if)# ip nat outside
```

Note that IP packets that do not match the addresses of 10.0.0.1 and 10.0.0.2 will be passed through the router without being translated. If you want to prevent other packets from leaving, you will need to configure an **access-list** and apply it to the router. Referring to the preceding example, if you only wanted 10.0.0.1 and 10.0.0.2 to leave your network, you would use the following configuration:

```
Router(config)# access-list 1 permit 10.0.0.1 0.0.0.0
Router(config)# access-list 1 permit 10.0.0.2 0.0.0.0
Router(config)# interface serial 0
Router(config-if)# ip access-group 1 out
Router(config-if)# exit
```

Dynamic NAT

For dynamic NAT, three sets of commands are required. First, you need to specify the list of inside local IP addresses that will be translated. This is done with the **ip nat inside source list** command. The syntax of this command is as follows:

```
Router(config)# ip nat inside source
                    list standard_IP_access_list_number
                    pool NAT_pool_name
```

Note that the command uses a standard IP **access-list**. The **access-list** contains all of the source addresses that will be translated.

Next, you must create a pool of inside global IP addresses that the router can use to map the local addresses to as the IP packets leave your network. This is accomplished with the **ip nat pool** global Configuration mode command:

```
Router(config)# ip nat pool NAT_pool_name
                    beginning_inside_global_IP_address
                    ending_inside_global_IP_address
                    netmask subnet_mask_of_addresses
```

You need to give the pool a name that matches that used by the **ip nat inside source** command. You must also list the beginning and ending IP addresses in the pool and the associated subnet mask for this address space.

Last, you must specify which interface(s) is on the inside of the network and which interface(s) is on the outside of the network—the interface connected to the Internet. This is done with the **ip nat inside** and **ip nat outside** interface Configuration mode commands, as was done with the static configuration:

```
Router(config)# interface type [module_number/]port_number
Router(config-if)# ip nat inside|outside
```

13

The following is an example of dynamic NAT, translating addresses for two machines—10.0.0.1 and 10.0.0.2—to a public address space when they access the outside world (you can view a picture of this network by referring back to Figure 13.8). This is the same example as before, except that dynamic NAT is used instead:

```
Router(config)# ip nat inside source list 1 pool nat-pool
Router(config)#
Router(config)# access-list 1 permit 10.0.0.1
Router(config)# access-list 1 permit 10.0.0.2
Router(config)#
Router(config)# ip nat pool nat-pool 200.200.200.1 200.200.200.2
                        netmask 255.255.255.0
Router(config)#
Router(config)# interface ethernet 0
Router(config-if)# ip address 10.0.0.254 255.255.255.0
Router(config-if)# ip nat inside
Router(config-if)# exit
Router(config)#
Router(config)# interface serial 0
Router(config-if)# ip address 192.168.1.1 255.255.255.0
Router(config-if)# ip nat outside
```

Note that IP packets that do not match the addresses of 10.0.0.1 and 10.0.0.2 will be passed through the router without being translated. If you want to prevent other packets from leaving, you will need to configure an **access-list** and apply it to the router.

Configuration of PAT

The configuration of PAT, or *address overloading*, is similar to the configuration of dynamic NAT. For PAT, three sets of commands are required. First, you need to specify the list of inside local IP addresses that will be translated. This is done with the **ip nat inside source list** command, the same command used for NAT. The syntax of this command is as follows:

```
Router(config)# ip nat inside source
                    list standard_IP_access_list_number
                    pool NAT_pool_name overload
```

There is one difference in this configuration, however; you need to specify the **overload** parameter with this command.

Next, you must create a pool of inside global IP addresses that the router can use to map the local addresses to. This is accomplished with the **ip nat pool** global Configuration mode command:

```
Router(config)# ip nat pool NAT_pool_name
                    beginning_inside_global_IP_address
                    ending_inside_global_IP_address
                    netmask subnet_mask_of_addresses
```

Again, this is the same command as is used with dynamic NAT. You can specify more than one IP address to be used for the overloading—or you can specify the same public address for both the beginning and ending number.

And last, you must specify which interface(s) is on the inside of the network and which interface(s) is on the outside of the network—the interface connected to the Internet. This is done with the **ip nat inside** and **ip nat outside** interface Configuration mode commands:

```
Router(config)# interface type [module_number/]port_number
Router(config-if)# ip nat inside|outside
```

The following is an example of dynamic PAT, translating addresses for two machines —10.0.0.1 and 10.0.0.2—to a public address space when they access the outside world (you can view a picture of this network by referring back to Figure 13.9):

```
Router(config)# ip nat inside source list 1 pool nat-pool overload
Router(config)#
Router(config)# access-list 1 permit 10.0.0.1
Router(config)# access-list 1 permit 10.0.0.2
Router(config)#
Router(config)# ip nat pool nat-pool 200.200.200.1 200.200.200.1
                    netmask 255.255.255.0
Router(config)#
Router(config)# interface ethernet 0
Router(config-if)# ip address 10.0.0.254 255.255.255.0
Router(config-if)# ip nat inside
Router(config-if)# exit
Router(config)#
Router(config)# interface serial 0
Router(config-if)# ip address 192.168.1.1 255.255.255.0
Router(config-if)# ip nat outside
```

13

Note that IP packets that do not match the addresses of 10.0.0.1 and 10.0.0.2 will be passed through the router without being translated. If you want to prevent other packets from leaving, you will need to configure an **access-list** and apply it to the router.

Configuration of Traffic Distribution

The configuration of traffic distribution, or *load distribution*, is similar to the configuration of dynamic NAT and PAT. For traffic distribution, three sets of commands are required. First, you need to specify the list of inside local IP addresses that will handle the traffic that is received from the outside world and is destined to one global IP address inside your network. This is done with the **ip nat inside pool** command, the same command used for PAT. The syntax of this command is as follows:

```
Router(config)# ip nat pool pool_name
                    beginning_inside_local_IP_address
                    ending_inside_local_IP_address
                    prefix-length subnet_mask_length_in_bits
                    type rotary
```

You assign an arbitrary name to the pool, which will reference the single global IP address that Internet machines are sending their traffic to. Next, you list the range of IP addresses of the inside machines that will handle this traffic, along with the number of bits in their subnet mask. Last, the **type rotary** parameter will have the router round-robin the traffic connections within the beginning and ending inside local IP addresses that you just listed.

You then need to specify the single global IP address that Internet machines are trying to reach. This is done with the **ip nat inside destination list** command:

```
Router(config)# ip nat inside destination
                    list standard_IP_access_list_number
                    pool pool_name
```

Here, *pool_name* must match the name listed in the **ip nat pool** command. The standard IP **access-list** needs to contain the global IP address.

And last, you must specify which interface(s) is on the inside of the network and which interface(s) is on the outside of the network—the interface connected to the Internet. This is done with the **ip nat inside** and **ip nat outside** interface Configuration mode commands:

```
Router(config)# interface type [module_number/]port_number
Router(config-if)# ip nat inside|outside
```

The following is an example of traffic distribution. You can view a picture of this network by referring back to Figure 13.10. In this example, the outside world is trying to access a Web server with a public address of 200.200.200.5. With traffic distribution, the two inside machines—10.0.0.1 and 10.0.0.2—will handle this load. Here's the code:

```
Router(config)# ip nat pool inside-hosts 10.0.0.1 10.0.0.2
                         prefix-length 24 type rotary
Router(config)#
Router(config)# ip nat inside destination list 1 pool inside-hosts
Router(config)#
Router(config)# access-list 1 permit 200.200.200.5
Router(config)#
Router(config)# interface ethernet 0
Router(config-if)# ip address 10.0.0.254 255.255.255.0
Router(config-if)# ip nat inside
Router(config-if)# exit
Router(config)#
Router(config)# interface serial 0
Router(config-if)# ip address 192.168.1.1 255.255.255.0
Router(config-if)# ip nat outside
```

Verifying Address Translation

Once you have configured address translation, you will want to verify that it is working properly. The **show ip nat translations** command is used to list the address translations that the router has either statically configured or dynamically created. The following is a display of a router performing NAT:

```
Router# show ip nat translations
Pro  Inside global    Inside local   Outside local  Outside global
-    200.200.200.1    10.0.0.1         -              -
-    200.200.200.2    10.0.0.2         -              -
```

In the preceding output, two addresses are being translated: 10.0.0.1 and 10.0.0.2.

If the router is performing PAT, the display will look similar to the following:

```
Router# show ip nat translations
Pro Inside global        Inside local   Outside local   Outside global
tcp 200.200.200.1:1074   10.0.0.1:1074  201.17.39.55:23  201.17.39.55:23
tcp 200.200.200.1:1067   10.0.0.2:1067  201.17.39.55:23  201.17.39.55:23
```

You can also examine the router's address-translation statistics with the **show ip nat statistics** command. For more detailed troubleshooting, you can use the **debug ip nat** command. This command will display the actual translation that the router is performing on packets that are being translated. You should *only* use this command to perform troubleshooting, because the router will display the header of every packet that is translated, which is very CPU-intensive.

13

If you need to remove an entry from the translation table, you can use one of the following **clear** commands:

```
Router# clear ip nat translation *
Router# clear ip nat translation inside
                    global_IP_address local_IP_address
Router# clear ip nat translation outside
                    global_IP_address local_IP_address
Router# clear ip nat translation protocol inside
                    global_IP_address global_port
                    local_IP_address local_port
```

The first **clear** command clears all the entries in the table. The second one clears inside entries, and the third one clears outside entries. The last **clear** command is used to clear PAT entries from the address-translation table.

Configuration of PAT for 700 Series Routers

With the 700 series of routers, only PAT is supported for address translation. This makes sense when you examine the role of the 700 series router—it is a SOHO (Small Office/Home Office) router with one PC, or possibly a handful of PCs, sitting behind it. In this scenario, a single public address is sufficient to represent the machines in the office when they access the Internet. If a company has a resource that the Internet may want to access, such as a Web server, the 700 series supports a feature called *porthandler*. With porthandler, you can redirect traffic sent to a particular port of the public IP address to a particular machine on the LAN segment connected to the 700 series router.

The configuration of PAT is done in the user profile for the BRI interface. Use the following command to set this up:

```
> set system 760
760> set user WAN_profile
760:WAN_profile> set ip pat on
```

As you can see, this is even simpler than configuring PAT on an IOS router.

To configure the porthandler feature, use the following user profile command:

```
> set system 760
760> set user WAN_profile
760:WAN_profile> set ip pat porthandler default|telnet|ftp|
                    smtp|wins|http|port_number ip_address|off
```

If you specify **default**, all traffic sent to the specified IP address is redirected to the IP address listed at the end of the command. You can specify one of the key words, such as **telnet**, or a TCP or UDP port number, to have the specified inbound Internet traffic forwarded to a specific file server, which you list at the end of the command. If you use the **off** parameter, the entry is removed from the list. You can have up to a maximum of 15 entries for your porthandler feature for a WAN user profile.

Once you have configured PAT, and possibly porthandler, you will want to verify your configuration with the **show ip pat** command:

```
700> show ip pat
Dropped - icmp 0, udp 0, tcp 0, map 0, frag 0
Timeout - udp 5 minutes, tcp 30 minutes


Port   Handler       Service
----   -------       -------
21     192.168.1.1   FTP
23     Router        TELNET
67     Router        DHCP Server
68     Router        DHCP Client
69     Router        TFTP
80     Router        HTTP
161    Router        SNMP
162    Router        SNMP-TRAP
520    Router        RIP
```

In the preceding example, the first entry is a porthandler redirecting FTP traffic to 192.168.1.1, a file server sitting behind the 700 series router. The other entries are the default configuration for porthandler: This type of traffic will be handled by the router itself.

13

Chapter Summary

When faced with using private IP addresses and requiring access to the Internet, you will need to perform at least PAT, and possibly NAT, to help with your addressing needs. Cisco supports these features, as well as many more. For both the small and home office, Cisco offers the 700 series router to assist you with your addressing problems. For medium-sized networks, Cisco offers the IOS router software, and for enterprise-sized networks, Cisco offers the PIX firewall.

Because of the shortage of addresses, companies are forced to use IP addresses from the private address space. These include 10.0.0.0 to 10.255.255.255, 172.16.0.0 to 172.31.255.255, and 192.168.0.0 to 192.168.255.255. However, the problem of using private IP addresses is that packets containing them in either the source or destination field of the IP address cannot be propagated out onto the Internet. To solve this problem, some type of address translation is required.

RFC 1631 defines how address translation is to be performed. Address translation contains different variations: NAT, PAT, and traffic distribution. With NAT, addresses are translated on a one-to-one basis. Each inside IP address is translated to a unique outside IP address. For Internet connectivity, the outside IP address must be from the public address space. NAT is typically used for connections that originate from the Internet and that access resources inside your internal network.

PAT, or *address overloading*, allows devices from your network to access the Internet, as does NAT. However with PAT, all inside machines will share the same inside global IP address. For Internet connectivity, this IP address must be from the public address space. PAT allows you to conserve your public address space while still allowing access to the Internet.

If you are running into performance problems when Internet machines access a particular resource in your network, you can employ traffic distribution on your address-translation device. With traffic distribution, traffic destined to one specific IP address on the inside of your network can be redirected to another IP address. Using this scheme, you can spread the load of multiple connections across a multitude of machines while still maintaining the illusion to the Internet users that only one machine is processing their requests.

Review Questions

1. Which of the following is not a private address?

   a. 10.255.255.1

   b. 172.30.37.5

   c. 192.168.255.254

   d. 172.32.79.84

2. What is a reason to employ NAT? [Choose the two best answers]

   a. Your ISP has not assigned you enough private addresses to give to all your computers.

   b. You are merging two networks that have unique address spaces.

   c. You have changed ISPs, where your new ISP will not support your old public address space.

   d. Because of the growing demands for resources on a critical machine, you need to duplicate those resources on redundant computers and spread the access requests that are sent to the original machine to all these redundant machines.

3. What is an advantage of using NAT? [Choose the two best answers]

    a. It gives you an abundant choice of addresses to use.

    b. It gives you tighter control over your traffic.

    c. It introduces no latency into the traffic stream.

    d. It works with all types of application traffic.

4. What is a disadvantage of NAT? [Choose the two best answers]

    a. It requires the recalculation of the CRC for both the TCP segment and IP packet.

    b. It introduces delay into the traffic stream.

    c. It provides end-to-end traceability of a connection.

    d. It gives you less control over your traffic going through the translation device.

5. A private IP address would be an example of what type of address?

    a. Inside local

    b. Inside global

    c. Outside local

    d. Outside global

6. What allows all the inside local IP addresses to share a single global IP address? [Choose the two best answers]

    a. NAT

    b. Address overloading

    c. Traffic distribution

    d. Porthandler

    e. PAT

7. An IOS router supports which of the following address-translation features? [Choose the three best answers]

    a. PAT

    b. Porthandler

    c. NAT

    d. Traffic distribution

13

8. What IOS address-translation feature would you use if you had an overloaded Web server?

   a. NAT

   b. PAT

   c. Porthandler

   d. Traffic distribution

9. NAT is supported by which of the following traffic types? [Choose the two best answers]

   a. SNMP

   b. ICMP

   c. Routing updates

   d. HTTP

10. Which commands are used to configure static NAT? [Choose all correct answers]

    a. **ip nat inside source static**

    b. **ip nat outside source static**

    c. **ip nat inside**

    d. **ip nat outside**

11. Which commands enable NAT or PAT on an interface of an IOS router?

    a. **ip nat**

    b. **ip nat outside**

    c. **ip nat translation**

    d. **ip nat inside**

12. You are required to set up dynamic NAT. You have already defined the inside local IP addresses with standard **access-list 5**. The name of the address pool for the inside global IP addresses is "nat-pool". Type in the dynamic NAT command to associate the inside local IP addresses to the global IP addresses:

    _____

13. Which parameter is added to the dynamic NAT address command **ip nat inside source list** *standard_IP_access_list* **pool** *pool_name* to perform PAT?

    a. **pat**

    b. **overload**

    c. **rotary**

    d. **prefix**

14. You are required to set up PAT on an IOS router. You have been given a single global inside IP address: 200.200.200.1/24. You have already configured the following:

```
ip nat inside source list 1 pool nat-pool overload
access-list 1 permit 10.0.0.0 0.255.255.255
interface ethernet 0
 ip nat inside
interface serial 0
 ip nat outside
```

Type in the command to create your address pool:

_____

15. Which parameter is added to the **ip nat pool** command in order to perform traffic distribution?

    a. **type pat**

    b. **type rotary**

    c. **address–overload**

    d. **rotary**

16. What IOS router command would you use to verify that your router is performing address translation?

    a. **show nat**

    b. **show ip nat**

    c. **show ip nat translations**

    d. **show nat translations**

17. The 700 series router supports which address-translation features? [Choose the two best answers]

    a. NAT

    b. PAT

    c. Traffic distribution

    d. Porthandler

18. Which feature redirects traffic sent to a particular port to a particular machine?

    a. PAT

    b. Address overloading

    c. Traffic distribution

    d. NAT

    e. Porthandler

13

19. Enter the profile command that enables PAT for the ISDN interface on a 700 series router:

_____

20. Type in the profile command to redirect WWW traffic (port 80) to 192.168.1.2 using the porthandler feature on a Cisco 700 series router:

_____

Real-World Projects

Creative Technologies, a company located in Orlando, FL, has decided to connect its network to the Internet. The current network layout can be seen in Figure 13.11.

Creative Technologies currently has two 7500 series routers for its internal Ethernet connections, is using the private address space of network 10.0.0.0, and is using EIGRP as its routing protocol.

Creative Technologies' ISP has assigned it an IP address of 200.200.200.2/32 for its Internet router connection. It has been given a C class subnet for its internal use: 200.200.201.0/29. Creative Technologies has hired Noah Trimpey, who worked with Sarah Davis at WFY but left and started his own network consulting company, to handle the configuration.

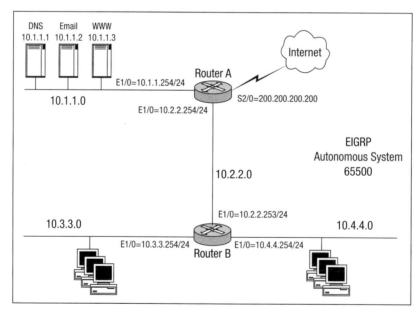

Figure 13.11   Creative Technologies' network layout.

One of his tasks is to handle any IP addressing issues with this new connection. Three servers—DNS, email, and WWW—need to be available to users on the Internet. He has decided to use three addresses (from a pool of six) and use static NAT to solve this problem. He has decided to use PAT and a fourth IP address to handle Creative Technologies' users' access to the Internet. Creative Technologies has placed one additional restriction—no one from 10.4.4.0 should be able to access the Internet, but anyone from any other internal segment should.

Project 13.1

Noah Trimpey will need to complete the following tasks to configure Creative Technologies' Internet access on RouterA. Once he examines Router A's current configuration, he will need to set up frame relay access to Creative Technology's ISP. He will configure his routing information, including a default route to the Internet, and redistribute it into EIGRP. He will set up security to prevent unnecessary/unwanted traffic from the Internet from entering their network. He will also ensure that no packets with private addresses leave Creative Technologies' network for the Internet, and also ensure that 10.4.4.0 cannot access the Internet. After he has completed these tasks, he will be ready to configure NAT on Router A. He will configure static NAT for the three file servers and PAT for the user's inside Creative Technologies. He will then test and verify the configuration.

To configure frame relay access to connect to the ISP on RouterA:

1. Examine the current routing configuration:

```
RouterA# show run
Building Configuration ...

hostname RouterA

router eigrp 65500
 network 10.0.0.0

interface ethernet 1/0
 ip address 10.1.1.254 255.255.255.0
 no shutdown

interface ethernet 1/1
 ip address 10.2.2.254 255.255.255.0
 no shutdown

interface serial 2/0
 no ip address
 shutdown

<output omitted>
```

13

2. Set up frame relay access to the ISP:

```
RouterA# config t
RouterA(config)#
RouterA(config)# interface serial 2/0
RouterA(config-if)# encapsulation frame-relay ietf
RouterA(config-if)# ip address 200.200.200.2 255.255.255.252
RouterA(config-if)# frame-relay lmi-type cisco
RouterA(config-if)# frame-relay map ip 200.200.200.1 100
RouterA(config-if)# no shutdown
RouterA(config-if)# end
RouterA#
RouterA# copy run start
RouterA#
RouterA# show frame-relay lmi
LMI Statistics for interface Serial2/0 (Frame Relay DTE) LMI TYPE=CISCO
  Invalid Unnumbered info 0          Invalid Prot Disc 0
  Invalid dummy Call Ref 0           Invalid Msg Type 0
  Invalid Status Message 0           Invalid Lock Shift 0
  Invalid Information ID 0           Invalid Report IE Len 0
  Invalid Report Request 0           Invalid Keep IE Len 0
  Num Status Enq. Sent 3             Num Status msgs Rcvd 2
  Num Update Status Rcvd 0           Num Status Timeouts 1
RouterA#
RouterA# show frame-relay pvc 100
PVC Statistics for interface Serial2/0 (Frame Relay DTE)
DLCI = 100, DLCI USAGE = LOCAL,
                        PVC STATUS = ACTIVE, INTERFACE=Serial2/0
      input pkts 3           output pkts 5          in bytes 304
      out bytes 358          dropped pkts 0         in FECN pkts 0
      in BECN pkts 0         out FECN pkts 0        out BECN pkts 0
      in DE pkts 0           out DE pkts 0
      out bcast pkts 0       out bcast bytes 0
      pvc create time 00:01:01, last time pvc status changed 00:01:01
RouterA#
RouterA# ping 200.200.200.1
Type escape sequence to abort.
Sending 5, 100-byte ICMP Echos to 200.200.200.1, timeout is 2 seconds:
!!!!!
Success rate is 100 percent, round-trip min/avg/max = 1/2/4 ms
RouterA#
```

3. Configure the default route and redistribute it into EIGRP for RouterB:

```
RouterA# config t
RouterA(config)#
RouterA(config)# ip route 0.0.0.0 0.0.0.0 200.200.200.1
```

```
RouterA(config)#
RouterA(config)# router eigrp 65500
RouterA(config-router)# redistribute static
RouterA(config-router)# default-metric 1544 2000 1 255 1500
RouterA(config-router)# end
RouterA#
RouterA# copy run start
RouterA#
```

4. Set up an **access-list** to prevent any Internet traffic from entering the network, with the exception of traffic destined for the three servers. Also, ensure that connections that start on the inside are allowed back into the network and that DNS replies can be returned to users. Be sure to deny any traffic that has a source address from the public address space that originates from outside of the network:

```
RouterA# config t
RouterA(config)# access-list 100 deny ip 200.200.201.0 0.0.0.7 any
RouterA(config)# access-list 100 permit tcp any any established
RouterA(config)# access-list 100 permit udp any eq 53 any
RouterA(config)# access-list 100 permit udp any
                          200.200.201.1 0.0.0.0 eq 53
RouterA(config)# access-list 100 permit tcp any
                          200.200.201.2 0.0.0.0 eq 25
RouterA(config)# access-list 100 permit tcp any
                          200.200.201.3 0.0.0.0 eq 80
RouterA(config)#
RouterA(config)# interface serial 2/0
RouterA(config-if)# ip access-group 101 in
RouterA(config-if)# end
RouterA#
RouterA# copy run start
RouterA#
```

5. Deny any private addresses from leaving the network—only those that have been translated via address translation should be allowed:

```
RouterA# config t
RouterA(config)# access-list 101 permit ip 200.200.201.0 0.0.0.7 any
RouterA(config)#
RouterA(config)# interface serial 2/0
RouterA(config-if)# ip access-group 101 out
RouterA(config-if)# end
RouterA#
RouterA# copy run start
RouterA#
```

To configure RouterA for address translation:

1. Configure static NAT for the three file servers.

   a. Set up the static translations for the DNS, email, and WWW servers:

   ```
   RouterA# config t
   RouterA(config)#
   RouterA(config)# ip nat inside source static 10.1.1.1 200.200.201.1
   RouterA(config)# ip nat inside source static 10.1.1.2 200.200.201.2
   RouterA(config)# ip nat inside source static 10.1.1.3 200.200.201.3
   RouterA(config)#
   ```

   b. Set up the inside and outside interfaces for NAT for the three file servers:

   ```
   RouterA(config)# interface ethernet 1/0
   RouterA(config-if)# description  Inside file servers
   RouterA(config-if)# ip nat inside
   RouterA(config-if)# exit
   RouterA(config)#
   RouterA(config)# interface serial 1/0
   RouterA(config-if)# description  Internet connection
   RouterA(config-if)# ip nat outside
   RouterA(config-if)# end
   RouterA#
   RouterA# copy run start
   RouterA#
   ```

2. Configure PAT for the users' Internet access.

   a. Set up address overload and the addresses that will be translated—use 200.200.201.4 as the inside global IP address. Remember to not include the 10.4.4.0 subnet:

   ```
   RouterA# config t
   RouterA(config)#
   RouterA(config)# ip nat inside source list 1 pool nat-pool overload
   RouterA(config)#
   RouterA(config)# access-list 1 permit 10.2.2.0 0.0.0.255
   RouterA(config)# access-list 1 permit 10.3.3.0 0.0.0.255
   RouterA(config)#
   RouterA(config)# ip nat pool nat-pool 200.200.201.4 200.200.201.4
                            netmask 255.255.255.248
   RouterA(config)#
   ```

b. Set up the inside NAT interface for the users:

```
RouterA(config)#
RouterA(config)# interface ethernet 1/1
RouterA(config-if)# description User connections
RouterA(config-if)# ip nat inside
RouterA(config-if)# end
RouterA#
RouterA# copy run start
RouterA#
```

3. Test the address translation configuration.

a. Check your static NAT translations:

```
Router# show ip nat translations
Pro Inside            Inside        Outside      Outside
    Global            local         local        global
 -  200.200.201.1     10.1.1.1       -            -
 -  200.200.201.2     10.1.1.2       -            -
 -  200.200.201.3     10.1.1.3       -            -
Router#
```

b. From 10.2.2.1—a PC—telnet out to the Internet and check the translation table. Make sure the Telnet shows up with an inside global IP address of 200.200.201.4:

```
Router# show ip nat translations
Pro Inside            Inside        Outside      Outside
    Global            local         local        global
 -  200.200.201.1     10.1.1.1       -            -
 -  200.200.201.2     10.1.1.2       -            -
 tcp 200.200.201.4:1074 10.2.2.1:1074 130.1.3.7:23 130.1.3.7.55:23
Router#
```

c. From a computer with a source address from network 10.4.4.0, try to access the Internet using a Web browser or telnet—it should fail because of your **access-list**.

CHAPTER FOURTEEN

Using AAA to Secure Remote Access

After completing this chapter, you will be able to:

✓ Know the components of CiscoSecure

✓ Understand the advantages of virtual profiles

✓ Know the components of AAA

✓ Understand the purpose of TACACS+

✓ Configure AAA on your access server or router

An Overview

A complete security system for remote access involves many components, including dial-up client software and hardware, access servers and routers, security servers, security protocols, authentication, authorization, and accounting. Dial-up clients such as Windows 95, 98, and NT machines require dial-up software, which will usually use the PPP protocol. Typically, PAP or CHAP will be used as one type of authentication mechanism when the dial-up client dials into the access server or router. On top of this, there may be additional security, such as the use of token cards by the clients. Some vendors that produce the cards are CryptoCards, Enigma, and SDI. The access server or router will have to authenticate the user based on their mode of access to the router. As was discussed in Chapter 4, this can be done locally with the access device's username database.

Of course, if you have many access servers and routers in your network, it would be much easier to centralize the management of your security on a central security server. A security server should be able to verify who users are and which resources they can access or manipulate as well as keep a record of the users' actions. Cisco offers a product called *CiscoSecure* that can perform these tasks as well as integrate with any external security device, such as a token card server, to provide a more secure solution. Typically, one of three secure protocols is used between the access server/router and the security server: TACACS+, RADIUS, or Kerberos V. This chapter will briefly discuss many of these items; however, an in-depth discussion of the design, configuration, and implementation of network security is beyond the scope of this book. This chapter will focus on the integration of your access servers and routers with a security server such as CiscoSecure. For more information concerning network security, Cisco has dedicated a whole class, titled *Managing Cisco Network Security* (MCNS), to this topic.

CiscoSecure

At the heart of a manageable security system is the security server. It centralizes all security—from authenticating dial-up users as they access the network, to verifying which resources they are allowed to access and manipulate. The security server should also have the ability to gather and report on detailed actions that a user performs on the different devices in the network, including routers, access servers, switches, hubs, firewalls, and even file servers. Cisco's product, CiscoSecure, performs all these functions—and many, many more.

Components of CiscoSecure

CiscoSecure is built on a foundation of three components: an AAA (authentication, authorization, and accounting) server, a Netscape Fasttrack server, and a relational database management system (RDBMS). CiscoSecure is supported on both Windows NT and Sun Solaris Unix platforms. The Netscape Fasttrack server product provides a Graphical User Interface (GUI) for easy configuration and management. The GUI interface requires that either a Netscape Navigator or Microsoft Internet Explorer client with Java enabled be used. The database included with CiscoSecure is SQLAnywhere; however, CiscoSecure is compatible with any ODBC database interface, including scalable database products like Oracle and Sybase SQL Server.

For an additional layer of security, CiscoSecure can be integrated with other security products, such as token card servers. Cisco includes CryptoCard Authentication Server software (but not hardware) with CiscoSecure, but other token card vendors are supported, including Security Dynamics Technologies, Axent Technologies, and Enigma Logics. Token cards are hardware devices that are synchronized with a central token card server. Generally, they display a Personal Identification Number (PIN) or key that a user enters, along with his username, when accessing the network. The key continuously changes, providing a more secure solution than the standard username/password authentication.

Features of CiscoSecure

The following are some of CiscoSecure's enhanced features:

➤ Support for secure protocols, including Terminal Access Controller Access Control System (TACACS+) and Remote Access Dial-In User Service (RADIUS)

➤ A single login for Windows users accessing their Windows NT domain

➤ Dial-up Virtual Private Networks (VPNs)

➤ Password aging

➤ Access restriction based on time of day

➤ Password support with PAP, CHAP, ARA (AppleTalk), and MS-CHAP (Microsoft clients)

➤ SSL support for the client browsers to provide security for remote management

➤ User and group administration

➤ Limitations as to the number of sessions allowed to a user

➤ Restrictions that bar a user from accessing network resources or limit the commands that the user can execute on a network resource

Besides these features, CiscoSecure has many, many more, providing you with a key component in your enterprise-capable centralized security solution. One of the more interesting features of CiscoSecure is *virtual profiles*.

14

Virtual Profiles

Virtual profiles are an extension of Point-to-Point Protocol (PPP) security for dial-up access. PPP has a limitation in that Challenge Handshake Authentication Protocol (CHAP) and Packet Authentication Protocol (PAP) only perform authentication. Once a user passes the authentication, the user has access to the entire network. You could implement **access-lists** and other types of security features to limit the user from gaining access to certain resources; however, the downside of this approach is that this type of restriction on the particular physical interface will affect all users. As an example, an **access-list** is applied to an interface such as a BRI, serial, or a dialer interface (if profiles are being used). Any user who dials into this interface has those same restrictions applied to him.

Virtual profiles overcome this limitation by allowing per-user configuration information to be applied to a specific user when he accesses the network. A virtual profile is basically a virtual interface that is created for a user when he dials into the network. All the properties that can be associated with a physical interface, such as **access-lists**, addressing, queuing, and so on, can be applied to the virtual interface. When the user disconnects, this virtual interface is removed. Therefore, on the same physical interface, the configuration properties can change based on the user who dials into it.

With virtual profiles, you are not limited to the type of dial-up method the user employs to access the network. This gives you extensive and flexible security controls in governing dial-up access to your network.

How Virtual Profiles Work

Virtual profiles are created on the AAA server. Virtual profiles are basically templates that define what a user is allowed to use. A user is then associated with a specific template. Note that you can create a template that will be applied to a group of people who should have the same type of network restrictions. When a user dials into the network and is authenticated, the virtual profile associated with the user is passed from the AAA server to the access server/router. The access server/router then applies this information to the dialed-in interface. This information can be in the form of an **access-list** that will be applied to the user's current dial-up interface or a specific layer-3 address that the user should be assigned. When the user disconnects, the configuration information is then removed from the physical interface by the access server/router.

AAA

Once you have purchased your security server, your work has just begun. The security server is the mechanism that you will use to deploy your security policies. Careful planning and configuration are required to provide a secure network. You will need to examine all avenues of entry into your network and evaluate your resources to determine how critical each of them is, and then you must decide upon an appropriate level of security for each resource. When going through this process, you will definitely want to weigh these factors:

➤ Level of security required

➤ Amount of monitoring necessary

➤ Ease of management

➤ Transparency of security to the users

➤ Cost

Components of AAA

AAA contains three components:

➤ Authentication

➤ Authorization

➤ Accounting

Together, these three items are referred to as *AAA*. People pronounce this not as "A, A, A", but usually as "triple-A", like the automotive organization.

Authentication

The first component, *authentication*, checks a user's identification and verifies whether the user can gain access to the network. Cisco has different mechanisms that can accomplish this. The access server/router can verify this information locally or forward it to a security server for verification. If performed locally, the security check can be a local password on the access router or a username and password located in the local **username** database. If a security server is used, the user information—whether it be a static password, username and password, one-time password, or token card authentication—is passed from the access server/router to the security server for verification.

Authorization

Authorization defines what the user is allowed to do once he has been authenticated to the network. Authorization might restrict which networking services a user can access or which commands a user can execute on a particular network resource.

Accounting

Accounting keeps a record of everything that the user does and a timestamp of when the user performs his different actions. This information can be used for many things—from keeping an audit trail to access damages or attempted break-ins, to

14

keeping a record for billing purposes to charge a user for resources that have been used and/or consumed.

AAA, the Security Server, and the Access Server/Router

The security server serves as a central point of control for AAA. With one point of control, it is easy to implement, maintain, and enforce your security policies. This chapter is concerned with securing access on your access server or router. On your access devices (routers and access servers), there are different methods that users may use to access the them, whether they are dialing into your network using PPP or attempting to access your network access device via Telnet, the console port, the auxiliary port, or a tty line.

Access Modes

The two basics modes in which a user can access your access server/router are *character* mode and *packet* mode. In character mode, the user is attempting to gain access to an EXEC shell, whether it be User or Privileged EXEC mode. In packet mode, the user is attempting to establish a network connection to the access device using a data link layer protocol, such as PPP, Appletalk Remote Access Protocol (ARAP is Apple's proprietary dial-up solution), or NetWare Asynchronous Services Interface (NASI is NetWare's proprietary dial-up solution).

Entry Points

When implementing security on your access device, you will have to carefully examine every possible avenue that a user might take in order to gain access to it (or to gain access to services behind your access device). The following are different types of lines that might provide a user access to your access server/router or to your network:

➤ line con

➤ line aux

➤ line vty

➤ line tty

These modes are typically used by a user to gain character mode access to your networking device. The following are interfaces on the router that a user might attempt to use to establish a dial-up network connection:

➤ interface async

➤ interface group-async

➤ interface bri

➤ interface serial

➤ interface dialer

Note that a serial interface could be connected to an analog modem, a terminal adapter for ISDN, or a logical interface used for ISDN dial-up access for a PRI interface.

AAA allows you to secure all these types of access. You can even define methods as to how a certain type of access should perform a security check. For instance, you could have a default method that has the router first try to use the central security server to perform authentication, and if this is not available, to use the access device's local **username** database. You could set up a different method for the console port and have the user enter a password that must match the **password** line Configuration mode command on the local console port. This type of configuration gives you a lot of flexibility in implementing your security policies.

RADIUS and TACACS+

To provide a more secure environment, a special protocol is used between the access device and the security server. This ensures that any communication between these two devices, when sent across a LAN or WAN, is encrypted and therefore cannot be deciphered by anyone tapping into your network (like your users' passwords). Plus, some process is needed to define how AAA should be implemented on a security server: How authentication is performed, how authorization is checked, and how accounting information should be gathered. CiscoSecure supports two different protocols to accomplish this: RADIUS and TACACS+.

RADIUS

RADIUS is a standards-based protocol based on a client/server system. One function of RADIUS is that it allows for the reliable and secure delivery of AAA information between the security server and access server/router. RADIUS also defines the implementation of AAA on the security server itself. Typically, the server code is freeware. One problem with RADIUS is that many proprietary extensions have been added to it because of its "free" nature, making implementation of the protocol difficult in a mixed-vendor environment. Cisco supports certain RADIUS extensions in its CiscoSecure security server.

TACACS+

TACACS+ is also a client/server system that provides a reliable and secure delivery of AAA information. TACACS, its predecessor, was developed by the U.S. Defense Department and later defined in RFC 1492. Cisco has taken this protocol and added enhancements to it, thus producing TACACS+. Like RADIUS, TACACS+ defines

14

how AAA is implemented on a security server. The following are some enhanced features of TACACS+ that Cisco has engineered:

➤ Authentication, authorization, and accounting can be tied to independent databases, providing more flexibility and scalability.

➤ Messages can be presented to users when they are logging in, telling them about expiring passwords, prompting for additional security information such as a mother's maiden name or social security number, displaying a customized login banner, or other types of information.

➤ The command levels that the user can gain access to on a Cisco device and/or the commands that a user can execute on a Cisco networking device can be restricted.

➤ Accounting information can be gathered. This information contains the starting and stopping times of access, the commands executed on Cisco networking devices by users, and the traffic statistics of dial-up users, including the number of packets and bytes for the user's connection.

Because of its robustness and Cisco's large market presence, the TACACS+ protocol specification is available in a draft RFC, which allows other vendors to implement TACACS+ in their networking devices or develop their own Cisco-compatible security server products.

Configuring AAA

Configuring AAA can become a complex task. Some of the AAA commands that will be discussed are very hard to interpret because of the many parameters associated with them. Besides configuring your access device, you will also have to set up your security policies on your security server, such as CiscoSecure. This section will cover only the commands necessary to have your access device send all authentication and authorization requests to the security server for verification as well as log all security events for your access device. Configuration of the Cisco's CiscoSecure security server is beyond the scope of this book. For information on the configuration of Cisco's CiscoSecure product, take the *Managing Cisco Network Security* class, which is offered by a variety of Cisco's training partners.

When configuring access to the security server, you will probably set up four sets of commands that fall under one of the these categories:

➤ Defining access to the AAA server

➤ Defining authentication

➤ Defining authorization

➤ Configuring accounting details

Enabling Access to the AAA

When configuring AAA, you must first decide whether you will use TACACS+ or RADIUS as the secure transport protocol between your access router and security server. Remember that these two protocols are used to provide for a secure transport of information between the router and the AAA server. The configuration of this component is fairly easy and straight-forward.

Configuring TACACS+ Access

If you decide to use TACACS+ as your transport protocol, use the following global Configuration commands to establish connectivity between your router and server:

```
Router(config)# aaa new-model
Router(config)# tacacs-server host ip_address [single-connection]
Router(config)# tacacs-server key security_key
```

The first command, **aaa new-model**, enables AAA on your access router.

The second command, **tacacs-server host**, lists the IP address of your security server. If you have more than one security server (for the purpose of redundancy), list each of these IP addresses with a *separate* **tacacs-server host** command. The access router will process these in the order you enter them—from the first to the last—until it is able to establish a connection. The **single-connection** option tells the access router that it will set up and maintain a single TCP session between itself and the security server. The advantage of this is that every time the access router needs to perform an AAA function, a connection is already established between the two devices, speeding up the verification and/or accounting function.

Last, you will need to specify the security key that is defined on the security server. This is done with the **tacacs-server key** command. This key is used to encrypt the access device's information when sent to the security server. This key must exactly match the key on the security server. Any leading spaces preceding the key are ignored; however, any spaces within or following the key *are* used as part of the key. If you use spaces in the key, you should not enclose the key in quotes—if you do, the quotes will become part of the key and therefore must also be configured on the security server. And as is common for passwords and keys on Cisco's products, the key is case-sensitive.

14

Configuring RADIUS Access

The configuration for RADIUS is just as simple as was the configuration for TACACS+. Use the following global Configuration commands to establish RADIUS connectivity between your router and server:

```
Router(config)# aaa new-model
Router(config)# radius-server host ip_address
Router(config)# radius-server key security_key
```

This configuration is very similar to that of TACACS+. The only major difference is the lack of the **single-connection** option for the **radius-server host** command. With RADIUS, unfortunately, a connection must be established from the access device to the security server *every* time a AAA event occurs, and then it gets immediately torn down. This means there will be more delay when processing security requests and performing accounting functions as compared to TACACS+.

Defining Authentication

After defining the secure connection between the access device and the security server(s), you will need to define your authentication commands. The list of these commands defines what type of authentication is to be performed when a user tries to access your network or resources on your access device. There are different access methods that the user can use when accessing the router—a simple login request to User EXEC mode, an attempt to access Privilege EXEC mode, a PPP dial-up connection, or a Novell or AppleTalk dial-up connection. You have a lot of flexibility in defining the method of authentication for each of these. The following sections explain this in more depth.

Login Authentication

You can restrict who gains User EXEC mode access with login authentication. The global Configuration command used to define login authentication to the access device is as follows:

```
Router(config)# aaa authentication login default|list_name
                    method1 [method2 [method3 [method4]]]
```

The **login** parameter specifies that every time a user tries to log into the access device, authentication should be performed. The **default** parameter specifies that if a specific list name is *not* specified for a particular type of login access, the listed methods should be used to perform the verification.

Note: The methods define what type of authentication should be performed, and in what order. The methods are listed in Table 14.1.

Looking at an example of AAA authentication code will help explain how this command is used:

```
Router(config)# aaa authentication login default group tacacs+
Router(config)# aaa authentication login consolecheck group tacacs+ line
Router(config)# line con 0
Router(config-line)# login authentication consolecheck
Router(config-line)# password emergency
Router(config-line)# exit
Router(config)# line vty 0 4
Router(config-line)#
```

Table 14.1   Methods for authentication.

Method	Definition	Type of Access
enable	Uses the enable password defined by the **enable password** or **enable secret** global Configuration command.	User EXEC, Privileged EXEC, NASI
line	Uses the password defined on the line (console, vty, tty, or aux) with the **password** line Configuration command.	User EXEC, Privileged EXEC, ARAP, NASI
local	Uses the local username database on the access router by finding a match with the username and password in the **username** global Configuration command(s).	User EXEC, ARAP, PPP, NASI
none	Performs no authentication.	User EXEC, Privileged EXEC, PPP, NASI
group tacacs+	Uses the list of TACACS+ servers listed in the **tacacs-server host** global Configuration command(s).	All*
group radius	Uses the list of RADIUS servers listed in the **radius-server host** global Configuration command(s).	User EXEC, Privileged EXEC, PPP*
if-needed	Does not authenticate a user if the user has already been authenticated on the line	PPP
krb5	Uses Kerberos V for authentication (only used for PPP PAP).	PPP
guest	Allows guest logins for AppleTalk users using Apple's remote-access software. It must be the first method listed.	ARAP
auth-guest	Allows guest logins for AppleTalk users using Apple's remote-access software only if the user has already gained an EXEC shell.	ARAP

* Note that the group parameter is not necessary in older versions of the IOS (but is required in newer versions) when specifying authentication by a security server. For the purpose of the CCNP Remote Access test, you can omit the group parameter.

The first **aaa authentication login** command indicates that if a particular type of access does not define how security should be performed, TACACS+ will be used. Because the line vtys do not specify the type of security to be performed with a **login** command, the **aaa authentication login default** command is used. In this command example, only one method is listed: TACACS+. If the security server(s) is not available, access would be *denied* to the user. To overcome this problem, you can list multiple methods.

Note: Typically, you will want to have at least two methods defined for your console port. This way, if your security server is not available, you will still be able to log into your access device.

The second **aaa authentication login** command is an example of having multiple login authentication methods for the different ways of accessing the access device. Note that the parameter **default** is not used; instead, a list name, *consolecheck*, is defined. This allows you to override the default authentication. This can be seen by the **login authentication** command on the console line. The access router will

14

first attempt to verify authentication using the TACACS+ security server. If the security server(s) is not available, however, the fallback security check is the password defined by the **password** command on the console line. This ensures that you will not be locked out of the router's console port if you lose access to the security server. When listing multiple methods, the access device tries each of these, in order, until one of them works.

Enable Authentication

You will also probably want to restrict who can gain access to Privileged EXEC mode on your access router. The global Configuration command used to define Privileged EXEC authentication to the access router is as follows:

```
Router(config)# aaa authentication enable default
                   method1 [method2 [method3 [method4]]]
```

The **enable** parameter specifies that every time a user tries to access Privileged EXEC mode, authentication should be performed. Unlike the **aaa authentication login** command, there is no *list_name* parameter, only **default**, because there is only one way to gain access to Privileged EXEC mode: by executing the **enable** command from User EXEC mode. The methods define what type of authentication should be performed, and in what order. All the methods listed in Table 14.1 are valid for authenticating Privileged-level access, with the exception of **local**.

The following is an example of setting up Privileged EXEC authentication:

```
Router(config)# aaa authentication enable default group tacacs+ enable
Router(config)# enable secret backdoor
```

In this example, the router will first try to use the security server to perform authentication. If the security server cannot be reached, the password specified by the **enable secret** or **enable password** global Configuration command is used. In the preceding example, "backdoor" would be the backdoor into the router.

PPP Authentication

For remote access, you can restrict users access when they attempt to establish an analog or ISDN dial-up PPP session with your access router. The global Configuration command used to define PPP authentication to the access router is as follows:

```
Router(config)# aaa authentication ppp default|list_name
                   method1 [method2 [method3 [method4]]]
```

The **ppp** parameter specifies that every time a user tries to establish a dial-up PPP session to your access router, authentication should be performed. The methods define what type of authentication should be performed, and in what order. The valid methods are listed previously in Table 14.1.

The **default** parameter indicates that if a specific list name is not specified for a particular type of line access, the listed methods that follow the parameter should be used to perform the verification. To override the default method, specify a list name in the **aaa authentication ppp** command and reference it with the line or interface **ppp authentication** command, as follows:

```
Router(config-if)# ppp authentication pap|chap|ms-chap list_name
```

Note that the list name listed here must match the list name in the **aaa authentication ppp** command. If you do not specify a list name, the **aaa authentication ppp default** methods are used. This configuration is helpful in situations in which you have two different groups dialing into your access device and you need to define different methods: one method for a set of lines reserved for your network administrators and another method for the remaining lines that are used by your user population.

Looking at an example will help explain how this command is implemented:

```
Router(config)# aaa authentication ppp default group tacacs+
```

The **aaa authentication ppp** command states that the default authentication method is the TACACS+ security server(s). If this is not available, authentication will fail and the access device will disconnect the PPP session. Note that when the user performs a dial-up session to the access router, he needs to use the username and password specified in the TACACS+ security server's database.

Here is another example that uses both a default and list configuration:

```
Router(config)# aaa authentication ppp default group tacacs+
Router(config)# aaa authentication ppp pppcheck if-needed group tacacs+
Router(config)# interface async1
Router(config-if)# ppp authentication chap pppcheck
Router(config-if)# exit
Router(config)# interface async2
Router(config-if)# ppp authentication chap
Router(config-if)# exit
```

In this example, interface async1 will use the **aaa authentication ppp pppcheck** statement to perform authentication. Note that because interface async2 does not specify a list, it will use the **aaa authentication ppp default** statement to perform authentication.

14

Other Types of Dial-up Authentication

Besides authentication for PPP dial-up access, you can also perform dial-up access for AppleTalk and NetWare clients. These are performed by using the following commands:

```
Router(config)# aaa authentication arap default|list_name
                    method1 [method2 [method3 [method4]]]
Router(config)# aaa authentication nasi default|list_name
                    method1 [method2 [method3 [method4]]]
```

The **arap** parameter specifies that every time a user tries to establish a dial-up AppleTalk session to your access device, authentication should be performed. This is needed only if the AppleTalk user is using Apple's proprietary remote-access software. The **nasi** parameter is used by NetWare dial-up users who are not using PPP, but rather Novell's proprietary remote-access software. The **default** parameter specifies that if a specific list name is not specified for a particular type of line access, the listed methods should be used to perform the verification. The methods define what type of authentication should be performed, and in what order. The valid methods are defined previously in Table 14.1.

Defining Authorization

Once a user has been successfully authenticated, you can then restrict what type of functions the user can perform with the following **aaa authorization** global Configuration mode command:

```
Router(config)# aaa authorization access_type
                    method1 [method2 [method3 [method4]]]
```

You can restrict five types of access. These are specified in Table 14.2.

Table 14.3 defines the methods for the type of security check to be performed for authorization.

Table 14.2   The types of access you can check for authorization.

Access Type	Definition
network	Checks for authorization for any type of network request, including PPP, PPP NCPs, ARA (AppleTalk), and SLIP.
exec	Checks to see whether a user is allowed an EXEC shell.
command *level*	Checks to see whether a user can execute commands at a certain level specified by the *level* parameter. With Cisco devices, level 1 is User EXEC and level 15 is Privileged EXEC, but you can assign level numbers between these two values for specific commands.
config-commands	Checks to see whether a user can execute Configuration mode commands.
reverse-access	Checks to see whether a user can perform a reverse Telnet.

Table 14.3   Methods you can use for authorization.

Method	Definition
local	Uses the local username database on the access device by finding a match with the username and password in the **username** global Configuration command(s).
none	Performs no authorization check.
group tacacs+	Uses the TACACS+ servers listed in the **tacacs-server host** global Configuration command(s).*
group radius	Uses the RADIUS servers listed in the **radius-server host** global Configuration command(s).*
if-authenticated	Does not perform an authorization check if the user has already been authenticated (for instance, if the user has already been authenticated during the setup of a PPP connection).
krb5-instance	Uses the Kerberos 5 instance defined in the **kerberos instance map** command to perform authorization.
guest	Allows guest logins for AppleTalk users using Apple's remote-access software. It must be the first method listed. This is only used with the ARAP method.
auth-guest	Allows guest logins for AppleTalk users using Apple's remote-access software only if the user has already gained an EXEC shell. This is only used with the ARAP method.

Note that the group parameter is not necessary in older versions of the IOS (but is required in newer versions) when specifying authentication by a security server. For the purpose of the CCNP Remote Access test, you can omit the group parameter.

The following is an example of using AAA authorization:

```
Router(config)# username emergency password backdoor
Router(config)# aaa authorization config-commands group tacacs+ local
```

In this example, when a user tries to execute a global Configuration command, the router will verify this with the TACACS+ security server. If it receives no response from the server, the router will then use the local **username** database. In this case, the user must type in the username "emergency" and the password "backdoor" if the security server is unavailable.

Configuring Accounting Details

To keep an audit trail or tracking of a user's actions, you can enable AAA accounting. To set up accounting, use the **aaa accounting** global Configuration command:

```
Router(config)# aaa accounting access_type
                    accounting_method group tacacs+|radius
```

You can define auditing for five types of access. These are specified in Table 14.4.

The *accounting_method* parameter defines when accounting should be started and/ or stopped. These methods are listed in Table 14.5.

One issue with using the **wait-start** parameter is that each accounting record must be logged *before* the user can execute the command—this means that if you use this

Table 14.4 Types of auditing you can perform.

Access Type	Definition
network	Audits all types of network connections, including PPP, ARAP, SLIP, and NASI.
exec	Audits all EXEC requests.
command *level*	Audits all commands at the specified command level.
connection	Audits any Telnet/rlogin, LAT, PAD, and tn3270 connections that the user makes from the router.
system	Audits all system events not associated with a user, including the changing status of an interface, reloads, and so on.

Table 14.5 When accounting should start and/or stop.

Accounting Method	Definition
start-stop	Sends a "start accounting" record at the beginning of the auditing and a "stop accounting" record at the end of the user's process; however, if the security server is not available, the user is *still* allowed to proceed with his/her process.
stop-only	Sends a "stop accounting" record only at the end of the user's process.
wait-start	Acts like **start-stop**, with the exception that the user is not allowed to proceed with his/her process unless the accounting record can be logged on the security server.

option with the **commands** *level* access type, each command must be recorded before it can be executed, thus introducing a noticeable delay at the CLI. Plus, if the TACACS+ server is not available, you will not be able to execute commands on the access device at the specified command level.

Finally, you must specify either **tacacs+** or **radius** for your accounting configuration, based on the type of security server you are connecting to. Note that the **group** parameter is only required by newer versions of the IOS and is omitted in older versions.

The following is an example of implementing AAA accounting:

```
Router(config)# aaa accounting exec start-stop group tacacs+
Router(config)# aaa accounting command 15 start-stop group tacacs+
Router(config)# aaa accounting system start-stop group tacacs+
```

In this example, any EXEC access, all commands executed at Privileged EXEC mode, and all system events will be logged; plus, a start and stop accounting record is generated for each user's process.

Chapter Summary

Implementing security can be very complex because of the multitude of components involved—users dialing into your network, authentication of those users, authorization of the types of actions they can perform, and keeping audit trails of their actions.

A centralized security system should address all these issues. AAA (or *authentication, authorization,* and *accounting*) is the main function of any security server. Integrating this with your existing network infrastructure can become a complex task. Securing dial-up access, protecting your networking devices, and implementing policies on your firewalls are just some of the tasks you will have to perform.

Cisco's CiscoSecure server software helps centralize all these functions for your network devices—whether they be a PIX firewall, an access server, a Catalyst switch, a router, or any other type of Cisco networking device. With its support of TACACS+ and RADIUS, as well as its support for ODBC-compliant databases, virtual profiles, and two different operating system platforms, CiscoSecure provides you with a lot of flexibility in the implementation of your security solution.

Configuring your access server/router to interact with the security server can become a daunting task because of all the parameters the necessary commands support. You will have to perform four basic tasks. First, you will have to set up access to the AAA server. You will need to specify that you will be using AAA with the **aaa new-model** command. Next, you will need to decide whether you will be using TACACS+ or RADIUS when accessing your AAA server. No matter which of these you decide to use, you will have to specify the server's IP address that you will access and the key to use for secure transmissions. The commands to do this are **tacacs-server host** and **tacacs-server key** for TACACS+ and **radius-server host** and **radius-server key** for RADIUS.

After this, you will need to enter your AAA commands. To define your authentication methods, use the **aaa authentication** commands. For authorization, use the **aaa authorization** commands, and for accounting and auditing, use the **aaa accounting** commands.

Review Questions

1. CiscoSecure is built on a foundation of which three components? [Choose the three best answers]

   a. IOS

   b. AAA

   c. Netscape Fasttrack server

   d. RDBMS

   e. Microsoft Internet Explorer

14

2. Which token card server does CiscoSecure not support?

   a. Crytpocard

   b. Cisco EncryptoCard

   c. Enigma Logics

   d. Security Dynamics Technologies

3. CiscoSecure uses what feature to enable per-user network restrictions?

   a. Virtual profiles

   b. Dialer profiles

   c. PPP

   d. **access-lists**

4. AAA contains all the following except which ones? [Choose the two best answers]

   a. Authentication

   b. Accounting

   c. Authorization

   d. Auditing

   e. Access

5. Which of the following items checks a user's identification and verifies whether he can gain access to the network?

   a. Authentication

   b. Authorization

   c. **access-lists**

   d. Virtual profiles

6. What restricts either what a user is allowed to do or the functions a user can perform?

   a. Authentication

   b. Virtual profiles

   c. Dialer profiles

   d. Authorization

7. What keeps a record of everything a user does after being permitted into the network?

   a. Audit

   b. Access

   c. Accounting

   d. Authorization

8. What are the two modes a user can use to gain access to your network? [Choose the two best answers]

    a. Packet

    b. Character

    c. Login

    d. Frame

9. What protocols does Cisco support between the access server/router and the security server? [Choose the two best answers]

    a. IPSec

    b. RADIUS

    c. TACACS+

    d. Kerberos

10. Which of the following tasks is not something you would do in setting up AAA on your access server/router? [Choose the two best answers]

    a. Defining user policies for accessing and using resources

    b. Defining access to the AAA server

    c. Defining what users can do on the access server/router

    d. Configuring accounting

11. Which of the following commands is not required to establish connectivity to the TACACS+ AAA server?

    a. **tacacs–server host**

    b. **aaa authentication**

    c. **tacacs–server key**

    d. **aaa new–model**

12. What AAA command restricts User EXEC mode access?

    a. **aaa authorization login**

    b. **aaa authentication enable**

    c. **aaa authorization enable**

    d. **aaa authentication login**

13. When using the **aaa authentication** command, what method parameter would you use to check the access server/router's username database for authentication?

    a. **enable**

    b. **line**

    c. **local**

    d. **group tacacs+**

14

14. Examine the following AAA router code:

```
Router(config)# username administrator password keepout
Router(config)# aaa authentication login default line group tacacs+
Router(config)# aaa authentication login consolecheck
                         group tacacs+ local
Router(config)# line con 0
Router(config-line)# login authentication consolecheck
Router(config-line)# password emergency
Router(config-line)# exit
Router(config)# line vty 0 4
Router(config-line)# password cisco
Router(config-line)# exit
```

When a user attempts to telnet into the router, which access method will be used?

a. TACACS+

b. Username database

c. Line password

d. None of the above

15. Examine the following AAA router code:

```
Router(config)# aaa authentication enable default enable group tacacs+
Router(config)# enable secret backdoor
```

How will the router check for Privileged EXEC access?

a. It will use TACACS+.

b. It will use the **enable secret** command.

16. Which command cannot be used to restrict a dial-up network session with the access server/router?

a. **aaa authentication ppp**

b. **aaa authentication nasi**

c. **aaa authentication login**

d. **aaa authentication arap**

17. Which command is used to verify what commands a user can execute?

a. **aaa authorization**

b. **aaa authentication**

c. **aaa command**

d. **aaa accounting**

18. When checking authorization for a user with the **aaa authorization** command, which parameters can you use to check the type of access the user is allowed? [Choose all that apply]

    a. **command**

    b. **reverse-access**

    c. **exec**

    d. **network**

19. When using the **aaa authorization** command, what method is used to skip the authorization check if the user has already been authenticated?

    a. **group tacacs+**

    b. **if-authenticated**

    c. **if-needed**

    d. **krb5-instance**

20. Which methods are valid for the **aaa accounting** command? [Choose the two best answers]

    a. **local**

    b. **group radius**

    c. **group tacacs+**

    d. **line**

21. If you are setting up accounting for AAA, which parameter would you use to track reloads of a router?

    a. **command**

    b. **system**

    c. **exec**

    d. **network**

22. Which accounting method should be used for the **aaa accounting** command if you are only interested in sending a record at the end of a user's process?

    a. **start-stop**

    b. **stop-only**

    c. **wait-start**

    d. **at-stop**

14

Real-World Projects

Remote Systems, Inc., located in Oviedo, FL, is a software-development company that creates add-on components to popular database products. Remote Systems has recently experienced a large amount of growth in its network because of the addition of 200 employees. Many of these employees are telecommuters and will be using ISDN for their connectivity. Because of the huge demand to support remote dial-up connections, security has become a concern. Kevin Davis is in charge of the current network infrastructure, including security issues. He has decided to purchase CiscoSecure for NT to centralize the security policies and to handle the dial-up security issues. The current network is shown in Figure 14.1.

Remote Systems currently has a 3640 series router for its remote access connections. The router's configuration is as follows:

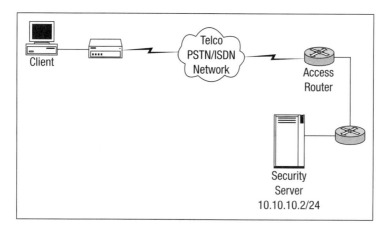

Figure 14.1   High-level overview of Remote Systems' network.

```
version 11.3

hostname RemoteInc
enable password san-fran

username rem_user password 0 cisco
username admin password 0 san-fran
no ip domain-lookup
ip host modem 2097 10.10.10.1

isdn switch-type primary-5ess
```

```
controller t1 1/0
 framing esf
 linecode b8zs
 pri-group timeslots 1-24

interface ethernet 0/0
 ip address 10.10.10.1 255.255.255.0

interface serial 1/0:23
 no ip address
 encapsulation ppp
 dialer pool-member 1
 isdn switch-type primary-5ess
 isdn incoming-voice modem
 ppp multilink
 hold-queue 75 in

interface serial 3/0
 physical-layer async
 encapsulation ppp
 ip unnumbered ethernet0/0
 async mode interactive
 peer default ip address pool ip-pool
 no cdp enable
 ppp authentication chap

interface serial 3/1
 no ip address
 shutdown

interface serial 3/2
 no ip address
 shutdown

interface serial 3/3
 no ip address
 shutdown

interface group-async1
 encapsulation ppp
 ip unnumbered ethernet 0/0
 dialer in-band
 dialer idle-timeout 60
 dialer-group 1
 async mode interactive
```

14

```
    peer default ip address pool ip-pool
    no cdp enable
    ppp authentication chap
    group-range 65 76

router igrp 10
    network 10.0.0.0
    passive-interface dialer1

ip local pool ip-pool 10.200.1.1 10.200.1.254
ip classless

line con 0

line 65 76
    autoselect during-login
    autoselect ppp
    login local
    modem inout
    modem autoconfigure type mica
    transport input all
    stopbits 1
    flowcontrol hardware

line 97
    autoselect during-login
    autoselect ppp
    login local
    modem inout
    modem autoconfigure type usr_courier
    transport input all
    stopbits 1
    flowcontrol hardware
    speed 115200

line aux 0

line vty 0 4
    login local

end
```

Currently, Remote Systems has an ISDN PRI on serial 1/0 that handles its dial-up needs. Some of the users dial up via BRIs, whereas others use analog. To handle the analog connections, Kevin has installed two internal MICA digital modem cards in slot 2. Security is handled via PPP CHAP and the local username database.

Remote Systems also has a single analog connection on Serial 3/1—a USR Courier modem is attached here. This is used in emergency situations when the primary line, the ISDN PRI, is out of service. Security is handled on this dial-up line via PPP CHAP and the local username database.

For User EXEC access coming from the MICA modems, USR Courier modem, and telnets, the local username database is used. For Privileged EXEC mode, the local enable password is used. Because Remote Systems has been growing rapidly and their dial-up connectivity has tripled over the last year, Kevin purchased CiscoSecure to help alleviate some of his security management headaches.

Project 14.1

Kevin will need to complete the following tasks to configure Remote Systems, Inc.'s router to authenticate to the CiscoSecure AAA server. First, enable AAA and, using TACACS+, specify the security server's IP address and the key that the two devices will use. For this project, use the key "secureplus".

After setting up the security server connection, configure your AAA authentication. For Privilege EXEC access and User EXEC access to the console port, set the primary method to TACACS+ and the secondary method to the local **username** database. For any other type of login access, use TACACS+ as the only security method. When users attempt to set up a PPP connection to the router, use only TACACS+ as the security method. Next, you will set up AAA authorization. If a user sets up a connection via PPP, then it will not be necessary to check EXEC access at the security server. Once all of this is completed, you are ready to configure your AAA accounting commands. Use the **start–stop** method for recording purposes for all system events and when users attempt to execute an EXEC command.

Configure authentication:

1. Use TACACS+ as the primary authentication for the Privileged EXEC mode and the local username database as a backup:

```
RemoteInc(config)# aaa authentication enable default
                   group tacacs+ local
```

2. Use TACACS+ as the primary authentication for User EXEC mode via the console port and the local username as a backup:

```
RemoteInc(config)# aaa authentication login consolecheck
                   group tacacs+ local
RemoteInc(config)# line con 0
RemoteInc(config-line) login authentication consolecheck
```

14

3. Use TACACS+ as the only authentication for User EXEC mode access via any other line:

```
RemoteInc(config)# aaa authentication login default group tacacs+
```

4. Use TACACS+ as the only authentication for PPP access:

```
RemoteInc(config)# aaa authentication ppp default group tacacs+
```

Configure authorization:

Configure the authorization command such that a user automatically gains access to the EXEC shell if the user has already been authenticated (using PPP):

```
RemoteInc(config)# aaa authorization exec
                          if-authenticated group tacacs+
```

Configure accounting:

1. Turn on accounting for all system-level events (use a start–stop accounting method):

```
RemoteInc(config)# aaa accounting system start-stop group tacacs+
```

2. Turn on accounting for all EXEC requests (use a start–stop accounting method):

```
RemoteInc(config)# aaa accounting exec start-stop group tacacs+
```

Project 14.2

After the implementation, AppleTalk was added to the network. Because of the secure nature of the application that the dial-up AppleTalk clients were using, Kevin had to purchase a separate security server that only runs RADIUS. You will need to configure AAA on the 3640 router so that it can also access the RADIUS server, whose IP address is 10.10.10.3. The key that you will use is "KeyApple". The Apple-Talk devices are using ARAP as their dial-up solution. Ensure that ARAP uses the RADIUS server for authentication.

Also, Kevin has been dealing with problems from some of his network administrators who have been misconfiguring some of his routers when they should not have been performing any changes. He still needs all of his administrators to access Privileged EXEC mode to use troubleshooing tools like the extended **ping** and **debug** commands, but he wants to restrict who can perform configuration commands. He also wants to log every command that is executed on the 3640 and who logs into the router (and for how long). These modes of access should be sent to CiscoSecure, and should fail if the security server is unavailable.

Confiure AAA for the AppleTalk users:

1. Enable AAA:

```
RemoteInc(config)# aaa new-model
```

2. Assign the server's IP address:

```
RemoteInc(config)# radius-server host 10.10.10.3
```

3. Assign the server's key, using "KeyApple" as the key:

```
RemoteInc(config)# radius-server key KeyApple
```

4. Use RADIUS as the only authentication for ARAP access:

```
RemoteInc(config)# aaa authentication arap default group radius
```

Configure authorization for the network administrators:

1. Configure the authorization command to restrict who can execute Configuration mode commands:

```
RemoteInc(config)# aaa authorization config-commands group tacacs+
```

2. Turn on accounting for all the execution of all commands:

```
RemoteInc(config)# aaa accounting command 1 start-stop group tacacs+
RemoteInc(config)# aaa accounting command 15 start-stop group tacacs+
```

3. Turn on accounting for all EXEC requests:

```
RemoteInc(config)# aaa accounting exec start-stop group tacacs+
```

14

CHAPTER FIFTEEN

Sample Test

Question 1

An X.25 DTE is which of the following?

○ a. Protocol Assember/Disassembler

○ b. Packetizer and Depacketizer

○ c. Packet Analyzer/Disanalyzer

○ d. Packet Assember/Disassembler

Question 2

An "M" listed after the 700 series model number refers to what amount of DRAM that the router has?

○ a. 500KB

○ b. 1MB

○ c. 1.5MB

○ d. 2MB

○ e. 3MB

Question 3

Type in the interface Configuration mode command to allow X.25 window sizes larger than 7:

_____

Question 4

Examine the following commands:

```
Router(config)# ip nat inside source static 10.0.0.1 200.200.200.1
Router(config)# ip nat inside source static 10.0.0.2 200.200.200.2
Router(config)# interface ethernet 0
Router(config-if)# ip address 10.0.0.254 255.255.255.0
Router(config-if)# ip nat inside
Router(config-if)# exit
Router(config)# interface serial 0
Router(config-if)# ip address 192.168.1.1 255.255.255.0
```

10.0.0.1 sends a packet to the preceding router and it arrives on ethernet 0, which is then routed out of serial 0. What is 10.0.0.1's IP address changed to?

○ a. 10.0.0.254.

○ b. 200.200.200.1.

○ c. 200.200.200.2.

○ d. It is not changed.

Question 5

Which of the following is an LMI standard? [Choose the two best answers]

❏ a. Annex A

❏ b. Annex B

❏ c. Annex C

❏ d. Annex D

Question 6

The _____ ISDN reference point is where the telephone company's network arrives at your doorstep, up to your NT1 device.

○ a. U

○ b. S

○ c. T

○ d. R

Question 7

Which values can you specify when configuring traffic shaping for frame relay? [Choose the two best answers]

❏ a. Access rate

❏ b. CIR

❏ c. BC

❏ d. BE

❏ e. DE

Question 8

Which of the following queuing mechanisms is enabled, by default, on T1/E1 or slower speed serial interfaces?

○ a. CQ

○ b. PQ

○ c. FIFO

○ d. WFQ

15

Question 9

What is not a reason to perform frame relay traffic shaping?

○ a. Mismatch in access rates between different DTEs

○ b. Carrier dropping nonconforming frames

○ c. To prevent one type of traffic from affecting other types on the interface

○ d. Split horizon problems

Question 10

Which of the following commands are necessary to configure backup interfaces? [Choose the two best answers]

❏ a. **backup load**

❏ b. **backup interface**

❏ c. **backup delay**

❏ d. **backup enable**

Question 11

Which of the following statements are true of X.121 addresses? [Choose the two best answers]

❏ a. X.121 addresses contain both a DNIC and NTN.

❏ b. X.121 addresses are only required for SVCs.

❏ c. The DNIC represents the country of the destination device.

❏ d. The DNIC is four digits in length.

❏ e. The X.121 address must be 15 digits in length.

Question 12

What types of compression are supported in X.25? [Choose the two best answers]

❑ a. Link

❑ b. Payload

❑ c. Header

❑ d. MPPC

Question 13

The load for the **backup load** command is specified as what range of values?

○ a. 1-255

○ b. 1-100

○ c. 1-10

○ d. Any range

Question 14

The 700 series supports which of the following address-translation features? [Choose the two best answers]

❑ a. NAT

❑ b. PAT

❑ c. Traffic distribution

❑ d. Overlapping networks

❑ e. Porthandler

15

Question 15

Which of the following uses DDR and a dynamic routing protocol?

○ a. Backup interfaces

○ b. Floating static routes

○ c. Dialer Watch

○ d. All of the above

Question 16

Which type of queuing uses **queue-list** commands to assign traffic to queues?

○ a. PQ

○ b. CQ

○ c. FIFO

○ d. WFQ

Question 17

What command is used to apply a Priority Queue to an interface?

○ a. **fair-queue**

○ b. **custom-queue-list**

○ c. **priority-group**

○ d. **priority-list**

Question 18

What command is used to authenticate a user's Privilege-level access?

○ a. **aaa authentication login**

○ b. **aaa authentication ppp**

○ c. **aaa authentication enable**

○ d. **aaa authentication privilege**

Question 19

AAA stands for what?

○ a. Authentication, application, accounting

○ b. Authorization, access, audit

○ c. Authentication, authorization, audit

○ d. Authentication, authorization, accounting

Question 20

Enter the command to enable a backup interface after a one-minute delay when the primary interface fails and is disabled one-minute after the primary is reactivated: _____

Question 21

Network Address Translation should be used for all the following situations except which one?

○ a. You are merging two networks together and have an overlapping address space.

○ b. You are changing ISPs, and your new ISP will not support your old private addresses.

○ c. You need to load balance connections across multiple computers.

○ d. You do not have enough public addresses for your internal network.

○ e. None of the above.

15

Question 22

You need to configure an X.25 PVC. The provider has assigned you a VC number of 89. Your source IP address is 172.16.7.10, with a subnet mask of 255.255.255.240, and your X.121 address is 1230. The destination IP address is 172.16.7.9, with a subnet mask of 255.255.255.240, and the destination X.121 address is 1234. Which of the following is the correct statement to perform this configuration?

○ a. **Router(config)# x25 pvc 89 172.16.7.10 1234**

○ b. **Router(config-if)# x25 map ip 172.16.7.9 255.255.255.240 1234**

○ c. **Router(config-if)# x25 pvc 89 ip 172.16.7.9 1234**

○ d. **Router(config-if)# x25 map ip 172.16.7.10 1230**

○ e. **Router(config-if)# x25 pvc 89 ip 172.16.7.10 1230**

Question 23

What commands are required for legacy DDR to define interesting traffic that will initiate phone calls? [Choose the two best answers]

❑ a. **dialer map**

❑ b. **dialer-group**

❑ c. **dialer-list**

❑ d. **access-list**

❑ e. **dialer idle-time**

Question 24

Examine the following code:

```
Router(config)# ip nat inside source list 1 pool nat-pool overload
Router(config)# access-list 1 permit 10.0.0.1 0.0.0.0
Router(config)# access-list 1 permit 10.0.0.2 0.0.0.0
Router(config)# access-list 2 permit 192.168.2.0 0.0.0.255
Router(config)# ip nat pool nat-pool 200.200.200.1 200.200.200.1
                        netmask 255.255.255.0
Router(config)# interface ethernet 0
Router(config-if)# ip address 10.0.0.254 255.255.255.0
Router(config-if)# ip nat inside
Router(config-if)# exit
Router(config)# interface serial 0
Router(config-if)# ip address 192.168.1.1 255.255.255.0
Router(config-if)# ip nat outside
```

A packet with a source IP address of 192.168.2.2 is received on ethernet 0 and forwarded to serial 0. What will the source IP address be when it exits serial 0's interface?

○ a. 200.200.200.1

○ b. 192.168.1.1

○ c. 10.0.0.254

○ d. 192.168.2.2

Question 25

Which of the following allow for one global IP address to represent many local IP addresses? [Choose the two best answers]

❏ a. NAT

❏ b. PAT

❏ c. Traffic distribution

❏ d. Overlapping networks

15

Question 26

> Which 700 series router supports a four-port integrated hub?
>
> ○ a. 761
>
> ○ b. 762
>
> ○ c. 771
>
> ○ d. 776

Question 27

> Which of the following is not a component of CiscoSecure?
>
> ○ a. Netscape Fasttrack
>
> ○ b. IOS
>
> ○ c. RDBMS
>
> ○ d. AAA

Question 28

> Type in the command to enable AAA on your IOS router: _____

Question 29

> Which modem standard initially defined a maximum rate of 28.8Kbps and then changed it to 33.6Kbps?
>
> ○ a. V.21
>
> ○ b. V.32bis
>
> ○ c. V.34
>
> ○ d. V.42bis

Question 30

Which of the following commands checks to see whether a user can execute a specific command on a router?

○ a. **aaa authentication**

○ b. **aaa authorization**

○ c. **aaa accounting**

○ d. **aaa authenticate**

Question 31

You should consider all the following when choosing a solution for remote access, with the exception of

_____.

○ a. security

○ b. scalability and flexibility

○ c. bandwidth needs

○ d. cost

○ e. LAN infrastructure

○ f. availability

○ g. manageability

○ h. reliability

Question 32

A floating static route should have an administrative distance _____ that of the dynamic routing protocol.

○ a. less than

○ b. equal to

○ c. greater than

○ d. greater than or equal to

15

Question 33

Which of the following are not features of the 700 series routers? [Choose the two best answers]

❏ a. NAT

❏ b. Caller-ID screening

❏ c. Stacker and Predictor compression

❏ d. Access-lists

Question 34

Type in the interface Configuration mode command to use the RFC 1490 standard encapsulation for a frame relay WAN connection: _____

Question 35

Which 700 series profile affects only dial-up connections?

○ a. LAN

○ b. Internal

○ c. User

○ d. System

Question 36

Which 700 series command is used for PPP CHAP to assign the password that will be sent to the challenger?

○ a. **set ppp secret client**

○ b. **set ppp secret host**

○ c. **set ppp client**

○ d. **set ppp host**

Question 37

Which of the following is not a packet-switched WAN solution?

○ a. ISDN

○ b. X.25

○ c. Frame relay

○ d. SMDS

Question 38

Which queuing method has 16 user-defined queues?

○ a. FIFO

○ b. WFQ

○ c. CQ

○ d. PQ

Question 39

If you have an asynchronous connection, what type of DCE device would you deploy?

○ a. NT1

○ b. CSU

○ c. Modem

○ d. DSU

15

Question 40

Which of the following routers are recommended for a SOHO environment? [Choose the two best answers]

❑ a. 760

❑ b. 2500

❑ c. 5200

❑ d. 3600

❑ e. 1000

Question 41

Which of the following is the only thing that SLIP defines?

○ a. Link testing

○ b. Dynamic address assignment

○ c. Compression

○ d. Encapsulation method

○ e. Security

Question 42

Cisco uses what type of serial WAN connector for its DTE EIA/TIA-232 serial cables to connect to a Cisco router?

○ a. DB-15

○ b. DB-25

○ c. DB-37

○ d. Winchester 34-pin

○ e. DB-60

Question 43

Which of the following provides a permanent end-to-end connection, where a company has complete control over how the bandwidth is used?

○ a. X.25

○ b. Frame relay

○ c. Dedicated circuits

○ d. ISDN

Question 44

Which commands can be used to determine whether the data link layer, using PPP, is up and operational? [Choose the two best answers]

❑ a. **show interface**

❑ b. **debug modem**

❑ c. **debug ppp authentication**

❑ d. **debug ppp negotiation**

❑ e. **show ppp status**

Question 45

Which of the following 2500 series routers provide eight low-speed analog connections? [Choose the two best answers]

❑ a. 2501

❑ b. 2509

❑ c. 2511

❑ d. 2522

15

Question 46

Which Cisco router would be the smallest available router that supports frame relay for WAN connectivity?

○ a. 760

○ b. 770

○ c. 1000

○ d. 1600

Question 47

Which 700 series command performs the same task as **erase start** and **reload** on an IOS-based router?

○ a. **upload**

○ b. **set default**

○ c. **clear nvram**

○ d. **delete nvram**

Question 48

You need to establish a reverse-Telnet connection to TTY5 using the router's loopback address of 10.10.10.1. What would you type in next after **telnet 10.10.10.1**?

○ a. **2000**

○ b. **2005**

○ c. **2006**

○ d. None of the above

Question 49

Which of the following LEDs on a 1600 series router, when green, indicates that the router has booted successfully?

- ○ a. SYSTEM PWR

- ○ b. SYSTEM OK

- ○ c. LAN ACT

- ○ d. WIC CD

Question 50

You have a 28.8Kbps modem attached to the first asynchronous serial port on a Cisco 2500 router. What command would you use to assign the clock rate of the connection between the router and the modem?

- ○ a. **clock rate 115200**

- ○ b. **flowcontrol hardware**

- ○ c. **speed 115200**

- ○ d. None of the above

Question 51

Which PPP protocol negotiates whether AppleTalk is to be used on the connection?

- ○ a. LCP

- ○ b. NCP

- ○ c. CHAP

- ○ d. LQR

15

Question 52

When the DTE becomes available and wants to establish a connection to a remote device, which control lead does it signal, at first, to the DCE?

○ a. DTR

○ b. DCD

○ c. TD

○ d. RTS

Question 53

What command assigns a physical interface into a dialer pool when using dialer profiles?

○ a. **interface dialer**

○ b. **dialer pool**

○ c. **dialer-group**

○ d. **dialer-list**

○ e. **dialer pool-member**

Question 54

For a European E1 PRI, how many B channels are available?

○ a. 23

○ b. 24

○ c. 30

○ d. 31

○ e. 32

Question 55

What is the absolute line number of the auxiliary port on a 2509 series router?

○ a. 0

○ b. 1

○ c. 8

○ d. 9

Question 56

What command is used to allow the user logging into the router to assign the encapsulation method?

○ a. **encapsulation**

○ b. **async mode-interactive**

○ c. **autoselect**

○ d. **async mode-dedicated**

Question 57

Which items does a Cisco router running PAP send across the link?

○ a. Hostname

○ b. Hash

○ c. Password

○ d. Answers a and b

○ e. Answers a and c

○ f. Answers a, b, and c

15

Question 58

Which commands would you use to troubleshoot ISDN layer-2 issues? [Choose the two best answers]

○ a. **show controllers**

○ b. **show isdn status**

○ c. **debug isdn q931**

○ d. **debug isdn q921**

○ e. **debug dialer**

Question 59

When configuring dialer profiles, you use the _____ command to assign the phone number to be called on the dialer interface.

○ a. **dialer map**

○ b. **dialer remote-name**

○ c. **dialer string**

○ d. **dialer pool**

Question 60

Which of the following do you not see in Windows 95/98 when using the Make A New Connection Wizard to create a new dial-up connection?

○ a. Phone number

○ b. Connection icon

○ c. Name

○ d. PPP configuration

○ e. Modem type

○ f. None of the above

Question 61

Which of the following protocols is not supported by Windows 95/98 for Dial-up Networking in the standard Server Type window?

○ a. AppleTalk

○ b. TCP/IP

○ c. NetBEUI

○ d. IPX/SPX

Question 62

Which command do you use to see the results of the modem autodiscovery process?

○ a. **debug modem config**

○ b. **modem autoconfigure discovery**

○ c. **show modemcap**

○ d. **debug confmodem**

Question 63

A(n) _____ is any type of device that does not have a native ISDN interface.

○ a. NT1

○ b. NT2

○ c. TE1

○ d. TE2

○ e. TA

15

Question 64

Which command would you use for PPP to allow the user to assign his/her own IP address on the link?

○ a. **peer default ip address**

○ b. **async dynamic**

○ c. **peer dynamic ip address**

○ d. **async mode-interactive**

Question 65

Which ISDN standard is responsible for setting up and tearing down phone calls?

○ a. Q.931

○ b. TEI

○ c. SPID

○ d. Q.921

Question 66

Which of the following tasks will LCP always perform? [Choose the two best answers]

❑ a. Negotiate optimal packet sizes

❑ b. Implement data compression

❑ c. Authenticate the identity of the peer at the other side of the link

❑ d. Determine encapsulation format options

Question 67

The _____ command is used to assign B8ZS to an ISDN PRI T1.

○ a. **controller t1**

○ b. **framing**

○ c. **linecode**

○ d. **clock source**

○ e. **pri-group timeslots**

○ f. **interface serial** *slot/port*:23

Question 68

When troubleshooting frame relay, you use which command to display the address resolution table?

○ a. **show frame-relay pvc**

○ b. **show frame-relay map**

○ c. **show frame-relay lmi**

○ d. **show interfaces**

Question 69

You have configured DDR and now are experiencing problems with routing updates triggering phone calls and keeping your DDR connection up 24 hours a day, 7 days a week. What solution(s) could you use to stop this problem?

○ a. Static routes

○ b. Passive interfaces

○ c. **dialer-list** with an **access-list**

○ d. Answers a and b

○ e. Answers a and c

○ f. Answers a, b, and c

15

Question 70

Which of the following commands is not required for the configuration of X.25 PVCs?

○ a. **encapsulation x25**

○ b. **x25 pvc**

○ c. **x25 address**

○ d. **x25 map**

CHAPTER SIXTEEN

Answer Key

1. d
2. c
3. **x25 modulo 128**
4. d
5. a, d
6. a
7. b, d
8. d
9. d
10. b, c
11. a, d
12. b, c
13. b
14. b, e
15. d
16. b
17. c
18. c
19. d
20. **backup delay 60 60**
21. b
22. c
23. b, c
24. d

25. b, c
26. d
27. b
28. **aaa new-model**
29. c
30. b
31. e
32. c
33. a, c
34. **encapsulation frame-relay ietf**
35. c
36. a
37. a
38. c
39. c
40. a, e
41. d
42. e
43. c
44. a, d
45. b, d
46. c
47. b

48. b
49. b
50. c
51. b
52. a
53. e
54. c
55. d
56. b
57. e
58. b, d
59. c
60. d
61. a
62. d
63. d
64. b
65. a
66. a, d
67. c
68. b
69. f
70. d

Question 1

The correct answer is d. The X.25 DTE is called a *Packet Assembler/Disassember* (PAD). Therefore, answers a, b, and c are incorrect. This name (PAD) defines the basic function of the X.25 DTE. The PAD performs three basic functions. First, when a user has data to send, it segments that data to fit into X.25 packets—the disassembler part. Second, as X.25 packets are coming in, the switch needs to extract the contents from the packets and place them into a buffer. And third, once it has received all the original packets (be they IP, IPX, or some other type), the PAD will then reassemble all the pieces.

Question 2

The correct answer is c. The 700 series routers come in two categories: Those with the letter *M* in their model name, such as the 761*M*, and those that don't. The *M* means that this router model has 1.5MB of DRAM. Those without the *M* only have 1MB of DRAM. Therefore, answers a, b, d, and e are incorrect.

Question 3

The correct answer is **x25 modulo 128**. Three commands affect window size. These are shown in the following code example:

```
Router(config)# interface serial [module_number/]port_number
Router(config-if)# x25 win window_size
Router(config-if)# x25 wout window_size
Router(config-if)# x25 modulo window_modulus
```

The **win** and **wout** parameters define the window size in both directions on the VCs, just like the packet size parameters—how many X.25 packets can be sent before the source PAD has to wait for an acknowledgement from the destination. However, you cannot change these values haphazardly because they are dependent on the **modulo** value. By default, the modulus is set to 8. This means that you can have window sizes from 1 to 7. If you change the modulus to its only other value, 128, you can increase your window size from 8 to 127. The default window size for your VCs is 2. Based on the value of the modulus, the window size can be any value between 1 and 127.

Question 4

The correct answer is d. 10.0.0.1's IP address is not changed because there is no **ip nat outside** command on serial 0. Therefore, answers a, b, and c are incorrect. If this command were configured on serial 0, the address would be changed to 200.200.200.1. In this situation, the router would never use 200.200.200.2 because of the **ip nat inside source static** statements. Also, it would never use 10.0.0.254 because that is the IP address of the router's ethernet 0 interface.

Question 5

The correct answers are a and d. Frame relay defines three different signaling protocols, referred to as *LMI*. The three different standards for LMI are:

➤ *Cisco*—Developed jointly by Cisco, DEC, Nortel, and StrataCom (now owned by Cisco). This is sometimes referred to as the "gang of four" protocol.

➤ *Annex D*—Specified by ANSI's T1.617 standard.

➤ *Annex A*—Specified by ITU-T's Q.933 standard.

Answers b and c are incorrect because these are nonexistent standards.

Question 6

The correct answer is a. ISDN reference points define the communication between the different devices and the parameters for the functional devices. The four protocol reference points that are commonly defined for ISDN are called R, S, T, and U. Understanding ISDN reference points is important because most CPE vendors refer to their equipment in terms of the reference points it embodies. The U reference point is where the telephone company's network arrives at your doorstep, up to the NT1 device. The U interface is also called the *U-Loop* because it represents the loop between your premises and the telephone company. ISDN devices made for the U interface include a built-in NT1 function. The S reference point lies between ISDN user equipment (TEI or TE2 with a TA) and the NT1 device. Therefore, answer b is incorrect. The T reference point lies between customer site switching equipment and the local loops termination (NT1), thus making answer c incorrect. The user-network reference point is usually the S/T reference point. The S/T reference point is one of two reference points that most ISDN equipment vendors incorporate in their devices. An S/T device requires a standalone NT1 device to work with your ISDN connection. The R reference point lies between the Terminal Equipment 2 (TE2) device and a Terminal Adapter. There are no specific standards for the R reference point, so the TA manufacturer determines and specifies how a TE2 and TA communicate with each other. Therefore, answer d is incorrect.

16

Question 7

The correct answers are b and d. When configuring traffic shaping within your map-class, you must specify the average rate (CIR) and the peak rate (BE). Answer a is incorrect because the access rate defines the clocked speed of the connection between the DTE and DCE (such as a T1). Answer c is incorrect because the BC is the average rate over a smaller time period than CIR that a provider guarantees for a VC. Answer e is incorrect because DE prioritizes the frame relay frame as either a normal or a low-priority frame.

Question 8

The correct answer is d. Weighted Fair Queuing is enabled on all serial interfaces clocked at T1/E1 speeds or less, by default. Answers a and b are incorrect because Custom and Priority Queuing require manual configuration. Answer c is incorrect because FIFO queuing is the default for everything else, except for serial interfaces clocked at T1/E1 speeds or less.

Question 9

The correct answer is d. If you are experiencing split horizon problems in an NBMA environment, using subinterfaces or static routes is your best solution in solving this issue. Answers a, b, and c list reasons for performing traffic shaping and are therefore incorrect answers.

Question 10

The correct answers are b and c. To configure basic redundancy for a primary interface, you will need to execute two commands on the *primary* serial interface: **backup interface** and **backup delay**. Answer a is incorrect because this command is optional—and it's only used to solve temporary congestion problems. Answer d is incorrect because this is a nonexistent command.

Question 11

The correct answers are a and d. X.25 uses X.121 addresses to identify PADs. X.121 addresses must be unique throughout the network (and unique throughout the world if you are connected to a public X.25 network). X.121 addresses are made up two components: The Data Network Identification Code (DNIC) and the National Terminal Number (NTN). The DNIC, which is optional, identifies the country and carrier where the X.25 DTE resides. The DNIC is four decimal digits in length. The DNIC is made of two subfields—one is the global region, the other is the X.25 carrier's number within that region. Therefore, answer c is incorrect. The NTN is the identifier used to uniquely identify your X.25 PAD in an X.25 carrier's network. When you connect to a provider's network, you will be assigned a value to use for your PAD. The NTN can range from 8 to 10 or 11 decimal digits, dependent on the provider's X.25 software on its switches. Actually, X.121 addresses can be a minimum of one digit and a maximum of 15 digits in length, thus making answer e incorrect. However, for public connections, addresses will be typically 14 or 15 digits in length. Whether you are employing SVCs or PVCs, each PAD needs a unique address, thus making answer b incorrect.

Question 12

The correct answers are b and c. X.25 supports both payload and TCP header compression. Link compression is only used on point-to-point links using either HDLC, LAPB, or PPP as an encapsulation type on your serial interfaces, thus making answer a incorrect. Answer d is incorrect because MPPC is a link compression method used between a Cisco router and Microsoft clients.

Question 13

The correct answer is b. The thresholds here are defined as percentages (1 through 100). Therefore answers a, c, and d are incorrect.

Question 14

The correct answers are b and e. The 700 router series supports only the PAT and Porthandler features. The 700 cannot perform NAT, thus making answer a incorrect. Overlapping networks require NAT, thus making answer d also incorrect. Traffic distribution is only supported on the IOS routers, thus making answer c incorrect.

Question 15

The correct answer is d. A dynamic routing protocol and DDR are used with all the backup methods: backup interfaces, floating static routes, and Dialer Watch. Note that floating static routes can be used with normal static routes.

Question 16

16

The correct answer is b. Custom Queuing uses **queue-list** commands to assign traffic to queues. To apply the CQ configuration to the interface, you use the **custom-queue-list** interface Configuration mode command. Answer a is incorrect because the **priority-list** command is used for Priority Queuing. Answers c and d are incorrect because you have no control on how traffic is assigned to queues with these queuing policies.

Question 17

The correct answer is c. To assign a Priority Queue list to a serial interface, use the **priority-group** command. Answer a is incorrect because the **fair-queue** command is used to assign the discard threshold limit for WFQ high-volume conversations. Answer b is incorrect because the **custom-queue-list** command is used to apply a CQ policy to an interface. Answer d is incorrect because the **priority-list** command is used to build your policy for Priority Queuing.

Question 18

The correct answer is c. You can restrict access to Privileged EXEC mode on your access router with the **aaa authentication enable** global Configuration command. Answer a is incorrect because the **aaa authentication login** global Configuration command is used to restrict access to User EXEC mode. For remote access, you can restrict users access when they attempt to establish an analog or ISDN dial-up PPP session with your access router. The global Configuration command used to define PPP authentication is **aaa authentication ppp**. Therefore, answer b is incorrect. There is no such command as **aaa authentication privilege**, thus making answer d incorrect.

Question 19

The correct answer is d. AAA contains three components: authentication, authorization, and accounting. Together, these three items are referred to as *AAA*. The first component, authentication, checks a user's identification and verifies whether the user can gain access to the network. Authorization defines what the user is allowed to do once he gains access to the network. Authorization might restrict which networking services a user can access or which commands a user can execute on a particular network resource. Accounting keeps a record of everything the user does and a timestamp of when the user performs his actions. Answer a is incorrect because "application" is not a component. Answers b is incorrect because "access" and "audit" are not components. Answer c is incorrect because "audit" is not a component.

Question 20

The correct answer is **backup delay 60 60**.

Question 21

The correct answer is b. You will have to employ NAT when you change ISPs and your new ISP will not support your old *public* address space, *not* private address space. Answers a, c, and d are reasons to use NAT and are therefore incorrect answers. Because there is a correct answer, answer e is incorrect.

Question 22

The correct answer is c. If you are configuring PVCs, use the following interface command:

```
Router(config-if)# x25 pvc circuit_number
                   protocol protocol_destination_address
                   [protocol2 protocol_destination_address2]...
                   destination_x.121_address
                   [broadcast]
```

Here, *circuit_number* is the value that the switch is expecting for the PVC. The *protocol* field is the protocol that you wish to carry across this VC. Next, you must specify the destination PAD's protocol address and its X.121 address. Answer a is incorrect because the command is being executed in global Configuration mode. Answers b and d are incorrect because **x25 map** is used for SVC resolution. Answer e is incorrect because it uses the source's addressing information instead of the destination's.

Question 23

The correct answers are b and c. The **dialer-list** command defines interesting traffic, whereas the **dialer-group** interface command activates the **dialer-list** on a specified interface. The syntax of these two commands is as follows:

```
Router(config)# dialer-list dialer_list_number
                protocol protocol_name
                permit| deny [list access_list_number]
Router(config)# interface type [module_number/]port_number
Router(config-if)# dialer-group dialer_list_number
```

Answer a is incorrect because the **dialer map** statement is used to define the destination that an interface will connect to. This command specifies things such as the destination's layer-3 address, the destination phone number, and the destination hostname for PPP authentication. Answer d is incorrect because an **access-list** is *optional* when defining interesting traffic. In most cases, you will use an **access-list**

16

to be specific about what types of traffic are or are not allowed to make phone calls. Answer e is incorrect because the **dialer idle-time** command specifies the amount of time, in seconds, that a phone connection will remain up while no interesting traffic is seen on the interface. The default is 120 seconds (2 minutes).

Question 24

The correct answer is d. This example implements PAT, or *address overloading*. The combination of **access-list 1** and the **ip nat inside source list** command will only translate 10.0.0.1 and 10.0.0.2. Note that the third **access-list** statement is a *different* list number and therefore does not apply to this configuration. Therefore, answer a is incorrect. Answers b and c are incorrect because these are addresses on the router's serial 0 and ethernet 0 interfaces, respectively.

Question 25

The correct answer are b and c. *Address overloading*, sometimes referred to as *Port Address Translation* (or PAT for short), allows all the inside local IP addresses to share a single global IP address. With this ability, the translation router can handle thousands of machines with a single global IP address. Traffic distribution presents one IP address for a computer to the outside world. The computers on the Internet use this IP address to access their resource. The translation box will take this and redirect it to a specific internal computer, load-balancing the connections across a multitude of computers. NAT performs a one-to-one translation of IP addresses—each inside local IP address is matched to a unique inside global IP address. Overlapping networks use NAT to solve their duplication problems. Therefore, answers a and d are incorrect.

Question 26

The correct answer is d. The 776 router supports a four-port hub as well as integrated NT1 and RJ-11 ports. Answers a and b are incorrect because the 760 models have a single Ethernet port. Answer c is incorrect because there is no such 700 series model.

Question 27

The correct answer is b. CiscoSecure is built on a foundation of three components: an AAA (authentication, authorization, and accounting) server, a Netscape Fasttrack server, and a relational database management system (RDBMS). Answers a, c, and d are all valid components and therefore incorrect answers. CiscoSecure is supported on both Windows NT and Sun Solaris Unix platforms. Netscape Fasttrack provides a GUI interface for easy configuration and management. The GUI interface requires that either a Netscape Navigator or Microsoft Internet Explorer client with Java enabled be used. The database included with CiscoSecure is SQLAnywhere; however, CiscoSecure is compatible with any ODBC database interface, including Oracle and Sybase SQL Server.

Question 28

The correct answer is **aaa new-model**. Besides enabling AAA, you will need to choose between TACACS+ or RADIUS as your security protocol and application for your security server. If you are using TACACS+, use the following two commands to establish connectivity to your security server:

```
Router(config)# tacacs-server host ip_address [single-connection]
Router(config)# tacacs-server key security_key
```

The first command, **tacacs-server host**, lists the IP address of your security server. If you have more than one security server—for the purpose of redundancy—then list each of these IP addresses with a separate **tacacs-server host** command. The access router will process these in the order that you enter them—from the first to the last—until it is able to establish a connection. The **single-connection** option tells the access router that it will set up and maintain a single TCP session between itself and the security server. The advantage of this is that every time the access router needs to perform an AAA function, a connection is already established between the two devices, speeding up the verification or accounting function.

Next, you will need to specify the security key that is defined on the security server. This is done with the **tacacs-server key** command. This key is used to encrypt information when sent from the access router to the security server. This key must exactly match the key on the security server. Any leading spaces preceding the key are ignored; however, any spaces within or following the key are used as part of the key. If you use spaces in the key, you should not enclose the key in quotes—if you do, the quotes will become part of the key and therefore must also be configured on the security server.

If you are using RADIUS, replace the **tacacs-server** command with **radius-server**.

16

Question 29

The correct answer is c. The V.34 protocol is the standard for 33.6Kbps connections. This standard was initially ratified as 28.8Kbps but was updated to include 33.6Kbps in 1996. Answer a is incorrect because V.21 is the standard for 300bps communications. It is very rarely used anymore. Answer b is incorrect because V.32bis is the standard for 14.4Kbps modem speeds. Answer d is incorrect because V.42bis does not define connection rates; instead, it defines compression (up to 4-to-1) and error correction.

Question 30

The correct answer is b. To verify what resources a user can access once authenticated, or what commands a user can execute (again, once the user is authenticated), use the **aaa authorization** commands. Answer a is incorrect because the **aaa authentication** commands are used to initially authenticate the user's identity. Answer c is incorrect because the **aaa accounting** commands are used to keep an audit trail of a user's actions. Answer d is incorrect because **aaa authenticate** is a nonexistent command.

Question 31

The correct answer is e. The infrastructure of your LAN should not have an impact on the solution you choose for your remote access needs. The general factors a business should consider when choosing a solution for remote-access sites are security, cost, scalability and flexibility, bandwidth needs, availability, manageability, and reliability. Security is always a major factor in any component of a network. Your users are your customers, and you must design your network to minimize your security risks, yet still make it functional. Finding the right mix of security, performance, and cost can be very difficult. Therefore, answer a is incorrect. Businesses can no longer afford to discard technology as they expand. Scalability and modularity are key requirements so that as a company grows, it can leverage its investment in existing equipment. For telecommuting and remote-access solutions, it is critical that the central office solution allow system administrators to scale their network capacities. Therefore, answer b is incorrect. WAN bandwidth is one of the most critical aspects of selecting a WAN solution. Because bandwidth is expensive, it is important to make sure you don't select too much capacity, thereby wasting precious resources. You will also need to forecast future bandwidth needs to keep up with expected business growth. The kinds of traffic expected on the WAN link should be taken into consideration. If you have small-sized, time-sensitive packets, your needs are much different than if you need to move large blocks of data for file transfers. Therefore, answer c is incorrect. As with any technology, there is a cost/

benefit relationship. As the technology becomes more beneficial, it becomes more expensive. In order to minimize costs, you can utilize circuit-switched networks, and you can bring up a network connection when it's needed and tear it down when you don't need it. Cost isn't always the same in all geographic locations for the same service. Tariffs differ from state to state; WAN circuits cost differing amounts from vendor to vendor, and personnel should always be factored into your cost model analysis, thus making answer d incorrect. When selecting a WAN service, you will want to find all the solutions that are available within your geographic region. Although asynchronous connections are available throughout the world, frame relay is not. If a service isn't offered at both ends of your connection, you may not be able to use it. Therefore, answer f is incorrect. The ability to manage the WAN service should also play a key role in your selection. In many cases, the remote offices will may not have access to local IT support. Therefore, it is important to be able to control and administer the remote sites from the central office with solutions that are all designed to facilitate easy management from the central office. Many solutions have built-in monitoring and reporting, which makes it easy to monitor the levels and the nature of the remote-access traffic. Therefore, answer g is incorrect. If your business requires a connection to your remote site at all times, reliability will be a very important factor when determining the appropriate service. It may be necessary to design a backup solution in case the dedicated WAN link goes down, thus making answer h incorrect.

Question 32

The correct answer c. A floating static route should have an administrative distance greater than that of the dynamic routing protocol. Therefore, answers a, b, and d are incorrect.

Question 33

The correct answers are a and c. PAT, not NAT, is a supported form of address translation. Also, only the Stacker form of compression is supported—not Predictor. Answers b and d are incorrect because Caller-ID and **access-list**s are supported features. Other features that are supported are DHCP relay agent and server, IP RIP versions 1 and 2, IPX RIP, IPX spoofing of Watchdog and SPX keepalives, static routes and static IPX SAPs, DDR routing, bandwidth on demand (BOD) for meeting increased bandwidth needs, snapshot routing, and PPP features such as multilink, PAP and CHAP authentication, and dial callback.

16

Question 34

The correct answer is **encapsulation frame-relay ietf**.

Question 35

The correct answer is c. The user and standard profiles are used for dial-up connections. The 700 series uses profiles to perform configuration tasks that are necessary to pass traffic between the Ethernet LAN interface and the ISDN WAN interface. *Profiles* are grouped sets of commands that allow you to customize your connections to different destinations. There are four different types of profiles, with a possible total of 20 different profiles in the 700 series routers. The LAN profile defines how information is passed to and from the Ethernet interface, thus making answer a incorrect. The internal profile is used to pass traffic through the bridge/route engine between the LAN and ISDN BRI interface, thus making answer b incorrect. The system profile defines system-level configurations that affect the router as a whole, thus making answer d incorrect.

Question 36

The correct answer is a. The **set ppp secret client** command assigns the password that the 700 router will use to authenticate to the destination router. The **set ppp secret host** command assigns the password that the 700 router will use to authenticate the incoming connection. Therefore, answer b is incorrect. Answers c and d are incorrect because these commands are nonexistent.

Question 37

The correct answer is a. ISDN is a circuit-switched, not a packet-switched, solution. X.25, frame relay, and SMDS are all packet-switched solutions. Therefore, answers b, c, and d are incorrect.

Question 38

The correct answer is c. Custom Queuing has 16 user-defined queues. Answer a is incorrect because FIFO has one queue. Answer b is incorrect because the number of queues for Weighed Fair Queuing is based on the number of conversations. Answer d is incorrect because Priority Queuing has four queues: high, medium, normal, and low.

Question 39

The correct answer is c. Modems are required for asynchronous serial connections. NT1s, CSUs, and DSUs are required for synchronous serial connections, thus making answers a, b, and d incorrect.

Question 40

The correct answers are a and e. Cisco's 700 and 1000 series of routers are recommended for SOHO usage. The Cisco 700 series ISDN access routers offer a cost-effective solution for telecommuters. The Cisco 760 and 770 series contain two analog telephone interfaces that allow devices such as standard telephones, fax machines, and modems to share one ISDN BRI line. This eliminates the need for multiple telephone lines or other expensive ISDN telephones. The Cisco 1000 series of compact, easily installed and managed, fixed-configuration desktop routers provide low-cost, high-speed connectivity for small offices as well as telecommuters. The Cisco 1000 series routers are the lowest-cost IOS-based routers available. All 1000 models contain an RJ-45 console port and one Ethernet 10Base-T (RJ-45) port. The 1003 and 1004 use ISDN BRI for their WAN connections, whereas the 1005 uses a serial port capable of both synchronous and asynchronous communications. Designed for use with external serial-device WAN connections, the 1005's singular WAN port (DB-60) supports asynchronous serial communications at speeds up to 115.2Kbps. Also supported are synchronous connections, such as leased lines, frame relay, switched 56Kbps, Switched Multimegabit Data Services (SMDS), and X.25 at speeds up to 2.048Mbps. Answer b is incorrect because the 2500 series of routers is recommended for branch office environments. Answers c and d are incorrect because the 5200 and 3600 series of access servers are recommended for central site environments.

Question 41

The correct answer is d. Serial Line IP (SLIP), documented in RFC 1055, was the first protocol for relaying IP packets over dial-up lines. It defines an encapsulation mechanism, but little else. There is no support for dynamic address assignment, link testing, security, compression, and multiplexing different protocols over a single link. SLIP has been largely supplanted by PPP because PPP supports all these features. Therefore answers a, b, c, and e are incorrect.

16

Question 42

The correct answer is e. Cisco uses a proprietary DB-60 interface for its DTE serial interface. Answer a is incorrect because a DB-15 connector is used on an X.21 DCE connector. Answer b is incorrect because a DB-25 connector is used on an EIA/TIA-232 DCE connector. Answer c is incorrect because a DB-37 connector is used on an EIA/TIA-449 DCE connector. V.35 uses a 34-pin Winchester-type cable for its DCE connections, thus making answer d incorrect.

Question 43

The correct answer is c. *Dedicated circuits* are fixed connections that do not involve establishing new connections each time the link is used. They are permanent end-to-end connections, and the company using them has full control over how the bandwidth is used. The telecommunications company provides a dedicated high-speed connection between the two desired locations, at speeds ranging from as low as 9600bps to as high as 45Mbps. The higher the speed, the greater the monthly fixed cost of the line. The connection is available 24 hours a day, 7 days a week, and it's thus suited to companies that want permanent connections between their office branches, or perhaps to companies that want permanent connections to the Internet. Answers a and b are incorrect because a user of frame relay or X.25 services must share bandwidth inside a carrier's network—other users might inadvertently affect other companies' traffic. Answer d is incorrect because ISDN is circuit switched and is therefore a temporary (not permanent) connection.

Question 44

The correct answers are a and d. To see the layer 2 status of an interface, use the **show interface** command. For PPP, you should see that LCP is in an OPEN state—this indicates that LCP has successfully performed its negotiations and that the two sides can now communicate using PPP. You can also view the mechanics of this interaction by using the **debug ppp negotiation** command. This is useful if the LCP status shows CLOSED, indicating a failed negotiation. Answer b is incorrect because **debug modem** shows the interaction between the router and the modem at the physical layer and has nothing to do with PPP. Answer c is incorrect because the **debug ppp authentication** command only shows the authentication negotiation, not the final status of the LCP negotiation. Answer e is incorrect because there is no such command as **show ppp status**.

Question 45

The correct answers are b and d. The following 2500 series routers support eight low-speed analog connections: 2509, 2510, 2522, and 2523. The major difference between the 2509 and 2510 is that the 2509 has a fixed Ethernet port, whereas the 2510 has a token ring port. The 2522 and 2523 routers also have this difference. Both of these routers, however, also have two high-speed serial connections as well as an additional BRI port. Answer a is incorrect because the 2501 has a single Ethernet port and two high-speed serial ports. Answer c is incorrect because the 2511 has 16 low-speed analog ports, not eight.

Question 46

The correct answer is c. The Cisco 1000 series of compact, easily installed and managed, fixed-configuration desktop routers provide low-cost, high-speed connectivity for small offices as well as telecommuters. The Cisco 1000 series includes the lowest-cost IOS-based routers available. Only three variants are available: the 1003, 1004, and 1005. All 1000 models contain an RJ-45 console port and one Ethernet 10Base-T (RJ-45) port. The 1003 and 1004 use ISDN BRI for their WAN connections, whereas the 1005 uses a serial port capable of both synchronous and asynchronous communications. Designed for use with external serial-device WAN connections, the 1005's singular WAN port (DB-60) supports asynchronous serial communications at speeds up to 115.2Kbps. Also supported are synchronous connections such as leased lines, frame relay, switched 56Kbps, Switched Multimegabit Data Services (SMDS), and X.25 at speeds up to 2.048Mbps. Answers a and b are incorrect because the 700 series routers only support ISDN WAN connectivity, not frame relay. The 1600 series supports frame relay, but the lower-cost 1000 does as well, thus making answer d incorrect.

Question 47

The correct answer is b. To set the router back to its factory defaults, use the **set default** command. The **set default** command is similar to executing **erase start/write erase** and **reload** on an IOS router. Answer a is incorrect because the **upload** command displays the commands currently configured on the router. Answers c and d are incorrect because these two commands do not exist on the 700 series routers.

16

Question 48

The correct answer is b. To establish a reverse-Telnet connection, issue the following command: **telnet** *x.x.x.x* **200***y*. Here, *x.x.x.x* represents the IP address of any interface on the Cisco router. The loopback is a good choice because the interface needs to be up/up. Also, *y* is the absolute line number of the line to which you want to connect. If the TTY line has already been configured, you can issue the **telnet** command from anywhere on the network that can ping the *x.x.x.x* interface. The console is line 0, the TTYs (async lines) start at 1, and the AUX port of any router is the last TTY line number plus 1. You can use the **show line** command to see the respective absolute line numbers. Therefore answers a, c, and d are incorrect.

Question 49

The correct answer is b. The SYSTEM OK LED will blink green as the 1600 series router boots and will stay a steady green once the 1600 router has successfully booted. The SYSTEM PWR LED, when green, indicates that the router is turned on and power is being supplied, thus making answer a incorrect. The LAN ACT LED will blink green as data is being sent to or received from the local Ethernet LAN, thus making answer c incorrect. The WIC CD LED, when green, indicates that there is an active connection on the WAN Interface Card serial port. Therefore, answer d is incorrect.

Question 50

The correct answer is c. You use the **speed** command in line Configuration mode to assign the data rate between the DTE and DCE. You always want to set this at the highest possible rate that the DTE/DCE cable supports in case the modems can negotiate compression and handle higher data rates. This is very true for modems that support V.42bis. The DTE and DCE will use RTS/CTS to implement flow control to ensure that they do not overrun their respective buffers. Answer a is incorrect because **clock rate** is used to assign the speed of a DCE synchronous interface (not asynchronous). Answer b is incorrect because **flowcontrol** defines flowcontrol—hardware or software (XON or XOFF). Finally, because there is a correct answer, answer d is incorrect.

Question 51

The correct answer is b. NCP negotiates the protocols to be carried across the connection. This includes protocols such as IP, IPX, and AppleTalk. Answer a is incorrect because LCP negotiates the encapsulation format options, an optimal packet size, authentication, link quality monitoring, data compression, and so on. Answer c is incorrect because CHAP is an authentication mechanism for PPP. Answer d is incorrect because LQR provides a dynamic reconfiguration when errors are present on the line.

Question 52

The correct answer is a. When a DTE (router or PC) wants to send data, it sets the data terminal ready line. This DTR signal goes into the DTR line of the DCE, the modem. The DCE recognizes that the DTE is requesting a connection. If an open phone line exists for the DCE, it sets the Data Set Ready (DSR) and Data Carrier Detected (DCD). Therefore, answer b is incorrect. When the router sees the DSR input line, it sets the request to send (RTS) line, which says that the router has data to send to the DCE. Therefore, answer d is incorrect. If the DCE is clear to accept data, it sets the clear to send (CTS) line, which tells the router that the DCE is free to receive, and the router begins transmitting data over the TD line, where it is received on the corresponding line on the DCE. Therefore, answer c is incorrect. Remember that the first thing that needs to happen is for the modem to detect a carrier—that is, the modem needs to connect to another modem before anything else can happen.

Question 53

The correct answer is e. You can use a combination of synchronous, serial, BRIs, or PRIs with dialer pools. To specify that a physical interface is a member of a specific DDR dialer profile pool, use the **dialer pool-member** command on the specified physical interface. Answer a is incorrect because the **interface dialer number** command creates a logical dialer interface for dialer profiles. Answer b is incorrect because the **dialer pool** command is used to specify the physical interfaces that can be used for incoming and outgoing telephone calls. Answers c and d are incorrect because the **dialer-list** command is used to specify what types of interesting traffic are allowed to make phone calls, and the **dialer-group** command binds this to the logical dialer profile interface.

Question 54

The correct answer is c. ISDN PRI in Europe, Australia, and other parts of the world provides 30 B channels plus one 64Kbps D channel, and one 64Kbps framing and clocking channel (for maintaining the E1 itself), giving a total interface rate of 2.048Mbps. Therefore, answers d and e are incorrect. The ISDN Primary Rate Interface (PRI) service offers 23 B channels and one D channel in North America, yielding a total bit rate of 1.544Mbps (the PRI D channel runs at 64Kbps). Therefore, answers a and b are incorrect.

16

Question 55

The correct answer is d. Cisco devices have four types of lines: console, auxiliary, asynchronous, and virtual terminal lines. Different routers have different numbers of these line types. There are two kinds of numbering systems: The relative line numbering within each set of line types and the absolute line number for the entire router. Each relative set starts at zero. For example, the first Async interface has a line number of zero, and the first VTY line has a number of zero. You need to know the way each line type is numbered and when to use absolute line numbering so you can make accurate reference to every line that is used in a router's configuration. The following is a list of line types, their command abbreviations, and their functions:

➤ *CON or CTY Console*—Typically used to log into the router for configuration purposes. This line is numbered as line 0.

➤ *AUX Auxiliary*—This is a RS-232 DTE port used as a backup asynchronous port (TTY). This port should not be used as a second console port. This port is numbered such that its absolute line number is equal to the last TTY line number plus 1. So, if a router has eight asynchronous ports, the AUX has an absolute line numbered equal to 9. On a 2501 router, which has no asynchronous ports, the AUX is numbered as absolute line 1 (0+1=1).

➤ *TTY Asynchronous*—This line type refers to an asynchronous interface. It's used typically for remote-node dial-in sessions that use such protocols as SLIP, PPP, and XRemote. The numbering varies widely among platforms.

➤ *VTY Virtual Terminal*—The VTY line is used for incoming Telnet, LAT, X.25 Packet Assembler/Disassembler (PAD), and protocol-translation connections into synchronous ports (such as Ethernet and serial interfaces) on the router. The absolute line numbers for VTY lines start at the last TTY line number plus 2 through the maximum number of VTY lines specified. Relative line numbers, of course, start at VTY 0 and go to the maximum number of VTY lines for that particular router model.

When you enter the line configuration mode, you can designate either an absolute line number or a relative line number. For example, in a Cisco 2509 router, the absolute line number 8 is TTY8, line 0 is the console port, and line 9 is the auxiliary port. Answer a is incorrect because line 0 is the console port. Answer b is incorrect because line 1 is the first TTY (the first asynchronous interface). Answer c is incorrect because line 8 is the last asynchronous interface (TTY). Note that a 2509 router has one ethernet interface and eight asynchronous interfaces.

Question 56

The correct answer is b. The **async mode-interactive** command allows a user to make selections as to the type of encapsulation used—you need to do this before using the **autoselect** command. Answer a is incorrect because the **encapsulation** command hard-codes the encapsulation type to be used on the interface (such as HDLC or PPP). The **autoselect** command automatically senses the encapsulation selection made by the user, which could be a simple shell prompt, PPP, or even SLIP, thus making answer c incorrect. The **async mode-dedicated** command forces the interface to use the configured encapsulation method—the user cannot change the encapsulation method. Therefore, answer d is incorrect.

Question 57

The correct answer is e. PAP works basically the same way as the normal login procedure. The client authenticates itself by sending a username and password to the server, which the server compares to its secrets database. This technique is vulnerable to eavesdroppers, who may try to obtain the password by listening in on the serial line, and to repeated trial-and-error attacks. CHAP does not have these deficiencies. CHAP instead exchanges a hash value, which is then used to create an encrypted password. Therefore answers b, d, and f are incorrect. Answers a and c are correct, but *both* are required, making them, individually, technically incorrect answers.

Question 58

The correct answers are b and d. BRI or PRI problems can be diagnosed by using **show** and **debug** commands. You can categorize the ISDN troubleshooting commands by the OSI layers. The **show isdn status** and **debug isdn q921** commands can be used to troubleshoot layer-2 ISDN problems between your Cisco router and the telco's ISDN switch. Answer a, **show controllers**, is incorrect because this only displays layer-1 information, not layer-2. Answer c, **debug isdn q931**, and answer e, **debug dialer**, are incorrect because these commands are used to troubleshoot layer-3 issues, with the setting up (or tearing down) of a phone connection.

16

Question 59

The correct answer is c. The **dialer string** command assigns the phone number that the **dialer** interface should use when making phone calls to the specified destination. Answer a, **dialer map**, is incorrect because this command is used with legacy DDR to specify the destination's phone number. Answer b is incorrect because the **dialer remote-name** command is used to specify the destination's hostname when performing PAP/CHAP authentication with PPP on a dialer profile interface. Answer d is incorrect because the **dialer pool** command specifies which physical interface(s) the dialer profile can use for its phone calls.

Question 60

The correct answer is d. To configure PPP for a dial-up connection, you must first create it and then right-click your new icon and choose Properties to change your PPP configuration as well as any addressing information. To create a new connection, follow these steps: In the first screen of the Make A New Connection Wizard, you need to enter a name for the connection icon (for example, Router1). Therefore, answers b and c are incorrect. If your modem has been set up properly, it should already be selected in the Select A Modem window, and you should not have to click Configure, thus making answer e incorrect. Click Next, and the phone number screen should appear. Enter the number of the router you are calling and then click Next. Therefore, answer a is incorrect. You should get a Success screen, indicating that your new connection has been successfully created. Click Finish. However, you may have to go back and configure the connection icon to provide additional configuration information (such as IP and its settings). As there is a correct answer, answer f is incorrect.

Question 61

The correct answer is a. AppleTalk is not a standard protocol supported by Windows 95/98 for Dial-up Networking. To select or change the protocols for a dial-up connection, first open the Dial-up Networking window. Click once on the icon you wish to change and then select Properties from the File menu (or right-click the icon and select Properties). Then click Server Type. In the Allowed Network Protocols section, you will find TCP/IP, NetBEUI, and IPX/SPX. Therefore, answers b, c, and d are incorrect.

Question 62

The correct answer is d. To see the results of the modem autodiscovery process, use the **debug confmodem** command. Modem autoconfiguration is used to automate the configuration of modems attached to a Cisco Access Server. Cisco Access Servers come with a number of preconfigured initialization strings for some of the most commonly used modems. These preconfigured initialization strings are stored in the modemcap database. Using the command **show modemcap** (without a specific modemcap name) will list the entries in the modemcap database. Therefore, answer c is incorrect. To have the access server automatically discover the modem attached to its asynchronous interface, you can use the command **modem autoconfigure discover**y. Therefore, answer b is incorrect. By using the **debug confmodem** command, you can see the results of the autodiscovery process. The command instructs the access server to send the AT string at various baud rates until it receives an OK. Then it tells the router to send a variety of AT commands to receive the identification of the modem and match that with the modem capabilities database. Answer a is incorrect because there is no such command.

Question 63

The correct answer is d. The Terminal Equipment 2 (TE2) includes any device that isn't ISDN ready. This category includes the equipment you now use for analog communications, such as the phone at your home. Any device in this class, such as a modem, requires an adapter to work with ISDN. A growing number of ISDN equipment vendors offer products that consolidate TE2 adapter and NT1 devices into a single unit (such as the 700 series routers with their analog phone support). The NT1 represents the boundary of the ISDN network from the end-user side. An NT1 is a device that physically connects the customer site to the telephone company local loop. An NT1 can be embodied in a standalone device or included in a specific device. For PRI access, the NT1 is a CSU/DSU device, whereas for BRI access, the device is simply called by its reference name, *NT1*. It provides a 4-wire connection to the customer site and a 2-wire connection to the network. Therefore, answer a is incorrect. An NT2 device provides customer site switching, multiplexing, and concentration, such as a PBX for voice and data switching. An NT2 device is not needed in every installation and will most likely be used with PRIs rather than BRIs. NT2s are needed for PRI multiplexing. The NT2 works with the NT1 and is on the customer side of the NT1. Therefore, answer b is incorrect. The Terminal Equipment 1 (TE1) refers to ISDN devices that support the standard ISDN interface directly, including digital phones, digital faxes, and integrated voice/data terminal devices. These TE1 devices provide direct access to an ISDN connection without adapters. Therefore, answer c is incorrect. Terminal Adapters (TAs) translate signaling from non-ISDN TE2 devices into a format compatible with ISDN. TAs are usually standalone physical devices. The TA device is a protocol converter that adapts equipment that's not designed for ISDN. ISDN equipment vendors market terminal adapter devices that include the NT1 function as well as support other devices. For example, using a Terminal Adapter, you can plug an analog telephone, a fax, and an ISDN adapter into your PC. This type of product, which controls the traffic from different devices sharing the same ISDN line, is called an *NT1 Plus device*. Therefore, answer e is incorrect.

16

Question 64

The correct answer is b. The **async dynamic** command allows a user to enter his/her own IP address at the EXEC line. Answer a is incorrect because the **peer default ip address** command has the router directly assign an IP address to the user either with a specific IP address, by using a pool, or via DHCP. Answer c is incorrect because there is no such command as **peer dynamic ip address**. The **async mode–interactive** command allows a user to make selections as to the type of encapsulation used, thus making answer d incorrect.

Question 65

The correct answer is a. The Q.931 layer-3 protocol is responsible for the actual setup and teardown of ISDN calls. Q.931 defines the layer-3 specifications for ISDN. Actually, the ISDN network layer is specified by the ITU Q series documents Q.930 through Q.939. Layer 3 is used for the establishment, maintenance, and termination of logical network connections between two devices. The emphasis here is on the word *logical*. The network layer provides procedures to make end-to-end connections on the network. The ISDN data link layer is specified by the ITU Q series documents Q.920 through Q.923. All the signaling on the D channel is defined in the Q.921 protocol specification. Therefore answer d is incorrect. The Q.921 recommendation defines layer 2 for ISDN lines. In the OSI reference model, layer 2 provides for procedures established to maintain communication between two network components. In the case of ISDN, the two components are the ISDN terminal, such as a router, and the ISDN switch. This means that ISDN terminals are in constant communication with the ISDN switch. Q.921 defines the frame structure of the data packets, the format of the fields in the frame, and procedures known as Link Access Procedures D Channel (LAPD). The LAPD procedures describe items such as flags, sequence control, flow control, and retransmission. So, Q.921 can also be referred to as LAPD. Also, LAPD is almost identical to the X.25 LAPB protocol. The LAPD frame has 16 bits of control information that contain a command/response (C/R) field, a SAPI (Service Access Point Identifier), and a TEI (Terminal Endpoint Identifier). TEIs are used to distinguish between several different devices using the same ISDN links. TEIs are unique IDs given to each device (TE) on an ISDN S/T bus. These numbers can be preassigned (TEIs 0 through 63) or dynamically assigned (TEIs 64 through 126). TEI 127 is broadcast. Before any higher-level (Q.931) functions can be performed, each ISDN device must be assigned at least one unique TEI value. Most TEI assignment is done dynamically, using the TEI management protocol. The user broadcasts an Identity request, and the network (the telco switch) responds with an Identity assigned containing the TEI value. Functions are also provided to verify and release TEI assignments. Therefore, answer b is incorrect. Service Profile IDs (SPIDs) are used to identify what services and features the telco switch provides to the attached

ISDN device. SPIDs are not always required by the telco. When they are used, they are only accessed at device-initialization time, before the call is set up. The format of the SPID is usually the 10-digit phone number of the ISDN line, plus an optional seven-digit local directory number (LDD). If an ISDN line requires an SPID, but it is not correctly supplied, then layer-2 initialization will take place, but layer-3 initialization will not, and the device will not be able to place or accept calls. Therefore, answer c is incorrect.

Question 66

The correct answers are a and d. LCP will always determine the encapsulation format options as well as negotiate an optimal packet size for the link. Data compression and authentication are optional—they are negotiated, but both sides must have these options enabled for the two respective processes to occur.

Question 67

The correct answer is c. To configure the line coding for your ISDN PRI T1, use the following controller Configuration mode command:

```
Router(config-controller)# linecode [ami | b8zs | hdb3]
```

To perform this command, you must be in the T1 controller Configuration mode. Use the following command to enter the controller mode:

```
Router(config)# controller [t1 | e1] [0 | 1]
Router(config-controller)#
```

Therefore, answer a is incorrect. You will also need to specify the framing on your T1/E1 controller with the following command:

```
Router(config-controller)# framing [esf | sf | crc4 | nocrc4]
```

Typically, an ISDN PRI T1 circuit uses Extended Super Frame (ESF) framing and Bipolar Eight Zero Substitution (B8ZS) or Alternate Mark Inversion for line coding. ISDN PRI E1 uses high-density bipolar 3 (HDB3) for line coding, and the framing type is CRC4. Therefore, answer b is incorrect. To change the clock source for the controller, use the **clock source** controller command. Typically, you will be deriving clocking from the provider, so this command is not necessary unless you have two different clock sources from the provider and you wish to rank them. Therefore, answer d is incorrect. The **pri-group timeslots** command is used on the T1/E1 controller to specify the timeslots that are usable (that you have purchased). For all the channels on a T1, you would specify 1-24; for an E1, 1-31.

16

Therefore, answer e is incorrect. All DDR operations are not performed on the channelized E1 or T1 controller line but on the line's corresponding logical serial interface that corresponds to the PRI group timeslots. You create this with one of the two following commands for a T1:

```
Router(config)# interface serial slot/port:23
Router(config)# interface serial number:23
```

Or one of the two following commands for an E1:

```
Router(config)# interface serial slot/port:15
Router(config)# interface serial number:15
```

Note that "23" and "15" represent the D (or *signaling*) channel. Therefore, answer f is incorrect.

Question 68

The correct answer is b. To see the address resolution table, use the **show frame-relay map** command. Answer a is incorrect because the **show frame-relay pvc** command shows the status of the VCs. Answers c and d are incorrect because the **show frame-relay lmi** and **show interfaces** commands display information concerning the operation of LMI.

Question 69

The correct answer is f. To stop the routing traffic from triggering phone calls, you could implement one of two solutions: use static routes with a passive dialer interface or use a **dialer-list** with an **access-list** to prohibit routing traffic from triggering phone calls. Answers a, b, and c are technically incorrect because all three can be used to solve the routing problem. Answers d and e are also technically incorrect because they omit one of the three answers.

Question 70

The correct answer is d. The **x25 map** command is used with the configuration of SVCs, not PVCs. All the configuration of X.25 is done on your serial interfaces that connect to your X.25 provider. When configuring X.25 on a Cisco router, you will need to perform three required tasks in order for X.25 to work correctly:

➤ Set up your X.25 encapsulation

➤ Define your X.121 address provided by your carrier

➤ Set up your resolution statements to access destination PADs

To accomplish the first, you must use the **encapsulation x25** command. To perform the second, you use the **x25 address** command. Last, you need your resolution statement. For PVCs, the command is **x25 pvc**; for SVCs, **x25 map**. Answers a, b, and c are all valid commands in this situation and therefore incorrect.

16

Appendix A
Answers to Review Questions

Chapter 1 Solutions

1. **b.** The ISDN D channel uses LAPD for its framing protocol.

2. **b, e.** T1/PRI uses 23 B channels and one D channel, each channel operating at 64Kbps.

3. **b, c.** ISDN and POTS are circuit-switching services.

4. **a,d .** Frame relay and X.25 are packet-switching services.

5. **a, d, e.** Synchronous connections use idle bits, sampling, and clocking for identifying where packets begin and end.

6. **b, c.** Asynchronous connections use start and stop bits for identifying where packets begin and end.

7. **c, d.** Only backup and interesting traffic are specifically DDR. Multilink PPP, Quality of Service, and traffic shaping can be used without DDR.

8. **d.** The price of a WAN increases from analog to ISDN to frame relay to T1.

9. **a.** X.25 uses LAPB, and ISDN uses LAPD.

10. **c.** Both SLIP and PPP can relay IP packets.

11. **c.** Branch office users are validated at the central site.

12. **e.** Basic user accounts and passwords are still the most important elements in remote access security.

13. **d.** The size of a central site is more likely to grow than the size of one branch office.

14. **a.** Both telecommuters and branch office users should log into the central site for validation.

15. **b.** ISDN has an advantage over DSL and other WAN types because it can perform both telephone and data transmission.

16. **d.** The central site to accommodate all users and their equipment.

17. **b.** PRI ISDN can accept multiple connections at the central site.

Chapter 2 Solutions

1. **c, d.** The 1601 and 1602 can use ISDN WICs, but the 1603 and 1604 have built-in ISDN interfaces.

2. **a, b, e.** If a 1600 series has a built in ISDN, it cannot have an ISDN WIC.

3. **b.** The 2509 and 25010 have 8 low-speed asynchronous interfaces, whereas the 2511 and 2512 have 16.

4. **c.** Most 1600 series–compatible WICs are also compatible with the 2600 and 3600 series.

5. **a.** The 4000 series uses NPMs instead of NMs.

6. **a.** All WICs compatible with the 1600 series have only one interface.

7. **d.** The AS5200 series is a central office router. The 2600 series is a branch office router; 700 and 1000 are for SOHO.

8. **e.** If the T1/PRI interface has an RJ-45 port, it must have a built-in CSU.

9. **d.** The 3620 has two NM slots and the 3640 has four NM slots, and both have no built-in LAN and WAN ports.

10. **d, e, f, g.** The 2600, 3600, 4000, and AS5200 series can have a T1/PRI interface.

11. **a.** The 1601 has a built-in sync/async interface and the 1602 has a built-in 56K interface.

12. **c.** Each individual cable at the other end of the Octal cable will be connected to a modem and has an EIA/TIA-232 connector.

13. **a.** The LAN COL LED indicates packet collisions when flashing yellow.

14. **c.** Modems are never considered as DTE equipment.

15. **b.** The 700 series is used for telecommuting and SOHO.

16. **b.** The 'U' reference point indicates that there is a built-in NT1.

17. **d.** The 2600 series is limited to two models: 2610 and 2611.

18. **e.** The 'R' series comes with two Ethernet ports but at the expense of not having other ports such as a built-in WAN.

19. **a, b.** Both the 3600 and 4000 series are completely modular.

20. **a.** A T1 can be a channelized T1 line used for multiplexing.

21. **c.** If you are using a NT1 or CSU/DSU with the 4000 series, these devices will have to be external.

22. **b.** Certain NMs have slots for WICs, and these NMs are typically used with the 3600 series.

23. **e.** The 700 series does not use the typical IOS software.

24. **b.** The 760 router contains an ISDN interface.

Chapter 3 Solutions

1. **c,e** . The **modem autoconfigure discovery** command detects which modem you have and initializes the modem.

2. **b.** The maximum speed for the AUX is slower—38400bps.

3. **c.** A modem translates digital signals to analog.

4. **a, c, d.** You can initialize a modem with the **modem autoconfigure type** command, which eliminates the need to reverse Telnet.

5. **b.** The **show line** command shows the status of the line and most of its parameters.

6. **modem autoconfigure discovery**

7. **a.** You can use the **IP Host** command to create a variable, which then can be used in the reverse Telnet command.

8. **c.** The V.25 standard is used for in-band signaling to bit synchronous DCE devices.

9. **e.** When DTR is up, the DTE is ready to accept data.

10. **b.** Use **physical-async layer** to turn on async in an async/sync interface.

11. **a.** The RTS/CTS pair are responsible for flow control.

12. **a.** The absolute line number for the AUX port on a router is equal to that router's last TTY line number plus 1.

13. **c.** The **modem-script** command calls a chat script, which dials a modem.

14. **a.** The async/sync serial interface is different from the regular serial interface found on a 2500 series.

15. **a, c.** The V.90 standard is a merge of X2 and K56flex. Download speeds are higher.

16. **c.** The speed between the router or PC and the modem is higher than the speed between the sending and receiving modems.

17. **d.** The VTY is Telnet; the TTY is asynchronous.

18. **d.** The **reverse telnet** command does not transfer data; it is only used to talk to the router's modem.

19. **a.** The MNP-5 and CCITT V.42bis are for compression, whereas MNP-4 and V.42 are for error control.

20. **b, c.** The MNP-5 and CCITT V.42bis are for compression, whereas MNP-4 and V.42 are for error control.

21. **c.** Router's are considered DTEs, and the modems are DCEs.

22. **b, d.** Because the AUX can transfer data, it uses more pins than the console port; both ports are DTE (specifically for flow control).

23. **f.** The Octal cable has a large DB-68 SCSI interface at the router end.

24. **c.** The 1600, 2500, 2600, and 1000 series use an RJ-45 interface for the AUX port, and other routers use an AUI interface.

Chapter 4 Solutions

1. **a.** Remember the correct syntax; DHCP here refers to a server.

2. **a, c, d.** Cisco uses Stacker, Predictor, and TCP header compression.

3. **c.** The correct syntax is **pool dhcp** after **peer default ip address**.

4. **a. peer default ip address 10.2.2.2** is how you assign a known IP address to a client.

5. **d.** The pool of addresses is created in global configuration and then referred to by the interface.

6. **ppp multilink**

7. **a.** The term dynamic means that the client is providing the IP instead from the router.

8. **a.** The command parameters are **request** and **accept**.

9. **d.** Don't confuse this with host or hostname. The name in this command must match the name of the other router.

10. **d.** You need to memorize the exact syntax for this set of commands.

11. **c.** This looks like an easy "give-away" question, but watch out for mistakes.

12. **a.** PAP uses clear text, and CHAP uses a form of encryption.

13. **d.** If the other router can perform both PAP and CHAP, the server router will use CHAP. If the other router can only use PAP, the server router will use PAP.

14. **c.** Both PAP and CHAP can be used with callback and multilink.

15. **a.** After the LCP communication level is complete, the IPCP configures IP at the NCP level.

16. **d.** The IPCP packet is encapsulated in the PPP information field of the PPP frame.

17. **b.** CHAP uses a three-way handshake with secret strings and hashing values.

18. **b.** Authentication is performed early at the LCP level.

19. **c.** The server router will not call back and it will drop the connection if the client router is not listed.

20. **a, c, d.** If the user inputs the IP address, the interactive mode must be set.

21. **b.** Negotiation comes before authentication.

22. **b, c, d.** Mutilink is dependent on DDR. Without configuring DDR, you cannot perform Multilink.

23. **d.** The actual timeout is equal to the **dialer hold-queue** plus the default timeout.

Chapter 5 Solutions

1. **b.** The TAPI device links the connection to the Dial-Up Adapter.

2. **b.** Dial-Up Adapter binds the protocols to the modem and global protocol configuration. Dial-Up Networking is responsible for more detailed protocol configuration and dialing configuration.

3. **a.** CHAP uses encryption; when encryption is unchecked, you are using PAP.

4. **c.** Dial-Up Networking is configured after Dial-Up Adapter.

5. **d.** One Dial-Up Networking icon represents one phonebook entry.

6. **b.** If no modem is installed, modem installation is automatic when running Dial-Up Networking.

7. **a.** The PPP selection option is found under the Server Type tab in the main configuration window.

8. **c.** From the Server Type window, you choose TCP/IP Settings and in the TCP/IP Setting window, you can select TCP Header Compression.

9. **d.** The Continue button or F7 closes the terminal window.

10. **d.** The /Admin/Apptools/ subdirectory on the Windows 95/98 CD contains the Scripting Tool.

11. **a.** The upgrade allows Multilink PPP for analog modems.

12. **b.** The Microsoft ISDN Accelerator Pack is needed to obtain 128K bandwidth for ISDN Multilink.

13. **b.** There are three main versions of the Cisco 200 series; the Cisco 202 includes a built-in NT1 device.

14. **d.** The Cisco 200 needs to have a MAC address manually assigned to it.

15. **b.** The throughput speed for a 28800 modem is 57600.

Chapter 6 Solutions

1. **b.** One job of the NT1 is to convert the existing four wires on the ST reference point to two wires on the U reference point.

2. **b.** Floating static route is a static route with a high administrative distance.

3. **e.** The valid line coding protocol for E1 PRI is HDB3.

4. **a, d.** The valid line coding protocols for T1 PRI are B8ZS and AMI.

5. **b.** You may need **isdn not-end-to-end (56|64)** in order to ensure a certain speed.

6. **a.** When the second B channel is used, you are actually starting another circuit-switched connection.

7. **a.** The threshold number is a "percentage" of the total bandwidth where the value 255 represents the total bandwidth. The value 65 would represent one-fourth of the total bandwidth.

8. **d.** North America uses Basic-5ess, Basic-nil, and Basic-dms100 switch types.

9. **b.** Snapshot routing uses user-defined intervals with distance-vector protocols only.

10. **a.** Use **show interface BRI 0 1 2** to show information on both channels.

11. **c.** Use **isdn calling-number** to identify the caller's number used for billing.

12. **c.** One PRI with T1 interface uses 23 B channels and 1 D channel.

13. **b, c.** The B channels for both BRI and PRI are 64K, the D channel for BRI is 16k, and the D channel for PRI is 64k.

14. **a.** ISDN uses out-of-band signaling because the D channel is separate and doesn't usually carry data.

15. **b, d.** The receiver does not need to know the SPIDs of the sender. Only DMS-100 and NI-1 switch types must have SPIDs; AT&T is optional.

16. **a.** The **dialer-list** command contains specifications for interesting traffic.

17. **a.** The R reference point is between the TE2 and the TA.

18. **b.** The CRC-4 is the valid frame type for E1 PRI.

19. **a, e, f.** Call teardown includes Disconnect, Release, and Release Complete messages.

20. **a. debug isdn q921** is used for layer 2, and **debug isdn q931** is used for layer 3.

21. **b, d, e.** Snapshot routing, static routing, and default static routing provide routing information without regular updates.

22. **c.** After the receiver is notified by its adjacent switch, the receiver sends an ALERTING message to the switch.

23. **c.** The **dialer map** command contains a lot of related parameters including the dial string.

24. **c.** Switches at the telco office communicate with each other using the SS7 protocol.

Chapter 7 Solutions

1. **b.** A dialer interface contains a set of elements used for making or receiving calls.

2. **b.** The dialer map class enhances the dial string or dialer map with further characteristics.

3. **c.** The dialer pool enables the dialer interface to include physical interfaces when using dialer profiles.

4. **e.** The **map-class** statement can be used with rotary groups or dialer profile groups and with asynchronous physical interfaces or ISDN interfaces.

5. **a.** The **dialer rotary-group** statement assigns a particular physical interface to a particular logical interface.

6. **a.** The **dialer-group 1** is connected to the **dialer-list** that determines interesting traffic.

7. **c.** The **interface dialer** statement creates a logical interface for collecting physical interfaces.

8. **b.** Only the dialer profile groups allow you to assign a physical interface to multiple dialer interfaces.

9. **a, b, c, e.** The map-class includes a dialer idle-timeout, dialer fast-idle, dialer wait-for-carrier-time, dialer isdn speed, and dialer enable-timeout.

10. **a, b.** Dialer profiles can have one physical interface belonging to multiple dialer pools; more than one dialer interface can operate one dialer pool.

11. **b, d. Encapsulation ppp** command and **ppp authentication pap chap** command are specified in the physical interface and are enabled in the dialer interface.

12. **b.** You need to make the dialer interface with all its elements before you can assign a physical interface to the dialer interface.

13. **a, c.** An interface with a higher priority assignment has precedence over another interface within the same pool. The **min-link** parameter sets the minimum number of B channels.

14. **d.** The **dialer string** command refers to a map class named 56K. The map class would contain elements such as the **isdn speed 56** command.

15. **b, c, d.** The **dialer in-band** statement and V.25bis are needed when using a serial interface for DDR; the router will disconnect calls by deactivating DTR, and V.25bis can be used with a variety of devices, including synchronous modems, ISDN terminal adapters, and Switched 56 DSU/CSUs.

Chapter 8 Solutions

1. **c.** Some 700 series have an "M" after their model number. This denotes that the router has 1.5MB of RAM. The standard amount of RAM on a 700 series router is 1MB.

2. **b, d.** The 762, 766, 775, and 776 have both an S/T and a U interface. U interfaces contain an integrated NT1. The 761 and 765 have only an S/T interface.

3. **d.** Stacker compression is a purchasable option for the 700 series routers.

4. **a.** The 700 series routers support IPX spoofing of Watchdog and SPX keepalives. The 700 series does not support IP spoofing.

5. **b.** The 700 series supports Stacker compression only, not Predictor.

6. The **?** command brings up the CLI context-sensitive help.

7. The **set default** command sets the router back to its factory defaults and reboots the router.

8. **d.** All changes made to the 700 series router are *automatically* saved to NVRAM—you do *not* need to execute **copy running-config startup-config** or **write memory**, as you must do on the IOS-based routers.

9. **d.** Once you have made changes to your router's configuration, you can use the **upload** command to examine your changes

10. **upload tftp** *server's_ip_address config_file_name*

11. **d.** The 700 series routers use profiles to perform configuration tasks that are necessary to pass traffic between the Ethernet LAN interface and the ISDN WAN interface. Profiles are grouped sets of commands that allow you to customize your connections to different destinations. There are four different types of profiles, with a possible total of 20 different profiles in the 700 series routers: LAN, internal, system, standard, and 16 user profiles.

12. **b.** The system profile affects all components of the system, including other profiles.

13. The **cd** command returns you from a profile to the system profile.

14. The **set user** *profile_name* command creates a user profile.

15. **a.** For the router to initiate a phone call using DDR, the profile it wishes to use must be active. However, this is not true for an incoming phone call. Whenever the router receives an incoming phone call, where the connection is using PAP or CHAP for authentication, the router looks for the incoming connection's name in its list of profiles. If it finds a match and the profile is active, it uses this profile. If the profile is inactive, the router will activate it for the connection and then deactivate it once the connection is broken. Inactive profiles, therefore, are very useful for situations where you want your 700 series router to handle incoming connections from various destinations but do not want your router making phone calls to these destinations.

16. **a.** The **set systemname** command changes the name of the router. This is then used with PPP's PAP and/or CHAP.

17. **b, c.** To assign an IP address and subnet mask to a LAN or user profile, use both the **set ip address** and **set ip netmask** commands.

18. **a.** To have the central site router challenge the 700 series router in one-way authentication, use the **set ppp auth incoming** command. The two parameters, **incoming** and **outgoing**, refer to the direction of the request for the

challenge. The **incoming** parameter sets the 700 router as a client, where the remote router (usually your corporate router) will initiate the challenge. The **outgoing** parameter, on the other hand, has the 700 router sending the challenge to the connecting router.

19. **b.** The **set ppp secret host** command assigns the password that the 700 router will use to authenticate the incoming connection. The **set ppp secret client** command assigns the password that the 700 router will use to authenticate to the destination router.

20. The **set number** *phone_number_to_dial* command assigns a phone number to a user profile.

21. **c.** To have your router dynamically acquire an IP address from the ISDN router that it is connecting to as well as use a default router, you will need use the following user profile command:

```
set ip route destination 0.0.0.0/0 gateway default_gateway's_IP_address
```

22. **e.** If you want to run a dynamic routing protocol across the WAN link, use the **set ip address**, **set ip routing on**, **set ip rip update periodic**, and **set bridging off** commands in your user profile.

23. A 700 series router can perform the function of a DHCP server or relay agent if it has at least software version 4.1 running. To configure the 700 series router as a relay agent, use the following system profile command:

```
set dhcp relay destination_IP_address
```

For the destination IP address, you can list a server's specific IP address or the directed broadcast address of a specific segment. Note that the DHCP relay agent performs the same function as the IP Helper feature of IOS-based routers.

24. **b.** As a DHCP server, the 700 series router can assign the client an IP address and subnet mask, a default gateway, a DNS and/or WINS server address(es), and a domain name. It cannot assign the client a hostname—this must be manually configured on the client.

Chapter 9 Solutions

1. **d.** Because of its extensive error correction and flow control capabilities at layers 3 and 2, X.25 incurs a lot of latency.

2. **c.** X.25 uses LAPB (Link Access Procedure Balanced) as a layer-2 protocol.

3. **d.** PLP supports five different modes: call setup, data transfer, idle, call clearing, and restarting. Call cancel is not a valid mode.

4. **b.** The LCI (Logical Channel Identifier) is the address of the VC. Note that the VC address is locally significant and can change on a segment-by-segment basis.

5. **a.** The frame structure that LAPB uses has its roots with ISO's HDLC frame format. One major difference between the two protocols is that LAPB supports error correction and flow control, whereas HDLC does not.

6. **b.** An X.25 DTE is a PAD. An example of this would be a Cisco router.

7. **d.** PAD stands for packet assembler/disassembler. The PAD performs three basic functions: First, when a user has data to send, the PAD segments the data to fit into X.25 packets—the disassembler part. Second, as X.25 packets are coming in, the DTE needs to extract the contents from the packets and place them into a buffer. Third, once it has received all the original packets (be they IP, IPX, and so on), the PAD must then reassemble all the pieces.

8. **c.** The X.25 DCE is the X.25 switch. Its main function is to pull in packets from the DTE and switch them out the correct destination port based on VC information inside the X.25 packet header.

9. **b.** SVCs are temporary connections, similar to the circuit-switched connections that a carrier's telephone network uses. When a user has information to send, his or her DTE requests a SVC to be set up. Once the SVC is operational, the user sends his information and, when finished, requests the SVC to be torn down.

10. **d.** Cisco routers support up to 4,095 X.25 VCs (PVCs or SVCs) on a single interface.

11. **a, c.** X.121 addresses are made up of two components: the Data Network Identification Code (DNIC) and the National Terminal Number (NTN). The DNIC, which is optional, identifies the country and carrier where the X.25 DTE resides. The DNIC is four decimal digits in length. The DNIC is made of two subfields—one is the global region, and the other is the X.25 carrier's number within that region. The NTN is the identifier used to uniquely identify your X.25 PAD in an X.25 carrier's network. The NTN can range from 8 to 10 or 11 decimal digits, depending on the providers' X.25 software on their switches.

12. **d.** X.121 addresses have a maximum length of 15 decimal digits. The DNIC consists of four digits, and the NTN is typically 8 to 10 or 11 digits in length.

13. **a, b.** Address resolution in X.25 requires manual configuration. If you are using PVCs, you specify this with the **x25 pvc** interface command. If you are using SVCs, you would use the **x25 map** interface command.

14. **c.** Cisco allows up to eight SVCs per protocol for each destination that you wish to connect to on an interface.

15. **a.** All the configuration of X.25 is done on your serial interfaces that connect to your X.25 provider. When configuring X.25 on a Cisco router, you must perform three required tasks in order for X.25 to work correctly: Set up your X.25 encapsulation, define your X.121 address provided by your carrier, and set up your statements for resolution to destination addresses.

16. **c.** To configure your router as an X.25 switch, first enter the interface and then enter the **encapsulation x25 dce** command.

17. **x25 address 30017898015763**

18. **d.** All resolution commands—**map** statements for SVCs and **pvc** statements for PVCs—are performed on the serial interface of the router. The syntax is as follows:

```
Router(config)# interface serial [module_number/]port_number
Router(config-if)# x25 map protocol protocol_destination_address
                  [protocol2 protocol_destination_address2]...
                  destination_x.121_address
                  [broadcast]
```

Therefore, the correct syntax is:

```
Router(config-if)# x25 map ipx 1301.1122.a579.89ef 30117123905891
```

19. **b.** By default, Cisco uses a packet size of 128 bytes at layer 3. You can change this with the following configuration commands:

```
Router(config)# interface serial [module_number/]port_number
Router(config-if)# x25 ips packet_size_in_bytes
Router(config-if)# x25 ops packet_size_in_bytes
```

Remember that X25 uses bidirectional VCs. These two commands allow you to create different packet sizes in both directions: **ips** represents the packet size for incoming packets, and **ops** represents the packet size for outgoing packets. The incoming size on one PAD must match the outgoing size on the destination PAD, and vice versa. Normally, you would configure the values the same. Valid values for this command are 16, 32, 64, 128, 256, 512, 1024, 2048, and 4096.

20. **c.** By default, the window size you can use ranges from 1 to 7. This is based on the modulo value of 8. You can create larger window sizes (up to 127) but must use the following interface command to do this:

```
x25 modulo 128
```

21. **b.** For SVCs, you can set limits to the ranges of VC numbers that can be used to identify your VCs. It is preferred that your PVC circuit numbers be lower than the ones that you will employ for your SVCs. The following commands are used to implement this restriction:

```
Router(config)# interface serial [module_number/]port_number
Router(config-if)# x25 lic circuit_number
Router(config-if)# x25 hic circuit_number
Router(config-if)# x25 ltc circuit_number
Router(config-if)# x25 htc circuit_number
Router(config-if)# x25 loc circuit_number
Router(config-if)# x25 hoc circuit_number
```

For these parameters to function correctly, both the PAD and switch must have the same restrictions defined. The preceding commands are broken into three categories: incoming SVC call setup requests by the switch (**lic** and **hic**), two-way SVC call setup requests by either the PAD or switch (**ltc** and **htc**), and outgoing SVC call setup requests by the PAD (**loc** and **hoc**). Here, "l" stands for *lowest*, and "h" stands for *highest* when representing VC numbers.

Chapter 10 Solutions

1. **a.** Each VC needs a unique address. In frame relay, this is called a *Data Link Connection Identifier* (DLCI). Like its sister protocol, X.25, a DLCI is locally significant. This means that the DLCI could be a different value on a segment-by-segment basis between the source and destination DTEs.

2. **b.** Annex D is specified by ANSI's T1.617 standard.

3. **c.** In the frame relay implementation in Cisco's routers, the status enquiry is generated once every 10 seconds. For every StEnq sent to the DCE, the DTE expects an acknowledgement back. Periodically, the DTE will ask for a status update of the VCs that terminate at its interface. This is called a *full status report*. Cisco routers do this on every sixth StEnq (60 seconds).

4. **b, d.** Before your DTE can start sending information across the VC, your DTE needs to know who it is connected to at the other end. To perform manual resolution, you use **frame-relay map** statements. Inverse-ARP, however, will do this resolution for you dynamically. When your DTE receives the full status report, for all VCs that are active, it will generate an inverse-ARP across those VCs. Inside the inverse-ARP it includes its layer-3 addressing information. When the destination DTE receives the inverse-ARP, it examines the VC that it came from—more specifically, the DLCI number of the VC—and the layer 3 address and adds this information to its resolution table.

5. **a.** The one required command is the **encapsulation frame-relay** command. For auto-sensing routers, the LMI configuration command can be omitted. Also, for routers that support inverse-ARP, **map** statements are not necessary.

6. **d.** The command to specify the encapsulation type to connect to non-Cisco routers is **encapsulation frame-relay ietf**. If you omit **ietf**, the encapsulation defaults to **cisco.**

7. **b.** To set the LMI type to Annex A, use the **frame-relay lmi-type q933i** interface command.

8. **a.** When inverse-ARP does not work, you will have to perform manual resolution by configuring a **frame-relay map** statement for each destination that you want to connect to.

9. **a.** The **show interfaces** command displays the LMI type, the DLCI that it uses, and the number of status enquiries sent by the router and the replies sent back by the switch.

10. **b, d.** To verify whether the DCE is sending full status reports, use either the **show frame-relay lmi** command and look at the "Num Update Status Rcvd" field or use the **debug frame-relay lmi** command.

11. **c.** The **show frame-relay pvc** command shows you the status of all the VCs on your router.

12. **d.** The **show frame-relay map** command will show information such as the layer-3 address and DLCI to use to get to a destination, the status of the VC and the interface it is associated with, whether or not broadcasts are allowed, and whether the resolution was dynamic or static for the VC.

13. **b, c.** With IPX, you can either use static routes or subinterfaces; IPX does not permit you to disable split horizon.

14. **b, d.** A subinterface is basically a logical interface that is associated with a physical one. You can have up to 256 subinterfaces associated with a single physical interface in IOS versions earlier than 12.x and up to 1,024 in version

12. x. The advantage of this approach is that you can assign a separate VC to each point-to-point subinterface, thus solving your split horizon problems. The problem of this type of subinterface, however, is that it uses a lot of network numbers. If your network is fully meshed, a multipoint (sub)interface is more manageable.

15. **d.** A point-to-point subinterface is like a dedicated leased line—there are only two devices at the ends of the VC. Each point-to-point connection is a separate subnet. Also, each subinterface will support only *one* VC. This type of design is very good for partially meshed or hub-and-spoke topologies, but it requires a separate subnet for each point-to-point link

16. **a, c.** If you are using inverse-ARP, you need to specify the DLCI used on the subinterface with the **frame-relay interface-dlci** command. If you are using manual resolution, this is not necessary—you need only the **frame-relay map** command.

17. **c.** Discard eligibility (DE) is used to indicate whether a frame relay frame is normal or high priority. This is indicated in the DE bit in the frame relay header.

18. **c.** To enable traffic shaping on your router, use the **frame-relay traffic-shaping** interface command. Any map-classes that you have configured and applied to either an interface or a VC will then have traffic shaping performed on them.

19. **b, c.** Backward Explicit Congestion Notification (BECN) is set by the destination DTE to indicate congestion (when it receives FECNs) to the source DTE or set by the switch to indicate congestion back to the source. The source DTE can then adjust its rate down to accommodate the congestion. Once the congestion disappears, the DTE can ramp the speed of the VC back up.

20. **d.** Cisco routers adjust their rate based on the presence or absence of BECNs, not FECNs.

Chapter 11 Solutions

1. **a.** X.25 is a primary WAN service. Backup interfaces, floating static routes with DDR, and Dialer Watch are used for the backup of WAN services.

2. **b.** In a traditional configuration, a backup interface is in a reserved state—this means that once you configure it, the interface can be used only for backup purposes. In other words, interesting traffic for DDR will *not* trigger a phone call on a backup interface. If you need it for other purposes, you will want to configure your setup with dialer profiles, which removes this restriction.

3. **a, d.** A floating static route is used in conjunction with DDR and a dynamic routing protocol. So that the router uses the dynamic routing protocol's routes, set the administrative distance of the static route higher than the routing protocol's.

4. **d.** RIP has an administrative distance of 120; the floating static route must have a higher value than this.

5. **d.** There is a problem with floating static routes when the primary path is restored. In this situation, the router will still use the floating static route as well as the primary path—load balancing across the two. It will not bring down the backup interface that the floating static route uses until your DDR idle-timer expires for interesting traffic. This is not a very good situation if the backup solution requires you to make a long distance telephone call because your floating static route interface could be up for minutes, if not hours, after your primary service is restored.

6. **b.** Dialer Watch is affected by what happens in the routing table. Dialer Watch monitors routes that you specify and will activate a DDR interface if these disappear. Floating statics do not monitor the routing table and a line is not brought up solely on the fact of a dynamic route disappearing. If a dynamic route disappears and a packet comes in destined for the network specified by the static, then the line is brought up.

7. **a.** Dialer Watch only works with the IP protocol stack.

8. **b, d.** The **backup interface** command specifies the interface you will use as your backup in case the primary interface fails. The **backup delay** command defines how long to wait before activating the backup interface when the primary fails and how long to wait to deactivate the backup interface when the primary is reactivated.

9. **b, c.** When configuring backup interfaces, only do so on one side of the WAN connection—do not do this on both sides. An interface that is specified as a backup interface can make a call *only* when the primary interface fails. It cannot make any other type of call, nor can it accept any incoming calls. If you configured backup interfaces on both sides, your backup solution would fail.

10. **c.** The **dialer load-threshold** is used only for dial-up links, whereas the **backup load** command is used with a mixture of links (dial-up and frame relay, for example).

11. **c.** Unlike the **dialer load-threshold** values of 1 to 255, the threshold with the **backup load** command is defined as a percentage.

12. **b, d.** For EIGRP and IGRP, you use the **variance** and **traffic-share balance** routing protocol commands to load-balance across unequal metric paths.

13. **a.** One problem of using legacy DDR employing a backup interface is that it precludes you from using the physical backup interface for other purposes. The advantage of using a dialer profile configuration over a standard configuration is that with a dialer profile, you associate the backup interface with a dialer interface, not a physical one. The dialer interface is, in turn, tied to a pool of physical interfaces. This gives you much more flexibility—with a small number of physical interfaces, you can back up a larger number of primary interfaces.

14. **c.** To verify that your backup interface is ready to perform its job, use the **show interfaces** command.

15. **a. ip route 172.16.10.0 255.255.255.0 192.168.1.1 200**

16. **f.** Answers a through d are required for creating redundancy in your WAN when using floating static routes. The use of a floating static route requires that you run a dynamic routing protocol over your primary link. The floating static route, which has a worse administrative distance than the routing protocol, will not be used unless the primary path fails. You will need to configure DDR for your backup connection, making sure that routing traffic will not trigger a phone call on it. One way to ensure this is to use **deny** entries in your **access-list**, which your **dialer-list** then specifies. Another option is to make sure that your backup interface is placed in a "passive" mode for your routing protocol. When the interface is configured this way, routing updates will not be sent out the interface, preventing the router from making a DDR phone call.

17. **a.** One of the interesting things about the Dialer Watch is that the router that is doing the "watching" does not have to have the primary WAN interface upon which the routes are arriving. It's required to have a dial-up interface and some other connection to the router with the primary WAN connection.

18. **b, c.** You must specify which routes or specific IP addresses you wish to monitor with the **dialer watch-list** command. You must also apply the **dialer watch-list** to the DDR interface with the **dialer watch-group** command. One optional interface command is to set a delay that determines how long the backup link will remain up once the primary WAN connection is back in action. This is done with the **dialer watch-disable** command.

Chapter 12 Solutions

1. **d.** Issues faced in queuing include choosing a queuing mechanism and determining the number of queues employed, the size of the queues, how information is placed into the queues, and how information is taken out of the queues and forwarded out of the interface.

2. **d.** You should implement queuing when you have limited bandwidth. Here are some questions you should examine when thinking about queuing as a congestion-management solution: Do you have time-sensitive applications such as SNA, video conferencing, or voice traffic? Are users complaining about the slowness of their interactive applications, such as Telnet and SNA sessions? Are you experiencing high bursts of data traffic, causing temporary congestion problems? Are your current bandwidth connections running at T1/E1 speeds or less? Do you even have a congestion problem?

3. **c.** Queuing will reorder the forwarding of traffic, thus incurring more delay for some types of traffic. It does *not* solve your congestion problems.

4. **b.** Queuing works best on T1/E1 lines or *slower*.

5. **b, c.** The CQ and PQ queuing mechanisms give you very specific control over processing, whereas FIFO and WFQ are completely left to the router to decide. With the CQ and PQ queuing mechanisms, you will have to perform the configuration manually, whereas FIFO and WFQ are done automatically.

6. **b.** Custom Queuing processes all its queues in a round-robin fashion.

7. **a, b.** Custom and Priority Queuing require manual configuration; WFQ and FIFO Queuing occur dynamically.

8. **d.** WFQ is the default queuing mechanism on all of Cisco's serial interfaces: It requires no configuration on your part to enable it. WFQ will dynamically sort traffic into *conversations*. A conversation is uniquely identified by the following components inside the packet: Source and destination address (network layer or MAC), protocol, protocol type, source and destination port numbers, QoS, and ToS. To allocate bandwidth, each conversation is assigned a weight that is used to differentiate between the low- and high-volume conversations. This is then used to determine how much bandwidth a conversation is allowed compared to other conversations that are using the serial interface. WFQ gives a higher preference to low-volume conversations over high-volume conversations; however, within the same conversation type, such as two Telnet sessions, the conversations are treated equally by the router.

9. **b.** The **fair-queue** interface Configuration mode command is used to define the maximum number of packets that a conversation can keep in the queue space. This is used to make sure one conversation does not use up all the queue space on the interface. This value defaults to 64 packets. You can set it from 1 to 512 messages.

10. **d.** CQ employs 17 queues, 0 through 16. Queue 0 is a reserved queue and is always processed first. This queue is referred to as the *system queue*. High-priority information, such as signaling packets (LMI for frame relay), keepalives, and other system information, is placed in this queue. Queues 1 through 16 are used for user traffic.

11. **b.** To build a Custom Queuing list to define your queuing policies, use the **queue-list** global Configuration mode commands.

12. **d.** To define a threshold for a queue in Custom Queuing, use the following command:

```
Router(config)# queue-list list_number queue queue_number
                    byte-count threshold_in_bytes
```

13. **a.** Only WFQ can dynamically adjust to changes in your traffic patterns; FIFO, PQ, and CQ cannot. Therefore, you will need to monitor Custom Queuing and Priority Queuing on an ongoing basis.

14. **d.** The high queue has the highest priority, and your most critical and delay-sensitive traffic should be placed here. The low queue has the lowest priority, and your least important delay-insensitive traffic should be placed here.

15. **b, c, d.** Traffic in the high-priority queue is always guaranteed to get serviced. There are no guarantees for the other queues. In other words, if the high-priority queue always contains packets, the other queues do not get serviced. Therefore, care must be taken when setting up your priority scheme to ensure that you don't inadvertently starve some of your important traffic that might be placed in a lower queue.

16. **d.** Once you have created your PQ list, you will need to activate it on your serial interface with the **priority-group** command. Once you have performed this, the router will process your traffic using your PQ list.

17. **b.** The default queue sizes for the high, medium, normal, and low priority queues are 20, 40, 60, and 80 packets, respectively.

18. **c.** Once you have configured your queuing policy, you will want to verify its operation. To examine the configuration, use the following **show** command:

```
Router# show queueing [custom|fair|priority]
```

Remember that **queueing** is misspelled by Cisco. You can optionally qualify the output of the command by listing the type of queuing policies that you wish to see, using either **custom** for CQ, **fair** for WFQ, or **priority** for PQ.

19. **a, b.** X.25 supports both payload and TCP header compression.

20. **b.** Link compression is used on point-to-point links using either HDLC, LAPB, or PPP as an encapsulation type on your serial interfaces. With link compression, the entire frame—header, payload, and trailer—are compressed. This type of compression is not supported in WAN environments that use VCs. The reason for this is that these environments need to see the header to make switching decisions—frame relay switches need to see the DLCI number, and X.25 switches need to see the VC address.

21. **c.** Cisco supports three types of link-compression algorithms. Stacker, developed by STAC Electronics, uses Lempel-Ziv, a compression algorithm based on a dictionary method. Predictor is a compression algorithm that is also based on a dictionary method. Cisco implements this in a proprietary fashion. Microsoft Point-to-Point Compression (MPPC) is used on dial-up (point-to-point) links between Cisco routers and Microsoft clients. Van Jacobson is used for TCP header compression.

22. **e.** Cisco's current header compression implementation supports PPP, HDLC, frame relay, ATM, and X.25 interfaces.

23. **a, b.** Software compression works well when a router has low CPU utilization—preferably below 50 percent. Software compression does not work well with modem compression and encryption.

Chapter 13 Solutions

1. **d.** RFC 1918 was developed to meet every company's growing address needs. RFC 1918 has set aside a range of addresses, called *private addresses*, for any company to use. There are three different private address spaces that have been set aside for use by anybody within a particular company: 10.0.0.0 to 10.255.255.255, 172.16.0.0 to 172.31.255.255, and 192.168.0.0 to 192.168.255.255.

2. **c, d.** RFC 1631 defines the process of translating private IP addresses to a public space address. This process is called *Network Address Translation*, or *NAT* for short. There are many reasons why you might want to, or need to, design a network with private addresses: Your ISP has not assigned you enough *public* addresses to give to all your computers, you are merging two networks together that have an overlapping address space (perhaps the two companies are using the same private address space), you have changed ISPs, where your new ISP will not support your old public address space, and because of the growing demands for resources on a critical machine, you need to duplicate those resources on redundant computers and spread the access requests that are sent to the original machine to all these redundant machines.

3. **a, b.** One of the obvious advantages of NAT is that it you no longer have to worry about your ISP assigning you enough public addresses. With one A class network, 16 B class networks, and 256 C class networks, you have over 17,000,000 private addresses at your disposal—more than enough for you addressing needs. And if you have to change ISPs, you will only have to reconfigure your NAT device instead of having to readdress your entire network. Also, because it is illegal to propagate packets with private addresses into the Internet, using private addresses provides additional security—all traffic leaving or entering your network will have to pass through your NAT device, thus giving you tight control over traffic patterns.

4. **a, b.** By performing NAT, additional delay is introduced into your traffic streams: Your NAT device will have to manipulate the addresses in the IP packet and possibly the port numbers in the TCP/UDP headers, as well as calculate a new CRC for the IP packet and, possibly, the TCP segment. Because NAT changes IP addresses, it becomes more difficult to troubleshoot problems—you really don't know whether the address you are examining is the real address of the machine. This, ironically, can create security problems. In some instances, certain applications may stop working when NAT is introduced into the data stream. Some applications use IP addresses instead of domain names, or some applications may embed IP addresses inside the data payload—which NAT does not translate. Sometimes the NAT device can handle this. Cisco's PIX firewall has the ability to change IP addresses embedded in the data of certain applications. In other instances, this can be overcome by static address mappings on the NAT device.

5. **a.** An inside local IP address is an end-station address located inside a private network with an address that is typically from the RFC 1918 address space. This type of address is seen only by other computers inside the private network.

6. **b, e.** Address overloading, sometimes referred to as *Port Address Translation*, or *PAT* for short, allows all the inside local IP addresses to share a single global IP address. With this ability, the translation router can handle thousands of machines with a single global IP address.

7. **a, c, d.** Cisco IOS routers support the following address translation features: NAT, PAT, traffic distribution, and overlapping networks.

8. **d.** Address translation devices can help out with an overloaded server that computers on the Internet are accessing on the inside of your network. Most people would assume that when your server becomes overloaded, you would have to upgrade it to handle the new load that Internet users are placing on it. Address translation provides an alternate and more flexible solution. Using

traffic distribution, users on the Internet send their traffic to a single inside global IP address. This single inside global IP address is represented by a group of inside machines, each with a unique inside local IP address.

9. **b, d.** NAT will not work with all types of IP communication. Some applications embed IP addresses in their data, which may cause problems when this information passes through the translation device, which, by default, is not looking for these types of situations. Types of traffic that typically cause problems are ICMP, encryption, SNMP, and routing protocols.

10. **a, b, c, d.** You need the **ip nat inside | outside source static** command(s) in order to define the static address translations. You must also specify the interfaces involved in the address translation with the **ip nat inside | outside** command(s).

11. **b, d.** You must specify which interface(s) is on the inside of the network and which interface(s) is on the outside of the network—the interface connected to the Internet. This is done with the **ip nat inside** and **ip nat outside** interface Configuration mode commands.

12. **ip nat inside source list 5 pool nat-pool**

13. **b.** Use the following command to set up the address overloading for your address translation router (note that the only difference between dynamic NAT and PAT is the **overload** parameter):

```
Router(config)# ip nat inside source
               list standard_IP_access_list_number
               pool NAT_pool_name overload
```

14. **ip nat pool nat-pool 200.200.200.1 200.200.200.1 netmask 255.255.255.0**

15. **b.** The configuration of traffic distribution, or *load distribution*, is similar to the configuration of dynamic NAT and PAT. For traffic distribution, three sets of commands are required. First, you need to specify the list of inside local IP addresses that will handle the traffic that is received from the outside world and is destined to one global IP address inside your network. This is done with the **ip nat inside pool** command, the same command used for PAT. The syntax of this command is as follows:

```
Router(config)# ip nat pool pool_name
               beginning_inside_local_IP_address
               ending_inside_local_IP_address
               prefix-length subnet_mask_length_in_bits
               type rotary
```

16. **c.** Once you have configured address translation, you will want to verify that it is working properly. The **show ip nat translations** command is used to list the address translations that the router has either statically configured or dynamically created.

17. **b, d.** With the 700 series of routers, only PAT is supported for address translation. This makes sense when you examine the role of the 700 series router—it is a SOHO (Small Office/Home Office) router with one PC, or possibly a handful of PCs, sitting behind it. In this scenario, a single public address is sufficient to represent the machines in the office when they access the Internet. If they have a resource that the Internet may want to access, such as a Web server, the 700 series supports a feature called *porthandler*. With porthandler, you can redirect traffic sent to a particular port of the public IP address to a particular machine on the LAN segment connected to the 700 series router.

18. **e.** Porthandler allows you to redirect traffic sent to a particular port of one of your public IP addresses to a particular machine on the LAN segment connected to the 700 series router.

19. **set ip pat on**

20. **set ip pat porthandler http 192.168.1.2**

Chapter 14 Solutions

1. **b, c, d.** CiscoSecure is built on a foundation of three components: a AAA (authentication, authorization, and accounting) server, a Netscape Fasttrack server, and a relational database management system (RDBMS). CiscoSecure is supported on both Windows NT and Sun Solaris Unix platforms. The database included with CiscoSecure is SQLAnywhere; however, CiscoSecure is compatible with any ODBC database interface, including Oracle and Sybase SQL Server.

2. **b.** For an additional layer of security, CiscoSecure can be integrated with other security products, such as token card servers. Cisco includes CryptoCard Authentication Server software (not hardware) with CiscoSecure, but other token card vendors are supported, including Security Dynamics Technologies, Axent Technologies, and Enigma Logics. Token cards are hardware devices that are synchronized with a central token card server. Generally, they display a PIN or key that a user enters, along with his username, when accessing the network.

3. **a.** Virtual profiles are an extension of PPP security for dial-up access. PPP has a limitation in that CHAP and PAP only perform authentication. Once a user passes the authentication, the user has access to the entire network. You could implement **access–lists** and other types of security features to limit the user

from gaining access to certain resources; however, the downside of this approach is that this type of restriction will affect all users. Virtual profiles overcome this limitation by allowing per-user configuration information to be applied to a specific user when he accesses the network. All the properties that can be associated with a physical interface, such as **access-lists**, addressing, queuing, and so on, can be applied to the virtual interface. When the user disconnects, this virtual interface is removed. Therefore, the properties of the physical interface can change based on the user who dials into it.

4. **d, e.** AAA contains three components: authentication, authorization, and accounting. Collectively, these three items are referred to as *AAA*.

5. **a.** Authentication checks a user's identification and verifies whether he can gain access to the network. Cisco has different mechanisms that can accomplish this. The access server/router can verify this information locally or forward it to a security server. If performed locally, the security check can be a local password on the access device or a username and password located in the local **username** database. If a security server is used, the user information—whether it be a static password, username and password, one-time password, or token card authentication—is passed from the access server/router to the security server for verification.

6. **d.** Authorization defines what the user is allowed to do once he gains access to the network. Authorization might restrict which networking services a user can access or which commands he can execute on a particular network resource. Virtual profiles restrict what resources a user can access (using **access-lists**), but they cannot restrict what a user can do once he has access to a particular resource (such as the type of commands the user can execute).

7. **c.** Accounting keeps a record of everything a user does and a timestamp of when the user performs his actions. This information can be used for many purposes—from keeping an audit trail to access damages or attempted break-ins, to keeping a record for billing purposes to charge a user for resources that have been used and/or consumed.

8. **a, b.** There are two basics modes in which a user can access your access server/router: character mode and packet mode. In character mode, the user is attempting to gain access to an EXEC shell, whether it be User or Privileged EXEC mode. In packet mode, the user is attempting to establish a network connection to the access device using a data link layer protocol such as PPP, ARAP (Apple dial-up client software), or NASI (NetWare dial-up client software).

9. **b, c.** Cisco supports two protocols for securing transmissions between the access server/router and the security server as well as how AAA should be implemented on the security server: TACACS+ and RADIUS.

10. **a, c.** When configuring access to the security server, you will probably set up four sets of commands, which involves defining access to the AAA server, defining authentication, defining authorization, and configuring accounting details. The definition of user policies (such as what they can do) is done on the security server.

11. **b.** When configuring TACACS+ access to your AAA security server, use the following three commands: **aaa new-model**, **tacacs-server host**, and **tacacs-server key**. The first command, **aaa new-model**, enables AAA on your access router. The second command, **tacacs-server host**, lists the IP address of your security server. The **tacacs-server key** command specifies the security key that is defined on the security server.

12. **d.** You can restrict who gains User EXEC mode access with login authentication. The global Configuration command used to define login authentication to the access router is **aaa authentication login**. This can be placed on lines such as the console or auxiliary lines, vty lines, or tty lines.

13. **c.** The **local** parameter uses the local **username** database on the access device by finding a match with the username and password in the **username** global Configuration command(s). This parameter is applicable for User EXEC, ARAP, PPP, and NASI types of access.

14. **c.** The first **aaa authentication login** command indicates that if a particular type of access does not define how security should be performed, the first type of authentication to be performed is to use the password specified with the **password** command on the vtys. Remember that methods are checked from left to right. In this example, the order would be **line** and then **tacacs+**.

15. **b.** In this example, the router will use the first method: the **enable secret** command's password.

16. **c.** For remote access, you can restrict users' access when they attempt to establish an analog or ISDN dial-up network session with your access router. To authenticate PPP sessions, use the **aaa authentication ppp** command. For Apple devices using Apple's remote-access software, use the **aaa authentication arap** command. For NetWare clients using Novell's remote-access software, use the **aaa authentication nasi** command.

17. **a.** Once a user has been successfully authenticated, you can then restrict what type of functions he can perform with the **aaa authorization** global Configuration mode command.

18. **a, b, c, d.** The types of access you can check for authorization include the following: The **network** parameter checks for authorization for any type of network request, including PPP, PPP NCPs, ARA (AppleTalk), and SLIP. The

exec parameter checks to see whether a user is allowed an EXEC shell. The **command** parameter checks to see whether a user can execute commands specified by the *level* parameter. The **config-commands** parameter checks to see whether a user can execute Configuration mode commands. The **reverse-access** parameter checks to see whether a user can perform a reverse telnet.

19. **b.** The **if-authenticated** parameter has the access router bypass authorization if the user has already been authenticated. The **if-needed** parameter applies to authentication, not authorization. This is used if the user has already established a login connection and then manually starts up PPP—in this case the use of the **if-needed** parameter would not cause another security check.

20. **b, c.** To track or keep an audit trail of a user's actions, you can enable AAA accounting. To set up accounting, use the **aaa accounting** global Configuration command. With this command, you have two different methods you can specify: **group tacacs+** and **group radius**.

21. **b.** The **system** parameter audits all system events not associated with a user, including the changing status of an interface, reloads, and so on, on the access server or router.

22. **b.** The **stop-only** accounting method parameter sends a "stop accounting" record only at the end of the user's process.

Appendix B
Objectives for Exam 640-505

Using ISDN and DDR Technologies to Enhance Remote Connectivity	Chapter
Identify when to use ISDN BRI and PRI services and select the service that best suits a set of given requirements	6, 8
Identify the Q.921 and Q.931 signaling and call setup sequences	6
Specify the commands to configure ISDN BRI and PRI	6, 8
Specify the commands to configure DDR	6, 8

Optimizing the use of DDR Interfaces	Chapter
Specify or select appropriate dialup capabilities to place a call	7
Specify the commands and procedures to configure rotary groups and dialer profiles	7
Specify the commands to verify proper dialer profile or rotary group configuration and troubleshoot an incorrect configuration	7

Using X.25 for Remote Access	Chapter
Specify the commands and procedures to configure an X.25 WAN connection between the central office and branch office	9
Specify proper X.121 addresses and the commands to assign them to router interfaces	9
Specify the commands and procedures used to verify proper X.25 configuration and troubleshoot incorrect X.25 configuration	9

Establishing a Dedicated Frame Relay Connection and Control Traffic Flow	Chapter
Specify the commands and procedures to configure a frame relay WAN connection between the central office and branch office	10
Specify the commands to configure subinterfaces on virtual interfaces to solve split horizon problems	10
Specify the commands to configure frame relay traffic shaping	10
Specify the commands and procedures to verify proper frame relay configuration and troubleshoot an incorrect configuration	10

Enabling a Backup to the Permanent Connection	Chapter
Specify the procedure and commands to configure a backup connection that activates upon primary line failure	11
Specify the procedure and commands to configure a backup connection to activate when the primary line reaches a specified threshold	11
Specify the procedure and commands to configure a dialer to function as backup to the primary interface	11

Managing Network Performance with Queuing and Compression	Chapter
Determine why queuing is enabled, identify alternative queuing protocols that Cisco products support, and determine the best queuing method to implement	12
Specify the commands to configure weighted-fair, priority, and custom queuing, and the commands and procedures used to verify proper queuing configuration, troubleshoot incorrect configuration, and effectively select and implement compression	12

Scaling IP Addresses with Network Address Translation	Chapter
Describe how NAT and PAT operate, specify the commands and procedures to configure NAT and PAT to allow reuse of registered IP addresses in a private network, and verify proper configuration of NAT and PAT with available Cisco verification commands	13

Using AAA to Scale Access Control in an Expanding Network	Chapter
Specify, recognize, or describe the security features of CiscoSecure and the operation of a CiscoSecure server, specify the commands and procedures to configure a router to access a CiscoSecure server and to use AAA, and specify the commands to configure AAA on a router to control access from remote access clients	14

Appendix C
Study Resources

Books

Held, Gilbert. *The Complete Modem Reference: The Technicians Guide to Installation, Testing, and Trouble-Free Communications.* New York, NY: John Wiley & Sons, 1996. ISBN: 047115457. This definitive guide to maximizing your modem connections closely examines the hardware, communication, and protocols involved in an analog connection.

Kessler, Gary C. and Peter Southwick. *ISDN Concepts, Facilities, and Services.* New York, NY: McGraw-Hill, 1997. ISBN: 0070342490. This book is an in-depth technical book describing the standards, implementation, and operation of ISDN in a broadband market.

Kumar, Balaji. *Broadband Communications: A Professional Guide to ATM, Frame Relay, SMDS, SONET, and B-ISDN.* New York, NY: McGraw-Hill, 1995. ISBN: 0070359687. This book provides a well-covered overview of differnet WAN solutions and their implementations.

Smith, Philip. *Frame Relay: Prinicples and Applications.* Reading: MA: Addison-Wesley, 1996. ISBN: 0201624001. This easy-to-read book explains, in layman's terms, the standards for frame relay as well as its operation.

Online Resources

Standards Bodies

www.ansi.org/ is the home site of ANSI, an international standards body.

www.arin.net/rfc/ is a site that contains the complete list of Request For Comments (RFCs).

www.itu.int/ is the home site of ITU-T, an international standards body formerly known as CCITT.

Modems

www.cisco.com/pcgi-bin/Support/PSP/psp_view.pl?p=Internetworking: ASYNC provides information on the configuration of modems for dialup.

ISDN

www.cisco.com/univercd/cc/td/doc/cisintwk/ito_doc/isdn.htm and

www.cisco.com/pcgi-bin/Support/PSP/psp_view.pl?p=Internetworking: ISDN are overviews of ISDN provided by Cisco.

PPP

www.cisco.com/univercd/cc/td/doc/cisintwk/ito_doc/ppp.htm and

www.cisco.com/pcgi-bin/Support/PSP/psp_view.pl?p=Internetworking: PPP provide an overview of the PPP protocol on Cisco's web site.

DDR

www.cisco.com/pcgi-bin/Support/PSP/psp_view.pl?p=Internetworking: DDR provides an overview of DDR on Cisco routers.

www.cisco.com/univercd/cc/td/doc/cisintwk/ics/cs002.htm provides case studies on DDR using Cisco routers.

www.cisco.com/univercd/cc/td/doc/product/software/ios120/ 12supdoc/dsqcg3/index.htm provides real "quick" solutions for dial-up on Cisco's routers.

www.cisco.com/warp/public/793/access_dial/index.html provides examples of configurations of DDR on Cisco's routers.

700 Series Routers

www.cisco.com/univercd/cc/td/doc/product/access/acs_fix/750/ index.htm provides information on the configuration of the 700 series routers.

www.cisco.com/warp/public/779/smbiz/service/configs/700_configs. htm and **www.cisco.com/warp/cpropub/67/sample.html** provide sample configurations of dialup for Cisco's 700 series routers.

www.cisco.com/warp/public/cc/pd/rt/700/ provides product information on Cisco's 700 series routers.

X.25

www.cisco.com/pcgi-bin/Support/PSP/psp_view.pl?p=Internetworking: X25 provides information on the theory and configuration of X.25 on Cisco's router products.

Frame Relay

www.cisco.com/pcgi-bin/Support/PSP/psp_view.pl?p=Internetworking: Frame_Relay provides information on the configuration of frame relay on Cisco's routers.

www.cisco.com/univercd/cc/td/doc/cisintwk/ito_doc/frame.htm provides an overview of frame relay.

Dial Backup

www.cisco.com/univercd/cc/td/doc/cisintwk/idg4/nd2010. htm#xtocid2988430 provides an overview of dial backup.

www.cisco.com/univercd/cc/td/doc/product/software/ios121/121cgcr/ dialts_c/dtsprt6/index.htm provides information on configuring dial backup solutions.

Queuing

www.cisco.com/univercd/cc/td/doc/cisintwk/ito_doc/qos.htm provides an overview of different Cisco queuing technologies.

www.cisco.com/univercd/cc/td/doc/product/software/ios121/121cgcr/ qos_c/qcprt2/index.htm provides information on configuring different queuing technologies on Cisco's router line.

Compression

www.cisco.com/univercd/cc/td/doc/product/software/ios121/121cgcr/ inter_r/irdacces.htm#xtocid2700941 provides information on configuring compression on Cisco routers.

Network Address Translation

www.cisco.com/pcgi-bin/Support/PSP/psp_view.pl?p=Internetworking: NAT provides information on the implementation of NAT on Cisco routers.

Security

www.cisco.com/pcgi-bin/Support/PSP/psp_view.pl?p=Internetworking: Radius provides information on the RADIUS security protocol.

www.cisco.com/pcgi-bin/Support/PSP/psp_view.pl?p=Internetworking: Tacacs_plus provides information on TACACS+ security protocol.

www.cisco.com/univercd/cc/td/doc/cisintwk/ics/cs003.htm provides an overview of security on Cisco's web site.

www.cisco.com/warp/public/cc/pd/sqsw/sq/index.shtml provides information on Cisco's security product, CiscoSecure.

Glossary

AAA

AAA contains three components: authentication, authorization, and accounting. Authentication checks a user's identification and verifies whether the user can gain access to the network. Authorization defines what the user is allowed to do once he gains access to the network. Accounting keeps a record of everything that the user does and a timestamp of when the user performs his actions.

access rate

Access rate is a frame relay term used to describe the clocked speed of the connection between the DTE and DCE (such as a T1).

address overloading

See *Port Address Translation*.

administrative distance

Each routing protocol is assigned an administrative distance, or *ranking*. This is used in situations where two routing protocols, perhaps a static route and IGRP, are telling your router information about the same network number. The router will choose the routing protocol that has the lowest administrative distance value.

asynchronous serial communication

Asynchronous serial communication uses the existing telephone network with its associated low cost. Asynchronous means *no synchronization* and therefore does not require sending and receiving idle characters. However, the beginning and end of each byte of data must be identified by start and stop bits. Asynchronous communication happens when using the existing dial-up telephone network and when a connection is made between two modems dialing the number associated with the other modem. These types of connections are suitable for low-speed access that occurs only periodically.

Asynchronous Transmission (AT) commands

The most basic commands used to configure and troubleshoot a modem are from the AT command set. The AT command set was originally developed by Hayes to work with its Smartmodem 300. The AT command set can be broken down into two different kinds of instructions: configuration commands and operation commands (usually called the *S-Registers*). Configuration commands include how to define flow control and set data compression, whereas the operations commands include how to dial a phone number or hang up the phone.

B channel

B channels are logical digital pipes that exist on a single ISDN line. Each B channel provides a 64Kbps clear channel. The term *clear* means that the entire bandwidth is available for data because call setup and other signaling is done through a separate D channel. B channels typically form circuit-switched connections. Just like a regular telephone connection, a B-channel connection is an end-to-end physical circuit that is temporarily dedicated to transferring data between two devices. The circuit-switched nature of B-channel connections, combined with their reliability and relatively high bandwidth, is what makes ISDN suitable for a range of applications, including voice, video, fax, and data. They can be used to transfer any layer-2 or higher protocols across a link. B channels are normally used for dial-on-demand connections, taking full advantage of the circuit-switched networks upon which they are based.

Backward Explicit Congestion Notification (BECN)

Backward Explicit Congestion Notification is a frame relay term used to describe the process by which either the destination DTE indicates congestion to the source DTE or the carrier switch indicates congestion directly back to the source DTE.

backup interface

A backup interface is an interface that is reserved as a backup in case your primary serial interface fails or the load on the primary interface exceeds a certain threshold. In this sense, it can serve two roles: It can provide your redundancy and can give you a bandwidth boost when your primary link becomes temporarily saturated.

Basic Rate Interface (BRI)

An ISDN BRI is the most basic ISDN interface. It provides a customer with two 64Kbps B channels and a single 16Kbps

D channel, all of which may be shared by numerous ISDN devices. It is the ideal service for homes and small offices, which, in the interest of controlling expenses, require a service that can integrate multiple communication needs (voice, video, data, and fax).

callback

Callback allows a router to initiate a circuit-switched WAN link to a second device and request that device to call it back. This can be configured for Async as well as ISDN. The second device (for example, a central site router) responds to the callback request by calling the device that made the initial call. Besides being used as an added security feature, callback is useful for minimizing costs. Callback provides centralized billing for synchronous dial-up services. It also allows you to take advantage of tariff disparities on both a national and an international basis. Because callback requires a circuit-switched connection to be established before the callback request can be passed, a small charge is always incurred by the router initiating the call that requests a callback. Ideally, for maximum security, the callback should occur on a different modem at the server end from the line used by the incoming call. When using ISDN, callback uses the D channel, which usually incurs no charge at all, whereas callback using modems will always incur a small charge while the authentication process occurs.

Challenge Handshake Authentication Protocol (CHAP)

CHAP is used to verify the identity of the peer using a three-way handshake. This is done upon initial link establishment and may be repeated any time after the link has been established. With CHAP, the authenticator (that is, the server) sends a randomly generated "challenge" string to the client, along with its hostname. The client uses the hostname to look up the appropriate secret, combines it with the challenge, and encrypts the string using a one-way hashing function. The result is returned to the server along with the client's hostname. The server now performs the same computation and acknowledges the client if it arrives at the same result. CHAP is more commonly used rather than PAP because it can encrypt the password. Each end of the link shares the same CHAP secret, and each end is given its own local name. The secret is used as an input variable to a "hashing" algorithm, which produces a *hash value*, which is sent across the link. This algorithm is called *Message Digest 5 (MD5)*. The other end uses the hash value to calculate a secret and compares it to its own secret; upon success, the other end sends back a new hash value. Once this has been successful, the authentication phase is complete.

Channel Service Unit (CSU)

This unit provides the interface to a channelized (T1/E1) circuit. It is common to find both the CSU and DSU in a single component.

character mode

In character mode, the user is attempting to gain access, via a dial-up connection to an EXEC shell, whether it be User or Privileged EXEC mode. Character mode is a term used in AAA.

chat script

Chat scripts are strings of text used to send commands for initializing modems, modem dialing, and logging into remote systems— although chat scripts are mainly used for dialing out on asynchronous lines. Each script is defined for a different event. The chat script is used by the router to send commands to the modem. It can send initialization strings each time the modem hangs up. It can send login information that a called system may require.

circuit switching

Circuit switching is a WAN switching method in which a dedicated physical circuit is established, maintained, and terminated through a carrier network for each communication session. The telephone companies' phone and ISDN networks are examples of circuit-switched networks.

CiscoSecure

CiscoSecure is a centralized security platform built on a foundation of three components: a AAA (authentication, authorization, and accounting) server, a Netscape Fasttrack server, and a relational database management system (RDBMS). CiscoSecure is supported on both Windows NT and Sun Solaris Unix platforms. The Netscape Fasttrack server provides a GUI interface for easy configuration and management and provides security for dial-up access and networking devices.

Clear To Send (CTS)

CTS is asserted by the modem (DCE) after receiving an RTS signal, indicating that the computer (DTE) can now transmit. When this signal is active, it tells the DTE that it can now start transmitting (on the Transmitted Data line). When this signal is "On" and Request To Send, Data Set Ready, and Data Terminal Ready are all "On," the DTE is assured that its data will be sent to the communications link. When "Off," it is an indication to the DTE that the DCE is not ready, and therefore data should not be sent.

Committed Burst Rate (BC)

Committed Burst Rate is a frame relay term used to describe the average rate (over a smaller time period than CIR) that a provider guarantees for a VC.

Committed Information Rate (CIR)

Committed Information Rate is a frame relay term used to describe the average rate over time that the provider guarantees for a VC.

Custom Queuing (CQ)

CQ allows you to allocate bandwidth based on traffic classifications—classifications that you have very strict control over. You determine what traffic is placed into a queue and then how the queue will be serviced. With this type of control, you can break up your allotted bandwidth, giving one type of traffic a certain amount of bandwidth compared to others. CQ employs 17 queues (0 through 16). Queue 0 is a reserved queue and is always processed first. This queue is referred to as the *system queue*. High-priority information, such as signaling packets (LMI for frame relay), keepalives, and other system information, is placed in this queue. Queues 1 through 16 are used for user traffic. In CQ, every queue is guaranteed to be serviced. The queues are processed in a round-robin fashion, starting with queue 0. After queue 0 is emptied, the router will then start processing queue 1. When processing a queue, the router will forward packets from the queue until it reaches the queue's threshold. Once a queue has been processed, the router proceeds to the next queue. It will process all the queues in order and then return to the system queue.

D channel

The D channel for ISDN is used mostly for administrative signaling, such as instructing the ISDN carrier to set up or tear down a call along a B channel, to ensure that a B channel is available to receive an incoming call or to provide the signaling information that is required for such features as caller identification. Depending on the ISDN service subscription, the D channel transmits at either 16Kbps (for BRI service) or 64Kbps (for PRI service). Unlike the B channel, which can function as a simple pipe, the D channel is associated with higher-level protocols at layers 2 and 3 of the OSI model, which form the packet-switched connections. The ITU-T layer-3 protocol specifications for use on the D channel are described within the Digital Subscriber Signaling System No. 1 (DSS1) network-layer definition. DSS1 is the network access signaling protocol for users connecting to ISDN. It includes the ITU-T Q.931 and Q.932 standards.

Data Carrier Detect (DCD or CD)

This control line is asserted by the modem, informing the computer that it has established a physical connection to another modem. It is sometimes known as *Carrier Detect* (CD). The DCE uses this line to signal the DTE that a good signal is being received (a *good signal* means a good analog connection that can ensure demodulation of received data). DCD and DSR work together.

Data Communications Equipment (DCE)

A DCE is a device, such as a modem, NT1, or CSU/DSU, that connects a DTE to a WAN. The DCE's primary responsibility is to either supply or derive clocking from its connected wire.

Data Link Connection Identifier (DLCI)

Each frame relay VC needs a unique address. In frame relay, this is called a *Data Link Connection Identifier* (DLCI). Like its sister protocol, X.25, the DLCI is locally significant. This means that the DLCI could be a different value on a segment-by-segment basis between the source and destination frame relay DTEs. It is the responsibility of the switch to handle this conversion of the DLCI number between the two segments.

Data Service Unit (DSU)

This unit interfaces between the CSU and the customer's equipment. It is common to find both the CSU and DSU in a single component.

Data Set Ready (DSR)

This signal line is asserted by the modem in response to a DTR signal from the computer. The computer will monitor the state of this line after asserting DTR to detect whether the modem is turned on.

Data Terminal Equipment (DTE)

A DTE is any end-station device, such as a computer or router, that is connected to a WAN.

Data Terminal Ready (DTR*)*

This signal line is asserted by the computer or router and informs the modem that the computer or router is ready to receive data. This signal must be "On" before the DCE can turn Data Set Ready "On," thereby indicating that it is connected to the communications link. The Data Terminal Ready and Data Set Ready signals deal with the readiness of the equipment, as opposed to the Clear To Send and Request To Send signals, which deal with the readiness of the communication channel.

When "Off," DTR causes the DCE to finish any transmission in progress and to be removed from the communication channel.

dedicated leased line

Dedicated leased lines are fixed connections that do not involve establishing a new connection each time the link is used. They are permanent end-to-end connections.

DHCP relay agent

The DHCP relay agent takes all DHCP client requests for addressing information and changes the destination address from a local broadcast to either a destination unicast address or a directed broadcast. It will then forward the DHCP request to a destination DHCP server to handle the addressing request. This is similar to the IP Helper feature of the IOS-based routers.

Dial-on-Demand Routing (DDR)

One of the most attractive features for both asynchronous and ISDN dial-up connections is DDR. DDR provides session control for WAN connectivity over circuit-switched networks, which in turn provide on-demand services and decreased network costs. DDR starts and stops connections based on "interesting traffic" or data that needs to be sent. DDR can also start a connection when a backup connection is needed or temporary additional bandwidth is required.

dialer interface

A dialer interface is a logical interface on a router used for DDR purposes with dialer profiles and rotary groups. A dialer interface configuration is a group of settings that a router uses to connect to a remote network. One dialer interface can use multiple dial strings (telephone numbers).

Each dial string can be associated with its own dialer **map-class**. The dialer **map-class** defines all the characteristics for any call to the specified dial string. For example, the dialer **map-class** for one destination might specify the amount of idle time as 4 seconds before calls are disconnected, and the **map-class** for a different destination might specify 12 seconds.

dialer profile

As with rotary groups, you can use dialer profiles to configure the router's physical interfaces apart from the logical configuration with parameters needed for making a call. In addition, these logical and physical configurations can be dynamically bound together on a per-call basis. The dialer profile becomes the recognized interface by the destination and not the physical serial or asynchronous interface, and all calls going to or from a destination subnetwork use the same dialer profile. Dialer profiles use dialer interfaces to accomplish this. The dialer interface uses one group of physical interfaces called a *dialer pool*. However, one physical interface can belong to multiple dialer pools. If you use dialer profiles to configure dial-on-demand routing (DDR), physical interfaces are configured only for encapsulation and the identification of the dialer pool or dialer pools to which the interface belongs. The other characteristics used for making calls, which would have been configured under the physical interface if there were no dialer interfaces, are defined in the **dialer map** of the dialer interface. If needed, there is a method for adding additional parameters in an extended optional **map-class**. The **map-class** acts as an extension to the **dialer map**, containing further call parameters.

Dialer Watch

Dialer Watch is a Cisco feature that builds upon dial backup by integrating it with special route-tracking capabilities that can overcome the problems of backup interfaces and floating static routes. Dialer Watch works hand-in-hand with your dynamic routing protocol. You will need to tell the router which routes are important to watch—those that are associated with your primary WAN interface. Dialer Watch then closely examines the contents of the routing table, keeping track of the "watched" routes that are deleted *and* added. If a watched route is deleted or does not exist in the routing table, Dialer Watch will activate your secondary interface. If your primary interface becomes active and your router relearns the original route from the primary interface, Dialer Watch will deactivate the secondary interface.

Discard Eligibility (DE)

Discard Eligibility is a frame relay term used to describe the prioritization of a frame relay frame as a normal- or low-priority frame.

Dynamic Host Configuration Protocol (DHCP)

DHCP is used to assign IP addressing information dynamically to end stations. This addressing information can include the IP address, subnet mask, default gateway address, DNS server address, and WINS server address. DHCP makes it easier for administrators to administer their address space(s).

Electronic Industries Association and the Telecommunications Industry Association (EIA/TIA)

The EIA/TIA is a standards body responsible for developing standards for telecommunications wiring within buildings. It is responsible for the definition of the wire types to be used, the connectors on the wires, and the interfaces that they attach to. Some common standards are EIA/TIA-232 and EIA/TIA-449.

EIA/TIA-232

The EIA/TIA-232 standard supports unbalanced circuits at signal speeds up to 64Kbps. The EIA/TIA-232 serial transition cable has a DB-60 connector for connection to a Cisco serial port. The opposite end has a DB-25 connector. The DB-25 connector can be male for DTE or female for DCE. This type of connection is commonly deployed between a DTE and a modem.

EIA/TIA-422

The EIA/TIA-422 is an electrical specification that allows communications speeds of up to 10Mbps at distances up to 40 ft. (12 m) or communications speeds of 100Kbps at distances up to 4,000 ft. (1,222 m). These speeds are possible because EIA/TIA-422–specified balanced circuits.

EIA/TIA-449

The EIA/TIA-449 standard was intended to replace the EIA/TIA-232 standard, but it was not widely adopted primarily because of the large installed base of DB-25 hardware and because of the larger size of the 37-pin EIA/TIA-449 connectors, which limited the number of connections possible (fewer than are possible with the smaller, 25-pin EIA/TIA-232 connector). The EIA/TIA-449 standard, which supports balanced and unbalanced transmissions, is a faster (up to 2Mbps) version of the EIA/TIA-232 standard that provides more functions and supports transmission over greater distances.

EIA/TIA-530

The EIA/TIA-530 standard, which supports balanced transmission, provides the increased functionality, speed, and distance of EIA/TIA-449 on the smaller, DB-25 connector used for EIA/TIA-232. Like EIA/TIA-449, EIA-530 refers to the electrical specifications of EIA/TIA-422 and EIA/TIA-423. Although the specification recommends a maximum speed of 2Mbps, EIA-530 is used successfully at 4Mbps or faster speeds over short distances. The EIA-530 serial transition cable has a DB-60 connector for connection to a Cisco serial port. The opposite end has a DB-25 connector. The DB-25 connector can be male for DTE or female for DCE.

Excessive Burst Rate (BE)

Excessive Burst Rate is a frame relay term used to describe the fastest rate, at any given moment, that the provider will service the VC.

First-In, First-Out Queuing (FIFO)

FIFO queuing does not reprioritize any of your traffic. When traffic traverses the backplane of the router and reaches your serial interface, it is queued up in the order upon which it arrives. In other words, the first packet that reaches the interface will be the first packet sent across your WAN. All the packets are treated equally.

floating static route

A floating static route is usually used in conjunction with a dynamic routing protocol. The floating static route is only used if the primary route fails. One advantage this provides over dial backup is that, in this situation, the router is monitoring layer-3 routing information. If your router loses sight of its WAN neighbor and its associated network numbers, your router can use the backup static route. Basically, a floating static route is a static route that has a lower preference over the dynamic routing protocol running on the router.

Forward Explicit Congestion Notification (FECN)

Forward Explicit Congestion Notification is a frame relay term used to describe the process by which the carrier switch(es) indicates congestion to the destination DTE device.

frame relay

Frame relay is a data service specified by ITU-T that defines how a DTE and DCE interact and transfer frames containing user and management information. Frame relay is a layer-2 protocol in the OSI model and has been designed to be simple and effective. It is based on the core aspects of the link-access procedure for the D channel (LAPD), in which error detection is carried out in the network, but no acknowledgment frames are exchanged between nodes in the network. If a frame is erroneous, it is discarded; the retransmission is done by the end system. This reduces processing at the nodes and thus provides a higher speed than the X.25 network.

full status report

Periodically, a frame relay DTE will ask for a status update of the VCs that terminate at its interface. This is called a *full status report*. Cisco routers do this on every sixth status enquiry (60 seconds). When the DCE (switch) receives this update, it responds back with the statuses of the different VCs connected to the DTE. If a VC is added or deleted (or operational or nonoperational), the DCE passes this information on to the DTE.

functional devices

Functional devices are definitions for specific tasks performed in an ISDN connection. These functional devices reside on the user side of the connection. Actual ISDN equipment often embodies multiple functional devices but may include only one.

header compression

Header compression uses the Van Jacobson algorithm defined in RFC 1144. Currently, only TCP is defined. TCP headers are typically 40 bytes in length, most of which is repetitive or predictable in nature. The Van Jacobson algorithm, using intelligent prediction and pattern-finding processes, can reduce the size of the header to 2 or 4 bytes in length in the most optimal of conditions. Cisco's current header compression implementation supports PPP, HDLC, frame relay, ATM, and X.25 interfaces.

I.430

The ITU-T I.430 describes the physical layer and lower data link layers of the ISDN BRI interface. The specification defines a number of ISDN reference points between the telco switch and the end system. The protocol also contains descriptions of the devices at the end system, which are called ISDN *functional devices*.

inside global IP address

An end-station address located inside a private network with a publicly registered IP address.

inside local IP address

An end-station address located inside a private network with an address from the RFC 1918 address space.

Integrated Services Digital Network (ISDN)

ISDN stands for *Integrated Services Digital Network.* The term represents a telecommunications service package, consisting of digital facilities from end to end. In most cases, analog dial-up service providers will not guarantee support for specific data rates even if users purchase analog modems capable of handling up to 56Kbps transmission rates. Little or no diagnostic information is available from the service provider other than normal testing performed on residential and business lines. Also, line quality varies widely, and the amount of noise on a line has a direct bearing on the maximum data-transmission rate. ISDN is completely digital. Digital circuits are typically characterized by very low error rates and high reliability. ISDN can support voice, video, and data transmissions. ISDN uses a circuit-switching network. Individual channels can transmit at speeds up to 64Kbps, and these channels can sometimes be combined to support even higher speeds. In general, ISDN has been more rapidly deployed and accepted in countries such as Australia, France, and Japan, with the U.S. lagging somewhat behind. ISDN is now available in essentially all major metropolitan areas in the U.S., but not in many outlying areas. ISDN connections, like asynchronous serial connections, are circuit-switched connections. They are intended to compete with the analog-based POTS by providing voice, data, and other traffic across a reliable digital telephone network. Logically, ISDN consists of two types of communications channels: bearer service B channels, which carry data and services at 64Kbps, and a single D channel, which carries signaling and control information that is used to set up, monitor, and tear down calls.

inverse-ARP

Frame relay supports a dynamic address-resolution process, alleviating the need to configure manual resolution statements. In frame relay, this process is called *inverse-ARP.* When your DTE receives the full status report, for all VCs that are active, it will generate an inverse-ARP across those VCs. Inside the inverse-ARP, your DTE includes its layer-3 addressing information. When the destination DTE receives the inverse-ARP, it examines the VC that it came from—more specifically, the DLCI number of the VC—and the layer-3 address and adds this information to its address resolution table.

Link Access Procedure, Balanced (LAPB)

The X.25 protocol stack uses Link Access Procedure, Balanced (LAPB) as its data-link–layer protocol. This is used to provide communication between two directly connected devices, such as a router and a carrier's X.25 switch. LAPB also defines the frame type to use, which it heavily borrows from ISO's HDLC frame format. LAPB provides a reliable connection—it uses error *and* flow control to maintain the integrity of the information between the two connected devices.

link compression

Link compression is used on point-to-point links using either HDLC, LAPB, or PPP as an encapsulation type on your serial interfaces. With link compression, the entire frame—header, payload, and trailer—are compressed. This type of compression is not supported in WAN environments that use VCs. The reason for this is that these environments need to see the header to make switching decisions—frame relay switches need to see the DLCI number, and X.25 switches need to see the VC address. If you used link compression on this, the switch would drop the traffic because it wouldn't know how to switch it. Therefore, only point-to-point connections are supported.

Link Control Protocol (LCP)

In order to be portable to a wide variety of environments, PPP provides the Link Control Protocol (LCP) for establishing, configuring, and testing the data link connection. LCP is used to automatically agree upon the encapsulation format options, handle varying limits on sizes of packets, detect common misconfiguration errors, and terminate the link. Other optional facilities provided are authentication of the identity of its peer on the link and determination of when a link is functioning properly and when it is failing. LCP is responsible for opening, configuring, and terminating the link. In addition to providing procedures for establishing, configuring, testing, and terminating data link connections, LCP also negotiates other nondefault LCP options, such as Maximum Receive Unit (MRU), Magic Number, Link Quality Monitoring (LQM), and authentication. MRU defines the optimal packet size for both ends of the serial link, which increases the transmission efficiency of the link. Magic Number identifies each peer so that loopback conditions can be recognized and corrected. Additionally, Link Quality Monitoring (LQM) can be configured along with Password Authentication Protocol (PAP) or Challenge Handshake Authentication Protocol (CHAP). The peer may be authenticated after the link has been established, using the authentication protocol decided on. If authentication is used, it must take place prior to starting the network-layer protocol phase.

Local Management Interface (LMI)

The frame relay signaling protocol is referred to as *LMI*. The three different standards for LMI are: *Cisco*, developed jointly by Cisco, DEC, Nortel, and StrataCom, now owned by Cisco (this is sometimes referred to as the "gang of four" protocol); *Annex D*, specified by ANSI's T1.617 standard; and *Annex A*, specified by ITU-T's Q.933 standard. LMI serves two basic purposes. First, it is used to ensure that communication between the DTE and DCE is ongoing. In this sense, it functions as a keepalive. Second, it is used by the DTE to gather status information about the VCs that are connected to it.

Microcom Networking Protocols (MNP)

Microcom, a maker of modems, designed error-checking protocols and compression protocols that many modems support. Microcom Networking Protocols (MNP) 1 through 4 are error-checking protocols, whereas MNP-5 is a compression protocol. MNP-5 modems include at least some of the MNP-1-4 error-checking protocols (usually 4). Some of these protocols are included in the ITU standards.

modem

A modem converts digital signals from your computer into audible tones, which can be transmitted over ordinary analog phone lines. This process is called *modulation*. On the receiving end, a modem demodulates the analog signals arriving over the phone line into electrical signals, which are then fed to the computer. MOdulation and DEModulation accurately describe what modems do.

modemcap database

Modem autoconfiguration is used to automate the configuration of modems attached to a Cisco Access Server. Cisco Access Servers come with a number of preconfigured initialization strings for some of the most commonly used modems. These preconfigured initialization strings are stored in the modemcap database. Cisco IOS maintains a set of built-in modemcaps for various internal and external modems. Each modemcap database entry uses the specific vendor's own unique set of commands that is represented within a set of attributes.

Multilink PPP (MLP)

The Multilink PPP Protocol (RFC 1717) is a standardized extension of the Point-to-Point (PPP) standard. It allows you to combine channels into a "multilink bundle" so that data can be sent at higher rates and it uses packet sequencing to order packets and ensure compatibility between manufacturers of internetworking equipment. You may also enable a feature known as *packet fragmentation*, where larger individual packets are chopped into smaller fragments. MLP works by splitting and reassembling upper-layer protocol data units (PDUs) between the participating devices. That is, datagrams are split, sequenced, transmitted, and reassembled. PPP Multilink is advantageous because it ensures packet ordering. It also guarantees compatibility with other vendors' equipment because it is an open standard. Packet fragmentation over a number of links is beneficial because it reduces latency (the length of time a packet waits to receive an acknowledgement from the other end of the link), which decreases transit times and therefore speeds up transmission.

Network Address Translation (NAT)

RFC 1631 defines the process of translating private IP addresses to a public space address. NAT maps one IP address to another IP address—a one-to-one mapping. It is typically used when devices outside your network want to access a specific machine on the inside, such as an email or Web server.

Network Control Protocols (NCP)

The last component of PPP involved in the connection negotiation process is the Network Control Protocols (NCPs). After the link has been established and optional facilities have been negotiated as needed by the LCP, PPP must send NCP packets to choose and configure one or more network-layer protocols. NCPs are a series of independently defined protocols that encapsulate network-layer protocols such as TCP/IP, DECnet, AppleTalk, IPX, and XNS. Each NCP has individual requirements for addressing and advertising connectivity for its network-layer protocol. Each NCP is defined in a separate RFC. Future protocols can be supported by defining new NCPs. NCP opens, configures, and terminates network-layer protocol communication—for example, IP, IPX, AppleTalk, and DECnet. Both LCP and NCP operate at layer 2.

Network Module (NM)

A network module is inserted into its available slot, and it is larger and can contain more interfaces than a WAN Interface Card (WIC). WICs typically have one or two interfaces, whereas NMs may have many interfaces (and these interfaces can be WAN, LAN, or a mixture of the two types).

Network Processor Module (NPM)

A network processor module is much like a network module (NM) but includes more circuitry, which is used for supplementary processing power that assists the router's central processing unit (CPU).

Network Termination 1 (NT1)

The NT1 represents the boundary of the ISDN network from the end-user side. An NT1 is a device that physically connects the customer site to the telephone company local loop. Because the ISDN line doesn't provide power as an analog line does, the NT1 also includes the power function for operating the ISDN line. Each BRI access has only one NT1 device. An NT1 can be embodied in a standalone device or included in a specific device. For PRI access, the NT1 is a CSU/DSU device, whereas for BRI access, the device is simply called by its reference name, NT1. It provides a 4-wire connection to the customer site and a 2-wire connection to the network. In Europe, the NT1 is owned by the telecommunications carrier and considered part of the network. In North America, the NT1 is located on the customer premises.

Network Termination 2 (NT2)

An NT2 device provides customer site switching, multiplexing, and concentration, such as a PBX for voice and data switching in an ISDN environment. An NT2 device is not needed in every installation and will most likely be used with PRIs rather than BRIs. NT2s are needed for PRI multiplexing. The NT2 works with the NT1 and is on the customer side of the NT1.

oversubscription

Oversubscription is a frame relay term used to describe a situation in which the sum of the CIR rates of all your VCs on an interface exceeds the access rate of that interface. In this situation, you are betting that all of your VCs will be be fully used simultaneously.

outside global IP address

This is an end-station address located outside the private network with a publicly registered IP address.

Packet Layer Protocol (PLP)

The X.25 (or PLP) layer is responsible for managing circuits between the two DTEs at layer 3 of the OSI reference model.

Packet Assembler/Disassembler (PAD)

The X.25 DTE is called a *Packet Assembler/ Disassembler* (PAD). This name defines the basic function of the X.25 DTE. The PAD performs three basic functions: First, when a user has data to send, it segments that data to fit into X.25 packets—the disassembler part. Second, as X.25 packets are coming in, the switch needs to extract the contents from the packets and place them into a buffer. And third, once it has received all the original packets (be they IP, IPX, or some other type), the PAD must then reassemble all the pieces.

packet mode

In packet mode, the user is attempting to establish a network connection to the access device using a data link layer protocol, such as PPP, Appletalk Remote Access Protocol (ARAP is Apple's proprietary dial-up solution), or NetWare Asynchronous Services Interface (NASI is NetWare's proprietary dial-up solution). Packet mode is a AAA term.

packet switching

Packet switching in a WAN environment supports the multiplexing of multiple connections, called *virtual circuits* (VCs), on a single physical line. Packet-switched connections use synchronous serial connections. They usually share bandwidth in the carrier's network with other companies VCs and are therefore less costly than leased lines.

Password Authentication Protocol (PAP)

PAP provides a simple method for a remote node to establish its identity using a two-way handshake. This is done only upon initial link establishment. After the PPP link establishment phase is complete, a username/password pair is repeatedly sent by the remote node across the link until authentication is acknowledged or the connection is terminated. Passwords are sent across the link in clear text, and there is no protection from playback or trial-and-error attacks. The remote node is in control of the frequency and timing of the login attempts. When a connection is established, each end can request the other to authenticate itself, regardless of whether it is the caller or the callee. A PPP device can ask its peer for authentication by sending yet another LCP configuration request identifying the desired authentication protocol. PAP works basically the same way as the normal login procedure. The client authenticates itself by sending a username and password to the server, which the server compares to its secrets database. This technique is vulnerable to eavesdroppers, who may try to obtain the password by listening in on the serial line, and to repeated trial-and-error attacks.

payload compression

Payload compression compresses only the payload of the frame—the header and trailer are left intact. This type of compression is most often used in VC switching environments such as X.25, frame relay, SMDS, and ATM. In these environments, the VC switches need to see the headers of the frames in order to make their switching decisions. They also need to see the trailer, which typically carries the checksum of the frame.

Permanent Virtual Circuit (PVC)

A PVC is similar to a dedicated leased line. Because the circuit already exists, the transfer of data can occur at any time. One disadvantage that SVCs have over PVCs is that they have additional latency because they must initially set up a VC before transferring data. However, PVCs usually cost more and therefore should be used only when you are constantly moving information between two sites.

Plain Old Telephone System (POTS)

POTS is the traditional analog telephone network that people use every day to place telephone calls.

Point-to-Point Protocol (PPP)

PPP originally emerged as an encapsulation protocol for transporting IP traffic over point-to-point links. PPP also established a standard for the assignment and management of IP addresses, asynchronous (start/stop) and bit-oriented synchronous encapsulation, network protocol multiplexing, link configuration, link quality testing, error detection, and option negotiation for such capabilities as network-layer address negotiation and data-compression negotiation. PPP supports these functions by providing an extensible Link Control Protocol (LCP) and a family of Network Control Protocols (NCPs) to negotiate optional configuration parameters and facilities. PPP is based on the High-Level Data Link Control (HDLC) protocol and provides a standard for sending data over data terminal equipment (DTE) and data communications equipment (DCE) interfaces, such as V.35, T1, E1, HSSI, EIA-

Glossary

232-D, and EIA-449. PPP can also simultaneously transmit multiple protocols across a single serial link, eliminating the need to set up a separate link for each protocol. PPP is also ideal for interconnecting dissimilar devices, such as hosts, bridges, and routers, over serial links. For example, a standalone TCP/IP host can communicate with a router across a serial PPP link. As a universal standard, PPP enables multivendor interoperability across serial links, dedicated links, dial-up links, and/or switched ISDN links, traditionally restricted to equipment supplied by the same manufacturer. PPP was first proposed as a standard in 1990 to replace an older de facto standard known as SLIP (Serial Line Internet Protocol), which requires links to be established and torn down manually. However, unlike SLIP, which supports only IP, PPP is not limited in protocol support. PPP provides the flexibility to add support for other protocols through software upgrades. In addition to IP, PPP supports other protocols, including Novell's Internetwork Packet Exchange (IPX) and DECnet. Point-to-Point Protocol (PPP) is a complete specification for transmitting datagrams between data communications equipment from different manufacturers over dial-up and dedicated serial point-to-point links. It is a recommended standard of the Internet Advisory Board (IAB) and is represented by a number of RFCs (Request for Comments) produced by the Point-to-Point Protocol Working Group.

Port Address Translation (PAT)

All inside devices are translated to one public IP address, where each inside machine is given a different source port number for uniqueness. This is used to help conserve your public address space assigned to you by your ISP. PAT is sometimes referred to as *address overloading*.

Porthandler

Porthandler is a feature of the 700 series routers. You can redirect traffic sent to the 700 series router that is destined for a particular port and forward it to a computer on the LAN segment of the 700 router.

predictor compression

Predictor examines data to see whether it is already compressed and then sends it. It does not waste time compressing data that is already compressed. Predictor tends to be more memory intensive and less CPU intensive.

Primary Rate Interface (PRI)

ISDN PRI includes one 64Kbps D channel and 23 64Kbps B channels in North America, and 30 64Kbps B channels in Europe. The number of B channels is limited to the size of the standard line used in the region (T1 in North America and E1 in Europe). There is also a single 64 Kbps D channel used for signalling.

Priority Queuing (PQ)

PQ gives you control over how traffic is to be prioritized before it is sent out of your serial interface. You define a set of queuing policies that defines your traffic prioritization. With PQ, you are given four queues: high, medium, normal, and low. The high queue has the highest priority and is where your most critical traffic should be placed. The low queue has the lowest priority and is where your least important traffic should be placed. Traffic in the high-priority queue is always guaranteed to get serviced. There are no guarantees for the other lower-priority queues.

private addresses

RFC 1918 has set aside a range of addresses, called *private addresses*, for any company to use. Three different private address spaces have been set aside for use by anyone within a local company: 10.0.0.0 through 10.255.255.255, 172.16.0.0 through 172.31.255.255, and 192.168.0.0 through 192.168.255.255. There are many reasons why you might want to, or need to, design a network with private addresses: Your ISP does not assign you enough public addresses to assign to all your computers, you are merging two networks together that have an overlapping address space (perhaps the two companies are using the same private address space), or you have changed ISPs, and your new ISP will not support your old public address space. However, when using private addresses, you cannot forward these packets to a public network—you will first have to perform address translation on them.

profiles (700 series routers)

The 700 series use profiles to perform configuration tasks that are necessary to pass traffic between the Ethernet LAN interface and the ISDN WAN interface. Profiles are grouped sets of commands that allow you to customize your connections to different destinations. There are four different types of profiles, with a possible total of 20 different profiles in the 700 series routers: LAN profile, internal profile, system profile, and two types of dialup profiles: standard and user. The LAN profile defines how information is passed to and from the Ethernet interface. There is only one LAN profile. The internal profile is used to pass traffic through the bridge/route engine between the LAN and ISDN BRI interface. There is only one internal

profile. The system profile defines system-level configurations that affect the router as a whole. There is only one system profile. The standard profile defines a default configuration connection for ISDN dial-up. There is only one standard profile. The user profiles define user-configured connections for ISDN dial-up. You can have up to 16 user profiles. A better way to view profiles and their usage is to examine how the router processes information between the LAN and WAN interfaces. The LAN profile is used to handle all traffic to/from the Ethernet port. All changes performed on this profile affect only the LAN interface. The standard and user profiles are used to handle all traffic to/from the ISDN BRI WAN interface. If traffic meets the criteria for a destination specified by a user profile, the router uses the user profile to process the traffic; otherwise, it uses the standard profile. To move traffic between the LAN and WAN profiles, the internal profile is used. It handles all routing and/or bridging functions between these two sets of profiles.

Public Switched Telephone Network (PSTN)

PSTN is the traditional analog circuit-switched telephone system that people use when they make telephone, fax, or modem calls.

Q.921

The ITU-T Q.921 recommendation defines layer 2 for ISDN lines. In the OSI reference model, layer 2 provides for procedures established to maintain communication between two network components. In the case of ISDN, the two components are the ISDN terminal (for example, a router) and the ISDN switch. This means that ISDN terminals are in constant communication with the ISDN switch. Q.921 defines the frame structure of the data packets, the format of the fields in the frame, and procedures known as *Link Access Procedures D Channel* (LAPD). The LAPD procedures describe flags, sequence control, flow control, retransmission, and so on. Therefore, Q.921 can also be referred to as *LAPD*. Also, LAPD is almost identical to the X.25 LAP-B protocol.

Q.931

Q.931, defined by ITU-T, is the call-control signal protocol component for network access for users connecting to ISDN. This layer-3 signaling protocol is transferred on the D channel using Link Access Procedure-D channel (LAPD), a layer-2 HDLC-like protocol. This layer 3 protocol is responsible for the actual setup and teardown of ISDN calls. Q.931 defines the layer-3 specifications for ISDN. Actually, the ISDN network layer is specified by the ITU Q series documents Q.930 through Q.939. Layer 3 is used for the establishment, maintenance, and termination of logical network connections between two devices. The emphasis here is on the word *logical*. The network layer provides procedures to make end-to-end connections on the network. Remember that the ISDN connections established are for circuit-switched voice and data connections. Connections that involve Q.931 procedures use packetized messages to initiate, monitor, and release circuit-switched connections. These call control messages are relayed between the ISDN terminal and the ISDN switch as the "information" part of the Q.921 information frame. Each message can be identified by type. The Message Type is a single byte (octet) that indicates what type of message is being sent/received. There are four general categories of messages that might be present: Call Establishment, Call Information, Call Clearing, and Miscellaneous.

R reference point

The R reference point lies between the Terminal Equipment 2 (TE2) device and a terminal adapter. There are no specific standards for the R reference point, so the TA manufacturer determines and specifies how a TE2 and TA communicate with each other.

Remote Access Dial-In User Service (RADIUS)

RADIUS is a standards-based protocol based on a client/server system that allows for the reliable and secure delivery of AAA information between the security server and access server/router. RADIUS also defines the implementation of AAA on a security server. Typically, the server code is freeware. One problem with RADIUS is that many proprietary extensions have been added to it because of its "free" nature, making implementation of the protocol difficult in a mixed-vendor environment. Cisco supports certain RADIUS extensions in its CiscoSecure security server.

Request To Send (RTS)

This signal line is asserted by the computer (DTE) to inform the modem (DCE) that it wants to transmit data. If the modem decides this is okay, it will assert the CTS line. When CTS is asserted by the modem, the computer will begin to transmit data. The DCE will receive data from the DTE and transmit it to the communication link.

reverse telnet

Reverse telnet is a telnet that sets up a data connection to one of the line connections on the router. This is normally done in order to configure an external device such as a modem attached to a serial interface. Typically, telnet uses port 23 for communication. Reverse telnets on Cisco routers have port numbers greater than 23. To perform a reverse telnet, you must specify the appropriate port number of the line that you wish to establish communications with. Cisco's nomenclature is to set the port number to 2000 plus the number of the line, where the console is 0 and the physical lines are numbered after this. The auxiliary port number is the number after the last line number.

rolled cable

In order to reverse the pinouts on the connectors, you can change the pins in one of two locations: in the cable or in the physical interface. When the pins have been changed through the cable, it is called a *rolled cable*. When it is implemented in the adapter, it is called a *rolled adapter*. Because most Cisco products come with a cable with RJ-45 connectors at both ends and either a RJ-45-to-DB25 or RJ-45-to-DB9 adapter, you need to be careful that you don't mix a rolled cable with a rolled adapter. Two rolled devices equal a straight device, and you would end up with what you started with—a DTE-to-DCE cable. Also, when connecting a DTE to a DCE, you do not use rolled cables or adapters. Therefore, you need to be careful of which adapter you use.

rotary group

When you use a single interface with multiple **dialer map**s, competition for the interface can occur. This conflict starts a fast-idle timer that causes lines to remain connected for a shorter idle time than usual, allowing other destinations to shut down the first call and use the interface.

Dialer rotary groups prevent contention by creating a set of interfaces to draw from to be used for dialing out. Instead of statically assigning an interface to a destination, dialer rotary groups allow dynamic allocation of interfaces to telephone numbers. When a call is placed, the rotary group is searched for an interface that is not in use to place the call. It is not until all the interfaces in the rotary group are in use that the fast-idle timer is started. Rotary groups can be used in a hub-and-spoke topology, in which a central site is connected to two or more remote sites. In this design, the remote sites communicate only with the central site directly and do not call any of the other remote sites. The central site has several interfaces that map to the remote sites. These interfaces are placed into a rotary group. A rotary group allows several sites to share several interfaces without dedicating an interface to each site. This is handled with a dialer interface. When a rotary group is used for placing calls, a free interface is selected out of all the physical interfaces in the rotary group. When a rotary group is used for incoming calls, the incoming call can be received by any of the physical interfaces, and packets will still be routed correctly. If an interface is already connected, incoming or outgoing calls can be received or placed by the next available interface in the rotary group.

S and T reference points

The S reference point lies between ISDN user equipment (TEI or TE2 with a TA) and the NT2 device. The T reference point lies between customer site switching equipment (NT2) and the local loop's termination (NT1). The user-network reference point is usually the S/T reference point. The S/T reference point is one of

Glossary

two reference points that most ISDN equipment vendors incorporate in their devices. An S/T device requires a standalone NT1 device to work with your ISDN connection. The most important of these are S/T and U. The U interface is the local loop between the telephone company and the customer premises. At the customer site, the 2-wire U interface is converted to a 4-wire S/T interface by an NT1. Originally, the T interface was a point-to-point interface and could be converted to a point-to-multipoint S interface by an NT2. However, the electrical specifications of the S and T interfaces were almost identical, so most modern NT1s include built-in NT2 functionality and can support either single or multiple ISDN devices on what is now called the *S/T interface*.

Serial Line IP (SLIP)

SLIP, documented in RFC 1055, was the first protocol for relaying IP packets over dial-up connections. It defines the encapsulation mechanism, but little else. There is no support for dynamic address assignment, link testing, security, compression, and multiplexing different protocols over a single link. SLIP has been largely supplanted by PPP.

Service Access Point Identifier (SAPI)

SAPIs play the role of a protocol or port number in ISDN, and identify the higher-layer protocol being used in the data field. The Service Access Point Identifier (SAPI) is a 6-bit field that identifies the point where layer 2 provides a service to layer 3. Q.931 messages are sent using SAPI 0. SAPI 16 means X.25, and SAPI 63 is used for TEI assignment procedures.

Service Profile ID (SPID)

SPIDs are used to identify what services and features the telco switch provides to the attached ISDN device. SPIDs are not always required. When they are used, they are only accessed at device initialization time, before the call is set up. The format of the SPID is usually the 10-digit phone number of the ISDN line, plus an optional seven-digit local directory number (LDN). Service providers may use different numbering schemes, but it all amounts to one large telephone-like number. If an ISDN line requires a SPID, but it is not correctly supplied, then layer 2 initialization will take place, but layer 3 will not, and the device will not be able to place or accept calls.

Small Office/Home Office (SOHO)

More and more organizations are either outsourcing or using a staff based at home. All the office costs are avoided, and the staff can be more flexible over working hours. Members of the IT staff—from programmers to support staff—can then choose their own hours of work. This is typically referred to as a *SOHO environment*. These people's work requirements are usually for occasional access to the corporate system, rather than a permanent link. Teleworkers can be anyone—for example, senior managers, executives, and professionals who telework for one or two days a week to get work done without interruption.

split horizon

Distance vector protocols use a mechanism called *split horizon* to ensure that routing loops do not occur. Split horizon restricts how routing information is sent to other routers: If a router receives knowledge about a network on an interface, it will not propagate that network back out the same interface.

stacker compression

Stacker compression examines data and sends each data type only once, and it sends information indicating to the other end where each type occurs within the data stream. The other end reassembles the data into the various data types from the data stream. Stacker tends to be more CPU intensive and less memory intensive.

status enquiry

Frame relay LMI operates on a special VC between the DTE and DCE. On a DTE-to-DCE connection, the DTE, by default, will be the one to initiate communication. It does this by generating a Status Enquiry (StEnq) frame. In the frame relay implementation in Cisco's routers, this is performed every 10 seconds. For every StEnq sent to the DCE, the DTE expects an acknowledgement back.

subinterface

A subinterface is basically a logical interface that is associated with a physical one. You can have up to 256 subinterfaces associated with a single physical interface in version 11.x of the IOS; this has been increased to 1,024 in version 12.0. The advantage of this approach is that you can assign a separate WAN VC to each subinterface. From the router's perspective, it treats the subinterface like any other physical interface in its chassis. If a routing update is received on one subinterface, the network numbers contained in this can be propagated out any other interface, including other subinterfaces, thereby solving your split horizon problems with distance vector protocols.

Switched Virtual Circuit (SVC)

SVCs are temporary connections used in packet-switched networks, like X.25 and frame relay. They are similar to the circuit-switched connections that a carrier's telephone network uses. When a user has information to send, the router requests a SVC to be set up. Once the SVC is operational, the user sends his information and, when finished, requests the SVC to be torn down

Terminal Access Controller Access Control System (TACACS+)

TACACS+ is a client/server system that provides a reliable and secure delivery of AAA information. TACACS, its predecessor, was developed by the U.S. Defense Department and later defined in RFC 1492. Cisco has taken this protocol and added enhancements to it, thus producing TACACS+. Like RADIUS, TACACS+ defines how AAA is implemented on a security server.

Terminal Adapter (TA)

TAs translate signaling from non-ISDN TE2 devices into a format compatible with ISDN. TAs are usually standalone physical devices. The TA device is a protocol converter that adapts equipment that's not designed for ISDN. ISDN equipment vendors market Terminal Adapter devices that include the NT1 function as well as support other devices. For example, using a Terminal Adapter, you can plug an analog telephone, a fax, and an ISDN adapter into your PC. This type of product, which controls the traffic from different devices sharing the same ISDN line, is called an *NT1 Plus device*.

Terminal Endpoint Identifier (TEI)

TEIs are used to distinguish between several different devices using the same ISDN links. TEIs are unique IDs given to each device (TE) on an ISDN S/T bus. These numbers can be preassigned (TEIs 0 through 63) or dynamically assigned (TEIs 64 through 126). TEI 127 is broadcast. Before any higher-level (Q.931) functions can be performed, each ISDN device must be assigned at least one unique TEI value. Most TEI assignment is done dynamically, using the TEI management protocol. The user broadcasts an identity request, and the network (the telco switch) responds with an Identity assigned containing the TEI value. Functions are also provided to verify and release TEI assignments.

Terminal Equipment (TE)

Terminal Equipment (TE) refers to any end-user device connected to an ISDN line—both TE1 and TE2. This is the general class of equipment that covers both ISDN-ready equipment and non–ISDN equipment, such as analog telephones, faxes, and modems. The encompassing term for any equipment on the customer side of the ISDN connection is *customer premise equipment* (CPE). ISDN can support up to eight pieces of CPE to perform multiple tasks using a single line.

Terminal Equipment 1 (TE1)

TE1 refers to ISDN devices that support the standard ISDN interface directly, including digital phones, digital faxes, and integrated voice/data terminal devices. These TE1 devices provide direct access to an ISDN connection without adapters. Currently, most ISDN-ready equipment is too expensive to be practical.

Terminal Equipment 2 (TE2)

TE2 includes any device that isn't ISDN ready. This category includes the equipment you now use for analog communications. Any device in this class, such as a modem, requires an adapter to work with ISDN. A growing number of ISDN equipment vendors offer products that consolidate a TE2 adapter and NT1 devices into a single unit.

traffic distribution

Address-translation devices can help out with an overloaded server that computers on the Internet are accessing inside your network. Most people assume that when a server becomes overloaded, you have to upgrade it to handle the new load that Internet users are placing on it. Address translation provides an alternate and more flexible solution. Using traffic distribution, users on the Internet send their traffic to a single inside global IP address. This single inside global IP address is represented by a group of inside machines, each with their own unique inside local IP addresses.

U Reference Point

The U reference point is where the telephone company's network arrives at your doorstep, up to the NT1 device. The U interface is also called the *U-Loop* because it represents the loop between your premises and the telephone company. ISDN devices made for the U interface include a built-in NT1 function.

Universal Asynchronous Receiver/Transmitter (UART)

The UART, which is a component in a PC, is a significant part of the communication process between a dial-up computer and remote device. The UART controls the process of breaking parallel data from the

PC down into serial data that can be transmitted, and vice versa for receiving data. The type of UART chip you have will be the factor determining how fast you can transmit and receive data for devices such as modems. A UART chip is an electronic circuit that transmits and receives data through the PC's serial port. It converts bytes into serial bits for transmission, and vice versa. It also generates and strips the start and stop bits appended to each character. The original PC serial interface specification utilized the 8250 Programmable Communications Interface, or *UART*. This device converts data from the microprocessor into a format that is easily transmittable via a single-wire connection. To accomplish this task, the UART takes data from the computer in a parallel format (that is, the bits are presented side by side) and shifts them out via a single pin in a serial (one bit directly after another, daisy-chain fashion) data stream. Various extra bits are added, such as the start, parity, and stop bits, to provide the UART on the other end of the serial data connection with an accurate means for the reassembly of the original data format.

V.21

V.21 is the standard for 300bps modem communications. It is very rarely used anymore.

V.22 and V.22bis

V.22 and V.22bis are standard modulation protocols for 1.2Kbps and 2.4Kbps modems, respectively. They do not have fallback speeds, but they can adjust to the lower modulation speed for poor line conditions.

V.23

V.23 is the standard for 1.2Kbps modem communications. This protocol was developed with terminal operators in mind. It has a download speed of 1.2Kbps but an upload speed of only 700bps. The upload speed was considered adequate for typing.

V.32

V.32 is the standard for 9.6Kbps modem communications. It also supports the fallback speed of 4.8Kbps.

V.32bis

V.32bis is the standard for 14.4Kbps modems. A V.32bis modem can also fall back to 12Kbps and then to 9.6Kbps, 7.2Kbps, and 4.8Kbps. Therefore, V.32bis is downward compatible with V.32.

V.34

The V.34 protocol is the standard for 33.6Kbps modem connections. This standard was initially ratified as 28.8Kbps but was updated to include 33.6Kbps in 1996.

V.35

The V.35 standard is the recommended cable for speeds up to 48Kbps, although in practice it is used successfully at 4Mbps. Cisco's products support speeds up to 2.048Mbps. The V.35 serial transition cable has a DB-60 connector for connection to a Cisco serial port (which is proprietary in nature). The opposite end has a standard 34-pin Winchester-type connector. The 34-pin Winchester-type connector can be male for DTE or female for DCE.

V.42

Error correction is an important feature in the fastest modems. It allows fast and reliable connections over standard phone lines, even those with some noise. All

Glossary

phone lines have noise, which degrades the data connection. Therefore, error correction is necessary. All modems in a network must be using the same error-correction protocols for it to work. Fortunately, most modems use the same protocol, V.42. With it, modems can detect damaged data streams, and the data will be resent. The V.42bis protocol is just like V.42, but it incorporates data compression. Data compression allows modems to use higher bps levels. A 14.4 modem, with data compression, can boast transmission rates of 57,600bps. A 28.8 modem can boast transmission rates up to 115,200bps.

V.90

The 56Kbps modem technology broke ground when it first came to market. It was released as a faster solution for end users and SOHOs. After this technology was originally introduced, two technologies emerged—X2, which was developed by U.S. Robotics, and Lucent and Rockwell's K56flex. Unfortunately, however, the two types of technologies and the lack of a standard created a problem for end users and Internet Service Providers. For example, if an end user had an X2 modem, but the Internet service provider only had Kflex modems, the end user would be unable to achieve optimal performance. Because of this dilemma, the V.90 standard was developed. This standard took both the X2 and Kflex technologies and merged them into one standard. This allowed end users to achieve maximum performance if they were with an ISP that was providing a different technology.

Virtual Circuit (VC)

A VC is a bidirectional, full-duplexed, logical connection between two devices. Note that a physical connection between two devices can hold many VCs. A VC is not bound to a specific physical connection—it can traverse many segments between the source and destination. Basically, VCs provide a multiplexing function—on one interface, you can connect to a multitude of destinations.

virtual profiles

A virtual profile is basically a virtual interface that is created for a user when he dials into the network. All the properties that can be associated with a physical interface, such as **access-list**s, addressing, queuing, and so on, can be applied to the virtual interface. When the user disconnects, this virtual interface configuration is removed. The physical interface's properties can change based on the user who dials into the router.

WAN Interface Card (WIC)

A WIC is a small card containing one or two WAN ports, and it is inserted into a WAN slot found in the chassis of certain modular routers or in the WAN slot found on certain network modules.

Weighted Fair Queuing (WFQ)

WFQ is the default queuing mechanism on all of Cisco's serial T1/E1 and slower interfaces: No configuration on your part is required to enable it. WFQ will dynamically sort traffic into *conversations*. To allocate bandwidth, each conversation is assigned a weight that is used to differentiate between the low- and high-volume conversations. This is then used to determine how much bandwidth a conversation is allowed compared to other conversations that are using the serial interface. There are two types of conversations. Interactive traffic, such as telnet and SNA sessions, are considered low-volume conversations. File transfers are considered high-volume conversations. WFQ gives a higher preference to low-volume conversations over high-volume conversations; however, within the same conversation type, such as two telnet sessions, the conversations are treated equally by the router.

X.121 Address

X.121 addresses are used to identify a PAD in an X.25 network. X.121 addresses must be unique throughout the network (and unique throughout the world if you are connected to a public X.25 network). X.121 addresses are made up of two components: Data Network Identification Code (DNIC) and National Terminal Number (NTN). The DNIC, which is optional, identifies the country and carrier where the X.25 DTE resides. The DNIC is four decimal digits in length. The NTN is the identifier used to uniquely identify your X.25 PAD in an X.25 carrier's network. When you connect to a provider's network, you will be assigned a value to use for your PAD. The NTN can range from 8 to 10 or 11 decimal digits, depending on the provider's X.25 software on its switches.

X.21

The X.21 is a connector that uses a 15-pin connector for balanced circuits, and it's commonly used in the United Kingdom to connect to the public data network. X.21 relocates some of the logic functions to the DTE and DCE interfaces and, as a result, requires fewer circuits and a smaller connector than EIA/TIA-232. The X.21 serial transition cable (not included) has a DB-60 connector for connection to a Cisco serial port. The opposite end has a DB-15 connector. The DB-15 connector can be male for DTE or female for DCE.

X.25

X.25 is based on a set of standards that the International Telecommunication Union-Telecommunication Standardization Sector (ITU-T) is responsible for. Developed in the early 1970s, X.25 was designed to cope with the unreliable, high-latency analog connections in WAN environments in a cost-effective manner. It gave telephone companies and carriers a standards-based mechanism to allow the flow of data across their analog networks.

Glossary

Index

M

O

P

The leading resource for IT certification!

This groundbreaking, e-learning Web destination for test preparation and training incorporates an innovative suite of personalized training technologies to help you pass your exams. Besides providing test preparation resources and an array of training products and services, **ExamCram.com** brings together an extensive community of professionals and students who can collaborate online.

ExamCram.com is designed with one overridi philosophy in mind—great access!

Review industry news, study tips, questions an answers, training courses and materials, ment programs, discussion groups, real-world practi questions, and more.

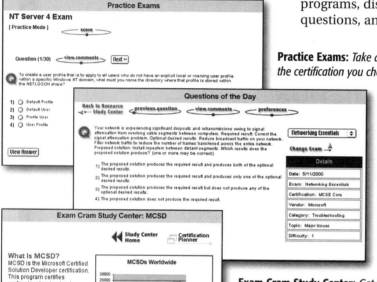

Practice Exams: *Take a FREE practice exam for the certification you choose.*

Questions of the Day: *Study questions are posted every day. Or, sign up to have them emailed to you daily.*

Exam Cram Study Center: *Get the facts on an exam, review study resources, read study tips, and more.*

OTHER HIGHLIGHTS:

Ask the Mentors: Ask questions and search the archives for answers.

Certification Planner: Discover the variety of certification programs offered.

Open Forum: Post your thoughts on weekly top and see what others thi

Certification Resource Cen Quickly find out about the newest certification programs.

Join the thousands who have already discovered ExamCram.com. Visit ExamCram.com today!

What's on the CD-ROM

What's on the CD-ROM

The *CCNP Remote Access Exam Prep's* companion CD-ROM contains the testing system for the book, which includes 50 questions. Additional questions are available for free download from **ExamCram.com**; simply click on the Update button in the testing engine. You can choose from numerous testing formats, including Fixed-Length, Random, Test All, and Review.

System Requirements

Software

➤ Your operating system must be Windows 95, 98, NT 4, or higher.

➤ To view the practice exams, you need Internet Explorer 5.x.

Hardware

➤ An Intel Pentium, AMD, or comparable 100MHz processor or higher is recommended for best results.

➤ 32MB of RAM is the minimum memory requirement.

➤ Available disk storage space of at least 10MB is recommended.

Software developed by Dreamtech Software, India